Customer service analysis	Database design Database querying and reporting	Chapter 9
Sales lead and customer analysis	Database design Database querying and reporting	Chapter 12
Blog creation and design	Blog creation tool	Chapter 4

Internet Skills

Using online software tools for job hunting and career development	Chapter 1
Using online interactive mapping software to plan efficient transportation routes	Chapter 2
Researching product information Evaluating Web sites for auto sales	Chapter 3
Using Internet newsgroups for marketing	Chapter 4
Researching travel costs using online travel sites	Chapter 5
Searching online databases for products and services	Chapter 6
Using Web search engines for business research	Chapter 7
Researching and evaluating business outsourcing services	Chapter 8
Researching and evaluating supply chain management services	Chapter 9
Evaluating e-commerce hosting services	Chapter 10
Using shopping bots to compare product price, features, and availability	Chapter 11
Analyzing Web site design	Chapter 12

Analytical, Writing, and Presentation Skills *

Business Problem	Chapter
Management analysis of a business	Chapter 1
Value chain and competitive forces analysis Business strategy formulation	Chapter 3
Formulating a corporate privacy policy	Chapter 4
Employee productivity analysis	Chapter 7
Disaster recovery planning	Chapter 8
Locating and evaluating suppliers	Chapter 9
Developing an e-commerce strategy	Chapter 10

B

Essentials of Management Information Systems

Eleventh Edition

Global Edition

Kenneth C. Laudon
New York University

Jane P. Laudon
Azimuth Information Systems

PEARSON

Boston   Columbus   Indianapolis   New York   San Francisco   Upper Saddle River
Amsterdam   Cape Town   Dubai   London   Madrid   Milan   Munich   Paris   Montreal   Toronto
Delhi   Mexico City   São Paulo   Sydney   Hong Kong   Seoul   Singapore   Taipei   Tokyo

Editor in Chief: Stephanie Wall
Executive Editor: Bob Horan
Program Manager Team Lead: Ashley Santora
Program Manager: Denise Vaughn
Editorial Assistant: Kaylee Rotella
Executive Marketing Manager: Anne K. Fahlgren
Senior Acquisitions Editor, Global Edition: Steven Jackson
Project Editor, Global Edition: Laura Thompson
Project Manager Team Lead: Judy Leale
Project Manager: Karalyn Holland
Operations Specialist: Michelle Klein
Creative Director: Blair Brown
Sr. Art Director: Janet Slowik
Cover Designer: John Christiana

Cover Image: DT10 / Shutterstock
VP, Director of Digital Strategy & Assessment: Paul Gentile
Digital Editor: Brian Surette
Digital Development Manager: Robin Lazrus
MyLab Project Manager: Joan Waxman
Digital Project Manager: Alana Coles
Media Project Manager: Lisa Rinaldi
Full-Service Project Management: Azimuth Interactive, Inc.
Composition: Azimuth Interactive, Inc.
Printer/Binder: Courier/Kendallville
Cover Printer: Lehigh-Phoenix Color/Hagerstown
Text Font: 10.5/12.5 Times LT Std, 9.5pt

Pearson Education Limited
Edinburgh Gate
Harlow
Essex CM20 2JE
England

and Associated Companies throughout the world

Visit us on the World Wide Web at:
www.pearson.com/uk

British Library Cataloguing-in-Publication Data
A catalogue record for this book is available from the British Library
10 9 8 7 6 5 4 3 2 1
15 14 13 12 11

ISBN-13: 978-1-292-01957-4
ISBN-10: 1-292-01957-3

Typeset in 10.5/12.5 Times LT Std, 9.5pt by Azimuth Interactive, Inc.
Printed and bound by Courier/Kendallville in United States of America

About the Authors

Kenneth C. Laudon is a Professor of Information Systems at New York University's Stern School of Business. He holds a B.A. in Economics from Stanford and a Ph.D. from Columbia University. He has authored twelve books dealing with electronic commerce, information systems, organizations, and society. Professor Laudon has also written over forty articles concerned with the social, organizational, and management impacts of information systems, privacy, ethics, and multimedia technology.

Professor Laudon's current research is on the planning and management of large-scale information systems and multimedia information technology. He has received grants from the National Science Foundation to study the evolution of national information systems at the Social Security Administration, the IRS, and the FBI. Ken's research focuses on enterprise system implementation, computer-related organizational and occupational changes in large organizations, changes in management ideology, changes in public policy, and understanding productivity change in the knowledge sector.

Ken Laudon has testified as an expert before the United States Congress. He has been a researcher and consultant to the Office of Technology Assessment (United States Congress), Department of Homeland Security, and to the Office of the President, several executive branch agencies, and Congressional Committees. Professor Laudon also acts as an in-house educator for several consulting firms and as a consultant on systems planning and strategy to several Fortune 500 firms.

At NYU's Stern School of Business, Ken Laudon teaches courses on Managing the Digital Firm, Information Technology and Corporate Strategy, Professional Responsibility (Ethics), and Electronic Commerce and Digital Markets. Ken Laudon's hobby is sailing.

Jane Price Laudon is a management consultant in the information systems area and the author of seven books. Her special interests include systems analysis, data management, MIS auditing, software evaluation, and teaching business professionals how to design and use information systems.

Jane received her Ph.D. from Columbia University, her M.A. from Harvard University, and her B.A. from Barnard College. She has taught at Columbia University and the New York University Stern School of Business. She maintains a lifelong interest in Oriental languages and civilizations.

The Laudons have two daughters, Erica and Elisabeth, to whom this book is dedicated.

Brief Contents

Complete Contents

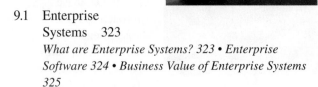

IV Building and Managing Systems   427

Preface

The Global Edition is written for business school students in Europe, the Middle East, South Africa, Australia, and the Pacific Asian region. Case studies and examples focus on how firms in these regions use information systems. We wrote this book for global business school students who wanted an in-depth look at how today's business firms use information technologies and systems to achieve corporate objectives. Information systems are one of the major tools available to business managers for achieving operational excellence, developing new products and services, improving decision making, and achieving competitive advantage. Students will find here the most up-to-date and comprehensive overview of information systems used by business firms today. After reading this book, we expect students will be able to participate in, and even lead, management discussions of information systems for their firms.

When interviewing potential employees, business firms often look for new hires who know how to use information systems and technologies for achieving bottom-line business results. Our hope is that after reading this book and completing the course, you will be able to participate in, and even lead, management discussions of information systems and technologies at your firm. Regardless of whether you are an accounting, finance, management, operations management, marketing, or information systems major, the knowledge and information you find in this book will be valuable throughout your business career.

What's New in This Edition

CURRENCY

The 11th edition features all new opening, closing, and Interactive Session cases. The text, figures, tables, and cases have been updated through October 2013 with the latest sources from industry and MIS research.

NEW FEATURES

- Chapter-opening cases have added new case study questions.
- More online cases: MIS Classic Cases, consisting of five outstanding cases from previous editions on companies such as Kmart or Blockbuster/Netflix, will be available on the book's Web site. In addition, all of the chapter-ending cases from the previous edition (Ess10e) will be available online.
- The chapter on Ethical and Social Issues in Information Systems has been positioned earlier in the text as Chapter 4 to highlight the importance of this topic.
- Learning Tracks and Video Cases for each chapter are listed at the beginning of each chapter.

NEW TOPICS

- **Social Business:** Extensive coverage of social business, introduced in Chapter 2 and discussed throughout the text. Detailed discussions of enterprise (internal corporate) social networking as well as social networking in e-commerce.

- **Social, Mobile, Local:** New e-commerce content in Chapter 10 describing how social tools, mobile technology, and location-based services are transforming marketing and advertising.

- **Big Data:** Chapter 6 on Databases and Information Management rewritten to provide in-depth coverage of Big Data and new data management technologies, including Hadoop, in-memory computing, non-relational databases, and analytic platforms.
- **Cloud Computing:** Expanded and updated coverage of cloud computing in Chapter 5 (IT Infrastructure), with more detail on types of cloud services, private and public clouds, hybrid clouds, managing cloud services, and a new chapter-ending case on Amazon's cloud services. Cloud computing also covered in Chapter 6 (databases in the cloud); Chapter 8 (cloud security); Chapter 9 (cloud-based CRM); Chapter 10 (e-commerce); and Chapter 12 (cloud-based systems development).
- Consumerization of IT and BYOD
- Internet of Things
- Visual Web
- Location analytics
- Location-based services (geosocial, geoadvertising, geoinformation services)
- Social graph, social marketing, social search, social CRM
- Building an e-commerce presence
- Mobile device management
- Responsive Web design
- Expanded coverage of business analytics including big data analytics
- Mobile and native apps
- Cyberlockers
- Software-defined networking
- 3-D printing
- Quantum computing

What's New in MIS?

Plenty. In fact, there's a whole new world of doing business using new technologies for managing and organizing. What makes the MIS field the most exciting area of study in schools of business is the continuous change in technology, management, and business processes. (Chapter 1 describes these changes in more detail.)

A continuing stream of information technology innovations is transforming the traditional business world. Examples include the emergence of cloud computing, the growth of a mobile digital business platform based on smartphones and tablet computers, and not least, the use of social networks by managers to achieve business objectives. Most of these changes have occurred in the last few years. These innovations are enabling entrepreneurs and innovative traditional firms to create new products and services, develop new business models, and transform the day-to-day conduct of business. In the process, some old businesses, even industries, are being destroyed while new businesses are springing up.

For instance, the emergence of online video stores like Netflix for streaming, and Apple iTunes for downloading, has forever changed how premium video is distributed, and even created. Netflix in 2013 attracted 30 million subscribers to its DVD rental and streaming movie business. Netflix now accounts for 90% of streaming premium movies and TV shows, and consumes an estimated 33% of Internet bandwidth in the United States. Netflix has moved into premium TV show production with House of Cards, and Arrested Development, challenging cable networks like HBO, and potentially disrupting the cable industry dominance of TV show production. Apple's iTunes now accounts for 67% of movie and TV show downloads and has struck deals with major Hollywood studios to obtain the right to distribute recent movies and TV shows. A trickle of viewers are unplugging from cable and using only the Internet for entertainment.

E-commerce is back, generating over $420 billion in revenues in 2013, and estimated to grow to over $637 billion in 2017. Amazon's revenues grew 27 percent to $61 billion in the 12-month period ending June 30, 2013, despite the recession, while offline retail grew by 5 percent. E-commerce is changing how firms design, produce and deliver their products and services. E-commerce has reinvented itself again, disrupting the traditional marketing and advertising industry and putting major media and content firms in jeopardy. Facebook and other social networking sites such as YouTube, Twitter, and Tumblr, exemplify the new face of e-commerce in the 21st Century. They sell services. When we think of e-commerce we tend to think of a selling physical products. While this iconic vision of e-commerce is still very powerful and the fastest growing form of retail in the U.S., growing up alongside is a whole new value stream based on selling services, not goods. It's a services model of e-commerce. Growth in social commerce is spurred by powerful growth of the mobile platform: 35% of Facebook's users access the service from mobile phones and tablets. Information systems and technologies are the foundation of this new services-based e-commerce.

Likewise, the management of business firms has changed: With new mobile smartphones, high-speed wireless Wi-Fi networks, and wireless laptop computers, remote salespeople on the road are only seconds away from their managers' questions and oversight. Managers on the move are in direct, continuous contact with their employees. The growth of enterprise-wide information systems with extraordinarily rich data means that managers no longer operate in a fog of confusion, but instead have online, nearly instant, access to the really important information they need for accurate and timely decisions. In addition to their public uses on the Web, wikis and blogs are becoming important corporate tools for communication, collaboration, and information sharing.

The 11th Edition: The Comprehensive Solution for the MIS Curriculum

Since its inception, this text has helped to define the MIS course around the globe. This edition continues to be authoritative, but is also more customizable, flexible, and geared to meeting the needs of different colleges, universities, and individual instructors.

This book is now part of a complete learning package that includes the core text and an extensive offering of supplemental materials on the Web.

The core text consists of 12 chapters with hands-on projects covering the most essential topics in MIS. An important part of the core text is the Video Case Study and Instructional Video Package: 24 video case studies (2 per chapter) plus 16 instructional videos that illustrate business uses of information systems, explain new technologies, and explore concepts. Videos are keyed to the topics of each chapter.

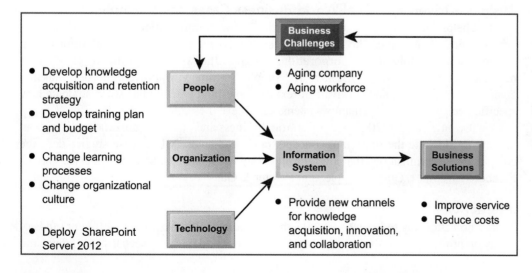

A diagram accompanying each chapter-opening case graphically illustrates how people, organization, and technology elements work together to create an information system solution to the business challenges discussed in the case.

In addition, for students and instructors who want to go deeper into selected topics, there are 49 online Learning Tracks that cover a variety of MIS topics in greater depth.

MyMISLab™ provides more in-depth coverage of chapter topics, career resources, additional case studies, supplementary chapter material, and data files for hands-on projects.

THE CORE TEXT

The core text provides an overview of fundamental MIS concepts using an integrated framework for describing and analyzing information systems. This framework shows information systems composed of people, organization, and technology elements and is reinforced in student projects and case studies.

Chapter Organization

Each chapter contains the following elements:

- A Chapter Outline that includes lists of all the supplemental Learning Tracks and Video Cases for each chapter
- A chapter-opening case describing a real-world organization to establish the theme and importance of the chapter
- A diagram analyzing the opening case in terms of the people, organization, and technology model used throughout the text
- A series of Learning Objectives
- Two Interactive Sessions with Case Study Questions
- A Review Summary keyed to the Student Learning Objectives
- A list of Key Terms that students can use to review concepts
- Review questions for students to test their comprehension of chapter material
- Discussion questions raised by the broader themes of the chapter
- A series of Hands-on MIS Projects consisting of two Management Decision Problems, a hands-on application software project, and a project to develop Internet skills
- A Collaboration and Teamwork Project to develop teamwork and presentation skills, with options for using open source collaboration tools
- A chapter-ending case study for students to apply chapter concepts

KEY FEATURES

We have enhanced the text to make it more interactive, leading-edge, and appealing to both students and instructors. The features and learning tools are described in the following sections:

Business-Driven with Real-World Business Cases and Examples

The text helps students see the direct connection between information systems and business performance. It describes the main business objectives driving the use of information systems and technologies in corporations all over the world: operational excellence; new products and services; customer and supplier intimacy; improved decision making; competitive advantage; and survival. In-text examples and case studies show students how specific companies use information systems to achieve these objectives.

We use only current (2013) examples from business and public organizations throughout the text to illustrate the important concepts in each chapter. All the case studies describe companies or organizations that are familiar to students, such as the San Francisco Giants, Facebook, Walmart, Google, Apple, and Procter & Gamble.

Interactivity

There's no better way to learn about MIS than by doing MIS! We provide different kinds of hands-on projects where students can work with real-world business scenarios and data, and learn firsthand what MIS is all about. These projects heighten student involvement in this exciting subject.

- **Online Video Case Package.** Students can watch short videos online, either in-class or at home or work, and then apply the concepts of the book to the analysis of the video. Every chapter contains at least two business video cases that explain how business firms and managers are using information systems, describe new management practices, and explore concepts discussed in the chapter. Each video case consists of a video about a real-world company, a background text case, and case study questions. These video cases enhance students' understanding of MIS topics and the relevance of MIS to the business world. In addition, there are 16 Instructional Videos that describe developments and concepts in MIS keyed to respective chapters.

- **Interactive Sessions.** Two short cases in each chapter have been redesigned as Interactive Sessions to be used in the classroom or online to stimulate student interest and active learning. Each case concludes with case study questions. The case study questions provide topics for class discussion, Internet discussion, or written assignments.

INTERACTIVE SESSION: PEOPLE **The Pleasures and Pitfalls of BYOD**

Just about everyone who has a smartphone wants to be able to bring it to work and use it on the job. And why not? Employees using their own smartphones would allow companies to enjoy all of the same benefits of a mobile workforce without spending their own money to purchase these devices. Smaller companies are able to go mobile without making large investments in devices and mobile services. According to Gartner Consultants, BYOD will be embraced by 38 percent of companies by 2016 and half of all companies will mandate BYOD by 2017. BYOD is becoming the "new normal."

But...wait a minute. Nearly three out of five enterprises believe that BYOD represents a growing problem for their organizations, according to a survey of 162 enterprises conducted by Osterman Research on behalf of Dell Inc. Although BYOD can improve employee job satisfaction and productivity, it also can cause a number of problems if not managed properly: Support for personally owned devices is more diffi-

transfer programs like Apple's iCloud; instead, employees use an IBM-hosted version called MyMobileHub. IBM even turns off Siri, the voice-activated personal assistant, on employees' iPhones because the spoken queries are uploaded to Apple servers.

Each employee's device is treated differently, depending on the model and the job responsibilities of the person using it. Some people are only allowed to receive IBM e-mail, calendars, and contacts on their portable devices, while others can access internal IBM applications and files (see Chapter 8). IBM equips the mobile devices of the latter category of employees with additional software, such as programs that encrypt information as it travels to and from corporate networks.

One company that has successfully implemented BYOD is Intel Corporation, the giant semiconductor company. About 70 percent of the 39,000 devices registered on its network are personal devices. Intel approached BYOD in a positive manner, trying to find

Each chapter contains two Interactive Sessions on People, Organizations, or Technology using real-world companies to illustrate chapter concepts and issues.

CASE STUDY QUESTIONS

1. What are the advantages and disadvantages of allowing employees to use their personal smartphones for work?

2. What people, organization, and technology factors should be addressed when deciding whether to allow employees to use their personal smartphones for work?

3. Compare the BYOD experiences of IBM and Intel. Why did BYOD at Intel work so well?

4. Allowing employees to use their own smartphones for work will save the company money. Do you agree? Why or why not?

Case Study Questions encourage students to apply chapter concepts to real-world companies in class discussions, student presentations, or writing assignments.

- **Hands-on MIS Projects.** Every chapter concludes with a Hands-on MIS Projects section containing three types of projects: two Management Decision Problems, a hands-on application software exercise using Microsoft Excel, Access, or Web page and blog creation tools, and a project that develops Internet business skills. A Dirt Bikes USA running case in MyMISLab provides additional hands-on projects for each chapter.

2. Dollar General Corporation operates deep-discount stores offering housewares, cleaning supplies, clothing, health and beauty aids, and packaged food, with most items selling for $1. Its business model calls for keeping costs as low as possible. The company has no automated method for keeping track of inventory at each store. Managers know approximately how many cases of a particular product the store is supposed to receive when a delivery truck arrives, but the stores lack technology for scanning the cases or verifying the item count inside the cases. Merchandise losses from theft or other mishaps have been rising and now represent over 3 percent of total sales. What decisions have to be made before investing in an information system solution?

Store & Region Sales Database

II	Store N	Sales Region	Item N	Item Descriptic	Unit Pric	Units Sol	Week Ending	Click to Add
1	1	South	2005	17" Monitor	$229.00	28	10/27/2013	
2	1	South	2005	17" Monitor	$229.00	30	11/24/2013	
3	1	South	2005	17" Monitor	$229.00	9	12/29/2013	
4	1	South	3006	101 Keyboard	$19.95	30	10/27/2013	
5	1	South	3006	101 Keyboard	$19.95	35	11/24/2013	
6	1	South	3006	101 Keyboard	$19.95	39	12/29/2013	
7	1	South	6050	PC Mouse	$8.95	28	10/27/2013	
8	1	South	6050	PC Mouse	$8.95	3	11/24/2013	
9	1	South	6050	PC Mouse	$8.95	38	12/29/2013	
10	1	South	8500	Desktop CPU	$849.95	25	10/27/2013	
11	1	South	8500	Desktop CPU	$849.95	27	11/24/2013	
12	1	South	8500	Desktop CPU	$849.95	33	12/29/2013	
13	2	South	2005	17" Monitor	$229.00	8	10/27/2013	
14	2	South	2005	17" Monitor	$229.00	8	11/24/2013	
15	2	South	2005	17" Monitor	$229.00	10	12/29/2013	
16	2	South	3006	101 Keyboard	$19.95	8	10/27/2013	

IMPROVING DECISION MAKING: USING WEB TOOLS TO CONFIGURE AND PRICE AN AUTOMOBILE

Software skills: Internet-based software
Business skills: Researching product information and pricing

In this exercise, you will use software at car-selling Web sites to find product information about a car of your choice and use that information to make an important purchase decision. You will also evaluate two of these sites as selling tools.

You are interested in purchasing a new Ford Escape (or some other car of your choice). Go to the Web site of CarsDirect (www.carsdirect.com) and begin your investigation. Locate the Ford Escape. Research the various Escape models, choose one you prefer in terms of price, features, and safety ratings. Locate and read at least two reviews. Surf the Web site of the manufacturer, in this case Ford (www.ford.com). Compare the information available on Ford's Web site with that of CarsDirect for the Ford Escape. Try to locate the lowest price for the car you want in a local dealer's inventory. Suggest improvements for CarsDirect.com and Ford.com.

- **Collaboration and Teamwork Projects.** Each chapter features a collaborative project that encourages students working in teams to use Google Drive, Google Docs, or other open-source collaboration tools. The first team project in Chapter 1 asks students to build a collaborative Google site.

Assessment and AACSB Assessment Guidelines

The Association to Advance Collegiate Schools of Business (AACSB) is a not-for-profit corporation of educational institutions, corporations and other organizations that seeks to improve business education primarily by accrediting university business programs. As a part of its accreditation activities, the AACSB has developed an Assurance of Learning Program designed to ensure that schools do in fact teach students what they promise. Schools are required to state a clear mission, develop a coherent business program, identify student learning objectives, and then prove that students do in fact achieve the objectives.

We have attempted in this book to support AACSB efforts to encourage assessment-based education. The front end papers of this edition identify student learning objectives and anticipated outcomes for our Hands-on MIS projects. On the Laudon Web site is a more inclusive and detailed assessment matrix that identifies the learning objectives of each chapter and points to all the available assessment tools for ensuring students in fact do achieve the learning objectives. Because each school is different and may have different missions and learning objectives, no single document can satisfy all situations. The authors will provide custom advice on how to use this text in colleges with different missions and assessment needs. Please e-mail the authors or contact your local Pearson Prentice Hall representative for contact information.

For more information on the AACSB Assurance of Learning Program, and how this text supports assessment-based learning, please visit the Web site for this book.

Customization and Flexibility: New Learning Track Modules

Our Learning Tracks feature gives instructors the flexibility to provide in-depth coverage of the topics they choose. There are 49 Learning Tracks available to instructors and students. A Learning Tracks list at the beginning of each chapter directs students to short essays or additional chapters in MyMISLab. This supplementary content takes students deeper into MIS topics, concepts and debates; reviews basic technology concepts in hardware, software, database design, telecommunications, and other areas; and provide additional hands-on software instruction. The 11th Edition includes new Learning Tracks on E-Commerce Payment Systems, LAN Topologies, Building an E-Commerce Web Site, 4th Generation Languages, and Occupational and Career Outlook for Information Systems Majors 2012–2018.

Author-Certified Test bank and Supplements

- **Author-Certified Test Bank.** The authors have worked closely with skilled test item writers to ensure that higher level cognitive skills are tested. Test bank multiple choice questions include questions on content, but also include many questions that require analysis, synthesis, and evaluation skills.
- **Annotated Slides.** The authors have prepared a comprehensive collection of fifty PowerPoint slides to be used in your lectures. Many of these slides are the same as used by Ken Laudon in his MIS classes and executive education presentations. Each of the slides is annotated with teaching suggestions for asking students questions, developing in-class lists that illustrate key concepts, and recommending other firms as examples in addition to those provided in the text. The annotations are like an Instructor's Manual built into the slides and make it easier to teach the course effectively.

Student Learning-Focused

Student Learning Objectives are organized around a set of study questions to focus student attention. Each chapter concludes with a Review Summary and Review Questions organized around these study questions.

MYMISLAB

MyMISLab is a Web-based assessment and tutorial tool that provides practice and testing while personalizing course content and providing student and class assessment and reporting. Your course is not the same as the course taught down the hall. Now, all the resources both you and your students need for course success are in one place – flexible and easily organized and adapted for your individual course experience. Visit www.pearsonglobaleditions.com/mymislab to see how you can teach, learn, experience MIS.

Career Resources

The Instructor's Resource section of the Laudon Web site also provides extensive Career Resources, including job-hunting guides and instructions on how to build a Digital Portfolio demonstrating the business knowledge, application software proficiency, and Internet skills acquired from using the text. The portfolio can be included in a resume or job application or used as a learning assessment tool for instructors.

Instructional Support Materials

Instructor's Resource

The support materials described in the following sections are conveniently available for adopters on the Instructor's Resource Center.

Image Library

The Image Library is an impressive resource to help instructors create vibrant lecture presentations. Almost every figure and photo in the text is provided and organized by chapter for convenience. These images and lecture notes can be imported easily into Microsoft PowerPoint to create new presentations or to add to existing ones.

Instructor's Manual

The Instructor's Manual features not only answers to review, discussion, case study, and group project questions but also an in-depth lecture outline, teaching objectives, key terms, teaching suggestions, and Internet resources.

Test Item File

The Test Item File is a comprehensive collection of true–false, multiple-choice, fill-in-the-blank, and essay questions. The questions are rated by difficulty level and the answers are referenced by section. The test item file also contains questions tagged to the AACSB learning standards. An electronic version of the Test Item File is available in TestGen and TestGen conversions are available for BlackBoard or WebCT course management systems. All TestGen files are available for download at the Instructor Resource Center.

PowerPoint Slides

Electronic color slides created by Azimuth Interactive Corporation, Inc., are available in Microsoft PowerPoint. The slides illuminate and build on key concepts in the text.

Video Cases and Instructional Videos

Instructors can download step-by-step instructions for accessing the video cases from the Instructor Resources Center. See page 19 for a list of video cases and instructional videos.

Learning Track Modules

49 Learning Tracks provide additional coverage topics for students and instructors. See page 20 for a list of the Learning Tracks available for this edition.

VIDEO CASES AND INSTRUCTIONAL VIDEOS

Chapter	Video
Chapter 1: Business Information Systems in Your Career	Case 1: UPS Global Operations with the DIAD Case 2: Google Data Center Efficiency Best Practices Instructional Video 1: Green Energy Efficiency in a Data Center Using Tivoli Architecture (IBM) Instructional Video 2: Tour IBM's Raleigh Data Center
Chapter 2: Global E-business and Collaboration	Case 1: Walmart's Retail Link Supply Chain Case 2: Salesforce.com: The Emerging Social Enterprise Instructional Video 1: US Foodservice Grows Market with Oracle CRM on Demand
Chapter 3: Achieving Competitive Advantage with Information Systems	Case 1: National Basketball Association: Competing on Global Delivery With Akamai OS Streaming Case 2: IT and Geo-Mapping Help a Small Business Succeed Case 3: Materials Handling Equipment Corp: Enterprise Systems Drive Corporate Strategy for a Small Business Instructional Video 1: SAP BusinessOne ERP: From Orders to Final Delivery and Payment
Chapter 4: Ethical and Social Issues in Information Systems	Case 1: What Net Neutrality Means for You Case 2: Facebook Privacy Case 3: Data Mining for Terrorists and Innocents Instructional Video 1: Viktor Mayer Schönberger on The Right to Be Forgotten
Chapter 5: IT Infrastructure: Hardware and Software	Case 1: ESPN.com: Getting to eXtreme Scale On the Web Case 2: Salesforce.com: SFA on the iPhone and iPod Touch Case 3: Hudson's Bay Company and IBM: Virtual Blade Platform Instructional Video 1: Google and IBM Produce Cloud Computing Instructional Video 2: IBM Blue Cloud Is Ready-to-Use Computing
Chapter 6: Foundations of Business Intelligence: Databases and Information Management	Case 1: Dubuque Uses Cloud Computing and Sensors to Build a Smarter City Case 2: Maruti Suzuki Business Intelligence and Enterprise Databases
Chapter 7: Telecommunications, the Internet, and Wireless Technology	Case 1: Telepresence Moves Out of the Boardroom and Into the Field Case 2: Virtual Collaboration With Lotus Sametime
Chapter 8: Securing Information Systems	Case 1: Stuxnet and Cyberwarfare Case 2: Cyberespionage: The Chinese Threat Case 3: IBM Zone Trusted Information Channel (ZTIC) Instructional Video 1: Sony PlayStation Hacked; Data Stolen from 77 Million Users Instructional Video 2: Zappos Working to Correct Online Security Breach Instructional Video 3: Meet the Hackers: Anonymous Statement on Hacking SONY
Chapter 9: Achieving Operational Excellence and Customer Intimacy: Enterprise Applications	Case 1: Workday: Enterprise Cloud Software-as-a-Service (SaaS) Case 2: Evolution Homecare Manages Patients with Microsoft Dynamics CRM Instructional Video 1: GSMS Protects Products and Patients By Serializing Every Bottle of Drugs
Chapter 10: E-commerce: Digital Markets, Digital Goods	Case 1: Groupon: Deals Galore Case 2: Etsy: A Marketplace and Community Case 3: Ford AutoXchange B2B Marketplace
Chapter 11: Improving Decision Making and Managing Knowledge	Case 1: How IBM's Watson Became a Jeopardy Champion Case 2: Alfresco: Open Source Document Management and Collaboration Case 3: FreshDirect Uses Business Intelligence to Manage Its Online Grocery. Case 4: Business Intelligence Helps the Cincinnati Zoo Work Smarter Instructional Video 1: Analyzing Big Data: IBM Watson: Watson After Jeopardy
Chapter 12: Building Information Systems and Managing Projects	Case 1: IBM: BPM in a Service-Oriented Architecture Case 2: IBM Helps the City of Madrid With Real-Time BPM Software Instructional Video 1: BPM: Business Process Management Customer Story Instructional Video 2: Workflow Management Visualized

LEARNING TRACKS

Chapter	Learning Tracks
Chapter 1: Business Information Systems in Your Career	How Much Does IT Matter?
	The Changing Business Environment for IT
	The Business Information Value Chain
	The Mobile Digital Platform
	Occupational and Career Outlook for Information Systems Majors 2012-2020
Chapter 2: Global E-business and Collaboration	Systems From a Functional Perspective
	IT Enables Collaboration and Teamwork
	Challenges of Using Business Information Systems
	Organizing the Information Systems Function
Chapter 3: Achieving Competitive Advantage with Information Systems	Challenges of Using Information Systems for Competitive Advantage
	Primer on Business Process Design and Documentation
	Primer on Business Process Management
Chapter 4: Ethical and Social Issues in Information Systems	Developing a Corporate Code of Ethics for IT
Chapter 5: IT Infrastructure: Hardware and Software	How Computer Hardware and Software Work
	Service Level Agreements
	Cloud Computing
	The Open Source Software Initiative
	The Evolution of IT Infrastructure
	Technology Drivers of IT Infrastructure
	Fourth Generation Languages
Chapter 6: Foundations of Business Intelligence: Databases and Information Management	Database Design, Normalization, and Entity-Relationship Diagramming
	Introduction to SQL
	Hierarchical and Network Data Models
Chapter 7: Telecommunications, the Internet, and Wireless Technology	Broadband Network Services and Technologies
	Cellular System Generations
	Wireless Applications for Customer Relationship Management, Supply Chain Management, and Healthcare
	Introduction to Web 2.0
	LAN Topologies
Chapter 8: Securing Information Systems	The Booming Job Market in IT Security
	The Sarbanes-Oxley Act
	Computer Forensics
	General and Application Controls for Information Systems
	Management Challenges of Security and Control
	Software Vulnerability and Reliability
Chapter 9: Achieving Operational Excellence and Customer Intimacy: Enterprise Applications	SAP Business Process Map
	Business Processes in Supply Chain Management and Supply Chain Metrics
	Best-Practice Business Processes in CRM Software
Chapter 10: E-commerce: Digital Markets, Digital Goods	E-Commerce Challenges: The Story of Online Groceries
	Build an E-commerce Business Plan
	Hot New Careers in E-Commerce
	E-commerce Payment Systems
	Building an E-commerce Web Site
Chapter 11: Improving Decision Making and Managing Knowledge	Building and Using Pivot Tables
	The Expert System Inference Engine
	Challenges of Knowledge Management Systems
Chapter 12: Building Information Systems and Managing Projects	Capital Budgeting Methods for Information Systems Investments
	Enterprise Analysis: Business Systems Planning and Critical Success Factors
	Unified Modeling Language
	Information Technology Investments and Productivity

Acknowledgments

The production of any book involves valued contributions from a number of persons. We would like to thank all of our editors for encouragement, insight, and strong support for many years. We thank Bob Horan for guiding the development of this edition and Karalyn Holland for her role in managing the project.

Our special thanks go to our supplement authors for their fine work. We are indebted to Robin Pickering for her assistance with writing and to William Anderson and Megan Miller for their help during production. We thank Diana R. Craig for her assistance with database and software topics.

Special thanks to colleagues at the Stern School of Business at New York University; to Professor Werner Schenk, Simon School of Business, University of Rochester; to Robert Kostrubanic, CIO and Director of Information Technology Services, Indiana - Purdue, University Fort Wayne; to Professor Lawrence Andrew of Western Illinois University; to Professor Detlef Schoder of the University of Cologne; to Professors Walter Brenner of the University of St. Gallen; to Professor Lutz Kolbe of the University of Gottingen; to Professor Donald Marchand of the International Institute for Management Development; and to Professor Daniel Botha of Stellenbosch University who provided additional suggestions for improvement. Thank you to Professor Ken Kraemer, University of California at Irvine, and Professor John King, University of Michigan, for more than a decade's long discussion of information systems and organizations. And a special remembrance and dedication to Professor Rob Kling, University of Indiana, for being my friend and colleague over so many years.

We also want to especially thank all our reviewers whose suggestions helped improve our texts. Reviewers for this edition include the following:

Amita Chin - Virginia Commonwealth University
Gail Ann Edwards - Brown Mackie College Fort Wayne
Jennifer Grant - Augsburg College
Monique L. Herard - Robert Morris University
Rick Herschel - Saint Joseph's University
Steven Hunt - Morehead State University
Bernard W. Merkle - California Lutheran University
Timothy Stanton - Mount St. Mary's University

Information Systems in the Digital Age

PART I

Part I introduces the major themes and the problem-solving approaches that are used throughout this book. While surveying the role of information systems in today's businesses, this part raises several major questions: What is an information system? Why are information systems so essential in businesses today? How can information systems help businesses become more competitive? What do I need to know about information systems to succeed in my business career? What ethical and social issues are raised by widespread use of information systems?

Business Information Systems in Your Career

CHAPTER 1

STUDENT LEARNING OBJECTIVES

After completing this chapter, you will be able to answer the following questions:

1. How are information systems transforming business, and what is their relationship to globalization?

2. Why are information systems so essential for running and managing a business today?

3. What exactly is an information system? How does it work? What are its people, organizational, and technology components?

4. How will a four-step method for business problem solving help you solve information system-related problems?

5. How will information systems affect business careers, and what information systems skills and knowledge are essential?

LEARNING TRACKS

1. How Much Does IT Matter?
2. The Changing Business Environment for Information Technology
3. The Business Information Value Chain
4. The Mobile Digital Platform
5. Occupational and Career Outlook for Information Systems Majors 2012-2020

VIDEO CASES

Case 1: UPS Global Operations with the DIAD
Case 2: Google Data Center Efficiency Best Practices
Instructional Video 1: Green Energy Efficiency in a Data Center Using Tivoli Architecture (IBM)
Instructional Video 2: Tour IBM's Raleigh Data Center

CHAPTER OUTLINE

RUGBY FOOTBALL UNION TRIES BIG DATA

In 1871, twenty-one English clubs decided that their sport, officially called rugby union but commonly referred to simply as rugby, needed an administrative body. The clubs formed The Rugby Football Union (RFU), which today manages the English national team (England Rugby) in partnership with Premier Rugby Limited. Responsible for the promotion of rugby at all levels, the RFU organizes the Six Nations Championship, the unofficial northern hemisphere championship featuring teams from England, Scotland, Wales, Italy, Ireland and France, and the Heineken Cup, its club-level counterpart. Owned by its member clubs, the RFU's mission is to maximize profits from international ticket sales and vending so that it can support the more than 60,000 volunteers who organize matches and seminars, help secure loans and insurance policies, fundraise, write grant proposals, provide medical advice and support, and perform the clerical duties that keep the lower-level clubs operating.

To succeed in this complicated mission, the RFU entered into a five year deal with IBM to capture and analyze Big Data that will be useful to both fans, and later—it is hoped—the players themselves. The system is called TryTracker. In rugby, a try, worth five points, is the highest scoring opportunity. Teams get possession of the ball through a scrum, a contest for the ball where eight players bind together and push against eight

© Fabrique/Fotolia

players from the other team. The outcome determines who can control the ball. To score a try, a team must break through the opposition's defenses, move into their in-goal area, and "ground" the ball. This is done in one of two ways. A player can either hold the ball in one or both hands or arms and then touch it to the ground in the in-goal area, or exert downward pressure on a ball already on the ground using one or both hands or arms or the upper front of the body (from the neck to the waistline).

The IBM TryTracker does not just track tries, however. It uses predictive analytics to track three categories of data: keys to the game, momentum, and key players. Traditional rugby statistics on team and individual performance, and live text commentary, complement the TryTracker data. The keys to the game are determined ahead of a specific contest by analyzing a historical database of past matchups between a pair. For example, factors that contributed to victory may have included achieving a certain percentage of successful kicks on goal or scrums won, a specific number of lineouts, or a particular conversion rate. Fans can keep track on their mobile devices of how their favorite team is faring, concentrating on game elements that will increase its winning chances. Key players for each team are selected after the game by comparing a single score compiled using different criteria for each position. Goal scoring is currently excluded so as not to overvalue kickers and under-value players who contribute to creating scoring opportunities.

Like the IBM SlamTracker used at the Grand Slam tennis tournaments, the goal of TryTracker is to provide data visualization and real time statistics to draw in fans. To compete with more popular sports such as Premier League football and expand rugby's fan base before England hosts the 2015 Rugby World Cup, the RFU hopes that enhanced communication will increase fan engagement. As their understanding of game mechanics and emotional investment in what their team needs to do in order to prevail grows, casual fans will become dedicated fans who return again and again. Beyond marketing strategy, the long-term potential of predictive analysis is that it may provide tactical insights to players and coaches that will improve match play and thus the overall product offered to fans.

Sources: "IBM's Live 'TryTracker' IS New RFU Online Insights Tool," activative.co.uk, February 5, 2013; "About Us," rfu.com, accessed December, 14, 2013; Simon Creasey, "Rugby Football Union uses IBM predictive analytics for Six Nations," computerweekly.com, February, 2013; Steve McCaskill, "IBM TryTracker Brings Big Data To Rugby," tech-weekeurope.co.uk, February 11, 2013; Caroline Baldwin, "Rugby Football Union uses analytics to educate and engage with users," computerweekly.com, October 8, 2013; "Rugby Tries," rugby-sidestep-central.com, accessed December 13, 2013.

The challenges facing the RFU demonstrate why information systems are so essential today. The RFU is classified as a "Friendly Society," somewhere between a true company and a charity. It receives both government support and corporate sponsorship money. But it must maximize revenues from ticket sales, hospitality and catering, television rights, and its travel company in order to support both grassroots and elite rugby in England.

The chapter-opening diagram calls attention to important points raised by this case and this chapter. The RFU entered into a strategic partnership with IBM to educate and engage fans. It has a big opportunity with the 2015 Rugby World Cup to bring in additional funds to support and grow its organization. Using the data collected by sports data company Opta and the analytics developed by IBM, it may also be able to improve coaching and game performance as an additional way of cultivating customers. Football clubs have already used data provided by Opta to scout prospects based on filling a specific set of skills the team is lacking.

IBM is also helping the RFU to develop a customer relationship management (CRM) system integrated with its Web site. The goal is to move beyond one-size-fits-all mass e-mailing to a system that can provide targeted responses to specific user input. Full implementation is expected by the end of 2014 along with a revamped England Rugby mobile application designed to enrich the TryTracker experience and available for the first time in an Android as well as an iOS version.

Here are some questions to think about: What role does technology play in the RFU's success as the administrative head of rugby union in England? Assess the contributions which these systems make to the future of RFU.

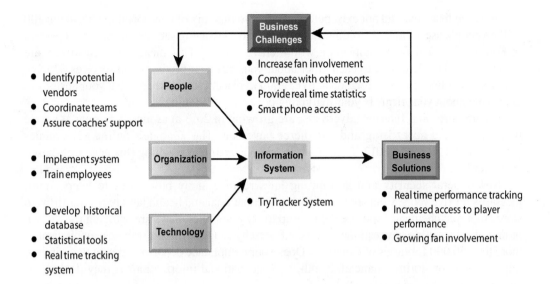

1.1 The Role of Information Systems in Business Today

It's not business as usual in the global economy. In 2013, worldwide expenditures for information technology will exceed €2.7 trillion, a 2% increase over 2012. This includes €685 billion in IT consulting services. Global investment in IT represents about one-third of all private capital investment in the world. In the United States, IT investment constitutes about 52% of all investment. IT investment in the United States is growing at about 4% annually in 2013, more than twice as fast as the entire economy (BEA, 2013; Gartner 2013). .

HOW INFORMATION SYSTEMS ARE TRANSFORMING BUSINESS

You can see the results of this massive spending around you every day by observing how people conduct business. Cell phones, smartphones, tablet computers, e-mail, and online conferencing over the Internet have all become essential tools of business. In 2012, more than 102 million businesses had dot-com Internet sites registered. Approximately 193 million adult Americans are online, 19 million purchase something every day on the Internet, 40 million research a product, and 116 million use a search engine. What this means is that if you and your business aren't connected to the Internet and wireless networks, chances are you are not being as effective as you could be (Pew Internet and American Life, 2013).

Despite the economic downturn, in 2012 FedEx moved over one billion packages in the United States, mostly overnight, and United Parcel Service (UPS) moved more than 4 billion packages, as businesses sought to sense and respond to rapidly changing customer demand, reduce inventories to the lowest possible levels, and achieve higher levels of operational efficiency. The growth of e-commerce has had a significant impact on UPS's shipping volume. Supply chains have become more fast paced, with companies of all sizes depending on the delivery of just-in-time inventory to help them compete. Companies today manage their inventories in near real time in order to reduce their overhead costs and get to market faster. If you are not a part of this new supply chain management economy, chances are your business is not as efficient as it could be.

As newspaper readership continues to decline, 150 million people read at least some of their news online, 110 million read actual newspapers online, and 170 million use a social networking site like Facebook, Tumblr, or Google+. Over 100 million bank online, and around 74 million now read blogs, creating an explosion of new writers, readers, and new forms of customer feedback that did not exist before. Adding to this mix of new social media, about 100 million people use Twitter, the online and cellular text messaging service, including 80 percent of Fortune 500 firms communicating with their customers. This means your customers are empowered and able to talk to each other about your business products and services. Do you have a solid online customer relationship program in place? Do you know what your customers are saying about your firm? Is your marketing department listening?

E-commerce and Internet advertising are growing in 2013 at around 7 percent at a time when traditional advertising and commerce have been flat. Google's online ad revenues surpassed $50 billion in 2012. Is your advertising department reaching this new Web-based customer?

New federal security and accounting laws require many businesses to keep e-mail messages for five years. Coupled with existing occupational and health laws requiring firms to store employee chemical exposure data for up to 60 years, these laws are spurring the growth of digital information now estimated to be 1.8 zettabytes (1.8 trillion gigabytes), equivalent to more than 50,000 Libraries of Congress. Does your compliance department meet the minimal requirements for storing financial, health, and occupational information? If they don't, your entire business may be at risk.

Briefly, it's a new world of doing business, one that will greatly affect your future business career. Along with the changes in business come changes in jobs and careers. No matter whether you are a finance, accounting, management, marketing, operations management, or information systems major, how you work, where you work, and how well you are compensated will all be affected by business information systems. The purpose of this book is to help you understand and benefit from these new business realities and opportunities.

WHAT'S NEW IN MANAGEMENT INFORMATION SYSTEMS?

Lots! What makes management information systems the most exciting topic in business is the continual change in technology, management use of the technology, and the impact on business success. New businesses and industries appear, old ones decline, and successful firms are those that learn how to use the new technologies. Table 1.1 summarizes the major new themes in business uses of information systems. These themes will appear throughout the book in all the chapters, so it might be a good idea to take some time now and discuss these with your professor and other students.

In the technology area are three interrelated changes: (1) the mobile digital platform composed of smartphones and tablet devices, (2) the growing business use of "big data," and (3) the growth in "cloud computing," where more and more business software runs over the Internet.

IPhones, Android phones, BlackBerrys, and high definition tablet computers are not just gadgets or entertainment outlets. They represent new emerging computing and media platforms based on an array of new hardware and software technologies. More and more business computing is moving from PCs and desktop machines to these mobile devices. Managers are increasingly using these devices to coordinate work, communicate with employees, and provide information for decision making. In 2013, more than half of Internet users will access the Web through mobile devices. To a large extent these devices change the character of corporate computing.

Managers routinely use online collaboration and social technologies in order to make better, faster decisions. As management behavior changes, how work gets organized, coordinated, and measured also changes. By connecting employees working on teams and projects, the social network is where work gets done, where plans are executed, and where managers manage. Output from social networks as well as from Web traffic and machine-generated data from sensors is creating vast pools of Big Data, with the potential for much more fine-grained data analysis and insights.

The strength of cloud computing, and the growth of the mobile digital platform, mean that organizations can rely more on telework, remote work, and distributed decision making.

TABLE 1.1

What's New in MIS

Change	Business Impact
TECHNOLOGY	
Cloud computing platform emerges as a major business area of innovation	A flexible collection of computers on the Internet begins to perform tasks traditionally performed on corporate computers. Major business applications are delivered online as an Internet service (Software as a Service-SaaS).
Big Data	Businesses look for insights from huge volumes of data from Web traffic, e-mail messages, social media content, and machines (sensors).
A mobile digital platform emerges to compete with the PC as a business system	The Apple iPhone and Android mobile devices are able to download hundreds of thousands of applications to support collaboration, location-based services, and communication with colleagues. Small tablet computers, including the iPad and Kindle Fire, challenge conventional laptops as platforms for consumer and corporate computing.
MANAGEMENT	
Managers adopt online collaboration and social networking software to improve coordination, collaboration, and knowledge sharing.	Google Apps, Google Sites, Microsoft's Windows SharePoint Services, and IBM's Lotus Connections are used by over 100 million business professionals worldwide to support blogs, project management, online meetings, personal profiles, social bookmarks, and online communities.
Business intelligence applications accelerate.	More powerful data analytics and interactive dashboards provide real-time performance information to managers to enhance decision making.
Virtual meetings proliferate.	Managers adopt telepresence, video conferencing, and Web conferencing technologies to reduce travel time, and cost, while improving collaboration and decision making.
ORGANIZATIONS	
Social business	Businesses use social networking platforms, including Facebook, Twitter, and internal corporate social tools, to deepen interactions with employees, customers, and suppliers. Employees use blogs, wikis, e-mail texting, and messaging to interact in online communities.
Telework gains momentum in the workplace.	The Internet, wireless laptops, smartphones, and tablet computers make it possible for growing numbers of people to work away from the traditional office. 55 percent of U.S. businesses have some form of remote work program.
Co-creation of business value	Sources of business value shift from products to solutions and experiences and from internal sources to networks of suppliers and collaboration with customers. Supply chains and product development become more global and collaborative; customer interactions help firms define new products and services.

This same platform means firms can outsource more work, and rely on markets (rather than employees) to build value. It also means that firms can collaborate with suppliers and customers to create new products, or make existing products more efficiently.

You can see some of these trends at work in the Interactive Session on People. Millions of managers and employees rely heavily on the mobile digital platform to coordinate suppliers

How much of your job can you do from the palm of your hand? Probably more than you think. There are many job functions today that can be performed using an iPad, iPhone, BlackBerry, or Android mobile device, both for rank-and-file employees and their managers. Businesses large and small are benefiting.

The BlackBerry used to be the favorite mobile handheld for business because it was optimized for e-mail and messaging, with strong security and tools for accessing internal corporate systems. Now that's changing. Companies large and small are starting to deploy Apple's iPhone and iPad as well as Android devices to conduct more of their work. They are enhancing their security systems so that mobile users can remotely access corporate systems with confidence. And they are developing more far-reaching applications to take advantage of the stunning mobile and graphic capabilities.

Many of the recent mobile applications have been for e-mailing, or for supplementing existing workplace tasks, like digital flight manuals for airplane pilots on iPads or checking in guests at hotels. But now, as mobile technology becomes more affordable and easy to use, it's spreading core work functions as well, such as marketing materials for pharmaceutical reps, customer account software for service technicians, and apps for farmers to test the quality of cow's milk.

Jackson Kayak is the leading whitewater kayak manufacturer. Its president, Eric Jackson, is a champion kayaker who spends half of each year following competitions and events throughout North America. Eric's job requires that he participate in athletic events, monitor industry trends in the field, and meet directly with dealers and customers. With the iPhone and iPad, Jackson claims he can run the entire 120-person company from afar.

Jackson's Wi-Fi-equipped RV connects wirelessly to company headquarters in Sparta, Tennessee. When Jackson's not on Wi-Fi, he uses his iPad 3G cellular connection. The iPad gives him instant access to his entire operation, so he can analyze customer data, refresh Website content, or approve new designs. Jackson's iPad includes calendars, e-mail, contact management, and the ability to create and edit documents, spreadsheets, and presentations—all the tools this executive needs to communicate with the home office, dealers, and customers.

Back at the shop, Jackson Kayak's managers and employees find iPad and iPhone equally invaluable. In the factory, Chief Operations Officer John Ratliff can compare Jackson Kayak's manufacturing equipment side-by-side with images of replacement parts on the iPad to make sure he's getting the correct pieces. The iPhone and iPad have become so indispensable that the company outfitted its entire workforce, from customer service, to design, to quality control, with iPhones. Many have iPads as well.

Using handhelds to run the business is not limited to small companies. PepsiCo manufactures and sells brands including Pepsi, Gatorade, Mountain Dew, Tropicana, Quaker, and Frito-Lay worldwide and has over 300,000 employees. The company uses a complex web of interlocking distribution systems to move its products from its manufacturing and warehouse facilities onto trucks and then into stores in time to meet customer demand. PepsiCo runs about 17,000 distribution routes each day. The iPhone and iPad help employees of PepsiCo's North America Beverages division ensure that the right products arrive in the right locations as quickly and efficiently as possible.

In the past, PepsiCo drivers and merchandisers began each day by picking up printed schedules with order quantities and tasks to be performed at each outlet, from unloading cases of soda to setting up new product displays. It was difficult to accommodate last-minute changes in orders because communicating with the delivery drivers was difficult when they were on the road.

PepsiCo North America Beverages created a custom in-house app for the iPhone called Power4Merch, which immediately notifies merchandisers when a driver has arrived at a store. The merchandiser's iPhone has an electronic timecard, and he can see his schedule, the store details, the account profiles, and everything he needs to know to service the store.

PepsiCo managers use iPads with custom applications to monitor their teams' performance; pull up pricing, planograms, and contracts; and help coordinate deliveries with merchandising. The Manager's Briefcase app provides territory sales managers with electronic versions of all the paperwork and resources they need to manage their teams, including store audits, employee coaching forms, and automated notifications to merchandisers. A manager can make manpower assignments directly on the iPad. The iPad automatically sends a notification to the merchandiser's iPhone informing him he has an additional stop to make, for example. In the past, managers had to spend much of their time on the phone, checking e-mail in the office, and checking paperwork. With the iPad, the manager starts and ends his day with his team.

The second iPad app, called SPOTLight, gives managers instant access to their Web-based SharePoint content. They can pull out pricing, display planograms, customer development agreements, or new contracts.

PepsiCo's iPhone and iPad systems are integrated with its established corporate information systems. The company uses Mobile Device Management from AirWatch to securely deploy and manage its mobile applications and also takes advantage of the built-in security on iPhone and iPad to protect them from unauthorized access.

PepsiCo's main competitor, beverage-bottling company Coca-Cola Enterprises Inc. (CCE), is benefiting from mobile technology as well. CCE uses mobile field service software from ServiceMax Inc. to streamline the work activities of its technicians, who service restaurant soda fountains and fix vending machines. Previously, after a technician visited a customer on site, he would go back to his car, transfer information from paper notes into a database on his laptop, and transmit it to Coca-Cola's aging centralized software system. Many technicians spent an extra half hour at the end of each day polishing their paperwork.

In 2012 about 100 CCE employees started using ServiceMax apps on iPhones to dispatch technicians to a day's worth of service calls, provide detailed customer information, automatically update lists of service parts stored in their vans, and transfer information to the billing department. The new system cut administration time for service technicians by a third, and employees are freed up to service other companies' equipment in addition to CCE's own. ServiceMax charges about $1000 per person per year for a subscription.

Sources: Shira Ovide, "Meet the New Mobile Workers," *The Wall Street Journal*, March 11, 2013; "Apple iPad in Business," www.apple.com, accessed April 18, 2013; and Aaron Freimark, "Apple Offers More iPad Management Features Than You Might Think," searchconsumerization.com, April 2, 2013.

CASE STUDY QUESTIONS

1. What kinds of applications are described here? What business functions do they support? How do they improve operational efficiency and decision making?

2. Identify the problems that businesses in this case study solved by using mobile digital devices.

3. What kinds of businesses are most likely to benefit from equipping their employees with mobile digital devices such as iPhones and iPads?

4. One company deploying iPhones has said, "The iPhone is not a game changer, it's an industry changer. It changes the way that you can interact with your customers" and "with your suppliers." Discuss the implications of this statement.

iPhone and iPad Business Applications

1. *Salesforce Mobile*
2. *Cisco WebEx*
3. *SAP Business ByDesign*
4. *iWork*
5. *QuickBooks Online*
6. *Adobe Reader*
7. *Oracle Business Intelligence*
8. *Dropbox*

© STANCA SANDA/Alamy.

Whether it's attending an online meeting, checking orders, working with files and documents, or obtaining business intelligence, Apple's iPhone and iPad offer unlimited possibilities for business users. A stunning multitouch display, full Internet browsing, and capabilities for messaging, video and audio transmission, and document management, make each an all-purpose platform for mobile computing.

and shipments, satisfy customers, and organize work activities. A business day without these mobile devices or Internet access would be unthinkable. As you read this case, note how the mobile platform has changed the way people do their work and make decisions.

GLOBALIZATION CHALLENGES AND OPPORTUNITIES: A FLATTENED WORLD

Prior to 1492 and the voyages of Columbus and others to the Americas, there was no truly global economic system of trade that connected all the continents on earth. After the fifteenth century, a global trading system began to emerge. The world trade that ensued after these voyages has brought the peoples and cultures of the world much closer together. The "industrial revolution" was really a worldwide phenomenon energized by expansion of trade among nations. Until the Internet was invented and refined, the global economy was inefficient because it was difficult and costly to communicate from one corner of the earth to another.

By 2005, journalist Thomas Friedman wrote an influential book declaring the world was now "flat," by which he meant that the Internet and global communications had greatly expanded the opportunities for people to communicate with one another, and reduced the economic and cultural advantages of developed countries. U.S. and European countries were in a fight for their economic lives, competing for jobs, markets, resources, and even ideas with highly educated, motivated populations in low-wage areas in the less developed world (Friedman, 2007). This "globalization" presents you and your business with both challenges and opportunities.

A growing percentage of the economy of the United States and other advanced industrial countries in Europe and Asia depends on imports and exports. In 2013, more than 33 percent of the U.S. economy resulted from foreign trade, both imports and exports. In Europe and Asia, the number exceeds 50 percent. Half of the Fortune 500 U.S. firms derive at least half their revenues from foreign operations. For instance, more than 50 percent of Intel's revenues in 2012 came from overseas sales of its microprocessors, and the same is true for General Electric, Ford Motor Company, IBM, Dow Chemical, and McDonald's. Toys for chips: 80 percent of the toys sold in the United States are manufactured in China, while about 90 percent of the PCs manufactured in China use American-made Intel or Advanced Micro Design (AMD) chips.

It's not just goods that move across borders. So too do jobs, some of them high-level jobs that pay well and require a college degree. In the past decade, the United States lost several million manufacturing jobs to offshore, low-wage producers. But manufacturing is now a very small part of U.S. employment (less than 12 percent). In a normal year, about 300,000 service jobs move offshore to lower-wage countries, many of them in less-skilled information system occupations, but also include "tradable service" jobs in architecture, financial services, customer call centers, consulting, engineering, and even radiology.

On the plus side, the U.S. economy creates over 3.5 million new jobs in a normal year. Employment in information systems and the other service occupations listed previously have expanded in sheer numbers, wages, productivity, and quality of work. Outsourcing has actually accelerated the development of new systems in the United States and worldwide. In the midst of an economic recession, jobs in information systems are among the most in demand.

The challenge for you as a business student is to develop high-level skills through education and on-the-job experience that cannot be outsourced. The challenge for your business is to avoid markets for goods and services that can be produced offshore much less expensively. The opportunities are equally immense. You can learn how to profit from the lower costs available in world markets and the chance to serve a marketplace with billions of customers. You have the opportunity to develop higher-level and more profitable products and services. You will find throughout this book examples of companies and individuals who either failed or succeeded in using information systems to adapt to this new global environment.

What does globalization have to do with management information systems? That's simple: everything. The emergence of the Internet into a full-blown international communications system has drastically reduced the costs of operating and transacting on a global scale. Communication between a factory floor in Shanghai and a distribution center in Sioux Falls, South Dakota, is now instant and virtually free. Customers now can shop in a worldwide marketplace, obtaining price and quality information reliably 24 hours a day. Firms producing goods and services on a global scale achieve extraordinary cost reductions by finding low-cost suppliers and managing production facilities in other countries. Internet service firms, such as Google and eBay, are able to replicate their business models and services in multiple countries without having to redesign their expensive fixed-cost information systems infrastructure.

BUSINESS DRIVERS OF INFORMATION SYSTEMS

What makes information systems so essential today? Why are businesses investing so much in information systems and technologies? They do so to achieve six important business objectives: operational excellence; new products, services, and business models; customer and supplier intimacy; improved decision making; competitive advantage; and survival.

Operational Excellence

Businesses continuously seek to improve the efficiency of their operations in order to achieve higher profitability. Information systems and technologies are some of the most important tools available to managers for achieving higher levels of efficiency and productivity in business operations, especially when coupled with changes in business practices and management behavior.

Walmart, the largest retailer on Earth, exemplifies the power of information systems coupled with brilliant business practices and supportive management to achieve world-class operational efficiency. In fiscal year 2013, Walmart achieved more than $469 billion in sales—nearly one-tenth of retail sales in the United States—in large part because of its Retail Link system, which digitally links its suppliers to every one of Walmart's 9,600 stores worldwide. As soon as a customer purchases an item, the supplier monitoring the item knows to ship a replacement to the shelf. Walmart is the most efficient retail store in the industry, achieving sales of more than $450 per square foot, compared to its closest competitor, Target, at $425 a square foot, with other large retail firms producing less than $12 a square foot.

Amazon, the largest online retailer on earth, generating $61 billion in sales in 2012, invested $2.1 billion in information systems so that when one of its estimated 170 million customers searches for a product, Amazon can respond in milliseconds with the correct product displayed (and recommendations for other products).

New Products, Services, and Business Models

Information systems and technologies are a major enabling tool for firms to create new products and services, as well as entirely new business models. A **business model** describes how a company produces, delivers, and sells a product or service to create wealth. Today's music industry is vastly different from the industry a decade ago. Apple Inc. transformed an old business model of music distribution based on vinyl records, tapes, and CDs into an online, legal distribution model based on its own operating system and iTunes store. Apple has prospered from a continuing stream of innovations, including the original iPod, iPod nano, iTunes music service, iPhone, and iPad.

Customer and Supplier Intimacy

When a business really knows its customers and serves them well, the way they want to be served, the customers generally respond by returning and purchasing more. This raises revenues and profits. Likewise with suppliers: the more a business engages its suppliers, the better the suppliers can provide vital inputs. This lowers costs. How to really know your customers, or suppliers, is a central problem for businesses with millions of offline and online customers.

The Mandarin Oriental in Manhattan and other high-end hotels exemplify the use of information systems and technologies to achieve customer intimacy. These hotels use computers to keep track of guests' preferences, such as their preferred room temperature, check-in time, frequently dialed telephone numbers, and television programs, and store these data in a giant data repository. Individual rooms in the hotels are networked to a central network server computer so that they can be remotely monitored or controlled. When a customer arrives at one of these hotels, the system automatically changes the room conditions, such as dimming the lights, setting the room temperature, or selecting appropriate music, based on the customer's digital profile. The hotels also analyze their customer data to identify their best customers and to develop individualized marketing campaigns based on customers' preferences.

JCPenney exemplifies the benefits of information systems-enabled supplier intimacy. Every time a dress shirt is bought at a JCPenney store in the United States, the record of the sale appears immediately on computers in Hong Kong at TAL Apparel Ltd., a giant contract manufacturer that produces one in eight dress shirts sold in the United States. TAL runs the numbers through a computer model it developed and decides how many replacement shirts to make, and in what styles, colors, and sizes. TAL then sends the shirts to each JCPenney store, completely bypassing the retailer's warehouses. In other words, JCPenney's surplus shirt inventory is near zero, as is the cost of storing it.

Improved Decision Making

Many business managers operate in an information fog bank, never really having the right information at the right time to make an informed decision. Instead, managers rely on forecasts, best guesses, and luck. The result is over- or underproduction of goods and services, misallocation of resources, and poor response times. These poor outcomes raise costs and lose customers. In the past 10 years, information systems and technologies have made it possible for managers to use real-time data from the marketplace when making decisions.

For instance, Verizon Corporation, one of the largest regional Bell operating companies in the United States, uses a Web-based digital dashboard to provide managers with precise real-time information on customer complaints, network performance for each locality served, and line outages or storm-damaged lines. Using this information, managers can immediately allocate repair resources to affected areas, inform consumers of repair efforts, and restore service fast.

Competitive Advantage

When firms achieve one or more of these business objectives—operational excellence; new products, services, and business models; customer/supplier intimacy; and improved decision making—chances are they have already achieved a competitive advantage. Doing things better than your competitors, charging less for superior products, and responding to customers and suppliers in real time all add up to higher sales and higher profits that your competitors cannot match. Apple Inc., Walmart, and UPS are industry leaders because they know how to use information systems for this purpose.

Survival

Business firms also invest in information systems and technologies because they are necessities of doing business. Sometimes these necessities are driven by industry-level changes. For instance, after Citibank introduced the first automated teller machines (ATMs) in the New York region to attract customers through higher service levels, its competitors rushed to provide ATMs to their customers to keep up with Citibank. Today, virtually all banks in the United States have regional ATMs and link to national and international ATM networks, such as CIRRUS. Providing ATM services to retail banking customers is simply a requirement of being in and surviving in the retail banking business.

Many federal and state statutes and regulations create a legal duty for companies and their employees to retain records, including digital records. For instance, the Toxic Substances Control Act (1976), which regulates the exposure of U.S. workers to more than 75,000 toxic chemicals, requires firms to retain records on employee exposure for 30 years. The Sarbanes-Oxley Act (2002), which was intended to improve the accountability of public firms and their auditors, requires public companies to retain audit working papers and records, including all e-mails, for five years. Firms turn to information systems and technologies to provide the capability to respond to these information retention and reporting requirements. The Dodd–Frank Act (2010) requires financial service firms to greatly expand their public reporting on derivatives and other financial instruments.

1.2 Perspectives on Information Systems and Information Technology

So far we've used *information systems and technologies* informally without defining the terms. **Information technology (IT)** consists of all the hardware and software that a firm needs to use in order to achieve its business objectives. This includes not only computer machines, disk drives, and mobile handheld devices but also software, such as the Windows or Linux operating systems, the Microsoft Office desktop productivity suite, and the many thousands of computer programs that can be found in a typical large firm. "Information systems" are more complex and can be best understood by looking at them from both a technology and a business perspective.

WHAT IS AN INFORMATION SYSTEM?

An **information system (IS)** can be defined technically as a set of interrelated components that collect (or retrieve), process, store, and distribute information to support decision making, coordinating, and control in an organization. In addition, information systems may also help managers and workers analyze problems, visualize complex subjects, and create new products.

Information systems contain information about significant people, places, and things within the organization or in the environment surrounding it. By **information** we mean data that have been shaped into a form that is meaningful and useful to human beings. **Data**, in contrast, are streams of raw facts representing events occurring in organizations or the physical environment before they have been organized and arranged into a form that people can understand and use.

A brief example contrasting information and data may prove useful. Supermarket checkout counters scan millions of pieces of data, such as bar codes, that describe the product. Such pieces of data can be totaled and analyzed to provide meaningful information, such as the total number of bottles of dish detergent sold at a particular store, which brands of dish detergent were selling the most rapidly at that store or sales territory, or the total amount spent on that brand of dish detergent at that store or sales region (see Figure 1.1).

Three activities in an information system produce the information that organizations need to make decisions, control operations, analyze problems, and create new products or services. These activities are input, processing, and output (see Figure 1.2). **Input** captures or collects raw data from within the organization or from its external environment. **Processing** converts this raw input into a meaningful form. **Output** transfers the processed information to the people who will use it or to the activities for which it will be used. Information systems also require **feedback**, which is output that is returned to appropriate members of the organization to help them evaluate or correct the input stage.

In the San Francisco Giants system for selling tickets, the raw input consists of order data for tickets, such as the purchaser's name, address, credit card number, number of tickets ordered, and the date of the game for which the ticket is being purchased. Another input would be the ticket price, which would fluctuate based on computer analysis of how much could optimally be charged for a ticket for a particular game. Computers store these data and process them to calculate order totals, to track ticket purchases, and to send requests for payment to credit card companies. The output consists of tickets to print out, receipts for orders, and reports on online ticket orders. The system provides meaningful information, such as

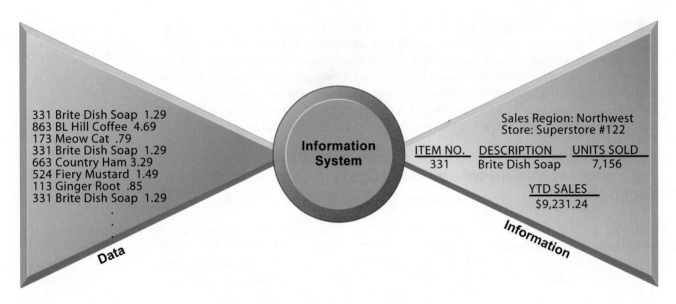

Figure 1.1
Data and Information
Raw data from a supermarket checkout counter can be processed and organized to produce meaningful information, such as the total unit sales of dish detergent or the total sales revenue from dish detergent for a specific store or sales territory.

the number of tickets sold for a particular game or at a particular price, the total number of tickets sold each year, and frequent customers.

Although computer-based information systems use computer technology to process raw data into meaningful information, there is a sharp distinction between a computer and a computer program and an information system. Electronic computers and related

Figure 1.2
Functions of an Information System
An information system contains information about an organization and its surrounding environment. Three basic activities—input, processing, and output—produce the information organizations need. Feedback is output returned to appropriate people or activities in the organization to evaluate and refine the input. Environmental actors, such as customers, suppliers, competitors, stockholders, and regulatory agencies, interact with the organization and its information systems.

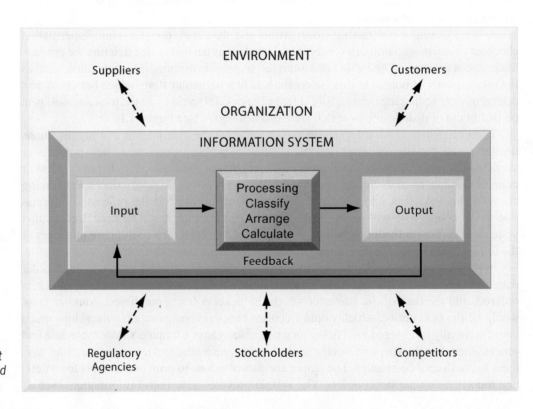

software programs are the technical foundation, the tools and materials, of modern information systems. Computers provide the equipment for storing and processing information. Computer programs, or software, are sets of operating instructions that direct and control computer processing. Knowing how computers and computer programs work is important in designing solutions to organizational problems, but computers are only part of an information system.

A house is an appropriate analogy. Houses are built with hammers, nails, and wood, but these alone do not make a house. The architecture, design, setting, landscaping, and all of the decisions that lead to the creation of these features are part of the house and are crucial for solving the problem of putting a roof over one's head. Computers and programs are the hammer, nails, and lumber of computer-based information systems, but alone they cannot produce the information a particular organization needs. To understand information systems, you must understand the problems they are designed to solve, their architectural and design elements, and the organizational processes that lead to these solutions.

IT ISN'T SIMPLY TECHNOLOGY: THE ROLE OF PEOPLE AND ORGANIZATIONS

To fully understand information systems, you will need to be aware of the broader organization, people, and information technology dimensions of systems (see Figure 1.3) and their power to provide solutions to challenges and problems in the business environment. We refer to this broader understanding of information systems, which encompasses an understanding of the people and organizational dimensions of systems as well as the technical dimensions of systems, as **information systems literacy**. Information systems literacy includes a behavioral as well as a technical approach to studying information systems. **Computer literacy**, in contrast, focuses primarily on knowledge of information technology.

The field of **management information systems (MIS)** tries to achieve this broader information systems literacy. MIS deals with behavioral issues as well as technical issues surrounding the development, use, and impact of information systems used by managers and employees in the firm.

DIMENSIONS OF INFORMATION SYSTEMS

Let's examine each of the dimensions of information systems—organizations, people, and information technology.

Figure 1.3
Information Systems Are More Than Computers
Using information systems effectively requires an understanding of the organization, people, and information technology shaping the systems. An information system provides a solution to important business problems or challenges facing the firm.

Organizations

Information systems are an integral part of organizations. And although we tend to think about information technology changing organizations and business firms, it is, in fact, a two-way street: The history and culture of business firms also affects how the technology is used and how it should be used. In order to understand how a specific business firm uses information systems, you need to know something about the structure, history, and culture of the company.

Organizations have a structure that is composed of different levels and specialties. Their structures reveal a clear-cut division of labor. A business firm is organized as a hierarchy, or a pyramid structure, of rising authority and responsibility. The upper levels of the hierarchy consist of managerial, professional, and technical employees, whereas the lower levels consist of operational personnel. Experts are employed and trained for different business functions, such as sales and marketing, manufacturing and production, finance and accounting, and human resources. Information systems are built by the firm in order to serve these different specialties and different levels of the firm. Chapter 2 provides more detail on these business functions and organizational levels and the ways in which they are supported by information systems.

An organization accomplishes and coordinates work through this structured hierarchy and through its **business processes**, which are logically related tasks and behaviors for accomplishing work. Developing a new product, fulfilling an order, and hiring a new employee are examples of business processes.

Most organizations' business processes include formal rules that have been developed over a long time for accomplishing tasks. These rules guide employees in a variety of procedures, from writing an invoice to responding to customer complaints. Some of these business processes have been written down, but others are informal work practices, such as a requirement to return telephone calls from coworkers or customers, that are not formally documented. Information systems automate many business processes. For instance, how a customer receives credit or how a customer is billed is often determined by an information system that incorporates a set of formal business processes.

Each organization has a unique **culture**, or fundamental set of assumptions, values, and ways of doing things, that has been accepted by most of its members. Parts of an organization's culture can always be found embedded in its information systems. For instance, the United Parcel Service's concern with placing service to the customer first is an aspect of its organizational culture that can be found in the company's package tracking systems.

Different levels and specialties in an organization create different interests and points of view. These views often conflict. Conflict is the basis for organizational politics. Information systems come out of this cauldron of differing perspectives, conflicts, compromises, and agreements that are a natural part of all organizations.

People

A business is only as good as the people who work there and run it. Likewise with information systems—they are useless without skilled people to build and maintain them, and without people who can understand how to use the information in a system to achieve business objectives.

For instance, a call center that provides help to customers using an advanced customer relationship management system (described in later chapters) is useless if employees are not adequately trained to deal with customers, find solutions to their problems, and leave the customer feeling that the company cares for them. Likewise, employee attitudes about their jobs, employers, or technology can have a powerful effect on their abilities to use information systems productively.

Business firms require many different kinds of skills and people, including managers as well as rank-and-file employees. The job of managers is to make sense out of the many situations faced by organizations, make decisions, and formulate action plans to solve organizational problems. Managers perceive business challenges in the environment, they set the organizational strategy for responding to those challenges, and they allocate the human and financial resources to coordinate the work and achieve success. Throughout, they must exercise responsible leadership.

But managers must do more than manage what already exists. They must also create new products and services and even re-create the organization from time to time. A substantial part of management responsibility is creative work driven by new knowledge and information. Information technology can play a powerful role in helping managers develop novel solutions to a broad range of problems.

As you will learn throughout this text, technology is relatively inexpensive today, but people are very expensive. Because people are the only ones capable of business problem solving and converting information technology into useful business solutions, we spend considerable effort in this text looking at the people dimension of information systems.

Technology

Information technology is one of many tools managers use to cope with change and complexity. **Computer hardware** is the physical equipment used for input, processing, and output activities in an information system. It consists of the following: computers of various sizes and shapes; various input, output, and storage devices; and telecommunications devices that link computers together.

Computer software consists of the detailed, preprogrammed instructions that control and coordinate the computer hardware components in an information system. Chapter 5 describes the contemporary software and hardware platforms used by firms today in greater detail.

Data management technology consists of the software governing the organization of data on physical storage media. More detail on data organization and access methods can be found in Chapter 6.

Networking and telecommunications technology, consisting of both physical devices and software, links the various pieces of hardware and transfers data from one physical location to another. Computers and communications equipment can be connected in networks for sharing voice, data, images, sound, and video. A **network** links two or more computers to share data or resources, such as a printer.

The world's largest and most widely used network is the **Internet**. The Internet is a global "network of networks" that uses universal standards (described in Chapter 7) to connect millions of different networks in over 230 countries around the world.

The Internet has created a new "universal" technology platform on which to build new products, services, strategies, and business models. This same technology platform has internal uses, providing the connectivity to link different systems and networks within the firm. Internal corporate networks based on Internet technology are called **intranets**. Private intranets extended to authorized users outside the organization are called **extranets**, and firms use such networks to coordinate their activities with other firms for making purchases, collaborating on design, and performing other interorganizational work. For most business firms today, using Internet technology is a business necessity and a competitive advantage.

The **World Wide Web** is a service provided by the Internet that uses universally accepted standards for storing, retrieving, formatting, and displaying information in a page format on the Internet. Web pages contain text, graphics, animations, sound, and video and are linked to other Web pages. By clicking on highlighted words or buttons on a Web page, you can link to related pages to find additional information and links to other locations on the Web. The Web can serve as the foundation for new kinds of information systems such as UPS's Web-based package tracking system.

All of these technologies, along with the people required to run and manage them, represent resources that can be shared throughout the organization and constitute the firm's **information technology (IT) infrastructure**. The IT infrastructure provides the foundation, or *platform*, on which the firm can build its specific information systems. Each organization must carefully design and manage its information technology infrastructure so that it has the set of technology services it needs for the work it wants to accomplish with information systems. Chapters 5 through 8 of this text examine each major technology component of information technology infrastructure and show how they all work together to create the technology platform for the organization.

The Interactive Session on Technology describes some of the typical technologies used in computer-based information systems today. UPS invests heavily in information systems technology to make its business more efficient and customer oriented. It uses an array of information technologies including bar code scanning systems, wireless networks, large mainframe computers, handheld computers, the Internet, and many different pieces of software for tracking packages, calculating fees, maintaining customer accounts, and managing logistics. As you read this case, try to identify the problem this company was facing, what alternative solutions were available to management, and how well the chosen solution worked.

Let's identify the organization, people, and technology elements in the UPS package tracking system we have just described. The organization element anchors the package tracking system in UPS's sales and production functions (the main product of UPS is a service—package delivery). It specifies the required procedures for identifying packages with both sender and recipient information, taking inventory, tracking the packages en route, and providing package status reports for UPS customers and customer service representatives.

The system must also provide information to satisfy the needs of managers and workers. UPS drivers need to be trained in both package pickup and delivery procedures and in how to use the package tracking system so that they can work efficiently and effectively. UPS customers may need some training to use UPS in-house package tracking software or the UPS Web site.

UPS's management is responsible for monitoring service levels and costs and for promoting the company's strategy of combining low cost and superior service. Management decided to use automation to increase the ease of sending a package using UPS and of checking its delivery status, thereby reducing delivery costs and increasing sales revenues.

The technology supporting this system consists of handheld computers, bar code scanners, wired and wireless communications networks, desktop computers, UPS's central computer, storage technology for the package delivery data, UPS in-house package tracking software, and software to access the World Wide Web. The result is an information system solution to the business challenge of providing a high level of service with low prices in the face of mounting competition.

1.3 Understanding Information Systems: A Business Problem-Solving Approach

Our approach to understanding information systems is to consider information systems and technologies as solutions to a variety of business challenges and problems. We refer to this as a "problem-solving approach." Businesses face many challenges and problems, and information systems are one major way of solving these problems. All of the cases in this book illustrate how a company used information systems to solve a specific problem.

The problem-solving approach has direct relevance to your future career. Your future employers will hire you because you are able to solve business problems and achieve business objectives. Your knowledge of how information systems contribute to problem solving will be very helpful to both you and your employers.

THE PROBLEM-SOLVING APPROACH

At first glance, problem solving in daily life seems to be perfectly straightforward: A machine breaks down, parts and oil spill all over the floor, and, obviously, somebody has to do something about it. So, of course, you find a tool around the shop and start repairing the

INTERACTIVE SESSION: TECHNOLOGY   UPS Competes Globally with Information Technology

United Parcel Service (UPS) started out in 1907 in a closet-sized basement office. Jim Casey and Claude Ryan—two teenagers from Seattle with two bicycles and one phone—promised the "best service and lowest rates." UPS has used this formula successfully for more than a century to become the world's largest ground and air package-delivery company. It's a global enterprise with nearly 400,000 employees, 96,000 vehicles, and the world's ninth largest airline.

Today UPS delivers 16.3 million packages and documents each day in the United States and more than 220 other countries and territories. The firm has been able to maintain leadership in small-package delivery services despite stiff competition from FedEx and Airborne Express by investing heavily in advanced information technology. UPS spends more than $1 billion each year to maintain a high level of customer service while keeping costs low and streamlining its overall operations.

It all starts with the scannable bar-coded label attached to a package, which contains detailed information about the sender, the destination, and when the package should arrive. Customers can download and print their own labels using special software provided by UPS or by accessing the UPS Web site. Before the package is even picked up, information from the "smart" label is transmitted to one of UPS's computer centers in Mahwah, New Jersey, or Alpharetta, Georgia and sent to the distribution center nearest its final destination.

Dispatchers at this center download the label data and use special software to create the most efficient delivery route for each driver that considers traffic, weather conditions, and the location of each stop. In 2009, UPS began installing sensors in its delivery vehicles that can capture the truck's speed and location, the number of times it's placed in reverse and whether the driver's seat belt is buckled. At the end of each day, this information is uploaded to a UPS central computer and analyzed overnight. By combining GPS information and data from fuel-efficiency sensors installed on more than 46,000 vehicles, UPS in 2011 reduced fuel consumption by 8.4 million gallons and cut 85 million miles off its routes.

The first thing a UPS driver picks up each day is a handheld computer called a Delivery Information Acquisition Device (DIAD), which can access a wireless cell phone network. As soon as the driver logs on, his or her day's route is downloaded onto the handheld. The DIAD also automatically captures customers' signatures along with pickup and delivery information. Package tracking information is then transmitted to UPS's com-

puter network for storage and processing. From there, the information can be accessed worldwide to provide proof of delivery to customers or to respond to customer queries. It usually takes less than 60 seconds from the time a driver presses "complete" on the DIAD for the new information to be available on the Web.

Through its automated package tracking system, UPS can monitor and even reroute packages throughout the delivery process. At various points along the route from sender to receiver, bar code devices scan shipping information on the package label and feed data about the progress of the package into the central computer. Customer service representatives are able to check the status of any package from desktop computers linked to the central computers and respond immediately to inquiries from customers. UPS customers can also access this information from the company's Web site using their own computers or mobile phones. UPS now has mobile apps and a mobile Web site for iPhone, BlackBerry, and Android smartphone users.

Anyone with a package to ship can access the UPS Web site to track packages, check delivery routes, calculate shipping rates, determine time in transit, print labels, and schedule a pickup. The data collected at the UPS Web site are transmitted to the UPS central computer and then back to the customer after processing. UPS also provides tools that enable customers, such as Cisco Systems, to embed UPS functions, such as tracking and cost calculations, into their own Web sites so that they can track shipments without visiting the UPS site.

A Web-based Post Sales Order Management System (OMS) manages global service orders and inventory for critical parts fulfillment. The system enables high-tech electronics, aerospace, medical equipment, and other companies anywhere in the world that ship critical parts to quickly assess their critical parts inventory, determine the most optimal routing strategy to meet customer needs, place orders online, and track parts from the warehouse to the end user. An automated e-mail or fax feature keeps customers informed of each shipping milestone and can provide notification of any changes to flight schedules for commercial airlines carrying their parts.

UPS is now leveraging its decades of expertise managing its own global delivery network to manage logistics and supply chain activities for other companies. It created a UPS Supply Chain Solutions division that provides a complete bundle of standardized services to subscribing companies at a fraction of what it would cost to build their own systems and infrastructure. These services include supply-chain design and management, freight forwarding, customs brokerage, mail services, multimodal transportation, and financial services, in addition to logistics services.

In 2006 UPS started managing the supply chains of medical device and pharmaceutical companies. For example, at UPS's Louisville, Kentucky headquarters, company pharmacists fill 4,000 orders a day for insulin pumps and other supplies from customers of Medtronic Inc., the Minneapolis-based medical-device company. UPS pharmacists in Louisville log into Medtronic's system, fill the orders with devices stocked on site, and arrange for UPS to ship them to patients. UPS's service has allowed Medtronic to close its own distribution warehouse and significantly reduce the costs of processing each order. UPS and other parcel-delivery companies are investing in giant warehouses that service multiple pharmaceutical companies at once, with freezers for medicines and high-security vaults for controlled substances.

UPS has partnered with Pratt & Whitney, a world leader in the design, manufacture, and service of aircraft engines, space propulsion systems, and industrial gas turbines, to run its Georgia Distribution Center, which processes 98 percent of the parts used to overhaul Pratt & Whitney jet engines for shipment around the world. UPS and Pratt & Whitney employees together keep track of about 25,000 different kinds of parts and fulfill up to 1,400 complex orders each day – ranging from a few nuts and bolts to kits comprising all the parts needed to build an entire engine. On the receiving side of the 250,000-square-foot building, UPS quality inspectors check newly arrived parts against blueprints.

Sources: Steve Rosenbush and Michael Totty, "How Big Data Is Transforming Business," *The Wall Street Journal*, March 10, 2013; Thomas H. Davenport, "Analytics That Tell You What to Do," *The Wall Street Journal*, April 3, 2013; Elana Varon, "How UPS Trains Front-Line Workers to Use Predictive Analytics," DataInformed, January 31, 2013; www.ups.com, accessed April 17, 2013; Jennifer Levitz and Timothy W. Martin, "UPS, Other Big Shippers, Carve Health Care Niches," *The Wall Street Journal*, June 27, 2012; and "Logistics in Action: At Pratt & Whitney Facility, Silence Is Golden," *UPS Compass*, August 2012.

CASE STUDY QUESTIONS

1. What are the inputs, processing, and outputs of UPS's package tracking system?

2. What technologies are used by UPS? How are these technologies related to UPS's business strategy?

3. What strategic business objectives do UPS's information systems address?

4. What would happen if UPS's information systems were not available?

Using a handheld computer called a Delivery Information Acquisition Device (DIAD), UPS drivers automatically capture customers' signatures along with pickup, delivery, and time card information. UPS information systems use these data to track packages while they are being transported.

© Bill Aron/PhotoEdit.

machine. After a cleanup and proper inspection of other parts, you start the machine, and production resumes.

No doubt some problems in business are this straightforward. But few problems are this simple in the real world of business. In real-world business firms, a number of major factors are simultaneously involved in problems. These major factors can usefully be grouped into three categories: *organization, technology,* and *people.* In other words, a whole set of problems is usually involved.

A MODEL OF THE PROBLEM-SOLVING PROCESS

There is a simple model of problem solving that you can use to help you understand and solve business problems using information systems. You can think of business problem-solving as a four-step process (see Figure 1.4). Most problem solvers work through this model on their way to finding a solution. Let's take a brief look at each step.

Problem Identification

The first step in the problem-solving process is to understand what kind of problem exists. Contrary to popular beliefs, problems are not like basketballs on a court simply waiting to be picked up by some "objective" problem solver. Before problems can be solved, there must be agreement in a business that a problem exists, about what the problem is, about what its causes are, and about what can be done about the problem given the limited resources of the organization. Problems have to be properly defined by people in an organization before they can be solved.

For instance, what at first glance what might seem like a problem with employees not adequately responding to customers in a timely and accurate manner might in reality be a result of a older, out-of-date information system for keeping track of customers. Or it might be a combination of both poor employee incentives for treating customers well and an outdated system. Once you understand this critical fact, you can start to solve problems creatively. Finding answers to these questions will require fact gathering, interviews with people involved in the problem, and analysis of documents.

In this text, we emphasize three different and typical dimensions of business problems: organizations, technology, and people (see Table 1.2). Typical organizational problems include poor business processes (usually inherited from the past), unsupportive culture,

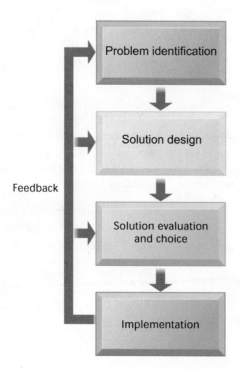

Figure 1.4
Problem Solving Is a Continuous Four-Step Process
During implementation and thereafter, the outcome must be continually measured and the information about how well the solution is working is fed back to the problem solvers. In this way, the identification of the problem can change over time, solutions can be changed, and new choices made, all based on experience.

political in-fighting, and changes in the organization's surrounding environment. Typical technology problems include insufficient or aging hardware, outdated software, inadequate database capacity, insufficient telecommunications capacity, and the incompatibility of old systems with new technology. Typical people problems include employee training, difficulties of evaluating performance, legal and regulatory compliance, ergonomics, poor or indecisive management, and employee support and participation. When you begin to analyze a business problem, you will find these dimensions are helpful guides to understanding the kind of problem with which you are working.

Solution Design

The second step is to design solutions to the problem(s) you have identified. As it turns out, there are usually a great many "solutions" to any given problem, and the choice of solution often reflects the differing perspectives of people in an organization. You should try to consider as many different solutions as possible so that you can understand the range of possible solutions. Some solutions emphasize technology; others focus on change in the organization and people aspects of the problem. As you will find throughout the text, most successful solutions result from an integrated approach in which new technologies are accompanied by changes in organization and people.

Solution Evaluation and Choice

Choosing the "best" solution for your business firm is the next step in the process. Some of the factors to consider when trying to find the "best" single solution are the cost of the solution, the feasibility of the solution for your business given existing resources and skills, and the length of time required to build and implement the solution. Also very important at this point are the attitudes and support of your employees and managers. A solution that does not have the support of all the major interests in the business can quickly turn into a disaster.

TABLE 1.2 Dimensions of Business Problems	Dimension	Description
	Organizational dimensions	Outdated business processes
		Unsupportive culture and attitudes
		Political conflict
		Turbulent business environment, change
		Complexity of task
		Inadequate resources
	Technology dimensions	Insufficient or aging hardware
		Outdated software
		Inadequate database capacity
		Insufficient telecommunications capacity
		Incompatibility of old systems with new technology
		Rapid technological change and failure to adopt new technology
	People dimensions	Lack of employee training
		Difficulties of evaluating performance
		Legal and regulatory compliance
		Work environment
		Lack of employee support and participation
		Indecisive management
		Poor management
		Wrong incentives

Implementation

The best solution is one that can be implemented. Implementation of an information system solution involves building the solution and introducing it into the organization. This includes purchasing or building the software and hardware—the technology part of the equation. The software must be tested in a realistic business setting; then employees need to be trained, and documentation about how to use the new system needs to be written.

You will definitely need to think about change management. **Change management** refers to the many techniques used to bring about successful change in a business. Nearly all information systems require changes in the firm's business processes and, therefore, changes in what hundreds or even thousands of employees do every day. You will have to design new, more efficient business processes, and then figure out how to encourage employees to adapt to these new ways of doing business. This may require meeting sessions to introduce the change to groups of employees, new training modules to bring employees quickly up to speed on the new information systems and processes, and, finally, some kind of rewards or incentives to encourage people to enthusiastically support the changes.

Implementation also includes the measurement of outcomes. After a solution has been implemented, it must be evaluated to determine how well it is working and whether any additional changes are required to meet the original objectives. This information is fed back to the problem solvers. In this way, the identification of the problem can change over time, solutions can be changed, and new choices made, all based on experience.

Problem Solving: A Process, Not an Event

It is often assumed that once a problem is "solved," it goes away and can be forgotten about. And it is easy to fall into the trap of thinking about problem solving as an event that is "over" at some point, like a relay race or a baseball game. Often in the real world this does not happen. Sometimes the chosen solution does not work, and new solutions are required.

For instance, the U.S. National Aeronautics and Space Administration (NASA) spent more than $1 billion to fix a problem with shedding foam on the space shuttle. Experience proved the initial solution did not work. More often, the chosen solution partially works but needs a lot of continuous changes to truly "fit" the situation. Initial solutions are often rough approximations at first of what ultimately "works." Sometimes, the nature of the problem changes in a way that makes the initial solution ineffective. For instance, hackers create new variations on computer viruses that require continually evolving antivirus programs to hold them in check. For all these reasons, problem solving is a continuous process rather than a single event.

THE ROLE OF CRITICAL THINKING IN PROBLEM SOLVING

It is amazingly easy to accept someone else's definition of a problem or to adopt the opinions of some authoritative group that has "objectively" analyzed the problem and offers quick solutions. You should try to resist this tendency to accept existing definitions of any problem. Through the natural flow of decision making, it is essential that you try to maintain some distance from any specific solution until you are sure you have properly identified the problem, developed understanding, and analyzed alternatives. Otherwise, you may leap off in the wrong direction, solve the wrong problem, and waste resources. You will have to engage in some critical-thinking exercises.

Critical thinking can be briefly defined as the sustained suspension of judgment with an awareness of multiple perspectives and alternatives. It involves at least four elements:
- Maintaining doubt and suspending judgment
- Being aware of different perspectives
- Testing alternatives and letting experience guide
- Being aware of organizational and personal limitations

Simply following a rote pattern of decision making, or a model, does not guarantee a correct solution. The best protection against incorrect results is to engage in critical thinking throughout the problem-solving process.

First, maintain doubt and suspend judgment. Perhaps the most frequent error in problem solving is to arrive prematurely at a judgment about the nature of the problem. By doubting all solutions at first and refusing to rush to a judgment, you create the necessary mental conditions to take a fresh, creative look at problems, and you keep open the chance to make a creative contribution.

Second, recognize that all interesting business problems have many dimensions and that the same problem can be viewed from different perspectives. In this text, we have emphasized the usefulness of three perspectives on business problems: technology, organizations, and people. Within each of these very broad perspectives are many subperspectives, or views. The *technology perspective*, for instance, includes a consideration of all the components in the firm's IT infrastructure and the way they work together. The *organization perspective* includes a consideration of a firm's business processes, structure, culture, and politics. The *people perspective* includes consideration of the firm's management, as well as employees as individuals and their interrelationships in workgroups.

You will have to decide for yourself which major perspectives are useful for viewing a given problem. The ultimate criterion here is usefulness: Does adopting a certain perspective tell you something more about the problem that is useful for solving the problem? If not, reject that perspective as being not meaningful in this situation and look for other perspectives.

The third element of critical thinking involves testing alternatives, or modeling solutions to problems, letting experience be the guide. Not all contingencies can be known in advance, and much can be learned through experience. Therefore, experiment, gather data, and reassess the problem periodically.

THE CONNECTION BETWEEN BUSINESS OBJECTIVES, PROBLEMS, AND SOLUTIONS

Now let's make the connection between business information systems and the problem-solving approach. At the beginning of this chapter we talked about the six reasons business firms invest in information systems and technologies. We identified six business objectives of information systems: operational excellence; new products, services, and business models; customer/supplier intimacy; improved decision making; strategic advantage; and survival. When firms cannot achieve these objectives, they become "challenges" or "problems" that receive attention. Managers and employees who are aware of these challenges often turn to information systems as one of the solutions, or the entire solution.

Review the diagram at the beginning of this chapter. The diagram shows how rugby clubs have solved the business problem presented by the need to analyze big data in a highly competitive industry. The TryTracker tool is an innovative way to improve fan engagement and develop a competitive edge against other sports and athletic contests. Each chapter of this text begins with a diagram similar to this one to help you analyze the chapter-opening case. You can use this diagram as a starting point for analyzing any information system or information system problem you encounter.

1.4 Information Systems and Your Career

Looking out to 2020, the U.S. economy will create 20 million new jobs and 24 million existing jobs will open up as their occupants retire. More than 95 percent of the new jobs will be created in the service sector. The vast majority of these new jobs and replacement jobs will require a college degree to perform (Statistical Abstract, 2013; U.S. Bureau of Labor Statistics, 2013).

What this means is that U.S. business firms are looking for candidates who have a broad range of problem-solving skills—the ability to read, write, and present ideas—as well as the technical skills required for specific tasks. Regardless of your business school major, or your future occupation, information systems and technologies will play a major and expanding role in your day-to-day work and your career. Your career opportunities, and your compensation, will in part depend on your ability to help business firms use information systems to achieve their objectives.

HOW INFORMATION SYSTEMS WILL AFFECT BUSINESS CAREERS

In the following sections, we describe how specific occupations will be affected by information systems and what skills you should be building in order to benefit from this emerging labor market based on the research of the Bureau of Labor Statistics (Bureau of Labor Statistics, 2013; U.S. Census, 2011).

Accounting

There are about 2 million accountants in the U.S. labor force today, and the field is expected to expand by 16 percent by the year 2020, adding nearly 200,000 new jobs, and a similar number of jobs to replace retirees. This above-average growth in accounting is in part driven by new accounting laws for public companies, greater scrutiny of public and private firms by government tax auditors, and a growing demand for management and operational advice.

Accountants rely heavily on information systems to summarize transactions, create financial records, organize data, and perform financial analysis. As a result of new public laws, accountants require an intimate knowledge of data bases, reporting systems, and networks in order to trace financial transactions. Because so many transactions are occurring over the Internet, accountants need to understand online transaction and reporting systems, and how systems are used to achieve management accounting functions in an online, wireless, and mobile business environment.

Finance

If you include financial analysts, stock analysts, insurance underwriters, and related financial service occupations, there are currently about 2.2 million managers and employees in finance. Financial managers develop financial reports, direct investment activities, and implement cash management strategies. These financial occupations are expected to grow by about 20 percent by the year 2020, and add over 400,000 new jobs.

Financial managers play important roles in planning, organizing, and implementing information system strategies for their firms. Financial managers work directly with a firm's board of directors and senior management to ensure investments in information systems help achieve corporate goals and achieve high returns. The relationship between information systems and the practice of modern financial management and services is so strong that many advise finance majors to also co-major in information systems (and vice versa).

Marketing

No field has undergone more technology-driven change in the past five years than marketing and advertising. The explosion in e-commerce activity described earlier means that eyeballs are moving rapidly to the Internet. As a result, Internet advertising is the fastest growing form of advertising, reaching $40 billion in 2013. Product branding and customer communication are moving online at a fast pace.

There are about 1.5 million public relations, marketing analysts, and marketing and sales managers in the U.S. labor force. This field is growing faster than average at about 12 percent, and is expected to add more than 300,000 jobs by 2020. There is a much larger group of 2.6 million nonmanagerial employees in marketing-related occupations (art, design, entertainment, sports, and media) and more than 15.9 million employees in sales. These occupations together are expected to create an additional 3.1 million jobs by 2020. Marketing and advertising managers deal with large databases of customer behavior both online and offline in the process of creating brands and selling products and services. They develop reports on product performance, retrieve feedback from customers, and manage product development. These managers need an understanding of how enterprise-wide systems for product management, sales force management, and customer relationship management are used to develop products that consumers want, to manage the customer relationship, and to manage an increasingly mobile sales force.

Operations Management in Services and Manufacturing

The growing size and complexity of modern industrial production and the emergence of huge global service companies have created a growing demand for employees who can coordinate and optimize the resources required to produce goods and services. Operations management as a discipline is directly relevant to three occupational categories: industrial production managers, administrative service managers, and operations analysts.

Production managers, administrative service managers, and operations analysts will be employing information systems and technologies every day to accomplish their jobs, with extensive use of database and analytical software.

Management

Management is the largest single group in the U.S. business labor force with more than 15 million members, not including an additional 627,000 management consultants. Overall, the management corps in the United States is expected to expand at an average pace of 15 percent, adding about 3.2 million new jobs by 2020. There are more than twenty different types of managers tracked by the Bureau of Labor Statistics, all the way from chief executive officer, to human resource managers, production managers, project managers, lodging managers, medical managers, and community service managers.

The job of management has been transformed by information systems. Arguably, it would be impossible to manage business firms today, even very small firms, without the extensive use of information systems. Nearly all U.S. managers use information systems and technologies every day to accomplish their jobs, from desktop productivity tools to applications coordinating the entire enterprise. Managers today manage through a variety of information technologies without which it would be impossible to control and lead the firm.

Information Systems

The information systems field is arguably one of the most fast-changing and dynamic of all the business professions because information technologies are among the most important tools for achieving business firms' key objectives. The explosive growth of business information systems has generated a growing demand for information systems employees and managers who work with other business professionals to design and develop new hardware and software systems to serve the needs of business. Of the top 20 fastest growing occupations through 2020, five are information systems occupations.

There are about 307,000 information system managers in the United States, with an estimated growth rate of 15 percent through 2020, expanding the number of new jobs by more than 55,000 new positions. As businesses and government agencies increasingly rely on the Internet for communication and computing resources, system and network security management positions are growing very rapidly. One of the fastest growing U.S. occupational groups is network systems and data communications analysts, with a projected growth rate of 21 percent.

© Kzenon/Shutterstock.

The job of management requires extensive use of information systems to support decision making and to monitor the performance of the firm.

Outsourcing and Offshoring The Internet has created new opportunities for outsourcing many information systems jobs, along with many other service sector and manufacturing jobs. There are two kinds of outsourcing: outsourcing to domestic U.S. firms and offshore outsourcing to low-wage countries, such as India, China, and eastern European countries. Even this distinction blurs as domestic service providers, such as IBM, develop global outsourcing centers in India.

The most common and successful offshore outsourcing projects involve production programming and system maintenance programming work, along with call center work related to customer relationship management systems. However, inflation in Indian and Chinese wages for technology work, coupled with the additional management costs incurred in outsourcing projects, is leading to a counter movement of jobs back to the United States. Moreover, although routine technical IS jobs like software maintenance can be outsourced easily, all those management and organizational tasks required in systems development—including business process design, customer interface, and supply chain management—often remain in the United States. Software design and new programming efforts are rarely outsourced because of their strategic importance to firms, and because domestic software designers are much closer to the American marketplace and customer base. Software outsourcing of routine IS work to low-wage countries lowers the cost of building and maintaining systems in the United States. As systems become less expensive, more are built. The net result is that offshore outsourcing will increase demand in the United States for managerial IS positions, as well as many of the IS occupations described above.

Given all these factors in the IT labor market, on what kinds of skills should information system majors focus? Following is a list of general skills we believe will optimize employment opportunities:

- An in-depth knowledge of how new and emerging hardware and software can be used by business firms to make them more efficient and effective, enhance customer and supplier intimacy, improve decision making, achieve competitive advantage, and ensure firm survival. This includes an in-depth understanding of databases, database design, implementation, and management.
- An ability to take a leadership role in the design and implementation of new information systems, work with other business professionals to ensure systems meet business objectives, and work with software packages providing new system solutions.

INFORMATION SYSTEMS AND YOUR CAREER: WRAP-UP

Looking back at the information system skills required for specific majors, there are some common themes that affect all business majors. Following is a list of these common requirements for information system skills and knowledge:

- All business students, regardless of major, should understand how information systems and technologies can help firms achieve business objectives such as achieving operational efficiency, developing new products and services, and maintaining customer intimacy.
- Perhaps the most dominant theme that pervades this review of necessary job skills is the central role of databases in a modern firm. Each of the careers we have just described relies heavily in practice on databases.
- With the pervasive growth in databases comes inevitably an exponential growth in digital information and a resulting challenge to managers trying to understand all this information. Regardless of major, business students need to develop skills in analysis of information and helping firms understand and make sense out of their environments. Business analytics and intelligence are important skill sets to analyze the mountains of big data being produced by the online environment of business firms.
- All business majors need to be able to work with specialists and system designers who build and implement information systems. This is necessary to ensure that the systems that are built actually service business purposes and provide the information and understanding required by managers and employees.
- Each of the business majors will be impacted by changes in the ethical, social, and legal environment of business. Business school students need to understand how information systems can be used to meet business requirements for reporting to government regulators and the public and how information systems impact the ethical issues in their fields.

HOW THIS BOOK PREPARES YOU FOR THE FUTURE

This book is explicitly designed to prepare you for your future business career. It provides you with the necessary knowledge and foundational concepts for understanding the role of information systems in business organizations. You will be able to use this knowledge to identify opportunities for increasing the effectiveness of your business. You will learn how to use information systems to improve operations, create new products and services, improve decision making, increase customer intimacy, and promote competitive advantage.

Equally important, this book develops your ability to use information systems to solve problems that you will encounter on the job. You will learn how to analyze and define a business problem and how to design an appropriate information system solution. You will deepen your critical-thinking and problem-solving skills. The following features of the text and the accompanying learning package reinforce this problem-solving and career orientation.

A Framework for Describing and Analyzing Information Systems

The text provides you with a framework for analyzing and solving problems by examining the people, organizational, and technology components of information systems. This framework is used repeatedly throughout the text to help you understand information systems in business and analyze information systems problems.

A Four-Step Model for Problem Solving

The text provides you with a four-step method for solving business problems, which we introduced in this chapter. You will learn how to identify a business problem, design alternative solutions, choose the correct solution, and implement the solution. You will be asked to use this problem-solving method to solve the case studies in each chapter. Chapter 12 will show you how to use this approach to design and build new information systems.

Hands-On MIS Projects for Stimulating Critical Thinking and Problem Solving

Each chapter concludes with a series of hands-on MIS projects to sharpen your critical-thinking and problem-solving skills. These projects include two Management Decision Problems, hands-on application software problems, and projects for building Internet skills. For each of these projects, we identify both the business skills and the software skills required for the solution.

Career Resources

To make sure you know how the text is directly useful in your future business career, we've added a full set of Career Resources to help you with career development and job hunting.

Digital Portfolio MyMISLab™ includes a template for preparing a structured digital portfolio to demonstrate the business knowledge, application software skills, Internet skills, and analytical skills you have acquired in this course. You can include this portfolio in your resume or job applications. Your professors can also use the portfolio to assess the skills you have learned.

Career Resources A Career Resources section in MyMISLab shows you how to integrate what you have learned in this course in your resume, cover letter, and job interview to improve your chances for success in the job market.

Review Summary

1 **How are information systems transforming business, and what is their relationship to globalization?** E-mail, online conferencing, smartphones, and tablet computers have become essential tools for conducting business. Information systems are the foundation of fast-paced supply chains. The Internet allows businesses to buy, sell, advertise, and solicit customer feedback online. The Internet has stimulated globalization by dramatically reducing the costs of producing, buying, and selling goods on a global scale.

2 **Why are information systems so essential for running and managing a business today?** Information systems are a foundation for conducting business today. In many industries, survival and even existence is difficult without extensive use of information technology. Businesses use information systems to achieve six major objectives: operational excellence; new products, services, and business models; customer/supplier intimacy; improved decision making; competitive advantage; and day-to-day survival.

3 **What exactly is an information system? How does it work? What are its people, organization, and technology components?** From a technical perspective, an information system collects, stores, and disseminates information from an organization's environment and internal operations to support organizational functions and decision making, communication, coordination, control, analysis, and visualization. Information systems transform raw data into useful information through three basic activities: input, processing, and output. From a business perspective, an information system provides a solution to a problem or challenge facing a firm and represents a combination of people, organization, and technology elements.

The people dimension of information systems involves issues such as training, job attitudes, and management behavior. The technology dimension consists of computer hardware, software, data management technology, and networking/telecommunications technology, including the Internet. The organization dimension of information systems involves issues such as the organization's hierarchy, functional specialties, business processes, culture, and political interest groups.

4 **How will a four-step method for business problem solving help you solve information system-related problems?** Problem identification involves understanding what kind of problem is being presented, and identifying people, organizational, and technology factors. Solution design involves designing several alternative solutions to the problem that has been identified. Evaluation and choice entails selecting the best solution, taking into account its cost and the available resources and skills in the business. Implementation of an information system solution entails purchasing or building hardware and software, testing the software, providing employees with training and documentation, managing change as the system is introduced into the organization, and measuring the outcome. Problem solving requires critical thinking in which one suspends judgment to consider multiple perspectives and alternatives.

5 **How will information systems affect business careers, and what information system skills and knowledge are essential?** Business careers in accounting, finance, marketing, operations management, management and human resources, and information systems all will need an understanding of how information systems help firms achieve major business objectives; an appreciation of the central role of databases; skills in information analysis and business intelligence; sensitivity to the ethical, social, and legal issues raised by systems; and the ability to work with technology specialists and other business professionals in designing and building systems.

Key Terms

Business model, 33
Business processes, 38
Change management, 45
Computer hardware, 39
Computer literacy, 37
Computer software, 39
Critical thinking, 45
Culture, 38
Data, 35
Data management technology, 39

Extranets, 39
Feedback, 35
Information, 35
Information system (IS), 35
Information systems literacy, 37
Information technology (IT), 35
Information technology (IT) infrastructure, 39
Input, 35

Internet, 39
Intranets, 39
Management information systems (MIS), 37
Network, 39
Networking and telecommunications technology, 39
Output, 35
Processing, 35
World Wide Web, 39

Review Questions

1-1 How are information systems transforming business, and what is their relationship to globalization?
- Describe the business impact of cloud computing, Big Data, and the mobile platform.
- Explain what globalization has to do with management information systems.

1-2 Why are information systems so essential for running and managing a business today?
- List and describe the six reasons why information systems are so important for business today.

1-3 What exactly is an information system? How does it work? What are its people, organization, and technology components?
- List and describe the organizational, people, and technology dimensions of information systems.
- Distinguish between information technology and an information system.
- Distinguish between data and information and between information systems literacy and computer literacy.

- Explain how the Internet and the World Wide Web are related to the other technology components of information systems.

1-4 How will a four-step method for business problem solving help you solve information system-related problems?
- List and describe each of the four steps for solving business problems.
- Give some examples of people, organizational, and technology problems found in businesses.
- Define critical thinking and list four elements that are involved in critical thinking.
- Describe the role of information systems in business problem solving.

1-5 How will information systems affect business careers, and what information system skills and knowledge are essential?
- Describe the role of information systems in careers in accounting, finance, marketing, management, and operations management, and explain how careers in information systems have been affected by new technologies and outsourcing.
- List and describe the information system skills and knowledge that are essential for all business careers.

Discussion Questions

1-6 What are the implications of globalization when you have to look for a job? What can you do to prepare yourself for competing in a globalized business environment? How would knowledge of information systems help you compete?

1-7 If you were setting up the Web site for the Rugby Football Union, what people, organizational, and technology issues might you encounter?

1-8 Identify some of the people, organizational, and technology issues that UPS had to address when creating its successful information systems.

Hands-On MIS Projects

The projects in this section give you hands-on experience in analyzing financial reporting and inventory management problems, using data management software to improve management decision making about increasing sales, and using Internet software for researching job requirements.

MANAGEMENT DECISION PROBLEMS

1-9 Warbenton Snack Foods is a manufacturer of potato crisps and savoury snacks in the U.K. Warbenton's financial department uses spreadsheets and manual processes for much of its data gathering and reporting. Warbenton's financial analyst would spend the entire final week of every month collecting spreadsheets from the heads of various departments. She would then consolidate and re-enter all the data into another spreadsheet, which would serve as the company's monthly profit-and-loss statement. If a department needed to update its data after submitting the spreadsheet to the main office, the analyst had to return the original spreadsheet and then wait for the department to resubmit its data before finally submitting the updated data in the consolidated document. Assess the impact of this situation on business performance and management decision making.

1-10 Rabatt operates deep-discount stores offering housewares, cleaning supplies, cloth-ing, health and beauty aids, and packaged food throughout Germany, with most items selling for 1 euro. Its business model calls for keeping costs as low as possible. The company has no automated method for keeping track of inventory at each store. Managers know approximately how many cases of a particular product the store is supposed to receive when a delivery truck arrives, but the stores lack technology for scanning the cases or verifying the item count inside the cases. Merchandise losses from theft or other mishaps have been rising and now represent over 3 percent of total sales. What decisions have to be made before investing in an information sys-tem solution?

IMPROVING DECISION MAKING: USING DATABASES TO ANALYZE SALES TRENDS

Software skills: Database querying and reporting
Business skills: Sales trend analysis

1-11 In this project, you will start out with raw transactional sales data and use Microsoft Access database software to develop queries and reports that help managers make bet-ter decisions about product pricing, sales promotions, and inventory replenishment. In MyMISLab, you can find a Store and Regional Sales Database developed in Microsoft Access. The database contains raw data on weekly store sales of computer equipment in various sales regions. The database includes fields for store identification number, sales region, item number, item description, unit price, units sold, and the weekly sales period when the sales were made. Use Access to develop some reports and queries to make this information more useful for running the business. Sales and production managers want answers to the following questions:

- Which products should be restocked?
- Which stores and sales regions would benefit from a promotional campaign and additional marketing?
- When (what time of year) should products be offered at full price, and when should discounts be used?

You can easily modify the database table to find and report your answers. Print your reports and results of queries.

IMPROVING DECISION MAKING: USING THE INTERNET TO LOCATE JOBS REQUIRING INFORMATION SYSTEMS KNOWLEDGE

Software skills: Internet-based software
Business skills: Job searching

1-12 The Interactive Session on page 41 examines how UPS competes globally with infor-mation technology. Use the Internet to identify a company that competes with UPS. Assume that your company needs to ship a package with a value of 500 euros from Rome, Italy to Paris, France. Which company would you choose and why? Write a one page report explaining your decision.

Collaboration and Teamwork Project

1-13 In MyMISLab, you will find a Collaboration and Teamwork Project dealing with the concepts in this chapter. You will be able to use Google Drive, Google Docs, Google Sites, Google+, or other open-source tools to complete the assignment.

BUSINESS PROBLEM-SOLVING CASE

A New Look at Electronic Medical Records

During a typical trip to the doctor, you'll often see shelves full of folders and papers devoted to the storage of medical records. Every time you visit, your records are created or modified, and often duplicate copies are generated throughout the course of a visit to the doctor or a hospital. The majority of medical records are currently paper-based, making these records very difficult to access and share. It has been said that the U.S. health care industry is the world's most inefficient information enterprise.

Inefficiencies in medical record keeping are one reason why health care costs in the United States are the highest in the world. In 2012 health care costs reached $2.8 trillion, representing 18 percent of the U.S. gross domestic product (GDP). Left unchecked, by 2037 health care costs will rise to 25% of GDP and consume approximately 40 percent of total federal spending. Since administrative costs and medical recordkeeping account for nearly 13 percent of U.S. health care spending, improving medical recordkeeping systems has been targeted as a major path to cost savings and even higher health care quality. Enter electronic medical record (EMR) systems.

An electronic medical record system contains all of a person's vital medical data, including personal information, a full medical history, test results, diagnoses, treatments, prescription medications, and the effect of those treatments. A physician would be able to immediately and directly access needed information from the EMR without having to pore through paper files. If the record holder went to the hospital, the records and results of any tests performed at that point would be immediately available online. Having a complete set of patient information at their fingertips would help physicians prevent prescription drug interactions and avoid redundant tests. Many experts believe that electronic records will reduce medical errors and improve care, create less paperwork, and provide quicker service, all of which will lead to dramatic savings in the future, as much as $80 billion per year.

The U.S. government's short-term goal is for all health care providers in the United States to have EMR systems in place that meet a set of basic functional criteria by the year 2015. Its long-term goal is to have a fully functional nationwide electronic medical recordkeeping network. The consulting firm Accenture estimated that 50 percent of U.S. hospitals are potentially at risk of incurring penalties by 2015 for failing to meet federal requirements.

Evidence of EMR systems in use today suggests that electronic records offer significant advantages to hospitals and patients alike. The U.S. Veterans Affairs (VA) system of doctors and hospitals is considered a leading example. The VA system switched to digital records years ago, and far exceeds the private sector and Medicare in quality of preventive services and chronic care. The VA also provides the lowest cost health care in the nation. The 1,400 VA facilities use VistA, record-sharing software developed by the government that allows doctors and nurses to share patient history. A typical VistA record lists all of the patient's health problems; their weight and blood pressure since beginning treatment at the VA system; images of the patient's x-rays, lab results, and other test results; lists of medications; and reminders about upcoming appointments.

VistA has many features that improve quality of care. For example, nurses scan tags for patients and medications to ensure that the correct dosages of medicines are going to the correct patients. This feature reduces medication errors, which is one of the most common and costly types of medical errors, and speeds up treatment as well. The system also generates automatic warnings based on specified criteria. It can notify providers if a patient's blood pressure goes over a certain level or if a patient is overdue for a regularly scheduled procedure like a flu shot or a cancer screening. Devices that measure patients' vital signs can automatically transmit their results to the VistA system, which automatically updates doctors at the first sign of trouble. The 40,000 patients in the VA's in-home monitoring program reduced their hospital admissions by 25 percent and the length of their hospital stays by 20 percent.

Patients also report that the process of being treated at the VA is effortless compared to paper-based providers. That's because instant processing of claims and payments are among the benefits of EMR systems. Insurance companies traditionally pay claims around two weeks after receiving them, despite quickly processing them soon after they are received; governmental regulations only require insurers to pay claims within fifteen days of their receipt. Additionally, today's paper-based health care providers must assign the appropriate diagnostic codes and procedure codes to claims. Because there are thousands of these codes, the process is even slower, and most providers employ someone solely to perform this task. Electronic systems hold the promise of immediate processing, or "real-time claims adjudication" just like when you pay using a credit card, because claim data would be sent immediately and diagnostic and procedure code information are automatically entered.

Economic stimulus money provided by the American Recovery and Reinvestment Act has been available to health care providers in two ways. First, $2 billion was provided up front to hospitals and physicians to help set up electronic records. Another $17 billion was available to reward providers that successfully implement electronic records by 2015. To qualify for these rewards, providers must demonstrate "meaningful use" of electronic health record systems. The bill defines this as the successful implementation of certified e-record products, the ability to write at least 40 percent of all prescriptions electronically, and the ability to exchange and report data to government health agencies.

In addition to stimulus payments, the federal government plans to assess penalties on practices that fail to comply with the new electronic recordkeeping standards. Providers that cannot meet the standards by 2015 will have their Medicare and Medicaid reimbursements slowly reduced by 1% per year until 2018, with further, more stringent penalties coming beyond that time if a sufficiently low number of providers are using electronic health records.

Is all this effort to automate healthcare recordkeeping worth the cost? So far, the results are mixed. Electronic medical recordkeeping systems typically cost around $30,000 to $50,000 per doctor. Only a small amount of funds are available up front. This would burden many providers, especially medical practices with fewer than four doctors and hospitals with fewer than fifty beds. The expenditure of overhauling recordkeeping systems represents a significant increase in the short-term budgets and workloads of health care providers—as much as 80 percent, according to Accenture. Smaller providers are also less likely to have done any preparatory work digitizing their records compared to their larger counterparts.

Implementing an EMR system also requires physicians and other health care workers to change the way they work. Answering patient phone calls, examining patients, and writing prescriptions will need to incorporate procedures for accessing and updating electronic medical records. Paper-based records will have to be converted into electronic form, most likely with codes assigned for various treatment options and data structured to fit the record's format. Training can take up to 20 hours of a doctor's time, and doctors are extremely time-pressed. Your doctor may be spending a considerable of time entering your previous medical history to an EMR. In order to get the system up and running, physicians themselves may have to enter some of the data, taking away time they could be spending with their

patients. A study of 49 physician practices in Massachusetts showed an average loss of nearly $44,000 over five years, even though these practices received free EHR systems and implementation support. Small practices, especially those that continued to use paper records alongside their EHRs, suffered the greatest losses. Although the cost of recordkeeping was lowered, there were higher ongoing costs for additional physician time.

Many health technology companies are eagerly awaiting the coming spike in demand for their EMR products and have developed a variety of different health record structures. Humana, Aetna, and other health-insurance companies are helping to defray the cost of setting up EMR systems for some doctors and hospitals.

There are two problems with the plethora of options available to health care providers. First, there are likely to be many issues with the sharing of medical data between different systems. While the majority of EMR systems will satisfy the specified criteria of reporting data electronically to governmental agencies, they may not be able to report the same data to one another, a key requirement for a nationwide system. It's unlikely that the many different types of EMR systems being developed and implemented right now will be compatible with one another in 2015 and beyond, jeopardizing the goal of a national system where all health care providers can share information. No nationwide software standards for organizing and exchanging medical information have been put in place. This means that if you go to one medical practice for a diagnosis, and then go to another hospital to receive treatment, these providers generally will not be able to share your medical records electronically.

The second problem is that there is a potential conflict of interest for the insurance companies involved in the creation of health record systems. Insurers are often accused of seeking ways to avoid or delay paying health care claims. Unfortunately, it is not in their interests to have electronic systems that can process payments too smoothly and efficiently.

The RAND Corporation, which had predicted in 2005 that improvements in information systems could save the U.S. healthcare system $81 billion per year, recently turned more cautious. It found that since 2005, even with an increase in digital healthcare systems, annual U.S. health spending had soared to $2.8 trillion, with only marginal improvements in quality and efficiency. RAND researchers believe the lack of interoperability in electronic health record systems is a major barrier.

Evidence is mounting that electronic health records may be contributing to rising Medicare costs by making it easier for hospitals and physicians to bill for services that were not actually provided, or to bill for services that in the past they did not charge for but are suggested by the EMR. Some electronic health record programs allow doctors to automatically cut and paste the same examination findings for multiple patients or bill for procedures that never took place. More controls and federal oversight are required to make electronic medical record systems produce the results that were originally intended.

Although most insurers are adamant that only doctors and patients will be able to access data in these systems, many prospective patients are skeptical. A May 2012 survey conducted by Harris Interactive found that only 26 percent of U.S. adults wanted their medical records converted from paper to electric. Most of those surveyed worried about the security of electronic records, the potential for misuse of personal information, and the inability of physicians to access patient records during a power or computer outage. Worries about privacy and security could affect the success of EMR systems and quality of care provided. One in eight Americans have skipped doctor visits or regular tests, asked a doctor to change a test result, or paid privately for a test, motivated mostly by privacy concerns. A poorly designed EMR network would amplify these concerns.

Sources: Paul Cerrato, "Healthcare IT: Savior or Sinkhole? *Information Week*, January 11, 2013; Ken Terry, "Some Physicians See Revenue Loss After EHR, Study Says," *Information Week*, March 14, 2003; Reed Abelson and Julie Cresswell, "In 2nd Look, Few Savings from Digital Health Records," *The New York Times*, January 10, 2013; Reed Abelson, Julie Cresswell, and Griffin J. Palmer, "Medicare Bills Rise as Records Turn Electronic," *The New York Times*, September 21, 2012; Nicole Lewis, "Healthcare Cost Cutting Hinges on IT," *Information Week*, August 10, 2012; Neil Versel, "Consumers Still Wary of Electronic Health Records," *Information Week*, August 9, 2012; Ken Terry, "Docs May Overestimate EHR Capabilities," Information Week *Health Care*, August 2012; Steve Lohr, "Seeing Promise and Peril in Digital Records," *The New York Times*, July 17, 2011; Marianne Kolbasuk McGee, "Better Clinical Analytics Means Better Clinical Care," Information Week, May 21, 2011; Jeff Goldman, "Implementing Electronic Health Records: Six Best Practices," *CIO Insight*, March 7, 2011; Robin Lloyd, "Electronic Health Records Face Human Hurdles More than Technological Ones," Scientific American, April 16, 2011; Katherine Gammon, "Connecting Electronic Medical Records," and Technology Review, August 9, 2010.

Case Study Questions

1-14 Identify and describe the problem in this case.

1-15 What people, organization, and technology factors are responsible for the difficulties in building electronic medical record systems? Explain your answer.

1-16 What is the business, political, and social impact of not digitizing medical records (for individual physicians, hospitals, insurers, patients, and the U.S. government)?

1-17 What are the business and social benefits of digitizing medical recordkeeping?

1-18 Are electronic medical record systems a good solution to the problem of rising health care costs in the United States? Explain your answer.

Global E-business and Collaboration

STUDENT LEARNING OBJECTIVES

After completing this chapter, you will be able to answer the following questions:

1. What major features of a business are important for understanding the role of information systems?

2. How do systems serve different management groups in a business?

3. How do systems that link the enterprise improve organizational performance?

4. Why are systems for collaboration and social business so important and what technologies do they use?

5. What is the role of the information systems function in a business?

LEARNING TRACKS

1. Systems from a Functional Perspective
2. IT Enables Collaboration and Teamwork
3. Challenges of Using Business Information Systems
4. Organizing the Information Systems Function

VIDEO CASES

Case 1: Walmart's Retail Link Supply Chain

Case 2: Salesforce.com: The Emerging Social Enterprise

Case 3: How FedEx Works: Inside the Memphis Super Hub

Instructional Video 1: US Foodservice Grows Market with Oracle CRM on Demand

Chapter Outline

SOCIAL NETWORKING TAKES OFF AT KLUWER

Wolters Kluwer is a market-leading global information services and publishing company focused on professionals working in law, taxation, finance, and healthcare. Kluwer provides information, software, and services that deliver vital insights, intelligent tools, and guidance from subject-matter experts. Headquartered in Alphen aan den Rijn, the Netherlands, the company in 2012 had 19,000 employees, revenue of €3.6 billion, and operations in 40 different countries across Europe, North America, Asia Pacific, and Latin America.

Although Kluwer has been able to provide professionals in the specialties it served with the up-to-date information they needed to do their jobs efficiently and effectively, it was unable to do so for its own employees. Management believed the company was not making the most of its own internal knowledge resources. So in early 2012 the company initiated a study of its communications channels. The study found that employees were not using Kluwer's existing corporate intranet, and that they were not meeting management goals for collaboration and knowledge sharing. The existing intranet was "static." Kluwer's intranet published information about the company for internal use, but the information was not updated quickly enough and the intranet lacked tools to

© iQoncept/Shutterstock.

help staff have dialogues, share ideas, and work with other members of the company, including people that they might not know. In addition, it was unclear which department or individual was responsible for maintaining this content, making it more difficult for people to add new information or updates.

What Kluwer needed was a central resource that would support dynamic knowledge-sharing. The entire staff would be able to easily locate information about the company as well as updates on the latest developments of current initiatives and projects. Tools that would help employees work more closely together-including the ability to locate employees in other parts of the company who were experts in specific subjects- would help streamline operations and speed up key business functions.

Kluwer decided to base its solution on Microsoft Yammer, an enterprise social networking platform used by over 200,000 organizations worldwide. Yammer enables employees to create groups to collaborate on projects and share and edit documents. The service can be accessed through the Web, desktop, and mobile devices and can be integrated with other systems such as Microsoft SharePoint, to make other applications more "social."

Management saw that early adopters of this software tool were indeed sharing information and ideas, and that Yammer could provide the foundation for a dynamic social network linking the entire company. Yammer quickly became Kluwer's central resource for sharing company news and updates. Employees are using Yammer to collaborate on projects, share ideas, and discover people in other departments with useful expertise that could help them in their work. Yammer has even encouraged more employee interaction offline, as employees get to know their fellow workers better from their online experiences.

Management believes Yammer has been hugely successful. Over 80 percent of employees, including managers, regularly log onto Yammer to locate and share information. Staff members are creating their own work spaces and groups on their own to further pool their experience and expertise. Kluwer today boasts over 21 active groups, including ones dealing with the legal field, customer experience, and innovation. The social network has been especially helpful as an incubator for new business ideas. And it is obvious that internal social networking has helped transform corporate culture into one that genuinely fosters openness and a strong sense of community. Many more employees feel closely involved with the business as a whole—something that could not have been achieved with the old system.

Sources: "TELUS Telecom Company Embraces Social Computing, Streamlines Formal Learning," www.microsoft. com, accessed April 25, 2013; www.telus.com, accessed April 25, 2013; and Sharon Gaudin, "Telus Links Social, Traditional Training," *Computerworld*, March 27, 2012.

The experience of Kluwer illustrates how much organizations today rely on information systems to improve their performance and remain competitive. It also shows how much systems supporting collaboration and teamwork make a difference in an organization's ability to innovate, execute, and grow profits.

The chapter-opening diagram calls attention to important points raised by this case and this chapter. Kluwer itself is very much a knowledge-intensive company, but it was hampered by outdated processes and tools for managing information that prevented employees and managers from working efficiently and effectively. This impacted the company's ability to create and deliver leading-edge knowledge products and services.

Kluwer management decided that the best solution was to deploy new technology to move from a static corporate knowledge and work environment to one in which actively engaged employees and enabled them to obtain more knowledge from colleagues. The company implemented Microsoft Yammer as a company-wide platform for collaboration, knowledge acquisition, and knowledge transfer, and it took advantage of the software's new "social" tools to increase employee collaboration and engagement. Kluwer now relies on its internal enterprise social network for much of employee learning and problem-solving, and Yammer integrates all of the ways employees share knowledge. There is more effective

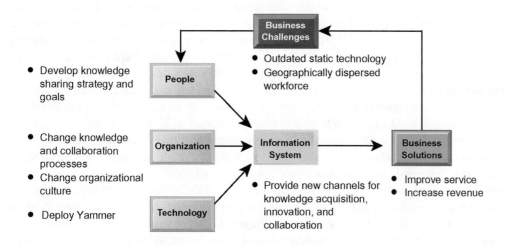

sharing of institutional knowledge and the company has become more innovative and efficient.

New technology alone would not have solved Kluwer's problem. To make the solution effective, Kluwer had to change its organizational culture and business processes for knowledge dissemination and collaborative work, and the new technology made these changes possible.

Here are some questions to think about: How are collaboration and employee engagement keeping Kluwer competitive? How did using Yammer change the way work was performed at Kluwer?

2.1 Components of a Business

A **business** is a formal organization whose aim is to produce products or provide services for a profit—that is, to sell products at a price greater than the costs of production. Customers are willing to pay this price because they believe they receive a value greater than or equal to the sale price. Business firms purchase inputs and resources from the larger environment (suppliers who are often other firms). Employees of the business firm transform these inputs by adding value to them in the production process.

There are, of course, nonprofit firms and government agencies that are complex formal organizations that produce services and products but do not operate in order to produce a profit. Nevertheless, even these organizations consume resources from their environments, add value to these inputs, and deliver their outputs to constituents and customers. In general, the information systems found in government and nonprofit organizations are remarkably similar to those found in private industry.

ORGANIZING A BUSINESS: BASIC BUSINESS FUNCTIONS

Imagine you want to set up your own business. Simply deciding to go into business is the most important decision, but next is the question of what product or service to produce (and hopefully sell). The decision of what to produce is called a *strategic choice* because it determines your likely customers, the kinds of employees you will need, the production methods and facilities needed, the marketing themes, and many other choices.

Once you decide what to produce, what kind of organization do you need? First, you need to develop a production division—an arrangement of people, machines, and business processes (procedures) that will produce the product. Second, you need a sales and marketing group who will attract customers, sell the product, and keep track of after-sales issues, such as warranties and maintenance. Third, once you generate sales, you will need a finance and accounting group to keep track of financial transactions, such as orders, invoices, disbursements, and payroll. In addition, this group will seek out sources of credit and finance. Finally, you will need a group of people to focus on recruiting, hiring, training, and retaining employees. Figure 2.1 summarizes the four basic functions found in every business.

If you were an entrepreneur or your business was very small with only a few employees, you would not need, and probably could not afford, all these separate groups of people. Instead, in small firms, you would be performing all these functions yourself or with a few others. No wonder small firms have a high mortality rate! In any event, even in small firms, the four basic functions of a firm are required. Larger firms often will have separate departments for each function: production and manufacturing, sales and marketing, finance and accounting, and human resources.

Figure 2.1 is also useful for thinking about the basic entities that make up a business. The five basic entities in a business with which it must deal are: suppliers, customers, employees, invoices/payments, and, of course, products and services. There are many other entities that a business must manage and monitor, but these are the basic ones at the foundation of any business.

BUSINESS PROCESSES

Once you identify the basic business functions and entities for your business, your next job is to describe exactly how you want your employees to perform these functions. What specific tasks do you want your sales personnel to perform, in what order, and on what schedule? What steps do you want production employees to follow as they transform raw resources into finished products? How will customer orders be fulfilled? How will vendor bills be paid?

The actual steps and tasks that describe how work is organized in a business are called **business processes**. A business process is a logically related set of activities that define how

Figure 2.1
The Four Major Functions of a Business
Every business, regardless of its size, must perform four functions to succeed. It must produce the product or service; market and sell the product or service; keep track of accounting and financial transactions; and perform basic human resources tasks, such as hiring and retaining employees.

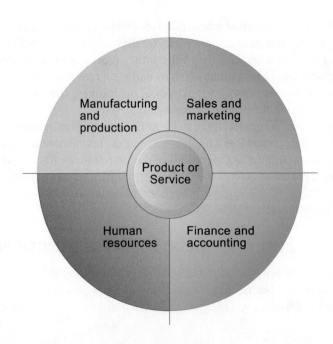

TABLE 2.1

Examples of Functional
Business Processes

Functional Area	Business Process
Manufacturing and production	Assembling the product
	Checking for quality
	Producing bills of materials
Sales and marketing	Identifying customers
	Making customers aware of the product
	Selling the product
Finance and accounting	Paying creditors
	Creating financial statements
	Managing cash accounts
Human resources	Hiring employees
	Evaluating employees' job performance
	Enrolling employees in benefits plans

specific business tasks are performed. Business processes also refer to the unique ways in which work, information, and knowledge are coordinated in a specific organization.

Every business can be seen as a collection of business processes. Some of these processes are part of larger encompassing processes. Many business processes are tied to a specific functional area. For example, the sales and marketing function would be responsible for identifying customers, and the human resources function would be responsible for hiring employees. Table 2.1 describes some typical business processes for each of the functional areas of business.

Other business processes cross many different functional areas and require coordination across departments. Consider the seemingly simple business process of fulfilling a customer order (see Figure 2.2). Initially, the sales department receives a sales order. The order goes to accounting to ensure the customer can pay for the order either by a credit verification or

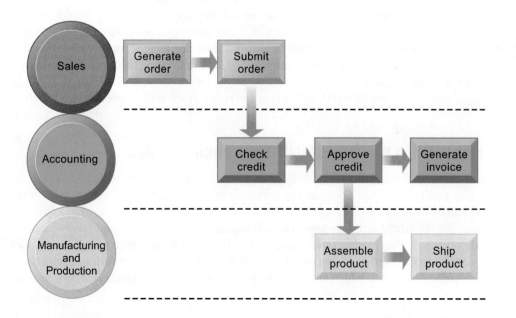

Figure 2.2
The Order
Fulfillment Process
Fulfilling a customer order involves a complex set of steps that requires the close coordination of the sales, accounting, and manufacturing functions.

request for immediate payment prior to shipping. Once the customer credit is established, the production department has to pull the product from inventory or produce the product. Next, the product needs to be shipped (and this may require working with a logistics firm, such as UPS or FedEx). A bill or invoice is then generated by the accounting department, and a notice will be sent to the customer indicating that the product has shipped. Sales has to be notified of the shipment and prepare to support the customer by answering calls or fulfilling warranty claims.

What at first appears to be a simple process—fulfilling an order—turns out to be a very complicated series of business processes that require the close coordination of major functional groups in a firm. Moreover, to efficiently perform all these steps in the order fulfillment process requires a great deal of information and the rapid flow of information within the firm, with business partners such as delivery firms, and with the customer. The particular order fulfillment process we have just described is not only *cross-functional*, it is also *interorganizational* because it includes interactions with delivery firms and customers who are outside the boundaries of the organization. Ordering raw materials or components from suppliers would be another interorganizational business process.

To a large extent, the efficiency of a business firm depends on how well its internal and interorganizational business processes are designed and coordinated. A company's business processes can be a source of competitive strength if they enable the company to innovate or to execute better than its rivals. Business processes can also be liabilities if they are based on outdated ways of working that impede organizational responsiveness and efficiency.

How Information Technology Enhances Business Processes

Exactly how do information systems enhance business processes? Information systems automate many steps in business processes that were formerly performed manually, such as checking a client's credit, or generating an invoice and shipping order. But today, information technology can do much more. New technology can actually change the flow of information, making it possible for many more people to access and share information, replacing sequential steps with tasks that can be performed simultaneously, and eliminating delays in decision making. It can even transform the way the business works and drive new business models. Ordering a book online from Amazon.com and downloading a music track from iTunes are entirely new business processes based on new business models that are inconceivable without information technology.

That's why it's so important to pay close attention to business processes, both in your information systems course and in your future career. By analyzing business processes, you can achieve a very clear understanding of how a business actually works. Moreover, by conducting a business process analysis, you will also begin to understand how to change the business to make it more efficient or effective. Throughout this book we examine business processes with a view to understanding how they might be changed, or replaced, by using information technology to achieve greater efficiency, innovation, and customer service. Chapter 3 discusses the business impact of using information technology to redesign business processes, and MyMISLab™ has a Learning Track with more detailed coverage of this topic.

MANAGING A BUSINESS AND FIRM HIERARCHIES

What is missing from Figures 2.1 and 2.2 is any notion of how to coordinate and control the four major functions, their departments, and their business processes. Each of these functional departments has its own goals and processes, and they obviously need to cooperate in order for the whole business to succeed. Business firms, like all organizations, achieve coordination by hiring managers whose responsibility is to ensure all the various parts of an organization work together. Firms coordinate the work of employees in various divisions by developing a hierarchy in which authority (responsibility and accountability) is concentrated at the top.

The hierarchy of management is composed of **senior management**, which makes long-range strategic decisions about products and services as well as ensures financial performance of the firm; **middle management**, which carries out the programs and plans of senior management; and **operational management**, which is responsible for monitoring the daily activities of the business. **Knowledge workers**, such as engineers, scientists, or architects, design products or services and create new knowledge for the firm, whereas **data workers**, such as secretaries or clerks, assist with administrative work at all levels of the firm. **Production or service workers** actually produce the product and deliver the service (Figure 2.3).

Each of these groups has different needs for information given their different responsibilities. Senior managers need summary information that can quickly inform them about the overall performance of the firm, such as gross sales revenues, sales by product group and region, and overall profitability. Middle managers need more specific information on the results of specific functional areas and departments of the firm, such as sales contacts by the sales force, production statistics for specific factories or product lines, employment levels and costs, and sales revenues for each month or even each day. Operational managers need transaction-level information, such as the number of parts in inventory each day or the number of hours logged on Tuesday by each employee. Knowledge workers may need access to external scientific databases or internal databases with organizational knowledge. Finally, production workers need access to information from production machines, and service workers need access to customer records in order to take orders and answer questions from customers.

THE BUSINESS ENVIRONMENT

So far we have talked about business as if it operated in a vacuum, but nothing could be further from the truth. In fact, business firms depend heavily on their environments to supply capital, labor, customers, new technology, services and products, stable markets and legal systems, and general educational resources. Even a pizza parlor cannot survive long without a supportive environment that delivers the cheese, tomato sauce, and flour!

Figure 2.4 summarizes the key actors in the environment of every business. To stay in business, a firm must monitor changes in its environment and share information with the key entities in that environment. For instance, a firm must respond to political shifts, respond to changes in the overall economy (such as changes in labor rates and price inflation), keep track of new technologies, and respond to changes in the global business environment (such

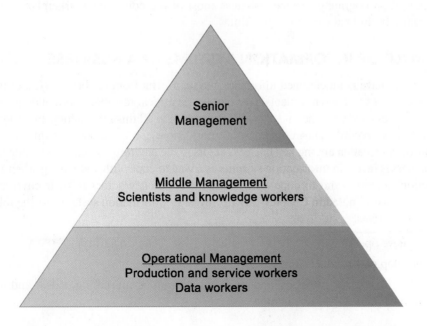

Figure 2.3
Levels in a Firm
Business organizations are hierarchies consisting of three principal levels: senior management, middle management, and operational management. Information systems serve each of these levels. Scientists and knowledge workers often work with middle management.

Figure 2.4
The Business Environment
To be successful, an organization must constantly monitor and respond to—or even anticipate—developments in its environment. A firm's environment includes specific groups with which the business must deal directly, such as customers, suppliers, and competitors as well as the broader general environment, including socioeconomic trends, political conditions, technological innovations, and global events.

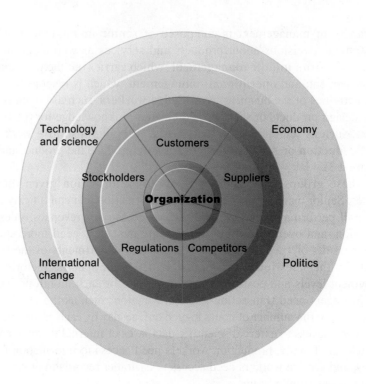

as foreign exchange rates). In its immediate environment, firms need to track and share information with suppliers, customers, stockholders, regulators, and logistic partners (such as shipping firms).

Business environments are constantly changing: New developments in technology, politics, customer preferences, and regulations happen all the time. In general, when businesses fail, it is often because they failed to respond adequately to changes in their environments.

Changes in technology, such as the Internet, are forcing entire industries and leading firms to change their business models or suffer failure. Apple's iTunes and other online music download services are making the music industry's traditional business model based on distributing music on CDs obsolete. Another example is the photography business. Digital photography has forced Eastman Kodak to downsize and move into digital cameras and Internet photography services because most of the consumer marketplace no longer wants to use traditional cameras with film.

THE ROLE OF INFORMATION SYSTEMS IN A BUSINESS

Until now we have not mentioned information systems. But from the brief review of business functions, entities, and environments, you can see the critical role that information plays in the life of a business. Up until the mid 1950s, firms managed all this information and information flow with paper records. During the past 50 years, more and more business information and the flow of information among key business actors in the environment has been computerized.

Businesses invest in information systems as a way to cope with and manage their internal production functions and to cope with the demands of key actors in their environments. Specifically, as we noted in Chapter 1, firms invest in information systems for the following business objectives:

- To achieve operational excellence (productivity, efficiency, agility)
- To develop new products and services
- To attain customer intimacy and service (continuous marketing, sales, and service; customization and personalization)

- To improve decision making (accuracy and speed)
- To achieve competitive advantage
- To ensure survival

2.2 Types of Business Information Systems

Now it is time to look more closely at how businesses use information systems to achieve these goals. Because there are different interests, specialties, and levels in an organization, there are different kinds of systems. No single system can provide all the information an organization needs.

A typical business organization will have systems supporting processes for each of the major business functions—sales and marketing, manufacturing and production, finance and accounting, and human resources. You can find examples of systems for each of these business functions in the Learning Tracks for this chapter. Functional systems that operated independently of each other are becoming a thing of the past because they cannot easily share information to support cross-functional business processes. They are being replaced with large-scale cross-functional systems that integrate the activities of related business processes and organizational units. We describe these integrated cross-functional applications later in this section.

A typical firm will also have different systems supporting the decision-making needs of each of the main management groups described earlier. Operational management, middle management, and senior management each use a specific type of system to support the decisions they must make to run the company. Let's look at these systems and the types of decisions they support.

SYSTEMS FOR DIFFERENT MANAGEMENT GROUPS

A business firm has systems to support decision making and work activities at different levels of the organization. They include transaction processing systems and systems for business intelligence.

Transaction Processing Systems

Operational managers need systems that keep track of the elementary activities and transactions of the organization, such as sales, receipts, cash deposits, payroll, credit decisions, and the flow of materials in a factory. **Transaction processing systems (TPS)** provide this kind of information. A transaction processing system is a computerized system that performs and records the daily routine transactions necessary to conduct business, such as sales order entry, hotel reservations, payroll, employee record keeping, and shipping.

The principal purpose of systems at this level is to answer routine questions and to track the flow of transactions through the organization. How many parts are in inventory? What happened to Mr. Williams's payment? To answer these kinds of questions, information generally must be easily available, current, and accurate.

At the operational level, tasks, resources, and goals are predefined and highly structured. The decision to grant credit to a customer, for instance, is made by a lower-level supervisor according to predefined criteria. All that must be determined is whether the customer meets the criteria.

Figure 2.5 illustrates a TPS for payroll processing. A payroll system keeps track of money paid to employees. An employee time sheet with the employee's name, social security number, and number of hours worked per week represents a single transaction for this system. Once this transaction is input into the system, it updates the system's file (or database—see Chapter 6) that permanently maintains employee information for the

Figure 2.5
A Payroll TPS
*A TPS for payroll
processing captures
employee payment
transaction data (such
as a timecard). System
outputs include online
and hard copy reports
for management and
employee paychecks.*

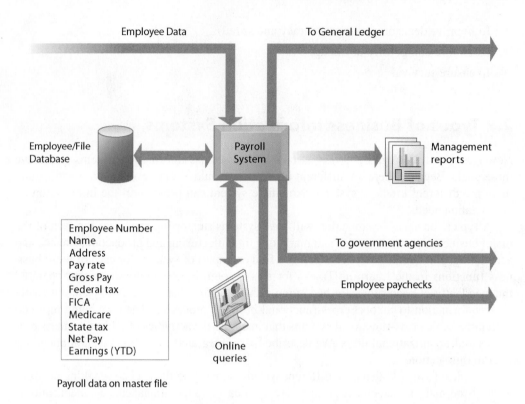

Payroll data on master file

organization. The data in the system are combined in different ways to create reports of interest to management and government agencies and to send paychecks to employees.

Managers need TPS to monitor the status of internal operations and the firm's relations with the external environment. TPS are also major producers of information for the other systems and business functions. For example, the payroll system illustrated in Figure 2.5, along with other accounting TPS, supplies data to the company's general ledger system, which is responsible for maintaining records of the firm's income and expenses and for producing reports such as income statements and balance sheets. It also supplies employee payment history data for insurance, pension, and other benefits calculations to the firm's human resources function, and employee payment data to government agencies such as the U.S. Internal Revenue Service and Social Security Administration.

Transaction processing systems are often so central to a business that TPS failure for a few hours can lead to a firm's demise and perhaps that of other firms linked to it. Imagine what would happen to UPS if its package tracking system were not working! What would the airlines do without their computerized reservation systems?

Systems for Business Intelligence

Firms also have business intelligence systems that focus on delivering information to support management decision making. **Business intelligence** is a contemporary term for data and software tools for organizing, analyzing, and providing access to data to help managers and other enterprise users make more informed decisions. Business intelligence addresses the decision-making needs of all levels of management. This section provides a brief introduction to business intelligence. You'll learn more about this topic in Chapters 6 and 11.

Business intelligence systems for middle management help with monitoring, controlling, decision-making, and administrative activities. In Chapter 1, we defined management information systems as the study of information systems in business and management. The term **management information systems (MIS)** also designates a specific category of information systems serving middle management. MIS provide middle managers with reports on the organization's current performance. This information is used to monitor and control the business and predict future performance.

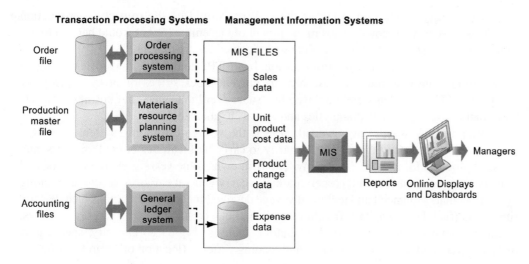

Figure 2.6
How Management Information Systems Obtain Their Data from the Organization's TPS
In the system illustrated by this diagram, three TPS supply summarized transaction data to the MIS reporting system at the end of the time period. Managers gain access to the organizational data through the MIS, which provides them with the appropriate reports.

MIS summarize and report on the company's basic operations using data supplied by transaction processing systems. The basic transaction data from TPS are compressed and usually presented in reports that are produced on a regular schedule. Today, many of these reports are delivered online. Figure 2.6 shows how a typical MIS transforms transaction-level data from inventory, production, and accounting into MIS files that are used to provide managers with reports. Figure 2.7 shows a sample report from this system.

MIS typically provide answers to routine questions that have been specified in advance and have a predefined procedure for answering them. For instance, MIS reports might list the total pounds of lettuce used this quarter by a fast-food chain or, as illustrated in Figure 2.7, compare total annual sales figures for specific products to planned targets. These systems generally are not flexible and have little analytical capability. Most MIS use simple routines, such as summaries and comparisons, as opposed to sophisticated mathematical models or statistical techniques.

Other types of business intelligence systems support more non-routine decision making. **Decision-support systems (DSS)** focus on problems that are unique and rapidly changing, for which the procedure for arriving at a solution may not be fully predefined in advance.

Consolidated Consumer Products Corporation Sales by Product and Sales Region: 2014

PRODUCT CODE	PRODUCT DESCRIPTION	SALES REGION	ACTUAL SALES	PLANNED	ACTUAL versus PLANNED
4469	Carpet Cleaner	Northeast	4,066,700	4,800,000	0.85
		South	3,778,112	3,750,000	1.01
		Midwest	4,867,001	4,600,000	1.06
		West	4,003,440	4,400,000	0.91
	TOTAL		16,715,253	17,550,000	0.95
5674	Room Freshener	Northeast	3,676,700	3,900,000	0.94
		South	5,608,112	4,700,000	1.19
		Midwest	4,711,001	4,200,000	1.12
		West	4,563,440	4,900,000	0.93
	TOTAL		18,559,253	17,700,000	1.05

Figure 2.7
Sample MIS Report
This report, showing summarized annual sales data, was produced by the MIS in Figure 2.6.

They try to answer questions such as these: What would be the impact on production schedules if we were to double sales in the month of December? What would happen to our return on investment if a factory schedule were delayed for six months?

Although DSS use internal information from TPS and MIS, they often bring in information from external sources, such as current stock prices or product prices of competitors. These systems are employed by "super-user" managers and business analysts who want to use sophisticated analytics and models to analyze data.

An interesting, small, but powerful, DSS is the voyage-estimating system of a large global shipping company that exists primarily to carry bulk cargoes of coal, oil, ores, and finished products for its parent company. The firm owns some vessels, charters others, and bids for shipping contracts in the open market to carry general cargo. A voyage-estimating system calculates financial and technical voyage details. Financial calculations include ship/time costs (fuel, labor, capital), freight rates for various types of cargo, and port expenses. Technical details include a myriad of factors, such as ship cargo capacity, speed, port distances, fuel and water consumption, and loading patterns (location of cargo for different ports).

The system can answer questions such as the following: Given a customer delivery schedule and an offered freight rate, which vessel should be assigned at what rate to maximize profits? What is the optimal speed at which a particular vessel can optimize its profit and still meet its delivery schedule? What is the optimal loading pattern for a ship bound for the U.S. West Coast from Malaysia? Figure 2.8 illustrates the DSS built for this company. The system operates on a powerful desktop personal computer, providing a system of menus that makes it easy for users to enter data or obtain information.

The voyage-estimating DSS we have just described draws heavily on models. Other business intelligence systems are more data-driven, focusing instead on extracting useful information from massive quantities of data. For example, large ski resort companies such as Intrawest and Vail Resorts collect and store large amounts of customer data from call centers, lodging and dining reservations, ski schools, and ski equipment rental stores. They use special software to analyze these data to determine the value, revenue potential, and loyalty of each customer to help managers make better decisions about how to target their marketing programs.

The Interactive Session on Organizations provides more detail on how Vail Resorts uses these data to cultivate customers and improve the customer experience. As you read this case, try to identify the problems solved by Vail Resorts' information systems and how the systems improve business operations and decision making.

Figure 2.8
Voyage-Estimating
Decision-Support
System
This DSS operates on a powerful PC. It is used daily by managers who must develop bids on shipping contracts.

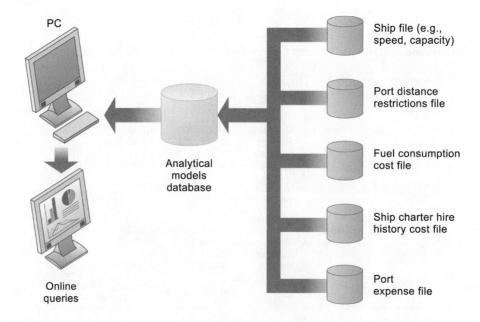

Vail Ski Resorts Goes High-Tech for High Touch

Vail Ski Resort is the largest single mountain ski resort in the United States, with 5,289 acres of the most diverse and expansive skiing in the world. To match its world-class skiing, Vail is also trying to offer world-class customer care—fine dining; spas and ski valets ready to haul, stow, and retrieve your equipment; heated boots; and hand-warming packets. Vail's season pass is a top value industry-wide, and its free PEAKS Rewards membership program further inculcates customer loyalty. Members can purchase the most economical lift tickets online, link the PEAKS card to a credit card, and accumulate points that can be redeemed for free lift tickets, ski school lessons, and various discounts.

In 2012, Vail Ski Resort installed the fastest, highest capacity gondola in the United States. Seating ten people per cabin, and with an uphill speed of 1,200 feet per minute, the state-of-the-art gondola carries 3,600 skiers per hour while decreasing ride time from 9 to 7.5 minutes. Heated seats and Wi-Fi access make it one of the world's most customer-friendly ski lifts as well.

Long lift lines have always created a big headache for skiers. In the past, the only way to gauge the flow of the crowd was to ask lift operators or check postings on bulletin boards at the bottom of the lifts. Now Vail skiers are able to obtain accurate up-to-the minute lift line information by using social networking, streaming alerts, and the resort's own Twitter account. Slope congestion can be alleviated by offering special pins or prizes to coax guests to move to a different slope. Guests can be directed to on-mountain dining locations at lunch time.

Vail now uses radio frequency identification (RFID) lift tickets and ski passes. Part of the EpicMix social media program, the tickets and passes are scanned at the base of each lift so that skiers and snowboarders can track how many lifts they ride and the vertical feet ascended each day. The scanned data are automatically transferred to an EpicMix application which can be accessed from either a smartphone or a computer. The basic program is free and confers various pins and virtual awards based on user statistics. For example, you earn the "Connoisseur" pin after 75 lifts and the "Over the Moon" pin when you surpass 350,000 vertical feet skied. After you create your EpicMix account, you can view and share stats by linking to your Facebook and Twitter accounts.

The EpicMix Racing program provides additional fun. At one of six race courses, you can compete against friends and family, all skiers, and even 2010

Olympic women's downhill gold medalist Lindsey Vonn. At the beginning of each season, the four-time overall World Cup champion establishes a course time for race courses at Vail, Beaver Creek, Breckenridge, Keystone, Heavenly and Northstar. Race pros then ski the courses to establish their "seconds behind Lindsey." To factor in changing course conditions, every day one of the race pros skis each course and uses his or her "seconds behind Lindsey" to determine a course time for Vonn on that particular day. When you ski a course, your actual time is automatically recorded and then adjusted for gender, age, and discipline. Snowboarders, telemark skiers, and adaptive skiers with disabilities and special needs can also participate. Scores are computed based on each skier's "seconds behind Lindsey," and gold, silver, and bronze medals are awarded to the top three daily. Race results and leaderboards are accessed on EpicMix.com or the EpicMix mobile app, available for Apple and Android smartphones. Your dashboard tallies your Lindsey Vonn Race Series points, EpicMix Racing medals, total number of resort check-ins, total days on a mountain, vertical feet, pins earned, and number of EpicMix photos taken.

The six race course mountains are staffed by 140 professional photographers. Photos are automatically identified and uploaded by scanning the intelligent chip embedded in the skier's lift ticket. Photos can be captioned and shared for free on Facebook and Twitter, or you can purchase prints at a number of locations, including, of course, the Children's Ski Schools. You can also purchase a $30 season package for unlimited downloads of all images taken at all locations and print them out later. All of these amenities turn a ski vacation into an "experience" that can be shared with family and friends, increasing emotional attachment and promoting customer retention.

Still, to ensure that it is fully leveraging the wealth of customer data it collects, Vail Ski Resorts' parent company Vail Resorts implemented SAS Customer Intelligence software. Customer data were previously collected and stored in a number of unrelated systems. Now, the data are compiled in a single database that includes all customer points of contact, allowing a complete picture of customer habits and preferences to emerge. Rather than one or two versions of a marketing campaign, Vail Resorts now runs 30 to 50, targeted to specific groups. In the future, the company expects to expand to hundreds or even thousands of personalized, individual communications. SAS predictive analytics will help Vail Resorts to identify guest motivations and anticipate customer desires, while customer segmentation models identify profitable segments to which they might be steered. Vail Resorts plans to further personalize its engagement with its guests and enrich their mountain experiences before they have even begun.

Sources: "EpicMix," snow.com (http://www.snow.com/epic-pass/pass-benefits/epicmix.aspx), accessed May 30, 2013; Bill Pennington, "Getting Comfortable With the New Vail," *New York Times*, March 1, 2013; "EpicMix FAQ," epicmix.com (http://www.epicmix.com/faq.aspx), accessed May 30, 2013; Spencer Reiss, "Vail Resorts Creates Epic Experiences with Customer Intelligence," *SAS Case Study*, March 20, 2013; Lauren Glendenning, "Vail's New Gondola Lifts Off," Vail Daily, November 16, 2012; and Nicole Perlroth, "Nine Ski Apps to Make the Most of the Mountain," *New York Times*, December 26, 2012.

CASE STUDY QUESTIONS

1. List and describe the types of systems described in this case study.

2. How do these systems improve the operation of the business?

3. How do these systems support decision-making? Identify 3 different decisions that can be supported by these systems.

4. Why is improving the guest experience so important at Vail Mountain Resort?

Business intelligence systems also address the decision-making needs of senior management. Senior managers need systems that focus on strategic issues and long-term trends, both in the firm and in the external environment. They are concerned with questions such as: What will employment levels be in five years? What are the long-term industry cost trends? What products should we be making in five years?

Executive support systems (ESS) help senior management make these decisions. They address non-routine decisions requiring judgment, evaluation, and insight because there is no agreed-on procedure for arriving at a solution. ESS present graphs and data from many sources through an interface that is easy for senior managers to use. Often the information is delivered to senior executives through a **portal**, which uses a Web interface to present integrated personalized business content.

ESS are designed to incorporate data about external events, such as new tax laws or competitors, but they also draw summarized information from internal MIS and DSS. They filter, compress, and track critical data, displaying the data of greatest importance to senior managers. Increasingly, such systems include business intelligence analytics for analyzing trends, forecasting, and "drilling down" to data at greater levels of detail.

For example, the CEO of Leiner Health Products, the largest manufacturer of private-label vitamins and supplements in the United States, has an ESS that provides on his desktop a minute-to-minute view of the firm's financial performance as measured by working capital, accounts receivable, accounts payable, cash flow, and inventory. The information is presented in the form of a **digital dashboard**, which displays on a single screen graphs and charts of key performance indicators for managing a company. Digital dashboards are becoming an increasingly popular tool for management decision makers.

Contemporary business intelligence and analytics technology have promoted data-driven management, where decision makers rely heavily on analytical tools and data at their fingertips to guide their work. Data captured at the factory or sales floor level are immediately available for high-level or detailed views in executive dashboards and reports. It's real-time management and highly visual. Procter & Gamble (P&G) is a world-class leader. The Interactive Session on People illustrates information-driven management at work in this company.

Procter and Gamble (P&G) is the world's largest and most profitable consumer products company, with 126,000 employees across 180 countries, 300 brands, and over $83 billion in revenues in 2012. P&G is regularly ranked near the top of lists of "most admired companies" for its ability to create, market and sell major consumer product brands. A major reason for P&G's success has been its robust information technology and willingness to pursue new IT innovations to maintain a competitive advantage in its industry.

To that end, P&G has made it its goal to digitize its processes from end to end and to fundamentally change the way it gathers, reports, and interprets data. While P&G is trimming costs from other areas of the business, its Global Business Services division is building analytics expertise and undertaking new analytical solutions such as Business Sufficiency, Business Sphere and Decision Cockpits.

These solutions eliminate time spent debating different data sets, and instead use a system that allows leaders to focus on immediate business decisions using the most accurate data available at that precise moment.

The solutions are based on a transformation in the way P&G uses data for decision-making across the company, from executives, to brand managers, to lower level employees. P&G's old decision-making model was to figure out what reports people wanted, capture the data and then deliver them to the key decision-makers days or weeks later. The new model is more instantaneous, with people huddling together in person or via video and pulling in the right experts to fix a problem the moment it arises. More real-time data and analytics expertise are required.

The Business Sufficiency program, launched in 2010, furnishes executives with predictions about P&G market share and other key performance metrics six to twelve months into the future. It is based on a series of analytic models showing what's occurring in the business right now (shipments, sales, market share), why it's happening, and what actions P&G can take. The "why" models highlight sales data at the country, territory, product line, and store levels, along with drivers such as advertising and consumer consumption, factoring in specific economic data at the regional and country levels. The "actions" show ways that P&G can adjust pricing, advertising, and product mix to respond to the predictions.

For example, when CEO Bob McDonald meets with his executive committee each Monday, they examine the top categories of products and country markets (such as Italy and hair care) that are responsible for 60 percent of sales. Data visualizations show changes in sales and market share. Executives may want more detailed data: Is the sales dip in detergent in Germany because of one large retailer? Is that retailer buying less only in Germany or across Europe? Did a rival take away market share because P&G raised prices or cut promotions, or is the product category overall losing sales?

P&G's Business Sphere is an interactive system designed to reveal insights, trends and opportunities for P&G's leaders and prompt them to ask focused business questions that can be addressed with data on the spot. Two giant 32-foot by 8-foot concave display screens physically surround these managers with the data on sales, market share, and ad spending required to make actionable decisions. Thousands of algorithms and analytical models aggregate data, organizing it by country, territory, product line, store level, and other categories, and monitor trends like response to advertising and consumer consumption within individual regions and countries. Everyone in the meeting sees the same information.

The program analyzes 200 terabytes of P&G data, equivalent to 200,000 copies of the Encyclopedia Britannica, and displays information quickly and clearly. The Business Sphere allows top executives to answer their own specific business questions, and to visualize data in a more intuitive way than a simple report allows. The Business Sphere was envisioned as a kind of command center, where top managers gather either in person or via high quality video conferencing technology like Cisco Telepresence, and immediately determine what are the biggest problems facing the business and who can fix those problems as soon as they arise. P&G now has more than 50 Business Spheres around the world.

The Business Sphere is mostly used by upper-level P&G managers and executives, but the company was determined to extend the same principles further across the business. That's where the Decision Cockpits come in. P&G has started to give more of its employees access to the same common data sources – over 58,000 employees now use the technology. These cockpits are dashboards displaying easy-to-read charts illustrating business status and trends. The cockpits feature automated alerts when important events occur, control charts, statistical analyses in real time, and the ability to "drill down" to more detailed levels of data.

One of the major goals of the Decision Cockpits was to eliminate time spent by P&G employees debating the validity of competing versions of data found in emails, spreadsheets, letters, and reports. By providing a one-stop source of accurate and detailed real-time business data, all P&G employees are able to focus instead on decisions for improving the business. Both the Business Sphere and Decision Cockpits encourage P&G employees and managers to "manage by exception." This means that by looking at the data and taking note of the exceptions, such as regions that are losing market share the fastest, or areas that are booming and require more resources, P&G can devote time and energy where it is most needed.

Managers and employees are now able to make faster and better decisions than were previously possible. Other benefits of the project have been the reduced complexity involved in generating a statistical report, as well as cost reductions from maintaining one stan-

dardized set of data across the enterprise instead of duplicated, redundant data. P&G has seen the number of e-mails generated by employees drop sharply, as more workers can answer their own questions and obtain their own information using Decision Cockpits. Better messaging and video will help employees pull in anyone needed to make a decision. The company is also able to better anticipate future events affecting the business and more quickly respond to market stimuli. P&G is now working on better messaging and video.

Sources: Chris Murphy, "P&G CEO Shares 3 Steps to Analytics-Driven Business," *Information Week*, February 7, 2013; Tom Davenport, "How P&G Presents Data to Decision-Makers," *Harvard Business Review*, April 4, 2013; Peter High, "Data Analytics Allows P&G to Turn on a Dime," CIO Insight, May 3, 2013; www.pg.com, accessed April 25, 2013; ShirishNetke and Ravi Kalakota, "Procter & Gamble - A Case Study in Business Analytics," *SmartAnalytics*, March 5, 2012; and Brian P. Watson, "Data Wrangling: How Procter and Gamble Maximizes Business Analytics," *CIO Insight*, January 30, 2012.

CASE STUDY QUESTIONS

1. What are the business benefits of Business Sufficiency, Business Sphere and Decision Cockpits?

2. What people, organization, and technology issues had to be addressed when implementing Business Sufficiency, Business Sphere, and Decision Cockpits?

3. How did these decision-making tools change the way the company ran its business? How effective are they? Why?

4. According to P&G CEO Bob McDonald, P&G's new approach to decision making represents a "cultural revolution." Discuss the implications of this statement.

5. How are these systems related to P&G's business strategy?

SYSTEMS FOR LINKING THE ENTERPRISE

Reviewing all the different types of systems we have just described, you might wonder how a business can manage all the information in these different systems. You might also wonder how costly it is to maintain so many different systems. Additionally, you might wonder how all these different systems can share information and how managers and employees are able to coordinate their work. In fact, these are all important questions for businesses today.

Enterprise Applications

Getting all the different kinds of systems in a company to work together has proven a major challenge. Typically, corporations are put together both through normal "organic" growth and through acquisition of smaller firms. Over a period of time, corporations end up with a collection of systems, most of them older, and face the challenge of getting them all to "talk" with one another and work together as one corporate system. There are several solutions to this problem.

One solution is to implement **enterprise applications**, which are systems that span functional areas, focus on executing business processes across the business firm, and include all levels of management. Enterprise applications help businesses become more flexible and productive by coordinating their business processes more closely and integrating groups of processes so they focus on efficient management of resources and customer service.

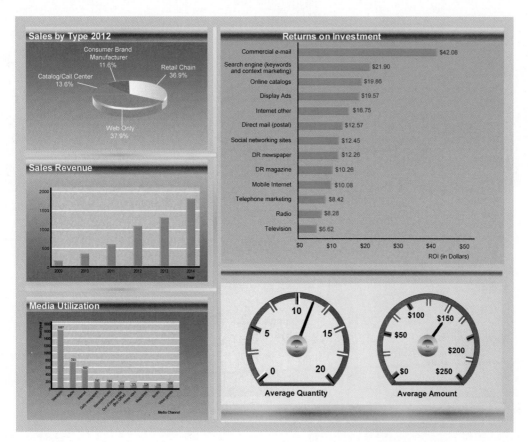

A digital dashboard delivers comprehensive and accurate information for decision making often using a single screen. The graphical overview of key performance indicators helps managers quickly spot areas that need attention.

There are four major enterprise applications: enterprise systems, supply chain management systems, customer relationship management systems, and knowledge management systems. Each of these enterprise applications integrates a related set of functions and business processes to enhance the performance of the organization as a whole. Figure 2.9 shows that the architecture for these enterprise applications encompasses processes spanning the entire organization and, in some cases, extending beyond the organization to customers, suppliers, and other key business partners.

Enterprise Systems Firms use **enterprise systems**, also known as *enterprise resource planning (ERP)* systems, to integrate business processes in manufacturing and production, finance and accounting, sales and marketing, and human resources into a single software system. Information that was previously fragmented in many different systems is stored in a single comprehensive data repository where it can be used by many different parts of the business.

For example, when a customer places an order, the order data flow automatically to other parts of the company that are affected by them. The order transaction triggers the warehouse to pick the ordered products and schedule shipment. The warehouse informs the factory to replenish whatever has been depleted. The accounting department is notified to send the customer an invoice. Customer service representatives track the progress of the order through every step to inform customers about the status of their orders. Managers are able to use firm-wide information to make more precise and timely decisions about daily operations and longer-term planning.

Supply Chain Management Systems Firms use **supply chain management (SCM) systems** to help manage relationships with their suppliers. These systems help suppliers, purchasing firms, distributors, and logistics companies share information about orders, production, inventory levels, and delivery of products and services so that they can source, produce, and deliver goods and services efficiently. The ultimate objective is to

Figure 2.9
Enterprise
Application
Architecture
*Enterprise applications
automate processes
that span multiple busi-
ness functions and
organizational levels and
may extend outside the
organization.*

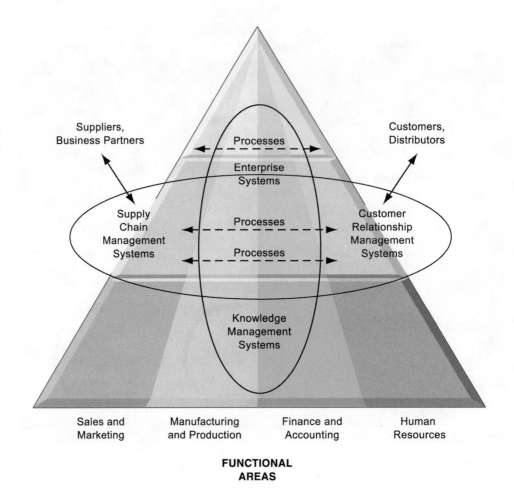

get the right amount of their products from their source to their point of consumption
in the least amount of time and at the lowest cost. These systems increase firm profitability by lowering the costs of moving and making products and by enabling managers
to make better decisions about how to organize and schedule sourcing, production, and
distribution.

Supply chain management systems are one type of **interorganizational system** because
they automate the flow of information across organizational boundaries. You will find
examples of other types of interorganizational information systems throughout this text
because such systems make it possible for firms to link electronically to customers and to
outsource their work to other companies.

Customer Relationship Management Systems Firms use **customer relationship
management (CRM) systems** to help manage their relationships with their customers.
CRM systems provide information to coordinate all of the business processes that deal
with customers in sales, marketing, and service to optimize revenue, customer satisfaction, and customer retention. This information helps firms identify, attract, and retain
the most profitable customers; provide better service to existing customers; and increase
sales.

Knowledge Management Systems Some firms perform better than others because they
have better knowledge about how to create, produce, and deliver products and services.
This firm knowledge is unique, difficult to imitate, and can be leveraged into long-term
strategic benefits. **Knowledge management systems (KMS)** enable organizations to better
manage processes for capturing and applying knowledge and expertise. These systems
collect all relevant knowledge and experience in the firm, and make it available wherever

and whenever it is needed to improve business processes and management decisions. They also link the firm to external sources of knowledge.

We examine enterprise systems and systems for supply chain management and customer relationship management in greater detail in Chapter 9. We discuss collaboration systems that support knowledge management in this chapter and cover other types of knowledge management applications in Chapter 11.

Intranets and Extranets

Enterprise applications create deep-seated changes in the way the firm conducts its business, offering many opportunities to integrate important business data into a single system. They are often costly and difficult to implement. Intranets and extranets deserve mention here as alternative tools for increasing integration and expediting the flow of information within the firm, and with customers and suppliers.

Intranets are simply internal company Web sites that are accessible only by employees. The term "intranet" refers to an internal network, in contrast to the Internet, which is a public network linking organizations and other external networks. Intranets use the same technologies and techniques as the larger Internet, and they often are simply a private access area in a larger company Web site. Extranets are company Web sites that are accessible to authorized vendors and suppliers, and often used to coordinate the movement of supplies to the firm's production apparatus.

For example, Six Flags, which operates 19 theme parks throughout North America, maintains an intranet for its 2,500 full-time employees that provides company-related news and information on each park's day-to-day operations, including weather forecasts, performance schedules, and details about groups and celebrities visiting the parks. We describe the technology for intranets and extranets in more detail in Chapter 7.

E-BUSINESS, E-COMMERCE, AND E-GOVERNMENT

The systems and technologies we have just described are transforming firms' relationships with customers, employees, suppliers, and logistic partners into digital relationships using networks and the Internet. So much business is now enabled by or based upon digital networks that we use the terms *electronic business* and *electronic commerce* frequently throughout this text.

Electronic business, or **e-business**, refers to the use of digital technology and the Internet to execute the major business processes in the enterprise. E-business includes activities for the internal management of the firm and for coordination with suppliers and other business partners. It also includes **electronic commerce**, or **e-commerce**. E-commerce is the part of e-business that deals with the buying and selling of goods and services over the Internet. It also encompasses activities supporting those market transactions, such as advertising, marketing, customer support, security, delivery, and payment.

The technologies associated with e-business have also brought about similar changes in the public sector. Governments on all levels are using Internet technology to deliver information and services to citizens, employees, and businesses with which they work. **E-government** refers to the application of the Internet and networking technologies to digitally enable government and public sector agencies' relationships with citizens, businesses, and other arms of government. In addition to improving delivery of government services, e-government can make government operations more efficient and also empower citizens by giving them easier access to information and the ability to network electronically with other citizens. For example, citizens in some states can renew their driver's licenses or apply for unemployment benefits online, and the Internet has become a powerful tool for instantly mobilizing interest groups for political action and fund-raising.

2.3 Systems for Collaboration and Social Business

With all these systems and information, you might wonder how is it possible to make sense of them? How do people working in firms pull it all together, work towards common goals, and coordinate plans and actions? Information systems can't make decisions, hire or fire people, sign contracts, agree on deals, or adjust the price of goods to the marketplace. In addition to the types of systems we have just described, businesses need special systems to support collaboration and teamwork.

WHAT IS COLLABORATION?

Collaboration is working with others to achieve shared and explicit goals. Collaboration focuses on task or mission accomplishment and usually takes place in a business or other organization, and between businesses. You collaborate with a colleague in Tokyo having expertise on a topic about which you know nothing. You collaborate with many colleagues in publishing a company blog. If you're in a law firm, you collaborate with accountants in an accounting firm in servicing the needs of a client with tax problems.

Collaboration can be short-lived, lasting a few minutes, or longer term, depending on the nature of the task and the relationship among participants. Collaboration can be one-to-one or many-to-many.

Employees may collaborate in informal groups that are not a formal part of the business firm's organizational structure or they may be organized into formal teams. **Teams** have a specific mission that someone in the business assigned to them. Team members need to collaborate on the accomplishment of specific tasks and collectively achieve the team mission. The team mission might be to "win the game," or "increase online sales by 10 percent." Teams are often short-lived, depending on the problems they tackle and the length of time needed to find a solution and accomplish the mission.

Collaboration and teamwork are more important today than ever for a variety of reasons.

- *Changing nature of work.* The nature of work has changed from factory manufacturing and pre-computer office work where each stage in the production process occurred independently of one another, and was coordinated by supervisors. Work was organized into silos. Within a silo, work passed from one machine tool station to another, from one desktop to another, until the finished product was completed. Today, the kinds of jobs we have require much closer coordination and interaction among the parties involved in producing the service or product. A recent report from the consulting firm McKinsey and Company argued that 41 percent of the U.S. labor force is now composed of jobs where interaction (talking, e-mailing, presenting, and persuading) is the primary value-adding activity. Even in factories, workers today often work in production groups, or pods.

- *Growth of professional work.* "Interaction" jobs tend to be professional jobs in the service sector that require close coordination, and collaboration. Professional jobs require substantial education, and the sharing of information and opinions to get work done. Each actor on the job brings specialized expertise to the problem, and all the actors need to take one another into account in order to accomplish the job.

- *Changing organization of the firm.* For most of the industrial age, managers organized work in a hierarchical fashion. Orders came down the hierarchy, and responses moved back up the hierarchy. Today, work is organized into groups and teams, who are expected to develop their own methods for accomplishing the task. Senior managers observe and measure results, but are much less likely to issue detailed orders or operating procedures. In part this is because expertise and decision making power have been pushed down in organizations.

- *Changing scope of the firm.* The work of the firm has changed a single location to multiple locations—offices or factories throughout a region, a nation, or even around the globe. For instance, Henry Ford developed the first mass-production automobile plant at a single Dearborn, Michigan factory. In 2012, Ford employed over 166,000 people at around 90 plants and facilities worldwide. With this kind of global presence, the need for close coordination of design, production, marketing, distribution, and service obviously takes on new importance and scale. Large global companies need to have teams working on a global basis.

- *Emphasis on innovation.* Although we tend to attribute innovations in business and science to great individuals, these great individuals are most likely working with a team of brilliant colleagues. Think of Bill Gates and Steve Jobs (founders of Microsoft and Apple), both of whom are highly regarded innovators, and both of whom built strong collaborative teams to nurture and support innovation in their firms. Their initial innovations derived from close collaboration with colleagues and partners. Innovation, in other words, is a group and social process, and most innovations derive from collaboration among individuals in a lab, a business, or government agencies. Strong collaborative practices and technologies are believed to increase the rate and quality of innovation.

- *Changing culture of work and business.* Most research on collaboration supports the notion that diverse teams produce better outputs faster than individuals working on their own. Popular notions of the crowd ("crowdsourcing," and the "wisdom of crowds") also provide cultural support for collaboration and teamwork.

WHAT IS SOCIAL BUSINESS?

Today many firms are enhancing collaboration by embracing **social business**, the use of social networking platforms, including Facebook, Twitter, and internal corporate social tools, to engage their employees, customers, and suppliers. These tools enable workers to set up profiles, form groups, and "follow" each other's status updates. The goal of social business is to deepen interactions with groups inside and outside the firm to expedite and enhance information-sharing, innovation, and decision-making.

A key word in social business is "conversations." Customers, suppliers, employees, managers, and even oversight agencies continually have conversations about firms, often without the knowledge of the firm or its key actors (employees and managers). Supporters of social business argue that, if firms could tune into these conversations, they will strengthen their bonds with consumers, suppliers and employees, increasing their emotional involvement in the firm.

All of this requires a great deal of information transparency. People need to share opinions and facts with others quite directly, without intervention from executives or others. Employees get to know directly what customers and other employees think; suppliers will learn very directly the opinions of supply chain partners; and even managers presumably will learn more directly from their employees how well they are doing. Nearly everyone involved in the creation of value will know much more about everyone else.

If such an environment could be created, it is likely to drive operational efficiencies, spur innovation, and accelerate decision making. If product designers can learn directly about how their products are doing in the market in real-time, based on consumer feedback, then they can speed up the re-design process. If employees can use social connections inside and outside the company to capture new knowledge and insights, they will be able to work more efficiently and solve more business problems.

Table 2.2 describes important applications of social business inside and outside the firm. This chapter focuses on enterprise social business - its internal corporate uses. Chapter 10 will describe social business applications relating to customers and suppliers outside the company.

TABLE 2.2

Applications of Social
Business

Business Application	Description
Social Networks	Connect through personal and business profiles
Crowdsourcing	Harness collective knowledge to generate new ideas and solutions
Shared workspaces	Coordinate projects and tasks, co-create content
Blogs and Wikis	Publish and rapidly access knowledge; discuss opinions and experiences
Social commerce	Share opinions about purchasing or purchase on social platforms
File sharing	Upload, share, and comment on photos, videos, audio, text documents
Social marketing	Use social media to interact with customers, derive customer insights
Communities	Discuss topics in open forums, share expertise

BUSINESS BENEFITS OF COLLABORATION AND SOCIAL BUSINESS

Although many articles and books have been written about collaboration, nearly all of the research on this topic is anecdotal. Nevertheless, among both business and academic communities there is a general belief that the more a business firm is "collaborative," the more successful it will be, and that collaboration within and among firms is more essential than in the past. A recent global survey of business and information systems managers found that investments in collaboration technology produced organizational improvements that returned over four times the amount of the investment, with the greatest benefits for sales, marketing, and research and development functions (Frost and White, 2009). Another study of the value of collaboration also found that the overall economic benefit of collaboration was significant: for every word seen by an employee in e-mails from others, $70 of additional revenue was generated (Aral, Brynjolfsson, and Van Alstyne, 2007). McKinsey & Company consultants predict that social technologies used within and across enterprises could potentially raise the productivity of interaction workers by 20 to 25 percent (McKinsey, 2012).

Table 2.3 summarizes some of the benefits of collaboration and social business that have been identified. Figure 2.10 graphically illustrates how collaboration is believed to impact business performance.

BUILDING A COLLABORATIVE CULTURE AND BUSINESS PROCESSES

Collaboration won't take place spontaneously in a business firm, especially if there is no supportive culture or business processes. Business firms, especially large firms, had in the past a reputation for being "command and control" organizations where the top leaders thought up all the really important matters, and then ordered lower level employees to execute senior management plans. The job of middle management supposedly was to pass messages back and forth, up and down the hierarchy.

TABLE 2.3

Business Benefits of Collaboration and Social Business

Benefit	Rationale
Productivity	People interacting and working together can capture expert knowledge and solve problems more rapidly than the same number of people working in isolation from one another. There will be fewer errors.
Quality	People work collaboratively can communicate errors, and corrective actions faster than if they work in isolation. Collaborative and social technologies help reduce time delays in design and production.
Innovation	People working collaboratively can come up with more innovative ideas for products, services, and administration than the same number working in isolation from one another. Advantages to diversity and the "wisdom of crowds."
Customer service	People working together using collaboration and social tools can solve customer complaints and issues faster and more effectively than if they were working in isolation from one another.
Financial performance (profitability, sales, and sales growth)	As a result of all of the above, collaborative firms have superior sales, sales growth, and financial performance.

Command and control firms required lower-level employees to carry out orders without asking too many questions, with no responsibility to improve processes, and with no rewards for teamwork or team performance. If your workgroup needed help from another work group, that was something for the bosses to figure out. You never communicated

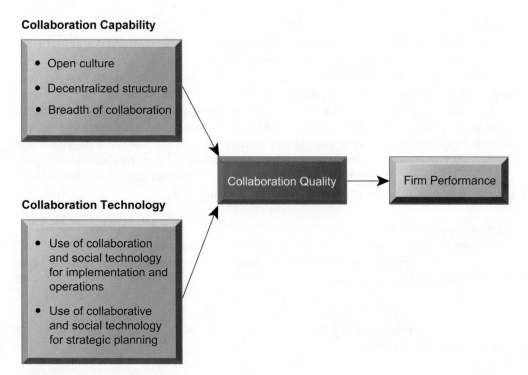

Figure 2.10
Requirements for Collaboration
Successful collaboration requires an appropriate organizational structure and culture, along with appropriate collaboration technology.

horizontally, always vertically, so management could control the process. Together, the expectations of management and employees formed a culture, a set of assumptions about common goals and how people should behave. Many business firms still operate this way.

A collaborative business culture and business processes are very different. Senior managers are responsible for achieving results, but rely on teams of employees to achieve and implement the results. Policies, products, designs, processes, and systems are much more dependent on teams at all levels of the organization to devise, to create, and to build. Teams are rewarded for their performance, and individuals are rewarded for their performance in a team. The function of middle managers is to build the teams, coordinate their work, and monitor their performance. The business culture and business processes are more "social." In a collaborative culture, senior management establishes collaboration and teamwork as vital to the organization, and it actually implements collaboration for the senior ranks of the business as well.

TOOLS AND TECHNOLOGIES FOR COLLABORATION AND SOCIAL BUSINESS

A collaborative, team-oriented culture won't produce benefits without information systems in place to enable collaboration and social business. Currently there are hundreds of tools designed to deal with the fact that, in order to succeed in our jobs, we are all much more dependent on one another, our fellow employees, customers, suppliers and managers. Some high-end tools like IBM's Lotus Notes are expensive, but powerful enough for global firms. Others are available online for free (or with premium versions for a modest fee) and are suitable for small businesses. Let's look more closely at some of these tools.

E-mail and Instant Messaging (IM)

E-mail and instant messaging (including text messaging) have been major communication and collaboration tools for interaction jobs. Their software operates on computers, cell phones, and other wireless handheld devices and includes features for sharing files as well as transmitting messages. Many instant messaging systems allow users to engage in real-time conversations with multiple participants simultaneously. In recent years, e-mail use has declined, with messaging and social media becoming preferred channels of communication.

Wikis

Wikis are a type of Web site that makes it easy for users to contribute and edit text content and graphics without any knowledge of Web page development or programming techniques. The most well-known wiki is Wikipedia, the largest collaboratively edited reference project in the world. It relies on volunteers, makes no money and accepts no advertising.

Wikis are very useful tools for storing and sharing corporate knowledge and insights. Enterprise software vendor SAP AG has a wiki that acts as a base of information for people outside the company, such as customers and software developers who build programs that interact with SAP software. In the past, those people asked and sometimes answered questions in an informal way on SAP online forums, but that was an inefficient system, with people asking and answering the same questions over and over.

Virtual Worlds

Virtual worlds, such as Second Life, are online 3-D environments populated by "residents" who have built graphical representations of themselves known as avatars. Organizations such as IBM and Insead, an international business school with campuses in France and Singapore, are using this virtual world to house online meetings, training sessions, and "lounges." Real-world people represented by avatars meet, interact, and exchange ideas at these virtual locations using gestures, chat box conversations, and voice communication (which requires microphones).

Collaboration and Social Business Platforms

There are now suites of software products providing multi-function platforms for collaboration and social business among teams of employees who work together from many different locations. The most widely used are Internet-based audio conferencing and video conferencing systems, cloud collaboration services such as Google's online tools and cyberlockers, corporate collaboration systems such as Lotus Notes and Microsoft SharePoint, and enterprise social networking tools such as Salesforce Chatter, Microsoft's Yammer, Jive, and IBM's Connections and SmartCloud for Business.

Virtual Meeting Systems　In an effort to reduce travel expenses, many companies, both large and small, are adopting videoconferencing and Web conferencing technologies. Companies such as Heinz, General Electric, and Pepsico are using virtual meeting systems for product briefings, training courses, strategy sessions, and even inspirational chats.

A videoconference allows individuals at two or more locations to communicate simultaneously through two-way video and audio transmissions. High-end videoconferencing systems feature **telepresence** technology, an integrated audio and visual environment which allows a person to give the appearance of being present at a location other than his or her true physical location. Free or low-cost Internet-based systems such as Skype group videoconferencing, Google+ Hangouts, Zoom, and ooVoo are of lower quality, but still useful for smaller companies. Apple's FaceTime and Google Chat are useful tools for one-to-one videoconferencing.

Companies of all sizes are finding Web-based online meeting tools such as Cisco WebEx, Microsoft Lync, and Adobe Connect especially helpful for training and sales presentations. These products enable participants to share documents and presentations in conjunction with audioconferencing and live video via Webcam.

Cloud Collaboration Services: Google Tools and Cyberlockers　Google offers many online tools and services, and some are suitable for collaboration. They include Google Drive, Google Docs, Google Apps, Google Sites, and Google +. Most are free of charge.

Google Drive is a file storage and synchronization service for cloud storage, file sharing and collaborative editing. Google Drive is an example of a cloud-based cyberlocker. **Cyberlockers** are online file-sharing services that allow users to upload files to secure online storage sites from which the files can be shared with others. Microsoft SkyDrive and Dropbox are other leading cyberlocker services. They feature both free and paid services, depending on the amount of storage space required. Users are able to synchronize their files stored online with their local PCs and other kinds of devices, with options for making the files private or public and for sharing them with designated contacts.

Google Drive and Microsoft SkyDrive are integrated with tools for document creation and sharing. Google Drive is now the home of Google Docs, a suite of productivity applications that offer collaborative editing on documents, spreadsheets, and presentations. SkyDrive provides online storage for Microsoft Office documents and other files and works with Office Web Apps, Microsoft's Web versions of Word, Excel, PowerPoint, and OneNote.

Google's cloud-based productivity suite for businesses (word processing, spreadsheets, presentations, calendars, and mail) called Google Apps also works with Google Drive. A Premier edition costs $50 per year for each user and offers 25 gigabytes of mail storage, a 99.9 percent uptime guarantee for e-mail, and tools for administration by the subscribing organization.

Google Sites allows users to quickly create online team-oriented sites where multiple people can collaborate and share files. Google Sites users are able to design and populate Web sites in minutes and, without any advanced technical skills, post a variety of files including calendars, text, spreadsheets, and videos for private, group, or public viewing and editing.

Google+ is Google's effort to make these tools and other products and services it offers more "social" for both consumer and business use. Google+ users can create a profile as well as "Circles," for organizing people into specific groups for sharing and collaborating.

"Hangouts" enable people to engage in group video chat, with a maximum of 10 people participating at any point in time. A feature available to Android, iPhone, and SMS devices called Messenger makes it possible to communicate through instant messaging within "Circles."

Microsoft SharePoint Microsoft SharePoint is a browser-based collaboration and document management platform, combined with a powerful search engine that is installed on corporate servers. SharePoint has a Web-based interface and close integration with everyday tools such as Microsoft Office desktop software products. SharePoint software makes it possible for employees to share their documents and collaborate on projects using Office documents as the foundation.

SharePoint can be used to host internal Web sites that organize and store information in one central workspace to enable teams to coordinate work activities, collaborate on and publish documents, maintain task lists, implement workflows, and share information via wikis and blogs. Users are able to control versions of documents and document security. Because SharePoint stores and organizes information in one place, users can find relevant information quickly and efficiently while working together closely on tasks, projects, and documents. Enterprise search tools help locate people, expertise, and content. As noted in the chapter-opening case, SharePoint has recently added social tools.

ASB Bank, based in Auckland, New Zealand, provides personal and business banking services for 25 percent of the population. Management wanted to increase employee collaboration, agility, and innovation while reducing paper usage by 40 percent over three years. The company implemented Microsoft Sharepoint 2013 because employees were already using other Microsoft software tools (Lync and Office2010), and Sharepoint works with tablet PCs, smartphones, and other mobile devices. ASB Bank built SharePoint 2013 Team Sites where individual departments can manage document scanning, storage, archiving, and security. Employees companywide are able to search for documents quickly and can easily locate the information and expertise they need through personal sites, team sites, blogs, and wiki sites. By organizing information using SharePoint 2013, ASB will be able to meet its paper reduction goals by 2015 (Microsoft, 2012).

Lotus Notes Lotus Notes was an early example of groupware, a collaborative software system with capabilities for sharing calendars, collective writing and editing, shared database access, and electronic meetings, with each participant able to see and display information from others and other activities. Notes software installed on desktop or laptop computers obtains applications stored on an IBM Lotus Domino server. Lotus Notes is now Web-enabled with a scripting and application development environment so that users can build custom applications to suit their unique needs.

Notes software installed on the user's client computer allows the machine to be used as a platform for e-mail, instant messaging (working with Lotus Sametime), Web browsing, and calendar/resource reservation work, as well as for interacting with collaborative applications. Today, Notes also has capabilities for blogs, microblogs, wikis, RSS aggregators, help desk systems, voice and video conferencing, and online meetings. A related IBM Lotus product called Lotus Quickr provides more specialized tools for teamwork (team spaces, content libraries, discussion forums, wikis) and is able to access information from Lotus Notes.

Large firms adopt IBM Lotus Notes because Notes promises high levels of security and reliability, and the ability to retain control over sensitive corporate information. For example, the Department of Clinical Biochemistry, a medical laboratory within Aarhus University Hospital in Denmark, conducts more than 10 million tests a year on more than one million patients. Its paper-based system was error prone, time consuming and difficult to audit. The Department started using an application called Sherlock based on IBM Lotus Notes for streamlining and documenting clinical processes and upgrades. The application contains all of the requirements, employee and supplier reports, operating procedures, confidentiality standards and calibration instructions that are needed to help the department meet ISO 15189 compliance. All emails related to quality management in Sherlock are generated in IBM Lotus Notes software, making it easier to track procedures. Sherlock sends out automatic notifications when specific procedures or calibrations need to be performed in order to remain in compliance. The system creates an audit trail to help the department verify that it is meeting all ISO 15189 requirements. Access control enables managers to decide who can—and cannot—access the system. Sherlock also leverages Lotus Notes capabilities to communicate in five different languages (IBM, 2012).

Enterprise Social Networking Tools   The tools we have just described include capabilities for supporting social business, but there are also more specialized social tools for this purpose, such as Salesforce Chatter, Microsoft's Yammer, Jive, and IBM Connections. Enterprise social networking tools create business value by connecting the members of an organization through profiles, updates, and notifications, similar to Facebook features, but tailored to internal corporate uses. IBM recently introduced a set of social business tools running on a cloud platform called SmartCloud for Social Business, featuring user profiles, communities, e-mail, instant messaging, Web meetings, calendars, personal dashboards, and file-sharing.

Table 2.4 provides more detail about these internal social capabilities.

Dallas-based 7-Eleven Inc. has about 2,000 employees using Yammer since May 2011. The convenience-store chain deployed the application to help field consultants, who work with local franchise owners, share their knowledge and learn best practices from one another. For example, someone might post a picture of a display that worked particularly well in one franchise location for others to see and try in their locations. The social software creates a "virtual water cooler" environment where people are able to talk about what's going on in an informal way yet have formal documentation to keep track of best practices.

Although 7-Eleven and other companies have benefited from enterprise social networking, internal social networking has not caught on as quickly as consumer uses of Facebook, Twitter, and other public social networking products.

Social Software Capability	Description
Profiles	Ability to set up member profiles describing who individuals are, educational background, interests. Includes work-related associations and expertise (skills, projects, teams).
Content Sharing	Share, store, and manage content including documents, presentations, images, and videos
Feeds and Notifications	Real-time information streams, status updates, and announcements from designated individuals and groups.
Groups and Team Workspaces	Establish groups to share information, collaborate on documents, and work on projects, with the ability to set up private and public groups and to archive conversations to preserve team knowledge.
Tagging and Social Bookmarking	Indicate preferences for specific pieces of content, similar to the Facebook "like" button. Tagging lets people add keywords to identify content they like.
Permissions and Privacy	Ability to make sure private information stays within the right circles, as determined by the nature of relationships. In enterprise social networks, there is a need to establish who in the company has permission to see what information.

TABLE 2.4

Enterprise Social Networking Software Capabilities

Checklist for Managers: Evaluating and Selecting Collaboration Software Tools

With so many collaboration tools and services available, how do you choose the right collaboration technology for your firm? To answer this question, you need a framework for understanding just what problems these tools are designed to solve. One framework that has been helpful for us to talk about collaboration tools is the time/space collaboration and social tool matrix developed by a number of collaborative work scholars (Figure 2.11).

The time/space matrix focuses on two dimensions of the collaboration problem: time and space. For instance, you need to collaborate with people in different time zones and you cannot all meet at the same time. Midnight in New York is noon in Bombay, so this makes it difficult to have a video conference. Time is clearly an obstacle to collaboration on a global scale.

Place (location) also inhibits collaboration in large global or even national and regional firms. Assembling people for a physical meeting is made difficult by the physical dispersion of distributed firms (firms with more than one location), the cost of travel, and the time limitations of managers.

The collaboration technologies described previously are ways of overcoming the limitations of time and space. Using this time/space framework will help you to choose the most appropriate collaboration and teamwork tools for your firm. Note that some tools are applicable in more than one time/place scenario. For example, Internet collaboration suites such as Lotus Notes have capabilities for both synchronous (instant messaging, electronic meeting tools) and asynchronous (e-mail, wikis, document editing) interactions.

Here's a "to-do" list to get started. If you follow these six steps, you should be led to investing in the correct collaboration software for your firm at a price you can afford, and within your risk tolerance.

1. What are the collaboration challenges facing the firm in terms of time and space? Locate your firm in the time/space matrix. Your firm can occupy more than one cell in the matrix. Different collaboration tools will be needed for each situation.

2. Within each cell of the matrix where your firm faces challenges, exactly what kinds of solutions are available? Make a list of vendor products.

3. Analyze each of the products in terms of their cost and benefits to your firm. Be sure to include the costs of training in your cost estimates, and the costs of involving the information systems department, if needed.

Figure 2.11
The Time/Space Collaboration and Social Tool Matrix
Collaboration technologies can be classified in terms of whether they support interactions at the same or different time or place, and whether these interactions are remote or co-located.

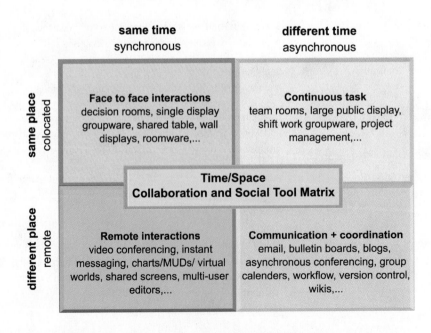

4. Identify the risks to security and vulnerability involved with each of the products. Is your firm willing to put proprietary information into the hands of external service providers over the Internet? Is your firm willing to risk its important operations to systems controlled by other firms? What are the financial risks facing your vendors? Will they be here in three to five years? What would be the cost of making a switch to another vendor in the event the vendor firm fails?

5. Seek the help of potential users to identify implementation and training issues. Some of these tools are easier to use than others.

6. Make your selection of candidate tools, and invite the vendors to make presentations.

2.4 The Information Systems Function in Business

We've seen that businesses need information systems to operate today and that they use many different kinds of systems. But who is responsible for running these systems? Who is responsible for making sure the hardware, software, and other technologies used by these systems are running properly and are up to date? End users manage their systems from a business standpoint, but managing the technology requires a special information systems function.

In all but the smallest of firms, the **information systems department** is the formal organizational unit responsible for information technology services. The information systems department is responsible for maintaining the hardware, software, data storage, and networks that comprise the firm's IT infrastructure. We describe IT infrastructure in detail in Chapter 5.

THE INFORMATION SYSTEMS DEPARTMENT

The information systems department consists of specialists, such as programmers, systems analysts, project leaders, and information systems managers. **Programmers** are highly trained technical specialists who write the software instructions for computers. **Systems analysts** constitute the principal liaisons between the information systems groups and the rest of the organization. It is the systems analyst's job to translate business problems and requirements into information requirements and systems. **Information systems managers** are leaders of teams of programmers and analysts, project managers, physical facility managers, telecommunications managers, or database specialists. They are also managers of computer operations and data entry staff. Also, external specialists, such as hardware vendors and manufacturers, software firms, and consultants, frequently participate in the day-to-day operations and long-term planning of information systems.

In many companies, the information systems department is headed by a **chief information officer (CIO)**. The CIO is a senior manager who oversees the use of information technology in the firm. Today's CIOs are expected to have a strong business background as well as information systems expertise, and to play a leadership role in integrating technology into the firm's business strategy. Large firms today also have positions for a chief security officer, chief knowledge officer, and chief privacy officer, all of whom work closely with the CIO.

The **chief security officer (CSO)** is in charge of information systems security for the firm and is responsible for enforcing the firm's information security policy (see Chapter 8). (Where information systems security is separated from physical security, this position is sometimes called the chief information security officer [CISO]). The CSO is responsible for educating and training users and information systems specialists about security, keeping management aware of security threats and breakdowns, and maintaining the tools and policies chosen to implement security.

Information systems security and the need to safeguard personal data have become so important that corporations collecting vast quantities of personal data have established positions for a **chief privacy officer (CPO)**. The CPO is responsible for ensuring that the company complies with existing data privacy laws.

The **chief knowledge officer (CKO)** is responsible for the firm's knowledge management program. The CKO helps design programs and systems to find new sources of knowledge or to make better use of existing knowledge in organizational and management processes. **End users** are representatives of departments outside of the information systems group for whom applications are developed. These users are playing an increasingly large role in the design and development of information systems.

In the early years of computing, the information systems group was composed mostly of programmers who performed highly specialized but limited technical functions. Today, a growing proportion of staff members are systems analysts and network specialists, with the information systems department acting as a powerful change agent in the organization. The information systems department suggests new business strategies and new information-based products and services, and coordinates both the development of the technology and the planned changes in the organization.

INFORMATION SYSTEMS SERVICES

Services provided by the information systems department include the following:

- Computing platforms provide computing services that connect employees, customers, and suppliers into a coherent digital environment, including large mainframes, desktop and laptop computers, and mobile handheld devices.
- Telecommunications services provide data, voice, and video connectivity to employees, customers, and suppliers.
- Data management services store and manage corporate data, and provide capabilities for analyzing the data.
- Application software services provide development and support services for the firm's business systems, including enterprise-wide capabilities, such as enterprise resource planning, customer relationship management, supply chain management, and knowledge management systems, that are shared by all business units.
- Physical facilities management services develop and manage the physical installations required for computing, telecommunications, and data management services.
- IT management services plan and develop the infrastructure, coordinate with the business units for IT services, manage accounting for the IT expenditure, and provide project management services.
- IT standards services provide the firm and its business units with policies that determine not only which information technology will be used, but when, and how.
- IT educational services provide training in system use to employees and offer managers training in how to plan for and manage IT investments.
- IT research and development services provide the firm with research on potential future information systems projects and investments that could help the firm differentiate itself in the marketplace.

In the past, firms generally built their own software and managed their own computing facilities. As our discussion of collaboration systems has shown, many firms are turning to external vendors to provide these services (see also Chapters 5 and 12) and are using their information systems departments to manage these service providers.

Review Summary

1 **What major features of a business are important for understanding the role of information systems?** A business is a formal complex organization producing products or services for a profit. Businesses have specialized functions, such as finance and accounting, human resources, manufacturing and production, and sales and marketing. Business organizations are arranged hierarchically into levels of management. A business process is a logically related set of activities that define how specific business tasks are performed. Business firms must monitor and respond to their surrounding environments.

2 **How do systems serve different management groups in a business?** Systems serving operational management are transaction processing systems (TPS), such as payroll or order processing, that track the flow of the daily routine transactions necessary to conduct business. Business intelligence systems serve multiple levels of management, and help employees make more informed decisions. Management information systems (MIS) and decision-support systems (DSS) support middle management. Most MIS reports condense information from TPS and are not highly analytical. DSS support management decisions that are unique and rapidly changing using advanced analytical models and data analysis capabilities. Executive support systems (ESS) support senior management by providing data that are often in the form of graphs and charts delivered via portals and dashboards using many sources of internal and external information.

3 **How do systems that link the enterprise improve organizational performance?** Enterprise applications are designed to coordinate multiple functions and business processes. Enterprise systems integrate the key internal business processes of a firm into a single software system to improve coordination and decision making. Supply chain management systems help the firm manage its relationship with suppliers to optimize the planning, sourcing, manufacturing, and delivery of products and services. Customer relationship management (CRM) systems coordinate the business processes surrounding the firm's customers. Knowledge management systems enable firms to optimize the creation, sharing, and distribution of knowledge. Intranets and extranets are private corporate networks based on Internet technology. Extranets make portions of private corporate intranets available to outsiders.

4 **Why are systems for collaboration and social business so important and what technologies do they use?** Collaboration is working with others to achieve shared and explicit goals. Social business is the use of internal and external social networking platforms to engage employees, customers, and suppliers, and it can enhance collaborative work. Collaboration and social business have become increasingly important in business because of globalization, the decentralization of decision making, and growth in jobs where interaction is the primary value-adding activity. Collaboration and social business enhance innovation, productivity, quality, and customer service. Tools for collaboration and social business include email and instant messaging, wikis, virtual meeting systems, virtual worlds, cloud-based services and cyberlockers, corporate collaboration platforms such Microsoft SharePoint and Lotus Notes, and enterprise social networking tools such as Chatter, Yammer, Jive, and IBM Connections.

5 **What is the role of the information systems function in a business?** The information systems department is the formal organizational unit responsible for information technology services. It is responsible for maintaining the hardware, software, data storage, and networks that comprise the firm's IT infrastructure. The department consists of specialists, such as programmers, systems analysts, project leaders, and information systems managers, and is often headed by a CIO.

Key Terms

Business, 61	Chief privacy officer (CPO), 87	Cyberlocker, 83
Business intelligence, 68		Data workers, 65
Business processes, 62	Chief security officer (CSO), 87	Decision-support systems (DSS), 69
Chief information officer (CIO), 87	Collaboration, 78	Digital dashboard, 72
Chief knowledge officer (CKO), 87	Customer relationship management (CRM) systems, 76	Electronic business (e-business), 77

Review Questions

2-1 What major features of a business are important for understanding the role of information systems?
- Define a business and describe the major business functions.
- Define business processes and describe the role they play in organizations.
- Explain how information technology and information systems enhance business processes.
- Explain why environments are important for understanding a business.

2-2 How do systems serve different management groups in a business?
- Identify the principal levels of management in a business and describe the different needs for information for each level.
- Describe the characteristics of transaction processing systems (TPS) and role they play in a business.
- Describe the characteristics of management information systems (MIS), decision support systems (DSS), and executive support systems (ESS) and explain how each type of system helps managers make decisions.

2-3 How do systems that link the enterprise improve organizational performance?
- Explain how enterprise applications improve organizational performance.
- Define enterprise systems, supply chain management systems, customer relationship management systems, and knowledge management systems and describe their business benefits.
- Explain how intranets and extranets help firms improve business performance.

2-4 Why are systems for collaboration and social business so important and what technologies do they use?
- Define collaboration and social business and explain why they have become so important in business today.
- List and describe the business benefits of collaboration and social business.
- List and describe the various types of collaboration and social business tools.
- Explain how you can evaluate and select collaboration software tools.

2-5 What is the role of the information systems function in a business?
- Describe the services provided by information systems departments.
- Compare the roles played by programmers, systems analysts, information systems managers, the chief information officer (CIO), chief security officer (CSO), and chief knowledge officer (CKO).

Discussion Questions

2-6 How could information systems be used to support the order fulfillment process illustrated in Figure 2.2? What are the most important pieces of information these systems should capture? Explain your answer.

2-7 Identify the steps that are performed in the process of selecting and checking out a book from your college library and the information that flows among these activities. Diagram the process. Are there any ways this process could be adjusted to improve the performance of your library or your school? Diagram the improved process.

2-8 Why do you think digital dashboards have become an increasingly popular tool for management decision makers?

Hands-On MIS Projects

The projects in this section give you hands-on experience analyzing opportunities to improve business processes with new information system applications, using a spreadsheet to improve decision making about suppliers, and using Internet software to plan efficient transportation routes.

MANAGEMENT DECISION PROBLEMS

2-9 Fulbert Timber Merchants in Brixton, UK features a large selection of building supplies, including timber, fencing and decking, mouldings, hardwood flooring, sheet materials, windows, doors, ironmongery, and other materials. The prices of building materials are constantly changing. When a customer asks about the price on fixtures, fittings, hangings, and other items of ironmongery, sales representatives consult a manual price sheet and then call the supplier for the most recent price. The supplier in turn uses a manual price sheet, which has been updated each day. Often, the supplier must call back Fulbert's sales reps because the company does not have the newest pricing information immediately on hand. Assess the business impact of this situation, describe how this process could be improved with information technology, and identify the decisions that would have to be made to implement a solution.

2-10 Quincaillerie is a small family hardware store in Paris, France. The owners must use every square foot of store space as profitably as possible. They have never kept detailed inventory or sales records. As soon as a shipment of goods arrives, the items are immediately placed on store shelves. Invoices from suppliers are only kept for tax purposes. When an item is sold, the item number and price are rung up at the cash register. The owners use their own judgment in identifying items that need to be reordered. What is the business impact of this situation? How could information systems help the owners run their business? What data should these systems capture? What decisions could the systems improve?

IMPROVING DECISION MAKING: USE A SPREADSHEET TO SELECT SUPPLIERS

Software skills: Spreadsheet date functions, data filtering, DAVERAGE function
Business skills: Analyzing supplier performance and pricing

2-11 In this exercise, you will learn how to use spreadsheet software to improve management decisions about selecting suppliers. You will filter transactional data on suppliers based on several different criteria to select the best suppliers for your company.

You run a company that manufactures aircraft components. You have many competitors who are trying to offer lower prices and better service to customers, and you are trying to determine whether you can benefit from better supply chain management. In MyMISLab, you will find a spreadsheet file that contains a list of all of the items that your firm has ordered from its suppliers during the past three months. The fields in the spreadsheet file include vendor name, vendor identification number, purchaser's order number, item identification number and item description (for each item ordered from the vendor), cost per item, number of units of the item ordered (quantity), total cost of each order, vendor's accounts payable terms, order date, and actual arrival date for each order.

Prepare a recommendation of how you can use the data in this spreadsheet database to improve your decisions about selecting suppliers. Some criteria to consider for identifying preferred suppliers include the supplier's track record for on-time deliveries, suppliers offering the best accounts payable terms, and suppliers offering lower pricing when the same item can be provided by multiple suppliers. Use your spreadsheet software to prepare reports to support your recommendations.

ACHIEVING OPERATIONAL EXCELLENCE: USING INTERNET SOFTWARE TO PLAN EFFICIENT TRANSPORTATION ROUTES

2-12 In this exercise, you will use Google Maps to map out transportation routes for a business and select the most efficient route.

You have just started working as a dispatcher for Trans-Europe Transport, a trucking and delivery service based in Brussels, Belgium. Your first assignment is to plan a shipment of paintings from the Museum Aan de Stroom in Antwerp, Belgium to the Royal Museums of Fine Arts of Belgium in Brussels. To guide your trucker, you need to know the most efficient route between the two cities. Use Google Maps to determine the route that is the shortest distance between the two cities, the route that takes the least time, and the estimated fuel cost for both routes Compare the results. Which route should Trans-Europe Transport use? Use MapQuest again to find the route that takes the least time. Compare the results. Which route should Cross-Country use?

Collaboration and Teamwork Project

2-13 In MyMISLab, you will find a Collaboration and Teamwork Project dealing with the concepts in this chapter. You will be able to use Google Drive, Google Docs, Google Sites, Google+, or other open-source tools to complete the assignment.

BUSINESS PROBLEM-SOLVING CASE

Modernization of NTUC Income

NTUC Income (Income), one of Singapore's largest insurers, has over 1.8 million policy holders with total assets of S$21.3 billion. The insurer employs about 3,400 insurance advisors and 1,200 office staff, with the majority located across an eight-branch network. On June 1, 2003, Income succeeded in the migration of its legacy insurance systems to a digital web-based system. The Herculean task required not only the upgrading of hardware and applications, it also required Income to streamline its decade-old business processes and IT practices.

Up until a few years ago, Income's insurance processes were very tedious and paper-based. The entire insurance process started with customers meeting an agent, filling in forms and submitting documents. The agent would then submit the forms at branches, from where they were sent by couriers to the Office Services department. The collection schedule could introduce delays of two to three days. Office Services would log documents, sort them, and then send them to departments for underwriting. Proposals were allocated to underwriting staff, mostly randomly. Accepted proposals were sent for printing at the Computer Services department and then redistributed. For storage, all original documents were packed and sent to warehouses where, over two to three days, a total of seven staff would log and store the documents. In all, paper policies comprising 45 million documents were stored in over 16,000 cartons at three warehouses. Whenever a document needed to be retrieved, it would take about two days to locate and ship it by courier. Refiling would again take about two days.

In 2002, despite periodic investments to upgrade the HP 3000 mainframe that hosted the core insurance applications as well as the accounting and management information systems, it still frequently broke down. According to James Kang, CIO at Income, "The system breakdowns were a real nightmare. Work would stop and the staff had to choose either data reconciliation, or backup. However, the HP 3000 backup system allowed restoration to only up to the previous day's backup data. If the daily backup was not completed at the end of the day, the affected day's data would be lost and costly and tedious reconciliation would be needed to bring the data up to date." In one of the hardware crashes, reconciliation took several months to restore the data loss. In all, the HP 3000 system experienced a total of three major hardware failures, resulting in a total of six days of complete downtime.

That was not enough. The COBOL programs that were developed in the early 1980s and maintained by Income's in-house IT team, also broke multiple times, halted the systems and caused temporary interruptions. In addition,

the IT team found developing new products in COBOL to be quite cumbersome and the time taken to launch new products ranged from a few weeks to months.

At the same time, transaction processing for policy underwriting was still a batch process and information was not available to agents and advisors in real-time. As a result, when staff processed a new customer application for motor insurance, they did not know if the applicant was an existing customer of Income, which led to the loss of opportunities for cross-product sales. Commenting on the problems faced by the agents, Kang said, "When the agents tried to submit the documents using notebooks, they ran into a lot of problems. HP 3000 was a terrible machine to connect to such devices. And with more of the advisors telecommuting, availability became an issue too." In addition, various departments did not have up-to-date information and had to pass physical documents among each other.

All this changed in June 2003, when Income switched to the Java based eBao LifeSystem from eBao Technology. The software comprised three subsystems – Policy Administration, Sales Management and Supplementary Resources. Commenting on its features, Kang said, "It has everything we are looking for - a customer-centric design, seamless integration with imaging and barcode technology, a product definition module that supports new products, new channels and changes in business processes."

Implementation work started in September 2002 and the project was completed in nine months. By May 2003, all the customization, data migration of Income's individual and group life insurance businesses and training were completed.

The new system was immediately operational on high-availability platform. All applications resided on two or more servers, each connected by two or more communication lines, all of which were "load balanced." This robust architecture minimized downtime occurrence due to hardware or operating system failures.

As part of eBao implementation, Income decided to replace its entire IT infrastructure with a more robust, scalable architecture. For example, all servicing branches were equipped with scanners; monitors were changed to 20 inches; PC RAM size was upgraded to 128 MB; and new hardware and software for application servers, database servers, web servers, and disk storage systems were installed. Furthermore, the LAN cables were replaced with faster cables, a fiber-optic backbone, and wireless capability.

In addition, Income also revamped its business continuity and disaster-recovery plans. A real-time hot backup disaster-recovery center was implemented, where the machines were always running and fully operational. Data was transmitted immediately on the fly from the primary datacenter to the backup machines' data storage. In the event of the datacenter site becoming unavailable, the operations could be switched quickly to the disaster-recovery site without the need to rely on restoration of previous day data.

Moving to a paperless environment, however, was not easy. Income had to throw away all paper records, including legal paper documents. Under the new system, all documents were scanned and stored on "trusted" storage devices – secured, reliable digital vaults that enabled strict compliance with stringent statutory requirements. Income had to train employees who had been accustomed to working with paper to use the eBao system and change the way they worked.

As a result of adopting eBao Life System, about 500 office staff and 3,400 insurance advisors could access the system anytime, anywhere. Staff members who would telecommute enjoyed faster access to information, almost as fast as those who accessed the information in the office.

According to Kang, "We got a singular view of every customer – across products and channels and even better life and general insurance business lines. That allowed us opportunities to cross-sell and improve customer service. In addition, because of the straight through processing workflow capabilities, we had 50 percent savings on both the time and cost needed to process policies. We had also cut the time needed to design and launch new products which was reduced from weeks to just days using the table-driven rule-based product-definition module."

Commenting on the benefits of eBao system, the former CEO Tan Kin Lian remarked, "…eBaoTech LifeSystem has the best straight through processing workflow and it is very flexible. It cuts our new product launch time from months to days. It also allows us to support agents, brokers, and customers to do online services easily. I got a fantastic deal: the best system with much lower cost and much shorter implementation time. I have to say that this is a revolution!"

Sources: Melanie Liew, Computerworld, July 2004; "NTUC Income of Singapore Successfully Implemented eBaoTech Lifesystem," ebaotech.com, accessed November 2008; Neerja Sethi & D G Allampallai, "NTUC Income of Singapore (A): Re-architecting Legacy Systems," asiacase.com, October 2005

Case Study Questions

1. What were the problems faced by Income in this case? How were the problems resolved by the new digital system?
2. What types of information systems and business processes were used by Income before migrating to the fully digital system?
3. Describe the Information systems and IT infrastructure at Income after migrating to the fully digital system?
4. What benefits did Income reap from the new system?
5. How well is Income prepared for the future? Are the problems described in the case likely to be repeated?

Case prepared by Neerja Sethi and Vijay Sethi, Nanyang Technological University.

Achieving Competitive Advantage with Information Systems

CHAPTER 3

STUDENT LEARNING OBJECTIVES

After completing this chapter, you will be able to answer the following questions:

1. How does Porter's competitive forces model help companies develop competitive strategies using information systems?

2. How do the value chain and value web models help businesses identify opportunities for strategic information system applications?

3. How do information systems help businesses use synergies, core competencies, and network-based strategies to achieve competitive advantage?

4. How do competing on a global scale and promoting quality enhance competitive advantage?

5. What is the role of business process management (BPM) in enhancing competitiveness?

LEARNING TRACKS

1. Challenges of Information Systems for Competitive Advantage
2. Primer on Business Process Design and Documentation
3. Primer on Business Process Management

VIDEO CASES

Case 1: National Basketball Association: Competing on Global Delivery with Akamai OS Streaming

Case 2: IT and Geo-Mapping Help a Small Business Succeed

Case 3: Materials Handling Equipment Corp: Enterprise Systems Drive Corporate Strategy for a Small Business

Instructional Video 1: SAP BusinessOne ERP: From Orders to Final Delivery and Payment

CHAPTER OUTLINE

GRUPO MODELO: COMPETING ON PROCESSES

If you drink beverages, chances are good you've tasted Grupo Modelo products. Grupo Modelo is Mexico's largest beverage maker, with a capacity of 1.5 billion gallons annually, placing it in the top ten beverage makers of the world. It's premiere brand is Corona which is exported to 180 countries. Grupo Model also makes beverages solely for the local market in Mexico. Anheuser-Busch InBev, one of the world's largest beverage makers, recently completed its acquisition of Grupo Modelo for a purchase price €14 billion. InBev already owned 50% of Grupo Modelo from a previous purchase. Like many firms that have grown from a collection of enterprises, to a regional powerhouse, and then to a global firm, Grupo Modelo needed to transform its administration so that managers could understand the complexity of the now larger firm, and compete with other global firms. In the future, Grupo Modelo would be competing with other firms on the basis of efficient business processes, and not just the taste of its beverages. The firm needed to become a process-oriented firm..

Grupo Modelo worked with the consulting firm Deloitte Consulting to implement an SAP enterprise management system, creating a single database for all the firm's business units. With nearly 100 different business units, from its seven manufacturing

© Jen Pham/Alamy.

97

facilities, to convenience stores, and distribution centers, the firm was hoping to integrate the disparate units and make it possible to manage them using a single software environment. The first step in building an enterprise system is to identify, document, and begin to measure the firm's business processes. This can take several years. Once identified, managers need to prioritize their efforts by focusing on the most important processes, and build an administrative apparatus to manage the processes. For instance, there are thousands of business processes in large firms. Who will govern these processes? Who will manage the risks associated with these processes? And who will ensure that employees conduct business in compliance with the firm's official processes? These are referred to as GRC challenges (for governance, risk, and compliance). Transforming a traditional organization into a modern competitive enterprise where managers can control their firm's myriad business processes requires both significant cultural change, and technology investment.

To address these challenges, Grupo Modelo organized a new program to bring about the transformation of Grupo Modelo into a process oriented firm. The new program, the Enterprise Model for Administration Transformation, worked with SAP enterprise software modules to build automated dashboards that would allow managers throughout the firm to visually observe how the firm's business processes were working.

SAP's Access Control module formalized security in the firm, ensuring that only authorized employees could define business processes and access process information, and that there was a proper "segregation of duties" in the firm. Segregation of duties is an auditing concept which attempts to prevent fraud and errors by spreading tasks and authorizations to specific business processes among multiple users. Having two people sign a check authorizing payment, for instance, is an example of separation of duties. SAP's Access Control module ensures that tasks and authorizations are precisely defined throughout the firm.

SAP's Process Control module contains the descriptions of processes, regulations that effect the processes, and the extent to which employees comply with the processes. Process Control is an enterprise software solution for compliance and policy management. The compliance management capabilities enable organizations to manage and monitor their internal control environment. This module allows firms to identify and correct compliance issues, document the necessary changes in processes, and then certify and report on the overall state of the corresponding compliance activities. These capabilities help reduce the cost of compliance and improve management transparency and confidence in overall compliance.

The Risk Management module measures and displays the change risks associated with each process, everything from supplier risk, to regulatory changes, and liability issues. The software tracks key risk indicators, and tries to estimate the potential losses and impacts of poor decisions, or adverse risk events. When regulations change, for instance, the software can trace the impact of these new regulations on business processes throughout the firm.

The result of Grupo Modelo's enterprise systems effort is a unification of a far flung company doing business on a global scale, giving management for the first time insights into the firm that had been hidden before. Among the benefits cited by managers are better security controls throughout the company, automating workflows, automated monitoring of processes and risk, and better decision-making based on the notion that all managers in the firm know the correct way of performing a business process no matter where they are located.

Sources: Bruce Romney, "Solutions for GRC Are Transformational for Grupo Modelo, SAP.com, June 24, 2013; Insider Profiles, "How Grupo Modelo Brews Up Process Change and Manages Risk," SAPInsider.com, April 1, 2013; Dana Cimilluca, "Stella, Bud—Meet Corona: AB InBev, Tapping Mexican Beer Market, Seals $20.1 Billion Deal for Modelo," Wall Street Journal, June 29, 2012. Dana Cimilluca, "Stella, Bud—Meet Corona: AB InBev, Tapping Mexican Beer Market, Seals $20.1 Billion Deal for Modelo," ," Wall Street Journal, June 29, 2012..

The story of Grupo Modelo illustrates some of the ways that information systems help businesses compete—and also the challenges of sustaining a competitive advantage. Success in the beer business depends on a number of factors. If Grupo Modelo was to compete in this environment, the firm's managers needed to have a much more fine-grained understanding of all its business processes, and build software tools in the form of desktop dashboards that

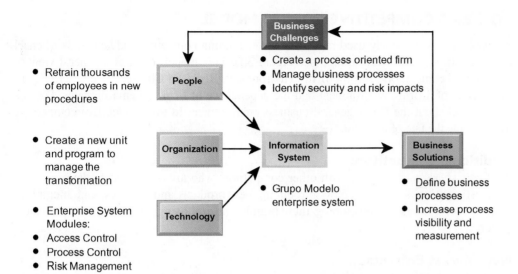

- Retrain thousands of employees in new procedures

- Create a new unit and program to manage the transformation

- Enterprise System Modules:
- Access Control
- Process Control
- Risk Management

Business Challenges

People

- Create a process oriented firm
- Manage business processes
- Identify security and risk impacts

Organization → Information System → Business Solutions

Technology

- Grupo Modelo enterprise system

- Define business processes
- Increase process visibility and measurement

would permit management to operate in real time. The firm also needed tools to ensure security, and understand and mitigate risk.

The chapter-opening diagram calls attention to important points raised by this case and this chapter. Grupo Modelo faced the challenge of becoming a "process oriented" firm, a firm where all the business processes were visible, measurable, and capable of being changed. The firm needed to identify, and then mitigate, security threats and understand the impact of other risks on the firm. New technology was one part of the solution: the firm built on the enterprise software of SAP by implementing process, security, and risk management modules. A successful implementation required that thousands of the firms employees had to be trained in the new software and the newly defined business processes. The result is an information system that defines and makes visible on managers' desktops the important business processes of the firm.

Here are some questions to think about: How do competitive forces and value chain models apply to Grupo Modelo? What do you think was the most difficult challenge Grupo Modelo faced when implementing its new system?

3.1 Using Information Systems to Achieve Competitive Advantage

In almost every industry you examine, you will find that some firms do better than most others. There's almost always a standout firm. In the automotive industry, Toyota is considered a superior performer. In pure online retail, Amazon is the leader; in offline retail, Walmart, the largest retailer on earth, has been the leader, as discussed in the chapter-opening case. In online music, Apple's iTunes is considered the leader with more than 60 percent of the downloaded music market, and in the related industry of digital music players, the iPod is the leader. In Web search, Google is considered the leader.

Firms that "do better" than others are said to have a competitive advantage over others: They either have access to special resources that others do not, or they are able to use commonly available resources more efficiently—usually because of superior knowledge and information assets. In any event, they do better in terms of revenue growth, profitability, or productivity growth (efficiency), all of which ultimately in the long run translate into higher stock market valuations than their competitors.

But why do some firms do better than others and how do they achieve competitive advantage? How can you analyze a business and identify its strategic advantages? How can you develop a strategic advantage for your own business? And how do information systems contribute to strategic advantages? One answer to these questions is Michael Porter's competitive forces model.

PORTER'S COMPETITIVE FORCES MODEL

Arguably, the most widely used model for understanding competitive advantage is Michael Porter's **competitive forces model** (see Figure 3.1). This model provides a general view of the firm, its competitors, and the firm's environment. Recall in Chapter 2 we described the importance of a firm's environment and the dependence of firms on environments. Porter's model is all about the firm's general business environment. In this model, five competitive forces shape the fate of the firm.

Traditional Competitors

All firms share market space with other competitors who are continuously devising new, more efficient ways to produce by introducing new products and services, and attempting to attract customers by developing their brands and imposing switching costs on their customers.

New Market Entrants

In a free economy with mobile labor and financial resources, new companies are always entering the marketplace. In some industries, there are very low barriers to entry, whereas in other industries, entry is very difficult. For instance, it is fairly easy to start a pizza business or just about any small retail business, but it is much more expensive and difficult to enter the computer chip business, which has very high capital costs and requires significant expertise and knowledge that is hard to obtain. New companies have several possible advantages: They are not locked into old plants and equipment, they often hire younger workers who are less expensive and perhaps more innovative, they are not encumbered by old worn-out brand names, and they are "more hungry" (more highly motivated) than traditional occupants of an industry. These advantages are also their weakness: They depend on outside financing for new plants and equipment, which can be expensive; they have a less-experienced workforce; and they have little brand recognition.

Substitute Products and Services

In just about every industry, there are substitutes that your customers might use if your prices become too high. New technologies create new substitutes all the time. Even oil has substitutes: Ethanol can substitute for gasoline in cars; vegetable oil for diesel fuel in trucks; and wind, solar, coal, and hydro power for industrial electricity generation. Likewise, Internet telephone service can substitute for traditional telephone service, and fiber-optic telephone lines to the home can substitute for cable TV lines. And, of course, an Internet music service

Figure 3.1
Porter's Competitive
Forces Model
In Porter's competitive forces model, the strategic position of the firm and its strategies are determined not only by competition with its traditional direct competitors but also by four forces in the industry's environment: new market entrants, substitute products, customers, and suppliers.

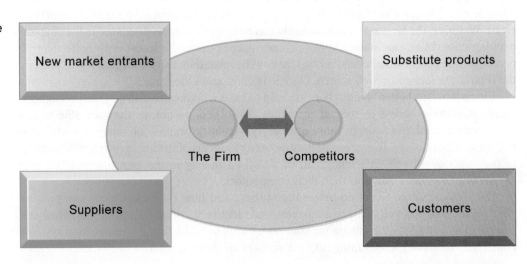

that allows you to download music tracks to an iPod is a substitute for CD-based music stores. The more substitute products and services in your industry, the less you can control pricing and the lower your profit margins.

Customers

A profitable company depends in large measure on its ability to attract and retain customers (while denying them to competitors), and charge high prices. The power of customers grows if they can easily switch to a competitor's products and services, or if they can force a business and its competitors to compete on price alone in a transparent marketplace where there is little product differentiation, and all prices are known instantly (such as on the Internet). For instance, in the used college textbook market on the Internet, students (customers) can find multiple suppliers of just about any current college textbook. In this case, online customers have extraordinary power over used-book firms.

Suppliers

The market power of suppliers can have a significant impact on firm profits, especially when the firm cannot raise prices as fast as suppliers can. The more suppliers a firm has, the greater control it can exercise over those suppliers in terms of price, quality, and delivery schedules. For instance, manufacturers of laptop PCs almost always have multiple competing suppliers of key components, such as keyboards, hard drives, and display screens.

INFORMATION SYSTEM STRATEGIES FOR DEALING WITH COMPETITIVE FORCES

What is a firm to do when faced with all these competitive forces? And how can the firm use information systems to counteract some of these forces? How do you prevent substitutes and inhibit new market entrants? How do you become the most successful firm in an industry in terms of profit and share price (two measures of success)?

Basic Strategy 101: Align the IT with the Business Objectives

The basic principle of IT strategy for a business is to ensure the technology serves the business, and not the other way around. The research on IT and business performance has found that (a) the more successfully a firm can align its IT with its business goals, the more profitable it will be, and (b) only about one-quarter of firms achieve alignment of IT with business. About half of a business firm's profits can be explained by alignment of IT with business (Luftman, 2003; Henderson, et al., 1996).

Most businesses get it wrong: IT takes on a life of its own and does not serve management and shareholder interests very well. Instead of business people taking an active role in shaping IT to the enterprise, they ignore it, claim to not understand IT, and tolerate failure in the IT area as just a nuisance to work around. Such firms pay a hefty price in poor performance. Successful firms and managers understand what IT can do and how it works, take an active role in shaping its use, and measure its impact on revenues and profits.

So how do you as a manager achieve this alignment of IT with business? In the following sections, we discuss some basic ways to do this, but here's a summary:
- Identify your business strategy and goals.
- Break these strategic goals down into concrete activities and processes.
- Identify how you will measure progress towards the business goals ((e.g., metrics).
- Ask yourself, "How can information technology help me achieve progress towards our business goals and how will it improve our business processes and activities?"
- Measure actual performance. Let the numbers speak.

Let's see how this works out in practice. There are four generic strategies, each of which often is enabled by using information technology and systems: low-cost leadership, product differentiation, focus on market niche, and strengthening customer and supplier intimacy.

Supermarkets and large retail stores such as Walmart use sales data captured at the checkout counter to determine which items have sold and need to be reordered. Walmart's continuous replenishment system transmits orders to restock directly to its suppliers. The system enables Walmart to keep costs low while fine-tuning its merchandise to meet customer demands.

© Bonnie Kamin/PhotoEdit.

Low-Cost Leadership

Use information systems to achieve the lowest operational costs and the lowest prices. The classic example is Walmart, described in the chapter-opening case. By keeping prices low and shelves well stocked using a legendary inventory replenishment system, Walmart became the leading retail business in the United States. Point-of-sale terminals record the bar code of each item passing the checkout counter and send a purchase transaction directly to a central computer at Walmart headquarters. The computer collects the orders from all Walmart stores and transmits them to suppliers. Suppliers can also access Walmart's sales and inventory data using Web technology.

Because the system replenishes inventory with lightning speed, Walmart does not need to spend much money on maintaining large inventories of goods in its own warehouses. The system also enables Walmart to adjust purchases of store items to meet customer demands. Competitors, such as Sears, have been spending 24.9 percent of sales on overhead. By using systems to keep operating costs low, Walmart pays only 16.6 percent of sales revenue for overhead. (Operating costs average 20.7 percent of sales in the retail industry.)

Walmart's continuous replenishment system is also an example of an **efficient customer response system**. An efficient customer response system directly links consumer behavior to distribution and production and supply chains. Walmart's continuous replenishment system provides such an efficient customer response.

Product Differentiation

Use information systems to enable new products and services, or greatly change the customer convenience in using your existing products and services. For instance, Google continuously introduces new and unique search services on its Web site, such as Google Maps. Apple created iPod, a unique portable digital music player, plus a unique online Web music service where songs can be purchased for $.69 to $1.29 each. Apple has continued to innovate with its multimedia iPhone, iPad tablet computer, and iPod video player.

Manufacturers and retailers are using information systems to create products and services that are customized and personalized to fit the precise specifications of

TABLE 3.1

IS-Enabled New Products and Services Providing Competitive Advantage

Amazon: One-click shopping	Amazon holds a patent on one-click shopping that it licenses to other online retailers
Online music: Apple iPod and iTunes	An integrated handheld player backed up with an online library of over 26 million songs
Golf club customization: Ping	Customers can select from more than 1 million different golf club options; a build-to-order system ships their customized clubs within 48 hours
Online person-to-person payment: PayPal.com	Enables transfer of money between individual bank accounts and between bank accounts and credit card accounts

individual customers. For example, Nike sells customized sneakers through its Nike iD program on its Web site. Customers are able to select the type of shoe, colors, material, outsoles, and even a logo of up to eight characters. Nike transmits the orders via computers to specially equipped plants in China and Korea. The sneakers cost only about $10 extra and take about three weeks to reach the customer. This ability to offer individually tailored products or services using the same production resources as mass production is called **mass customization**.

Table 3.1 lists a number of companies that have developed IS-based products and services that other firms have found difficult to copy.

Focus on Market Niche

Use information systems to enable a specific market focus, and serve this narrow target market better than competitors. Information systems support this strategy by producing and analyzing data for finely tuned sales and marketing techniques. Information systems enable companies to analyze customer buying patterns, tastes, and preferences closely so that they efficiently pitch advertising and marketing campaigns to smaller and smaller target markets.

The data come from a range of sources—credit card transactions, demographic data, purchase data from checkout counter scanners at supermarkets and retail stores, and data collected when people access and interact with Web sites. Sophisticated software tools find patterns in these large pools of data and infer rules from them that can be used to guide decision making. Analysis of such data drives one-to-one marketing where personal messages can be created based on individualized preferences. For example, Hilton Hotels' OnQ system analyzes detailed data collected on active guests in all of its properties to determine the preferences of each guest and each guest's profitability. Hilton uses this information to give its most profitable customers additional privileges, such as late checkouts. Contemporary customer relationship management (CRM) systems feature analytical capabilities for this type of intensive data analysis (see Chapters 2 and 9).

Strengthen Customer and Supplier Intimacy

Use information systems to tighten linkages with suppliers and develop intimacy with customers. Toyota, Ford, and other automobile manufacturers have information systems that give their suppliers direct access to their production schedules, enabling suppliers to decide how and when to ship supplies to the plants where cars are assembled. This allows suppliers more lead time in producing goods. On the customer side, Amazon.com keeps track of user preferences for book and music purchases, and can recommend titles purchased by others to its customers. Strong linkages to customers and suppliers increase **switching costs** (the cost of switching from one product or service to a competitor) and loyalty to your firm.

TABLE 3.2

Four Basic Competitive
Strategies

Strategy	Description	Example
Low-cost leadership	Use information systems to produce products and services at a lower price than competitors while enhancing quality and level of service	Walmart
Product differentiation	Use information systems to differentiate products, and enable new services and products	Google, eBay, Apple, Starbucks
Focus on market niche	Use information systems to enable a focused strategy on a single market niche; specialize	Hilton Hotels, Harrah's
Customer and supplier intimacy	Use information systems to develop strong ties and loyalty with customers and suppliers	Toyota Corporation, Amazon

Table 3.2 summarizes the competitive strategies we have just described. Some companies focus on one of these strategies, but you will often see firms pursuing several of them simultaneously. For example, Starbucks, the world's largest specialty coffee retailer, offers unique high-end specialty coffees and beverages, but it is also trying to compete by lowering costs.

Implementing any of these strategies is no simple matter. But it is possible, as evidenced by the many firms that obviously dominate their markets and that have used information systems to enable their strategies. As shown by the cases throughout this book, successfully using information systems to achieve a competitive advantage requires a precise coordination of technology, organizations, and people. Indeed, as many have noted with regard to Walmart, Apple, and Amazon, the ability to successfully implement information systems is not equally distributed, and some firms are much better at it than others.

THE INTERNET'S IMPACT ON COMPETITIVE ADVANTAGE

Because of the Internet, the traditional competitive forces are still at work, but competitive rivalry has become much more intense (Porter, 2001). Internet technology is based on universal standards that any company can use, making it easier for rivals to compete on price alone and for new competitors to enter the market. Because information is available to everyone, the Internet raises the bargaining power of customers, who can quickly find the lowest-cost provider on the Web. Profits have been dampened. Table 3.3 summarizes some of the potentially negative impacts of the Internet on business firms identified by Porter.

The Internet has nearly destroyed some industries and has severely threatened others. For instance, the printed encyclopedia industry and the travel agency industry have been nearly decimated by the availability of substitutes over the Internet. Likewise, the Internet has had a significant impact on the retail, music, book, retail brokerage, software, telecommunications, and travel industries. The chapter-ending case provides a detailed discussion of the Internet's impact on publishing.

However, the Internet has also created entirely new markets, formed the basis for thousands of new products, services, and business models, and provided new opportunities for building brands with very large and loyal customer bases. Amazon, eBay, iTunes, YouTube, Facebook, Travelocity, and Google are examples. In this sense, the Internet is "transforming" entire industries, forcing firms to change how they do business.

Competitive Force	Impact of the Internet
Substitute products or services	Enables new substitutes to emerge with new approaches to meeting needs and performing functions
Customers' bargaining power	Shifts bargaining power to customers due to the availability of global price and product information
Suppliers' bargaining power	Tends to raise bargaining power over suppliers in procuring products and services; however, suppliers can benefit from reduced barriers to entry and from the elimination of distributors and other intermediaries standing between them and their users
Threat of new entrants	Reduces barriers to entry, such as the need for a sales force, access to channels, and physical assets; it provides a technology for driving business processes that makes other things easier to do
Positioning and rivalry among existing competitors	Widens the geographic market, increasing the number of competitors and reducing differences among competitors; makes it more difficult to sustain operational advantages; puts pressure to compete on price

TABLE 3.3

Impact of the Internet on Competitive Forces and Industry Structure

THE BUSINESS VALUE CHAIN MODEL

Although the Porter model is very helpful for identifying competitive forces and suggesting generic strategies, it is not very specific about what exactly to do, and it does not provide a methodology to follow for achieving competitive advantages. If your goal is to achieve operational excellence, where do you start? Here's where the business value chain model is helpful.

The **value chain model** highlights specific activities in the business where competitive strategies can best be applied (Porter, 1985) and where information systems are most likely to have a strategic impact. This model identifies specific, critical leverage points where a firm can use information technology most effectively to enhance its competitive position. The value chain model views the firm as a series or chain of basic activities that add a margin of value to a firm's products or services. These activities can be categorized as either primary activities or support activities (see Figure 3.2).

Primary activities are most directly related to the production and distribution of the firm's products and services, which create value for the customer. Primary activities include inbound logistics, operations, outbound logistics, sales and marketing, and service. Inbound logistics includes receiving and storing materials for distribution to production. Operations transforms inputs into finished products. Outbound logistics entails storing and distributing finished products. Sales and marketing includes promoting and selling the firm's products. The service activity includes maintenance and repair of the firm's goods and services.

Support activities make the delivery of the primary activities possible and consist of organization infrastructure (administration and management), human resources (employee recruiting, hiring, and training), technology (improving products and the production process), and procurement (purchasing input).

You can ask at each stage of the value chain, "How can we use information systems to improve operational efficiency and improve customer and supplier intimacy?" This will force you to critically examine how you perform value-adding activities at each stage and how the business processes might be improved. For example, value chain analysis would

Figure 3.2
The Value Chain
Model
This figure provides
examples of systems
for both primary and
support activities of
a firm and of its value
partners that would
add a margin of value
to a firm's products or
services.

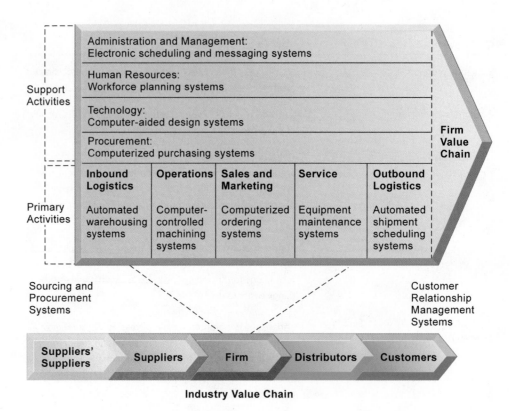

indicate that Walmart, described in the chapter-opening case, should improve its processes for inventory management and quality control. You can also begin to ask how information systems can be used to improve the relationship with customers and with suppliers who lie outside the firm value chain but belong to the firm's extended value chain where they are absolutely critical to your success. Here, supply chain management systems that coordinate the flow of resources into your firm, and customer relationship management systems that coordinate your sales and support employees with customers, are two of the most common system applications that result from a business value chain analysis. We discuss these enterprise applications in detail later in Chapter 9.

Using the business value chain model will also cause you to consider benchmarking your business processes against your competitors or others in related industries, and identifying industry best practices. **Benchmarking** involves comparing the efficiency and effectiveness of your business processes against strict standards and then measuring performance against those standards. Industry **best practices** are usually identified by consulting companies, research organizations, government agencies, and industry associations as the most successful solutions or problem-solving methods for consistently and effectively achieving a business objective.

Once you have analyzed the various stages in the value chain at your business, you can come up with candidate applications of information systems. Then, once you have a list of candidate applications, you can decide which to develop first. By making improvements in your own business value chain that your competitors might miss, you can achieve competitive advantage by attaining operational excellence, lowering costs, improving profit margins, and forging a closer relationship with customers and suppliers. If your competitors are making similar improvements, then at least you will not be at a competitive disadvantage—the worst of all cases!

In the Interactive Session on Technology, we can see how value chain analysis might have helped auto makers refine their competitive strategies. Ford, GM, and other leading auto makers are adding more value to their products by offering software interfaces and applications for improving vehicle performance, providing entertainment, and integrating with other systems for maintenance and future traffic control.

INTERACTIVE SESSION: TECHNOLOGY   Auto Makers Become Software Companies

As the smartphone market continues to expand, another industry has begun getting "smarter" with software and apps: the automobile industry. Ford, BMW, and other automobile companies are enhancing their vehicles with on-board software that improves the customer experience, and the auto industry is working on technology that will allow cars to be managed via the cloud.

Automakers are finding that software is a way of adding more "value" and freshness to their products without having to invest so heavily in new vehicle production. It takes Ford Motor Company, for example, about two and one-half years to plan, design, and build a new car. Design and production, including metal stamping equipment and assembly line setup, must be finalized long before the car rolls off the line. But the auto makers can create a new software interface for a car within months and update it again and again over the life of the car without much lead time. This enables Ford and other auto makers to significantly improve the driving experience and add new features to cars years after they are built.

Ford is perhaps the automaker doing the most to innovate with software and apps. Its MyFord Touch interface is an in-dash touchscreen available for select vehicles with controls for navigation, music, phone integration, and temperature. Ford has upgraded this interface and the Sync software behind the interface, adding tablet and smartphone integration and better voice response. In 2010 Ford added support for the online music streaming service Pandora, which is very popular among young potential buyers. This update enables drivers to connect their tablets and smartphones to the Sync system to access music and other apps using voice commands.

Chairman Bill Ford Jr. has championed the use of software to alleviate urban congestion by investing in technology that responds to the problems created by traffic in the biggest cities. Theoretically, technology might help cars to avoid traffic jams, recommend routes that drivers feel more comfortable with, reserve parking spaces in advance, and possibly to even drive themselves.

To manage vehicles in this way, cars need to be connected to some kind of central system, which would coordinate with public transit and other transportation methods, and to do this, cars need to be equipped with software that can monitor and enhance vehicle function at the most basic levels. The eventual system would require that cars feed increasing amounts of information to systems whose purpose would be to minimize highway congestion. The system would also require an industry standard, which does not exist as of yet. Ford has doubled its investment in vehicle-to-vehicle communication technologies and BMW is also continuing to develop ways for vehicles to communicate with one another on the road to avoid collisions.

With the inclusion of software in their cars, automakers are entering uncharted territory. They must now devote resources to updating and testing their software, as well as establishing ways to provide the updated software to their customers. Car companies need to coordinate their car development cycles more closely with their software development cycles. Also, many of the technologies included in automobile software packages raise the same privacy concerns surrounding location tracking that have often plagued smartphone manufacturers and app developers.

Ford is grappling with the best way to roll out software upgrades to its customers. The company has been mailing USB sticks to 250,000 customers whose cars have an advanced touchscreen control panel running the MyFord Touch interface. The stick contains a software upgrade that will improve navigation controls, the music and phone features, as well as the ability to control car temperature. The upgrade also contains code that will upgrade system speed and improve the interface based on common criticisms from Ford owners.

Although Ford says it plans to continue issuing software upgrades this way, the company hopes that customers will get into the habit of checking the Ford Web site for software upgrades on their own. Though most car owners are used to the technology in their cars remaining constant throughout the life of the car, newer cars are poised to change all of that.

Ford has hired "human-machine interface engineers," whose job is to analyze how their customers interact with the software in their cars. Often, these engineers use customer feedback to make changes to the software. Customers complained that too much information was available on each screen of the interface, so Ford moved the most commonly used features to more prominent positions on screen and increased their font size, relegating the rest to submenus. Feedback has been positive. Ford has also asked dealers to dedicate more time and personnel to hands-on technology training to help customers master its interface.

GM, Daimler, and other companies are all developing new features for their cars that operate online in the cloud. Users will be able to remotely track their cars (you'll never forget where you parked again) and diagnose problems with the car, such as low tire pressure or the need for an oil change. Corporations will be able to track employee use of company cars by interpreting car sensors and engine readouts. Manufacturers will be able to aggregate and analyze the data from customers' cars to identify quality problems and, if necessary, quickly issue recalls. Just as with apps, the possibilities are limited only by the imagination of automakers.

GM will allow its app developers to access its computer systems to improve app function, which raises a familiar set of privacy concerns. Auto analysts believe that automakers will make mistakes as they learn how to properly handle sensitive customer data and to provide robust privacy options. On the other hand, automakers are hoping that younger customers who have grown up using Facebook are less likely to care about privacy, and features that collect highly targeted information about a car's location and driving habits.

BMW is also investing a whopping $100 million in mobile apps, hoping to market them to their customers as "premium services." Some analysts are skeptical of the decision to invest that much money, but BMW believes that mobile apps will become an increasingly attractive selling point for customers of its BMWi electric and hybrid cars. Although the future of cars sharing information with other nearby cars is still years away, automakers are excited by the possibilities afforded by smart software and apps.

Sources: Jaclyn Trop, "Tired of Silicon Valley? Try Motor City," *The New York Times*, July 1, 2013; Ian Scherr and Mike Ramsey, "Drive into the Future," *The Wall Street Journal*, March 11, 2013; Michelle Maisto, "Ford, Google, Facebook Team Up to Reconsider Mobility," *eWeek*, March 28, 2013; Ian Sherr, "Cars Pump Up IQ To Get Edge," *The Wall Street Journal*, January 13, 2012; Chris Murphy, "4 Ways Ford Is Exploring Next-Gen Car Tech," *Information Week*, July 27, 2012; Mike Ramsey, "Avoiding Gridlock with Smart Autos," *The Wall Street Journal*, February 27, 2012; Joseph B. White, "New Driver's Ed: Tutors to Decode High-Tech Dashboards," *The Wall Street Journal*, May 8, 2012; and Chris Murphy, "Ford is Now a Software Company," *Information Week*, November 28, 2011; and "Why BMW Suddenly Loves Mobile Apps," *Information Week*, March 2, 2011.

CASE STUDY QUESTIONS

1. How is software adding value to automakers' products?

2. How are the automakers benefiting from software-enhanced cars? How are customers benefiting?

3. What value chain activities are involved in enhancing cars with software?

4. How much of a competitive advantage is software providing for automakers? Explain your answer.

Extending the Value Chain: The Value Web

Figure 3.2 shows that a firm's value chain is linked to the value chains of its suppliers, distributors, and customers. After all, the performance of most firms depends not only on what goes on inside a firm but also on how well the firm coordinates with direct and indirect suppliers, delivery firms (logistics partners, such as FedEx or UPS), and, of course, customers.

How can information systems be used to achieve strategic advantage at the industry level? By working with other firms, industry participants can use information technology to develop industry-wide standards for exchanging information or business transactions electronically, which force all market participants to subscribe to similar standards. Such efforts increase efficiency, making product substitution less likely and perhaps raising entry costs—thus discouraging new entrants. Also, industry members can build industry-wide, IT-supported consortia, symposia, and communications networks to coordinate activities concerning government agencies, foreign competition, and competing industries.

Looking at the industry value chain encourages you to think about how to use information systems to link up more efficiently with your suppliers, strategic partners, and customers. Strategic advantage derives from your ability to relate your value chain to the value chains of other partners in the process. For instance, if you are Amazon.com, you would want to build systems that

- Make it easy for suppliers to display goods and open stores on the Amazon site
- Make it easy for customers to pay for goods

- Develop systems that coordinate the shipment of goods to customers
- Develop shipment tracking systems for customers

In fact, this is exactly what Amazon has done to make it one of the Web's most satisfying online retail shopping sites.

Internet technology has made it possible to create highly synchronized industry value chains called value webs. A **value web** is a collection of independent firms that use information technology to coordinate their value chains to produce a product or service for a market collectively. It is more customer driven and operates in a less linear fashion than the traditional value chain.

Figure 3.3 shows that this value web synchronizes the business processes of customers, suppliers, and trading partners among different companies in an industry or in related industries. These value webs are flexible and adaptive to changes in supply and demand. Relationships can be bundled or unbundled in response to changing market conditions. Firms will accelerate time to market and to customers by optimizing their value web relationships to make quick decisions on who can deliver the required products or services at the right price and location.

SYNERGIES, CORE COMPETENCIES, AND NETWORK-BASED STRATEGIES

A large corporation is typically a collection of businesses. Often, the firm is organized financially as a collection of strategic business units, and the returns to the firm are directly tied to the performance of all the units. For instance, General Electric—one of the largest industrial firms in the world—is a collection of aerospace, heavy manufacturing, electrical appliance, medical imaging, electronics, and financial services firms called business units. Information systems can improve the overall performance of these business units by promoting communication, synergies, and core competencies among the units.

Synergies

Synergies develop when the output of some units can be used as inputs to other units, or two organizations can pool markets and expertise, and these relationships lower costs and

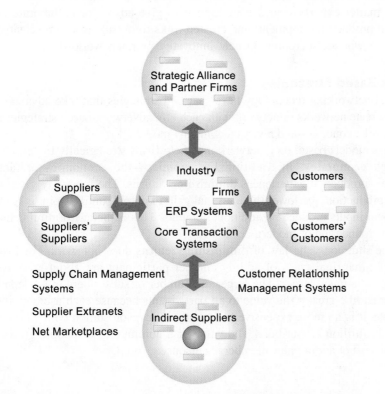

Figure 3.3
The Value Web
The value web is a networked system that can synchronize the value chains of business partners within an industry to respond rapidly to changes in supply and demand.

generate profits. Recent bank and financial firm mergers, such as the merger of Bank of America and Countrywide Financial as well as of JPMorgan Chase and Washington Mutual, occurred precisely for this purpose.

One use of information technology in these synergy situations is to tie together the operations of disparate business units so that they can act as a whole. For example, acquiring Countrywide Financial enabled Bank of America to expand its mortgage lending business and acquire a large pool of new customers that might be interested in its credit cards, consumer banking, and other financial products. Information systems would help the merged companies consolidate operations, lower retailing costs, and increase cross-marketing of financial products.

Enhancing Core Competencies

Another use of information systems for competitive advantage is to think about ways that systems can enhance core competencies. The argument is that the performance of all business units can increase insofar as these business units develop, or create, a central core of competencies. A **core competency** is an activity for which a firm is a world-class leader. Core competencies may involve being the world's best miniature parts designer, the best package delivery service, or the best thin-film manufacturer. In general, a core competency relies on knowledge that is gained over many years of experience and a first-class research organization, or simply key people who follow the literature and stay abreast of new external knowledge.

Any information system that encourages the sharing of knowledge across business units enhances competency. Such systems might encourage or enhance existing competencies and help employees become aware of new external knowledge; such systems might also help a business leverage existing competencies to related markets.

For example, Procter & Gamble (P&G), a world leader in brand management and consumer product innovation, uses a series of systems to enhance its core competencies. P&G uses an intranet called InnovationNet to help people working on similar problems share ideas and expertise. The system connects those working in research and development (R&D), engineering, purchasing, marketing, legal affairs, and business information systems around the world, using a portal to provide browser-based access to documents, reports, charts, videos, and other data from various sources. InnovationNet added a directory of subject matter experts who can be tapped to give advice or collaborate on problem solving and product development, and created links to outside research scientists and 150 entrepreneurs who are searching for new, innovative products worldwide.

Network-Based Strategies

Internet and networking technology have spawned strategies that take advantage of firms' abilities to create networks or network with each other. Network-based strategies include the use of network economics and a virtual company model.

Business models based on a network may help firms strategically by taking advantage of **network economics**. In traditional economics—the economics of factories and agriculture—production experiences diminishing returns. The more any given resource is applied to production, the lower the marginal gain in output, until a point is reached where the additional inputs produce no additional outputs. This is the law of diminishing returns, and it is one foundation of modern economics.

In some situations, the law of diminishing returns does not work. For instance, in a network, the marginal costs of adding another participant are about zero, whereas the marginal gain is much larger. The larger the number of subscribers in a telephone system or the Internet, the greater the value to all participants because each user can interact with more people. It is no more expensive to operate a television station with 1,000 subscribers than with 10 million subscribers. The value of a community of people grows with size, whereas the cost of adding new members is inconsequential.

From this network economics perspective, information technology can be strategically useful. Internet sites can be used by firms to build *communities of users*—like-minded customers who want to share their experiences. This can build customer loyalty and enjoyment, and build unique ties to customers. EBay, the giant online auction and retail site, and iVillage, an online community for women, are examples. Both businesses are based on networks of millions of users, and both companies have used the Web and Internet communication tools to build communities. The more people offering products on eBay, the more valuable the eBay site is to everyone because more products are listed, and more competition among suppliers lowers prices. Network economics also provide strategic benefits to commercial software vendors. The value of their software and complementary software products increases as more people use them, and there is a larger installed base to justify continued use of the product and vendor support.

Another network-based strategy uses the model of a virtual company to create a competitive business. A **virtual company**, also known as a *virtual organization*, uses networks to link people, assets, and ideas, enabling it to ally with other companies to create and distribute products and services without being limited by traditional organizational boundaries or physical locations. One company can use the capabilities of another company without being physically tied to that company. The virtual company model is useful when a company finds it cheaper to acquire products, services, or capabilities from an external vendor or when it needs to move quickly to exploit new market opportunities and lacks the time and resources to respond on its own.

Fashion companies, such as GUESS, Ann Taylor, Levi Strauss, and Reebok, enlist Hong Kong-based Li & Fung to manage production and shipment of their garments. Li & Fung handles product development, raw material sourcing, production planning, quality assurance, and shipping. Li & Fung does not own any fabric, factories, or machines, outsourcing all of its work to a network of more than 7,500 suppliers in 37 countries all over the world. Customers place orders to Li & Fung over its private extranet. Li & Fung then sends instructions to appropriate raw material suppliers and factories where the clothing is produced. The Li & Fung extranet tracks the entire production process for each order. Working as a virtual company keeps Li & Fung flexible and adaptable so that it can design and produce the products ordered by its clients in short order to keep pace with rapidly changing fashion trends.

DISRUPTIVE TECHNOLOGIES: RIDING THE WAVE

Sometimes a technology and resulting business innovation comes along to radically change the business landscape and environment. These innovations are loosely called "disruptive." (Christensen, 2003). In some cases, **disruptive technologies** are substitute products that perform as well or better than anything currently produced. The automobile substituted for the horse-drawn carriage; the Apple iPod for portable CD players; digital photography for process film photography. In these cases, entire industries are put out of business. The chapter-ending case study explores the impact of the Internet on retail bookstores.

In other cases, disruptive technologies simply extend the market, usually with less functionality and much less cost, than existing products. Eventually they turn into low-cost competitors for whatever was sold before. Disk drives are an example: Small hard disk drives used in PCs extended the market for computer disk drives by offering cheap digital storage for small files on small computers. Eventually, small PC hard disk drives became the largest segment of the disk drive marketplace.

Some firms are able to create these technologies and ride the wave to profits, whereas others learn quickly and adapt their business; still others are obliterated because their products, services, and business models become obsolete. There are also cases where no firms benefit, and all gains go to consumers (firms fail to capture any profits). Table 3.4 provides examples of some disruptive technologies.

TABLE 3.4

Disruptive
Technologies: Winners
and Losers

Technology	Description	Winners and Losers
Microprocessor chips (1971)	Thousands and eventually millions of transistors on a silicon chip	Microprocessor firms win (Intel, Texas Instruments) while transistor firms (GE) decline
Personal computers (1975)	Small, inexpensive, but fully functional desktop computers	PC manufacturers (HP, Apple, IBM), and chip manufacturers prosper (Intel), while mainframe (IBM) and minicomputer (DEC) firms lose
Digital photography 1975	Using charge-coupled device (CCD) image sensor chips to record images	CCD manufacturers and traditional camera companies win, manufacturers of film products lose
World Wide Web (1989)	A global database of digital files and "pages" instantly available	Owners of online content, news benefit while traditional publishers (newspapers, magazines, and broadcast television) lose
Internet music, video, TV services	Repositories of downloadable music, video, TV broadcasts on the Web	Owners of Internet platforms, telecommunications providers owning Internet backbone (AT&T, Verizon), local Internet service providers win, while content owners and physical retailers lose (Tower Records, Blockbuster)
PageRank algorithm	A method for ranking Web pages in terms of their popularity to supplement Web search by key terms	Google is the winner (they own the patent), while traditional key word search engines (Alta Vista) lose
Software as Web service	Using the Internet to provide remote access to online software	Online software services companies (Salesforce.com) win, while traditional "boxed" software companies (Microsoft, SAP, Oracle) lose

Disruptive technologies are tricky. Firms that invent disruptive technologies as "first movers" do not always benefit if they lack the resources to exploit the technology or fail to see the opportunity. The MITS Altair 8800 is widely regarded as the first PC, but its inventors did not take advantage of their first mover status. Second movers, so-called "fast followers" such as IBM and Microsoft, reaped the rewards. Citibank's ATMs revolutionized retail banking, but they were copied by other banks. Now all banks use ATMs, with the benefits going mostly to the consumers.

3.2 Competing on a Global Scale

Look closely at your jeans or sneakers. Even if they have a U.S. label, they were probably designed in California and stitched together in Hong Kong or Guatemala using materials from China or India. Call Microsoft Support, or Verizon Support, and chances are good you will be speaking to a customer service representative located in India.

Consider the path to market for an iPhone, which is illustrated in Figure 3.4. The iPhone was designed by Apple engineers in the United States, sourced with more than 100 high-tech components from around the world, and assembled in China. Among the iPhone 5's major suppliers, Samsung Electronics in South Korea supplied the applications processor. The iPhone 5's accelerator and gyroscope were made in Italy and France by STMicroelectronics, and its electronic compass was made by AKM Semiconductor in Japan. Germany's Dialog Semiconductor designed chips for power management. Texas Instruments (TI) and Broadcom in the United States supplied the touch screen controller, while Japan's Japan Display and Sharp Electronics and South Korea's LG Display made the high-definition display screen. Foxconn, a Chinese division of Taiwan's Hon Hai Group, is in charge of manufacturing and assembly.

Firms pursuing a global strategy benefit from economies of scale and resource cost reduction (usually wage cost reduction). Apple spread design, sourcing, and production for its iPhone over multiple countries overseas to reduce logistics, tariffs, and labor costs. Digital content firms that produce Hollywood movies are able to sell millions more copies of DVDs of popular films by using foreign markets.

THE INTERNET AND GLOBALIZATION

Up until the mid-1990s, competing on a global scale was dominated by huge multinational firms, such as General Electric, General Motors, Toyota, and IBM. These large firms could afford huge investments in factories, warehouses, and distribution centers in foreign countries and proprietary networks and systems that could operate on a global scale. The emergence of the Internet into a full-blown international communications system has drastically reduced the costs of operating on a global scale, deepening the possibilities for large companies but simultaneously creating many opportunities for small and medium-sized firms.

The global Internet, along with internal information systems, puts manufacturing firms in nearly instant contact with their suppliers. Internet telephony permits millions of service calls to U.S. companies to be answered in India and Jamaica, just as easily and cheaply as if the help desk were in New Jersey or California. Likewise, the Internet makes it possible to move very large computer files with hundreds of graphics, or complex industrial designs, across the globe in seconds.

Small and medium-sized firms have created an entirely new class of "micromultinational firms." For instance, CEO Brad Oberwager launched Sundia, a company that sells premium

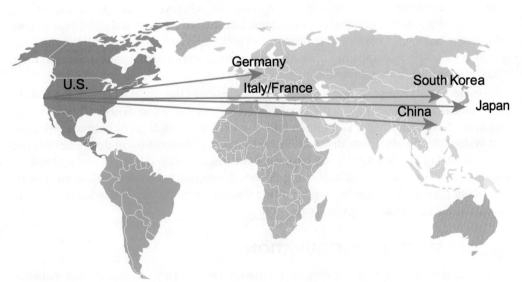

Figure 3.4
Apple iPhone's Global Supply Chain
Apple designs the iPhone in the United States, and relies on suppliers in the United States, Germany, Italy, France, and South Korea for other parts. Final assembly occurs in China.

cut fruit to more than 6,000 grocery and convenience stores in the United States and Canada out of his San Francisco home. Oberwager employees in other parts of the United States as well as in India and the Philippines use Web-based information systems to manage and coordinate. A Sundia employee in the Philippines is able to take orders from a Boston grocery store for watermelon juice made from Mexican fruit. The juice is squeezed in Washington State and payment goes to Oberwager in California.

GLOBAL BUSINESS AND SYSTEM STRATEGIES

There are four main ways of organizing businesses internationally: domestic exporter, multinational, franchiser, and transnational, each with different patterns of organizational structure or governance. In each type of global business organization, business functions may be centralized (in the home country), decentralized (to local foreign units), and coordinated (all units participate as equals).

The **domestic exporter** strategy is characterized by heavy centralization of corporate activities in the home country of origin. Production, finance/accounting, sales/marketing, human resources, and strategic management are set up to optimize resources in the home country. International sales are sometimes dispersed using agency agreements or subsidiaries, but foreign marketing is still totally reliant on the domestic home base for marketing themes and strategies. Caterpillar Corporation and other heavy capital equipment manufacturers fall into this category of firm.

A **multinational** strategy concentrates financial management and control out of a central home base while decentralizing production, sales, and marketing operations to units in other countries. The products and services on sale in different countries are adapted to suit local market conditions. The organization becomes a far-flung confederation of production and marketing facilities operating in different countries. Many financial service firms, along with a host of manufacturers such as Ford Motor Co. and Intel Corporation, fit this pattern.

Franchisers have the product created, designed, financed, and initially produced in the home country but rely heavily on foreign personnel for further production, marketing, and human resources. Food franchisers, such as McDonald's and Starbucks, fit this pattern. McDonald's created a new form of fast-food chain in the United States and continues to rely largely on the United States for inspiration of new products, strategic management, and financing. Nevertheless, local production of some items, local marketing, and local recruitment of personnel are required.

Transnational firms have no single national headquarters but instead have many regional headquarters and perhaps a world headquarters. In a **transnational** strategy, nearly all the value-adding activities are managed from a global perspective without reference to national borders, optimizing sources of supply and demand wherever they appear and taking advantage of any local competitive advantages. There is a strong central management core of decision making but considerable dispersal of power and financial muscle throughout the global divisions. Few companies have actually attained transnational status, but Citigroup, Sony, and Nestlé are attempting this transition.

Nestlé S.A., the largest food and beverage company in the world, is one of the world's most globalized companies, with nearly 328,000 employees at 500 facilities in 200 countries. Nestlé launched a $2.4 billion initiative to adopt a single set of business processes and systems for procurement, distribution, and sales management using mySAP enterprise software. All of Nestlé's worldwide business units use the same processes and systems for making sales commitments, establishing factory production schedules, billing customers, compiling management reports, and reporting financial results. Nestlé has learned how to operate as a single unit on a global scale.

GLOBAL SYSTEM CONFIGURATION

Figure 3.5 depicts four types of systems configurations for global business organizations. *Centralized systems* are those in which systems development and operation occur totally

SYSTEM CONFIGURATION	Strategy			
	Domestic Exporter	Multinational	Franchiser	Transnational
Centralized	X			
Duplicated			X	
Decentralized	x	X	x	
Networked		x		X

Figure 3.5
Global Business Organization and Systems Configurations
The large Xs show the dominant patterns, and the small Xs show the emerging patterns. For instance, domestic exporters rely predominantly on centralized systems, but there is continual pressure and some development of decentralized systems in local marketing regions.

at the domestic home base. *Duplicated systems* are those in which development occurs at the home base but operations are handed over to autonomous units in foreign locations. *Decentralized systems* are those in which each foreign unit designs its own unique solutions and systems. *Networked systems* are those in which systems development and operations occur in an integrated and coordinated fashion across all units.

As can be seen in Figure 3.5, domestic exporters tend to have highly centralized systems in which a single domestic systems development staff develops worldwide applications. Multinationals allow foreign units to devise their own systems solutions based on local needs with few, if any, applications in common with headquarters (the exceptions being financial reporting and some telecommunications applications). Franchisers typically develop a single system, usually at the home base, and then replicate it around the world. Each unit, no matter where it is located, has identical applications. Firms such as Nestle organized along transnational lines use networked systems that span multiple countries using powerful telecommunications networks and a shared management culture that crosses cultural barriers.

3.3 Competing on Quality and Design

Quality has developed from a business buzzword into a very serious goal for many companies. Quality is a form of differentiation. Companies with reputations for high quality, such as Lexus or Nordstrom, are able to charge premium prices for their products and services. Information systems have a major contribution to make in this drive for quality. In the services industries in particular, quality strategies are generally enabled by superior information systems and services.

WHAT IS QUALITY?

Quality can be defined from both producer and customer perspectives. From the perspective of the producer, quality signifies conformance to specifications or the absence of variation from those specifications. The specifications for a telephone might include one that states the strength of the phone should be such that it will not be dented or otherwise damaged by a drop from a four-foot height onto a wooden floor. A simple test will allow this specification to be measured.

A customer definition of quality is much broader. First, customers are concerned with the quality of the physical product—its durability, safety, ease of use, and installation. Second, customers are concerned with the quality of service, by which they mean the accuracy and truthfulness of advertising, responsiveness to warranties, and ongoing product support. Finally, customer concepts of quality include psychological aspects: the company's knowledge of its products, the courtesy and sensitivity of sales and support staff, and the reputation of the product.

Today, as the quality movement in business progresses, the definition of quality is increasingly from the perspective of the customer. Customers are concerned with getting value for their dollar and product fitness, performance, durability, and support.

Many companies have embraced the concept of **total quality management (TQM)**. Total quality management makes quality the responsibility of all people and functions within an organization. TQM holds that the achievement of quality control is an end in itself. Everyone is expected to contribute to the overall improvement of quality—the engineer who avoids design errors, the production worker who spots defects, the sales representative who presents the product properly to potential customers, and even the secretary who avoids typing mistakes. TQM derives from quality management concepts developed by American quality experts, such as W. Edwards Deming and Joseph Juran, but the Japanese popularized it.

Another quality concept that is widely implemented today is six sigma, which Amazon.com used to reduce errors in order fulfillment. **Six sigma** is a specific measure of quality, representing 3.4 defects per million opportunities. Most companies cannot achieve this level of quality but use six sigma as a goal to implement a set of methodologies and techniques for improving quality and reducing costs. Studies have repeatedly shown that the earlier in the business cycle a problem is eliminated, the less it costs the company. Thus, quality improvements not only raise the level of product and service quality but they can also lower costs.

HOW INFORMATION SYSTEMS IMPROVE QUALITY

Let's examine some of the ways companies face the challenge of improving quality to see how information systems can be part of the process.

Reduce Cycle Time and Simplify the Production Process

Studies have shown that one of the best ways to reduce quality problems is to reduce **cycle time**, which refers to the total elapsed time from the beginning of a process to its end. Shorter cycle times mean that problems are caught earlier in the process, often before the production of a defective product is completed, saving some of the hidden production costs. Finally, finding ways to reduce cycle time often means finding ways to simplify production steps. The fewer steps in a process, the less time and opportunity for an error to occur. Information systems help eliminate steps in a process and critical time delays.

800-Flowers, a multimillion-dollar company selling flowers by telephone or over the Web, used to be a much smaller company that had difficulty retaining its customers. It had poor service, inconsistent quality, and a cumbersome manual order-taking process. Telephone representatives had to write each order, obtain credit card approval, determine which participating florist was closest to the delivery location, select a floral arrangement, and forward the order to the florist. Each step in the manual process increased the chance of human error, and the whole process took at least a half hour. Owners Jim and Chris McCann installed a new information system that downloads orders taken in telecenters or over the Web to a central computer and electronically transmits them to local florists. As a result, orders are more accurate and arrive at the florist within two minutes.

Benchmark

Companies achieve quality by using benchmarking to set standards for products, services, and other activities, and then measuring performance against those standards. Companies may use external industry standards, standards set by other companies, internally developed standards, or some combination of the three. L.L.Bean, the Freeport, Maine, outdoor clothing company, used benchmarking to achieve an order-shipping accuracy of 99.9 percent. Its old batch order fulfillment system could not handle the surging volume and variety of items to be shipped. After studying German and Scandinavian companies with leading-edge order fulfillment operations, L.L.Bean carefully redesigned its order fulfillment process and information systems so that orders could be processed as soon as they were received and shipped within 24 hours.

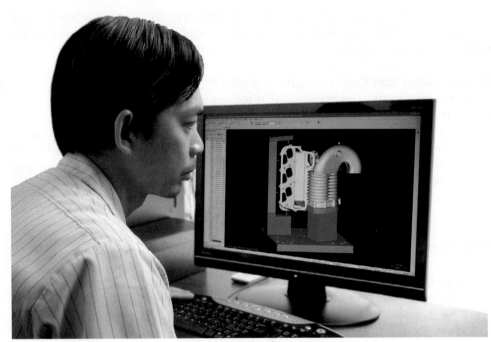

Computer-aided design (CAD) systems improve the quality and precision of product design by performing much of the design and testing work on the computer.

© Chuck Rausin/Shutterstock.

Use Customer Demands to Improve Products and Services

Improving customer service, and making customer service the number one priority, will improve the quality of the product itself. Delta Airlines decided to focus on its customers, installing a customer care system at its airport gates. For each flight, the airplane seating chart, reservations, check-in information, and boarding data are linked in a central database. Airline personnel can track which passengers are on board regardless of where they checked in and use this information to help passengers reach their destination quickly, even if delays cause them to miss connecting flights.

Improve Design Quality and Precision

Computer-aided design (CAD) software has made a major contribution to quality improvements in many companies, from producers of automobiles to producers of razor blades. A **computer-aided design (CAD) system** automates the creation and revision of designs, using computers and sophisticated graphics software. The software enables users to create a digital model of a part, a product, or a structure, and make changes to the design on the computer without having to build physical prototypes.

Troy Lee Designs, which makes sports helmets, recently invested in CAD design software that could create the helmets in 3-D. The technology defined the shapes better than traditional methods, which involved sketching an idea on paper, hand-molding a clay model, and shipping the model to Asian factories to create a plastic prototype. Production is now about six months faster and about 35 percent cheaper, with Asian factories about to produce an exact replica after receiving the digital design via e-mail.

CAD systems are able to supply data for **3-D printing**, also known as additive manufacturing, which uses machines to make solid objects, layer by layer, from specifications in a digital file. Unlike traditional techniques, where objects are cut or drilled from molds, resulting in some wasted materials, 3-D printing lets workers model an object on a computer and print it out with plastic, metal, or composite materials. 3-D printing is currently being used for producing prototypes and small items, such as jewelry, electronics, toys, and car parts. For example, Ford Motor Company is using 3-D printing to prototype automobile parts such as cylinder heads, brake rotors, and rear axles for test vehicles in less time than traditional manufacturing methods. Mattel uses 3-D printers to create parts for toys it manufactures, including popular brands such as Barbie, Max Steel, and Hot Wheels cars. 3-D printing is also starting to be used in medicine to create 3-D replicas of patients' organs to help physicians plan surgeries and increase their precision.

Improve Production Precision and Tighten Production Tolerances

For many products, quality can be enhanced by making the production process more precise, thereby decreasing the amount of variation from one part to another. CAD software often produces design specifications for tooling and manufacturing processes, saving additional time and money while producing a manufacturing process with far fewer problems. The user of this software is able to design a more precise production system, a system with tighter tolerances, than could ever be done manually. You can find out more about benefits of CAD in the Chapter 11 Interactive Session on Technology.

3.4 Competing on Business Processes

Technology alone is often not enough to make organizations more competitive, efficient, or quality-oriented. The organization itself needs to be changed to take advantage of the power of information technology. These changes may require minor adjustments in work activities, but, often, entire business processes will need to be redesigned. Business process management (BPM) addresses these needs.

WHAT IS BUSINESS PROCESS MANAGEMENT?

Business process management (BPM) is an approach to business that aims to continuously improve business processes. BPM uses a variety of tools and methodologies to understand existing processes, design new processes, and optimize those processes. BPM is never concluded because continuous improvement requires continual change. Companies practicing business process management need to go through the following steps:

1. **Identify processes for change:** One of the most important strategic decisions that a firm can make is not deciding how to use computers to improve business processes, but rather understanding what business processes need improvement. When systems are used to strengthen the wrong business model or business processes, the business can become more efficient at doing what it should not do. As a result, the firm becomes vulnerable to competitors who may have discovered the right business model. Considerable time and cost may also be spent improving business processes that have little impact on overall firm performance and revenue. Managers need to determine what business processes are the most important and how improving these processes will help business performance.

2. **Analyze existing processes:** Existing business processes should be modeled and documented, noting inputs, outputs, resources, and the sequence of activities. The process design team identifies redundant steps, paper-intensive tasks, bottlenecks, and other inefficiencies.

Figure 3.6 illustrates the "as-is" process for purchasing a book from a physical bookstore. Consider what happens when a customer visits a physical bookstore and searches its shelves for a book. If he or she finds the book, that person takes it to the checkout counter and pays for it via credit card, cash, or check. If the customer is unable to locate the book, he or she must ask a bookstore clerk to search the shelves or check the bookstore's inventory records to see if it is in stock. If the clerk finds the book, the customer purchases it and leaves. If the book is not available locally, the clerk inquires about ordering it for the customer, either from the bookstore's warehouse or from the book's distributor or publisher. Once the ordered book arrives at the bookstore, a bookstore employee telephones the customer with this information. The customer would have to go to the bookstore again to pick up the book

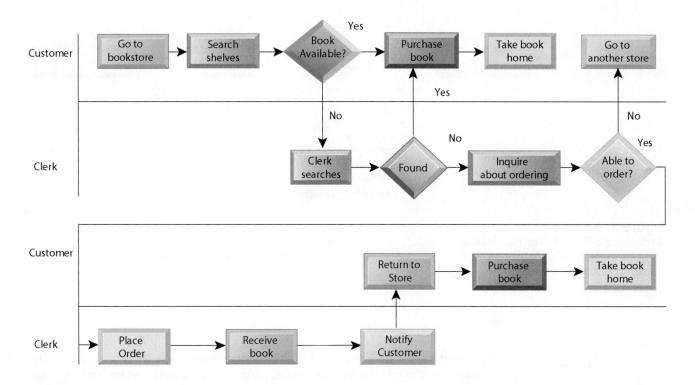

Figure 3.6
As-Is Business Process for Purchasing a Book from a Physical Bookstore
Purchasing a book from a physical bookstore requires many steps to be performed by both the seller and the customer.

and pay for it. If the bookstore is unable to order the book for the customer, the customer would have to try another bookstore. You can see that this process has many steps and might require the customer to make multiple trips to the bookstore.

3. Design the new process: Once the existing process is mapped and measured in terms of time and cost, the process design team will try to improve the process by designing a new one. A new streamlined "to-be" process will be documented and modeled for comparison with the old process.

Figure 3.7 illustrates how the book purchasing process can be redesigned by taking advantage of the Internet. The customer accesses an online bookstore over the Internet from his or her computer. He or she searches the bookstore's online catalog for the book he or she wants. If the book is available, the customer orders the book online, supplying credit card and shipping address information, and the book is delivered to the customer's home. If the online bookstore does not carry the book, the customer selects another online bookstore and searches for the book again. This process has far fewer steps than that for purchasing the book in a physical bookstore, requires much less effort on the part of the customer, and requires less sales staff for customer service. The new process is therefore much more efficient and time-saving.

The new process design needs to be justified by showing how much it reduces time and cost or enhances customer service and value. Management first measures the time and cost of the existing process as a baseline. In our example, the time required for purchasing a book from a physical bookstore might range from 15 minutes (if the customer immediately finds what he or she wants) to 30 minutes if the book is in stock but has to be located by sales staff. If the book has to be ordered from another source, the process might take one or two weeks and another trip to the bookstore for the customer. If the customer lives far away

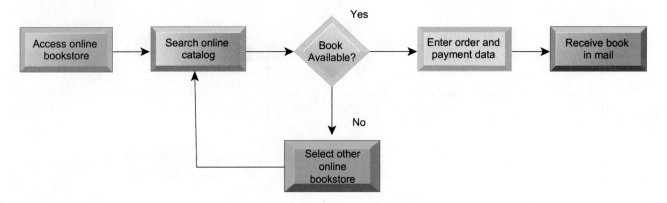

Figure 3.7
Redesigned Process for Purchasing a Book Online
Using Internet technology makes it possible to redesign the process for purchasing a book so that it only has a few steps and consumes much fewer resources.

from the bookstore, the time to travel to the bookstore would have to be factored in. The bookstore will have to pay the costs for maintaining a physical store and keeping the book in stock, for sales staff on site, and for shipment costs if the book has to be obtained from another location.

The new process for purchasing a book online might only take several minutes, although the customer might have to wait several days or weeks to receive the book in the mail and will have to pay a small shipping charge. But the customer saves time and money by not having to travel to the bookstore or make additional visits to pick up the book. Book sellers' costs are lower because they do not have to pay for a physical store location or for local inventory.

4. **Implement the new process:** Once the new process has been thoroughly modeled and analyzed, it must be translated into a new set of procedures and work rules. New information systems or enhancements to existing systems may have to be implemented to support the redesigned process. The new process and supporting systems are rolled out into the business organization. As the business starts using this process, problems are uncovered and addressed. Employees working with the process may recommend improvements.

5. **Continuous measurement:** Once a process has been implemented and optimized, it needs to be continually measured. Why? Processes may deteriorate over time as employees fall back on old methods, or they may lose their effectiveness if the business experiences other changes.

Over 100 software firms provide tools for various aspects of BPM, including IBM, Oracle, and Tibco. These tools help businesses identify and document processes requiring improvement, create models of improved processes, capture and enforce business rules for performing processes, and integrate existing systems to support new or redesigned processes. BPM software tools also provide analytics for verifying that process performance has been improved and for measuring the impact of process changes on key business performance indicators.

The Interactive Session on Organizations illustrates how a company can benefit from business process management. As with any company expanding globally, MoneyGram found that some of its business processes had become outdated. As you read this case, try to find out how changing business processes and their underlying technology improved MoneyGram's business performance and enabled it to compete on a global scale.

INTERACTIVE SESSION: ORGANIZATIONS New Systems and Business Processes Put MoneyGram "On the Money"

If you use PayPal, you may not have heard of MoneyGram, but millions of people around the globe use this service to send money anywhere within minutes. Dallas-headquartered MoneyGram is the second largest money transfer business in the world, with 293,000 agent locations and 2,350 employees in 197 countries and territories. Most of MoneyGram's money transfer services are provided through its worldwide network of third-party agents using MoneyGram's money transfer system, ranging from Walmart to tobacco shops in Paris. MoneyGram also operates its own outlets in key countries, including the United States, Belgium, France, and Germany. In 2012 MoneyGram generated over $1.3 billion in revenue.

Customers send cash at an agent location and within two minutes it is available for pick up by the recipient at a MoneyGram agent anywhere in the world. In many locations, consumers can collect funds in local currency, U.S. dollars or euros. In some markets, customers also have the option to send and receive money through alternative channels such as online services, mobile phones, ATMs, kiosks, call centers, and home delivery.

For a global money transfer company, it's essential to be able to move money between two points around the world within minutes. MoneyGram uses an automated financial management system to make this happen. The system handles hundreds of thousands of money transfer transactions each day and ensures that all of the retail stores, banks, and other MoneyGram agents receive proper financial settlement and commissions for each money transfer.

Despite many years of double-digit growth, MoneyGram's operations were not working well. The company was saddled with outdated systems that required the use of spreadsheets and time-consuming manual processes to calculate payments and close the books each month. Those systems were adequate for a long time, but eventually their complexity and lack of scalability constrained MoneyGram's ability to address market demands, add new products, and serve the sales team. Moreover, lack of a central data storehouse made it difficult to create reports, analyze market opportunities, and spot bottlenecks in the system.

Senior management decided to examine MoneyGram's business processes and legacy systems, some of which were redundant. It assembled the company's top business and technology managers, including the company's chief financial officer, controller, treasurer, head of sales, and executive vice president of operations and technology. They concluded that in addition to updating technology, MoneyGram needed to change some of its key business processes.

Culturally, MoneyGram's managers made changes in staff responsibilities to make employees more aware of the company's business processes and ways to improve them. Employees were instructed to understand each step in the business processes that they were part of, instead of their own individual job functions. The company used numerous Webinars and other tools to show employees how business processes were being altered.

To that end MoneyGram created a subset of managers called global process owners or GPOs. Each GPO is responsible for the performance of an individual process, such as cash management, customer onboarding, or credit processing. GPO's were asked to define the current state of their processes, how processes impacted each other, and how they felt they could be improved. They also defined how the success of their process could be measured, and were tasked with gathering performance data to gauge that improvement.

MoneyGram still uses GPOs in its operations, along with subprocess owners (SPOs), who are responsible for handling day-to-day activities and problems. This new process orientation has moved MoneyGram from the old siloed departments to cross-functional work groups that collaborate closely with a long-range view of what's best for the business.

For the technology to support its new global processes, MoneyGram selected Oracle's E-Business Suite with the Oracle Incentive Compensation module. Oracle E-Business Suite consists of enterprise resource planning (ERP), customer relationship management (CRM), and supply-chain management (SCM) applications using Oracle's relational database management system. Oracle Incentive Compensation module automates the process of designing, administering, and analyzing variable compensation programs. Management believed the Oracle software was capable of handling the customization work required to integrate with the processes used by the company's back-office and proprietary agents and to handle other unique business requirements. The Oracle system included capabilities for creating, viewing, and managing customer information online.

MoneyGram started implementing Oracle E-Business Suite in September 2012. The new software and business processes streamlined most of MoneyGram's back-office operations, making it easier to process more customer transactions and settlements with agents and billers and to update the company's General Ledger. New partners can be added at a much faster rate.

Commissions are critical for driving profitability in MoneyGram's existing and new products. MoneyGram must track a large number of different plans for calculating the commissions of its partner agents throughout the world. Its legacy system was unable to automate many of the commission plans, so MoneyGram had to use spreadsheets and manual processes to manage several hundred commission plans. MoneyGram built a flexible commission model using Oracle Incentive Compensation that has been able to automate more than 90 percent of its nonstandard commission plans.

MoneyGram business managers can also deliver new products faster to maintain their competitive edge in the global market. In the past new regional innovations took months to plan, but the Oracle implementation has cut that time by approximately 40%. This is because one of the bigger challenges with new product introductions is to ensure that they will integrate seamlessly with MoneyGram's backend processes so that new transactions are recorded and accounted for correctly. The new Oracle system allows MoneyGram

to configure the processes easily simply by adjusting currently existing parameters instead of coding or developing new software. MoneyGram is less likely to go to market with a product that has to be initially run on manual processes.

Having an enterprise-wide repository of data located centrally allows MoneyGram employees to better serve customers and agents conducting the money transfers. Centralized data are up-to-date and easily available. Reports used to take 40 hours and three employees to create, but now take 80% less time. Those workers can spend more time analyzing reports and less time putting them together.

The cost savings of consolidating more than 40 MoneyGram legacy IT systems into one enterprise-wide implementation of Oracle E-business Suite amount to millions of dollars. The company can now handle more transactions without having to hire additional staff. The company estimates that the Oracle software has paid for itself within one year.

Sources: www.moneygram.com, accessed March 19, 2013; www.businesswire.com, February 6, 2013; and Alan Joch, "On the Money" and "MoneyGram Exploits the Flexibility of Oracle Incentive Compensation," *Profit Magazine*, February 2012.

CASE STUDY QUESTIONS

1. Why was it so important for MoneyGram to pay attention to business processes? How were they related to the company's global growth plans?

2. What are the advantages of using an enterprise-wide software suite such as Oracle E-Business Suite in a global company such as MoneyGram?

3. How much did the new system and process improvements change the way MoneyGram ran its business? How did these changes help MoneyGram compete on a global scale?

Business Process Reengineering

Many business process improvements are incremental and ongoing, but occasionally, more radical change is required. Our example of a physical bookstore redesigning the book purchasing process so that it can be carried out online is an example of this type of radical, far-reaching change. This radical rethinking and redesign of business processes is called **business process reengineering (BPR)**.

When properly implemented, BPR can lead to dramatic gains in productivity and efficiency, even changing the way the business is run. In some instances, it drives a "paradigm shift" that transforms the nature of the business itself. This actually happened in book retailing when Amazon challenged traditional physical bookstores with its online retail model. By radically rethinking the way a book can be purchased and sold, Amazon and other online bookstores have achieved remarkable efficiencies, cost reductions, and a whole new way of doing business.

BPM poses challenges. Executives report that the largest single barrier to successful business process change is organizational culture. Employees do not like unfamiliar routines, and often try to resist change. This is especially true of business process reengineering projects because the organizational changes are so far-reaching. Managing change is neither simple nor intuitive, and companies committed to extensive process improvement need a good change management strategy (see Chapter 12).

Review Summary

1 **How does Porter's competitive forces model help companies develop competitive strategies using information systems?** In Porter's competitive forces model, the strategic position of the firm, and its strategies, are determined by competition with its traditional direct competitors. They are also greatly affected by new market entrants, substitute products and services, suppliers, and customers. Information systems help companies compete by maintaining low costs, differentiating products or services, focusing on market niche, strengthening ties with customer and suppliers, and increasing barriers to market entry with high levels of operational excellence. Information systems are most successful when the technology is aligned with business objectives.

2 **How do the value chain and value web models help businesses identify opportunities for strategic information system applications?** The value chain model highlights specific activities in the business where competitive strategies and information systems will have the greatest impact. The model views the firm as a series of primary and support activities that add value to a firm's products or services. Primary activities are directly related to production and distribution, whereas support activities make the delivery of primary activities possible. A firm's value chain can be linked to the value chains of its suppliers, distributors, and customers. A value web consists of information systems that enhance competitiveness at the industry level by promoting the use of standards and industry-wide consortia, and by enabling businesses to work more efficiently with their value partners.

3 **How do information systems help businesses use synergies, core competences, and network-based strategies to achieve competitive advantage?** Because firms consist of multiple business units, information systems achieve additional efficiencies or enhanced services by tying together the operations of disparate business units. Information systems help businesses leverage their core competencies by promoting the sharing of knowledge across business units. Information systems facilitate business models based on large networks of users or subscribers that take advantage of network economics. A virtual company strategy uses networks to link to other firms so that a company can use the capabilities of other companies to build, market, and distribute products and services. Disruptive technologies provide strategic opportunities, although "first movers" do not necessarily obtain long-term benefit.

4 **How do competing on a global scale and promoting quality enhance competitive advantage?** Information systems and the Internet can help companies operate internationally by facilitating coordination of geographically dispersed units of the company and communication with faraway customers and suppliers. Information systems can enhance quality by simplifying a product or service, facilitating benchmarking, reducing product development cycle time, and improving quality and precision in design and production.

5 **What is the role of business process management (BPM) in enhancing competitiveness?** Organizations often have to change their business processes in order to execute their business strategies successfully. If these business processes use technology, they can be redesigned to make the technology more effective. BPM combines and streamlines the steps in a business process to eliminate repetitive and redundant work and to achieve dramatic improvements in quality, service, and speed. BPM is most effective when it is used to strengthen a good business model and when it strengthens processes that have a major impact on firm performance.

Key Terms

3-D printing, 117	Core competency, 110	Quality, 115
Benchmarking, 106	Cycle time, 116	Six sigma, 116
Best practices, 106	Disruptive technologies, 111	Support activities, 107
Business process management (BPM), 118	Domestic exporter, 114	Switching costs, 103
Business process reengineering (BPR), 122	Efficient customer response system, 102	Total quality management (TQM), 116
Competitive forces model, 100	Franchiser, 114	Transnational, 114
Computer-aided design (CAD) system, 117	Mass customization, 103	Value chain model, 107
	Multinational, 114	Value web, 109
	Network economics, 110	Virtual company, 111
	Primary activities, 107	

Review Questions

3-1 How does Porter's competitive forces model help companies develop competitive strategies using information systems?
- Explain how new market entrants might impact the strategic position of a firm.
- Discuss the impact of the availability of substitute products and services on the strategic position of a firm.
- Describe some situations in which a firm's customers have market power.
- List and describe four competitive strategies enabled by information systems that firms can pursue.
- Describe how information systems can support each of these competitive strategies and give examples.
- Explain how management of a firm can achieve alignment of IT with with business objectives.

3-2 How do the value chain and value web models help businesses identify opportunities for strategic information system applications?
- Define and describe the value chain model.
- Explain how the value chain model can be used to identify opportunities for information systems.
- Define the value web and show how it is related to the value chain.
- Explain how the value web helps businesses identify opportunities for strategic information systems.
- Describe how the Internet has changed competitive forces and competitive advantage.

3-3 How do information systems help businesses use synergies, core competencies, and network-based strategies to achieve competitive advantage?
- Explain how information systems promote synergies and core competencies.
- Describe how promoting synergies and core competencies enhances competitive advantage.
- Explain how businesses benefit by using network economics.

- Define the law of diminishing returns and describe some situations in which the law does not work.
- Explain how disruptive technologies create strategic opportunities.

3-4 How do competing on a global scale and promoting quality enhance competitive advantage?
- Describe how globalization has increased opportunities for businesses.
- List and describe the four main ways of organizing a business internationally and the types of systems configuration for global business organizations.
- Define the concepts of total quality management (TQM) and six sigma.
- Describe the various ways in which information systems can improve quality.

3-5 What is the role of business process management (BPM) in enhancing competitiveness?
- Define BPM and explain how it helps firms become more competitive.
- Distinguish between BPM and business process reengineering (BPR).
- List and describe the steps companies should take to make sure BPM is successful.

Discussion Questions

3-6 It has been said that there is no such thing as a sustainable competitive advantage. Do you agree? Why or why not?

3-7 What are some of the issues to consider in determining whether the Internet would provide your business with a competitive advantage?

3-8 Why are disruptive technologies tricky?

Hands-On MIS Projects

The projects in this section give you hands-on experience identifying information systems to support a business strategy and to solve a customer retention problem, using a database to improve decision making about business strategy, and using Web tools to configure and price an automobile.

MANAGEMENT DECISION PROBLEMS

3-9 Marks & Spencer Group is a leading department store chain in the United Kingdom. Its retail stores sell a range of merchandise. Senior management has decided that Marks & Spencer should tailor merchandise more to local tastes, and that the colors, sizes, brands, and styles of clothing and other merchandise should be based on the sales patterns in each individual store. How could information systems help management implement this new strategy? What pieces of data should these systems collect to help management make merchandising decisions that support this strategy?

3-10 Despite aggressive campaigns to attract customers with lower mobile phone prices, T-Mobile has been losing large numbers of monthly contract subscribers. Management wants to know why so many customers are leaving T-Mobile and what can be done to entice them back. Are customers deserting because of poor customer service, uneven network coverage, or wireless service charges? How can the company use information systems to help find the answer? What management decisions could be made using information from these systems?

IMPROVING DECISION MAKING: USING A DATABASE TO CLARIFY BUSINESS STRATEGY

Software skills: Database querying and reporting; database design
Business skills: Reservation systems; customer analysis

3-11 In this exercise, you'll use database software to analyze the reservation transactions for a hotel and use that information to fine-tune the hotel's business strategy and marketing activities.

In MyMISLab™, you'll find a database for hotel reservation transactions developed in Microsoft Access with information about The President's Inn hotel in Cape May, New Jersey. At the Inn, 10 rooms overlook side streets, 10 rooms have bay windows with limited views of the ocean, and the remaining 10 rooms in the front of the hotel face the ocean. Room rates are based on room choice, length of stay, and number of guests per room. Room rates are the same for one to four guests. Fifth and sixth guests must pay an additional $20 per person per day. Guests staying for seven days or more receive a 10 percent discount on their daily room rates.

The owners currently use a manual reservation and bookkeeping system, which is unable to provide management with immediate data about the hotel's daily operations and revenue. Use the database to develop reports on average length of stay per room type, average visitors per room type, base revenue per room (i.e., length of visit multiplied by the daily rate) during a specified period of time, and strongest customer base. After answering these questions, write a brief report about the Inn's current business situation and suggest future strategies.

IMPROVING DECISION MAKING: USING WEB TOOLS TO CONFIGURE AND PRICE AN AUTOMOBILE

Software skills: Internet-based software
Business skills: Researching product information and pricing

3-12 In this exercise, you will use software at car-selling Web sites to find product information about a car of your choice and use that information to make an important purchase decision. You will also evaluate two of these sites as selling tools.

You are interested in purchasing a new Vauxhall Corsa (or some other car of your choice). Go to the Web site of AutoTrader.co.uk (www.autotrader.co.uk) and begin your investigation. Locate the Vauxhall Corsa. Research the various models, choose one you prefer in terms of price, features, and safety ratings. Locate and read at least two reviews. Surf the Web site of the manufacturer, in this case Vauxhall (www.vauxhall.co.uk). Compare the information available on Vauxhall's Web site with that of Autotrader.co.uk for the Vauxhall Corsa. Try to locate the lowest price for the car you want in a local dealer's inventory. Suggest improvements for Autotrader.co.uk and Vauxhall.co.uk.

Collaboration and Teamwork Project

3-13 In MyMISLab, you will find a Collaboration and Teamwork Project dealing with the concepts in this chapter. You will be able to use Google Drive, Google Docs, and Google Sites, Google+, or other open-source tools to complete the assignment.

BUSINESS PROBLEM-SOLVING CASE

Can This Bookstore Be Saved?

Borders Group (including many former Waldenbooks rebranded as Borders Express) liquidated its assets and closed all of its locations in the second half of 2011. The previous year had already seen the demise of B. Dalton, a Barnes & Noble subsidiary since 1987. Since 1991, eleven major U.S. bookstore chains have been whittled down to six, and nearly 3300 stores to just over 2200 in 2011.

Still in the lead after over 20 years of domination, Barnes & Noble was often painted as the bully, driving both regional chains and small independent bookstores out of business with its aggressive pricing tactics and unbeatable inventory. Before e-commerce reshaped the landscape, its superstores forced smaller rivals into "most titles offered" wars. As smaller chains struggled to keep pace, support from publishers was not forthcoming. This short-term, bottom-line strategy would come back to haunt publishers.

B&N kicked around the idea of selling books online, experimenting with Trintex, a 1980s Web-retail prototype, selling books on CompuServ in the mid-1990s, and opening an online shop on AOL. However, it was not until 1997, fully two years after the arrival of Amazon, that it launched its first Web site. Data from numerous emerging e-commerce markets now verifies that books are an ideal initial product to draw first-time buyers. B&N was already behind the curve.

Amazon, launched initially as an online bookstore, upended the titles war. While B&N might be able to offer over 200,000 titles in its bricks-and-mortar stores, Amazon offered an inventory limited only by publisher availability. Shrewd financial moves, including selling 50% of its Internet operation to German giant Bertelsmann in 1998, kept B&N in the game. It established a new industry standard of 750,000 titles on-hand and bragged that it could procure over 8 million new, out-of-print, and rare books for customers from suppliers. However, Amazon continued to trump B&N on innovation. When B&N launched its online music store in 1999, several months after taking barnesandnoble.com public and refurbishing its cash reserves, it was again playing catch-up with Amazon, which had pioneered the concept a year earlier.

In early 2009, when B&N purchased Fictionwise, one of the biggest electronic book proprietors in North America, it was again behind the technology curve. Amazon had already unveiled its Kindle e-reader sixteen months earlier. What's more, Amazon would offer New York Times bestsellers and other popular e-books for less than $10.

While publishers fretted that readers would be reconditioned to devalue the worth of the printed word and that offline stores would be strained to their limits discounting print books to compete, B&N scrambled. It took until July 2009 (two months after the Fictionwise purchase) to finally unveil B&N's e-bookstore. Its Nook e-reader was released in October, again more than two years behind Amazon. Ironically, as early as 1998, B&N had partnered with software companies such as Nuvo-Media to develop a prototype e-reader called the Rocket, but it had nixed the project in 2003 because there didn't appear to be any money in it. Now it had to hustle to refashion itself as a seller of e-books, e-readers, and apps to enhance the reading experience.

Critically well-received, the Nook began to scrape market share from the Kindle when it sparked a price war a year later. Dropping the price from $259 to $199 and releasing a WiFi-only model for $149, B&N took aim at the giant. Amazon quickly countered by slashing the Kindle to $189 eight hours later and releasing the WiFi-enabled 3G Kindle3 within a month, again at $10 below the Nook.

With titans such as Apple (iPad) and Google (originally with the iRiver Story and in 2012 with the Nexus 7) providing additional competition, the tables had been turned on the former bookstore baron. Will B&N be able to survive against these tech giants?

The answer remains to be seen. B&N was the only bookseller with the resources to complete the considerable task of developing an e-reader, marketing it, and setting up manufacturing and retail operations for the device. Its closest competitors were already succumbing to the contraction of the chain bookstore market, victims of both B&N and the e-commerce revolution. Books-A-Million, with approximately 250 stores compared to 1,363 (689 retail and 674 college) for B&N, is its closest remaining competitor.

While B&N still depends on its physical, brick-and-mortar stores to drive its business, the e-book market is a horse of a different color. The economics of e-book sales are very different from traditional book sales. Customers who visit B&N's Web site buy three digital books for every one physical book, but booksellers still make more money on print books than e-books. And while having a competitive e-reader seemed essential to successfully vying for market share, it came at a steep cost. Moreover, it is not the pivotal factor in controlling the e-book market. Content is.

Since the price war, the reality is that in order to compete with Amazon, e-reader hardware must sell at or near cost, with profits derived from the sale of digital content, including e-books, music, videos, apps, and games. Once Amazon had wrung all the profit it could from Kindle hardware, it quickly maneuvered into adding apps and app features and aggressively pursuing a cross-platform strategy. It began marketing its e-books for tablets, smartphones, and PCs using Android, Windows, and OS X operating systems. Moreover, Amazon, along with Apple, and another competitor, Kobo, are global competitors; B&N is not.

Despite spending hundreds of millions of dollars to compete with Amazon.com Inc. and Apple Inc. in the market for tablets and e-readers, B&N continued to lose money on the Nook, as well as e-book market share. Analysts estimated in 2011 that B&N controlled approximately 27% of the U.S. digital book market while Amazon led with 60%. Since then, Amazon has held steady, and B&N has steadily ceded ground to Apple. B&N's digital book market share has dropped to 25%, and is still falling.

On June 25, 2013 B&N announced that losses at its Nook digital business more than doubled in the quarter ending April 27, 2013, wiping out profits generated at its bookstores. As a result, the company decided to stop producing its own color tablets in favor of co-branded devices made by third-party manufacturers. Barnes & Noble will continue to design and make its own black-and-white Nook e-readers, which account for the majority of its e-book sales. But with e-reader sales declining, it is unclear how competitive Barnes & Noble can be long term without its own presence in the tablet market, which is forecast to keep growing.

B&N retail store closings continued to outpace new store openings as had been the case since 2009. CEO Michael Klipper projected a net reduction of one-third of B&N's stores over the next decade, reducing the total by about 20 stores per year until between 450 and 500 remain.

While B&N has its back against the wall, it does have a multipronged strategy for survival. It faces a principal opponent with an estimated value 121 times higher than its own (B&N has a market capitalization of $1.062 billion; Amazon's is $121.5 billion). But it also has allies. Publishing companies have a vested interest in B&N's survival. Physical book retailers are indispensable for effectively marketing and selling books. Bookstores spur publisher sales with the "browsing effect." Surveys show that just one-third of bookstore visitors who make a purchase walked in with a specific book in mind. According to Madeline McIntosh, Random House president of sales, operations, and digital, a bookstore's display space is one of the most valuable places that exists for communicating to the consumer that a book is a big deal. Brick-and-mortar retail stores are not only essential for selling physical books, but also stimulate sales of e-books

and audio books, bring traffic into malls, and serve as social gathering places. The more visibility a book has, the more likely readers will want to purchase it. With the demise of B. Dalton, Crown Books, and Borders, B&N is the only retailer offering an extensive inventory of physical books. Book publishers need a physical presence.

Without B&N, the likely candidate to fill the void is Amazon, and publishers are not eager for that to happen. Amazon's goal for e-books is to cut out the publishers and publish books directly, selling books at an extremely steep discount to drive sales of its Kindle devices. Editors, publicists, and other entities within the publishing business view Amazon as an enemy. Selling books at Amazon's discounted prices is not a tenable business model for publishers in the long-term.

If B&N is to survive it must capitalize on its profitable retail stores, develop small, local community-based shops, expand digital content, lead the digital education market, and develop marketing techniques to drive e-book readers to purchase print books. B&N has been experimenting with ways to drive traffic to its physical stores. For example, if you connect to a Wi-Fi network in a B&N store with your Nook, you can get free extras in many apps and games like Angry Birds, where you can unlock a bonus character that normally costs a dollar. B&N has also expanded its store space for toys and games, which have higher profit margins, while reducing the range of book titles it stocks. There are also plans to experiment with slightly smaller stores in malls. Although that strategy is boosting the company's bottom line, publishers worry it may also drive book lovers to Amazon.com Inc., which says its physical book sales are still growing.

What will the future hold? Will B&N be able to succeed as a digital company and is there a future for its brick-and-mortar stores? Is there a way for e-books to help sell print books, just as print books have stimulated demand for their digital versions? Although B&N has made a spirited effort to revamp its business and go toe-to-toe with several tech titans, it's possible that it might be too tall an order for the storied bookseller.

Sources: Jeffrey A. Trachtenberg, "How to Rescue Barnes & Noble? Here are Ideas from Five Experts," *Wall Street Journal*, July 1, 2013; Leslie Kaufman, "Barnes & Noble Rethinks Its Strategy for the Nook," *New York Times*, February 28, 2013; Tom Gara, "Barnes & Noble: Stores Are Bad, But E-Books Are Worse," *Wall Street Journal*, February 28, 2013; Jeffrey A. Trachtenberg, "B&N Aims To Whittle Its Stores For Years," *Wall Street Journal*, January 28, 2013; Horace Dediu, "Apple iBooks at 24% Worldwide Ebook Market Share? One Analyst Thinks So," *Digital Book World*, February 28, 2013; Michael J. De La Merced and Julie Bosman, "Microsoft Deal Adds to Battle over E-Books," *The New York Times*, May 1, 2012; Shira Ovide and Jeffrey A. Trachtenberg, "Microsoft Hooks Onto Nook," *The Wall Street Journal*, May 1, 2012; Julie Bosnan, "The Bookstore's Last Stand," *The New York Times*, January 29, 2012; Paul Vigna, "E-Books, Apple, Amazon: The Deadly Hallows for Publishers," *The New York Times*, April 11, 2012; Brian X. Chen, "Barnes & Noble Uses Apps to Lure Customers Into Stores," *The New York Times*, January 27, 2012; Alter, Alexandra, "Blowing Up the Book." *The Wall Street Journal*, January 20, 2012; Jim Milliot, "Tracking 20 Years of Bookstore Chains," *Publisher's Weekly*, August 26, 2011; and Jeffrey A. Trachtenberg and Martin Peers, "Barnes and Noble: The Next Chapter," *The Wall Street Journal*, January 6, 2011.

Case Study Questions

3-14 Use the value chain and competitive forces models to evaluate the impact of the Internet on book publishers and book retail stores such as Barnes & Noble.

3-15 How did Barnes and Noble change its business model to deal with the Internet and e-book technology?

3-16 Will Barnes & Noble's new strategy be successful? Explain your answer.

3-17 Is there anything else Barnes & Noble and the book publishers should be doing to stimulate more business?

Ethical and Social Issues in Information Systems

CHAPTER 4

STUDENT LEARNING OBJECTIVES

After completing this chapter, you will be able to answer the following questions:

1. What ethical, social, and political issues are raised by information systems?

2. What specific principles for conduct can be used to guide ethical decisions?

3. Why do contemporary information systems technology and the Internet pose challenges to the protection of individual privacy and intellectual property?

4. How have information systems affected everyday life?

CHAPTER OUTLINE

CONTENT PIRATES SAIL THE WEB

More than 11 million HBO subscribers watched each episode of Game of Thrones in 2012, but another 3.7 to 4.2 million were able to watch the same shows without paying a cent. They were watching pirated versions of each episode that were made available by companies specializing in distributing digital content for free without paying the owners and creators of that content for using it. Television shows, music, movies, and videogames have all been plundered this way.

Such "content pirates" have sailed the World Wide Web since its earliest days, but today they are bolder, faster and better equipped than ever. The antipiracy and security firm Irdeto detected 14 billion instances of pirated online content in 2012, up from 5.4 billion instances in 2009.

Pirated content threatens television industry profits, much of which comes from subscription fees on cable channels like HBO and USA. Viewers watching pirated versions of shows are less likely to pay for cable subscriptions or to buy movies or rent them from services such as Netflix. According to one estimate, pirated content costs the U.S. economy $58 billion a year, including theft of content, lost entertainment jobs and taxes lost to federal and state governments.

The explosion in pirated TV shows and movies has been made possible by faster Internet speeds. Longer videos can be downloaded within minutes from peer-to-peer

© eldeiv/Shutterstock.

networks and online cyberlockers. A great deal of illegal content, including live sports, is also available through instant streaming. Media companies also believe online ad networks help finance piracy by placing ads on sites that traffic in unauthorized content. A summer 2012 study commissioned in part by Google found that 86 percent of peer-to-peer sharing sites depend on advertising for income.

One of the biggest content pirate sites is The Pirate Bay, based in Sweden, which offers free access to millions of copyrighted songs and thousands of copyrighted movies. The Pirate Bay uses BitTorrent file-sharing technology, which breaks up large computer files into small pieces so they can zip across the Web. In June 2012, The Pirate Bay had 6 million registered users and was the 74th most trafficked site in the world. There have been many legal efforts to shut it down, but The Pirate Bay finds ways to keep going.

What can be done to stop this pirating? Google adjusted its search algorithm to obscure search results for sites with pirated content. NBCUniversal uses armies of automated "crawlers" to scour the Web for unauthorized videos and also applies "content recognition" technology to its programming, which it then passes on to video sites like YouTube to help block illegal uploads. NBC sends out digital snapshots of its shows to YouTube and other video sites to prevent users from putting up copyrighted shows. The five major Internet service providers, including NBC's parent company, Comcast, initiated an alert system which notifies users suspected of piracy and results in progressive penalties, including slowed Web access in some cases. The Ad Council, which handles ads for the Forest Service, said that any time its ads appear on questionable sites, it requests that they be taken down immediately.

New products and services have made pirated content less attractive. High-quality content now can be streamed for a small fee to both tethered and mobile devices. Apple's iTunes made buying individual songs inexpensive and easy, while new subscription-based services such as Spotify and Rhapsody have attracted 20 million paying subscribers. Netflix and other video services offer access to movies and television shows at low prices. Right now content pirates are still sailing, but new and better ways to listen to music and view videos may eventually put them out of business.

Sources: Christopher S. Stuart, "As TV Pirates Run Rampant, TV Studios Dial Up Pursuit," *The Wall Street Journal*, March 3, 2013; "Pirate Bay Sails to the Caribbean," I4U News, May 2, 2013; and L. Gordon Crovitz, "A Six-Strike Rule for Internet Privacy," *The Wall Street Journal*, March 3, 2013.

The prevalence and brazen activities of "content pirates" described in the chapter-opening case show that technology can be a double-edged sword. It can be the source of many benefits, including the ability to share and transmit legitimate photos, music, videos, and information over the Internet at high speeds. But, at the same time, digital technology creates new opportunities for breaking the law or taking benefits away from others, including owners of valuable intellectual property, such as music, videos, and television shows that are protected by copyright law.

The chapter-opening diagram calls attention to important points raised by this case and this chapter. Content pirating has become rampant because of opportunities created by broadband communications technology and the global nature of the Internet. Various policies and technology solutions have been put in place to put a stop to content piracy, but the practice still prevails. New technology-based products and services that make online content purchase and downloads very quick and inexpensive may eventually provide a solution.

This case illustrates an ethical dilemma because it shows two sets of interests at work— the interests of people and organizations that have worked to develop intellectual property and need to be rewarded versus those of groups who fervently believe the Internet should foster the free exchange of content and ideas. As a manager, you will need to be sensitive to both the positive and negative impacts of information systems for your firm, employees and customers. You will need to learn how to resolve ethical dilemmas involving information systems.

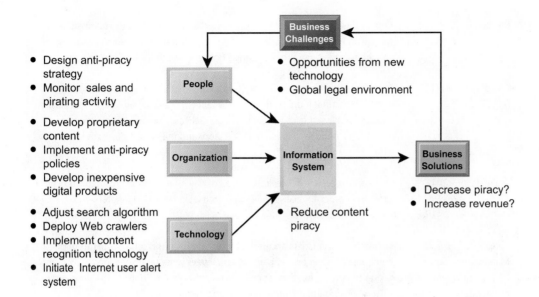

- Design anti-piracy strategy
- Monitor sales and pirating activity

- Develop proprietary content
- Implement anti-piracy policies
- Develop inexpensive digital products

- Adjust search algorithm
- Deploy Web crawlers
- Implement content reognition technology
- Initiate Internet user alert system

Business Challenges

- Opportunities from new technology
- Global legal environment

People

Organization

Information System

Technology

Business Solutions

- Decrease piracy?
- Increase revenue?

- Reduce content piracy

Here are some questions to think about: Does content piracy create an ethical dilemma? Why or why not? What would happen if no copyright laws were upheld, and everyone did not have to pay to view videos and television programs online?

4.1 Understanding Ethical and Social Issues Related to Systems

In the past 10 years, we have witnessed, arguably, one of the most ethically challenging periods for U.S. and global business. Table 4.1 provides a small sample of recent cases demonstrating failed ethical judgment by senior and middle managers. These lapses in ethical and business judgment occurred across a broad spectrum of industries.

In today's new legal environment, managers who violate the law and are convicted will most likely spend time in prison. U.S. federal sentencing guidelines adopted in 1987 mandate that federal judges impose stiff sentences on business executives based on the monetary value of the crime, the presence of a conspiracy to prevent discovery of the crime, the use of structured financial transactions to hide the crime, and failure to cooperate with prosecutors (U.S. Sentencing Commission, 2004).

Although business firms would, in the past, often pay for the legal defense of their employees enmeshed in civil charges and criminal investigations, firms are now encouraged to cooperate with prosecutors to reduce charges against the entire firm for obstructing investigations. These developments mean that, more than ever, as a manager or an employee, you will have to decide for yourself what constitutes proper legal and ethical conduct.

Although these major instances of failed ethical and legal judgment were not masterminded by information systems departments, information systems were instrumental in many of these frauds. In many cases, the perpetrators of these crimes artfully used financial reporting information systems to bury their decisions from public scrutiny in the vain hope they would never be caught.

We deal with the issue of control in information systems in Chapter 8. In this chapter, we will talk about the ethical dimensions of these and other actions based on the use of information systems.

Barclays Bank PLC (2012)	One of the world's largest banks admitted to manipulating its submissions for the LIBOR benchmark interest rates in order to benefit its trading positions and the media's perception of the bank's financial health. Fined $160 million.
GlaxoSmithKline LLC (2012)	The global health care giant admitted to unlawful and criminal promotion of certain prescription drugs, its failure to report certain safety data, and its civil liability for alleged false price reporting practices. Fined $3 billion, the largest health care fraud settlement in U.S. history and the largest payment ever by a drug company.
Walmart Inc. (2012)	Walmart executives in Mexico accused of paying millions in bribes to Mexican officials in order to receive building permits. Under investigation by the Department of Justice.
Minerals Management Service (U.S. Department of the Interior) (2010)	Government managers accused of accepting gifts and other favors from oil companies, letting oil company rig employees write up inspection reports, and failing to enforce existing regulations on offshore Gulf drilling rigs. Employees systematically falsified information record systems.
Yahoo! Inc. (2012)	Yahoo hired Scott Thompson, former head of PayPal, as a new CEO in 2012 to reverse the company's sagging fortunes. A shareholder activist group alleged that Thompson had embellished his resume by claiming he had a degree in computer science, along with an accounting degree. He only has an accounting degree. Thompson was fired in May 2012.
Galleon Group (2011)	Founder of the Galleon Group sentenced to 11 years in prison for trading on insider information. Found guilty of paying $250 million to Wall Street banks, and in return received market information that other investors did not get.
Siemens (2009)	The world's largest engineering firm paid over $4 billion to German and U.S. authorities for a decades-long, worldwide bribery scheme approved by corporate executives to influence potential customers and governments. Payments concealed from normal reporting accounting systems.
IBM (2011)	IBM settled SEC charges that it paid off South Korean and Chinese government officials with bags of cash over a 10-year period.
McKinsey & Company (2011)	CEO Rajat Gupta heard on tapes leaking insider information. The former CEO of prestigious management consulting firm McKinsey & Company was found guilty in 2012 and sentenced to two years in prison.
Bank of America (2012)	Federal prosecutors accused Bank of America and its affiliate Countrywide Financial of defrauding government-backed mortgage agencies by churning out loans at a rapid pace without proper controls. Prosecutors are seeking $1 billion in penalties from the bank as compensation for the behavior that they say forced taxpayers to guarantee billions in bad loans.

Ethics refers to the principles of right and wrong that individuals, acting as free moral agents, use to make choices to guide their behaviors. Information systems raise new ethical questions for both individuals and societies because they create opportunities for intense social change, and thus threaten existing distributions of power, money, rights, and obligations. Like other technologies, such as steam engines, electricity, the telephone, and the radio, information technology can be used to achieve social progress, but it can also be used to commit crimes and threaten cherished social values. The development of information technology will produce benefits for many and costs for others.

Ethical issues in information systems have been given new urgency by the rise of the Internet and electronic commerce. Internet and digital firm technologies make it easier than ever to assemble, integrate, and distribute information, unleashing new concerns about the appropriate use of customer information, the protection of personal privacy, and the protection of intellectual property.

Other pressing ethical issues raised by information systems include establishing accountability for the consequences of information systems, setting standards to safeguard system quality that protects the safety of the individual and society, and preserving values and institutions considered essential to the quality of life in an information society. When using information systems, it is essential to ask, "What is the ethical and socially responsible course of action?"

A MODEL FOR THINKING ABOUT ETHICAL, SOCIAL, AND POLITICAL ISSUES

Ethical, social, and political issues are closely linked. The ethical dilemma you may face as a manager of information systems typically is reflected in social and political debate. One way to think about these relationships is shown in Figure 4.1. Imagine society as a more or less calm pond on a summer day, a delicate ecosystem in partial equilibrium with individuals and with social and political institutions. Individuals know how to act in this pond because social institutions (family, education, organizations) have developed well-honed rules of behavior, and these are supported by laws developed in the political sector that prescribe behavior and promise sanctions for violations. Now toss a rock into the center of the pond. What happens? Ripples, of course.

Imagine instead that the disturbing force is a powerful shock of new information technology and systems hitting a society more or less at rest. Suddenly, individual actors are confronted with new situations often not covered by the old rules. Social institutions cannot respond overnight to these ripples—it may take years to develop etiquette, expectations,

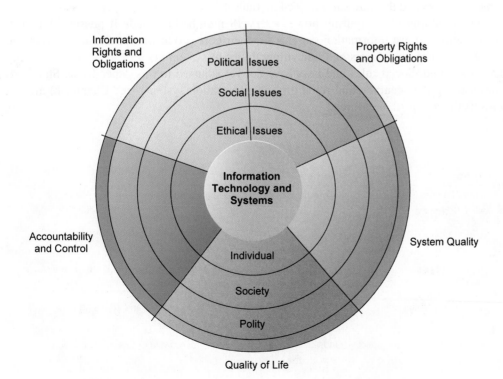

Figure 4.1
The Relationship Between Ethical, Social, and Political Issues in an Information Society
The introduction of new information technology has a ripple effect, raising new ethical, social, and political issues that must be dealt with on the individual, social, and political levels. These issues have five moral dimensions: information rights and obligations, property rights and obligations, system quality, quality of life, and accountability and control.

social responsibility, politically correct attitudes, or approved rules. Political institutions also require time before developing new laws and often require the demonstration of real harm before they act. In the meantime, you may have to act. You may be forced to act in a legal gray area.

We can use this model to illustrate the dynamics that connect ethical, social, and political issues. This model is also useful for identifying the main moral dimensions of the information society, which cut across various levels of action—individual, social, and political.

FIVE MORAL DIMENSIONS OF THE INFORMATION AGE

The major ethical, social, and political issues raised by information systems include the following moral dimensions:

- *Information rights and obligations.* What **information rights** do individuals and organizations possess with respect to themselves? What can they protect?
- *Property rights and obligations.* How will traditional intellectual property rights be protected in a digital society in which tracing and accounting for ownership are difficult and ignoring such property rights is so easy?
- *Accountability and control.* Who can and will be held accountable and liable for the harm done to individual and collective information and property rights?
- *System quality.* What standards of data and system quality should we demand to protect individual rights and the safety of society?
- *Quality of life.* What values should be preserved in an information- and knowledge-based society? Which institutions should we protect from violation? Which cultural values and practices are supported by the new information technology?

We explore these moral dimensions in detail in Section 4.3.

KEY TECHNOLOGY TRENDS THAT RAISE ETHICAL ISSUES

Ethical issues long preceded information technology. Nevertheless, information technology has heightened ethical concerns, taxed existing social arrangements, and made some laws obsolete or severely crippled. There are five key technological trends responsible for these ethical stresses and they are summarized in Table 4.2.

The doubling of computing power every 18 months has made it possible for most organizations to use information systems for their core production processes. As a result, our dependence on systems and our vulnerability to system errors and poor data quality have increased. Social rules and laws have not yet adjusted to this dependence. Standards for ensuring the accuracy and reliability of information systems (see Chapter 8) are not universally accepted or enforced.

TABLE 4.2	**Trend**	**Impact**
Technology Trends That Raise Ethical Issues	Computing power doubles every 18 months	More organizations depend on computer systems for critical operations.
	Data storage costs rapidly decline	Organizations can easily maintain detailed databases on individuals.
	Data analysis advances	Companies can analyze vast quantities of data gathered on individuals to develop detailed profiles of individual behavior.
	Networking advances	Copying data from one location to another and accessing personal data from remote locations are much easier.
	Mobile device growth Impact	Individual cell phones may be tracked without user consent or knowledge.

Advances in data storage techniques and rapidly declining storage costs have been responsible for the multiplying databases on individuals—employees, customers, and potential customers—maintained by private and public organizations. These advances in data storage have made the routine violation of individual privacy both cheap and effective. Enormous data storage systems for terabytes and petabytes of data are now available on-site or as online services for firms of all sizes to use in identifying customers.

Advances in data analysis techniques for large pools of data are another technological trend that heightens ethical concerns because companies and government agencies are able to find out highly detailed personal information about individuals. With contemporary data management tools (see Chapter 6), companies can assemble and combine the myriad pieces of information about you stored on computers much more easily than in the past.

Think of all the ways you generate computer information about yourself—credit card purchases, telephone calls, magazine subscriptions, video rentals, mail-order purchases, banking records, local, state, and federal government records (including court and police records), and visits to Web sites. Put together and mined properly, this information could reveal not only your credit information but also your driving habits, your tastes, your associations, what you read and watch, and your political interests.

Companies with products to sell purchase relevant information from these sources to help them more finely target their marketing campaigns. Chapters 6 and 11 describe how companies can analyze large pools of data from multiple sources to rapidly identify buying patterns of customers and suggest individual responses. The use of computers to combine data from multiple sources and create electronic dossiers of detailed information on individuals is called **profiling**.

For example, several thousand of the most popular Web sites allow DoubleClick (owned by Google), an Internet advertising broker, to track the activities of their visitors in exchange for revenue from advertisements based on visitor information DoubleClick gathers. DoubleClick uses this information to create a profile of each online visitor, adding more detail to the profile as the visitor accesses an associated DoubleClick site. Over time, DoubleClick can create a detailed dossier of a person's spending and computing habits on the Web that is sold to companies to help them target their Web ads more precisely.

Credit card purchases can make personal information available to market researchers, telemarketers, and direct mail companies. Advances in information technology facilitate the invasion of privacy.

ChoicePoint gathers data from police, criminal, and motor vehicle records, credit and employment histories, current and previous addresses, professional licenses, and insurance claims to assemble and maintain electronic dossiers on almost every adult in the United States. The company sells this personal information to businesses and government agencies. Demand for personal data is so enormous that data broker businesses such as ChoicePoint are flourishing. In 2011, the two largest credit card networks, Visa Inc. and MasterCard Inc., were planning to link credit card purchase information with consumer social network and other information to create customer profiles that could be sold to advertising firms. In 2012, Visa processed more than 45 billion transactions a year and MasterCard processed more than 23 billion transactions. Currently, this transactional information is not linked with consumer Internet activities.

A new data analysis technology called **nonobvious relationship awareness (NORA)** has given both the government and the private sector even more powerful profiling capabilities. NORA can take information about people from many disparate sources, such as employment applications, telephone records, customer listings, and "wanted" lists, and correlate relationships to find obscure hidden connections that might help identify criminals or terrorists (see Figure 4.2).

NORA technology scans data and extracts information as the data are being generated so that it could, for example, instantly discover a man at an airline ticket counter who shares a phone number with a known terrorist before that person boards an airplane. The technology is considered a valuable tool for homeland security but does have privacy implications because it can provide such a detailed picture of the activities and associations of a single individual.

An example of how government and private industry not only use the same data mining techniques to identify and track individuals, but in cases of national security, closely

Figure 4.2
Nonobvious
Relationship
Awareness (NORA)
*NORA technology can
take information about
people from disparate
sources and find
obscure, nonobvious
relationships. It might
discover, for example,
that an applicant for a
job at a casino shares a
telephone number with a
known criminal and issue
an alert to the hiring
manager.*

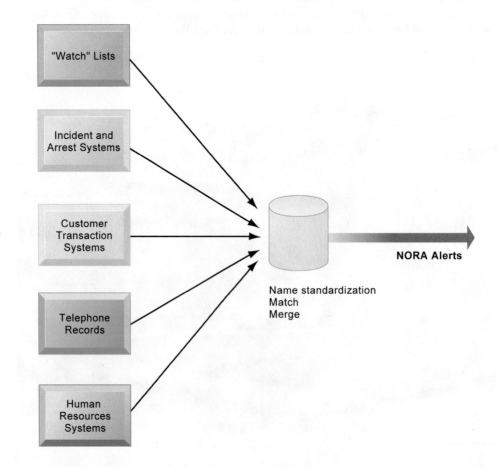

cooperate with one another in gathering data, was provided by the unauthorized release of documents describing the PRISM program of the U.S. National Security Agency (NSA). In June 2013, Edward Snowden, (one of five million people in the United States who have top security clearance) provided details of the NSA surveillance program called PRISM to the British newspaper The Guardian. He described how NSA collects information on telephone calls, e-mails, social network postings, search queries, and other Web communications of Internet users in the United States. The data are provided to the government by the data-gathering giants of Silicon Valley: Google, Facebook, Twitter, Microsoft, Yahoo, and other large Internet firms.

The purpose of PRISM is to identify terrorists and their plans before the plans can be executed. PRISM does not collect the contents of Internet communications, but only the meta-data (essentially who is communicating with whom). Using this data, PRISM constructs a social graph of Internet communications, identifies suspicious patterns, and then requests more detailed information from these firms that can include the contents of the communication. NSA and government officials claim the program is legal under existing statutes, has been in operation for many years with Congressional oversight, and provides for judicial review of active surveillance of specific people. While aimed at communications with and among foreign nationals, it is apparent that the entire U.S. population, citizens and non-citizens, is included in the data gathering effort. As commentators have noted, the government and Internet firms are interested in the same data and use the same data mining techniques, one to make money, the other to identify terrorists. Critics of the program describe it as a new level of surveillance heretofore imagined only in dystopian novels, and unprecedented in the United States or other democratic countries.

Finally, advances in networking, including the Internet, promise to greatly reduce the costs of moving and accessing large quantities of data and open the possibility of mining large pools of data remotely using small desktop machines, permitting an invasion of privacy on a scale and with a precision heretofore unimaginable.

4.2 Ethics in an Information Society

Ethics is a concern of humans who have freedom of choice. Ethics is about individual choice: When faced with alternative courses of action, what is the correct moral choice? What are the main features of ethical choice?

BASIC CONCEPTS: RESPONSIBILITY, ACCOUNTABILITY, AND LIABILITY

Ethical choices are decisions made by individuals who are responsible for the consequences of their actions. **Responsibility** is a key element of ethical action. Responsibility means that you accept the potential costs, duties, and obligations for the decisions you make. **Accountability** is a feature of systems and social institutions: It means that mechanisms are in place to determine who took responsible action, and who is responsible. Systems and institutions in which it is impossible to find out who took what action are inherently incapable of ethical analysis or ethical action. **Liability** extends the concept of responsibility further to the area of laws. Liability is a feature of political systems in which a body of laws is in place that permits individuals to recover the damages done to them by other actors, systems, or organizations. **Due process** is a related feature of law-governed societies and is a process in which laws are known and understood, and there is an ability to appeal to higher authorities to ensure that the laws are applied correctly.

These basic concepts form the underpinning of an ethical analysis of information systems and those who manage them. First, information technologies are filtered through social institutions, organizations, and individuals. Systems do not have impacts by themselves. Whatever information system impacts exist are products of institutional, organizational, and individual actions and behaviors. Second, responsibility for the consequences of technology falls clearly on the institutions, organizations, and individual managers who choose to use the technology. Using information technology in a socially responsible manner means that you can and will be held accountable for the consequences of your actions. Third, in an ethical, political society, individuals and others can recover damages done to them through a set of laws characterized by due process.

ETHICAL ANALYSIS

When confronted with a situation that seems to present ethical issues, how should you analyze it? The following five-step process should help:

1. *Identify and describe the facts clearly.* Find out who did what to whom, and where, when, and how. In many instances, you will be surprised at the errors in the initially reported facts, and often you will find that simply getting the facts straight helps define the solution. It also helps to get the opposing parties involved in an ethical dilemma to agree on the facts.

2. *Define the conflict or dilemma and identify the higher-order values involved.* Ethical, social, and political issues always reference higher values. The parties to a dispute all claim to be pursuing higher values (e.g., freedom, privacy, protection of property, and the free enterprise system). Typically, an ethical issue involves a dilemma: two diametrically opposed courses of action that support worthwhile values. For example, the chapter-opening case study illustrates two competing values: the need to improve access to digital content and the need to respect the property rights of the owners of that content.

3. *Identify the stakeholders.* Every ethical, social, and political issue has stakeholders: players in the game who have an interest in the outcome, who have invested in the situation, and usually who have vocal opinions. Find out the identity of these groups and what they want. This will be useful later when designing a solution.

4. *Identify the options that you can reasonably take.* You may find that none of the options satisfy all the interests involved, but that some options do a better job than others. Sometimes arriving at a good or ethical solution may not always be a balancing of consequences to stakeholders.

5. *Identify the potential consequences of your options.* Some options may be ethically correct but disastrous from other points of view. Other options may work in one instance but not in other similar instances. Always ask yourself, "What if I choose this option consistently over time?"

CANDIDATE ETHICAL PRINCIPLES

Once your analysis is complete, what ethical principles or rules should you use to make a decision? What higher-order values should inform your judgment? Although you are the only one who can decide which among many ethical principles you will follow, and how you will prioritize them, it is helpful to consider some ethical principles with deep roots in many cultures that have survived throughout recorded history:

1. Do unto others as you would have them do unto you (the **Golden Rule**). Putting yourself into the place of others, and thinking of yourself as the object of the decision, can help you think about fairness in decision making.

2. If an action is not right for everyone to take, it is not right for anyone (**Immanuel Kant's Categorical Imperative**). Ask yourself, "If everyone did this, could the organization, or society, survive?"

3. If an action cannot be taken repeatedly, it is not right to take at all (**Descartes' rule of change**). This is the slippery-slope rule: An action may bring about a small change now that is acceptable, but if it is repeated, it would bring unacceptable changes in the long

run. In the vernacular, it might be stated as "once started down a slippery path, you may not be able to stop."

4. Take the action that achieves the higher or greater value (**Utilitarian Principle**). This rule assumes you can prioritize values in a rank order and understand the consequences of various courses of action.

5. Take the action that produces the least harm or the least potential cost (**Risk Aversion Principle**). Some actions have extremely high failure costs of very low probability (e.g., building a nuclear generating facility in an urban area) or extremely high failure costs of moderate probability (speeding and automobile accidents). Avoid these high-failure-cost actions, paying greater attention to high-failure-cost potential of moderate to high probability.

6. Assume that virtually all tangible and intangible objects are owned by someone else unless there is a specific declaration otherwise. (This is the **ethical "no free lunch" rule.**) If something someone else has created is useful to you, it has value, and you should assume the creator wants compensation for this work.

Actions that do not easily pass these rules deserve close attention and a great deal of caution. The appearance of unethical behavior may do as much harm to you and your company as actual unethical behavior.

PROFESSIONAL CODES OF CONDUCT

When groups of people claim to be professionals, they take on special rights and obligations because of their special claims to knowledge, wisdom, and respect. Professional codes of conduct are promulgated by associations of professionals, such as the American Medical Association (AMA), the American Bar Association (ABA), the Association of Information Technology Professionals (AITP), and the Association for Computing Machinery (ACM). These professional groups take responsibility for the partial regulation of their professions by determining entrance qualifications and competence. Codes of ethics are promises by professions to regulate themselves in the general interest of society. For example, avoiding harm to others, honoring property rights (including intellectual property), and respecting privacy are among the General Moral Imperatives of the ACM's Code of Ethics and Professional Conduct.

SOME REAL-WORLD ETHICAL DILEMMAS

Information systems have created new ethical dilemmas in which one set of interests is pitted against another. For example, many of the large telephone companies in the United States are using information technology to reduce the sizes of their workforces. Voice recognition software reduces the need for human operators by enabling computers to recognize a customer's responses to a series of computerized questions. Many companies monitor what their employees are doing on the Internet to prevent them from wasting company resources on non-business activities. Facebook monitors its subscribers and then sells the information to advertisers and app developers (see the chapter-ending case study).

In each instance, you can find competing values at work, with groups lined up on either side of a debate. A company may argue, for example, that it has a right to use information systems to increase productivity and reduce the size of its workforce to lower costs and stay in business. Employees displaced by information systems may argue that employers have some responsibility for their welfare. Business owners might feel obligated to monitor employee e-mail and Internet use to minimize drains on productivity. Employees might believe they should be able to use the Internet for short personal tasks in place of the telephone. A close analysis of the facts can sometimes produce compromised solutions that give each side "half a loaf." Try to apply some of the principles of ethical analysis described to each of these cases. What is the right thing to do?

4.3 The Moral Dimensions of Information Systems

In this section, we take a closer look at the five moral dimensions of information systems first described in Figure 4.1. In each dimension, we identify the ethical, social, and political levels of analysis and use real-world examples to illustrate the values involved, the stakeholders, and the options chosen.

INFORMATION RIGHTS: PRIVACY AND FREEDOM IN THE INTERNET AGE

Privacy is the claim of individuals to be left alone, free from surveillance or interference from other individuals or organizations, including the state. Claims to privacy are also involved at the workplace: Millions of employees are subject to electronic and other forms of high-tech surveillance. Information technology and systems threaten individual claims to privacy by making the invasion of privacy cheap, profitable, and effective.

The claim to privacy is protected in the U.S., Canadian, and German constitutions in a variety of different ways and in other countries through various statutes. In the United States, the claim to privacy is protected primarily by the First Amendment guarantees of freedom of speech and association, the Fourth Amendment protections against unreasonable search and seizure of one's personal documents or home, and the guarantee of due process.

Table 4.3 describes the major U.S. federal statutes that set forth the conditions for handling information about individuals in such areas as credit reporting, education, financial records, newspaper records, and electronic communications. The Privacy Act of 1974 has been the most important of these laws, regulating the federal government's collection, use, and disclosure of information. At present, most U.S. federal privacy laws apply only to the federal government and regulate very few areas of the private sector.

Most American and European privacy law is based on a regime called **Fair Information Practices (FIP)** first set forth in a report written in 1973 by a federal government advisory committee and updated most recently in 2010 to take into account new privacy-invading technology (FTC, 2010; U.S. Department of Health, Education, and Welfare, 1973). FIP

TABLE 4.3

Federal Privacy Laws in the United States

General Federal Privacy Laws	Privacy Laws Affecting Private Institutions
Freedom of Information Act of 1966 as Amended (5 USC 552)	Fair Credit Reporting Act of 1970
Privacy Act of 1974 as Amended (5 USC 552a)	Family Educational Rights and Privacy Act of 1974
Electronic Communications Privacy Act of 1986	Right to Financial Privacy Act of 1978
Computer Matching and Privacy Protection Act of 1988	Privacy Protection Act of 1980
Computer Security Act of 1987	Cable Communications Policy Act of 1984
Federal Managers Financial Integrity Act of 1982	Electronic Communications Privacy Act of 1986
Driver's Privacy Protection Act of 1994	Video Privacy Protection Act of 1988
E-Government Act of 2002	The Health Insurance Portability and Accountability Act of 1996 (HIPAA)
	Children's Online Privacy Protection Act (COPPA) of 1998
	Financial Modernization Act (Gramm-Leach-Bliley Act) of 1999

is a set of principles governing the collection and use of information about individuals. FIP principles are based on the notion of a mutuality of interest between the record holder and the individual. The individual has an interest in engaging in a transaction, and the record keeper—usually a business or government agency—requires information about the individual to support the transaction. Once information is gathered, the individual maintains an interest in the record, and the record may not be used to support other activities without the individual's consent. In 1998, the FTC restated and extended the original FIP to provide guidelines for protecting online privacy. Table 4.4 describes the FTC's Fair Information Practice principles.

The FTC's FIP principles are being used as guidelines to drive changes in privacy legislation. In July 1998, the U.S. Congress passed the Children's Online Privacy Protection Act (COPPA), requiring Web sites to obtain parental permission before collecting information on children under the age of 13. The FTC has recommended additional legislation to protect online consumer privacy in advertising networks that collect records of consumer Web activity to develop detailed profiles, which are then used by other companies to target online ads. In 2010, the FTC added three practices to its framework for privacy. Firms should adopt "privacy by design," building products and services that protect privacy. Firms should increase the transparency of their data practices. And firms should require consumer consent and provide clear options to opt out of data collection schemes (FTC, 2010). Other proposed Internet privacy legislation focuses on protecting the online use of personal identification numbers, such as social security numbers; protecting personal information collected on the Internet that deals with individuals not covered by COPPA; and limiting the use of data mining for homeland security.

Beginning in 2009 and continuing through 2012, the FTC extended its FIP doctrine to address the issue of behavioral targeting. The FTC held hearings to discuss its program for voluntary industry principles for regulating behavioral targeting. The online advertising trade group Network Advertising Initiative (discussed later in this section), published its own self-regulatory principles that largely agreed with the FTC. Nevertheless, the government, privacy groups, and the online ad industry are still at loggerheads over two issues. Privacy advocates want both an opt-in policy at all sites and a national Do Not Track list. The industry opposes these moves and continues to insist on an opt-out capability being the only way to avoid tracking. In May 2011, Senator Jay D. Rockefeller (D-WV), Chairman of the Senate Commerce Subcommittee on Consumer Protection,

1. Notice/awareness (core principle). Web sites must disclose their information practices before collecting data. Includes identification of collector; uses of data; other recipients of data; nature of collection (active/inactive); voluntary or required status; consequences of refusal; and steps taken to protect confidentiality, integrity, and quality of the data.	**TABLE 4.4** Federal Trade Commission Fair Information Practice Principles
2. Choice/consent (core principle). There must be a choice regime in place allowing consumers to choose how their information will be used for secondary purposes other than supporting the transaction, including internal use and transfer to third parties.	
3. Access/participation. Consumers should be able to review and contest the accuracy and completeness of data collected about them in a timely, inexpensive process.	
4. Security. Data collectors must take responsible steps to assure that consumer information is accurate and secure from unauthorized use.	
5. Enforcement. There must be in place a mechanism to enforce FIP principles. This can involve self-regulation, legislation giving consumers legal remedies for violations, or federal statutes and regulations.	

Product Safety, and Insurance, held hearings to discuss consumer privacy concerns and to explore the possible role of the federal government in protecting consumers in the mobile marketplace. Rockefeller supports the Do-Not-Track Online Act of 2011 (reintroduced in 2013), which requires firms to notify consumers they are being tracked and allows consumers to opt out of the tracking (U.S. Senate, 2011). Nevertheless, there is an emerging consensus among all parties that greater transparency and user control (especially making opting out of tracking the default option) is required to deal with behavioral tracking.

Privacy protections have also been added to recent laws deregulating financial services and safeguarding the maintenance and transmission of health information about individuals. The Gramm-Leach-Bliley Act of 1999, which repeals earlier restrictions on affiliations among banks, securities firms, and insurance companies, includes some privacy protection for consumers of financial services. All financial institutions are required to disclose their policies and practices for protecting the privacy of nonpublic personal information and to allow customers to opt out of information-sharing arrangements with nonaffiliated third parties.

The Health Insurance Portability and Accountability Act (HIPAA) of 1996, which took effect on April 14, 2003, includes privacy protection for medical records. The law gives patients access to their personal medical records maintained by health care providers, hospitals, and health insurers, and the right to authorize how protected information about themselves can be used or disclosed. Doctors, hospitals, and other health care providers must limit the disclosure of personal information about patients to the minimum amount necessary to achieve a given purpose.

The European Directive on Data Protection

In Europe, privacy protection is much more stringent than in the United States. Unlike the United States, European countries do not allow businesses to use personally identifiable information without consumers' prior consent. On October 25, 1998, the European Commission's Directive on Data Protection went into effect, broadening privacy protection in the European Union (EU) nations. The directive requires companies to inform people when they collect information about them and disclose how it will be stored and used. Customers must provide their informed consent before any company can legally use data about them, and they have the right to access that information, correct it, and request that no further data be collected. **Informed consent** can be defined as consent given with knowledge of all the facts needed to make a rational decision. EU member nations must translate these principles into their own laws and cannot transfer personal data to countries, such as the United States, that do not have similar privacy protection regulations. In 2009, the European Parliament passed new rules governing the use of third-party cookies for behavioral tracking purposes. These new rules were implemented in May 2011 and require that Web site visitors must give explicit consent to be tracked by cookies. Web sites will be required to have highly visible warnings on their pages if third-party cookies are being used (European Parliament, 2009).

In January 2012, the E.U. issued significant proposed changes to its data protection rules, the first overhaul since 1995 (European Commission, 2012). The new rules would apply to all companies providing services in Europe, and require Internet companies like Amazon, Facebook, Apple, Google, and others to obtain explicit consent from consumers about the use of their personal data, delete information at the user's request (based on the "right to be forgotten"), and retain information only as long as absolutely necessary. The proposed rules provide for fines up to 2% of the annual gross revenue of offending firms. The requirement for user consent includes the use of cookies and super cookies used for tracking purposes across the Web (third-party cookies), and not for cookies used on a Web site. Like the FTC's proposed framework, the EU's new proposed rules have a strong emphasis on regulating tracking, enforcing transparency, limiting data retention periods, and obtaining user consent.

Working with the European Commission, the U.S. Department of Commerce developed a safe harbor framework for U.S. firms. A **safe harbor** is a private, self-regulating policy and enforcement mechanism that meets the objectives of government regulators and legislation but does not involve government regulation or enforcement. U.S. businesses would be allowed to use personal data from EU countries if they develop privacy protection policies that meet EU standards. Enforcement would occur in the United States using self-policing, regulation, and government enforcement of fair trade statutes.

Internet Challenges to Privacy

Internet technology has posed new challenges for the protection of individual privacy. Information sent over this vast network of networks may pass through many different computer systems before it reaches its final destination. Each of these systems is capable of monitoring, capturing, and storing communications that pass through it.

Web sites track searches that have been conducted, the Web sites and Web pages visited, the online content a person has accessed, and what items that person has inspected or purchased over the Web. This monitoring and tracking of Web site visitors occurs in the background without the visitor's knowledge. It is conducted not just by individual Web sites but by advertising networks such as Microsoft Advertising, Yahoo, and DoubleClick that are capable of tracking personal browsing behavior across thousands of Web sites. Both Web site publishers and the advertising industry defend tracking of individuals across the Web because doing so allows more relevant ads to be targeted to users, and it pays for the cost of publishing Web sites. In this sense, it's like broadcast television: advertiser-supported content that is free to the user. The commercial demand for this personal information is virtually insatiable. However, these practices also impinge on individual privacy, as discussed in the Interactive Session on Technology.

Cookies are small text files deposited on a computer hard drive when a user visits Web sites. Cookies identify the visitor's Web browser software and track visits to the Web site. When the visitor returns to a site that has stored a cookie, the Web site software will search the visitor's computer, find the cookie, and know what that person has done in the past. It may also update the cookie, depending on the activity during the visit. In this way, the site can customize its content for each visitor's interests. For example, if you purchase a book on Amazon.com and return later from the same browser, the site will welcome you by name and recommend other books of interest based on your past purchases. DoubleClick, described earlier in this chapter, uses cookies to build its dossiers with details of online purchases and to examine the behavior of Web site visitors. Figure 4.3 illustrates how cookies work.

Web sites using cookie technology cannot directly obtain visitors' names and addresses. However, if a person has registered at a site, that information can be combined with cookie data to identify the visitor. Web site owners can also combine the data they have gathered from cookies and other Web site monitoring tools with personal data from other sources, such as offline data collected from surveys or paper catalog purchases, to develop very detailed profiles of their visitors.

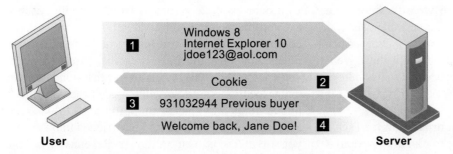

User   **Server**

1. The Web server reads the user's Web browser and determines the operating system, browser name, version number, Internet address, and other information.
2. The server transmits a tiny text file with user identification information called a cookie, which the user's browser receives and stores on the user's computer hard drive.
3. When the user returns to the Web site, the server requests the contents of any cookie it deposited previously in the user's computer.
4. The Web server reads the cookie, identifies the visitor, and calls up data on the user.

Figure 4.3
How Cookies Identify Web Visitors
Cookies are written by a Web site on a visitor's hard drive. When the visitor returns to that Web site, the Web server requests the ID number from the cookie and uses it to access the data stored by that server on that visitor. The Web site can then use these data to display personalized information.

Ever get the feeling somebody is trailing you on the Web, watching your every click? Do you wonder why you start seeing display ads and pop-ups just after you've been searching the Web for a car, a dress, or cosmetic product? Well, you're right: your behavior is being tracked, and you are being targeted on the Web as you move from site to site in order to expose you to certain "targeted" ads. It's Big Data's dark side.

Individual Web sites and companies whose business is identifying and tracking Internet users for advertisers and marketers are collecting data on your every online move. Google, which handles more than 500 million Web searches each day, knows more about you than your mother does. Many of the tracking tools gather incredibly personal information such as age, gender, race, income, marital status, health concerns (health topics you search on), TV shows and movies viewed, magazines and newspapers read, and books purchased. A $31 billion dollar online ad industry is driving this intense data collection. Facebook, which maintains detailed data on over 1 billion users, employs its Like button to follow users around the Web even if you log off. Its social networking site is one giant tracking system that remembers what you like, what your friends like, and whatever you reveal on your Wall. (See the chapter-ending case study.)

While tracking firms claim the information they gather is anonymous, this is true in name only. Scholars have shown that with just a few pieces of information, such as age, gender, zip code, and marital status, specific individuals can be easily identified. Moreover, tracking firms combine their online data with data they purchase from offline firms who track retail store purchases of virtually all Americans. Here, personal names and other identifiers are used.

Use of real identities across the Web is going mainstream at a rapid clip. A Wall Street Journal examination of nearly 1,000 top Websites found that 75% now include code from social networks, such as Facebook's "Like" or Twitter's "Tweet" buttons. Such code can match people's identities with their Web-browsing activities on an unprecedented scale and can even track a user's arrival on a page if the button is never clicked.

In separate research, the Journal examined what happens when people logged in to roughly 70 popular Websites that request a login and found that more than a quarter of the time, the sites passed along a user's real name, email address or other personal details to third-party companies.

Online advertising titans like Google, Microsoft, and Yahoo are all looking for ways to monetize their huge collections of online behavioral data. While search engine marketing is arguably the most effective form of advertising in history, untargeted banner display ad marketing is highly inefficient because it displays ads to everyone regardless of their interests. As a result, these firms cannot charge much for display ads. However, by tracking the online movements of 245 million U.S. Internet users, they can develop a very clear picture of who you are, and use that information to show you ads that might be of interest to you. This would make the marketing process more efficient, and more profitable for all the parties involved.

You're also being tracked closely when you use your mobile phone to access the Internet, visit your Facebook page, get Twitter feeds, watch video, and listen to music. The mobile Web is working hard to keep track of your whereabouts, locations, habits, and friends in the hope of selling you even more products and services.

New technologies found on smartphones can identify where you are located within a few yards. Performing routine actions using your smart phone makes it possible to locate you throughout the day, to report this information to corporate databases, retain and analyze the information, and then sell it to advertisers. Most of the popular apps report your location. Law enforcement agencies certainly have an interest in knowing the whereabouts of criminals and suspects. There are, of course, many times when you would like to report your location either automatically or on your command. If you were injured, for instance, you might like your cell phone to be able to automatically report your location to authorities, or, if you were in a restaurant, you might want to notify your friends where you are and what you are doing. But what about occasions when you don't want anyone to know where you are, least of all advertisers and marketers?

Location data gathered from cell phones has extraordinary commercial value because advertising companies can send you highly targeted advertisements, coupons, and flash bargains, based on where you are located. This technology is the foundation for many location-based services, which include smartphone maps and charts, shopping apps, and social apps that you can use to let your friends know where you are and what you are doing. Revenues from the global location-based services market are projected to reach reach $10.3 billion in 2015, according to Gartner.

Both Apple's iPhone and Google's Android phones collect personal, private location data, and both firms are building massive databases that can pinpoint your location. Advertising firms pay Apple and Google for that information and for distributing their mobile ads, and they are becoming increasingly important sources of revenue. (In 2012 Google earned $2.2 billion from its mobile ads.) Smartphone apps that provide location-based services are also sources of personal, private location information based on the smartphone GPS capability.

Expect those eyes to follow your movements even more in the future as behavioral targeting becomes even more precise. New software is being developed to help advertisers track users across devices by establishing cross-screen identities. That means that companies will be able to serve ads to your mobile phone based on what they learned about you from surfing the Web on your PC.

Sources: Natasha Singer, "Their Apps Track You, Will Congress Track Them?" *The New York Times*, January 5, 2013; Spencer E. Ante, "Online Ads Can Now Follow Your Home," *The Wall Street Journal*, April 29, 2013; Wendy Davis, "New App Lets Mobile Users Opt Out of Behavioral Targeting," Online Media Daily, April 11, 2013; Jennifer Valentino-Devries and Jeremy Singer, "They Know What You're Shopping For," *The Wall Street Journal*, December 7 , 2012; Julia Angwin, "Online Tracking Ramps Up," *The Wall Street Journal*, June 17, 2012; Christina DesMarais, "Location Tracking of Mobile Devices Gets Really Nosy," PC World, June 2, 2012; "This Smart Phone Tracking Tech Will Give You the Creeps," PC World, May 22, 2012; Julia Angwin, "Digital Privacy Rules Taking Shape," *The Wall Street Journal*, March 26, 2012; and Julia Angwin, "Latest inWeb Tracking: Stealthy 'Supercookies," *The Wall Street Journal*, August 18, 2011.

CASE STUDY QUESTIONS

1. Why is behavioral tracking such an important ethical dilemma today? Identify the stakeholders and interest groups in favor of and opposed to behavioral tracking.

2. How do businesses benefit from behavioral tracking? Do people benefit? Explain your answer.

3. What would happen if there were no behavioral tracking on the Internet?

There are now even more subtle and surreptitious tools for surveillance of Internet users. So-called "super cookies" or Flash cookies cannot be easily deleted and can be installed whenever a person clicks on a Flash video. These so-called "Local Shared Object" files are used by Flash to play videos and are put on the user's computer without their consent. Marketers use Web beacons as another tool to monitor online behavior. **Web beacons**, also called *Web bugs* (or simply "tracking files"), are tiny software programs that keep a record of users' online clickstream and report this data back to whomever owns the tracking file invisibly embedded in e-mail messages and Web pages that are designed to monitor the behavior of the user visiting a Web site or sending e-mail. Web beacons are placed on popular Web sites by third-party firms who pay the Web sites a fee for access to their audience. So how common is Web tracking? In a path-breaking series of articles in the *Wall Street Journal* in 2010 and 2011, researchers examined the tracking files on 50 of the most popular U.S Web sites. What they found revealed a very widespread surveillance system. On the 50 sites, they discovered 3,180 tracking files installed on visitor computers. Only one site, Wikipedia, had no tracking files. Some popular sites such as Dictionary.com, MSN, and Comcast, installed more than 100 tracking files! Two-thirds of the tracking files came from 131 companies whose primary business is identifying and tracking Internet users to create consumer profiles that can be sold to advertising firms looking for specific types of customers. The biggest trackers were Google, Microsoft, and Quantcast, all of whom are in the business of selling ads to advertising firms and marketers. A follow-up study in 2012 found the situation had worsened: tracking on the 50 most popular sites had risen nearly five fold! The cause: growth of online ad auctions where advertisers buy the data about users' Web browsing behavior.

Other **spyware** can secretly install itself on an Internet user's computer by piggybacking on larger applications. Once installed, the spyware calls out to Web sites to send banner ads and other unsolicited material to the user, and it can report the user's movements on the Internet to other computers. More information is available about intrusive software in Chapter 8.

About 83 percent of global Internet users use Google Search and other Google services, making Google the world's largest collector of online user data. Whatever Google does with its data has an enormous impact on online privacy. Most experts believe that Google possesses the largest collection of personal information in the world—more data on more people than any government agency. The nearest competitor is Facebook.

After Google acquired the advertising network DoubleClick in 2007, Google has been using behavioral targeting to help it display more relevant ads based on users' search activities and to target individuals as they move from one site to another in order to show them display or banner ads. Google allows tracking software on its search pages, and using DoubleClick, it is able to track users across the Internet. One of its programs enables advertisers to target ads based on the search histories of Google users, along with any other information the user submits to Google such as age, demographics, region, and other Web activities (such as blogging). Google's AdSense program enables Google to help advertisers select keywords and design ads for various market segments based on search histories, such as helping a clothing Web site create and test ads targeted at teen-age females. A recent study found that 88 percent of 400,000 Web sites had at least one Google tracking bug.

Google has also been scanning the contents of messages received by users of its free Web-based e-mail service called Gmail. Ads that users see when they read their e-mail are related to the subjects of these messages. Profiles are developed on individual users based on the content in their e-mail. Google now displays targeted ads on YouTube and on Google mobile applications, and its DoubleClick ad network serves up targeted banner ads.

The United States has allowed businesses to gather transaction information generated in the marketplace and then use that information for other marketing purposes without obtaining the informed consent of the individual whose information is being used. An **opt-out** model of informed consent permits the collection of personal information until the consumer specifically requests that the data not be collected. Privacy advocates would like to see wider use of an **opt-in** model of informed consent in which a business is prohibited from collecting any personal information unless the consumer specifically takes action to approve information collection and use. Here, the default option is no collection of user information.

The online industry has preferred self-regulation to privacy legislation for protecting consumers. The online advertising industry formed the Online Privacy Alliance to encourage self-regulation to develop a set of privacy guidelines for its members. The group promotes the use of online seals, such as that of TRUSTe, certifying Web sites adhering to certain privacy principles. Members of the advertising network industry, including Google's DoubleClick, have created an additional industry association called the Network Advertising Initiative (NAI) to develop its own privacy policies to help consumers opt out of advertising network programs and provide consumers redress from abuses.

Individual firms like Microsoft, Mozilla Foundation, Yahoo, and Google have recently adopted policies on their own in an effort to address public concern about tracking people online. Microsoft's new Internet Explorer 10 Web browser was shipped with the opt-out option as the default in 2013. Other browsers have opt out options but users need to turn them on, and most users fail to do this. AOL established an opt-out policy that allows users of its site to not be tracked. Yahoo follows NAI guidelines and also allows opt-out for tracking and Web beacons (Web bugs). Google has reduced retention time for tracking data.

In general, most Internet businesses do little to protect the privacy of their customers, and consumers do not do as much as they should to protect themselves. For commercial Web sites that depend on advertising to support themselves, most revenue derives from selling customer information. Of the companies that do post privacy polices on their Web sites, about half do not monitor their sites to ensure they adhere to these policies. The vast majority of online customers claim they are concerned about online privacy, but less than half read the privacy statements on Web sites. In general, Web site privacy policies require a law degree to understand and are ambiguous about key terms (Laudon and Traver, 2013).

In one of the more insightful studies of consumer attitudes towards Internet privacy, a group of Berkeley students conducted surveys of online users, and of complaints filed with the FTC involving privacy issues. Here are some of their results: people feel they have no control over the information collected about them, and they don't know who to complain to. Web sites collect all this information, but do not let users have access, the Web site policies are unclear, and they share data with "affiliates" but never identify who the affiliates are and how many there are. Web bug trackers are ubiquitous and users are not informed of trackers on the pages they visit. The results of this study and others suggest that consumers are not saying "Take my privacy, I don't care, send me the service for free." They are saying "We want access to the information, we want some controls on what can be collected, what is done with the information, the ability to opt out of the entire tracking enterprise, and some clarity on what the policies really are, and we don't want those policies changed without our participation and permission." (The full report is available at knowprivacy.org.)

Technical Solutions

In addition to legislation, there are a few technologies that can protect user privacy during interactions with Web sites. Many of these tools are used for encrypting e-mail, for making e-mail or surfing activities appear anonymous, for preventing client computers from accepting cookies, or for detecting and eliminating spyware. For the most part, technical solutions have failed to protect users from being tracked as they move from one site to another.

Because of growing public criticism of behavioral tracking, targeting of ads, and the failure of industry to self-regulate, attention has shifted to browsers. Many browsers have Do Not Track options. For users who have selected the Do Not Track browser option, their browser will send a request to Web sites requesting the user's behavior not be tracked. But Web sites are not obligated to honor their visitors' requests not to be tracked. There is no online advertising industry agreement on how to respond to Do Not Track requests, and currently no legislation requiring Web sites to stop tracking.

PROPERTY RIGHTS: INTELLECTUAL PROPERTY

Contemporary information systems have severely challenged existing laws and social practices that protect private intellectual property. **Intellectual property** is considered to be intangible property created by individuals or corporations. Information technology has made it difficult to protect intellectual property because computerized information can be so easily copied or distributed on networks. Intellectual property is subject to a variety of protections under three different legal traditions: trade secrets, copyright, and patent law.

Trade Secrets

Any intellectual work product—a formula, device, pattern, or compilation of data—used for a business purpose can be classified as a **trade secret**, provided it is not based on information in the public domain. Protections for trade secrets vary from state to state. In general, trade secret laws grant a monopoly on the ideas behind a work product, but it can be a very tenuous monopoly.

Software that contains novel or unique elements, procedures, or compilations can be included as a trade secret. Trade secret law protects the actual ideas in a work product, not only their manifestation. To make this claim, the creator or owner must take care to bind employees and customers with nondisclosure agreements and to prevent the secret from falling into the public domain.

The limitation of trade secret protection is that, although virtually all software programs of any complexity contain unique elements of some sort, it is difficult to prevent the ideas in the work from falling into the public domain when the software is widely distributed.

Copyright

Copyright is a statutory grant that protects creators of intellectual property from having their work copied by others for any purpose during the life of the author plus an additional 70 years after the author's death. For corporate-owned works, copyright protection lasts for 95 years after their initial creation. Congress has extended copyright protection to books, periodicals, lectures, dramas, musical compositions, maps, drawings, artwork of any kind, and motion pictures. The intent behind copyright laws has been to encourage creativity and authorship by ensuring that creative people receive the financial and other benefits of their work. Most industrial nations have their own copyright laws, and there are several international conventions and bilateral agreements through which nations coordinate and enforce their laws.

In the mid-1960s, the Copyright Office began registering software programs, and in 1980, Congress passed the Computer Software Copyright Act, which clearly provides protection for software program code and for copies of the original sold in commerce, and sets forth the rights of the purchaser to use the software while the creator retains legal title.

Copyright protects against copying of entire programs or their parts. Damages and relief are readily obtained for infringement. The drawback to copyright protection is that the underlying ideas behind a work are not protected, only their manifestation in a work. A competitor can use your software, understand how it works, and build new software that follows the same concepts without infringing on a copyright.

"Look and feel" copyright infringement lawsuits are precisely about the distinction between an idea and its expression. For instance, in the early 1990s, Apple Computer sued Microsoft Corporation and Hewlett-Packard for infringement of the expression of Apple's Macintosh interface, claiming that the defendants copied the expression of over-lapping windows. The defendants countered that the idea of overlapping windows can be expressed only in a single way and, therefore, was not protectable under the merger doctrine of copyright law. When ideas and their expression merge, the expression cannot be copyrighted.

In general, courts appear to be following the reasoning of a 1989 case—*Brown Bag Software v. Symantec Corp*—in which the court dissected the elements of software alleged to be infringing. The court found that similar concept, function, general functional features (e.g., drop-down menus), and colors are not protectable by copyright law (*Brown Bag Software v. Symantec Corp.*, 1992).

Patents

A **patent** grants the owner an exclusive monopoly on the ideas behind an invention for 20 years. The congressional intent behind patent law was to ensure that inventors of new machines, devices, or methods receive the full financial and other rewards of their labor and yet make widespread use of the invention possible by providing detailed diagrams for those wishing to use the idea under license from the patent's owner. The granting of a patent is determined by the United States Patent and Trademark Office and relies on court rulings.

The key concepts in patent law are originality, novelty, and invention. The Patent Office did not accept applications for software patents routinely until a 1981 Supreme Court decision that held that computer programs could be a part of a patentable process. Since that time, hundreds of patents have been granted and thousands await consideration.

The strength of patent protection is that it grants a monopoly on the underlying concepts and ideas of software. The difficulty is passing stringent criteria of nonobviousness (e.g., the work must reflect some special understanding and contribution), originality, and novelty, as well as years of waiting to receive protection.

In what some call the patent trial of the century, in 2011, Apple sued Samsung for violating its patents for iPhones, iPads, and iPods. On August 24, 2012, a California jury in federal district court delivered a decisive victory to Apple and a stunning defeat to Samsung. The jury awarded Apple $1 billion in damages. The decision established criteria for determining just how close a competitor can come to an industry-leading and standard-setting product like Apple's iPhone before it violates the design and utility patents of the leading firm. The same court ruled that Samsung could not sell its new tablet computer (Galaxy 10.1) in the United States. In a later patent dispute, Samsung won an infringement case against Apple. In June 2013, the United States International Trade Commission issued a ban for a handful of older iPhone and iPad devices because they violated Samsung patents from years ago. To make matters more complicated, Apple has been one of Samsung's largest customers for flash memory processors, graphic chips, solid-state drives and display parts that are used in Apple's iPhones, iPads, iPod Touch devices, and MacBooks. The Samsung and Apple patent cases are indicative of the complex relationships among the leading computer firms.

Challenges to Intellectual Property Rights

Contemporary information technologies, especially software, pose severe challenges to existing intellectual property regimes and, therefore, create significant ethical, social, and political issues. Digital media differ from books, periodicals, and other media in terms of ease of replication; ease of transmission; ease of alteration; difficulty in classifying a software work as a program, book, or even music; compactness—making theft easy; and difficulties in establishing uniqueness.

The proliferation of electronic networks, including the Internet, has made it even more difficult to protect intellectual property. Before widespread use of networks, copies of software, books, magazine articles, or films had to be stored on physical media, such as paper, computer disks, or videotape, creating some hurdles to distribution. Using networks, information can be more widely reproduced and distributed. The Ninth Annual Global Software Piracy Study conducted by International Data Corporation and the Business Software Alliance reported that the rate of global software piracy climbed to 42 percent in 2011, representing $63 billion in global losses from software piracy. Worldwide, for every $100 worth of legitimate software sold that year, an additional $75 worth was obtained illegally (Business Software Alliance, 2012).

The Internet was designed to transmit information freely around the world, including copyrighted information. With the World Wide Web in particular, you can easily copy and distribute virtually anything to thousands and even millions of people around the world, even if they are using different types of computer systems. Information can be illicitly copied from one place and distributed through other systems and networks even though these parties do not willingly participate in the infringement.

Individuals have been illegally copying and distributing digitized MP3 music files on the Internet for a number of years. File-sharing services such as Napster, and later Grokster, Kazaa, and Morpheus, sprung up to help users locate and swap digital music files, including those protected by copyright. Illegal file sharing became so widespread that it threatened the viability of the music recording industry and, at one point, consumed 20 percent of Internet bandwidth. The recording industry won the legal battles for shutting these services down, but it has not been able to halt illegal file sharing entirely. The motion picture and cable television industries are waging similar battles, as described in the chapter-opening case study.

As legitimate online music stores like the iTunes Store expanded, and more recently as Internet radio services like Pandora expanded, some forms of illegal file sharing have declined. Technology has radically altered the prospects for intellectual property protection from theft, at least for music, videos, and television shows (less so for software). The Apple iTunes Store legitimated paying for music and entertainment, and created a closed environment where music and videos could not be easily copied and widely distributed unless played on Apple devices. Amazon's Kindle also protects the rights of publishers and writers because its books cannot be copied to the Internet and distributed. Streaming of Internet radio, on services such as Pandora and Spotify, and Hollywood movies (at sites such as Hulu and Netflix) also inhibits piracy because the streams cannot be easily recorded on separate devices. Moreover, the large Web distributors like Apple, Google, and Amazon do not want to encourage piracy in music or videos simply because they need these properties to earn revenue.

The Digital Millennium Copyright Act (DMCA) of 1998 also provides some copyright protection. The DMCA implemented a World Intellectual Property Organization Treaty that makes it illegal to circumvent technology-based protections of copyrighted materials. Internet service providers (ISPs) are required to take down sites of copyright infringers they are hosting once the ISPs are notified of the problem. Microsoft and other major software and information content firms are represented by the Software and Information Industry Association (SIIA), which lobbies for new laws and enforcement of existing laws to protect intellectual property around the world. The SIIA runs an antipiracy hotline for individuals to report piracy activities, offers educational programs to help organizations combat software piracy, and has published guidelines for employee use of software.

ACCOUNTABILITY, LIABILITY, AND CONTROL

Along with privacy and property laws, new information technologies are challenging existing liability laws and social practices for holding individuals and institutions accountable. If a person is injured by a machine controlled, in part, by software, who should be held accountable and, therefore, held liable? Should a social network site like Facebook or Twitter be held liable and accountable for the posting of pornographic material or racial insults, or should they be held harmless against any liability for what users post (as is true of common carriers, such as the telephone system)? What about the Internet? If you outsource your information processing, to the Cloud, and the Cloud provider fails to provide adequate service, what can you do? Cloud providers often claim the software you are using is the problem, not the Cloud servers. Some real-world examples may shed light on these questions.

Computer-Related Liability Problems

For a week in October 2011, millions of BlackBerry users around the world began experiencing disruption to their e-mail service, the most vital service provided by the smartphone maker Research in Motion (RIM). The three-day blackout of e-mail involved users in Asia, Europe, the Middle East, and the Americas, a substantial part of BlackBerry's installed base of 70 million users. The BlackBerry, until recently, had the dominant position in the corporate smartphone market because it provided excellent e-mail security, and integrated well with corporate mail servers. The iPhone and Android smartphones championed by employees now account for more than half of all new corporate mobile devices. The outage is expected to encourage more corporations to abandon the BlackBerry. On the positive side, police departments around the world reported a significant drop in urban car accidents during the outage because drivers could no longer text or telephone using their BlackBerry (Austen, 2011).

After the outage, Research in Motion CTO for Software David Yach said a backlog of messages to Europe created a cascading outage effect around the world.

The company determined the root cause of the initial European BlackBerry e-mail service outage and said there was no evidence that a hack or security breach was involved.

RIM customers in Europe had been suffering from major outages for days, but it wasn't until the Americas caught the bug that BlackBerry customers started complaining on Twitter of mail delays and lack of access to their BlackBerry devices. Yach described the initial outage as a failure of one of RIM's core switches. However, the real trouble began when RIM's redundant systems failed as well. "The failover did not function as expected," Yach said, "despite the fact that we regularly test failover systems." This led to a significant backup of mail.

Who is liable for any economic harm caused to individuals or businesses that could not access their e-mail during this three-day period? If consumers pay for cell phone service, come to rely on it, and then are denied service for a significant period of time, is the cell phone provider liable for damages?

This case reveals the difficulties faced by information systems executives who ultimately are responsible for any harm done by systems they have selected and installed. Beyond IT managers, insofar as computer software is part of a machine, and the machine injures someone physically or economically, the producer of the software and the operator can be held liable for damages. Insofar as the software acts like a book, storing and displaying information, courts have been reluctant to hold authors, publishers, and booksellers liable for contents (the exception being instances of fraud or defamation), and hence courts have been wary of holding software authors liable for software.

In general, it is very difficult (if not impossible) to hold software producers liable for their software products that are considered to be like books, regardless of the physical or economic harm that results. Historically, print publishers of books and periodicals have not been held liable because of fears that liability claims would interfere with First Amendment rights guaranteeing freedom of expression. And the kind of harm caused by software failures is rarely fatal and typically inconveniences users but does not physically harm them (the exception being medical devices).

What about software as a service? ATM machines are a service provided to bank customers. Should this service fail, customers will be inconvenienced and perhaps harmed economically if they cannot access their funds in a timely manner. Should liability protections be extended to software publishers and operators of defective financial, accounting, simulation, or marketing systems?

Software is very different from books. Software users may develop expectations of infallibility about software; software is less easily inspected than a book, and it is more difficult to compare with other software products for quality; software claims to perform a task rather than describe a task, as a book does; and people come to depend on services essentially based on software. Given the centrality of software to everyday life, the chances are excellent that liability law will extend its reach to include software even when the software merely provides an information service.

Telephone systems have not been held liable for the messages transmitted because they are regulated common carriers. In return for their right to provide telephone service, they must provide access to all, at reasonable rates, and achieve acceptable reliability. But broadcasters and cable television stations are subject to a wide variety of federal and local constraints on content and facilities. In the United States, with few exceptions, Web sites are not held liable for content posted on their sites regardless if it was placed their by the Web site owners or users.

SYSTEM QUALITY: DATA QUALITY AND SYSTEM ERRORS

White Christmas turned into a black out for millions of Netflix customers, and social network users, on December 25th, 2012. The blackout was caused by the failure of Amazon's cloud computing service, which provides storage and computing power for all kinds of Web sites and services, including Netflix. The loss of service lasted for a day. Amazon blamed it on "Elastic Load Balancing," a software program that balances the loads on all its cloud servers to prevent overload. Outages at cloud computing services are rare, but are recurring. These outages have called into question the reliability and quality of cloud services. Are these outages acceptable?

The debate over liability and accountability for unintentional consequences of system use raises a related but independent moral dimension: What is an acceptable, technologically feasible level of system quality? At what point should system managers say, "Stop testing, we've done all we can to perfect this software. Ship it!" Individuals and organizations may be held responsible for avoidable and foreseeable consequences, which they have a duty to perceive and correct. The gray area is that some system errors are foreseeable and correctable only at very great expense, an expense so great that pursuing this level of perfection is not feasible economically—no one could afford the product.

For example, although software companies try to debug their products before releasing them to the marketplace, they knowingly ship buggy products because the time and cost of fixing all minor errors would prevent these products from ever being released. What if the product was not offered on the marketplace, would social welfare as a whole not advance and perhaps even decline? Carrying this further, just what is the responsibility of a producer of computer services—should it withdraw the product that can never be perfect, warn the user, or forget about the risk (let the buyer beware)?

Three principal sources of poor system performance are (1) software bugs and errors, (2) hardware or facility failures caused by natural or other causes, and (3) poor input data quality. A Chapter 8 Learning Track discusses why zero defects in software code of any complexity cannot be achieved and why the seriousness of remaining bugs cannot be estimated. Hence, there is a technological barrier to perfect software, and users must be aware of the potential for catastrophic failure. The software industry has not yet arrived at testing standards for producing software of acceptable but imperfect performance.

Although software bugs and facility catastrophes are likely to be widely reported in the press, by far the most common source of business system failure is data quality. Few companies routinely measure the quality of their data, but individual organizations report data error rates ranging from 0.5 to 30 percent.

QUALITY OF LIFE: EQUITY, ACCESS, AND BOUNDARIES

The negative social costs of introducing information technologies and systems are beginning to mount along with the power of the technology. Many of these negative social consequences are not violations of individual rights or property crimes. Nevertheless, these negative consequences can be extremely harmful to individuals, societies, and political institutions. Computers and information technologies potentially can destroy valuable elements of our culture and society even while they bring us benefits. If there is a balance of good and bad consequences of using information systems, who do we hold responsible for the bad consequences? Next, we briefly examine some of the negative social consequences of systems, considering individual, social, and political responses.

Balancing Power: Center Versus Periphery

An early fear of the computer age was that huge, centralized mainframe computers would centralize power in the nation's capital, resulting in a Big Brother society, as was suggested in George Orwell's novel *1984*. The shift toward highly decentralized computing, coupled with an ideology of empowerment of thousands of workers, and the decentralization of decision making to lower organizational levels, have reduced the fears of power centralization in government institutions. Yet much of the empowerment described in popular business magazines is trivial. Lower-level employees may be empowered to make minor decisions, but the key policy decisions may be as centralized as in the past. At the same time, corporate Internet behemoths like Google, Apple, Yahoo, Amazon, and Microsoft have come to dominate the collection and analysis of personal private information of all citizens. In this sense, power has become more centralized into the hands of a few private oligopolies.

Rapidity of Change: Reduced Response Time to Competition

Information systems have helped to create much more efficient national and international markets. Today's more efficient global marketplace has reduced the normal social buffers that permitted businesses many years to adjust to competition. Time-based competition has an ugly side: The business you work for may not have enough time to respond to global competitors and may be wiped out in a year, along with your job. We stand the risk of developing a "just-in-time society" with "just-in-time jobs" and "just-in-time" workplaces, families, and vacations.

Maintaining Boundaries: Family, Work, and Leisure

Parts of this book were produced on trains and planes, as well as on vacations and during what otherwise might have been "family" time. The danger to ubiquitous computing, telecommuting, nomad computing, mobile computing, and the "do anything anywhere" computing environment is that it is actually coming true. The traditional boundaries that separate work from family and just plain leisure have been weakened.

Although authors have traditionally worked just about anywhere (typewriters have been portable for nearly a century), the advent of information systems, coupled with the growth of knowledge-work occupations, means that more and more people are working when traditionally they would have been playing or communicating with family and friends. The work umbrella now extends far beyond the eight-hour day into commuting time, vacation time, and leisure time.

Even leisure time spent on the computer threatens these close social relationships. Extensive Internet use, even for entertainment or recreational purposes, takes people away from their family and friends. Among middle school and teenage children, it can lead to harmful anti-social behavior, such as the recent upsurge in cyberbullying.

Weakening these institutions poses clear-cut risks. Family and friends historically have provided powerful support mechanisms for individuals, and they act as balance points in a society by preserving private life, providing a place for people to collect their thoughts, allowing people to think in ways contrary to their employer, and dream.

Dependence and Vulnerability

Today, our businesses, governments, schools, and private associations, such as churches, are incredibly dependent on information systems and are, therefore, highly vulnerable if these systems fail. Secondary schools, for instance, increasingly use and rely on educational software. Test results are often stored off campus. If these systems were to shut down, there is no backup educational structure or content that can make up for the loss of the system. With systems now as ubiquitous as the telephone system, it is startling to remember that there are no regulatory or standard-setting forces in place that are similar to telephone, electrical, radio, television, or other public utility technologies. The absence of standards and the criticality of some system applications will probably call forth demands for national standards and perhaps regulatory oversight.

Computer Crime and Abuse

New technologies, including computers, create new opportunities for committing crime by creating new valuable items to steal, new ways to steal them, and new ways to harm others. **Computer crime** is the commission of illegal acts through the use of a computer or against a computer system. Computers or computer systems can be the object of the crime (destroying a company's computer center or a company's computer files), as well as the instrument of a crime (stealing computer lists by illegally gaining access to a computer system using a home computer). Simply accessing a computer system without authorization or with intent to do harm, even by accident, is now a federal crime. How common is computer crime? One source of information is the Internet Crime Complaint Center ("IC3"), a partnership between the National White Collar Crime Center and the Federal Bureau of Investigation. The IC3 data is useful for gauging the types of e-commerce crimes most likely to be reported by consumers. In 2012, the IC3 processed about 290,000 Internet crime complaints, the second-highest number in its 11-year history. Over half the complainants reported a financial loss, with the total reported amount at $525 million. The average amount of loss for those who reported a financial loss was more than $4,573. The most common complaints were for scams involving the FBI, identity theft, and advance fee fraud (National White Collar Crime Center and the Federal Bureau of Investigation, 2013). The Computer Security Institute's annual *Computer Crime and Security Survey* is another source of information. In 2011, the survey was based on the responses of 351 security practitioners in U.S. corporations, government agencies, financial institutions, medical institutions, and universities. The survey reported that 46 percent of responding organizations experienced a computer security incident within the past year. The most common type of attack experienced was a malware infection (67%), followed by phishing fraud (39%), laptop and mobile hardware theft (34%), attacks by botnets (29%), and insider abuse (25%). The true cost of all computer crime is estimated to be in the billions of dollars.

© Monkey Business Images/Shutterstock.

Computer abuse is the commission of acts involving a computer that may not be illegal but that are considered unethical. The popularity of the Internet and e-mail has turned one form of computer abuse—spamming—into a serious problem for both individuals and businesses. **Spam** is junk e-mail sent by an organization or individual to a mass audience of Internet users who have expressed no interest in the product or service being marketed. Spammers tend to market pornography, fraudulent deals and services, outright scams, and other products not widely approved in most civilized societies. Some countries have passed laws to outlaw spamming or to restrict its use. In the United States, it is still legal if it does not involve fraud and the sender and subject of the e-mail are properly identified.

Spamming has mushroomed because it costs only a few cents to send thousands of messages advertising wares to Internet users. The percentage of all e-mail that is spam was estimated at around 69 percent in 2012 (Symantec, 2013). Most spam originates from bot networks, which consist of thousands of captured PCs that can initiate and relay spam messages. Spam volume has declined somewhat since authorities took down the Rustock botnet in 2011. Spam is seasonally cyclical, and varies monthly due to the impact of new technologies (both supportive and discouraging of spammers), new prosecutions, and seasonal demand for products and services. Spam costs for businesses are very high (estimated at over $50 billion per year) because of the computing and network resources consumed by billions of unwanted e-mail messages and the time required to deal with them.

Internet service providers and individuals can combat spam by using spam filtering software to block suspicious e-mail before it enters a recipient's e-mail inbox. However, spam filters may block legitimate messages. Spammers know how to skirt around filters by continually changing their e-mail accounts, by incorporating spam messages in images, by embedding spam in e-mail attachments and electronic greeting cards, and by using other people's computers that have been hijacked by botnets (see Chapter 8). Many spam messages are sent from one country while another country hosts the spam Web site.

Spamming is more tightly regulated in Europe than in the United States. In 2002, the European Parliament passed a ban on unsolicited commercial messaging. Electronic marketing can be targeted only to people who have given prior consent.

The U.S. CAN-SPAM Act of 2003, which went into effect in 2004, does not outlaw spamming but does ban deceptive e-mail practices by requiring commercial e-mail messages to display accurate subject lines, identify the true senders, and offer recipients an easy way to remove their names from e-mail lists. It also prohibits the use of fake return addresses. A few people have been prosecuted under the law, but it has had a negligible impact on spamming in large part because of the Internet's exceptionally poor security and the use of offshore servers and botnets. In 2008, Robert Soloway, the so-called Seattle "Spam King," was sentenced to 47 months in prison for sending over 90 million spam messages in just three months off two servers. In 2011, the so-called Facebook "Spam King," Sanford Wallace, was indicted for sending over 27 million spam messages to Facebook users. He is facing a 40-year sentence because of prior spamming convictions.

Employment: Trickle-Down Technology and Reengineering Job Loss

Reengineering work is typically hailed in the information systems community as a major benefit of new information technology. It is much less frequently noted that redesigning business processes has caused millions of mid-level managers and clerical workers to lose their jobs. One economist has raised the possibility that we will create a society run by a small "high tech elite of corporate professionals . . . in a nation of the permanently unemployed" (Rifkin, 1993). In 2011, some economists have sounded new alarms about information and computer technology threatening middle-class, white-collar jobs (in addition to blue-collar factory jobs). Erik Brynjolfsson and Andrew P. McAfee argue that the pace of automation has picked up in recent years because of a combination of technologies including robotics, numerically controlled machines, computerized inventory control, pattern recognition, voice recognition, and online commerce. One result is that machines can now do a great many jobs heretofore reserved for humans including tech support, call center work, X-ray examiners, and even legal document review (Brynjolfsson and McAfee, 2011).

Other economists are much more sanguine about the potential job losses. They believe relieving bright, educated workers from reengineered jobs will result in these workers moving to better jobs in fast-growth industries. Missing from this equation are unskilled, blue-collar workers and older, less well-educated middle managers. It is not clear that these groups can be retrained easily for high-quality (high-paying) jobs. Careful planning and sensitivity to employee needs can help companies redesign work to minimize job losses.

Equity and Access: Increasing Racial and Social Class Cleavages

Does everyone have an equal opportunity to participate in the digital age? Will the social, economic, and cultural gaps that exist in the United States and other societies be reduced by information systems technology? Or will the cleavages be increased, permitting the better off to become even more better off relative to others?

These questions have not yet been fully answered because the impact of systems technology on various groups in society has not been thoroughly studied. What is known is that information, knowledge, computers, and access to these resources through educational institutions and public libraries are inequitably distributed along ethnic and social class lines, as are many other information resources. Several studies have found that poor and minority groups in the United States are less likely to have computers or online Internet access even though computer ownership and Internet access have soared in the past five years. Although the gap is narrowing, higher-income families in each ethnic group are still more likely to have home computers and Internet access than lower-income families in the same group.

A similar **digital divide** exists in U.S. schools, with schools in high-poverty areas less likely to have computers, high-quality educational technology programs, or Internet access availability for their students. Left uncorrected, the digital divide could lead to a society of information haves, computer literate and skilled, versus a large group of information have-nots, computer illiterate and unskilled. Public interest groups want to narrow this digital divide by making digital information services—including the Internet—available to virtually everyone, just as basic telephone service is now.

In recent years, ownership of computers and digital devices has broadened, but the digital divide still exists. Today's digital divide is not only based on access to digital technology but also on how that technology is being used.

INTERACTIVE SESSION: PEOPLE   Monitoring in the Workplace

There may be only 11 players on the pitch during a match, but the Blackburn Rovers Football Club in the UK employs more than 800 people. As with any modern organization, computers are at the heart of running an efficient business. Most of the club's computers are housed with the administration department at the Ewood Park office, but others can be found at the club's training center and soccer academy.

The club decided to install a software product called Spector 360, which it obtained from the Manchester-based company Snapguard. According to Snapguard's sales literature, the product enables company-wide monitoring of employee PC and Internet usage. Previously, the club had tried to introduce an acceptable use policy (AUP), but initial discussions with employees stalled, and the policy was never implemented. Early trials of Spector 360 showed that some employees were abusing the easygoing nature of the workplace to spend most of their day surfing the Web, using social networking sites, and taking up a huge amount of bandwidth for downloads.

Before officially implementing the monitoring software, the AUP was resurrected. The policy was also made part of the terms and conditions of employment. Understandably, some employees were annoyed at the concept of being watched, but the software was installed anyway. According to Ben Hayler, senior systems administrator at Blackburn Rovers, Spector 360 has definitely restored order, increasing productivity and reducing activity on non-business apps.

Reports provided by Spector 360 can show managers the following: excessive use of Facebook, Twitter, and other social networking sites; visits to adult sites or shopping sites; use of chat services; the printing or saving of confidential information; and staff login and logout times. Managers can also use the software to drill-down to look at patterns of usage, generate screen snapshots, or even log individual keystrokes.

The software can also be used to benefit employees. For example, because it can log exactly what an employee is doing, the system can help in staff training and troubleshooting, because it is easy to track exactly what caused a particular problem to occur.

Another important benefit of the software is that it helps the club to stay compliant with the Payment Card Industry (PCI) Data Security Standard. PCI standards require access to credit card information. As Spector 360 tracks and records all data to do with

credit card transactions, the information can be easily recovered.

However, what is the wider view of the monitoring of employees in the workplace? According to the Citizens Advice Bureau (a free information and advice service for UK residents), the following are some of the ways that employers monitor their employees in the workplace: recording the workplace on CCTV cameras; opening mail or e-mail; using automated software to check e-mail; checking telephone logs or recording telephone calls; checking logs of Web sites visited; videoing outside the workplace; getting information from credit reference agencies; and collecting information from point-of-sale terminals.

Although this list may look formidable, there is no argument that the employer has a right to ensure that his or her employees are behaving in a manner that is not illegal or harmful to the company. However, under UK data protection law, the employer must ensure that the monitoring is justified and take into account any negative effects the monitoring may have on staff. Monitoring for the sake of it is not allowed. Secret monitoring without employees' knowledge is usually illegal.

In a case that went before the European Court of Human Rights in 2007 (Copeland v the United Kingdom), Ms. Copeland, who was an employee of Carmarthenshire College, claimed that her privacy had been violated. She was a personal assistant to the principal and also worked closely with the deputy principal, who instigated monitoring and analysis of her telephone bills, Web sites visited, and e-mail communication. The deputy principal wanted to determine whether Copeland was making excessive use of the college's services. The European Court ruled in her favor, stating that her personal Internet usage was deemed to be under the definitions of the Convention for the Protection of Rights, covered as "private life."

The major fault of Carmarthenshire College was in not having a usage policy in place. Employers and employees should have an agreed-upon policy as part of the contract of employment that clarifies what is and is not acceptable computer usage in the workplace. The employer can then follow normal disciplinary procedures if an employee is using workplace equipment in a manner that is not permitted in the contract of employment.

Whatever the legal situation, it is clear where potential problems can occur in the workplace regarding information technology use. An e-mail, once sent, becomes a legally published document that can be produced as evidence in court cases involving issues of libel, breach of contract, and so on. Most businesses rely on their company data to keep ahead of the competition. Therefore, the loss, theft, or sabotage of data is potentially more dangerous than similar problems with hardware. If a USB memory stick is lost in a bar parking lot, replacing the hardware will cost a few dollars, but if it contains the company's confidential data, then its loss could put the company out of business!

Sources: Information Commissioners Office, "Employment Practices Data Protection Code-Supplementary Guidance" (www.ico.gov.uk/upload/documents/library/data_protection/ practical_application/coi_html/english/supplementary_guidance/monitoring_at_work_3.html, accessed October 25, 2010); "Spector 360 Helps Blackburn Rovers Show Red Card to PC and Internet Abuse," Snapguard (www.snapguard.co.uk/blackburn_fc.html, accessed October 25, 2010); "Citizens Advice Bureau Advice Guide, Basic Rights at Work," Adviceguide (www.adviceguide.org.uk/index/your_money/employment/basic_rights_at_work.htm, accessed October 25, 2010); "Employee Monitoring in the Workplace: What Constitutes 'Personal Data'?" Crowell and Moring (www.crowell.com/NewsEvents/Newsletter.aspx?id = 654, accessed October 25, 2010).

Case contributed by Andy Jones, Staffordshire University.

CASE STUDY QUESTIONS

1. How does information technology affect socioeconomic disparities? Explain your answer.

2. Why is access to technology insufficient to eliminate the digital divide?

3. How serious a problem is the "new" digital divide? Explain your answer.

4. Why is the digital divide problem an ethical dilemma?

Health Risks: RSI, CVS, and Technostress

The most common occupational disease today is **repetitive stress injury (RSI)**. RSI occurs when muscle groups are forced through repetitive actions often with high-impact loads (such as tennis) or tens of thousands of repetitions under low-impact loads (such as working at a computer keyboard).

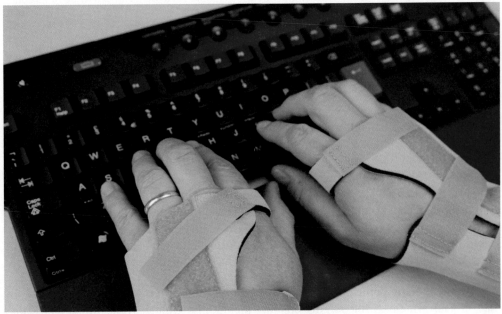

Repetitive stress injury (RSI) is the leading occupational disease today. The single largest cause of RSI is computer keyboard work.

© Stephen Barnes/Alamy.

The single largest source of RSI is computer keyboards. The most common kind of computer-related RSI is **carpal tunnel syndrome (CTS)**, in which pressure on the median nerve through the wrist's bony structure, called a carpal tunnel, produces pain. The pressure is caused by constant repetition of keystrokes: in a single shift, a word processor may perform 23,000 keystrokes. Symptoms of carpal tunnel syndrome include numbness, shooting pain, inability to grasp objects, and tingling. Millions of workers have been diagnosed with carpal tunnel syndrome.

RSI is avoidable. Designing workstations for a neutral wrist position (using a wrist rest to support the wrist), proper monitor stands, and footrests all contribute to proper posture and reduced RSI. Ergonomically correct keyboards are also an option. These measures should be supported by frequent rest breaks and rotation of employees to different jobs.

RSI is not the only occupational illness computers cause. Back and neck pain, leg stress, and foot pain also result from poor ergonomic designs of workstations. **Computer vision syndrome (CVS)** refers to any eyestrain condition related to display screen use in desktop computers, laptops, e-readers, smartphones, and handheld video games. CVS affects about 90 percent of people who spend three hours or more per day at a computer (Beck, 2010). Its symptoms, which are usually temporary, include headaches, blurred vision, and dry and irritated eyes.

The newest computer-related malady is **technostress**, which is stress induced by computer use. Its symptoms include aggravation, hostility toward humans, impatience, and fatigue. According to experts, humans working continuously with computers come to expect other humans and human institutions to behave like computers, providing instant responses, attentiveness, and an absence of emotion. Technostress is thought to be related to high levels of job turnover in the computer industry, high levels of early retirement from computer-intense occupations, and elevated levels of drug and alcohol abuse.

The incidence of technostress is not known but is thought to be in the millions and growing in the United States. Computer-related jobs now top the list of stressful occupations based on health statistics in several industrialized countries.

In addition to these maladies, computer technology may be harming our cognitive functions or at least changing how we think and solve problems. Although the Internet has made it much easier for people to access, create, and use information, some experts believe that it is also preventing people from focusing and thinking clearly.

The computer has become a part of our lives—personally as well as socially, culturally, and politically. It is unlikely that the issues and our choices will become easier as information technology continues to transform our world. The growth of the Internet and the information economy suggests that all the ethical and social issues we have described will be heightened further as we move into the first digital century.

Review Summary

1 **What ethical, social, and political issues are raised by information systems?** Information technology is introducing changes for which laws and rules of acceptable conduct have not yet been developed. Increasing computing power, storage, and networking capabilities—including the Internet—expand the reach of individual and organizational actions and magnify their impacts. The ease and anonymity with which information is now communicated, copied, and manipulated in online environments pose new challenges to the protection of privacy and intellectual property. The main ethical, social, and political issues raised by information systems center around information rights and obligations, property rights and obligations, accountability and control, system quality, and quality of life.

2 **What specific principles for conduct can be used to guide ethical decisions?** Six ethical principles for judging conduct include the Golden Rule, Immanuel Kant's

Categorical Imperative, Descartes' rule of change, the Utilitarian Principle, the Risk Aversion Principle, and the ethical "no free lunch" rule. These principles should be used in conjunction with an ethical analysis.

3 **Why do contemporary information systems technology and the Internet pose challenges to the protection of individual privacy and intellectual property?** Contemporary data storage and data analysis technology enables companies to easily gather personal data about individuals from many different sources and analyze these data to create detailed electronic profiles about individuals and their behaviors. Data flowing over the Internet can be monitored at many points. Cookies and other Web monitoring tools closely track the activities of Web site visitors. Not all Web sites have strong privacy protection policies, and they do not always allow for informed consent regarding the use of personal information. Traditional copyright laws are insufficient to protect against software piracy because digital material can be copied so easily and transmitted to many different locations simultaneously over the Internet.

4 **How have information systems affected everyday life?** Although computer systems have been sources of efficiency and wealth, they have some negative impacts. Computer errors can cause serious harm to individuals and organizations. Poor data quality is also responsible for disruptions and losses for businesses. Jobs can be lost when computers replace workers or tasks become unnecessary in reengineered business processes. The ability to own and use a computer may be exacerbating socioeconomic disparities among different racial groups and social classes. Widespread use of computers increases opportunities for computer crime and computer abuse. Computers can also create health problems, such as RSI, computer vision syndrome, and technostress.

Key Terms

Accountability, 139

Carpal tunnel syndrome (CTS), 160

Computer abuse, 156

Computer crime, 155

Computer vision syndrome (CVS), 160

Cookies, 145

Copyright, 150

Descartes' rule of change, 140

Digital divide, 157

Digital Millennium Copyright Act (DMCA), 152

Due process, 139

Ethical "no free lunch" rule, 141

Ethics, 134

Fair Information Practices (FIP), 142

Golden Rule, 140

Immanuel Kant's Categorical Imperative, 140

Information rights, 136

Informed consent, 134

Intellectual property, 149

Liability, 139

Nonobvious relationship awareness (NORA), 138

Opt-in, 148

Opt-out, 148

Patent, 150

Privacy, 142

Profiling, 137

Repetitive stress injury (RSI), 159

Responsibility, 139

Risk Aversion Principle, 141

Safe harbor, 144

Spam, 156

Spyware, 147

Technostress, 160

Trade secret, 149

Utilitarian Principle, 141

Web beacons, 147

Review Questions

4-1 What ethical, social, and political issues are raised by information systems?

- Define ethics and explain why information systems raise new ethical questions

- List and describe the issues raised by the five moral dimensions of the information age.

- Differentiate between responsibility, accountability, and liability.

4-2 What specific principles for conduct can be used to guide ethical decisions?

- List and describe the five steps in an ethical analysis.

- Identify and describe six ethical principles.

4-3 Why do contemporary information systems technology and the Internet pose challenges to the protection of individual privacy and intellectual property?

- Define privacy and fair information practices.

- Describe the European Directive on Data Protection and the 2012 proposed changes to EU data protection rules.

- Explain how informed consent, legislation, industry self-regulation, and technology tools help protect the individual privacy of Internet users.

- Define intellectual property and explain how contemporary information technologies pose challenges to the protection of intellectual property.

4-4 How have information systems affected everyday life?

- Explain why it is so difficult to hold software services liable for failure or injury.

- List and describe the principal causes of system quality problems.

- Name and describe four quality-of-life impacts of computers and information systems.

- Define and describe technostress and RSI and explain their relationship to information technology.

Discussion Questions

4-5 Should producers of software-based services, such as ATMs, be held liable for economic injuries suffered when their systems fail?

4-6 Should companies be responsible for unemployment caused by their information systems? Why or why not?

4-7 Is there a digital divide? If so, why does it matter?

Hands-On MIS Projects

The projects in this section give you hands-on experience in analyzing the privacy implications of using online data brokers, developing a corporate policy for employee Web usage, using blog creation tools to create a simple blog, and using Internet newsgroups for market research.

MANAGEMENT DECISION PROBLEMS

4-8 InfoFree's Web site is linked to massive databases that consolidate personal data on millions of people and businesses. Users can purchase marketing lists of consumers broken down by location, age, income level, home value, and interests. One could use this capability to obtain a list, for example, of everyone in Peekskill, New York, making $150,000 or more per year. Do data brokers such as InfoFree raise privacy issues? Why or why not? If your name and other personal information were in this database, what limitations on access would you want in order to preserve your privacy? Consider the following data users: government agencies, your employer, private business firms, other individuals.

4-9 As the head of a small insurance company with six employees, you are concerned about how effectively your company is using its networking and human resources.

Budgets are tight, and you are struggling to meet payrolls because employees are reporting many overtime hours. You do not believe that the employees have a sufficiently heavy work load to warrant working longer hours and are looking into the amount of time they spend on the Internet.

Each employee uses a computer with Internet access on the job. Review a sample of your company's weekly report of employee Web usage, which can be found in MyMISLab™.

- Calculate the total amount of time each employee spent on the Web for the week and the total amount of time that company computers were used for this purpose. Rank the employees in the order of the amount of time each spent online.
- Do your findings and the contents of the report indicate any ethical problems employees are creating? Is the company creating an ethical problem by monitoring its employees' use of the Internet?
- Use the guidelines for ethical analysis presented in this chapter to develop a solution to the problems you have identified.

ACHIEVING OPERATIONAL EXCELLENCE: CREATING A SIMPLE BLOG

Software skills: Blog creation
Business skills: Blog and Web page design

4-10 In this project, you'll learn how to build a simple blog of your own design using the online blog creation software available at Blogger.com. Pick a sport, hobby, or topic of interest as the theme for your blog. Name the blog, give it a title, and choose a template for the blog. Post at least four entries to the blog, adding a label for each posting. Edit your posts, if necessary. Upload an image, such as a photo from your hard drive or the Web to your blog. Add capabilities for other registered users, such as team members, to comment on your blog. Briefly describe how your blog could be useful to a company selling products or services related to the theme of your blog. List the tools available to Blogger that would make your blog more useful for business and describe the business uses of each. Save your blog and show it to your instructor.

IMPROVING DECISION MAKING: USING SOCIAL MEDIA FOR ONLINE MARKET RESEARCH

Software Skills: Web browser software
Business Skills: Using social media identify potential customers

4-11 This project will help develop your Internet skills in using social media for marketing. It will also ask you to think about the ethical implications of using information gleaned from social media for business purposes.

This project will help develop your Internet skills in using social media for marketing. It will also ask you to think about the ethical implications of using information gleaned from social media for business purposes. You are producing hiking boots that you sell through a few stores at this time. You would like to social media both to sell your boots and to make them well known. Visit a social network site of your choice (such as Facebook, Twitter, Pinterest or another of your choosing). Through the site you have chosen, search for posts that you think indicate the author might be interested in your products. Note all the information you can obtain, including information about the author.

- How could you use this information to market your boots?

- What ethical principles might you be violating if you use these messages to sell your boots? Do you think there are ethical problems in using social media posts this way? Explain your answer.

Collaboration and Teamwork Project

4-12 In MyMISLab, you will find a Collaboration and Teamwork Project dealing with the concepts in this chapter. You will be able to use Google Drive, Google Docs, Google Sites, Google+, or other open source collaboration tools to complete the assignment.

BUSINESS PROBLEM-SOLVING CASE

Facebook: It's About the Money

Over the course of less than a decade, Facebook has morphed from a small, niche networking site for mostly Ivy League college students into a publicly traded company with a market worth of $59 billion in 2013. Facebook boasts that it is free to join and always will be, so where's the money coming from to service 1 billion subscribers? Just like its fellow tech titan and rival Google, Facebook's revenue comes almost entirely from advertising. Facebook does not have a diverse array of hot new gadgets, a countrywide network of brick-and-mortar retail outlets, or a full inventory of software for sale; instead, it has your personal information, and the information of hundreds of millions of others with Facebook accounts.

Advertisers have long understood the value of Facebook's unprecedented trove of personal information. They can serve ads using highly specific details, like relationship status, location, employment status, favorite books, movies, or TV shows, and a host of other categories. For example, an Atlanta woman who posts that she has become engaged might be offered an ad for a wedding photographer on her Facebook page. When advertisements are served to finely targeted subsets of users, the response is much more successful than traditional types of advertising. A growing number of companies both big and small have taken notice: in 2013, Facebook made $4.2 billion in advertising revenue, which constituted 85 percent of its total revenue. The rest comes from the sale of virtual goods and services, principally Zynga games. Facebook's ad revenues in 2012 grew by 32 percent over the previous year, driven mostly by adding new users. Existing users are not clicking on more ads.

That was good news for Facebook, which launched its IPO (initial public stock offering) in May 2012, and is expected to continue to increase its revenue in coming years. But is it good news for you, the Facebook user? More than ever, companies like Facebook and Google, which made approximately $43 billion in advertising revenue in 2012, are using your online activity to develop a frighteningly accurate picture of your life. Facebook's goal is to serve advertisements that are more relevant to you than anywhere else on the Web, but the personal information they gather about you both with and without your consent can also be used against you in other ways.

Facebook has a diverse array of compelling and useful features. Facebook's partnership with the Department of Labor helps to connect job seekers and employers; Facebook has helped families find lost pets after natural disasters, such as when tornadoes hit the Midwest in 2012; Facebook allows active-duty soldiers to stay in touch with their families; it gives smaller companies a chance to further their e-commerce efforts and larger companies a chance to solidify their brands; and, perhaps most obviously, Facebook allows you to more easily keep in touch with your friends. These are the reasons why so many people are on Facebook.

However, Facebook's goal is to get its users to share as much data as possible, because the more Facebook knows about you, the more accurately it can serve relevant advertisements to you. Facebook CEO Mark Zuckerberg often says that people want the world to be more open and connected. It's unclear whether that is truly the case, but it is certainly true that Facebook wants the world to be more open and connected, because it stands to make more money in that world. Critics of Facebook are concerned that the existence of a repository of personal data of the size that Facebook has amassed requires protections and privacy controls that extend far beyond those that Facebook currently offers.

Facebook wanting to make more money is not a bad thing, but the company has a checkered past of privacy violations and missteps that raise doubts about whether it should be responsible for the personal data of hundreds of millions of people. There are no laws in the United States that give consumers the right to know what data companies like Facebook have compiled. You can challenge information in credit reports, but you can't even see what data Facebook has gathered about you, let alone try to change it. It's different in Europe: you can request Facebook to turn over a report of all the information it has about you. More than ever, your every move, every click, on social networks is being used by outside entities to assess your interests, and behavior, and then pitch you an ad based on this knowledge. Law enforcement agencies use social networks to gather evidence on tax evaders, and other criminals; employers use social networks to make decisions about prospective candidates for jobs; and data aggregators are gathering as much information about you as they can sell to the highest bidder.

In a recent study, Consumer Reports found that of 150 million Americans on Facebook, at least 4.8 million are willingly sharing information that could be used against them in some way. That includes plans to travel on a particular day, which burglars could use to time robberies, or Liking a page about a particular health condition or treatment, which insurers could use to deny coverage. 13 million users have never adjusted Facebook's privacy controls, which allow friends using Facebook applications to unwittingly transfer your data to a third party without your knowledge. Credit card companies and other similar organizations have begun engaging in "weblining", taken from the phrase redlining, by altering their treatment of you based on the actions of other people with profiles similar to yours.

Ninety-three percent of people polled believe that Internet companies should be forced to ask for permission before using your personal information, and 72 percent want the ability to opt out of online tracking. Why, then, do so many people share sensitive details of their life on Facebook? Often it's because users do not realize that their data are being collected and transmitted in this way. A Facebook user's friends are not notified if information about them is collected by that user's applications. Many of Facebook's features and services are enabled by default when they are launched without notifying users. And a study by Siegel+Gale found that Facebook's privacy policy is more difficult to comprehend than government notices or typical bank credit card agreements, which are notoriously dense. Next time you visit Facebook, click on Privacy Settings, and see if you can understand your options.

Facebook's value and growth potential is determined by how effectively it can leverage the personal data it aggregated about its users to attract advertisers. Facebook also stands to gain from managing and avoiding the privacy concerns raised by its users and government regulators. For Facebook users that value the privacy of their personal data, this situation appears grim. But there are some signs that Facebook might become more responsible with its data collection processes, whether by its own volition or because it is forced to do so. As a publicly traded company, Facebook now invites more scrutiny from investors and regulators because, unlike in the past, their balance sheets, assets, and financial reporting documents are readily available.

In August 2012, Facebook settled a lawsuit with the FTC in which they were barred from misrepresenting the privacy or security of users' personal information. Facebook was charged with deceiving its users by telling them they could keep their information on Facebook private, but then repeatedly allowing it to be shared and made public. Facebook agreed to obtain user consent before making any change to that user's privacy preferences, and to submit to bi-annual privacy audits by an independent firm for the next 20 years. Privacy advocate groups like the Electronic Privacy Information Center (EPIC) want Facebook to restore its more robust privacy settings from 2009, as well as to offer complete access to all data it keeps about its users. Facebook has also come under fire from EPIC for collecting information about users who are not even logged into Facebook or may not even have accounts on Facebook. Facebook keeps track of activity on other sites that have Like buttons or "recommendations" widgets, and records the time of your visit and your IP address when you visit a site with those features, regardless of whether or not you click on them.

While U.S. Facebook users have little recourse to access data that Facebook has collected on them, users from other countries have made inroads in this regard. An Austrian law student was able to get a full copy of his personal information from Facebook's Dublin office, due to the more stringent consumer privacy protections in Ireland. The full document was 1,222 pages long and covered three years of activity on the site, including deleted Wall posts and messages with sensitive personal information and deleted e-mail addresses.

It isn't just text-based data that Facebook is stockpiling, either. Facebook is also compiling a biometric database of unprecedented size. The company stores more than 60 billion photos on its servers and that number grows by 250 million each day. A recent feature launched by Facebook called Tag Suggest scans photographs using facial recognition technology. When Tag Suggest was launched, it was enabled for many users without opting in. This database has value to law enforcement and other organizations looking to compile profiles of users for use in advertising. EPIC also has demanded that Facebook stop creating facial recognition profiles without user consent.

In 2012, as part of the settlement of another class-action lawsuit, Facebook agreed to allow users to opt in to its Sponsored Stories service, which serves advertisements in the user's News Feed that highlight products and businesses that your Facebook friends are using. Now, users can control and see which of their actions on Facebook generate advertisements that their friends will see. Sponsored Stories are one of the most effective forms of advertising on Facebook because they don't seem like advertisements at all to most users. Facebook had previously argued that users were giving "implied consent" every time they clicked a Like button on a page. Users are now confronted with an opt-in notice that analysts speculate may cost Facebook up to $103 million in lost advertising revenues.

Additionally, in response to the increased scrutiny brought about by its IPO, Facebook has improved its archive feature to include more categories of information that the company makes available to users that request copies of their personal data. In Europe, 40,000 Facebook users have already requested their data, and European law requires that Facebook respond to these requests within 40 days. Still, even after Facebook's improvements, they will offer users access to 39 data categories, while the company supposedly maintains at least 84 categories about each user. And, despite the increased emphasis on privacy and data disclosure, European lawmakers are unlikely to hamper Facebook's ability to offer highly customized advertisements, which is the backbone of Facebook's business model.

Despite consumer protests and government scrutiny, Facebook continues to challenge its customers' sense of control over their personal information. In January 2013, Facebook launched its Graph Search program, a social network search engine intended to rival Google but based on a totally different approach. Rather than scour the Internet for information related to a user's search term, Graph Search responds to user queries with

information produced by all Facebook users on their personal pages, and their friends personal pages. For instance, Graph Search, without consent of the user, allows any Facebook user to type in your name, and click the link "Photos of..." which appears underneath the search bar. Complete strangers can find pictures of you. The person searched may not be able to control who sees personal photos: it depends on the privacy settings of other users with whom the photos were shared. If you shared your photos with friends who had less strict privacy settings, then those lesser settings determine who will have access to your photos. Graph Search results in new pages being created that contain the search results. These pages present Facebook with additional opportunities to sell ads, and to monetize the activities and information of its users.

The future of Facebook as a private corporation, and its stock price, will depend on its ability to monetize its most valuable asset, personal private information.

Sources: Sarah Perez, "Facebook Graph Search Didn't Break Your Privacy Settings, It Only Feels Like That," TechCrunch, February 4, 2013; Claire Cain Miller, "Tech Companies Concede to Surveillance Program," New York Times, June 7, 2013; "SEC Form 10K for the Fiscal Year Ending December 31, 2012," Facebook, March 31, 2013; "Selling You on Facebook," Julia Angwin and Jeremy Singer-Vine, The Wall Street Journal, April 7, 2012; Consumer Reports, "Facebook and Your Privacy," May 3, 2012; "Facebook Is Using You," Lori Andrews, The New York Times, Feb. 4, 2012; "Personal Data's Value? Facebook Set to Find Out," Somini Sengupta and Evelyn M. Rusli, The New York Times, Jan. 31, 2012; "Facebook, Eye on Privacy Laws, Offers More Disclosure to Users," Kevin J O'Brien, The New York Times, April 13, 2012; "To Settle Lawsuit, Facebook Alters Policy for Its 'Like' Button," Somini Sengupta, The New York Times, June 21, 2012.

Case Study Questions

4-13 Perform an ethical analysis of Facebook. What is the ethical dilemma presented by this case?

4-14 What is the relationship of privacy to Facebook's business model?

4-15 Describe the weaknesses of Facebook's privacy policies and features. What people, organization, and technology factors have contributed to those weaknesses?

4-16 Will Facebook be able to have a successful business model without invading privacy? Explain your answer. Are there any measures Facebook could take to make this possible?

Information Technology Infrastructure

PART II

Part II provides the technical foundation for understanding information systems by examining hardware, software, databases, networking technologies, and tools and techniques for security and control. This part answers questions such as these: What technologies and tools do businesses today need to accomplish their work? What do I need to know about these technologies to make sure they enhance the performance of my firm? How are these technologies likely to change in the future?

IT Infrastructure:
Hardware and Software

CHAPTER 5

STUDENT LEARNING OBJECTIVES

After completing this chapter, you will be able to answer the following questions:

1. What are the components of IT infrastructure?

2. What are the major computer hardware, data storage, input, and output technologies used in business and major hardware trends?

3. What are the major types of computer software used in business and major software trends?

4. What are the principal issues in managing hardware and software technology?

CHAPTER OUTLINE

PORTUGAL TELECOM OFFERS IT INFRASTURCTURE FOR SALE

Portugal Telecom SGPS SA (Portugal Telecom, also known as PT) is a Portugal-based holding company providing telecommunications and information technology services in Portugal, Brazil, Angola, Macao, and Namibia. The company serves more than 100 million business and residential customers worldwide and generates 58 percent of its revenue outside Portugal. The global telecommunications industry is unusually fast-changing and competitive, due to the end of state-owned or monopoly enterprises and the emergence of new services, including mobile phones, the Internet, and digital television.

PT today provides a range of telecommunications and multimedia services, including fixed line and mobile telephone services; pay television (TV) distribution; Internet Service Provider (ISP) services and data transmission. These services are delivered primarily over digital networks and are very information-technology intensive. Portugal Telecom has been able to leverage its technology expertise to provide information technology (IT) systems and services to other companies of all sizes.

Portugal Telecom's newest data center is in the mountain city of Covilhã, Portugal, where it can take advantage of "free cooling" from Covilhã's often-chilly mountain air 99 percent of the time, thereby reducing energy usage. The Covilhã center opened

Jakub Jirsák/Fotolia.

169

in September 2013. Large numbers of solar panels around the facility are an additional source of clean energy. The center boasts a power usage effectiveness (PUE) rating of just 1.25, compared to an industry average of 1.88, making it among the most energy-efficient data centers in the world. (PUE is a metric for determining the energy efficiency of a data center and is calculated by dividing the total amount of power consumed by a data center by the amount of power used to run the computer infrastructure within it. The closer PUE approaches 1.0, the greater the overall energy efficiency.) When it's completely built, the Covilhã data center will be the largest in the country and one of the largest in the world, capable of hosting more than 50,000 servers. The Covilhã data center is expected to achieve an annual availability of 99.98 percent.

PT management estimates that just one-sixth of the Covilhã's eventual capacity will be required for domestic needs. The rest will provide cloud-based applications and services to other countries, including Brazil and African nations, enabling the company to expand its services across the globe. The Covilhã data center and six other domestic data centers run cloud-based information technology services for other companies known as SmartCloudPT. These cloud services include cloud storage and file synchronization services, infrastructure as a service (IaaS), platform as a service (PaaS), and software as a service (SaaS). Companies who subscribe to SmartCloudPT pay only for the services they actually use. PT and Oracle are now working on incorporating Oracle software applications into SmartCloudPT. Customers need only to register at the SmartCloud PT Web site and log in to purchase the available services that they need, which are billed in the customers' PT invoice, together with other PT services.

PT claims the benefits of its cloud services include having the information protected in the country's largest data center network, the speed and reliability that customers' businesses need, access to PT's cutting-edge technology, and having certified security, advantages that only PT can provide.

Sources: www.telecom.pt/InternetResource/PTSIte/UK, accessed December 11, 2013; Archana Venkatraman, "Portugal Telecom Opens Modular Datacentre to Boost Cloud Offering," ComputerWeekly.com, September 24, 2013; and Fred Sandesmark, "Core Strengths,"Profit Magazine, November 2013.

The experience of Portugal Telecom illustrates the importance of information technology infrastructure in running a business today. The right technology at the right price will improve organizational performance. Because of the need to prevail in a highly competitive industry requiring leading-edge information technology, PT had world-class expertise in computer hardware, software, and networking technology that enabled it to run its business effectively. The company was then able to leverage its IT investment to sell some of its computing resources and expertise as on-line "cloud" services to other companies. This helped other companies achieve cost savings or acquire information technology resources that they were unable to manage on their own to make their businesses more competitive and efficient.

The chapter-opening case diagram calls attention to important points raised by this case and this chapter. Telecommunications services today are largely computer-based. As a leading telecommunications provider, Portugal Telecom had huge investments in hardware, software, and networking technology and a vast pool of internal IT experts. The company could then sell this expertise and its excess computing capacity as a service to other companies in need of such resources. These services appealed to small and medium-sized businesses as well as larger enterprises that were saddled with outdated or inappropriate information technology that prevented them from operating as efficiently and effectively as they could have.

PT created a global data center network for itself and its business customers on several continents. These data centers provide subscribing companies with cloud computing services featuring leading-edge information technologies at very affordable prices. PT's cloud services are easy to purchase and to use, the services are always available, and they include a high level of security protection. The solution is also serving important social goals: lower energy consumption and carbon emissions through more energy-efficient computing.

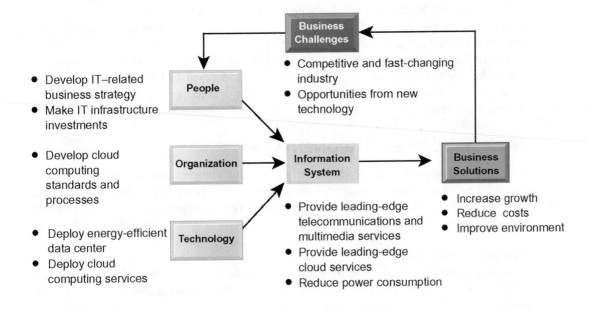

Here are some questions to think about: How does information technology help Portugal Telecom solve its own business problems? How does PT use technology to help other companies solve their business problems?

5.1 IT Infrastructure: Computer Hardware

If you want to know why businesses worldwide spend about $3.7 trillion every year on computing and information systems, just consider what it would take for you personally to set up a business or manage a business today. Businesses require a wide variety of computing equipment, software, and communications capabilities simply to operate and solve basic business problems. Obviously, you need computers, and, as it turns out, a wide variety of computers are available, including desktops, laptops, and handhelds.

Do your employees travel or do some work from home? You will want to equip them with laptop computers (and perhaps tablets or smartphones). If you are employed by a medium to large business, you will also need larger server computers, perhaps an entire data center or server farm with hundreds or even thousands of servers. A **data center** is a facility housing computer systems and associated components, such as telecommunications, storage, security systems, and backup power supplies.

You will also need plenty of software. Each computer will require an operating system and a wide range of application software capable of dealing with spreadsheets, documents, and data files. Unless you are a single-person business, you will most likely want to have a network to link all the people in your business together and perhaps your customers and suppliers. As a matter of fact, you will probably want several networks: a local area network connecting employees in your office, and remote access capabilities so employees can share e-mail and computer files while they are out of the office. You will also want all your employees to have access to landline phone systems, cell phone networks, and the Internet. Finally, to make all this equipment and software work harmoniously, you will also need the services of trained people to help you run and manage this technology.

All of the elements we have just described combine to make up the firm's *information technology (IT) infrastructure*, which we first defined in Chapter 1. A firm's IT infrastructure provides the foundation, or platform, for supporting all the information systems in the business.

INFRASTRUCTURE COMPONENTS

Today's IT infrastructure is composed of five major components: computer hardware, computer software, data management technology, networking and telecommunications technology, and technology services (see Figure 5.1). These components must be coordinated with each other.

Computer Hardware

Computer hardware consists of technology for computer processing, data storage, input, and output. This component includes large mainframes, servers, desktop and laptop computers, and mobile devices for accessing corporate data and the Internet. It also includes equipment for gathering and inputting data, physical media for storing the data, and devices for delivering the processed information as output.

Computer Software

Computer software includes both system software and application software. **System software** manages the resources and activities of the computer. **Application software** applies the computer to a specific task for an end user, such as processing an order or generating a mailing list. Today, most system and application software is no longer custom programmed

Figure 5.1
IT Infrastructure Components
A firm's IT infrastructure is composed of hardware, software, data management technology, networking technology, and technology services.

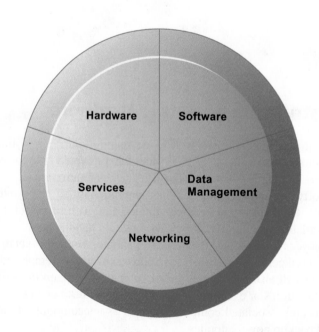

but rather is purchased from outside vendors. We describe these types of software in detail in Section 5.2.

Data Management Technology

In addition to physical media for storing the firm's data, businesses need specialized software to organize the data and make them available to business users. **Data management software** organizes, manages, and processes business data concerned with inventory, customers, and vendors. Chapter 6 describes data management software in detail.

Networking and Telecommunications Technology

Networking and telecommunications technology provides data, voice, and video connectivity to employees, customers, and suppliers. It includes technology for running a company's internal networks, services from telecommunications/telephone services companies, and technology for running Web sites and linking to other computer systems through the Internet. Chapter 7 provides an in-depth description of these technologies.

Technology Services

Businesses need people to run and manage the infrastructure components we have just described and to train employees in how to use these technologies for their work. Chapter 2 described the role of the information systems department, which is the firm's internal business unit set up for this purpose. Today, many businesses supplement their in-house information systems staff with external technology consultants to provide expertise that is not available internally. When businesses need to make major system changes or implement an entirely new IT infrastructure, they typically turn to external consultants to help them with systems integration.

Systems integration means ensuring that the new infrastructure works with the firm's older, so-called legacy systems and that the new elements of the infrastructure work with one another. **Legacy systems** are generally older transaction processing systems created for older computers that continue to be used to avoid the high cost of replacing or redesigning them.

There are thousands of technology vendors supplying IT infrastructure components and services and an equally large number of ways of putting them together. This chapter is about the hardware and software components of infrastructure you will need to run a business. Chapter 6 describes the data management component, and Chapter 7 is devoted to the networking and telecommunications technology component. Chapter 8 deals with hardware and software for ensuring that information systems are reliable and secure, and Chapter 9 discusses software for enterprise applications.

TYPES OF COMPUTERS

Business firms face many different challenges and problems that can be solved by computers and information systems. In order to be efficient, firms need to match the right computer hardware to the nature of the business challenge, neither overspending nor underspending for the technology.

Computers come in an array of sizes with differing capabilities for processing information, from the smallest handheld devices to the largest mainframes and supercomputers. If you're working alone or with a few other people in a small business, you'll probably be using a desktop or laptop **personal computer (PC).** You might carry around a mobile device with substantial computing capability, such as an iPhone, iPad, BlackBerry, or Android device. If you're doing advanced design or engineering work requiring powerful graphics or computational capabilities, you might use a **workstation**, which fits on a desktop but has more powerful mathematical and graphics-processing capabilities than a PC.

If your business has a number of computers networked together or maintains a Web site, it will need a **server**. Server computers are specifically optimized to support a computer network, enabling users to share files, software, peripheral devices (such as printers), or other network resources.

Servers provide the hardware platform for electronic commerce. By adding special software, they can be customized to deliver Web pages, process purchase and sale transactions, or exchange data with systems inside the company. You will sometimes find many servers linked together to provide all the processing needs for large companies. If your company has to process millions of financial transactions or customer records, you will need multiple servers or a single large mainframe to solve these challenges.

Mainframe computers first appeared in the mid-1960s, and are still used by large banks, insurance companies, stock brokerages, airline reservation systems, and government agencies to keep track of hundreds of thousands, or even millions, of records and transactions. A **mainframe** is a large-capacity, high-performance computer that can process large amounts of data very rapidly. Airlines, for instance, use mainframes to process upwards of 3,000 reservation transactions per second.

IBM, the leading mainframe vendor, has repurposed its mainframe systems so they can be used as giant servers for large-scale enterprise networks and corporate Web sites. A single IBM mainframe can run enough instances of Linux or Windows server software to replace thousands of smaller Windows-based servers.

A **supercomputer** is a specially designed and more sophisticated computer that is used for tasks requiring extremely rapid and complex calculations with thousands of variables, millions of measurements, and thousands of equations. Supercomputers traditionally have been used in engineering analysis of structures, scientific exploration and simulations, and military work, such as classified weapons research and weather forecasting. Some private business firms use supercomputers. For instance, Volvo and most other automobile manufacturers use supercomputers to simulate vehicle crash tests.

If you are a long-term weather forecaster, such as the National Oceanic and Atmospheric Administration (NOAA), or the National Hurricane Center, and your challenge is to predict the movement of weather systems based on hundreds of thousands of measurements, and thousands of equations, you would want access to a supercomputer or a distributed network of computers called a grid.

Grid computing involves connecting geographically remote computers into a single network to create a "virtual supercomputer" by combining the computational power of all computers on the grid. Grid computing takes advantage of the fact that most computers in the United States use their central processing units on average only 25 percent of the time, leaving 75 percent of their capacity available for other tasks. By using the combined power of thousands of PCs and other computers networked together, the grid is able to solve complicated problems at supercomputer speeds at far lower cost.

For example, Royal Dutch/Shell Group is using a scalable grid computing platform that improves the accuracy and speed of its scientific modeling applications to find the best oil reservoirs. This platform, which links 1,024 IBM servers running Linux, in effect creates one of the largest commercial Linux supercomputers in the world. The grid adjusts to accommodate the fluctuating data volumes that are typical in this seasonal business.

Computer Networks and Client/Server Computing

Unless you are in a small business with a stand-alone computer, you'll be using networked computers for most processing tasks. The use of multiple computers linked by a communications network for processing is called **distributed processing**. **Centralized processing**, in which all processing is accomplished by one large central computer, is much less common.

One widely used form of distributed processing is **client/server computing**. Client/server computing splits processing between "clients" and "servers." Both are on the network, but each machine is assigned functions it is best suited to perform. The **client** is the user point of entry for the required function and is normally a desktop or laptop computer. The user generally interacts directly only with the client portion of the application. The server provides the client with services. Servers store and process shared data and also perform functions such as managing printers, backup storage, and network activities such as security, remote access, and user authentication. Figure 5.2 illustrates

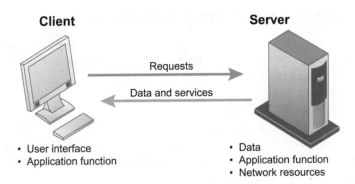

Client   **Server**

Requests →

← Data and services

- User interface   - Data
- Application function   - Application function
                                    - Network resources

Figure 5.2
Client/Server
Computing
*In client/server
computing, computer
processing is split
between client machines
and server machines
linked by a network.
Users interface with the
client machines.*

the client/server computing concept. Computing on the Internet uses the client/server model (see Chapter 7).

Figure 5.2 illustrates the simplest client/server network, consisting of a client computer networked to a server computer, with processing split between the two types of machines. This is called a *two-tiered client/server architecture*. Whereas simple client/server networks can be found in small businesses, most corporations have more complex, multitiered (often called **N-tier**) **client/server architectures**, in which the work of the entire network is balanced over several different levels of servers, depending on the kind of service being requested (see Figure 5.3).

For instance, at the first level a **Web server** will serve a Web page to a client in response to a request for service. Web server software is responsible for locating and managing stored Web pages. If the client requests access to a corporate system (a product list or price information, for instance), the request is passed along to an **application server.** Application server software handles all application operations between a user and an organization's back-end business systems. The application server may reside on the same computer as the Web server or on its own dedicated computer. Chapters 6 and 7 provide more detail on other pieces of software that are used in multitiered client/server architectures for e-commerce and e-business.

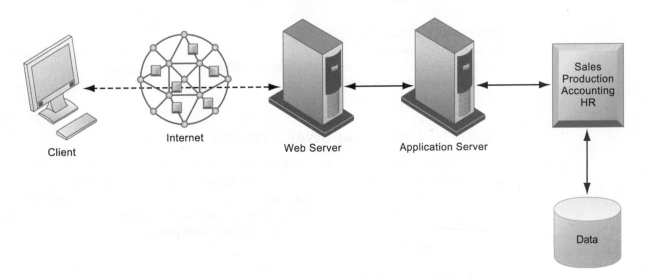

Client   Internet   Web Server   Application Server   Sales Production Accounting HR   Data

Figure 5.3
A Multitiered Client/Server Network (N-Tier)
In a multitiered client/server network, client requests for service are handled by different levels of servers.

STORAGE, INPUT, AND OUTPUT TECHNOLOGY

In addition to hardware for processing data, you will need technologies for data storage, and input and output. Storage and input and output devices are called *peripheral devices* because they are outside the main computer system unit.

Secondary Storage Technology

Electronic commerce and electronic business, and regulations such as Sarbanes-Oxley, have made storage a strategic technology. The amount of data that companies now need to store is doubling every 12 to 18 months. The principal storage technologies are magnetic disks, optical disc, magnetic tape, and storage networks.

Magnetic Disks The most widely used secondary storage medium today is the **magnetic disk.** Some PCs have *hard drives*, and large mainframe or midrange computer systems have multiple hard disk drives because they require immense disk storage capacity in the gigabyte and terabyte range. In lightweight PCs, such as the MacBook Air, smartphones, and tablets, hard drives have been replaced by **solid state drives (SSDs)**. SSDs use an array of semiconductors organized as an internal disk drive, while portable USB flash drives use similar technology for external storage.

Optical Discs These discs use laser technology to store large quantities of data, including sound and images, in a highly compact form. They are available for both PCs and large computers. **CD-ROM (compact disc read-only memory)** for PCs is a 4.75-inch compact disc that can store up to 660 megabytes. CD-ROM is read-only storage, but *CD-RW (CD-ReWritable)* discs are rewritable. **Digital video discs (DVDs)** are optical discs the same size as CD-ROMs but of even higher capacity, storing a minimum of 4.7 gigabytes of data. DVDs are now the favored technology for storing video and large quantities of text, graphics, and audio data, and rewritable *(DVD-RW)* discs are widely used in personal computer systems.

Magnetic Tape Some companies still use **magnetic tape,** an older storage technology that is used for secondary storage of large quantities of data that are needed rapidly but not instantly. It stores data sequentially and is slow compared to the speed of other secondary storage media.

Storage Networking Contemporary computer data storage technology is capable of dividing and replicating data among multiple physical drives or storage devices linked together. **Storage area networks (SANs)** connect multiple storage devices on a separate high-speed network dedicated to storage. The SAN creates a large central pool of storage that can be rapidly accessed and shared by multiple servers (see Figure 5.4).

Input and Output Devices

Human beings interact with computer systems largely through input and output devices. **Input devices** gather data and convert them into electronic form for use by the computer, whereas **output devices** display data after they have been processed. Table 5.1 describes the principal input and output devices.

CONTEMPORARY HARDWARE TRENDS

The exploding power of computer hardware and networking technology has dramatically changed how businesses organize their computing power, putting more of this power on networks and mobile handheld devices. Let's look at eight hardware trends: the mobile digital platform, consumerization of IT, nanotechnology and quantum computers, virtualization, cloud computing, green computing, high-performance/power-saving processors, and autonomic computing.

The Mobile Digital Platform

Chapter 1 pointed out that new mobile digital computing platforms have emerged as alternatives to PCs and larger computers. Mobile devices such as the iPhone, Android, and

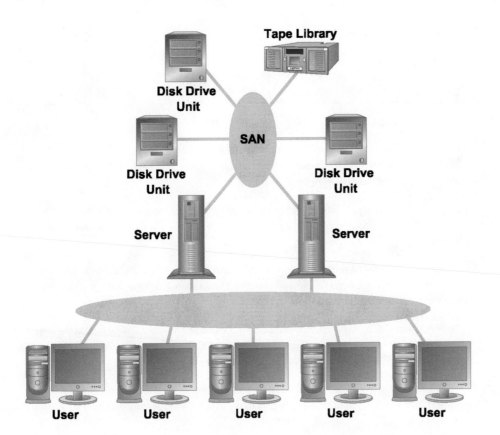

Figure 5.4
A Storage Area
Network (SAN)
*A typical SAN consists
of a server, storage
devices, and networking
devices, and is used
strictly for storage. The
SAN stores data on
many different types
of storage devices,
providing data to the
enterprise. The SAN
supports communication
between any server and
the storage unit as well
as between different
storage devices in the
network.*

BlackBerry smartphones have taken on many functions of PCs, including transmission of data, surfing the Web, transmitting e-mail and instant messages, displaying digital content, and exchanging data with internal corporate systems. The new mobile platform also includes small low-cost lightweight subnotebooks called netbooks optimized for wireless communication and Internet access, **tablet computers** such as the iPad, and digital e-book readers such as Amazon's Kindle with some Web access capabilities.

Smartphones and tablet computers are becoming the primary means of accessing the Internet. These devices are increasingly used for business computing as well as for consumer applications. For example, senior executives at General Motors are using smartphone applications that drill down into vehicle sales information, financial performance, manufacturing metrics, and project management status.

Consumerization of IT and BYOD

The popularity, ease of use, and rich array of useful applications for smartphones and tablet computers have created a groundswell of interest in allowing employees to use their personal mobile devices in the workplace, a phenomenon popularly called *"bring your own device"* (*BYOD*). **BYOD** is one aspect of the **consumerization of IT**, in which new information technology that first emerges in the consumer market spreads into business organizations. Consumerization of IT includes not only mobile personal devices but also business uses of software services that originated in the consumer marketplace as well, such as Google and Yahoo search, Gmail, Google Apps, Dropbox (see Chapter 2), and even Facebook and Twitter.

Consumerization of IT is forcing businesses to rethink the way they obtain and manage information technology equipment and services. Historically, at least in large firms, the IT department controlled selection and management of the firm's hardware and software. This ensured that information systems were protected and served the purposes of the firm. Today, employees and business departments are playing a much larger role in technology selection,

TABLE 5.1

Input and Output Devices

Input Device	Description
Keyboard	Principal method of data entry for text and numerical data.
Computer mouse	Handheld device with point-and-click capabilities for controlling a cursor's position on a computer display screen and selecting commands. Trackballs and touch pads often are used in place of the mouse as pointing devices on laptop PCs.
Touch screen	Device that allows users to interact with a computer by touching the surface of a sensitized display screen. Used in kiosks in airports, retail stores, and restaurants and in multitouch devices such as the iPhone, iPad, and multitouch PCs.
Optical character recognition	Device that can translate specially designed marks, characters, and codes into digital form. The most widely used optical code is the bar code. The codes can include time, date, and location data in addition to identification data.
Magnetic ink character recognition (MICR)	Technology used primarily in check processing for the banking industry. Characters on the bottom of a check identify the bank, checking account, and check number and are preprinted using special magnetic ink, for translation into digital form for the computer.
Pen-based input	Handwriting-recognition devices, such as pen-based tablets, notebooks, and notepads, that convert the motion made by an electronic stylus pressing on a touch-sensitive tablet screen into digital form.
Digital scanner	Device that translates images, such as pictures or documents, into digital form.
Audio input	Voice input devices that convert spoken words into digital form for processing by the computer. Microphones and tape cassette players can serve as input devices for music and other sounds.
Sensors	Devices that collect data directly from the environment for input into a computer system. For instance, today's farmers can use sensors to monitor the moisture of the soil in their fields to help them with irrigation.
Output Device	**Description**
Monitor	Display screen consisting of a flat-panel display or (in older systems) a cathode ray tube (CRT).
Printers	Devices that produce a printed hard copy of information output. They include impact printers (such as dot matrix printers) and nonimpact printers (such as laser, inkjet, and thermal transfer printers).
Audio output	Voice output devices that convert digital output data back into intelligible speech. Other audio output, such as music, can be delivered by speakers connected to the computer.

in many cases demanding that workers be able to use their own personal mobile devices to access the corporate network. Although consumer technologies provide new tools to foster creativity, collaboration, and productivity, they are more difficult for firms to manage and control. We provide more detail on this topic in Section 5.3.

Nanotechnology and Quantum Computing

Over the years, microprocessor manufacturers have been able to exponentially increase processing power while shrinking chip size by finding ways to pack more transistors into less space. They are now turning to nanotechnology to shrink the size of transistors down to the width of several atoms. **Nanotechnology** uses individual atoms and molecules to

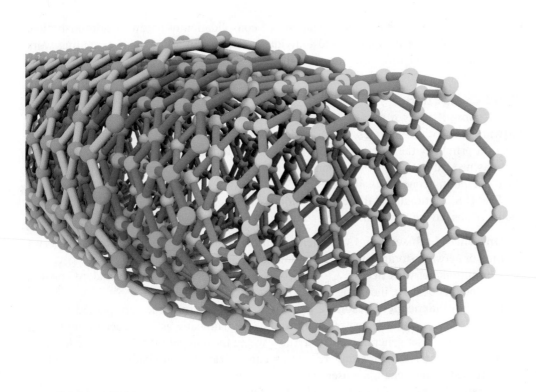

Figure 5.5
Examples of Nanotubes
Nanotubes are tiny tubes about 10,000 times thinner than a human hair. They consist of rolled up sheets of carbon hexagons and have potential uses as minuscule wires or in ultrasmall electronic devices and are very powerful conductors of electrical current.

© Tyler Boyes/Shutterstock.

create computer chips and other devices that are thousands of times smaller than current technologies permit. IBM and other research labs have created transistors from nanotubes (Figure 5.5).

Another new way of enhancing computer processing power is to use quantum computing. **Quantum computing** uses the principles of quantum physics to represent data and perform operations on these data. A quantum computer would gain enormous processing power through the ability to be in many different states at once, allowing it to perform many different computations simultaneously and solve some scientific and business problems millions of times faster than can be done today. Researchers at IBM, MIT, and the Los Alamos National Laboratory have been working on quantum computing, and the aerospace firm Lockheed Martin has purchased a quantum computer for commercial use.

Virtualization

Virtualization is the process of presenting a set of computing resources (such as computing power or data storage) so that they can all be accessed in ways that are not restricted by physical configuration or geographic location. Virtualization enables a single physical resource (such as a server or a storage device) to appear to the user as multiple logical resources. For example, a server or mainframe can be configured to run many instances of an operating system so that it acts like many different machines. Virtualization also enables multiple physical resources (such as storage devices or servers) to appear as a single logical resource, as would be the case with storage area networks or grid computing. Virtualization makes it possible for a company to handle its computer processing and storage using computing resources housed in remote locations. VMware is the leading virtualization software vendor for Windows and Linux servers.

By providing the ability to host multiple systems on a single physical machine, virtualization helps organizations increase equipment utilization rates, conserving data center space and energy usage. Most servers run at just 15–20 percent of capacity, and virtualization can boost server utilization rates to 70 percent or higher. Higher utilization rates translate into fewer computers required to process the same amount of work.

Virtualization also facilitates centralization and consolidation of hardware administration. It is now possible for companies and individuals to perform all of their computing work using a virtualized IT infrastructure, as is the case with cloud computing.

Cloud Computing

Cloud computing is a model of computing in which computer processing, storage, software, and other services are provided as a pool of virtualized resources over a network, primarily the Internet. These "clouds" of computing resources can be accessed on an as-needed basis from any connected device and location. Figure 5.6 illustrates the cloud computing concept.

The U.S. National Institute of Standards and Technology (NIST) defines cloud computing as having the following essential characteristics (Mell and Grance, 2009).

- **On-demand self-service:** Consumers can obtain computing capabilities such as server time or network storage as needed automatically on their own.
- **Ubiquitous network access:** Cloud resources can be accessed using standard network and Internet devices, including mobile platforms.
- **Location independent resource pooling:** Computing resources are pooled to serve multiple users, with different virtual resources dynamically assigned according to user demand. The user generally does not know where the computing resources are located.
- **Rapid elasticity:** Computing resources can be rapidly provisioned, increased, or decreased to meet changing user demand.
- **Measured service:** Charges for cloud resources are based on amount of resources actually used.

Cloud computing consists of three different types of services:

- **Cloud infrastructure as a service:** Customers use processing, storage, networking, and other computing resources from cloud service providers to run their information systems. For example, Amazon uses the spare capacity of its IT infrastructure to provide a broadly based cloud environment selling IT infrastructure services. These

Figure 5.6
Cloud Computing
Platform
*In cloud computing,
hardware and software
capabilities are a
pool of virtualized
resources provided over
a network, often the
Internet. Businesses and
employees have access
to applications and IT
infrastructure anywhere
and at any time.*

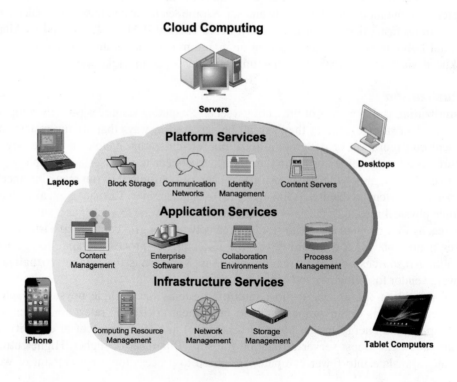

include its Simple Storage Service (S3) for storing customers' data and its Elastic Compute Cloud (EC2) service for running their applications. Users pay only for the amount of computing and storage capacity they actually use. (See the chapter-ending case study.)

- **Cloud platform as a service:** Customers use infrastructure and programming tools supported by the cloud service provider to develop their own applications. For example, IBM offers SmartCloud Application Services for software development and testing on the IBM Cloud. Another example is Salesforce.com's Force.com, which allows developers to build applications that are hosted on its servers as a service.
- **Cloud software as a service:** Customers use software hosted by the vendor on the vendor's cloud infrastructure and delivered over a network. Leading examples are **Google Apps**, which provides common business applications online and Salesforce.com, which also leases customer relationship management and related software services over the Internet. Both charge users an annual subscription fee, although Google Apps also has a pared-down free version. Users access these applications from a Web browser, and the data and software are maintained on the providers' remote servers.

A cloud can be private or public. A **public cloud** is owned and maintained by a cloud service provider, such as Amazon Web Services, and made available to the general public or industry group. A **private cloud** is operated solely for an organization. It may be managed by the organization or a third party and may exist on or off premise. Like public clouds, private clouds are able to allocate storage, computing power, or other resources seamlessly to provide computing resources on an as-needed basis. Companies that want flexible IT resources and a cloud service model while retaining control over their own IT infrastructure are gravitating toward these private clouds.

Since organizations using public clouds do not own the infrastructure, they do not have to make large investments in their own hardware and software. Instead, they purchase their computing services from remote providers and pay only for the amount of computing power they actually use (utility computing) or are billed on a monthly or annual subscription basis. The term **on-demand computing** has also been used to describe such services.

Cloud computing has some drawbacks. Unless users make provisions for storing their data locally, the responsibility for data storage and control is in the hands of the provider. Some companies worry about the security risks related to entrusting their critical data and systems to an outside vendor that also works with other companies. Companies expect their systems to be available 24/7 and do not want to suffer any loss of business capability if cloud infrastructures malfunction. Nevertheless, the trend is for companies to shift more of their computer processing and storage to some form of cloud infrastructure. You can find out more about cloud computing in the Learning Tracks for this chapter.

Green Computing

By curbing hardware proliferation and power consumption, virtualization has become one of the principal technologies for promoting green computing. **Green computing** or **green IT** refers to practices and technologies for designing, manufacturing, using, and disposing of computers, servers, and associated devices such as monitors, printers, storage devices, and networking and communications systems to minimize impact on the environment.

Reducing computer power consumption has been a very high "green" priority. Information technology is responsible for about 2 percent of total U.S. power demand and is believed to contribute about 2 percent of the world's greenhouse gases. Cutting power consumption in data centers has become a serious business and environmental challenge. The Interactive Session on Technology examines this problem.

High-Performance and Power-Saving Processors

Another way to reduce power requirements and hardware sprawl is to use more efficient and power-saving processors. Contemporary microprocessors now feature multiple processor cores (which perform the reading and execution of computer instructions) on a

What's too hot to handle? It might very well be your company's data center, which can easily consume more than 100 times more power than a standard office building. Data-hungry tasks such as video on demand, maintaining Web sites, or analyzing large pools of transactions or social media data require more and more power-hungry machines. Power and cooling costs for data centers have skyrocketed, with cooling a server requiring roughly the same number of kilowatts of energy as running one. All this additional power consumption has a negative impact on the environment as well as corporate operating costs.

Companies are now looking to green computing for solutions. The standard for measuring data center energy efficiency is Power Usage Effectiveness (PUE). This metric is a ratio of the total annual power consumed by a data center divided by how much is used annually by IT equipment. The lower the ratio, the better, with a PUE of 1.0 representing a desirable target. The PUE of traditional data centers has hovered around 2.0. That means the data center is using twice the amount of electricity that's actually needed to do the computing. (The extra power is consumed by lighting, cooling, and other systems.) PUE is influenced by many factors, including hardware efficiency, data center size, the types of servers and their uses, the proficiency of monitoring software, building architecture, and the climate outside the facility. New data center designs with PUEs of 1.5 or better are emerging.

Virtualization is a highly effective tool for cost-effective green computing because it reduces the number of servers and storage resources in the firm's IT infrastructure. About five years ago, Acorda, a $210 million-per-year maker of drugs to treat nervous disorders such as multiple sclerosis, found it needed more servers and was outgrowing its data center. The company invested $100,000 in virtual servers running on technology from VMware. Using virtualization, Acorda avoided spending an additional $1.5 million on more physical servers and increasing energy consumption. Moreover, when the company moved to a new building in 2012, it was able to significantly shrink the size of its data center, further lowering cooling costs.

Acorda took additional steps to boost energy efficiency at the new facility. The company installed motion sensors that shut off lights after five minutes if no movement is detected, and it invested in a more intelligent cooling system that automatically changes settings as conditions change. Current plans include replacing all of Acorda's host servers and taking advantage of a VMware feature that moves virtual servers from one cluster to another, thereby reducing the number of clusters that require power at any given time. Acorda is also preparing to test virtualized desktops, which will greatly reduce the power required to run workstations and laptops.

Other tools and techniques are also available to make data centers more energy-efficient. Google and Microsoft have built data centers that take advantage of hydroelectric power. In April 2011 Facebook publicly posted the specifications for the design of its data centers, including motherboards, power supply, server chassis, server rack, and battery cabinets, as well as data center electrical and mechanical construction specifications. Facebook hardware engineers re-thought the electric design, power distribution, and thermal design of its servers to optimize energy efficiency, reducing power usage by 13 percent. The power supply, which converts alternating current into direct current consumed by the motherboard, operates at 94.5 percent efficiency. Instead of using air conditioning or air ducts, the servers are cooled by evaporative cooling and misting machines, which flow air through grill-covered walls. The server racks are taller to provide for bigger heat sinks, and the data center's large fans can move air through the servers more efficiently. Facebook's engineers modified the programming in the servers to work with these larger fans and reduce their reliance on small, individual fans that consume more power. This data center design, which has a 1.07 PUE rating, was implemented at Facebook's Prineville, Oregon data center. All of these changes have reduced Facebook's energy consumption per unit of computing power by 38 percent and operating costs by nearly 25 percent. The Prineville data center reports its PUE is 1.07, one of the lowest.

By using ambient air cooling techniques and running warmer than average, Google's newest data centers deliver a PUE rating of 1.16. Yahoo's new Lockport, N.Y., data center has a PUE of 1.08. Lockport's cool climate, prevailing winds, and hydropower help cool Yahoo's 120 foot by 60 foot server buildings. FedEx located its energy-efficient Colorado data center at an elevation of 6000 feet so that the building can be cooled using outside air instead of internal air conditioning.

In addition to lowering IT costs, using cloud computing services may save energy as well. Cloud computing centers pack in servers that have been optimized for virtualization and for supporting as many different subscribing companies as possible. Cloud vendors are willing to invest heavily in cost-lowering virtualization software and energy-conserving server hardware because those efforts can produce major savings when doing the computing for large numbers of companies. A study by the Carbon Disclosure Project predicted that by 2020, large U.S. companies with revenues of more than $1 billion that used cloud computing would be able to achieve annual energy savings of $12.3 billion and annual carbon reductions equivalent to 200 million barrels of oil—enough to power 5.7 million cars for one year.

Experts note that it's important for companies to measure their energy use and inventory and track their information technology assets both before and after they start their green initiatives. And it isn't always necessary to purchase new technologies to achieve "green" goals. Organizations can achieve sizable efficiencies by better managing the computing resources they already have. Unfortunately, many information systems departments still aren't deploying their existing technology resources efficiently or using green measurement tools.

Sources: Tony Kontzer, "Energy Management Revamps the Data Center," Baseline, January 30, 2013; Charles Babcock, "Facebook's Data Center: Where Likes Live," Information Week, March 6 , 2013; Doug Mohney, "The Little Guys: Survival vs. Green," Green Data Center News, May 15, 2013; Chris Murphy, "FedEx's Strategic Tech Shift." Information Week, May 20, 2013; "How Facebook's Data Center Leads by Example," CIO Insight, August 20, 2012; Sam Greengard, "IT Gets Greener," Baseline, April 11, 2012; "New Study: Cloud Computing Can Dramatically Reduce Energy Costs and Carbon Emissions," AT&T, July 21, 2011; and Kenneth Miller, "The Data Center Balancing Act," Information Week, May 16, 2011.

CASE STUDY QUESTIONS

1. What business and social problems does data center power consumption cause?

2. What solutions are available for these problems? Are they people, organizational, or technology solutions? Explain your answer.

3. What are the business benefits and costs of these solutions?

4. Should all firms move toward green computing? Why or why not?

single chip. A **multicore processor** is an integrated circuit to which two or more processor cores have been attached for enhanced performance, reduced power consumption, and more efficient simultaneous processing of multiple tasks. This technology enables two or more processing engines with reduced power requirements and heat dissipation to perform tasks faster than a resource-hungry chip with a single processing core. Today you'll find PCs with dual-core, quad-core, six-core, and eight-core processors and servers with 16-core processors.

Intel and other chip manufacturers are working on microprocessors that minimize power consumption. Low power consumption is essential for prolonging battery life in smartphones, netbooks, and other mobile digital devices. You will now find highly power-efficient microprocessors, such as the A5 and A6 processors used in Apple's iPhone and iPad, and Intel's Atom in netbooks, digital media players, and smartphones. The Apple processors have about one-fiftieth of the power consumption of a laptop dual-core processor.

Autonomic Computing

With large systems encompassing many thousands of networked devices, computer systems have become so complex today that some experts believe they may not be manageable in the future. One approach to this problem is autonomic computing. **Autonomic computing** is an industry-wide effort to develop systems that can configure themselves, optimize and tune themselves, heal themselves when broken, and protect themselves from outside intruders and self-destruction.

You can glimpse a few of these capabilities in desktop systems. For instance, virus and firewall protection software are able to detect viruses on PCs, automatically defeat the viruses, and alert operators. These programs can be updated automatically as the need arises by connecting to an online virus protection service such as McAfee. IBM and other vendors are starting to build autonomic features into products for large systems.

Figure 5.7
The Major Types of
Software
*The relationship between
the system software,
application software,
and users can be illus-
trated by a series of
nested boxes. System
software—consisting
of operating systems,
language translators,
and utility programs—
controls access to the
hardware. Application
software, including
programming languages
and software packages,
must work through the
system software to
operate. The user inter-
acts primarily with the
application software.*

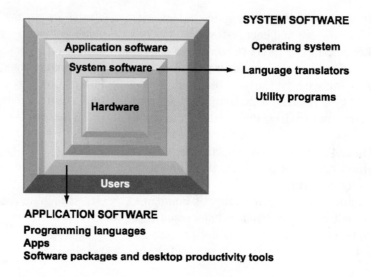

5.2 IT Infrastructure: Computer Software

In order to use computer hardware, you will need software, which provides the detailed instructions that direct the computer's work. System software and application software are interrelated and can be thought of as a set of nested boxes, each of which must interact closely with the other boxes surrounding it. Figure 5.7 illustrates this relationship. The system software surrounds and controls access to the hardware. Application software must work through the system software in order to operate. End users work primarily with application software. Each type of software must be designed for a specific machine to ensure its compatibility.

OPERATING SYSTEM SOFTWARE

The system software that manages and controls the computer's activities is called the **operating system**. Other system software consists of computer language translation programs that convert programming languages into machine language that can be understood by the computer and utility programs that perform common processing tasks, such as copying, sorting, or computing a square root.

The operating system is the computer system's chief manager, enabling the system to handle many different tasks and users at the same time. The operating system allocates and assigns system resources, schedules the use of computer resources and computer jobs, and monitors computer system activities. The operating system provides locations in primary memory for data and programs, and controls the input and output devices, such as printers, terminals, and telecommunication links. The operating system also coordinates the schedul-ing of work in various areas of the computer so that different parts of different jobs can be worked on at the same time. Finally, the operating system keeps track of each computer job and may also keep track of who is using the system, of what programs have been run, and of any unauthorized attempts to access the system.

PC, Server, and Mobile Operating Systems

The operating system controls the way users interact with the computer. Contemporary PC operating systems and many types of contemporary application software use a **graphical user interface**, often called a **GUI**, which makes extensive use of icons, buttons, bars, and boxes to perform tasks.

New interface technologies are emerging for both business and home systems. An increasingly popular interface technology is **multitouch**, which is now found in the iPhone and other smartphones and tablet computers, and is starting to be used in PCs. Multitouch interfaces allow you to use one or more fingers to perform special gestures to manipulate lists or objects on a screen without using a mouse or a keyboard.

Table 5.2 compares leading PC and server operating systems. These include the Windows family of operating systems (**Windows 7**, Windows 8, Windows Server), UNIX, Linux, and OS X, the operating system for the Macintosh computer.

The Microsoft Windows family of operating systems has both client and server versions and a streamlined GUI. Windows systems can perform multiple programming tasks simultaneously and have powerful networking capabilities, including the ability to access information from the Internet. At the client level, 90 percent of PCs use some form of Microsoft Windows operating system. The latest Windows client version is **Windows 8**. Its user interface is optimized for touch, but works equally well with a mouse and keyboard. The software runs on a wide array of devices including tablets as well as traditional desktops and laptops.

Windows operating systems for servers provide network management functions, including support for virtualization and cloud computing. Windows Server 2012 has multiple versions for small, medium, and large businesses.

Today there is a much greater variety of operating systems than in the past, with new operating systems for computing on handheld mobile digital devices or cloud-connected computers. Google's **Chrome OS** provides a lightweight operating system for cloud computing using a Web-connected computer or mobile device. Programs are not stored on the user's PC but are used over the Internet and accessed through the Chrome Web browser. User data reside on servers across the Internet. **Android** is an open source operating system for mobile devices such as smartphones and tablet computers developed by the Open Handset Alliance led by Google. It has become the most popular smartphone platform worldwide, competing with **iOS**, Apple's mobile operating system for the iPhone, iPad, and iPod Touch.

UNIX is a multiuser, multitasking operating system developed by Bell Laboratories in 1969 to connect various machines together and is highly supportive of communications and networking. UNIX is often used on workstations and servers, and provides the reliability and scalability for running large systems on high-end servers. UNIX can run on many different kinds of computers and can be easily customized. Application programs that run under UNIX can be ported from one computer to run on a different computer with little

Operating System	Features
Windows 8	Most recent Windows operating system, which supports multitouch and mobile devices as well as traditional PCs.
Windows Server 2012	Most recent Windows operating system for servers.
UNIX	Used for PCs, workstations, and network servers. Supports multitasking, multiuser processing, and networking. Is portable to different models of computer hardware.
Linux	Open source, reliable alternative to UNIX and Windows operating systems that runs on many different types of computer hardware and can be modified by software developers.
OS X	Operating system for the Macintosh computer that highly visual and user-friendly, with support for multitouch. Most recent version is OS X Mavericks. The iPhone's iOS operating system is derived from OS X.

TABLE 5.2

Leading PC and Server Operating Systems

modification. Graphical user interfaces have been developed for UNIX. Vendors have developed different versions of UNIX that are incompatible, thereby limiting software portability.

Linux is a UNIX-like operating system that can be downloaded from the Internet free of charge or purchased for a small fee from companies that provide additional tools for the software. It is free, reliable, compactly designed, and capable of running on many different hardware platforms, including servers, handheld computers, and consumer electronics.

Linux has become popular as a robust low-cost alternative to UNIX and the Windows operating systems. For example, E*Trade Financial saves $13 million annually with improved computer performance by running Linux on a series of small inexpensive IBM servers instead of large expensive Oracle Sun servers running a proprietary version of UNIX.

Linux plays a major role in the back office, running Web servers and local area networks in about 25 percent of the U.S. server market. Its use in cloud computing is growing steadily. IBM, HP, Dell, and Oracle have made Linux part of their offerings to corporations, and major software vendors are starting to provide versions of their products that can run on Linux.

Linux is an example of **open source software**, which provides all computer users with free access to its program code, so they can modify the code to fix errors or to make improvements. Open source software is not owned by any company or individual. A global network of programmers and users manages and modifies the software, usually without being paid to do so. Other popular open source software tools include the Apache HTTP Web server, the Mozilla Firefox Web browser, and the Apache OpenOffice desktop productivity suite.

APPLICATION SOFTWARE AND DESKTOP PRODUCTIVITY TOOLS

Today, businesses have access to an array of tools for developing their application software. These include traditional programming languages, application software packages, and desktop productivity tools; software for developing Internet applications; and software for enterprise integration. It is important to know which software tools and programming languages are appropriate for the work your business wants to accomplish.

Programming Languages for Business

Popular programming languages for business applications include C, C++, Visual Basic, and Java. **C** is a powerful and efficient language developed in the early 1970s that combines machine portability with tight control and efficient use of computer resources. C is used primarily by professional programmers to create operating systems and application software, especially for PCs. **C++** is a newer version of C that has all the capabilities of C plus additional features for working with software objects. Unlike traditional programs, which separate data from the actions to be taken on the data, a software **object** combines data and procedures. Chapter 12 describes object-oriented software development in detail. **Visual Basic** is a widely used visual programming tool and environment for creating applications that run on Microsoft Windows operating systems. A **visual programming language** allows users to manipulate graphic or iconic elements to create programs. COBOL (COmmon Business Oriented Language), was developed in the early 1960s for business processing and can still be found in large legacy systems in banking, insurance, and retail.

Java is an operating system-independent, processor-independent, object-oriented programming language created by Sun Microsystems that has become the leading interactive programming environment for the Web. Java allows programmers to create interactivity and active content that can be downloaded over the Web as applets that run on a client computer, thereby saving considerable load on the server.

The Java platform has migrated into cell phones, smartphones, automobiles, music players, game machines, and finally, into set-top cable television systems serving interactive content and pay-per-view services. Java software is designed to run on any computer or computing device, regardless of the specific microprocessor or operating system the device uses. Oracle Corporation estimates that 3 billion devices are running Java, and it is the most popular development platform for mobile devices running the Android operating system (Taft, 2012). For each of the computing environments in which Java is used, Sun created a Java Virtual Machine that interprets Java programming code for that machine. In this manner, the code is written once and can be used on any machine for which there exists a Java Virtual Machine.

Other popular programming tools for Web applications include Ruby and Python. Ruby is an object-oriented programming language known for speed and ease of use in building Web applications and Python (praised for its clarity) is being used for building cloud computing applications. Major Web sites such as Google, Facebook, Amazon, and Twitter use Python and Ruby as well as Java.

Software Packages and Desktop Productivity Tools

Much of the software used in businesses today is not custom programmed but consists of application software packages and desktop productivity tools. A **software package** is a prewritten, precoded, commercially available set of programs that eliminates the need for individuals or organizations to write their own software programs for certain functions. There are software packages for system software, but most package software is application software.

Software packages that run on mainframes and larger computers usually require professional programmers for their installation and support. Desktop productivity software packages for word processing, spreadsheets, data management, presentation graphics, and Web browsers are the most widely used software tools among business and consumer users.

Word Processing Software If you work in an office or attend school, you probably use word processing software every day. **Word processing software** stores text data electronically as a computer file rather than on paper. The word processing software allows the user to make changes in the document electronically, with formatting options to make changes in line spacing, margins, character size, and column width. Microsoft Word is a popular word processing software tool.

Businesses that need to create highly professional looking brochures, manuals, or books will likely use desktop publishing software for this purpose. Desktop publishing software provides more control over the placement of text, graphics, and photos in the layout of a page than does word processing software. Adobe InDesign and QuarkXpress are two professional publishing packages.

Spreadsheet Software Spreadsheets are valuable for applications in which numerous calculations with pieces of data must be related to each other. **Spreadsheet software** organizes data into a grid of columns and rows. When you change a value or values, all other related values on the spreadsheet will be automatically recomputed.

You will often see spreadsheets in applications that require modeling and "what-if" analysis. After the user has constructed a set of mathematical relationships, the spreadsheet can be recalculated instantaneously using a different set of assumptions. Spreadsheet packages include graphics functions to present data in the form of line graphs, bar graphs, or pie charts, and the ability to read and create Web files. The most popular spreadsheet package is Microsoft Excel. Figure 5.8 illustrates the output from a spreadsheet for a break-even analysis and its accompanying graph.

Data Management Software Although spreadsheet programs are powerful tools for manipulating quantitative data, data management software, which we defined earlier in this chapter, is more suitable for creating and manipulating lists and for combining information from different files. PC database management packages have programming features and easy-to-learn menus that enable nonspecialists to build small information systems.

Figure 5.8
Spreadsheet
Software
*Spreadsheet software
organizes data into
columns and rows for
analysis and manipula-
tion. Contemporary
spreadsheet software
provides graphing abili-
ties for a clear, visual
representation of the
data in the spread-
sheets. This sample
break-even analysis is
represented as numbers
in a spreadsheet as well
as a line graph for easy
interpretation.*

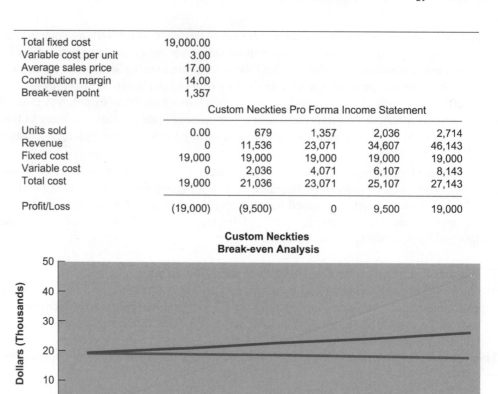

Total fixed cost	19,000.00
Variable cost per unit	3.00
Average sales price	17.00
Contribution margin	14.00
Break-even point	1,357

Custom Neckties Pro Forma Income Statement				
Units sold	0.00	679	1,357	2,036	2,714
Revenue	0	11,536	23,071	34,607	46,143
Fixed cost	19,000	19,000	19,000	19,000	19,000
Variable cost	0	2,036	4,071	6,107	8,143
Total cost	19,000	21,036	23,071	25,107	27,143
Profit/Loss	(19,000)	(9,500)	0	9,500	19,000

Data management software typically has facilities for creating files and databases and for storing, modifying, and manipulating data for reports and queries. Popular database management software for the personal computer includes Microsoft Access, which has been enhanced to publish data on the Web. We discuss data management software in greater detail in Chapter 6.

Presentation Graphics Users can create professional-quality graphics presentations with **presentation graphics software**. This software can convert numeric data into charts and other types of graphics and can include multimedia displays of sound, animation, photos, and video clips. The leading presentation graphics packages include capabilities for computer-generated slide shows and translating content for the Web. Microsoft PowerPoint is a popular presentation graphics tool.

Software Suites Typically, the major office productivity tools are bundled together as a software suite. Microsoft Office is an example. There are a number of different versions of Office for home and business users, but the core office tools include Word processing software, Excel spreadsheet software, Access database software, PowerPoint presentation graphics software, and Outlook, a set of tools for e-mail, scheduling, and contact management. Microsoft **Office 2013** is the latest version of this suite. Microsoft has added a hosted cloud version of its productivity and collaboration tools called Office 365. Competing with Microsoft Office are low-cost office productivity suites such as the open source OpenOffice (downloadable for free over the Internet) and cloud-based Google Apps (see Chapter 2).

Web Browsers Easy-to-use software tools called **Web browsers** are used for displaying Web pages and for accessing the Web and other Internet resources. Browsers can display or present graphics, audio, and video information, as well as traditional text, and they allow you to click (or touch) on-screen buttons or highlighted words to link to related Web sites. Web browsers have become the primary interface for accessing the Internet or for using networked systems based on Internet technology. The leading Web browsers today are Microsoft Internet Explorer, Mozilla Firefox, Apple Safari, Amazon Silk, and Google Chrome.

HTML AND HTML5

Hypertext Markup Language (HTML) is a page description language for specifying how text, graphics, video, and sound are placed on a Web page and for creating dynamic links to other Web pages and objects. Using these links, a user need only point at a highlighted keyword or graphic, click on it, and immediately be transported to another document. Table 5.3 illustrates some sample HTML statements.

HTML programs can be custom written, but they also can be created using the HTML authoring capabilities of Web browsers or of popular word processing, spreadsheet, data management, and presentation graphics software packages. HTML editors, such as Adobe Dreamweaver, are more powerful HTML authoring tool programs for creating Web pages.

HTML was originally designed to create and link static documents composed largely of text. Today, however, the Web is much more social and interactive, and many Web pages have multimedia elements—images, audio, and video. Third-party plug-in applications like Flash, Silverlight, and Java have been required to integrate these rich media with Web pages. However, these add-ons require additional programming and put strains on computer processing. This is one reason Apple dropped support for Flash on its mobile devices. The most recent version of HTML, called **HTML5,** solves this problem by making it possible to embed images, audio, video, and other elements directly into a document without processor-intensive add-ons. HTML5 also makes it easier for Web pages to function across different display devices, including mobile devices as well as desktops. Web pages will execute more quickly and Web-based mobile apps will work like Web pages.

WEB SERVICES

Web services refer to a set of loosely coupled software components that exchange information with each other using universal Web communication standards and languages. They can exchange information between two different systems regardless of the operating systems or programming languages on which the systems are based. They can be used to build open-standard, Web-based applications linking systems of two different organizations, and they can be used to create applications that link disparate systems within a single company. Different applications can use them to communicate with each other in a standard way without time-consuming custom coding.

The foundation technology for Web services is **XML**, which stands for **Extensible Markup Language**. This language was developed in 1996 by the World Wide Web Consortium (W3C, the international body that oversees the development of the Web) as a more powerful and flexible markup language than HTML for Web pages. Whereas HTML

Plain English	HTML
Subcompact	<TITLE>Subcompact</TITLE>
4 passenger	<LI>4 passenger</LI>
$16,800	<LI>$16,800</LI>

TABLE 5.3

Examples of HTML

is limited to describing how data should be presented in the form of Web pages, XML can perform presentation, communication, and storage of data. In XML, a number is not simply a number; the XML tag specifies whether the number represents a price, a date, or a zip code. Table 5.4 illustrates some sample XML statements.

By tagging selected elements of the content of documents for their meanings, XML makes it possible for computers to manipulate and interpret their data automatically and perform operations on the data without human intervention. XML provides a standard format for data exchange, enabling Web services to pass data from one process to another.

Web services communicate through XML messages over standard Web protocols. Companies discover and locate Web services through a directory much as they would locate services in the Yellow Pages of a telephone book. Using Web protocols, a software application can connect freely to other applications without custom programming for each different application with which it wants to communicate. Everyone shares the same standards.

The collection of Web services that are used to build a firm's software systems constitutes what is known as a service-oriented architecture. A **service-oriented architecture (SOA)** is set of self-contained services that communicate with each other to create a working software application. Software developers reuse these services in other combinations to assemble other applications as needed.

Virtually all major software vendors, such as IBM, Microsoft, Oracle, and HP, provide tools and entire platforms for building and integrating software applications using Web services. IBM includes Web service tools in its WebSphere e-business software platform, and Microsoft has incorporated Web services tools in its Microsoft .NET platform.

Dollar Rent-A-Car's systems use Web services to link its online booking system with the Southwest Airlines Web site. Although both companies' systems are based on different technology platforms, a person booking a flight on Southwest.com can reserve a car from Dollar without leaving the airline's Web site. Instead of struggling to get Dollar's reservation system to share data with Southwest's information systems, Dollar used Microsoft .NET Web services technology as an intermediary. Reservations from Southwest are translated into Web services protocols, which are then translated into formats that can be understood by Dollar's computers.

Other car rental companies have linked their information systems to airline companies' Web sites before. But without Web services, these connections had to be built one at a time. Web services provide a standard way for Dollar's computers to "talk" to other companies' information systems without having to build special links to each one. Dollar is now expanding its use of Web services to link directly to the systems of a small tour operator and a large travel reservation system as well as a wireless Web site for mobile phones and PDAs. It does not have to write new software code for each new partner's information systems or each new wireless device (see Figure 5.9).

SOFTWARE TRENDS

Today there are many more sources for obtaining software and many more capabilities for users to create their own customized software applications. Expanding use of open source software and cloud-based software tools and services exemplify this trend.

TABLE 5.4		
Examples of XML	**Plain English**	**XML**
	Subcompact	<AUTOMOBILETYPE="Subcompact">
	4 passenger	<PASSENGERUNIT="PASS">4</PASSENGER>
	$16,800	<PRICE CURRENCY="USD">$16,800</PRICE>

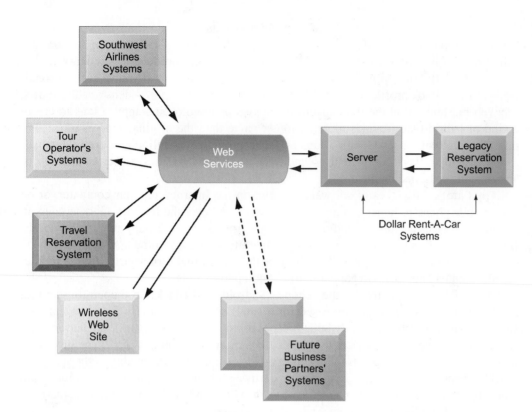

Figure 5.9
How Dollar Rent-A-Car Uses Web Services
Dollar Rent-A-Car uses Web services to provide a standard intermediate layer of software to "talk" to other companies' information systems. Dollar Rent-A-Car can use this set of Web services to link to other companies' information systems without having to build a separate link to each firm's systems.

Open Source Software

Arguably the most influential software trend is the movement towards open source software. As noted earlier, open source software is developed by a community of programmers around the world, who make their programs available to users under one of several different licensing schemes. Essentially, users of the software can use the software as is, modify it at will, and even include it in for-profit software applications.

The open source movement started out small in 1983, but it has since grown to be a major part of corporate computing infrastructure, as the foundation for programs such as Linux, and Apache, the most widely used Web server software. Today you can find thousands of open source computer programs to accomplish everything from e-commerce shopping carts and funds clearance to sales force management. Google's Android mobile operating system and Chrome Web browser are based on open source code.

Cloud-Based Software Services and Tools

In the past, software such as Microsoft Word or Adobe Illustrator came in a box and was designed to operate on a single machine. Today, you're more likely to download the software from the vendor's Web site, or to use the software as a cloud service delivered over the Internet. Services for delivering and providing access to software remotely as a Web-based service are now referred to as **Software as a Service (SaaS)**.

Cloud-based software and the data it uses are hosted on powerful servers in massive data centers, and can be accessed with an Internet connection and standard Web browser. In addition to free or low-cost tools for individuals and small businesses provided by Google or Yahoo!, enterprise software and other complex business functions are available as services from the major commercial software vendors. Instead of buying and installing software programs, subscribing companies rent the same functions from these services, with users paying either on a subscription or per transaction basis.

Mashups and Apps The software you use for both personal and business tasks may consist of large self-contained programs, or it may be composed of interchangeable components that integrate freely with other applications on the Internet. Individual users and entire companies mix and match these software components to create their own customized applications and to share information with others. The resulting software applications are called **mashups**. The idea is to take different sources and produce a new work that is "greater than" the sum of its parts. You have performed a mashup if you've ever personalized your Facebook profile or your blog with a capability to display videos or slide shows.

Web mashups combine the capabilities of two or more online applications to create a kind of hybrid that provides more customer value than the original sources alone. For instance, ZipRealty uses Google Maps and data provided by online real estate database Zillow.com to display a complete list of multiple listing service (MLS) real estate listings for any zip code specified by the user.

Apps are small pieces of software that run on the Internet, on your computer, or on your mobile phone or tablet and are generally delivered over the Internet. Google refers to its online services as apps, including the Google Apps suite of desktop productivity tools. But when we talk about apps today, most of the attention goes to the apps that have been developed for the mobile digital platform. It is these apps that turn smartphones and other mobile handheld devices into general-purpose computing tools.

Most of these apps are for the iPhone, Android, and BlackBerry operating system platforms. Many are free or purchased for a small charge, much less than conventional software. There are already nearly 800,000 apps for the Apple iPhone and iPad platform and about 700,000 that run on devices using Google's Android operating system. The success of these mobile platforms depends in large part on the quantity and the quality of the apps they provide. Apps tie the customer to a specific hardware platform: As the user adds more and more apps to his or her mobile phone, the cost of switching to a competing mobile platform (for instance from the iPhone to an Android phone) rises.

At the moment, the most commonly downloaded apps are games, music, social networking, news and weather, maps/navigation, and video/movies. But there are also serious apps for business users that make it possible to create and edit documents, connect to corporate systems, schedule and participate in meetings, and track shipments. There are also a huge number of e-commerce apps for researching and buying goods and services online.

5.3 Managing Hardware and Software Technology

Selection and use of computer hardware and software technology has a profound impact on business performance. We now describe the most important issues you will face when managing hardware and software technology: capacity planning and scalability; determining the total cost of technology assets; determining whether to own and maintain your own hardware, software, and other infrastructure components or lease them from an external technology service provider; and managing mobile platforms and software localization.

CAPACITY PLANNING AND SCALABILITY

E-commerce and e-business need much larger processing and storage resources to handle the surging digital transactions flowing between different parts of the firm, and between the firm and its customers and suppliers. Many people using a Web site simultaneously place great strains on a computer system, as does hosting large numbers of interactive Web pages with data-intensive graphics or video.

Managers and information systems specialists now need to pay more attention to hardware capacity planning and scalability than before. From an IT perspective, **capacity planning** is the process of predicting when a computer hardware system becomes saturated. It considers factors such as the maximum number of users that the system can accommodate at one time, the impact of existing and future software applications, and performance measures, such as minimum response time for processing business transactions. Capacity planning ensures that the firm has enough computing power for its current and future needs. For example, the Nasdaq Stock Market performs ongoing capacity planning to identify peaks in the volume of stock trading transactions and to ensure it has enough computing capacity to handle large surges in volume when trading is very heavy.

Scalability refers to the ability of a computer, product, or system to expand to serve a large number of users without breaking down. Electronic commerce and electronic business both call for scalable IT infrastructures that have the capacity to grow with the business as the size of a Web site and number of visitors increase. Organizations must make sure they have sufficient computer processing, storage, and network resources to handle surging volumes of digital transactions and to make such data immediately available online.

TOTAL COST OF OWNERSHIP (TCO) OF TECHNOLOGY ASSETS

When you calculate how much your hardware and software cost, their purchase price is only the beginning. You must also consider ongoing administration costs for hardware and software upgrades, maintenance, technical support, training, and even utility and real estate costs for running and housing the technology. The **total cost of ownership (TCO)** model can be used to analyze these direct and indirect costs to help determine the actual cost of owning a specific technology. Table 5.5 describes the most important TCO components to consider in a TCO analysis.

When all these cost components are considered, the "hidden costs" for support staff, downtime, and additional network management can make distributed client/server architectures—especially those incorporating handheld computers and wireless devices—more expensive than centralized mainframe architectures.

Many large firms are saddled with redundant, incompatible hardware and software because of poor planning. These firms could reduce their TCO through greater centralization and standardization of their hardware and software resources. Companies could reduce the size of the information systems staff required to support their infrastructure if the firm minimized the number of different computer models and pieces of software that employees are allowed to use.

USING TECHNOLOGY SERVICE PROVIDERS

Some of the most important questions facing managers are "How should we acquire and maintain our technology assets? Should we build software applications ourselves or outsource them to an external contractor? Should we purchase and run them ourselves or rent them from external service providers?" In the past, most companies ran their own computer facilities and developed their own software. Today, more and more companies are obtaining their hardware and software technology from external service vendors.

Hardware acquisition	Purchase price of computer hardware equipment, including computers, terminals, storage, and printers	**TABLE 5.5** TCO Cost Components
Software acquisition	Purchase or license of software for each user	
Installation	Cost to install computers and software	
Training	Cost to provide training to information systems specialists and end users	
Support	Cost to provide ongoing technical support, help desks, and so forth	
Maintenance	Cost to upgrade the hardware and software	
Infrastructure	Cost to acquire, maintain, and support related infrastructure, such as networks and specialized equipment (including storage backup units)	
Downtime	Lost productivity if hardware or software failures cause the system to be unavailable for processing and user tasks	
Space and energy	Real estate and utility costs for housing and providing power for the technology	

Outsourcing

A number of firms are **outsourcing** the maintenance of their IT infrastructures and the development of new systems to external vendors. They may contract with an external service provider to run their computer center and networks, to develop new software, or to manage all of the components of their IT infrastructures. For example, FedEx is outsourcing 30 percent of its IT system operations and software development to external IT service providers.

Specialized Web hosting services are available for companies that lack the financial or technical resources to operate their own Web sites. A **Web hosting service** maintains a large Web server, or a series of servers, and provides fee-paying subscribers with space to maintain their Web sites. The subscribing companies may create their own Web pages or have the hosting service, or a Web design firm, create them. Some services offer *co-location*, in which the firm actually purchases and owns the server computer housing its Web site but locates the server in the physical facility of the hosting service.

Firms often retain control over their hardware resources but outsource custom software development or maintenance to outside firms, frequently firms that operate offshore in low-wage areas of the world. When firms outsource software work outside their national borders, the practice is called **offshore software outsourcing**. Until recently, this type of software development involved lower-level maintenance, data entry, and call center operations, but with the growing sophistication and experience of offshore firms, particularly in India, more and more new program development is taking place offshore. Chapter 12 discusses offshore software outsourcing in greater detail.

In order to manage their relationship with an outsourcer or technology service provider, firms will need a contract that includes a **service level agreement (SLA)**. The SLA is a formal contract between customers and their service providers that defines the specific responsibilities of the service provider and the level of service expected by the customer. SLAs typically specify the nature and level of services provided, criteria for performance measurement, support options, provisions for security and disaster recovery, hardware and software ownership and upgrades, customer support, billing, and conditions for terminating the agreement.

Using Cloud Services

Firms now have the option of maintaining their own IT infrastructures or using cloud-based hardware and software services. Companies considering the cloud computing model need to carefully assess the costs and benefits of external services, weighing all people, organizational, and technology issues, including the level of service and performance that is acceptable for the business.

Cloud computing is more immediately appealing to small and medium-sized businesses that lack resources to purchase and own their own hardware and software. However, large corporations have huge investments in complex proprietary systems supporting unique business processes, some of which give them strategic advantages. Moreover, the cost savings from switching to cloud services are not always easy to determine for large companies that already have their own IT infrastructures in place.

Pricing for cloud services is usually based on a per-hour or other per-use charge. Even if a company can approximate the hardware and software costs to run a specific computing task on premises, it still needs to figure in how much of the firm's network management, storage management, system administration, electricity, and real estate costs should be allocated to a specific individual on-premises IT service. An information systems department may not have the right information to analyze those factors on a service-by-service basis.

Large firms are most likely to adopt a **hybrid cloud** computing model where they use their own infrastructure for their most essential core activities and adopt public cloud computing for less-critical systems or for additional processing capacity during peak business periods. In general, cloud computing will gradually shift firms from having a fixed infrastructure capacity toward a more flexible infrastructure, some of it owned by the firm, and some of it rented from cloud computing centers.

In order to achieve a global presence, firms need to efficiently translate their online interfaces to multiple languages. This process is called localization.

MANAGING MOBILE PLATFORMS

Gains in productivity from equipping employees with mobile computing devices must be balanced against increased costs from integrating these devices into the firm's IT infrastructure and from providing technical support. This is especially true when the organization allows employees to use their own personal devices for their jobs (BYOD).

In the past, companies tried to limit business smartphone use to a single platform. This made it easier to keep track of each mobile device and to roll out software upgrades or fixes, because all employees were using the same devices, or at the very least, the same operating system. Today, employees want to be able to use a variety of personally-owned mobile devices, including the iPad, iPhone, and Android handhelds to access corporate systems like e-mail, databases and applications.

For personal mobile devices to access company information, the company's networks must be configured to receive connections from that device. Firms need an efficient inventory management system that keeps track of which devices employees are using, where each device is located, and what software is installed on it. They also need to know what pieces of corporate data are on those personal devices, and this is not always easy to determine. It is more difficult to protect the company's network and data when employees access them from their privately owned devices.

If a device is stolen or compromised, companies need to ensure that sensitive or confidential company information isn't exposed. Companies often use technologies that allow them to wipe data from devices remotely, or encrypt data so that if stolen, they cannot be used. You'll find a detailed discussion of mobile security issues in Chapter 8.

Many companies only allow employee mobile devices access to a limited set of applications and noncritical corporate data. For more critical business systems, more-company control is required, and firms often turn to **mobile device management (MDM)** software. Mobile device management software monitors, manages, and secures mobile devices that are deployed across multiple mobile service providers and across multiple mobile operating systems being used in the organization. MDM tools enable the IT department to monitor mobile usage, install or update mobile software, back up and restore mobile

Just about everyone who has a smartphone wants to be able to bring it to work and use it on the job. And why not? Employees using their own smartphones would allow companies to enjoy all of the same benefits of a mobile workforce without spending their own money to purchase these devices. Smaller companies are able to go mobile without making large investments in devices and mobile services. According to Gartner Consultants, BYOD will be embraced by 38 percent of companies by 2016 and half of all companies will mandate BYOD by 2017. BYOD is becoming the "new normal."

But...wait a minute. Nearly three out of five enterprises believe that BYOD represents a growing problem for their organizations, according to a survey of 162 enterprises conducted by Osterman Research on behalf of Dell Inc. Although BYOD can improve employee job satisfaction and productivity, it also can cause a number of problems if not managed properly: Support for personally owned devices is more difficult than it is for company-supplied devices, the cost of managing mobile devices can increase, and protecting corporate data and networks becomes more difficult. Research conducted by the Aberdeen Group found that on average, an enterprise with 1,000 mobile devices spends an extra $170,000 per year when it allows BYOD. So it's not that simple.

IBM's CIO Jeanette Horan believes that BYOD may cause as many problems as it solves. BYOD is not saving IBM any money and is actually creating new challenges for the IT department because employees' devices are full of software that IBM doesn't control. IBM provides secure BlackBerrys for about 40,000 of its 400,000 workers while allowing 80,000 more employees to use their own smartphones or tablets to access IBM networks.

The IBM IT department found it had no grasp of which apps and services employees were using on their personal devices, and employees themselves were "blissfully unaware" of the security risks posed by popular apps. IBM decided to ban the use of such popular services as the Dropbox cloud-based cyberlocker, fearing that employees would put IBM-sensitive information in their personal Dropbox accounts, forward internal e-mail to public Web mail services, or use their smartphones as mobile Wi-Fi hotspots.

IBM will not allow an employee to access its corporate networks with his or her personal device unless it secures the device. The IT department configures the device so that its memory can be erased remotely if it is lost or stolen. The IT group also disables public file-transfer programs like Apple's iCloud; instead, employees use an IBM-hosted version called MyMobileHub. IBM even turns off Siri, the voice-activated personal assistant, on employees' iPhones because the spoken queries are uploaded to Apple servers.

Each employee's device is treated differently, depending on the model and the job responsibilities of the person using it. Some people are only allowed to receive IBM e-mail, calendars, and contacts on their portable devices, while others can access internal IBM applications and files (see Chapter 8). IBM equips the mobile devices of the latter category of employees with additional software, such as programs that encrypt information as it travels to and from corporate networks.

One company that has successfully implemented BYOD is Intel Corporation, the giant semiconductor company. About 70 percent of the 39,000 devices registered on its network are personal devices. Intel approached BYOD in a positive manner, trying to find ways to make it work rather than to defeat it. Diane Bryant, then Intel's CIO, didn't want to be dependent on a single mobile vendor or device.

Intel hammered out a BYOD strategy and created an end-user service-level agreement that clarified that end users were voluntarily using BYOD rather than being mandated by Intel. The company developed different policies, rules, and access limits for each type of device—smartphone, tablet, or laptop—with multiple levels of controls in place. Intel maintains a list of approved devices. If a device does not meet its requirements, it is blocked from the network. Intel's BYOD program today offers 40 proprietary applications, including travel tools to help schedule a flight and conference room finders. The company has an internal "app store" and uses a variety of software and security tools, including mobile device management (MDM) software and mobile app management (MAM) software.

Intel's goal for BYOD is not to save money but to make employees happier and more productive. Employees like being able to use their own device and apps alongside specialized Intel apps. On average, Intel workers report that bringing their own devices saves them about 57 minutes per day, which amounts to 5 million hours annually company-wide.

Canadian Tire decided not to allow BYOD at all and issued new BlackBerry Q10 and Z10 smartphones to its 3000 corporate employees. (Canadian Tire is one of Canada's largest companies, with an online e-commerce store and 1200 retail outlets selling automotive, sports, leisure, home products, and apparel; petroleum outlets; and financial services.) The company felt that for its purposes, the bring-your-own-device model was not sufficiently secure. Canadian Tire's chief technology officer (CTO) Eugene Roman worries that an e-mail could send a virus into the company's core infrastructure. At present, Canadian Tire's management thinks BYOD is interesting but is not yet ready for the company's mainstream business applications.

In order to successfully deploy mobile devices, companies need to carefully examine their business processes and determine whether or not mobility makes sense for them. Not every firm will benefit from mobil-

ity to the same degree. Without a clear idea of exactly how mobile devices fit into the long-term plans for the firm, companies will end up wasting their money on unnecessary devices and programs. One of the biggest worries that managers have about mobility is the difficulty of measuring return on investment. Many workers swear by their mobile devices, and the benefits are too significant to ignore, but quantifying how much money is earned or saved by going mobile can be difficult.

Sources: Fred Donovan, "The Growing BYOD Problem," *FierceMobileIT*, February 13, 2013; Brian Bergstein, "IBM Faces the Perils of 'Bring Your Own Device'," *MIT Technology Review*, May 21, 2013; Matt Hamblen, "Canadian Tire forgoes BYOD, issues BlackBerries to workers," *Computerworld*, May 20, 2013; and Boonsri Dickinson, "Security Headaches: BYOD Users Expected to Double by 2014," *Information Week*, August 8, 2012.

CASE STUDY QUESTIONS

1. What are the advantages and disadvantages of allowing employees to use their personal smartphones for work?

2. What people, organization, and technology factors should be addressed when deciding whether to allow employees to use their personal smartphones for work?

3. Compare the BYOD experiences of IBM and Intel. Why did BYOD at Intel work so well?

4. Allowing employees to use their own smartphones for work will save the company money. Do you agree? Why or why not?

devices, and remove software and data from devices that are stolen or lost. The Interactive Session on People provides more detail on how companies are handling the management challenges created by BYOD and consumerization of IT.

MANAGING SOFTWARE LOCALIZATION FOR GLOBAL BUSINESS

If you are operating a global company, all of the management issues we have just described will be affected by the need to create systems that can be realistically used by multiple business units in different countries. Although English has become a kind of standard business language, this is truer at higher levels of companies and not throughout the middle and lower ranks. Software may have to be built with local language interfaces before a new information system can be successfully implemented worldwide.

These interfaces can be costly and messy to build. Menu bars, commands, error messages, reports, queries, online data entry forms, and system documentation may need to be translated into all the languages of the countries where the system will be used. To be truly useful for enhancing productivity of a global workforce, the software interfaces must be easily understood and mastered quickly. The entire process of converting software to operate in a second language is called *software localization*.

Global systems must also consider differences in local cultures and business processes. Cross-functional systems such as enterprise and supply chain management systems are not always compatible with differences in languages, cultural heritages, and business processes in other countries. In a global systems environment, all of these factors add to the TCO and will influence decisions about whether to outsource or use technology service providers.

Review Summary

1 **What are the components of IT infrastructure?** IT infrastructure consists of the shared technology resources that provide the platform for the firm's specific information system applications. Major IT infrastructure components include computer hardware, software, data management technology, networking and telecommunications technology, and technology services.

2 **What are the major computer hardware, data storage, input, and output technologies used in business and major hardware trends?** Computers are categorized as mainframes, midrange computers, PCs, workstations, or supercomputers. Mainframes are the largest computers, midrange computers are servers, PCs are desktop or laptop machines, workstations are desktop machines with powerful mathematical and graphic capabilities, and supercomputers are sophisticated, powerful computers that can perform massive and complex computations rapidly. Computing power can be further increased by creating a computational grid that combines the computing power of all the computers on a network. In the client/server model of computing, computer processing is split between "clients" and "servers" connected via a network. The exact division of tasks between client and server depends on the application.

The principal secondary storage technologies are magnetic disk, optical disc, and magnetic tape. Optical CD-ROM and DVD discs can store vast amounts of data compactly and some types are rewritable. Storage area networks (SANs) connect multiple storage devices on a separate high-speed network dedicated to storage. The principal input devices are keyboards, computer mice, touch screens (including those with multitouch), magnetic ink and optical character recognition devices, pen-based instruments, digital scanners, sensors, audio input devices, and radio-frequency identification devices. The principal output devices are display monitors, printers, and audio output devices.

Major hardware trends include the mobile digital platform, nanotechnology, quantum computers, consumerization of IT, virtualization, cloud computing, green computing, high-performance/power-saving processors, and autonomic computing. Cloud computing provides computer processing, storage, software, and other services as virtualized resources over a network, primarily the Internet, on an as-needed basis.

3 **What are the major types of computer software used in business and major software trends?** The two major types of software are system software and application software. System software coordinates the various parts of the computer system and mediates between application software and computer hardware. Application software is used to develop specific business applications.

The system software that manages and controls the activities of the computer is called the operating system. Leading PC and server operating systems include, Windows 8, UNIX, Linux, and the Macintosh operating system OS X. Linux is a powerful, resilient open source operating system that can run on multiple hardware platforms and is used widely to run Web servers.

The principal programming languages used in business application software include Java, C, C++, and Visual Basic. PC and cloud-based productivity tools include word processing, spreadsheet, data management, presentation graphics, and Web browser software. Java is an operating-system- and hardware-independent programming language that is the leading interactive programming environment for the Web. HTML is a page description language for creating Web pages.

Web services are loosely coupled software components based on XML and open Web standards that can work with any application software and operating system. They can be used as components of Web-based applications to link the systems of two different organizations or to link disparate systems of a single company.

Software trends include the expanding use of open source software and cloud-based software tools and services (including SaaS, mashups, and apps).

4 **What are the principal issues in managing hardware and software technology?**
Managers and information systems specialists need to pay special attention to hardware capacity planning and scalability to ensure that the firm has enough computing power for its current and future needs. Businesses also need to balance the costs and benefits of building and maintaining their own hardware and software versus outsourcing or using an on-demand computing model. The total cost of ownership (TCO) of the organization's technology assets includes not only the original cost of computer hardware and software but also costs for hardware and software upgrades, maintenance, technical support, and training, including the costs for managing and maintaining mobile devices. Companies with global operations need to manage software localization.

Key Terms

Android, 185
Application server, 175
Application software, 172
Apps, 192
Autonomic computing, 183
BYOD, 177
C, 186
C++, 186
Capacity planning, 192
CD-ROM (compact disc read-only memory), 176
Centralized processing, 174
Chrome OS, 185
Client, 174
Client/server computing, 174
Cloud computing, 180
Consumerization of IT, 177
Data center, 171
Data management software, 173
Digital video disc (DVD), 176
Distributed processing, 174
Extensible Markup Language (XML), 189
Google Apps, 181
Graphical user interface (GUI), 184
Green computing (green IT), 181
Grid computing, 174
HTML5, 189
Hybrid cloud, 194

Hypertext Markup Language (HTML), 189
Input devices, 176
iOS, 185
Java, 186
Legacy systems, 173
Linux, 186
Magnetic disk, 176
Magnetic tape, 176
Mainframe, 174
Mashups, 192
Mobile device management (MDM), 195
Multicore processor, 183
Multitouch, 184
Nanotechnology, 178
N-tier client/server architectures, 175
Object, 186
Office 2035, 188
Offshore software outsourcing, 194
On-demand computing, 181
Open source software, 186
Operating system, 184
Output devices, 176
Outsourcing, 194
Personal computer (PC), 173
Presentation graphics software, 188
Private cloud, 181
Public cloud, 181
Quantum computing, 179

SaaS (Software as a Service), 191
Scalability, 193
Server, 173
Service level agreement (SLA), 194
Service-oriented architecture (SOA), 190
Software package, 187
Solid state drive (SSD), 176
Spreadsheet software, 187
Storage area networks (SANs), 176
Supercomputer, 174
System software, 172
Tablet computer, 177
Total cost of ownership (TCO), 193
UNIX, 185
Virtualization, 179
Visual Basic, 186
Visual programming language, 186
Web browsers, 188
Web hosting service, 194
Web server, 175
Web services, 189
Windows 29, 185
Windows 30, 185
Word processing software, 187
Workstation, 173

Review Questions

5-1 What are the components of IT infrastructure?
- Define information technology (IT) infrastructure and describe each of its components.

5-2 What are the major computer hardware, data storage, input, and output technologies used in business and major hardware trends?
- List and describe the various type of computers available to businesses today.
- Define the client/server model of computing, and describe the difference between two-tiered and n-tier client/server architecture.
- List the most important secondary storage media and the strengths and limitations of each.
- List and describe the major computer input and output devices.
- Define and describe the mobile digital platform, BYOD, nanotechnology, grid computing, cloud computing, autonomic computing, virtualization, green computing, and multicore processing.
- List the essential characteristics of cloud computing and distinguish between a public cloud and a private cloud.

5-3 What are the major types of computer software used in business and major software trends?
- Distinguish between application software and system software, and explain the role played by the operating system of a computer.
- List and describe the major PC and server operating systems.
- List and describe some popular programming languages for business applications.
- Name and describe the major desktop productivity software tools.
- Define Web services, describe the technologies they use, and explain how Web services benefit businesses.
- Explain why open source software is so important today and its benefits for business.
- Define HTML and explain how HTML5 provides additional functionality.

5-4 What are the principal issues in managing hardware and software technology?
- Explain why managers need to pay attention to capacity planning and scalability of technology resources.
- Describe some methods that firms can use to reduce the TCO of technology assets.
- Identify the benefits and challenges of using outsourcing, cloud computing services, and mobile platforms.
- Explain why software localization has become an important management issue for global companies.

Discussion Questions

5-5 Why is selecting computer hardware and software for the organization an important business decision? What people, organization, and technology issues should be considered when selecting computer hardware and software?

5-6 Should organizations use software service providers (including cloud services) for all their software needs? Why or why not? What people, organization, and technology factors should be considered when making this decision?

5-7 What are the advantages and disadvantages of the BYOD movement?

Hands-On MIS Projects

The projects in this section give you hands-on experience in developing solutions for managing IT infrastructures and IT outsourcing, using spreadsheet software to evaluate alternative desktop systems, and using Web research to budget for a sales conference.

MANAGEMENT DECISION PROBLEMS

5-8 Hischornklinik Group is a leading private medical clinic group in Germany. It relies on information systems to operate 14 hospitals, as well as hundreds of specialist institutes. Demand for additional servers and storage technology is growing by 20 percent each year. Hischornklinik was setting up a separate server for every application, and its servers and other computers were running a number of different operating systems, including several versions of UNIX and Windows. Hischornklinik had to manage technologies from many different vendors, including Hewlett-Packard (HP), Sun Microsystems, Microsoft, and IBM. Assess the impact of this situation on business performance. What factors and management decisions must be considered when developing a solution to this problem?

5-9 Qantas Airways, Australia's leading airline, faces cost pressures from high fuel prices and lower levels of global airline traffic. To remain competitive, the airline must find ways to keep costs low while providing a high level of customer service. Qantas had a 30-year-old data center. Management had to decide whether to replace its IT infrastructure with newer technology or outsource it. What factors should be considered by Qantas management when deciding whether to outsource? If Qantas decides to outsource, list and describe points that should be addressed in a service level agreement.

IMPROVING DECISION MAKING: USING A SPREADSHEET TO EVALUATE HARDWARE AND SOFTWARE OPTIONS

Software skills: Spreadsheet formulas
Business skills: Technology pricing

5-10 In this exercise, you will use spreadsheet software to calculate the cost of desktop systems, printers, and software.

Use the Internet to obtain pricing information on hardware and software for an office of 30 people. You will need to price 30 PC desktop systems (monitors, computers, and keyboards) manufactured by Lenovo, Dell, and HP/Compaq. (For the purposes of this exercise, ignore the fact that desktop systems usually come with preloaded software packages.) Obtain pricing on 15 desktop printers manufactured by HP, Canon, and Dell. Each desktop system must satisfy the minimum specifications shown in tables that you can find in MyMISLab™. Also obtain pricing on 30 copies of the most recent versions of Microsoft Office, Lotus SmartSuite, and OpenOffice, and on 30 copies of Microsoft Windows 8 Professional. Each desktop productivity package should contain programs for word processing, spreadsheets, database, and presentations. Prepare a spreadsheet showing your research results for the software and the desktop system, printer, and software combination offering the best performance and pricing per worker. Because every two workers share one printer (15 printers/30 systems), your calculations should assume only half a printer cost per worker.

IMPROVING DECISION MAKING: USING WEB RESEARCH TO BUDGET FOR A SALES CONFERENCE

Software skills: Internet-based software
Business skills: Researching transportation and lodging costs

5-11 In this exercise, you'll use software at various online travel sites to obtain pricing for total travel and lodging costs for a sales conference.

EuroPlastiques is a leading EU plastics company. EuroPlastiques is planning a two-day sales conference for June 19–20, starting with a reception on the evening of June 18. The conference consists of all-day meetings that the entire sales force, numbering 100 sales representatives and their 15 managers, must attend. Each sales representative requires his or her own room, and the company needs two common meeting rooms, one large enough to hold the entire sales force plus a few visitors (150 total) and the other able to hold half the force.. The company would like to hold the conference in either Zurich, Switzerland or Milan, Italy, at a Marriott - or Novotel-owned hotel. Use the Marriott and Novotel Web sites to select a hotel in whichever of these cities would enable the company to hold its sales conference within its budget and meet its sales conference requirements. Then locate flights arriving the afternoon prior to the conference.

Your attendees will be coming from Paris (44), London (22), Amsterdam (20), Stockholm (18), and Dublin (11). Determine costs of each airline ticket from these cities. When you are finished, create a budget for the conference. The budget will include the cost of each airline ticket, the room cost, and 60 euros per attendee per day for food.

Collaboration and Teamwork Project

5-12 In MyMISLab, you will find a Collaboration and Teamwork Project dealing with the concepts in this chapter. You will be able to use Google Drive, Google Docs, Google Sites, Google+, or other open-source tools to complete the assignment.

BUSINESS PROBLEM-SOLVING CASE

Is It Time for Cloud Computing?

Cloud computing has begun to take off in the business world. The biggest players in the cloud computing marketplace are Amazon Web Services (AWS) division, Microsoft, and Google. These companies have streamlined cloud computing and made it an affordable and sensible option for companies ranging from tiny Internet startups to established companies like FedEx. Amazon is the leader.

AWS provides subscribing companies with flexible computing power and data storage, as well as data management, messaging, payment, and other services that can be used together or individually as the business requires. Anyone with an Internet connection and a little bit of money can harness the same computing systems that Amazon itself uses to run its now $48 billion a year retail business. To make the process of harnessing the cloud simpler, Amazon added an automated service called Cloud Formation that helps customers determine the right amount of computing resources. Customers provide the amount of server space, bandwidth, storage, and any other services they require, and AWS can automatically allocate those resources.

Since its launch in March 2006, AWS has continued to grow in popularity, with $2 billion in business in 2012 and hundreds of thousands of customers in more than 190 countries. In fact, Amazon believes that Amazon Web Services will someday become more valuable than its vaunted retail operation. Amazon's sales pitch is that you don't pay a monthly or yearly fee to use their computing resources—instead, you pay for exactly what you use. For many businesses, this is an appealing proposition, because it allows Amazon to handle all of the maintenance and upkeep of IT infrastructures, leaving businesses to spend more time on higher-value work.

Zynga is a good example of a company using cloud computing to improve its business in a new way. With over 260 million monthly active users, Zynga is the developer of wildly popular Facebook applications such as FarmVille, Mafia Wars, and many others. When Zynga releases a new game, it has no way of knowing what amount of computing resources to dedicate to the game. The game might be a mild success, or a smash hit that adds millions of new users. Rather than Zynga spending on computing resources of its own before the launch of each game, it's much more cost-effective to use Amazon's cloud services until the company can more accurately predict the computing power it needs. Once game traffic stabilizes and reaches a steady number of users, Zynga moves the game onto its private zCloud, which is structurally similar to Amazon's cloud, but operates under Zynga's control in data centers on the East and West coasts.

Although the consequences for server downtime are not as catastrophic for Zynga as they would be for a financial services firm, Zynga still needs 99.9% uptime. On its own financial reports, Zynga recognized that a significant majority of its game traffic had been hosted by a single vendor and any failure or significant interruption in its network could negatively impact operations. An Amazon Web Services outage lasting several hours in April 2011 made it impossible for users to log into some of Zynga's games.

National Australia Bank (NAB), with $754 billion in assets, opted for an internal private cloud using IBM's infrastructure on demand. IBM had already been managing the bank's IT infrastructure under a seven-year contract signed in 2010. NAB is a third of the way into a ten-year transformation plan to overhaul business processes and core banking systems in order to increase its competitive edge and improve the customer and banker experience. The private cloud hosts the bank's main production environment, including its new Oracle banking system, and will support short-term computing-intense projects such as marketing campaigns. NAB pays only for what it uses so that it doesn't have to make large IT capital expenditures. The equipment is all hosted in NAB's data centers, which is unusual for on-demand environments.

State Street Bank expects to save $600 million from moving to a private cloud. A significant portion of these savings comes from lower software development costs, which used to constitute 20 to 25 percent of the bank's annual IT budget. State Street writes a lot of highly customized software to manage $2 trillion under direct management and $23.2 trillion in assets under custody and administration. State Street has simplified and standardized its IT infrastructure by replacing heterogeneous data centers with many best-of-breed systems with the private cloud. This makes it possible for all State Street developers to write software for the same cloud-based platform, so State Street does not need to write so much program code. The bank has reduced the cost of writing software by 30 to 40 percent.

InterContinental Hotels revamped its IT infrastructure to include both private and public cloud usage. To improve response time for customers, InterContinental moved its core room reservation transaction system onto a private cloud within its own data center, but it moved room availability and pricing Web site applications onto public cloud data centers on the East and West coasts. In fact, InterContinental hopes to put all of its publicly accessible information in these public clouds so that customers receive faster results to site queries. Customers receive data faster if the data are located on a server that is physically close to them, and cloud computing helps InterContinental to take advantage of this.

Startup companies and smaller companies are finding that they no longer need to build their own data center. With cloud infrastructures like Amazon's readily available, they have access to technical capability that was formerly available only to much larger businesses. For example, online crafts marketplace Etsy uses Amazon computers to analyze data from the 1 billion monthly views of its Web site. Etsy can then use its findings to create product recommendation systems that allow customers to rank which products they like best and to generate a list of 100 products each might enjoy. Etsy's engineers and managers are both excited about their ability to handle these types of activities on someone else's computer systems.

Low overhead and infrastructure management costs make cloud computing especially attractive to startups. However, according to Cliff Olson, director of infrastructure systems at FP International, Inc., a Fremont, California-based packaging company, the financial benefits of cloud computing for large and mid-sized organizations are less apparent. If a company pays a cloud provider a monthly service fee for 10,000 or more employees, that will be more expensive than having the company maintain its own IT infrastructure and staff. Companies also worry about unexpected "runaway costs" from using a pay-per-use model. Integrating cloud services with existing IT infrastructures, errors, mismanagement, or even a distributed denial-of-service attack, which floods a Web site with information requests (see Chapter 8), will run up the bill for cloud service users. Right now, it's cheaper for a very large company to own and manage its own data center. But as public clouds become more efficient and secure and the technology grows cheaper, large companies will start using cloud resources as well.

Many other companies share Zynga's concern about cloud reliability and security and this remains a major barrier to widespread cloud adoption. Amazon's cloud experienced significant outages in April and August 2011, on June 14 and 29, 2012, and on December 24, 2012. Normally, cloud networks are very reliable, and often more so than private networks operated by individual companies. But when a cloud of significant size like Amazon's goes down, it sends ripples across the entire Web.

According to Amazon, a simple network configuration error caused a major multiday service outage in Amazon's east coast region from April 21–24, 2011. Amazingly, the error was most likely a simple error made by a human being during a routine network adjustment. Sites affected included Reddit, Foursquare, Engine Yard, Hootsuite, Quora, Zynga, and many more. On June 14 and June 29, 2012, Amazon Web Services suffered outages due to power failures in its primary East Coast data center in North Virginia. Many popular Web sites, including Netflix, Heroku, Quora, and Pinterest, as well as Web sites of smaller companies, were knocked offline for hours. Netflix and other companies lost Amazon service again on Christmas Eve 2012.

The outages were proof that the vision of a cloud with 100 percent uptime is still far from reality. Experts have conflicting opinions on how serious this is. A June 2012 report issued by the Paris-based International Working Group on Cloud Computing Resiliency estimated that the major cloud computing services were down about 10 hours per year or more, with average availability at 99.9 percent or less. Even this small amount of downtime can lead to large revenue losses for firms that need 24/7 availability. Nevertheless, some large cloud users such as Netflix believe that overall cloud service availability has steadily improved. Neil Hunt, Netflix's chief product officer, believes the cloud is becoming more reliable, and that Amazon Web Services gives Netflix much larger scale and technical expertise than it would have otherwise. A number of experts recommend that companies for whom an outage would be a major risk consider using another computing service as a backup.

Wendell Thomas, director of IS and IT infrastructure operations at Safe Horizon, Inc., a New York-based victim advocacy agency, believes that most mid-sized and large companies will gravitate toward a hybrid approach. Safe Horizon uses a cloud provider for its e-mail system serving 700 employees. Premier Inc., a provider of health care data to a network of 2600 health care system providers and 400,000 doctors, keeps patient information in one of its two data centers, which is highly virtualized and owned by the company. The other data center is dedicated to disaster recovery and is at a hosting facility. An SaaS provider handles human resources and payroll systems, although Premier's staff manages these applications. At this point, Premier is unlikely to put its patient data on a public cloud unless security improves in hosted data centers.

Still, cloud computing has finally gone mainstream, and the major cloud providers have the sales numbers to prove it. Cloud providers will have to continue to work to avoid outages, while other companies must decide whether the cloud is right for them, and if so, how to most effectively use the cloud to enhance their businesses.

Sources: Charles Babcock, "Cloud Implementation Costs, Complexity Surprise Companies," *Information Week*, February 6, 2013; Christina Torode, Linda Tucci, and Karen Goulart, "Managing the Next-Generation Data Center," *Modern Infrastructure CIO Edition*, January 2013; Penny Crossman, "How New Core, Cloud Computing Are Transforming an Aussie Bank," Information Management, January 2, 2013; Spencer E. Ante, "CIA Chooses: Amazon or IBM?" *The Wall Street Journal*, June 12, 2013; Quentin Hardy, "Active in Cloud, Amazon Reshapes Computing," *The New York Times*, August 27, 2012; Charles Babcock, "Cloud's Thorniest Question: Does It Pay Off?" *Information Week*, June 4, 2012, "Cloud's Big Caveat: Runaway Costs," *Information Week*, June 7, 2012 and "State Street Sees $600 Million Silver Lining in Cloud," *Information Week*, July 9, 2012; ; Zack Whittaker, "Amazon Explains Latest Cloud Outage: Blame the Power," *ZDNet*, June 18, 2012; Stuart J. Johnston, "Cloud Outage of 13 Providers Reveals Downtime Costs," searchcloud-computing.com, June 22, 2012; Charles Babcock, "Amazon Launches Cloud Formation to Simplify App Development," *Information Week*, February 28, 2011; and Charles Babcock, "Zynga's Unusual Cloud Strategy is Key To Success," *Information Week*, July 1, 2011.

Case Study Questions

5-13 What business benefits do cloud computing services provide? What problems do they solve?

5-14 What are the disadvantages of cloud computing?

5-15 How do the concepts of capacity planning, scalability, and TCO apply to this case? Apply these concepts both to Amazon and to subscribers of its services.

5-16 What kinds of businesses are most likely to benefit from using cloud computing? Why?

Foundations of Business Intelligence: Databases and Information Management

CHAPTER 6

STUDENT LEARNING OBJECTIVES

After completing this chapter, you will be able to answer the following questions:

1. How does a relational database organize data?

2. What are the principles of a database management system?

3. What are the principal tools and technologies for accessing information from databases to improve business performance and decision making?

4. What is the role of information policy and data administration in the management of organizational data resources?

5. Why is data quality assurance so important for a business?

LEARNING TRACKS

1. Database Design, Normalization, and Entity-Relationship Diagramming

2. Introduction to SQL

3. Hierarchical and Network Data Models

VIDEO CASES

Case 1: Dubuque Uses Cloud Computing and Sensors to Build a Smarter City

Case 2: Maruti Suzuki Business Intelligence and Enterprise Databases

CHAPTER OUTLINE

BAE SYSTEMS

BAE Systems (BAE) is the United Kingdom's largest manufacturing company and one of the largest commercial aerospace and defence organisations in Europe. Its high-technology, information-driven products and services range from one of the world's most capable multi-role combat fighters, the Eurofighter Typhoon, to the Jetstream family of commercial aircraft, to the provision of information technology and information systems for e-business to develop and implement logistics, IT and e-capability services. With sales, manufacturing and support sites throughout the world, including the U.K., Europe, the United States, and Australia, BAE employs 88,000 people and generates more than €22 billion in annual revenue.

Although BAE has consolidated its competitive position in established markets, and continues to expand into new markets in the Middle East and Asia, its performance in the aircraft part of the business was being impeded by legacy information systems which support the computer-aided design (CAD) and computer-aided manufacturing (CAM) of its aircraft. The distributed nature of BAE's design and manufacturing sites meant that storing and analysing accurate sets of operational data describing the com-

© senohrabek/Fotolia

plex components of the various aircraft types to produce aircraft assembly reports for the production lines became increasingly challenging and resource-consuming. Data describing the same aircraft component parts might need resolution, such as in the case of various part naming conventions and codes.

Accessing the data from the many systems was a complex task involving many technical challenges. As the aircraft business of BAE grew so did the likelihood for delays in producing the aircraft assembly reports and other operations data sets necessary for aircraft production management decision making. In the worst case, the production of aircraft on the assembly line would stop until accurate information was available, with consequent schedule and cost implications. BAE's CAD/CAM staff were storing and analysing data sets sourced from 5 major aircraft design and manufacturing sites spread throughout the U.K., each host to thousands of staff involved in the design and manufacturing process, so that assembly reports and other operations data could be produced. Although the data that the legacy systems processed were held principally in computer files, there were numerous occasions when paper drawings with annotations containing component design and manufacturing information were used to reconcile ambiguities and inconsistencies in the assembly reports. When these data ambiguities and inconsistencies occurred, this gave rise to a sense of uncertainty in the assembly reports produced.

What BAE needed was a single repository for CAD/CAM data that would also facilitate the integration of data held in its legacy systems. The company decided to replace its legacy systems with an enterprise-wide knowledge management system which would bring the design and manufacturing data into a single database that could be concurrently accessed by the design and manufacturing engineers. BAE implemented Siemens' Teamcenter product lifecycle management software and Dassault Systemes' CATIA CAD/CAM software. Teamcenter can also be configured to take advantage of recent developments in cloud computing using Microsoft's Azure, IBM's SmartCloud Enterprise+, and Amazon Web Services.

Bringing together Siemens' Teamcenter and Dassault Systemes' CATIA has given BAE Systems powerful integrated data management tools. The Teamcenter database includes tools for component markup and rollup capabilities allowing users to visualise the effect of component design changes and configuration selections in real-time.

The new solution has produced significant cost savings at BAE in terms of its design and manufacturing data management and storage, while boosting performance. With fewer legacy systems and data files to manage, BAE has been able to meet quality, time and cost requirements by being able to produce complete and accurate aircraft component definitions and configurations. BAE's new design and manufacturing database technology has improved speed-to-market by synchronising upstream CAD and downstream CAM component definitions, thereby enabling better cross-discipline coordination. With these savings, the company has been able to spend more resources on improving data management across the entire enterprise.

Sources: "BAE Systems Half-Yearly Report and Presentation 2012" www.baesystems.com, accessed November 8, 2012; "Teamcenter supports aircraft through 50-year cycle: BAE Systems Military Air Solutions" www.plm.automation.siemens.com, accessed November 8, 2012; "CATIA V5 Fact Sheet" www.3ds.com, accessed November 8, 2012.

Case contributed by Robert Manderson, University of Roehampton

The experience of BAE Systems illustrates the importance of data management. Business performance depends on the accuracy and reliability of its data. The company has grown its business, but, both operational CAD/CAM efficiency and production management decision making were impeded by data stored in legacy systems that were difficult to access. How businesses store, organise, and manage their data has a huge impact on organisational effectiveness.

The chapter-opening diagram calls attention to important points raised by this case and this chapter. BAE Systems management decided that the firm needed to improve the man-

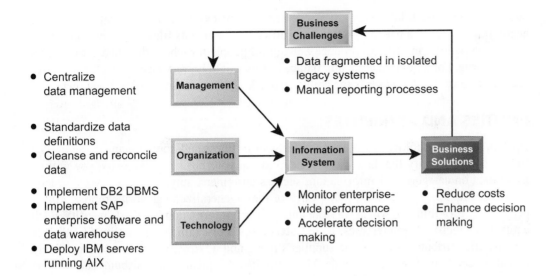

- Centralize data management

- Standardize data definitions
- Cleanse and reconcile data

- Implement DB2 DBMS
- Implement SAP enterprise software and data warehouse
- Deploy IBM servers running AIX

Business Challenges
- Data fragmented in isolated legacy systems
- Manual reporting processes

Management

Organization

Technology

Information System

Business Solutions

- Monitor enterprise-wide performance
- Accelerate decision making

- Reduce costs
- Enhance decision making

agement of its data. Pieces of data about design components, manufactured components, and their final assembly had been stored in many large legacy systems that made it extremely difficult for the data to be retrieved, correctly unified so that it could be used in the production line assembly of aircraft components. The data were often redundant and inconsistent, limiting their usefulness. Management was unable to obtain an enterprise-view of the company.

A state-of-the-art database management system suite of software helps BAE Systems boost efficiency by making it easier to locate and assemble data for management reporting and for processing day-to-day CAD/CAM transactions for final aircraft component assembly. The data are more accurate and reliable, and costs for managing and storing the data have been considerably reduced.

Here are some questions to think about: What kinds of data management problems did BAE Systems experience in its legacy database environment? What work had to be done before the company could effectively take advantage of the new data management technology?

6.1 The Database Approach to Data Management

A **database** is a collection of related files containing records on people, places, or things. One of the most successful databases in modern history is the telephone book. The telephone book is a collection of records on people and businesses who use telephones. The telephone book lists four pieces of information for each phone user: last name, first name, address, and phone number. It also contains information on businesses and business categories, such as auto dealers or plumbing suppliers. The telephone book draws its information from a database with files for customers, business classifications, and area codes and geographic regions.

Prior to the development of digital databases, a business would use large filing cabinets filled with paper files to store information on transactions, customers, suppliers, inventory, and employees. They would also use lists, laboriously collated and typed by hand, to quickly summarize the information in paper files. You can still find paper-based manual databases in most doctors' offices where patient records are stored in thousands of paper files.

Needless to say, paper-based databases are extremely inefficient and costly to maintain, often contain inaccurate data, are slow, and make it difficult to access the data in a timely fashion. Paper-based databases are also extremely inflexible. For instance, it would be nearly impossible for a paper-based doctor's office to combine its files on prescriptions with its files on patients in order to produce a list of all people for whom they had prescribed a specific drug. For a modern computer database, this would be very easy. In fact, a powerful feature of computer databases is the ability to quickly relate one set of files to another.

ENTITIES AND ATTRIBUTES

How do you start thinking about the data for your business and how to manage them? The first step is to identify the data you will need to run your business. Typically, you will be using data on categories of information, such as customers, suppliers, employees, orders, products, shippers, and perhaps parts. Each of these generalized categories representing a person, place, or thing on which we store and maintain information is called an **entity**. Each entity has specific characteristics, called **attributes**. For example, the entity SUPPLIER has specific attributes, such as the supplier's name and address, which would most likely include street, city, state, and zip code. The entity PART typically has attributes such as part description, price of each part (unit price), and supplier who produced the part.

ORGANIZING DATA IN A RELATIONAL DATABASE

If you stored this information in paper files, you would probably have a file on each entity and its attributes. In an information system, a database organizes the data much the same way, grouping related pieces of data together. The **relational database** is the most common type of database today. Relational databases organize data into two-dimensional tables (called *relations*) with columns and rows. Each table contains data on an entity and its attributes. For the most part, there is one table for each business entity. So, at the most basic level, you will have one table for customers, and a table each for suppliers, parts in inventory, employees, and sales transactions.

Let's look at how a relational database would organize data about suppliers and parts. Take the SUPPLIER table, which is illustrated in Figure 6.1. It consists of a grid of columns and rows of data. Each individual element of data about a supplier, such as the supplier name, street, city, state, and zip code, is stored as a separate **field** within the SUPPLIER table. Each field represents an attribute for the entity SUPPLIER. Fields in a relational database are also called *columns*.

The actual information about a single supplier that resides in a table is called a *row*. Rows are commonly referred to as **records**, or, in very technical terms, as **tuples**.

Note that there is a field for Supplier_Number in this table. This field uniquely identifies each record so that the record can be retrieved, updated, or sorted, and it is called a **key field**. Each table in a relational database has one field designated as its **primary key**. This

Figure 6.1
A Relational
Database Table
A relational database organizes data in the form of two-dimensional tables. Illustrated here is a table for the entity SUPPLIER showing how it represents the entity and its attributes. Supplier_Number is the key field.

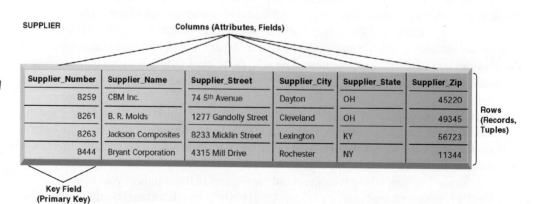

Supplier_Number	Supplier_Name	Supplier_Street	Supplier_City	Supplier_State	Supplier_Zip
8259	CBM Inc.	74 5th Avenue	Dayton	OH	45220
8261	B. R. Molds	1277 Gandolly Street	Cleveland	OH	49345
8263	Jackson Composites	8233 Micklin Street	Lexington	KY	56723
8444	Bryant Corporation	4315 Mill Drive	Rochester	NY	11344

SUPPLIER   Columns (Attributes, Fields)

Rows (Records, Tuples)

Key Field (Primary Key)

key field is the unique identifier for all the information in any row of the table, and this primary key cannot be duplicated.

We could use the supplier's name as a key field. However, if two different suppliers had the same name (which does happen from time to time), supplier name would not uniquely identify each, so it is necessary to assign a special identifier field for this purpose. For example, if you had two suppliers, both named "CBM," but one was based in Dayton and another in St. Louis, it would be easy to confuse them. However, if each has a unique supplier number, such confusion is prevented.

We also see that the address information has been separated into four separate fields: Supplier_Street, Supplier_City, Supplier_State, and Supplier_Zip. Data are separated into the smallest elements that one would want to access separately to make it easy to select only the rows in the table that match the contents of one field, such as all the suppliers in Ohio (OH). The rows of data can also be sorted by the contents of the Supplier_State field to get a list of suppliers by state regardless of their cities.

So far, the SUPPLIER table does not have any information about the parts that a particular supplier provides for your company. PART is a separate entity from SUPPLIER, and fields with information about parts should be stored in a separate PART table (see Figure 6.2).

Why not keep information on parts in the same table as suppliers? If we did that, each row of the table would contain the attributes of both PART and SUPPLIER. Because one supplier could supply more than one part, the table would need many extra rows for a single supplier to show all the parts that supplier provided. We would be maintaining a great deal of redundant data about suppliers, and it would be difficult to search for the information on any individual part because you would not know whether this part is the first or fiftieth part in this supplier's record. A separate table, PART, should be created to store these three fields and solve this problem.

The PART table would also have to contain another field, Supplier_Number, so that you would know the supplier for each part. It would not be necessary to keep repeating all the information about a supplier in each PART record because having a Supplier_ Number field in the PART table allows you to "look up" the data in the fields of the SUPPLIER table.

Notice that Supplier_Number appears in both the SUPPLIER and PART tables. In the SUPPLIER table, Supplier_Number is the primary key. When the field Supplier_Number appears in the PART table it is called a **foreign key** and is essentially a look-up field to find data about the supplier of a specific part. Note that the PART table would itself have its own primary key field, Part_Number, to uniquely identify each part. This key is not used to link PART with SUPPLIER but might be used to link PART with a different entity.

PART

Part_Number	Part_Name	Unit_Price	Supplier_Number
137	Door latch	22.00	8259
145	Side mirror	12.00	8444
150	Door molding	6.00	8263
152	Door lock	31.00	8259
155	Compressor	54.00	8261
178	Door handle	10.00	8259

Primary Key   **Foreign Key**

Figure 6.2
The PART Table
Data for the entity PART have their own separate table. Part_Number is the primary key and Supplier_Number is the foreign key, enabling users to find related information from the SUPPLIER table about the supplier for each part.

As we organize data into tables, it is important to make sure that all the attributes for a particular entity apply only to that entity. If you were to keep the supplier's address with the PART record, that information would not really relate only to PART; it would relate to both PART and SUPPLIER. If the supplier's address were to change, it would be necessary to alter the data in every PART record rather than only once in the SUPPLIER record.

ESTABLISHING RELATIONSHIPS

Now that we've broken down our data into a SUPPLIER table and a PART table, we must make sure we understand the relationship between them. A schematic called an **entity-relationship diagram** is used to clarify table relationships in a relational database. The most important piece of information provided by an entity-relationship diagram is the manner in which two tables are related to each other. Tables in a relational database may have one-to-one, one-to-many, and many-to-many relationships.

An example of a one-to-one relationship might be a situation where a human resources system must store confidential data about employees. It might store data, such as the employee name, date of birth, address, and job position in one table, and confidential data about that employee, such as salary or pension benefits, in another table. These two tables pertaining to a single employee would have a one-to-one relationship because each record in the EMPLOYEE table with basic employee data has only one related record in the table storing confidential data.

The relationship between the SUPPLIER and PART entities in our database is a one-to-many relationship: Each supplier can supply more that one part, but each part has only one supplier. For every record in the SUPPLIER table, there may be many related records in the PART table.

Figure 6.3 illustrates how an entity-relationship diagram would depict this one-to-many relationship. The boxes represent entities. The lines connecting the boxes represent relationships. A line connecting two entities that ends in two short marks designates a one-to-one relationship. A line connecting two entities that ends with a crow's foot preceded by a short mark indicates a one-to-many relationship. Figure 6.3 shows that each part has only one supplier, but many parts can be provided by the same supplier.

We would also see a one-to-many relationship if we wanted to add a table about orders to our database because one supplier services many orders. The ORDER table would contain only the Order_Number and Order_Date fields. Figure 6.4 illustrates a report showing an order of parts from a supplier. If you look at the report, you can see that the information on the top-right portion of the report comes from the ORDER table. The actual line items ordered are listed in the lower portion of the report.

Because one order can be for many parts from a supplier, and a single part can be ordered many times on different orders, this creates a many-to-many relationship between the PART and ORDER tables. Whenever a many-to-many relationship exists between two tables, it is necessary to link these two tables in a table that joins this information. Creating a separate table for a line item in the order would serve this purpose. This table is often called a *join table* or an *intersection relation*. This join table contains only three fields: Order_Number and Part_Number, which are used only to link the ORDER and PART tables, and Part_Quantity. If you look at the bottom-left part of the report, this is the information coming from the LINE_ITEM table.

Figure 6.3
A Simple Entity-Relationship Diagram
This diagram shows the relationship between the entities SUPPLIER and PART.

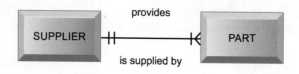

Order Number: 3502
Order Date: 1/15/2014

Supplier Number: 8259
Supplier Name: CBM Inc.
Supplier Address: 74 5th Avenue, Dayton, OH 45220

Order_Number	Part_Number	Part_Quantity	Part_Name	Unit_Price	Extended Price
3502	137	10	Door latch	22.00	$220.00
3502	152	20	Door lock	31.00	620.00
3502	178	5	Door handle	10.00	50.00
			Order Total:		$890.00

Figure 6.4
Sample Order Report
The shaded areas show which data came from the ORDER, SUPPLIER, and LINE_ITEM tables. The database does not maintain data on extended price or order total because they can be derived from other data in the tables.

We would thus wind up with a total of four tables in our database. Figure 6.5 illustrates the final set of tables, and Figure 6.6 shows what the entity-relationship diagram for this set of tables would look like. Note that the ORDER table does not contain data on the extended price because that value can be calculated by multiplying Unit_Price by Part_Quantity. This data element can be derived when needed using information that already exists in the PART and LINE_ITEM tables. Order_Total is another derived field calculated by totaling the extended prices for items ordered.

The process of streamlining complex groups of data to minimize redundant data elements and awkward many-to-many relationships, and increase stability and flexibility is called **normalization.** A properly designed and normalized database is easy to maintain, and minimizes duplicate data. The Learning Tracks at the end of this chapter direct you to more detailed discussions of database design, normalization, and entity-relationship diagramming in MyMISLab™.

Relational database systems enforce **referential integrity** rules to ensure that relationships between coupled tables remain consistent. When one table has a foreign key that points to another table, you may not add a record to the table with the foreign key unless there is a corresponding record in the linked table. In the database we have just created, the foreign key Supplier_Number links the PART table to the SUPPLIER table. We may not add a new record to the PART table for a part with supplier number 8266 unless there is a corresponding record in the SUPPLIER table for supplier number 8266. We must also delete the corresponding record in the PART table if we delete the record in the SUPPLIER table for supplier number 8266. In other words, we shouldn't have parts from nonexistent suppliers!

The example provided here for parts, orders, and suppliers is a simple one. Even in a very small business, you will have tables for other important entities, such as customers, shippers, and employees. A very large corporation might have databases with thousands of entities (tables) to maintain. What is important for any business, large or small, is to have a good data model that includes all of its entities and the relationships among them, one that is organized to minimize redundancy, maximize accuracy, and make data easily accessible for reporting and analysis.

It cannot be emphasized enough: If the business does not get its data model right, the system will not be able to serve the business properly. The company's systems will not be as effective as they could be because they will have to work with data that may be inaccurate, incomplete, or difficult to retrieve. Understanding the organization's data and how they should be represented in a database is perhaps the most important lesson you can learn from this course.

For example, Famous Footwear, a shoe store chain with more than 1,100 locations in 49 states, could not achieve its goal of having "the right style of shoe in the right store for sale

PART

LINE_ITEM

Order_Number	Part_Number	Part_Quantity
3502	137	10
3502	152	20
3502	178	5

Part_Number	Part_Name	Unit_Price	Supplier_Number
137	Door latch	22.00	8259
145	Side mirror	12.00	8444
150	Door molding	6.00	8263
152	Door lock	31.00	8259
155	Compressor	54.00	8261
178	Door handle	10.00	8259

ORDER

Order_Number	Order_Date
3502	1/15/2014
3503	1/16/2014
3504	1/17/2014

SUPPLIER

Supplier_Number	Supplier_Name	Supplier_Street	Supplier_City	Supplier_State	Supplier_Zip
8259	CBM Inc.	74 5th Avenue	Dayton	OH	45220
8261	B. R. Molds	1277 Gandolly Street	Cleveland	OH	49345
8263	Jackson Components	8233 Micklin Street	Lexington	KY	56723
8444	Bryant Corporation	4315 Mill Drive	Rochester	NY	11344

Figure 6.5
The Final Database Design with Sample Records
The final design of the database for suppliers, parts, and orders has four tables. The LINE_ITEM table is a join table that eliminates the many-to-many relationship between ORDER and PART.

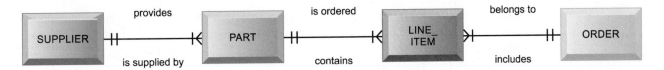

Figure 6.6
Entity-Relationship Diagram for the Database with Four Tables
This diagram shows the relationship between the entities SUPPLIER, PART, LINE_ITEM, and ORDER.

at the right price" because its database was not properly designed for a rapidly adjusting store inventory. The company had an Oracle relational database running on an IBM AS/400 midrange computer, but the database was designed primarily for producing standard reports for management rather than for reacting to marketplace changes. Management could not obtain precise data on specific items in inventory in each of its stores. The company had to work around this problem by building a new database where the sales and inventory data could be better organized for analysis and inventory management.

6.2 Database Management Systems

Now that you have started creating the files and identifying the data required by your business, you will need a database management system to help you manage and use the data. A **database management system (DBMS)** is a specific type of software for creating, storing, organizing, and accessing data from a database. Microsoft Access is a DBMS for desktop systems, whereas DB2, Oracle Database, and Microsoft SQL Server are DBMS for large mainframes and midrange computers. MySQL is a popular open-source DBMS. All of these products are relational DBMS that support a relational database.

The DBMS relieves the end user or programmer from the task of understanding where and how the data are actually stored by separating the logical and physical views of the data. The *logical view* presents data as end users or business specialists would perceive them, whereas the *physical view* shows how data are actually organized and structured on physical storage media, such as a hard disk.

The database management software makes the physical database available for different logical views required by users. For example, for the human resources database illustrated in Figure 6.7, a benefits specialist might require a view consisting of the employee's name,

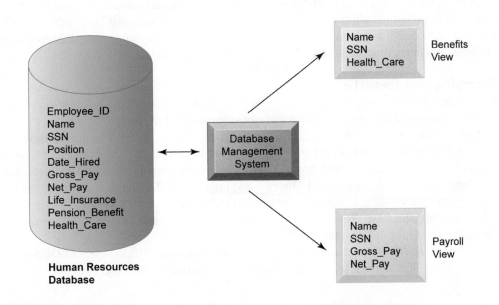

Human Resources Database

Figure 6.7
Human Resources Database with Multiple Views
A single human resources database provides many different views of data, depending on the information requirements of the user. Illustrated here are two possible views, one of interest to a benefits specialist and one of interest to a member of the company's payroll department.

social security number, and health insurance coverage. A payroll department member might need data such as the employee's name, social security number, gross pay, and net pay. The data for all of these views is stored in a single database, where it can be more easily managed by the organization.

OPERATIONS OF A RELATIONAL DBMS

In a relational database, tables can be easily combined to deliver data required by users, provided that any two tables share a common data element. Let's return to the database we set up earlier with PART and SUPPLIER tables illustrated in Figures 6.1 and 6.2.

Suppose we wanted to find in this database the names of suppliers who could provide us with part number 137 or part number 150. We would need information from two tables: the SUPPLIER table and the PART table. Note that these two tables have a shared data element: Supplier_Number.

In a relational database, three basic operations, as shown in Figure 6.8, are used to develop useful sets of data: select, project, and join. The *select* operation creates a subset consisting of all records in the file that meet stated criteria. Select creates, in other words, a subset of rows that meet certain criteria. In our example, we want to select records (rows) from the PART table where the Part_Number equals 137 or 150. The *join* operation combines relational tables to provide the user with more information than is available in individual tables. In our example, we want to join the now-shortened PART table (only parts 137 or 150 will be presented) and the SUPPLIER table into a single new table.

The *project* operation creates a subset consisting of columns in a table, permitting the user to create new tables that contain only the information required. In our example, we want to extract from the new table only the following columns: Part_Number, Part_Name, Supplier_Number, and Supplier_Name (see Figure 6.8).

CAPABILITIES OF DATABASE MANAGEMENT SYSTEMS

A DBMS includes capabilities and tools for organizing, managing, and accessing the data in the database. The most important are its data definition capability, data dictionary, and data manipulation language.

DBMS have a **data definition** capability to specify the structure of the content of the database. It would be used to create database tables and to define the characteristics of the fields in each table. This information about the database would be documented in a **data dictionary**. A data dictionary is an automated or manual file that stores definitions of data elements and their characteristics. Microsoft Access has a rudimentary data dictionary capability that displays information about the name, description, size, type, format, and other properties of each field in a table (see Figure 6.9). Data dictionaries for large corporate databases may capture additional information, such as usage, ownership (who in the organization is responsible for maintaining the data), authorization, security, and the individuals, business functions, programs, and reports that use each data element.

Querying and Reporting

DBMS include tools for accessing and manipulating information in databases. Most DBMS have a specialized language called a **data manipulation language** that is used to add, change, delete, and retrieve the data in the database. This language contains commands that permit end users and programming specialists to extract data from the database to satisfy information requests and develop applications. The most prominent data manipulation language today is **Structured Query Language**, or **SQL**. Figure 6.10 illustrates the SQL **query** that would produce the new resultant table in Figure 6.8. A query is a request for data from a database. You can find out more about how to perform SQL queries in our Learning Tracks for this chapter, which can be found in MyMISLab.

Users of DBMS for large and midrange computers, such as DB2, Oracle, or SQL Server, would employ SQL to retrieve information they needed from the database. Microsoft Access

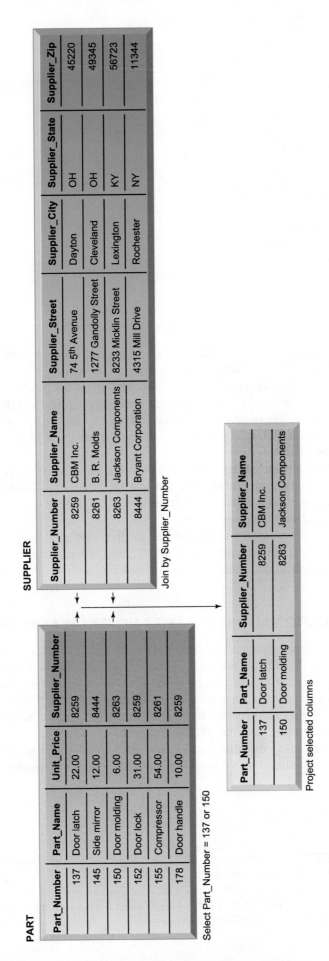

Figure 6.8
The Three Basic Operations of a Relational DBMS
The select, join, and project operations enable data from two different tables to be combined and only selected attributes to be displayed.

Figure 6.9
Access Data
Dictionary Features
*Microsoft Access has
a rudimentary data
dictionary capability
that displays information
about the size, format,
and other characteristics
of each field in a data-
base. Displayed here is
the information main-
tained in the SUPPLIER
table. The small key icon
to the left of Supplier_
Number indicates that it
is a key field.*

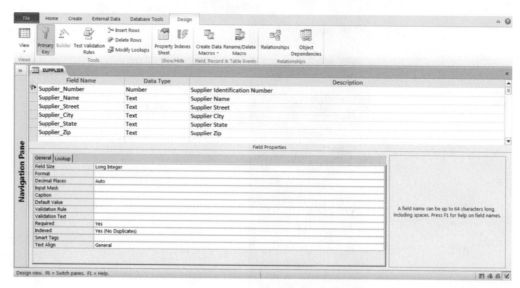

also uses SQL, but it provides its own set of user-friendly tools for querying databases and
for organizing data from databases into more polished reports.

Microsoft Access has capabilities to help users create queries by identifying the tables
and fields they want and the results, and then selecting the rows from the database that meet
particular criteria. These actions in turn are translated into SQL commands. Figure 6.11
illustrates how the SQL query to select parts and suppliers in Figure 6.10 would be constructed using Microsoft Access.

DBMS typically include capabilities for report generation so that the data of interest can
be displayed in a more structured and polished format than would be possible just by querying. Crystal Reports is a popular **report generator** for large corporate DBMS, although it
can also be used with Microsoft Access.

Microsoft Access also has capabilities for developing desktop system applications.
These include tools for creating data entry screens, reports, and developing the logic for
processing transactions. These capabilities are primarily used by information systems
specialists.

NON-RELATIONAL DATABASES AND DATABASES IN THE CLOUD

For over thirty years, relational database technology has been the gold standard. Cloud computing, unprecedented data volumes, massive workloads for Web services, and the need
to store new types of data require database alternatives to the traditional relational model
of organizing data in the form of tables, columns, and rows. Companies are turning to
"*NoSQL*" non-relational-database technologies for this purpose. **Non-relational database
management systems** use a more flexible data model and are designed for managing large
data sets across many distributed machines and for easily scaling up or down. They are
useful for accelerating simple queries against large volumes of structured and unstructured

Figure 6.10
Example of a SQL
Query
*Illustrated here are the
SQL statements for a
query to select suppliers
for parts 137 or 150.
They produce a list with
the same results as
Figure 6.8.*

SELECT PART.Part_Number, PART.Part_Name, SUPPLIER.Supplier_Number,
SUPPLIER.Supplier_Name
FROM PART, SUPPLIER
WHERE PART.Supplier_Number = SUPPLIER.Supplier_Number AND
Part_Number = 137 OR Part_Number = 150;

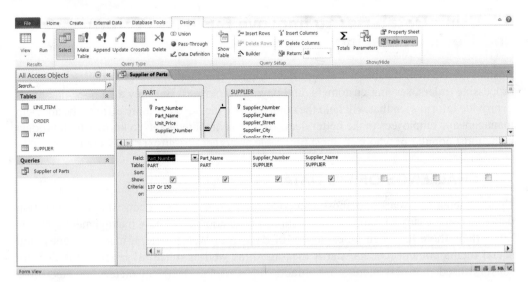

Figure 6.11
An Access Query
Illustrated here is how the query in Figure 6.10 would be constructed using Microsoft Access query-building tools. It shows the tables, fields, and selection criteria used for the query.

data, including Web, social media, graphics, and other forms of data that are difficult to analyze with traditional SQL-based tools.

There are several different kinds of NoSQL databases, each with its own technical features and behavior. Oracle NoSQL Database is one example, as is Amazon's SimpleDB, one of the Amazon Web Services that run in the cloud. SimpleDB provides a simple Web services interface to create and store multiple data sets, query data easily, and return the results. There is no need to pre-define a formal database structure or change that definition if new data sets are added later.

For example, MetLife decided to employ the MongoDB open source NoSQL database to quickly integrate disparate data and deliver a consolidated view of the customer. MetLife's database brings together data from more than 70 separate administrative systems, claims systems and other data sources, including semi-structured and unstructured data, such as images of health records and death certificates. The NoSQL database is able to ingest structured, semi-structured and unstructured information without requiring tedious, expensive and time-consuming database-mapping to normalize all data to a rigid schema, as required by relational databases (Henschen, 2013).

Cloud Databases

Among the services provided by Amazon and other cloud computing vendors are relational database engines. Amazon Relational Database Service (Amazon RDS) offers MySQL, Microsoft SQL Server, or Oracle Database as database engines. Pricing is based on usage. Oracle has its own Database Cloud Services using its relational Oracle Database and Microsoft Windows Azure SQL Database is a cloud-based relational database service based on Microsoft's SQL Server DBMS. Cloud-based data management services have special appeal for Web-focused start-ups or small to medium-sized businesses seeking database capabilities at a lower price than in-house database products.

In addition to public cloud-based data management services, companies now have the option of using databases in private clouds. For example, Sabre Holdings, the world's largest SaaS provider for the aviation industry, has a private database cloud that supports more than 100 projects and 700 users. A consolidated database spanning a pool of standardized servers running Oracle Database 11g provides database services for multiple applications. Workload management tools ensure sufficient resources are available to meet application needs even when the workload changes. The shared hardware and software platform reduces the number of servers, DBMS, and storage devices needed for these projects, which consist of custom airline travel applications along with rail, hotel, and other travel industry applications (Baum, 2011).

6.3 Using Databases to Improve Business Performance and Decision Making

Businesses use their databases to keep track of basic transactions, such as paying suppliers, processing orders, serving customers, and paying employees. But they also need databases to provide information that will help the company run the business more efficiently, and help managers and employees make better decisions. If a company wants to know which product is the most popular or who is its most profitable customer, the answer lies in the data.

THE CHALLENGE OF BIG DATA

Up until about five years ago, most data collected by organizations consisted of transaction data that could easily fit into rows and columns of relational database management systems. Since then, there has been an explosion of data from Web traffic, e-mail messages, and social media content (tweets, status messages), as well as machine-generated data from sensors (used in smart meters, manufacturing sensors, electrical meters, or electronic trading systems.) These data may be unstructured or semi-structured and thus not suitable for relational database products that organize data in the form of columns and rows. We now use the term **big data** to describe these datasets with volumes so huge that they are beyond the ability of typical DBMS to capture, store, and analyze.

Big data doesn't refer to any specific quantity, but usually refers to data in the petabyte and exabyte range—in other words, billions to trillions of records, all from different sources. Big data are produced in much larger quantities and much more rapidly than traditional data. For example, a single jet engine is capable of generating 10 terabytes of data in just 30 minutes, and there are more than 25,000 airline flights each day. Facebook has more than 250 billion photos on the site, and adds 350 million new photos every day. Even though "tweets" are limited to 140 characters each, Twitter generates over 8 terabytes of data daily. Digital information is growing exponentially, from 1.8 zettabytes in 2011 to an expected 35 zettabytes in 2020. According to a Cisco Systems report, if an 11-ounce cup of coffee represented one gigabyte, then one zettabyte would have the same volume as the Great Wall of China.

Businesses are interested in big data because they contain more patterns and interesting anomalies than smaller data sets, with the potential to provide new insights into customer behavior, weather patterns, financial market activity, or other phenomena. For example, Shutterstock, the global online image marketplace, stores 24 million images and adds 10,000 more each day. It analyzes its big data to find out where its Web site visitors place their cursors and how long they hover over an image before making a purchase in order to find ways to optimize the Shutterstock experience.

However, to derive business value from these data, organizations need new technologies and tools capable of managing and analyzing non-traditional data along with their traditional enterprise data. They also need to know what questions to ask of the data and limitations of big data. Capturing, storing, and analyzing big data can be expensive, and information from big data may not necessarily help decision-makers. It's important to have a clear understanding of the problem big data will solve for the business. The chapter-ending case study provides examples of companies using big data as it explores these issues.

BUSINESS INTELLIGENCE INFRASTRUCTURE

Suppose you wanted concise, reliable information about current operations, trends, and changes across the entire company. If you worked in a large company, the data you need might have to be pieced together from separate systems, such as sales, manufacturing in accounting, and even from external sources, such as demographic or competitor data. Increasingly, you might need to use big data. A contemporary infrastructure for business intelligence has an array of tools for obtaining useful information all the different types of data used by businesses today, including semi-structured and unstructured big data in vast quantities. These capabilities include data warehouses and data marts, Hadoop, in-memory computing, and analytical platforms. Some of these capabilities are now available as cloud services.

Data Warehouses and Data Marts

The traditional tool for analyzing corporate data for the past two decades has been the data warehouse. A **data warehouse** is a database that stores current and historical data of potential interest to decision makers throughout the company. The data originate in many core operational transaction systems, such as systems for sales, customer accounts, and manufacturing, and may include data from Web site transactions. The data warehouse extracts current and historical data from multiple operational systems inside the organization. These data are combined with data from external sources and transformed by correcting inaccurate and incomplete data and restructuring the data for management reporting and analysis before being loaded into the data warehouse.

The data warehouse makes the data available for anyone to access as needed, but it cannot be altered. A data warehouse system also provides a range of ad hoc and standardized query tools, analytical tools, and graphical reporting facilities.

Companies often build enterprise-wide data warehouses, where a central data warehouse serves the entire organization, or they create smaller, decentralized warehouses called data marts. A **data mart** is a subset of a data warehouse in which a summarized or highly focused portion of the organization's data is placed in a separate database for a specific population of users. For example, a company might develop marketing and sales data marts to deal with customer information. Bookseller Barnes & Noble used to maintain a series of data marts—one for point-of-sale data in retail stores, another for college bookstore sales, and a third for online sales.

Hadoop

Relational DBMS and data warehouse products are not well-suited for organizing and analyzing big data or data that do not easily fit into columns and rows used in their data models. For handling unstructured and semi-structured data in vast quantities, as well as structured data, organizations are starting to use **Hadoop**. Hadoop is an open-source software framework managed by the Apache Software Foundation that enables distributed parallel processing of huge amounts of data across inexpensive computers. It breaks a big data problem down into sub-problems, distributes them among up to thousands of inexpensive computer processing nodes, and then combines the result into a smaller data set that is easier to analyze. You've probably used Hadoop to find the best airfare on the Internet, get directions to a restaurant, or connect with a friend on Facebook.

Hadoop consists of several key services: the Hadoop Distributed File System (HDFS) for data storage and MapReduce for high-performance parallel data processing. HDFS links together the file systems on the numerous nodes in a Hadoop cluster to turn them into one big file system. Hadoop's MapReduce was inspired by Google's MapReduce system for breaking down processing of huge datasets and assigning work to the various nodes in a cluster. HBase, Hadoop's non-relational database, provides rapid access to the data stored on HDFS and a transactional platform for running high-scale real-time applications.

Hadoop can process large quantities of any kind of data, including structured transactional data, loosely structured data such as Facebook and Twitter feeds, complex data such as Web server log files, and unstructured audio and video data. Hadoop runs on a cluster of inexpensive servers, and processors can be added or removed as needed. Companies use Hadoop for analyzing very large volumes of data as well as for a staging area for unstructured and semi-structured data before they are loaded into a data warehouse. Facebook stores its data on its massive Hadoop cluster, which holds an estimated 100 petabytes, about 10,000 times more information than the Library of Congress. Yahoo! uses Hadoop to track user behavior so it can modify its home page to fit their interests. Life sciences research firm NextBio uses Hadoop and HBase to process data for pharmaceutical companies conducting genomic research. Top database vendors such as IBM, Hewlett-Packard, Oracle, and

Microsoft have their own Hadoop software distributions. Other vendors offer tools for moving data into and out of Hadoop or for analyzing data within Hadoop.

In-Memory Computing

Another way of facilitating big data analysis is to use **in-memory computing**, which relies primarily on a computer's main memory (RAM) for data storage. (Conventional DBMS use disk storage systems.) Users access data stored in system primary memory, thereby eliminating bottlenecks from retrieving and reading data in a traditional, disk-based database and dramatically shortening query response times. In-memory processing makes it possible for very large sets of data, amounting to the size of a data mart or small data warehouse, to reside entirely in memory. Complex business calculations that used to take hours or days are able to be completed within seconds, and this can even be accomplished on handheld devices.

The previous chapter details some of the advances in contemporary computer hardware technology that make in-memory processing possible, such as powerful high-speed processors, multicore processing, and falling computer memory prices. These technologies help companies optimize the use of memory and accelerate processing performance while lowering costs.

Leading commercial products for in-memory computing include SAP's High Performance Analytics Appliance (HANA) and Oracle Exalytics. Each provides a set of integrated software components, including in-memory database software and specialized analytics software, that run on hardware optimized for in-memory computing work.

McLaren Racing is regularly feeding gigabytes of data generated by sensors attached to its race cars into a SAP HANA in-memory computing system to analyze data while the cars are racing. Each McLaren Formula One car generates about 1 gigabyte of raw data during a race, and McLaren engineers can now query the data and receive a response in a tenth of a second. This process used to take two days. McLaren is able to use this information to make adjustments in real time to changing conditions on the race course (Vizard, 2013).

Analytic Platforms

Commercial database vendors have developed specialized high-speed **analytic platforms** using both relational and non-relational technology that are optimized for analyzing large datasets. These analytic platforms, such as IBM Netezza and Oracle Big Data Appliance, feature preconfigured hardware-software systems that are specifically designed for query processing and analytics. For example, IBM Netezza features tightly integrated database, server and storage components that handle complex analytic queries 10 to 100 times faster than traditional systems. Analytic platforms also include in-memory systems and NoSQL non-relational database management systems.

Figure 6.12 illustrates a contemporary business intelligence infrastructure using the technologies we have just described. Current and historical data are extracted from multiple operational systems along with Web data, machine-generated data, unstructured audio/visual data, and data from external sources and restructured and reorganized for reporting and analysis. Hadoop clusters pre-process big data for use in the data warehouse, data marts, or an analytic platform, or for direct querying by power users. Outputs include reports and dashboards as well as query results. Chapter 11 discusses the various types of BI users and BI reporting in greater detail.

ANALYTICAL TOOLS: RELATIONSHIPS, PATTERNS, TRENDS

Once data have been captured and organized using the business intelligence technologies we have just described, they are available for further analysis using software for database querying and reporting, multidimensional data analysis (OLAP), and data mining. This section will introduce you to these tools, with more detail about business intelligence analytics and applications in Chapter 11.

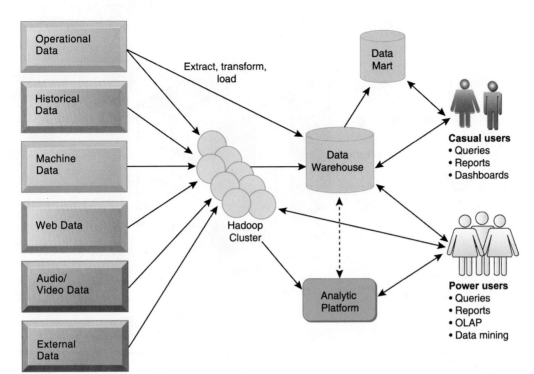

Figure 6.12
Contemporary
Business Intelligence
Infrastructure
*A contemporary busi-
ness intelligence
infrastructure features
capabilities and tools
to manage and analyze
large quantities and
different types of data
from multiple sources.
Easy-to-use query and
reporting tools for
casual business users
and more sophisticated
analytical toolsets
for power users are
included.*

Online Analytical Processing (OLAP)

Suppose your company sells four different products—nuts, bolts, washers, and screws—in the East, West, and Central regions. If you wanted to ask a fairly straightforward question, such as how many washers sold during the past quarter, you could easily find the answer by querying your sales database. But what if you wanted to know how many washers sold in each of your sales regions and compare actual results with projected sales?

To obtain the answer, you would need **online analytical processing (OLAP)**. OLAP supports multidimensional data analysis, enabling users to view the same data in different ways using multiple dimensions. Each aspect of information—product, pricing, cost, region, or time period—represents a different dimension. So, a product manager could use a multi-dimensional data analysis tool to learn how many washers were sold in the East in June, how that compares with the previous month and the previous June, and how it compares with the sales forecast. OLAP enables users to obtain online answers to ad hoc questions such as these in a fairly rapid amount of time, even when the data are stored in very large databases, such as sales figures for multiple years.

Figure 6.13 shows a multidimensional model that could be created to represent products, regions, actual sales, and projected sales. A matrix of actual sales can be stacked on top of a matrix of projected sales to form a cube with six faces. If you rotate the cube 90 degrees one way, the face showing will be product versus actual and projected sales. If you rotate the cube 90 degrees again, you will see region versus actual and projected sales. If you rotate 180 degrees from the original view, you will see projected sales and product versus region. Cubes can be nested within cubes to build complex views of data. A company would use either a specialized multidimensional database or a tool that creates multidimensional views of data in relational databases.

Data Mining

Traditional database queries answer such questions as, "How many units of product number 403 were shipped in February 2014?" OLAP, or multidimensional analysis, supports much more complex requests for information, such as, "Compare sales of product 403 relative to

Figure 6.13
Multidimensional Data Model
This view shows product versus region. If you rotate the cube 90 degrees, the face that will show is product versus actual and projected sales. If you rotate the cube 90 degrees again, you will see region versus actual and projected sales. Other views are possible.

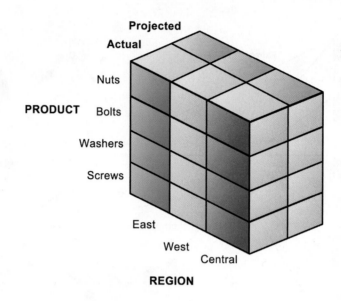

plan by quarter and sales region for the past two years." With OLAP and query-oriented data analysis, users need to have a good idea about the information for which they are looking.

Data mining is more discovery-driven. Data mining provides insights into corporate data that cannot be obtained with OLAP by finding hidden patterns and relationships in large databases and inferring rules from them to predict future behavior. The patterns and rules are used to guide decision making and forecast the effect of those decisions. The types of information obtainable from data mining include associations, sequences, classifications, clusters, and forecasts.

- *Associations* are occurrences linked to a single event. For instance, a study of supermarket purchasing patterns might reveal that, when corn chips are purchased, a cola drink is purchased 65 percent of the time, but when there is a promotion, cola is purchased 85 percent of the time. This information helps managers make better decisions because they have learned the profitability of a promotion.

- In *sequences*, events are linked over time. We might find, for example, that if a house is purchased, a new refrigerator will be purchased within two weeks 65 percent of the time, and an oven will be bought within one month of the home purchase 45 percent of the time.

- *Classification* recognizes patterns that describe the group to which an item belongs by examining existing items that have been classified and by inferring a set of rules. For example, businesses such as credit card or telephone companies worry about the loss of steady customers. Classification helps discover the characteristics of customers who are likely to leave and can provide a model to help managers predict who those customers are so that the managers can devise special campaigns to retain such customers.

- *Clustering* works in a manner similar to classification when no groups have yet been defined. A data mining tool can discover different groupings within data, such as finding affinity groups for bank cards or partitioning a database into groups of customers based on demographics and types of personal investments.

- Although these applications involve predictions, *forecasting* uses predictions in a different way. It uses a series of existing values to forecast what other values will be. For example, forecasting might find patterns in data to help managers estimate the future value of continuous variables, such as sales figures.

These systems perform high-level analyses of patterns or trends, but they can also drill down to provide more detail when needed. There are data mining applications for all the functional areas of business, and for government and scientific work. One popular use for data mining is to provide detailed analyses of patterns in customer data for one-to-one marketing campaigns or for identifying profitable customers. (See the chapter-ending case study.)

Caesars Entertainment, formerly known as Harrah's Entertainment, is the largest gaming company in the world. It continually analyzes data about its customers gathered when people play its slot machines or use its casinos and hotels. The corporate marketing department uses this information to build a detailed gambling profile, based on a particular customer's ongoing value to the company. For instance, data mining lets Caesars know the favorite gaming experience of a regular customer at one of its riverboat casinos, along with that person's preferences for room accommodations, restaurants, and entertainment. This information guides management decisions about how to cultivate the most profitable customers, encourage those customers to spend more, and attract more customers with high revenue-generating potential. Business intelligence improved Caesar's profits so much that it became the centerpiece of the firm's business strategy.

Another organization that has benefited from business intelligence and data mining is the Cincinnati Zoo, described in the Interactive Session on Organizations. As you read this case, think about how what problems were able to be solved by making better use of data available to the Zoo.

Text Mining and Web Mining

Unstructured data, most in the form of text files, is believed to account for over 80 percent of useful organizational information and is one of the major sources of big data that firms want to analyze. E-mail, memos, call center transcripts, survey responses, legal cases, patent descriptions, and service reports are all valuable for finding patterns and trends that will help employees make better business decisions. **Text mining** tools are now available to help businesses analyze these data. These tools are able to extract key elements from unstructured big data sets, discover patterns and relationships, and summarize the information.

Businesses might turn to text mining to analyze transcripts of calls to customer service centers to identify major service and repair issues or to measure customer sentiment about their company. **Sentiment analysis** software is able to mine text comments in an e-mail message, blog, social media conversation, or survey form to detect favorable and unfavorable opinions about specific subjects.

For example, the discount broker Charles Schwab uses Attensity Analyze software to analyze hundreds of thousands of its customer interactions each month. The software analyzes Schwab's customer service notes, e-mails, survey responses, and online discussions to discover signs of dissatisfaction that might cause a customer to stop using the company's services. Attensity is able to automatically identify the various "voices" customers use to express their feedback (such as a positive, negative, or conditional voice) to pinpoint a person's intent to buy, intent to leave, or reaction to a specific product or marketing message. Schwab uses this information to take corrective actions such as stepping up direct broker communication with the customer and trying to quickly resolve the problems that are making the customer unhappy.

The Web is another rich source of unstructured big data for revealing patterns, trends, and insights into customer behavior. The discovery and analysis of useful patterns and information from the World Wide Web is called **Web mining**. Businesses might turn to Web mining to help them understand customer behavior, evaluate the effectiveness of a particular Web site, or quantify the success of a marketing campaign. For instance marketers use Google Trends and Insights for Search services, which track the popularity of various words and phrases used in Google search queries, to learn what people are interested in and what they are interested in buying.

Web mining looks for patterns in data through content mining, structure mining, and usage mining. Web content mining is the process of extracting knowledge from the content of Web pages, which may include text, image, audio and video data. Web structure mining examines data related to the structure of a particular Web site. For example, links

Founded in 1873, the Cincinnati Zoo & Botanical Garden is one of the world's top-rated zoological institutions, and the second oldest zoo in the United States. It is also one of the nation's most popular attractions, a Top 10 Zagat-rated Zoo, and a Parents Magazine Top Zoo for Children. The zoo's 71 acre site is home to more than 500 animal and 3,000 plant species. About 1.2 million people visit this zoo each year.

Although the Zoo is a non-profit organization partially subsidized by Hamilton County, more than two thirds of its $26 million annual budget is paid from fundraising efforts, the remainder coming from tax support, admissions fees, food, and gifts. To increase revenue and improve performance, the Zoo's senior management team embarked on a comprehensive review of its operations. The review found that management had limited knowledge and understanding of what was actually happening in the Zoo on a day-to-day basis, other than how many people visited every day and the zoo's total revenue.

Who is coming to the Zoo? How often do they come? What do they do and what do they buy? Management had no idea. Each of the Zoo's four income streams- admissions, membership, retail and food service- had different point-of-sale platforms, and the food service business, which brings in $4 million a year, still relied on manual cash registers. Management had to sift through paper receipts just to understand daily sales totals.

The Zoo had compiled a spreadsheet that collected visitors' ZIP codes, hoping to use the data for geographic and demographic analysis. If the data could be combined with insight into visitor activity at the Zoo—what attractions they visited, what they ate and drank, and what they bought at the gift shops – the information would be extremely valuable for guiding marketing.

To achieve this, however, the Zoo needed to change its information systems to focus more on analytics and data management. The Zoo replaced its four legacy point of sale systems with a single platform—Galaxy POS from Gateway Ticketing Systems. It then enlisted IBM and BrightStar Partners (a consulting firm partnering with IBM) to build a centralized data warehouse and implement IBM Cognos Business Intelligence to provide real-time analytics and reporting.

Like all outdoor attractions, the zoo's business is highly weather-dependent. On rainy days, attendance falls off sharply, often leaving the Zoo overstaffed and overstocked. If the weather is unusually hot, sales of certain items such as ice cream and bottled water are likely to rise, and the Zoo may run out of these items.

The Zoo now feeds weather forecast data from the U.S. National Oceanic and Atmospheric Administration (NOAA) Website into its business intelligence system. By comparing current forecasts to historic attendance and sales data during similar weather conditions , the Zoo is able to make more accurate decisions about labor scheduling and inventory planning.

As visitors scan their membership cards at the Zoo's entrance, exit, attractions, restaurants, and stores, or use the Zoo's Loyalty Rewards card, the Zoo's system captures these data and analyzes them to determine usage and spending patterns down to the individual customer level. This information helps the Zoo segment visitors based on their spending and visitation behaviors and use this information to target marketing and promotions specifically for each customer segment.

One customer segment the Zoo identified consisted of people who spent nothing other than the price of admissions during their visit. If each of these people spent $20 on their next visit to the Zoo, the Zoo would take in an extra $260,000, which is almost 1 percent of its entire budget. The Zoo used its customer information to devise a direct mail marketing campaign in which this type of visitor would be offered a discount for some of the Zoo's restaurants and gift shops. Loyal customers are also rewarded with targeted marketing and recognition programs.

Instead of sending a special offer to its entire mailing list, the Zoo is able to tailor campaigns more precisely to smaller groups of people, increasing its chances of identifying the people who were most likely to respond to its mailings. More targeted marketing helped the Zoo cut $40,000 from its annual marketing budget.

Management had observed that food sales tend to tail off significantly after 3 PM each day, and started closing some of the Zoo's food outlets at that time. But more detailed data analysis showed that a big spike in soft-serve ice cream sales occurs during the last hour before the Zoo closes. As a result, the Zoo's soft-serve ice cream outlets are open for the entire day.

The Zoo's 'Beer Hut' concession features six different brands, which are typically rotated based on sales volume and the seasons. With IBM analytics, management can now instantly identify which beer is selling best, on what day, and at what time to make sure inventory meets demand. Previously, it took seven to 14 days to get this information, which required hiring part-time staff to sift through register tapes.

The Zoo's ability to make better decisions about operations has led to dramatic improvements in sales. Six months after deploying its business intelligence solution, the Zoo achieved a 30.7 percent increase in food sales, and a 5.9 percent increase in retail sales compared to the same period a year earlier.

Sources: "Zoo Wants Additional Revenue from Taxes," Cincinnati.com, January 18, 2013; www.cincinnatizoo.org, accessed March 5, 2012; IBM Corporation, "Cincinnati Zoo Improves Customer Experience and Enhances Performance," 2011; and Nucleus Research, "IBM ROI Case Study: Cincinnati Zoo," July 2011.

CASE STUDY QUESTIONS

1. What people, organization, and technology factors were behind Cincinnati Zoo losing opportunities to increase revenue?

2. Why was replacing legacy point-of-sale systems and implementing a data warehouse essential to an information system solution?

3. Describe the types of information gleaned from data mining that helped the Zoo better understand visitor behavior.

4. How did the Cincinnati Zoo benefit from business intelligence? How did it enhance operational performance and decision making?

5. The Zoo's management recently stated that it might have to ask for more revenue from taxes in order to provide the same level of quality and service in the future. How might business intelligence be used to prevent this from happening?

---

pointing to a document indicate the popularity of the document, while links coming out of a document indicate the richness or perhaps the variety of topics covered in the document. Web usage mining examines user interaction data recorded by a Web server whenever requests for a Web site's resources are received. The usage data records the user's behavior when the user browses or makes transactions on the Web site and collects the data in a server log. Analyzing such data can help companies determine the value of particular customers, cross marketing strategies across products, and the effectiveness of promotional campaigns.

The chapter-ending case study describes organizations' experiences as they use the analytical tools and business intelligence technologies we have described to grapple with "big data" challenges.

DATABASES AND THE WEB

Many companies are using the Web to make some of the information in their internal databases available to customers and business partners. Prospective customers might use a company's Web site to view the company's product catalog or to place an order. The company in turn might use the Web to check inventory availability for that product from its supplier. That supplier in turn may have to check with its own suppliers as well as delivery firms needed to ship the products on time.

These actions involve accessing and (in the case of ordering) updating corporate databases through the Web. Suppose, for example, a customer with a Web browser wants to search an online retailer's database for pricing information. Figure 6.14 illustrates how that customer might access the retailer's internal database over the Web. The user would access the retailer's Web site over the Internet using Web browser software on his or her client PC. The user's Web browser software would request data from the organization's database, using HTML commands to communicate with the Web server.

Because many "back-end" databases cannot interpret commands written in HTML, the Web server would pass these requests for data to software that translates HTML commands into SQL so that they can be processed by the DBMS working with the database. In a client/server environment, the DBMS resides on a dedicated computer called a **database server**. The DBMS receives the SQL requests and provides the required data. The information is transferred from the organization's internal database back to the Web server for delivery in the form of a Web page to the user.

Figure 6.14 shows that the software working between the Web server and the DBMS could be on an application server running on its own dedicated computer (see Chapter 5). The application server software handles all application operations, including transaction processing and data access, between browser-based computers and a company's back-end business applications or databases. The application server takes requests from the Web server, runs the business logic to process transactions based on those requests, and provides connectivity to the organization's back-end systems or databases. Alternatively, the software for handling these operations could be a custom program or a CGI script. A CGI script is a compact program using the *Common Gateway Interface (CGI)* specification for processing data on a Web server.

There are a number of advantages to using the Web to access an organization's internal databases. First, everyone knows how to use Web browser software, and employees require much less training than if they used proprietary query tools. Second, the Web interface requires few or no changes to the internal database. Companies leverage their investments in older systems because it costs much less to add a Web interface in front of a legacy system than to redesign and rebuild the system to improve user access. For this reason, most large Fortune 500 firms have back-end legacy databases running on mainframe computers that are linked to "front-end" software that makes the information available in the form of a Web page to users on request.

Accessing corporate databases through the Web is creating new efficiencies and opportunities, and, in some cases, it is even changing the way business is being done. ThomasNet.com provides an up-to-date directory of information from more than 600,000 suppliers of industrial products, such as chemicals, metals, plastics, rubber, and automotive equipment. Formerly called Thomas Register, the company used to send out huge paper catalogs with this information. Now, it provides this information to users online via its Web site and has become a smaller, leaner company.

Other companies have created entirely new businesses based on access to large databases through the Web. One is the social networking service Facebook, which helps users stay connected with each other and meet new people. Facebook features "profiles" with information on more than 1.1 billion active users with information about themselves, including interests, friends, photos, and groups with which they are affiliated. Facebook maintains a massive database to house and manage all of this content.

Figure 6.14
Linking Internal Databases to the Web
Users access an organization's internal database through the Web using their desktop PCs and Web browser software.

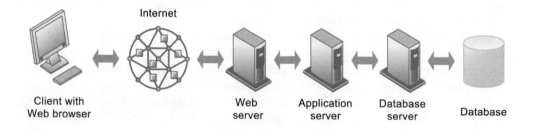

Client with Web browser   Internet   Web server   Application server   Database server   Database

6.4 Managing Data Resources

Setting up a database is only a start. In order to make sure that the data for your business remain accurate, reliable, and readily available to those who need it, your business will need special policies and procedures for data management.

ESTABLISHING AN INFORMATION POLICY

Every business, large and small, needs an information policy. Your firm's data are an important resource, and you don't want people doing whatever they want with them. You need to have rules on how the data are to be organized and maintained, and who is allowed to view the data or change them.

An **information policy** specifies the organization's rules for sharing, disseminating, acquiring, standardizing, classifying, and inventorying information. Information policies lay out specific procedures and accountabilities, identifying which users and organizational units can share information, where information can be distributed, and who is responsible for updating and maintaining the information. For example, a typical information policy would specify that only selected members of the payroll and human resources department would have the right to change and view sensitive employee data, such as an employee's salary or social security number, and that these departments are responsible for making sure that such employee data are accurate.

If you are in a small business, the information policy would be established and implemented by the owners or managers. In a large organization, managing and planning for information as a corporate resource often requires a formal data administration function. **Data administration** is responsible for the specific policies and procedures through which data can be managed as an organizational resource. These responsibilities include developing information policy, planning for data, overseeing logical database design and data dictionary development, and monitoring how information systems specialists and end-user groups use data.

A large organization will also have a database design and management group within the corporate information systems division that is responsible for defining and organizing the structure and content of the database, and maintaining the database. In close cooperation with users, the design group establishes the physical database, the logical relations among elements, and the access rules and security procedures. The functions it performs are called **database administration**.

ENSURING DATA QUALITY

A well-designed database and information policy will go a long way toward ensuring that the business has the information it needs. However, additional steps must be taken to ensure that the data in organizational databases are accurate and remain reliable.

What would happen if a customer's telephone number or account balance were incorrect? What would be the impact if the database had the wrong price for the product you sold? Data that are inaccurate, untimely, or inconsistent with other sources of information create serious operational and financial problems for businesses. When faulty data go unnoticed, they often lead to incorrect decisions, product recalls, and even financial losses.

Gartner Group consultants reported that more than 25 percent of the critical data in large Fortune 1000 companies' databases is inaccurate or incomplete, including bad product codes and product descriptions, faulty inventory descriptions, erroneous financial data, incorrect supplier information, and incorrect employee data.

Some of these data quality problems are caused by redundant and inconsistent data produced by multiple systems feeding a data warehouse. For example, the sales ordering system and the inventory management system might both maintain data on the organization's products. However, the sales ordering system might use the term *Item Number* and the inventory system might call the same attribute *Product Number.* The sales, inventory, or manufacturing systems of a clothing retailer might use different codes to represent values for an attribute. One system might represent clothing size as "extra large," whereas the other system might use the code "XL" for the same purpose. During the design process for the warehouse database, data describing entities, such as a customer, product, or order, should be named and defined consistently for all business areas using the database.

If a database is properly designed and enterprise-wide data standards established, duplicate or inconsistent data elements should be minimal. Most data quality problems, however, such as misspelled names, transposed numbers, or incorrect or missing codes, stem from errors during data input. The incidence of such errors is rising as companies move their businesses to the Web and allow customers and suppliers to enter data into their Web sites that directly update internal systems.

Think of all the times you have received several pieces of the same direct mail advertising on the same day. This is very likely the result of having your name maintained multiple times in a database. Your name may have been misspelled or you used your middle initial on one occasion and not on another or the information was initially entered onto a paper form and not scanned properly into the system. Because of these inconsistencies, the database would treat you as different people! We often receive redundant mail addressed to Laudon, Lavdon, Lauden, or Landon.

Before a new database is in place, organizations need to identify and correct their faulty data and establish better routines for editing data once their database is in operation. Analysis of data quality often begins with a **data quality audit**, which is a structured survey of the accuracy and level of completeness of the data in an information system. Data quality audits can be performed by surveying entire data files, surveying samples from data files, or surveying end users for their perceptions of data quality.

Data cleansing, also known as *data scrubbing*, consists of activities for detecting and correcting data in a database that are incorrect, incomplete, improperly formatted, or redundant. Data cleansing not only corrects data but also enforces consistency among different sets of data that originated in separate information systems. Specialized data-cleansing software is available to automatically survey data files, correct errors in the data, and integrate the data in a consistent company-wide format.

The Interactive Session on People illustrates American Water's experience with managing data as a resource. As you read this case, try to identify the policies, procedures, and technologies that were required to improve data management at this company.

Review Summary

1 **How does a relational database organize data?** The relational database is the primary method for organizing and maintaining data today in information system. It organizes data in two-dimensional tables with rows and columns called relations. Each table contains data about an entity and its attributes. Each row represents a record and each column represents an attribute or field. Each table also contains a key field to uniquely identify each record for retrieval or manipulation. An entity-relationship diagram graphically depicts the relationship between entities (tables) in a relational database. The process of breaking down complex groupings of data and streamlining them to minimize redundancy and awkward many-to-many relationships is called normalization. Non-relational databases are becoming popular for managing types of data that can't be handled easily by the relational data model.

2 **What are the principles of a database management system?** A DBMS consists of software that permits centralization of data and data management so that businesses have a single consistent source for all their data needs. A single database services multiple

American Water, founded in 1886, is the largest public water utility in the United States. Headquartered in Voorhees, N.J., the company employs more than 7,000 dedicated professionals who provide drinking water, wastewater and other related services to approximately 16 million people in 35 states, as well as Ontario and Manitoba, Canada. Most of American Water's services support locally-managed utility subsidiaries that are regulated by the U.S. state in which each operates as well as the federal government. American Water also owns subsidiaries that manage municipal drinking water and wastewater systems under contract and others that supply businesses and residential communities with water management products and services.

Until recently, American Water's systems and business processes were very localized, and many of these processes were manual. Over time, this information environment became increasingly difficult to manage. Many systems were not integrated, so that running any type of report that had to provide information about more than one region was a heavily manual process. Data had to be extracted from the systems supporting each region and then combined manually to create the desired output. When the company was preparing to hold an initial public offering of its stock in 2006, its software systems could not handle the required regulatory controls, so roughly 80 percent of this work had to be performed manually. It was close to a nightmare.

Management wanted to change the company from a decentralized group of independent regional businesses into a more centralized organization with standard company-wide business processes and enterprise-wide reporting. The first step toward achieving this goal was to implement an enterprise resource planning (ERP) system designed to replace disparate systems with a single integrated software platform. The company selected SAP as its ERP system vendor.

An important step of this project was to migrate the data from American Water's old systems to the new platform. The company's data resided in many different systems in various formats. Each regional business maintained some of its own data in its own systems, and a portion of these data were redundant and inconsistent. For example, there were duplicate pieces of materials master data because a material might be called one thing in the company's Missouri operation and another in its New Jersey business. These names had to be standardized so that the same name for a piece of data was used by every business unit. American Water's business users had to buy into this new company-wide view of data.

Data migration entails much more than just transferring data between old and new systems. Business users need to know that data are not just a responsibility of the information systems department: the business "owns" the data. It is business needs that determine the rules and standards for managing the data. Therefore, it is up to business users to inventory and review all the pieces of data in their systems to determine precisely which pieces of data from the old system will be used in the new system and which data do not need to be brought over. The data also need to be reviewed to make sure they are accurate and consistent and that redundant data are eliminated.

Most likely some type of data cleansing will be required. For example, American Water had data on more than 70,000 vendors in its vendor master data file. Andrew Clarkson, American Water's Business Intelligence Lead, asked business users to define an active vendor and to use that definition to identify which data to migrate. He also worked with various functional groups to standardize how to present address data.

One of the objectives of American Water's data management work was to support an enterprise-wide business intelligence program based on a single view of the business. An analytical system and data warehouse would be able to combine data from the SAP ERP System with data from other sources, including new customer information and enterprise asset management systems. That meant that American Water's business users had to do a lot of thinking about the kinds of reports they wanted. The company had originally planned to have the system provide 200 reports, but later reduced that number by half. Business users were trained to generate these reports and customize then. Most financial users initially tried to create their reports using Microsoft Excel spreadsheet software. Over time, however, they learned to do the same thing using SAP Business Objects Web Intelligence tools that came with the system. SAP Business Objects Web Intelligence is a set of tools that enables business users to view, sort, and analyze business intelligence data. It includes tools for generating queries, reports and interactive dashboards.

At present, American Water is focusing on promoting the idea that data must be "clean" to be effective and has poured an incredible amount of effort into its data cleansing work—identifying incomplete, incorrect, inaccurate, and irrelevant pieces of data and then replacing, modifying, or deleting the "dirty" data. According to Clarkson, just as water treatment plants have measurements and meters to check water quality as its being treated, data management needs to ensure the quality of data at every step to make sure the final product will be genuinely useful for the company.

Sources: David Hannon, "Clean Smooth-Flowing Data at American Water," SAP Insider Profiles, January-March 2013 and www.amwater.com, accessed March 2, 2013.

CASE STUDY QUESTIONS

1. Discuss the role of information policy, data administration, and efforts to ensure data quality in improving data management at American Water.

2. Describe roles played by information systems specialists and end users in American Water's systems transformation project.

3. Why was the participation of business users so important? If they didn't play this role, what would have happened?

4. How did implementing a data warehouse help American Water move toward a more centralized organization?

5. Give some examples of problems that would have occurred at American Water if its data were not "clean"?

6. How would American Water's data warehouse improve operations and management decision making?

applications. The DBMS separates the logical and physical views of data so that the user does not have to be concerned with the data's physical location. The principal capabilities of a DBMS includes a data definition capability, a data dictionary capability, and a data manipulation language.

3 **What are the principal tools and technologies for accessing information from databases to improve business performance and decision making?** Contemporary data management technology has an array of tools for obtaining useful information from all the different types of data used by businesses today, including semi-structured and unstructured big data in vast quantities. These capabilities include data warehouses and data marts, Hadoop, in-memory computing, and analytical platforms. OLAP represents relationships among data as a multidimensional structure, which can be visualized as cubes of data and cubes within cubes of data. Data mining analyzes large pools of data, including the contents of data warehouses, to find patterns and rules that can be used to predict future behavior and guide decision making. Text mining tools help businesses analyze large unstructured data sets consisting of text. Web mining tools focus on analyzing useful patterns and information from the World Wide Web, examining the structure of Web sites, activities of Web site users, and the contents of Web pages. Conventional databases can be linked to the Web or a Web interface to facilitate user access to an organization's internal data.

4 **What is the role of information policy and data administration in the management of organizational data resources?** Developing a database environment requires policies and procedures for managing organizational data as well as a good data model and database technology. A formal information policy governs the maintenance, distribution, and use of information in the organization. In large corporations, a formal data administration function is responsible for information policy, as well as for data planning, data dictionary development, and monitoring data usage in the firm.

5 **Why is data quality assurance so important for a business?** Data that are inaccurate, incomplete, or inconsistent create serious operational and financial problems for businesses if they lead to inaccurate decisions about the actions that should be taken by the firm. Assuring data quality involves using enterprise-wide data standards, databases designed to minimize inconsistent and redundant data, data quality audits, and data cleansing software.

Key Terms

Analytic platform, 222
Attributes, 210
Big data, 220
Data administration, 229
Data cleansing, 230
Data definition, 216
Data dictionary, 216
Data manipulation language, 216
Data mart, 221
Data mining, 224
Data quality audit, 230
Data warehouse, 221
Database, 209
Database administration, 229

Database management system (DBMS), 215
Database server, 228
Entity, 210
Entity-relationship diagram, 212
Field, 210
Foreign key, 211
Hadoop, 221
Information policy, 229
In-memory computing, 222
Key field, 210
Non-relational database management systems, 218
Normalization, 213

Online analytical processing (OLAP), 223
Primary key, 210
Query, 216
Records, 210
Referential integrity, 213
Relational database, 210
Report generator, 218
Sentiment analysis, 225
Structured Query Language (SQL), 216
Text mining, 225
Tuples, 210
Web mining, 225

Review Questions

6-1 How does a relational database organize data?
- Define and explain the significance of entities, attributes, and key fields.
- Define a relational database and explain how it organizes and stores information.
- Explain the role of entity-relationship diagrams and normalization in database design.
- Define referential integrity and explain its role in relational database systems.

6-2 What are the principles of a database management system?
- Define a database management system (DBMS), describe how it works, and explain how it benefits organizations.
- Define and compare the logical and a physical view of data.
- Define and describe the three operations of a relational database management system.
- Name and describe the three major capabilities of a DBMS.

6-3 What are the principal tools and technologies for accessing information from databases to improve business performance and decision making?
- Define big data and describe the technologies for managing and analyzing big data.
- List and describe the components of a contemporary business intelligence infrastructure.
- Define data warehouse and explain how it differs from a data mart.
- Define data mining, describe what types of information can be obtained from it, and explain how does it differs from online analytical processing (OLAP).
- Explain how text mining and Web mining differ from conventional data mining.
- Explain how users can access information from a company's internal databases through the Web.

6-4 What is the role of information policy and data administration in the management of organizational data resources?
- Explain why an organization needs an information policy.

6-5 Why is data quality assurance so important for a business?
- List and describe the most common data quality problems.
- Explain how data quality problems arise.
- List and describe the most important tools and techniques for assuring data quality.

Discussion Questions

6-6 It has been said that you do not need database management software to create a database environment. Discuss.

6-7 Why is big data so interesting to businesses? What challenges does big data present?

6-8 What are the consequences of an organization not having an information policy?

Hands-On MIS Projects

MANAGEMENT DECISION PROBLEMS

6-9 Iko Instruments Group, a global supplier of measurement, analytical, and monitoring instruments and services based in the Netherlands, had a new data warehouse designed to analyze customer activity to improve service and marketing. However, the data warehouse was full of inaccurate and redundant data. The data in the warehouse came from numerous transaction processing systems in the United States, Europe, Asia, and other locations around the world. The team that designed the warehouse had assumed that sales groups in all these areas would enter customer names, telephone numbers, and addresses the same way. In fact, companies in different countries were using multiple ways of entering quote, billing, shipping, contact information and other data. Assess the potential business impact of these data quality problems. What decisions have to be made and steps taken to reach a solution?

6-10 Your industrial supply company wants to create a data warehouse where management can obtain a single corporate-wide view of critical sales information to identify bestselling products, key customers, and sales trends. Your sales and product information are stored in several different systems: a divisional sales system running on a UNIX server and a corporate sales system running on an IBM mainframe. You would like to create a single standard format that consolidates these data from both systems. In MyMISLab, you can review the proposed format, along with sample files from the two systems that would supply the data for the data warehouse. Then answer the following questions:

- What business problems are created by not having these data in a single standard format?
- How easy would it be to create a database with a single standard format that could store the data from both systems? Identify the problems that would have to be addressed.
- Should the problems be solved by database specialists or general business managers? Explain.
- Who should have the authority to finalize a single company-wide format for this information in the data warehouse?

ACHIEVING OPERATIONAL EXCELLENCE: BUILDING A RELATIONAL DATABASE FOR INVENTORY MANAGEMENT

Software skills: Database design, querying, and reporting
Business skills: Inventory management

6-11 In this exercise, you will use database software to design a database for managing inventory for a small business. Sylvester's Bike Shop, located in San Francisco, California, sells road, mountain, hybrid, leisure, and children's bicycles. Currently, Sylvester's purchases bikes from three suppliers, but plans to add new suppliers in the near future. Using the information found in the tables in MyMISLab, build a simple relational database to manage information about Sylvester's suppliers and products. MyMISLab contains more details about the specifications for the database.

Once you have built the database, perform the following activities.
- Prepare a report that identifies the five most expensive bicycles. The report should list the bicycles in descending order from most expensive to least expensive, the quantity on hand for each, and the markup percentage for each.
- Prepare a report that lists each supplier, its products, the quantities on hand, and associated reorder levels. The report should be sorted alphabetically by supplier. Within each supplier category, the products should be sorted alphabetically.
- Prepare a report listing only the bicycles that are low in stock and need to be reordered. The report should provide supplier information for the items identified.
- Write a brief description of how the database could be enhanced to further improve management of the business. What tables or fields should be added? What additional reports would be useful?

IMPROVING DECISION MAKING: SEARCHING ONLINE DATABASES FOR OVERSEAS BUSINESS RESOURCES

Software skills: Online databases
Business skills: Researching services for overseas operations

6-12 This project develops skills in searching online Web-enabled databases with information about products and services in faraway locations.

Your company, Caledonian Furniture, is located in Cumbernauld, Scotland, and manufactures office furniture of various types. You are considering opening a facility to manufacture and sell your products in Australia. You would like to contact organizations that offer many services necessary for you to open your Australian office and manufacturing facility, including lawyers, accountants, import-export experts, and telecommunications equipment and support firms. Access the following online databases to locate companies that you would like to meet with during your upcoming trip: Australian Business Register, AustraliaTrade Now (www.australiatradenow.com), and the Nationwide Business Directory of Australia (www.nationwide.com.au). If necessary, use search engines such as Yahoo! and Google.
- List the companies you would contact on your trip to determine whether they can help you with these and any other functions you think are vital to establishing your office.
- Rate the databases you used for accuracy of name, completeness, ease of use, and general helpfulness.

Collaboration and Teamwork Project

6-13 In MyMISLab, you will find a Collaboration and Teamwork Project dealing with the concepts in this chapter. You will be able to use Google Drive, Google Docs, Google Sites, Google+, or other open-source tools to complete the assignment.

BUSINESS PROBLEM-SOLVING CASE

Does Big Data Bring Big Rewards?

Today's companies are dealing with an avalanche of data from social media, search, and sensors as well as from traditional sources. In 2012, an estimated 988 exabytes of digital information was generated, equivalent to a stack of books from the sun to Pluto and back. Making sense of "big data" has become one of the primary challenges for corporations of all shapes and sizes, but it also represents new opportunities. How are companies currently taking advantage of "big data?"

U.S. state and federal law enforcement agencies are analyzing big data to discover hidden patterns in criminal activity such as correlations between time, opportunity, and organizations, or non-obvious relationships (see Chapter 4) between individuals and criminal organizations that would be difficult to uncover in smaller data sets. New tools allow agencies to analyze data from a wide array of sources, including the Internet, and apply analytics to predict future crime patterns.

In New York City, the Real Time Crime Center data warehouse contains millions of data points on city crime and criminals. IBM and the New York Police Department (NYPD) worked together to create the warehouse, which contains data on over 120 million criminal complaints, 31 million national crime records, and 33 billion public records. The system's search capabilities allow the NYPD to quickly obtain data from any of these data sources. Information on criminals, such as a suspect's photo with details of past offenses or addresses with maps, can be visualized in seconds on a video wall or instantly relayed to officers at a crime scene.

Other organizations are using the data to go green, or, in the case of Vestas, to go even greener. Headquartered in Denmark, Vestas is the world's largest wind energy company, with over 43,000 wind turbines across 66 countries. Location data are important to Vestas so that it can accurately place its turbines for optimal wind power generation. Areas without enough wind will not generate the necessary power, but areas with too much wind may damage the turbines. Vestas relies on location-based data to determine the best spots to install their turbines.

To gather data on prospective turbine locations, Vestas's wind library combines data from global weather systems along with data from existing turbines. The company's previous wind library provided information in a grid pattern, with each grid measuring 27 x 27 kilometers (17x17 miles). Vestas engineers were able to bring the resolution down to about 10x10 meters (32x32 feet) to establish the exact wind flow pattern at a particular location. To further increase the accuracy of its turbine placement models, Vestas needed to shrink the grid area even more, and this required ten times as much data as the previous system and a more powerful data management platform.

The company implemented a solution consisting of IBM InfoSphereBigInsights software running on a high-performance IBM System x iDataPlex server. (InfoSphereBigInsights is a set of software tools for "big data" analysis and visualization and is powered by Apache Hadoop.) Using these technologies, Vestas increased the size of its wind library and is able to manage and analyze location and weather data with models that are much more powerful and precise.

Vestas's wind library currently stores 2.8 petabytes of data and includes approximately 178 parameters, such as barometric pressure, humidity, wind direction, temperature, wind velocity, and other company historical data. Vestas plans to add global deforestation metrics, satellite images, geospatial data, and data on phases of the moon and tides.

The company can now reduce the resolution of its wind data grids by nearly 90 percent, down to a 3x3 kilometer area (about 1.8x1.8 miles). This capability enables Vestas to forecast optimal turbine placement in 15 minutes instead of three weeks, saving a month of development time for a turbine site and enabling Vestas customers to achieve a return on investment much more quickly.

AutoZone uses big data to help it adjust inventory and product prices at some of its 5,000 stores. For example, a customer walking into an AutoZone store in Waco, Texas, might find a deal on Gabriel shocks which that person would not find in most other AutoZone stores. The Mulberry, Florida AutoZone store might feature a special on a bug deflector. To target these deals at the local level, the auto parts retailer analyzes information gleaned from a variety of databases, such as the types of cars driven by people living around its retail outlets. Software from NuoDB, which uses a cloud services model, makes it possible to quickly increase the amount of data analyzed without bringing down the system, or changing a line of code.

Companies are also using big data solutions to analyze consumer sentiment. For example, car-rental giant Hertz gathers data from Web surveys, e-mails, text messages, Web site traffic patterns, and data generated at all of Hertz's 8,300 locations in 146 countries. The company now stores all of that data centrally instead of within each branch, reducing time spent processing data and improving company response time to customer feedback and changes in sentiment. For example, by analyzing data generated from multiple sources, Hertz was able to determine that delays were occurring for returns in Philadelphia during specific times of the day. After investigating this anomaly, the company was able to quickly adjust staffing levels at its Philadelphia office during those peak times, ensuring a manager was present to resolve any issues. This enhanced Hertz's performance, and increased customer satisfaction.

There are limits to using big data. A number of companies have rushed to start big data projects without first establishing a business goal for this new information. Swimming in numbers doesn't necessarily mean that the right information is being collected or that people will make smarter decisions.

Several years ago, Google developed what it thought was a leading-edge algorithm using data it collected from Web searches to determine exactly how many people had influenza. It tried to calculate the number of people with flu in the United States by relating people's location to flu-related search queries on Google. According to Google Flu Trends, nearly 11 percent of the U.S. population was supposed to have had influenza at the flu season's peak in mid-January 2013. However, an article in the science journal Nature stated that Google's results were twice the actual amount estimated by the U.S. Centers for Disease Control and Prevention, which had 6 percent of the population coming down with the disease. Why did this happen? Several scientists suggested that Google was "tricked" by widespread media coverage of this year's severe flu season in the U.S, which was further amplified by social media coverage. Google's algorithm only looked at numbers, not the context of the search results.

Sears Holdings, the parent company of Sears and Kmart, is trying to use big data to get closer to its customers. Sears used to be the largest retailer in the United States, but for many years has steadily lost ground to discounters such as Walmart and Target and to competitively-priced specialty retailers such as Home Depot and Lowe's. The company has been slow to reduce operating costs, keep pace with current merchandising trends, and remodel its 2,173 U.S. stores, many of which are run-down and in undesirable locations.

Over the years, Sears had invested heavily in information technology. At one time it spent more on information technology and networking than all other non-computer firms in the United States except the Boeing Corporation. Sears used its huge customer databases of 60 million past and present Sears credit card holders to target groups such as tool buyers, appliance buyers, and gardening enthusiasts with special promotions. These efforts did not translate into competitive

advantage because Sears's cost structure remained one of the highest in its industry.

The Sears company has continued to embrace new technology to revive flagging sales: online shopping, mobile apps, and an Amazon.com-like marketplace with other vendors for 18 million products, along with heavy in-store promotions. So far, these efforts have not paid off, and sales have declined since the 2005 merger with Kmart. The company posted a loss of $930 million for 2012.

Sears Holdings CEO Lou D'Ambrosio thinks that even more intensive use of technology and mining of customer data will be the answer. The expectation is that deeper knowledge of customer preferences and buying patterns will make promotions, merchandising, and selling much more effective. Customers will flock to Sears stores because they will be carrying exactly what they want.

A customer loyalty program called Shop Your Way Rewards promises customers generous free deals for repeat purchases if they agree to share their personal shopping data with the company. Sears would not disclose how many customers have signed up for Shop Your Way Rewards, but loyalty-marketing firm Colloquy estimates around 50 million people are members.

Sears wants to personalize marketing campaigns, coupons, and offers down to the individual customer, but its legacy systems were incapable of supporting that level of activity. In order to use big models on large data sets, Sears turned to Apache Hadoop and big data technology. It used to take Sears six weeks to analyze marketing campaigns for loyalty club members using a mainframe, Teradata data warehouse software, and SAS servers. Using Hadoop, the processing can be completed weekly. Certain online and mobile commerce analyses can be performed daily and targeting is much more precise, in some cases down to the individual customer. Sears's old models were able to use 10 percent of available data, but the new models are able to work with 100 percent. In the past, Sears was only able to retain data from 90 days to two years, but with Hadoop, it can keep everything, increasing its chances of finding more meaningful patterns in the data.

What's more, Hadoop processing is much less costly than conventional relational databases. A Hadoop system handling 200 terabytes of data runs about one-third the cost of a 200-terabyte relational platform. With Hadoop's massively parallel processing power, processing 2 billion records takes Sears little more than one minute longer than processing 100 million records.

Hadoop is still an immature platform, and Hadoop expertise is scarce. Sears had to learn Hadoop largely by trial and error. But it now runs critical reports on the platform, including analyses of customers, financial data, products, and supply chains. Capitalizing on its experience as a big-data innovator, Sears set up a subsidiary called MetaScale to sell big data cloud and consulting services to other companies.

Sears can point to many conceptual uses of Hadoop, but the question still lingers about whether the company is effectively using Hadoop to solve its enormous business problems. Is it truly able to offer customers personalized promotions and are they working? What is the business impact? Where are the numbers to show that big data is helping Sears become more profitable? Sears may be able to generate revenue by selling big data expertise to MetaScale customers, but will Hadoop really help turn Sears around?

Jim Sullivan, a partner at loyalty marketing firm Colloquy, notes that a good loyalty program that gives a company better intelligence about what its customers really want can be a strategic advantage, but even the best loyalty programs can't fix a fundamentally broken brand.

Sources: Rachael King and Steven Rosenbush. "Big Data Broadens Its Range." *The Wall Street Journal* (March 13, 2013; Nick Bilton, "Disruptions: Data Without a Context Tells a Misleading Story," *The New York Times*, February 24, 2013; Shira Ovide, "Big Data, Big Blunders," *The Wall Street Journal*, March 11, 2013; Mark A. Smith, "Big Data Pointless without Integration," *Information Management*, February 25, 2013; Frank Konkel, "Fast Failure Could Lead to Big-Data Success," *Federal Computer Week*, January 30, 2013; Doug Henschen, "Why Sears Is Going All-in on Hadoop," *Information Week*, October 3, 2012; Samuel Greengard,"Big Data Unlocks Business Value." Baseline, January 2012; Paul S. Barth, "Managing Big Data: What Every CIO Needs to Know," *CIO Insight*, January 12, 2012; IBM Corporation, "Vestas: Turning Climate into Capital with Big Data," 2011; IBM Corporation, "Extending and Enhancing Law Enforcement Capabilities" and "How Big Data Is Giving Hertz a Big Advantage," 2010.

Case Study Questions

6-14 Describe the kinds of "big data" collected by the organizations described in this case.

6-15 List and describe the business intelligence technologies described in this case.

6-16 Why did the companies described in this case need to maintain and analyze big data? What business benefits did they obtain? How much were they helped by analyzing big data?

6-17 Identify three decisions that were improved by using big data.

6-18 Should all organizations try to analyze big data? Why or why not? What people, organization, and technology issues should be addressed before a company decides to work with big data?

Telecommunications, the Internet, and Wireless Technology

STUDENT LEARNING OBJECTIVES

After completing this chapter, you will be able to answer the following questions:

1. What are the principal components of telecommunications networks and key networking technologies?

2. What are the different types of networks?

3. How do the Internet and Internet technology work and how do they support communication and e-business?

4. What are the principal technologies and standards for wireless networking, communication, and Internet access?

5. Why are radio frequency identification (RFID) and wireless sensor networks valuable for business?

LEARNING TRACKS

1. Broadband Network Services and Technologies
2. Cellular System Generations
3. Wireless Applications for Customer Relationship Management, Supply Chain Management, and Healthcare
4. Introduction to Web 2.0
5. LAN Topologies

VIDEO CASES

Case 1: Telepresence Moves Out of the Boardroom and Into the Field

Case 2: Virtual Collaboration with Lotus Sametime

CHAPTER OUTLINE

RFID AND WIRELESS TECHNOLOGY SPEED UP PRODUCTION AT CONTINENTAL TIRES

Continental AG, headquartered in Hanover, Germany, is a global auto and truck parts manufacturing company, with about 170,000 employees in 46 countries. It is also the world's fourth largest tire manufacturer and one of the top five automotive suppliers in the world.

One of the factories for Continental's Tire Division is located in Sarreguemines, France. This facility produces 1,000 different kinds of tires and encompasses nearly 1.5 million square feet. The production process requires large wheeled carts loaded with sheets of rubber or other components to be transported from storage to work-stations as tires are being built. Until recently, if a carrier was not in its expected location, a worker had to look for it manually. Manual tracking was time-consuming and inaccurate, and the plant often lost track of tire components altogether.

Missing materials created bottlenecks and production delays at a time when business was growing and the company needed to increase production capacity. Continental

© Bastian / Alamy

found a solution in a new real-time location system based on a Wi-Fi wireless network using radio frequency identification (RFID) tags, AeroScout MobileView software, mobile computers, and Global Data Sciences' material inventory tracking system software.

The Sarreguemines plant mounted AeroScout T2-EB Industrial RFID tags on the sides of 1,100 of its carriers. As the carriers move from one manufacturing or storage station to another, location information about the cart is transmitted to nearby nodes of a Cisco Wi-Fi wireless network. AeroScout's MobileView software picks up the location and represents the carrier as an icon on a map of the facility displayed on computer screens. Fifteen Honeywell Dolphin 6500 and Motorola Solutions MC9190 handheld computers are used to confirm that a carrier has been loaded with components or has arrived at a specific workstation.

Seven of the plant's tuggers, which are small trucks for hauling the carriers around the plant, are equipped with DLOG mobile vehicle-mounted computers. When a tugger driver is looking for a specific component, he or she can use the mobile device to access the MobileView system, pull up a map of the facility, and see an icon indicating where that component's carrier is located. The location tracking system provides a real-time snapshot of all the components used in the factory.

A bar code label is attached to each component and carrier, and the system starts tracking that component as soon as it is placed in a carrier. Plant workers use one of the Motorola or Honeywell handhelds and the MobileView software to scan the bar code labels on both the component and its carrier, which is associated with the ID number transmitted by an RFID tag mounted on the carrier. The scanned bar code data are stored in a material inventory tracking system. The MobileView software tracks the carrier's location as it is being transported to a storage area, and also the location where it is placed in storage.

When components are needed for manufacturing, a tugger driver uses the DLOG mobile computer to identify the location of the carrier with those specific components, and then goes to that location. After the carrier has been retrieved and taken to a workstation, its bar code is scanned by an employee at that station using one of the handheld computers. This updates the system to show that the required components have been received.

By enabling tugger drivers to quickly locate components, the new system has increased productivity and ensures that materials are not overlooked or misplaced. Fewer materials are thrown away because they expired and were not used when they were needed. The system is able to send alerts of materials that have been sitting too long in one spot.

When AeroScout and the new material inventory tracking system were implemented in September 2011, Continental made sure all production employees, including truckers, tire builders, and management, received training in the new system functions. The company also provided workers with instruction cards with detailed descriptions of system functions that they could use for reference.

Thanks to the new system, the Sarreguemines tire factory has increased production from 33,000 to 38,000 tires per day. Wastage of tire components has been reduced by 20 percent.

Sources: www.aeroscout.com, accessed June 21, 2013; Claire Swedberg, "Continental Tire Plant Increases Productivity, Reduces Waste," *RFID Journal*, April 25, 2012 and www.conti-online.com, accessed June 21, 2013.

Continental Tires's experience illustrates some of the powerful capabilities and opportunities provided by contemporary networking technology. The company uses wireless networking, radio frequency identification (RFID) technology, mobile computers, and materials inventory management software to automate tracking of components as they move through the production process.

The chapter-opening diagram calls attention to important points raised by this case and this chapter. Continental Tires' production environment extends over a very large area, and requires intensive oversight and coordination to make sure that components are available when and where they are needed in the production process. Tracking components manually was very slow and cumbersome, increasing the possibility that components would be overlooked or lost.

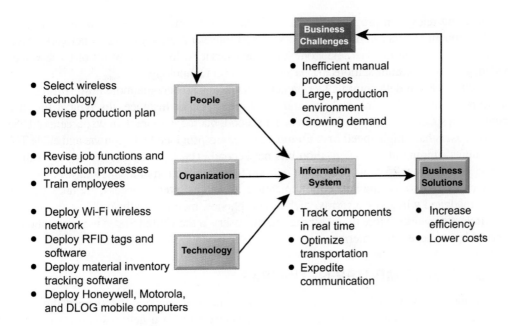

Management decided that wireless technology and RFID tagging provided a solution and arranged for the deployment of a wireless RFID network throughout the entire Sarreguemines production facility. The network made it much easier to track components and to optimize tugger truck movements. Continental Tires had to redesign its production and other work processes and train employees in the new system to take advantage of the new technology.

Here are some questions to think about: How did Continental's real-time location system transform operations? Why was training so important?

7.1 Telecommunications and Networking in Today's Business World

If you run or work in a business, you can't do without networks. You need to communicate rapidly with your customers, suppliers, and employees. Until about 1990, businesses used the postal system or telephone system with voice or fax for communication. Today, however, you and your employees use computers, e-mail, text messaging, the Internet, cell phones, and mobile computers connected to wireless networks for this purpose. Networking and the Internet are now nearly synonymous with doing business.

NETWORKING AND COMMUNICATION TRENDS

Firms in the past used two fundamentally different types of networks: telephone networks and computer networks. Telephone networks historically handled voice communication, and computer networks handled data traffic. Telephone networks were built by telephone companies throughout the twentieth century using voice transmission technologies (hardware and software), and these companies almost always operated as regulated monopolies throughout the world. Computer networks were originally built by computer companies seeking to transmit data between computers in different locations.

Thanks to continuing telecommunications deregulation and information technology innovation, telephone and computer networks are converging into a single digital network using shared Internet-based standards and equipment. Telecommunications providers today, such as AT&T and Verizon, offer data transmission, Internet access, cellular telephone service, and television programming as well as voice service. Cable companies, such as Cablevision and Comcast, offer voice service and Internet access. Computer networks have expanded to include Internet telephone and video services. Increasingly, all of these voice, video, and data communications are based on Internet technology.

Both voice and data communication networks have also become more powerful (faster), more portable (smaller and mobile), and less expensive. For instance, the typical Internet connection speed in 2000 was 56 kilobits per second, but today more than 96 percent of U.S. Internet users have high-speed **broadband** connections provided by telephone and cable TV companies running at 1 to 15 million bits per second. The cost for this service has fallen exponentially, from 25 cents per kilobit in 2000 to a tiny fraction of a cent today.

Increasingly, voice and data communication, as well as Internet access, are taking place over broadband wireless platforms, such as cell phones, mobile handheld devices, and PCs in wireless networks. More than half the Internet users in the United States use smartphones and tablets to access the Internet.

WHAT IS A COMPUTER NETWORK?

If you had to connect the computers for two or more employees together in the same office, you would need a computer network. Exactly what is a network? In its simplest form, a network consists of two or more connected computers. Figure 7.1 illustrates the major hardware, software, and transmission components used in a simple network: a client computer and a dedicated server computer, network interfaces, a connection medium, network operating system software, and either a hub or a switch.

Each computer on the network contains a network interface device to link the computer to the network. The connection medium for linking network components can be a telephone wire, coaxial cable, or radio signal in the case of cell phone and wireless local area networks (Wi-Fi networks).

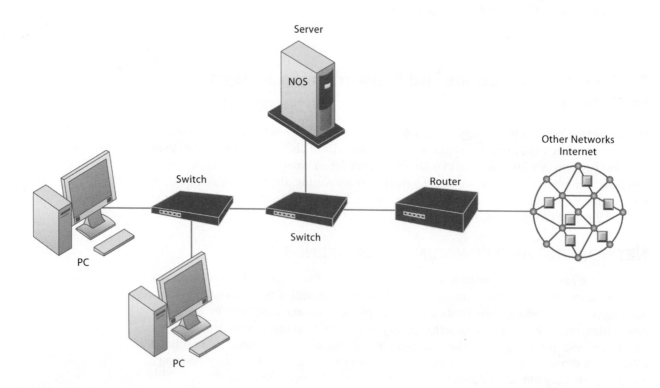

Figure 7.1
Components of a Simple Computer Network
Illustrated here is a very simple computer network, consisting of computers, a network operating system (NOS) residing on a dedicated server computer, cable (wiring) connecting the devices, switches, and a router.

The **network operating system (NOS)** routes and manages communications on the network and coordinates network resources. It can reside on every computer in the network, or it can reside primarily on a dedicated server computer for all the applications on the network. A server computer is a computer on a network that performs important network functions for client computers, such as serving up Web pages, storing data, and storing the network operating system (and hence controlling the network). Microsoft Windows Server, Linux, and Novell Open Enterprise Server are the most widely used network operating systems.

Most networks also contain a switch or a hub acting as a connection point between the computers. **Hubs** are very simple devices that connect network components, sending a packet of data to all other connected devices. A **switch** has more intelligence than a hub and can filter and forward data to a specified destination on the network.

What if you want to communicate with another network, such as the Internet? You would need a router. A **router** is a communications processor used to route packets of data through different networks, ensuring that the data sent gets to the correct address.

Network switches and routers have proprietary software built into their hardware for directing the movement of data on the network. This can create network bottlenecks and makes the process of configuring a network more complicated and time-consuming. **Software-defined networking (SDN)** is a new networking approach in which many of these control functions are managed by one central program, which can run on inexpensive commodity servers that are separate from the network devices themselves. This is especially helpful in a cloud computing environment with many different pieces of hardware because it allows a network administrator to manage traffic loads in a flexible and more efficient manner.

Networks in Large Companies

The network we've just described might be suitable for a small business. But what about large companies with many different locations and thousands of employees? As a firm grows, and collects hundreds of small local area networks, these networks can be tied together into a corporate-wide networking infrastructure. The network infrastructure for a large corporation consists of a large number of these small local area networks linked to other local area networks and to firmwide corporate networks. A number of powerful servers support a corporate Web site, a corporate intranet, and perhaps an extranet. Some of these servers link to other large computers supporting back-end systems.

Figure 7.2 provides an illustration of these more complex, larger scale corporate-wide networks. Here you can see that the corporate network infrastructure supports a mobile sales force using cell phones and smartphones, mobile employees linking to the company Web site, internal company networks using mobile wireless local area networks (Wi-Fi networks), and a videoconferencing system to support managers across the world. In addition to these computer networks, the firm's infrastructure may include a separate telephone network that handles most voice data. Many firms are dispensing with their traditional telephone networks and using Internet telephones that run on their existing data networks (described later).

As you can see from this figure, a large corporate network infrastructure uses a wide variety of technologies—everything from ordinary telephone service and corporate data networks to Internet service, wireless Internet, and cell phones. One of the major problems facing corporations today is how to integrate all the different communication networks and channels into a coherent system that enables information to flow from one part of the corporation to another, and from one system to another. As more and more communication networks become digital, and based on Internet technologies, it will become easier to integrate them.

KEY DIGITAL NETWORKING TECHNOLOGIES

Contemporary digital networks and the Internet are based on three key technologies: client/server computing, the use of packet switching, and the development of widely used

Figure 7.2
Corporate Network
Infrastructure
*Today's corporate
network infrastructure
is a collection of many
different networks from
the public switched
telephone network, to
the Internet, to corporate
local area networks
linking workgroups,
departments, or office
floors.*

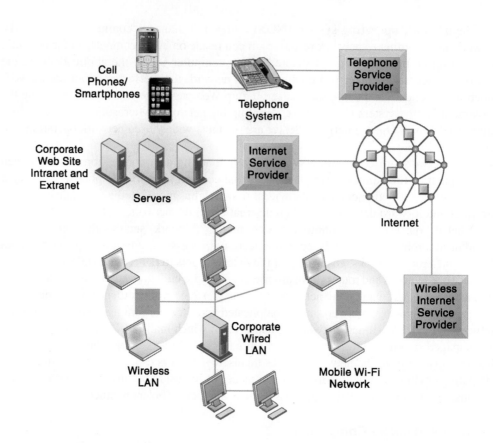

communications standards (the most important of which is Transmission Control Protocol/Internet Protocol, or TCP/IP) for linking disparate networks and computers.

Client/Server Computing

Client/server computing, introduced in Chapter 5, is a distributed computing model in which some of the processing power is located within small, inexpensive client computers, and resides literally on desktops, laptops, or in handheld devices. These powerful clients are linked to one another through a network that is controlled by a network server computer. The server sets the rules of communication for the network and provides every client with an address so others can find it on the network.

Client/server computing has largely replaced centralized mainframe computing in which nearly all of the processing takes place on a central large mainframe computer. Client/server computing has extended computing to departments, workgroups, factory floors, and other parts of the business that could not be served by a centralized architecture. The Internet is the largest implementation of client/server computing.

Packet Switching

Packet switching is a method of slicing digital messages into parcels called packets, sending the packets along different communication paths as they become available, and then reassembling the packets once they arrive at their destinations (see Figure 7.3). Prior to the development of packet switching, computer networks used leased, dedicated telephone circuits to communicate with other computers in remote locations. In circuit-switched networks, such as the telephone system, a complete point-to-point circuit is assembled, and then communication can proceed. These dedicated circuit-switching techniques were expensive and wasted available communications capacity—the circuit was maintained regardless of whether any data were being sent.

Packet switching makes much more efficient use of the communications capacity of a network. In packet-switched networks, messages are first broken down into small fixed

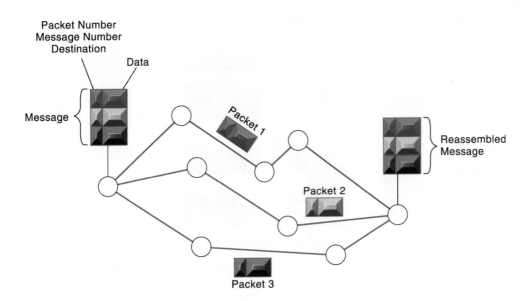

Packet Number
Message Number
Destination

Data

Message

Packet 1

Packet 2

Packet 3

Reassembled
Message

Figure 7.3
Packet-Switched
Networks and Packet
Communications
*Data are grouped into
small packets, which
are transmitted inde-
pendently over various
communications chan-
nels and reassembled at
their final destination.*

bundles of data called packets. The packets include information for directing the packet
to the right address and for checking transmission errors along with the data. The packets
are transmitted over various communications channels using routers, each packet traveling
independently. Packets of data originating at one source will be routed through many different paths and networks before being reassembled into the original message when they reach
their destinations.

TCP/IP and Connectivity

In a typical telecommunications network, diverse hardware and software components need
to work together to transmit information. Different components in a network communicate
with each other only by adhering to a common set of rules called protocols. A **protocol** is
a set of rules and procedures governing transmission of information between two points in
a network.

In the past, many diverse proprietary and incompatible protocols often forced business
firms to purchase computing and communications equipment from a single vendor. But today,
corporate networks are increasingly using a single, common, worldwide standard called
Transmission Control Protocol/Internet Protocol (TCP/IP). TCP/IP was developed during the early 1970s to support U.S. Department of Defense Advanced Research Projects
Agency (DARPA) efforts to help scientists transmit data among different types of computers
over long distances.

TCP/IP uses a suite of protocols, the main ones being TCP and IP. TCP refers to the
Transmission Control Protocol, which handles the movement of data between computers.
TCP establishes a connection between the computers, sequences the transfer of packets, and
acknowledges the packets sent. IP refers to the Internet Protocol (IP), which is responsible
for the delivery of packets and includes the disassembling and reassembling of packets during transmission. Figure 7.4 illustrates the four-layered Department of Defense reference
model for TCP/IP, and the layers are described as follows:

1. *Application layer.* The Application layer enables client application programs to access
   the other layers and defines the protocols that applications use to exchange data. One of
   these application protocols is the Hypertext Transfer Protocol (HTTP), which is used to
   transfer Web page files.
2. *Transport layer.* The Transport layer is responsible for providing the Application
   layer with communication and packet services. This layer includes TCP and other
   protocols.

Figure 7.4
The Transmission
Control Protocol/
Internet Protocol
(TCP/IP) Reference
Model
*This figure illustrates the
four layers of the TCP/
IP reference model for
communications.*

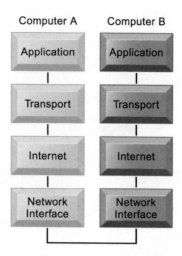

3. *Internet layer.* The Internet layer is responsible for addressing, routing, and packaging data packets called IP datagrams. The Internet Protocol is one of the protocols used in this layer.
4. *Network Interface layer.* At the bottom of the reference model, the Network Interface layer is responsible for placing packets on and receiving them from the network medium, which could be any networking technology.

Two computers using TCP/IP are able to communicate even if they are based on different hardware and software platforms. Data sent from one computer to the other passes downward through all four layers, starting with the sending computer's Application layer and passing through the Network Interface layer. After the data reach the recipient host computer, they travel up the layers and are reassembled into a format the receiving computer can use. If the receiving computer finds a damaged packet, it asks the sending computer to retransmit it. This process is reversed when the receiving computer responds.

7.2 Communications Networks

Let's look more closely at alternative networking technologies available to businesses.

SIGNALS: DIGITAL VS. ANALOG

There are two ways to communicate a message in a network: an analog signal or a digital signal. An *analog signal* is represented by a continuous waveform that passes through a communications medium and has been used for voice communication. The most common analog devices are the telephone handset, the speaker on your computer, or your iPod earphone, all of which create analog waveforms that your ear can hear.

A *digital signal* is a discrete, binary waveform, rather than a continuous waveform. Digital signals communicate information as strings of two discrete states: one bit and zero bits, which are represented as on-off electrical pulses. Computers use digital signals and require a modem to convert these digital signals into analog signals that can be sent over (or received from) telephone lines, cable lines, or wireless media that use analog signals (see Figure 7.5). **Modem** stands for modulator-demodulator. Cable modems connect your computer to the Internet using a cable network. DSL modems connect your computer to the Internet using a telephone company's landline network. Wireless modems perform the same function as traditional modems, connecting your computer to a wireless network that could be a cell phone network, or a Wi-Fi network. Without modems, computers could not communicate with one another using analog networks (which include the telephone system and cable networks).

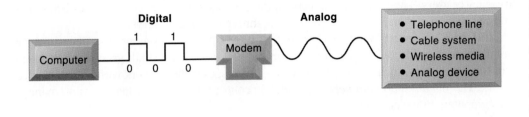

Figure 7.5
Functions of the Modem
A modem is a device that translates digital signals into analog form (and vice versa) so that computers can transmit data over analog networks such as telephone and cable networks.

TYPES OF NETWORKS

There are many different kinds of networks and ways of classifying them. One way of looking at networks is in terms of their geographic scope (see Table 7.1).

Local Area Networks

If you work in a business that uses networking, you are probably connecting to other employees and groups via a local area network. A **local area network (LAN)** is designed to connect personal computers and other digital devices within a half-mile or 500-meter radius. LANs typically connect a few computers in a small office, all the computers in one building, or all the computers in several buildings in close proximity. LANs also are used to link to long-distance wide area networks (WANs, described later in this section) and other networks around the world using the Internet.

Review Figure 7.1, which could serve as a model for a small LAN that might be used in an office. One computer is a dedicated network file server, providing users with access to shared computing resources in the network, including software programs and data files.

The server determines who gets access to what and in which sequence. The router connects the LAN to other networks, which could be the Internet or another corporate network, so that the LAN can exchange information with networks external to it. The most common LAN operating systems are Windows, Linux, and Novell. Each of these network operating systems supports TCP/IP as its default networking protocol.

Ethernet is the dominant LAN standard at the physical network level, specifying the physical medium to carry signals between computers, access control rules, and a standardized set of bits used to carry data over the system. Originally, Ethernet supported a data transfer rate of 10 megabits per second (Mbps). Newer versions, such as Gigabit Ethernet, support a data transfer rate of 1 gigabit per second (Gbps).

The LAN illustrated in Figure 7.1 uses a client/server architecture where the network operating system resides primarily on a single file server, and the server provides much of the control and resources for the network. Alternatively, LANs may use a peer-to-peer architecture. A peer-to-peer network treats all processors equally and is used primarily in small networks with

TABLE 7.1

Types of Networks

Type	Area
Local area network (LAN)	Up to 500 meters (half a mile); an office or floor of a building
Campus area network (CAN)	Up to 1,000 meters (a mile); a college campus or corporate facility
Metropolitan area network (MAN)	A city or metropolitan area
Wide area network (WAN)	A transcontinental or global area

10 or fewer users. The various computers on the network can exchange data by direct access and can share peripheral devices without going through a separate server.

In LANs using the Windows Server family of operating systems, the **peer-to-peer** architecture is called the *workgroup network model*, in which a small group of computers can share resources, such as files, folders, and printers, over the network without a dedicated server. The *Windows domain network model*, in contrast, uses a dedicated server to manage the computers in the network.

Larger LANs have many clients and multiple servers, with separate servers for specific services, such as storing and managing files and databases (file servers or database servers), managing printers (print servers), storing and managing e-mail (mail servers), or storing and managing Web pages (Web servers).

Metropolitan and Wide Area Networks

Wide area networks (WANs) span broad geographical distances—entire regions, states, continents, or the entire globe. The most universal and powerful WAN is the Internet. Computers connect to a WAN through public networks, such as the telephone system or private cable systems, or through leased lines or satellites. A **metropolitan area network (MAN)** is a network that spans a metropolitan area, usually a city and its major suburbs. Its geographic scope falls between a WAN and a LAN.

TRANSMISSION MEDIA AND TRANSMISSION SPEED

Networks use different kinds of physical transmission media, including twisted pair wire, coaxial cable, fiber-optic cable, and media for wireless transmission. Each has advantages and limitations. A wide range of speeds is possible for any given medium depending on the software and hardware configuration. Table 7.2 compares these media.

Bandwidth: Transmission Speed

The total amount of digital information that can be transmitted through any telecommunications medium is measured in bits per second (bps). One signal change, or cycle, is required to transmit one or several bits; therefore, the transmission capacity of each type of telecommunications medium is a function of its frequency. The number of cycles per second that can be sent through that medium is measured in **hertz**—one hertz is equal to one cycle of the medium.

The range of frequencies that can be accommodated on a particular telecommunications channel is called its **bandwidth**. The bandwidth is the difference between the highest and lowest frequencies that can be accommodated on a single channel. The greater the range of frequencies, the greater the bandwidth and the greater the channel's transmission capacity.

7.3 The Global Internet

We all use the Internet, and many of us can't do without it. It's become an indispensable personal and business tool. But what exactly is the Internet? How does it work, and what does Internet technology have to offer for business? Let's look at the most important Internet features.

WHAT IS THE INTERNET?

The Internet has become the world's most extensive, public communication system. It's also the world's largest implementation of client/server computing and internetworking, linking millions of individual networks all over the world. This global network of networks began in the early 1970s as a U.S. Department of Defense network to link scientists and university professors around the world.

Most homes and small businesses connect to the Internet by subscribing to an Internet service provider. An **Internet service provider (ISP)** is a commercial organization with a permanent connection to the Internet that sells temporary connections to retail subscribers. EarthLink,

TABLE 7.2

Physical Transmission Media

Transmission Medium	Description	Speed
Twisted pair wire (CAT 5)	Strands of copper wire twisted in pairs for voice and data communications. CAT 5 is the most common 10 Mbps LAN cable. Maximum recommended run of 100 meters.	10 Mbps to 1 Gbps
Coaxial cable	Thickly insulated copper wire, which is capable of high-speed data transmission and less subject to interference than twisted wire. Currently used for cable TV and for networks with longer runs (more than 100 meters).	Up to 1 Gbps
Fiber-optic cable	Strands of clear glass fiber, transmitting data as pulses of light generated by lasers. Useful for high-speed transmission of large quantities of data. More expensive than other physical transmission media and harder to install; often used for network backbone.	500 Kbps to 6+ Tbps
Wireless transmission media	Based on radio signals of various frequencies and includes both terrestrial and satellite microwave systems and cellular networks. Used for long-distance, wireless communication and Internet access.	Up to 600+ Mbps

NetZero, AT&T, and Time Warner are ISPs. Individuals also connect to the Internet through their business firms, universities, or research centers that have designated Internet domains.

There are a variety of services for ISP Internet connections. Connecting via a traditional telephone line and modem, at a speed of 56.6 kilobits per second (Kbps), used to be the most common form of connection worldwide, but it has been largely replaced by broadband connections. Digital subscriber line, cable, satellite Internet connections, and T lines provide these broadband services.

Digital subscriber line (DSL) technologies operate over existing telephone lines to carry voice, data, and video at transmission rates ranging from 385 Kbps all the way up to 40 Mbps, depending on usage patterns and distance. **Cable Internet connections** provided by cable television vendors use digital cable coaxial lines to deliver high-speed Internet access to homes and businesses. They can provide high-speed access to the Internet of up to 50 Mbps, although most providers offer service ranging from 1 Mbps to 6 Mbps. In areas where DSL and cable services are unavailable, it is possible to access the Internet via satellite, although some satellite Internet connections have slower upload speeds than other broadband services.

T1 and T3 are international telephone standards for digital communication. They are leased, dedicated lines suitable for businesses or government agencies requiring high-speed guaranteed service levels. **T1 lines** offer guaranteed delivery at 1.54 Mbps, and T3 lines offer delivery at 45 Mbps. The Internet does not provide similar guaranteed service levels, but simply "best effort."

INTERNET ADDRESSING AND ARCHITECTURE

The Internet is based on the TCP/IP networking protocol suite described earlier in this chapter. Every computer on the Internet is assigned a unique **Internet Protocol (IP) address**, which currently is a 32-bit number represented by four strings of numbers ranging from 0 to 255 separated by periods. For instance, the IP address of www.microsoft.com is 207.46.250.119.

When a user sends a message to another user on the Internet, the message is first decomposed into packets using the TCP protocol. Each packet contains its destination address.

The packets are then sent from the client to the network server and from there on to as many other servers as necessary to arrive at a specific computer with a known address. At the destination address, the packets are reassembled into the original message.

The Domain Name System

Because it would be incredibly difficult for Internet users to remember strings of 12 numbers, the **Domain Name System (DNS)** converts domain names to IP addresses. The **domain name** is the English-like name that corresponds to the unique 32-bit numeric IP address for each computer connected to the Internet. DNS servers maintain a database containing IP addresses mapped to their corresponding domain names. To access a computer on the Internet, users need only specify its domain name.

DNS has a hierarchical structure (see Figure 7.6). At the top of the DNS hierarchy is the root domain. The child domain of the root is called a top-level domain, and the child domain of a top-level domain is called a second-level domain. Top-level domains are two- and three-character names you are familiar with from surfing the Web, for example, .com, .edu, .gov, and the various country codes such as .ca for Canada or .it for Italy. Second-level domains have two parts, designating a top-level name and a second-level name—such as buy.com, nyu.edu, or amazon.ca. A host name at the bottom of the hierarchy designates a specific computer on either the Internet or a private network.

The most common domain extensions currently available and officially approved are shown in the following list. Countries also have domain names such as .uk, .au, and .fr (United Kingdom, Australia, and France, respectively), and there is a new class of "internationalized" top-level domains that use non-English characters. In the future, this list will expand to include many more types of organizations and industries.

.com	Commercial organizations/businesses
.edu	Educational institutions
.gov	U.S. government agencies
.mil	U.S. military
.net	Network computers
.org	Nonprofit organizations and foundations
.biz	Business firms
.info	Information providers

Figure 7.6
The Domain Name System
Domain Name System is a hierarchical system with a root domain, top-level domains, second-level domains, and host computers at the third level.

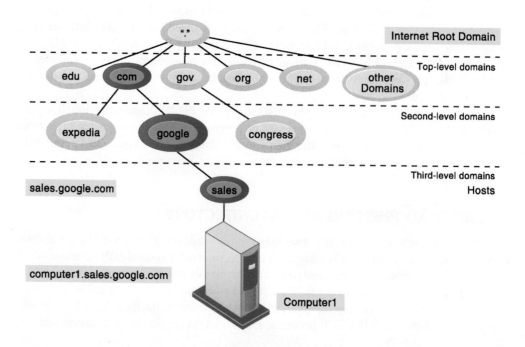

Internet Architecture and Governance

Internet data traffic is carried over transcontinental high-speed backbone networks that generally operate in the range of 45 Mbps to 2.5 Gbps (see Figure 7.7). These trunk lines are typically owned by long-distance telephone companies (called *network service providers*) or by national governments. Local connection lines are owned by regional telephone and cable television companies in the United States that connect retail users in homes and businesses to the Internet. The regional networks lease access to ISPs, private companies, and government institutions.

Each organization pays for its own networks and its own local Internet connection services, a part of which is paid to the long-distance trunk line owners. Individual Internet users pay ISPs for using their service, and they generally pay a flat subscription fee, no matter how much or how little they use the Internet. A debate is now raging on whether this arrangement should continue or whether heavy Internet users who download large video and music files should pay more for the bandwidth they consume. The Interactive Session on Organizations explores this topic, by examining the pros and cons of net neutrality.

No one "owns" the Internet, and it has no formal management. However, worldwide Internet policies are established by a number of professional organizations and government bodies, including the Internet Architecture Board (IAB), which helps define the overall structure of the Internet; the Internet Corporation for Assigned Names and Numbers (ICANN), which assigns IP addresses; and the World Wide Web Consortium (W3C), which sets Hypertext Markup Language and other programming standards for the Web.

These organizations influence government agencies, network owners, ISPs, and software developers with the goal of keeping the Internet operating as efficiently as possible. The Internet must also conform to the laws of the sovereign nation-states in which it operates, as well as the technical infrastructures that exist within the nation-states. Although in the early years of the Internet and the Web there was very little legislative or executive interference, this situation is changing as the Internet plays a growing role in the distribution of information and knowledge, including content that some find objectionable.

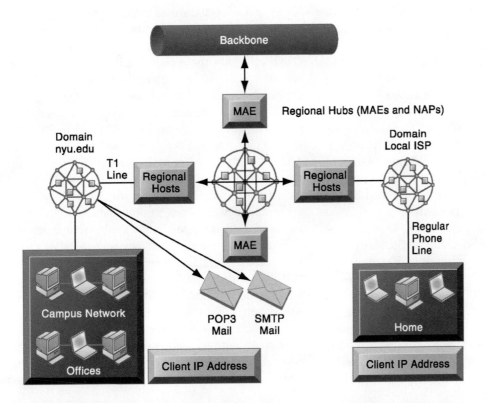

Figure 7.7
Internet Network Architecture
The Internet backbone connects to regional networks, which in turn provide access to Internet service providers, large firms, and government institutions. Network access points (NAPs) and metropolitan area exchanges (MAEs) are hubs where the backbone intersects regional and local networks and where backbone owners connect with one another.

What kind of Internet user are you? Do you primarily use the Net to do a little e-mail and online banking? Or are you online all day, watching YouTube videos, downloading music files, or playing online games? Do you use your iPhone to stream TV shows and movies on a regular basis? If you're a power Internet or smartphone user, you are consuming a great deal of bandwidth. Could hundreds of millions of people like you start to slow the Internet down?

Video streaming on Netflix accounts for nearly a third of all bandwidth use in the United States. AT&T's mobile network will carry more data in the first two months of 2015 than in all of 2010. If user demand overwhelms network capacity, the Internet might not come to a screeching halt, but users could face sluggish download speeds and video transmission. Heavy use of iPhones in urban areas such as New York and San Francisco has already degraded service on the AT&T wireless network. AT&T reported that 3 percent of its subscriber base accounted for 40 percent of its data traffic.

Internet service providers (ISPs) assert that network congestion is a serious problem, but claim that expanding their networks would require passing on burdensome costs to consumers. These companies believe differential pricing methods, which include data caps and metered use—charging based on the amount of bandwidth consumed—are the "fairest way" to finance necessary investments in their network infrastructures. But metering Internet use is not widely accepted, because of an ongoing debate about net neutrality.

Net neutrality is the idea that Internet service providers must allow customers equal access to content and applications, regardless of the source or nature of the content. Currently, the Internet is neutral: All Internet traffic is treated equally on a first-come, first-served basis by Internet backbone owners. However, this arrangement prevents telecommunications and cable companies from charging differentiated prices based on the amount of bandwidth consumed by the content being delivered over the Internet.

Comcast, the second largest U.S. Internet service provider, complained that illegal file sharing of copyrighted material was consuming 50 percent of its network capacity. In 2008 the company slowed down transmission of BitTorrent files used extensively for piracy and illegal sharing of copyrighted materials, including video. The Federal Communications Commission (FCC) ordered Comcast to stop discriminating against such Web sites. Comcast then filed a lawsuit challenging the FCC's authority to enforce net-

work neutrality. In April 2010, a federal appeals court ruled in favor of Comcast that the FCC had the power to regulate only the telecommunications portion of the Internet—the "wires"—not the information portion.

The strange alliance of net neutrality advocates includes MoveOn.org, the Christian Coalition, the American Library Association, data-intensive Web businesses such as Netflix and Google, every major consumer group, and a host of bloggers and small businesses. Net neutrality advocates argue that differentiated pricing would impose heavy costs on heavy bandwidth users such as YouTube, Skype, and other innovative services, preventing high-bandwidth startup companies from gaining traction. Net neutrality supporters also argue that without net neutrality, ISPs that are also cable companies, such as Comcast, might block online streaming video from Netflix or Hulu in order to force customers to use the cable company's on-demand movie rental services.

Network owners believe regulation to enforce net neutrality will impede U.S. competitiveness by discouraging capital expenditure for new networks and curbing their networks' ability to cope with the exploding demand for Internet and wireless traffic. U.S. Internet service lags behind that of many other nations in overall speed, cost, and quality of service, adding credibility to this argument. And with enough options for Internet access, dissatisfied consumers could simply switch to providers who enforce net neutrality and allow unlimited Internet use.

A December 2012 report by the nonprofit, nonpartisan, public policy institute, New America Foundation (NAF), disputes these claims. Like personal computers, the processing capacity of the routers and switches that comprise wired broadband networks has vastly expanded while the price has declined. Although total U.S. Internet data consumption rose 120% in 2012, the cost to transport the data decreased at a faster pace. The net cost to carriers was, at worst, flat and for the most part, down. The NAF report further asserts that lack of competition has enabled wired broadband carriers to charge higher rates, institute data caps, and spend less on the capital expenditures needed to upgrade and maintain their networks than they have in the past.

In December 2010, the FCC approved measures that would allow the federal government to regulate some aspects of Internet traffic. Broadband providers would be required to provide information regarding Internet speeds and service to their subscribers, and they could not block access to sites or products that compete against their own products. However, the regulations did not officially safeguard net neutrality, and wireless providers may block applications that use too much bandwidth.

Wireless providers have already moved to develop tiered plans that charge heavy bandwidth users larger service fees, and online content providers have struck exclusive deals with distributors that leave their competitors at a disadvantage. For example, in 2012, Comcast struck a deal with Microsoft to provide streaming video via its Xfinity TV service through the Xbox 360 that does not count against its broadband data cap of 250 gigabytes per month. This gives Comcast's television programming an edge over rival streaming shows, which will consume subscribers' data allotment. Netflix and other competitors are incensed, arguing that this represents an anti-competitive practice.

Currently, the net neutrality laws on the books are riddled with loopholes. For example, they allow broadband providers to allocate portions of their networks for special "managed" services. That may change with further court rulings, including the outcome of a major net neutrality case pitting Verizon Communications Inc. against the FCC.

Sources: Alina Selyukh, "S. Court to Hear Oral Arguments in Net Neutrality Case on September 9," Reuters, June 25, 2013; Edward Wyatt, "Backer of an Open Internet Steps Down as F.C.C. Chief," *New York Times*, March 22, 2013; Zach Walton, "Should The Government Regulate ISP Bandwidth Caps?", WebProNews, December 23, 2012; Hibah Hussain, Danielle Kehl, Benjamin Lennett, and Patrick Lucey, "Capping the Nation's Broadband Future? Dwindling Competition Is Fueling the Rise of Increasingly Costly and Restrictive Internet Usage Caps," New America Foundation, December 17, 2012; Kevin Fitchard, "AT&T's data traffic is actually doubling annually," Gigaom, Feb. 14, 2012; Eduardo Porter, "Keeping the Internet Neutral," *The New York Times*, May 8, 2012; Matt Peckham, "Netflix CEO Takes Swing at Comcast Xfinity over Net Neutrality," *Time Techland*, April 16, 2012; "FCC Approves Net Neutrality But With Concessions," *eWeek*, December 22, 2010; and Brian Stelter, "Comcast Fee Ignites Fight Over Videos on Internet," *New York Times*, November 30, 2010.

CASE STUDY QUESTIONS

1. What is network neutrality? Why has the Internet operated under net neutrality up to this point in time?

2. Who's in favor of net neutrality? Who's opposed? Why?

3. What would be the impact on individual users, businesses, and government if Internet providers switched to a tiered service model for transmission over land lines as well as wireless?

4. Are you in favor of legislation enforcing network neutrality? Why or why not?

The Future Internet: IPv6 and Internet2

The Internet was not originally designed to handle the transmission of massive quantities of data and billions of users. Because of sheer Internet population growth, the world is about to run out of available IP addresses using the old addressing convention. The old addressing system is being replaced by a new version of the IP addressing schema called **IPv6** (Internet Protocol version 6), which contains 128-bit addresses (2 to the power of 128), or more than a quadrillion possible unique addresses. IPv6 is not compatible with the existing Internet addressing system, so the transition to the new standard will take years.

Internet2 is an advanced networking consortium representing over 350 U.S. universities, private businesses, and government agencies working with 66,000 institutions across the United States and international networking partners from more than 100 countries. To connect these communities, Internet2 developed a high-capacity 100 Gbps network that serves as a testbed for leading-edge technologies that may eventually migrate to the public Internet, including telemedicine, distance learning, and other advanced applications not possible with consumer-grade Internet services. The fourth generation of this network is being rolled out to provide 8.8 terabits of capacity.

INTERNET SERVICES AND COMMUNICATION TOOLS

The Internet is based on client/server technology. Individuals using the Internet control what they do through client applications on their computers, such as Web browser software. The data, including e-mail messages and Web pages, are stored on servers. A client uses the Internet to request information from a particular Web server on a distant computer, and the server sends the requested information back to the client over the Internet. Chapters 5 and 6 describe how Web servers work with application servers and database servers to access information from an organization's internal information systems applications and their associated databases. Client platforms today include not only PCs and other computers but also smartphones and tablets.

Internet Services

A client computer connecting to the Internet has access to a variety of services. These services include e-mail, chatting and instant messaging, electronic discussion groups, **Telnet, File Transfer Protocol (FTP)**, and the Web. Table 7.3 provides a brief description of these services.

Each Internet service is implemented by one or more software programs. All of the services may run on a single server computer, or different services may be allocated to different machines. Figure 7.8 illustrates one way that these services can be arranged in a multitiered client/server architecture.

E-mail enables messages to be exchanged from computer to computer, with capabilities for routing messages to multiple recipients, forwarding messages, and attaching text documents or multimedia files to messages. Most e-mail today is sent through the Internet. The cost of e-mail is far lower than equivalent voice, postal, or overnight delivery costs, and e-mail messages arrive anywhere in the world in a matter of seconds.

Nearly 90 percent of U.S. workplaces have employees communicating interactively using **chat** or instant messaging tools. Chatting enables two or more people who are simultaneously connected to the Internet to hold live, interactive conversations. Chat systems now support voice and video chat as well as written conversations. Many online retail businesses offer chat services on their Web sites to attract visitors, to encourage repeat purchases, and to improve customer service.

Instant messaging is a type of chat service that enables participants to create their own private chat channels. The instant messaging system alerts the user whenever someone on his or her private list is online so that the user can initiate a chat session with other individuals. Instant messaging systems for consumers include Yahoo! Messenger, Google Talk, and Windows Live Messenger. Companies concerned with security use proprietary communications and messaging systems such as IBM Sametime.

Newsgroups are worldwide discussion groups posted on Internet electronic bulletin boards on which people share information and ideas on a defined topic, such as radiology or rock bands. Anyone can post messages on these bulletin boards for others to read. Many thousands of groups exist that discuss almost all conceivable topics.

Employee use of e-mail, instant messaging, and the Internet is supposed to increase worker productivity, but the accompanying Interactive Session on People shows that this may not always be the case. Many company managers now believe they need to monitor

---

TABLE 7.3

Major Internet Services

Capability	Functions Supported
E-mail	Person-to-person messaging; document sharing
Chatting and instant messaging	Interactive conversations
Newsgroups	Discussion groups on electronic bulletin boards
Telnet	Logging on to one computer system and doing work on another
File Transfer Protocol (FTP)	Transferring files from computer to computer
World Wide Web	Retrieving, formatting, and displaying information (including text, audio, graphics, and video) using hypertext links

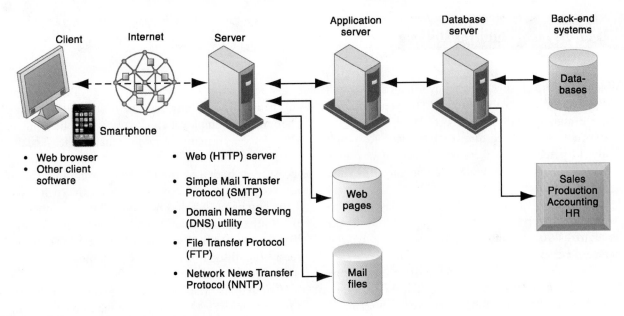

Figure 7.8
Client/Server Computing on the Internet
Client computers running Web browsers and other software can access an array of services on servers over the Internet. These services may all run on a single server or on multiple specialized servers.

and even regulate their employees' online activity. But is this ethical? Although there are some strong business reasons why companies may need to monitor their employees' e-mail and Web activities, what does this mean for employee privacy?

Voice over IP

The Internet has also become a popular platform for voice transmission and corporate networking. **Voice over IP (VoIP)** technology delivers voice information in digital form using packet switching, avoiding the tolls charged by local and long-distance telephone networks (see Figure 7.9). Calls that would ordinarily be transmitted over public telephone networks travel over the corporate network based on the Internet Protocol, or the public

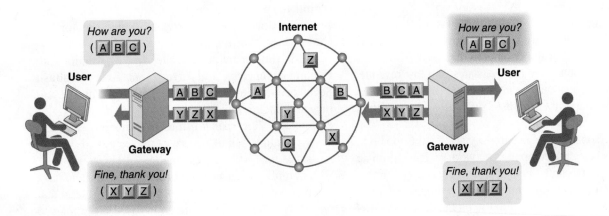

Figure 7.9
How Voice over IP Works
A VoIP phone call digitizes and breaks up a voice message into data packets that may travel along different routes before being reassembled at the final destination. A processor nearest the call's destination, called a gateway, arranges the packets in the proper order and directs them to the telephone number of the receiver or the IP address of the receiving computer.

When you were at work, how many minutes (or hours) did you spend on Facebook today? Did you send personal e-mail or visit some sports Web sites? If so, you're not alone. According to a Nucleus Research study, 77 percent of workers with Facebook accounts use them during work hours. A Ponemon Institute study reported that the average employee wastes approximately 30 percent of the workday on non-work-related Web browsing, while other studies report as many as 90 percent of employees receive or send personal e-mail at work.

This behavior creates serious business problems. Checking e-mail, responding to instant messages, or sneaking in a brief YouTube video creates a series of nonstop interruptions that divert employee attention from the job tasks they are supposed to be performing. According to Basex, a New York City business research company, these distractions result in $650 billion in lost productivity each year!

Many companies have begun monitoring employee use of e-mail and the Internet, sometimes without their knowledge. A 2010 study from Proofpoint Plus found that more than one in three large U.S corporations assign staff to read or analyze employee e-mail. Another recent survey from the American Management Association (AMA) and the ePolicy Institute found that two out of three of the small, medium, and large companies surveyed monitored Web use, including visits to social networking sites. Instant messaging and text message monitoring are also increasing. Although U.S. companies have the legal right to monitor employee Internet and e-mail activity while they are at work, is such monitoring unethical, or is it simply good business?

Managers worry about the loss of time and employee productivity when employees are focusing on personal rather than company business. Too much time on personal business translates into lost revenue. Some employees may even be billing time they spend pursuing personal interests online to clients, thus overcharging them.

If personal traffic on company networks is too high, it can also clog the company's network so that legitimate business work cannot be performed. Procter & Gamble (P&G) found that on an average day, employees were listening to 4,000 hours of music on Pandora and viewing 50,000 five-minute YouTube videos. These activities involved streaming huge quantities of data, which slowed down P&G's Internet connection.

When employees use e-mail or the Web (including social networks) at employer facilities or with employer equipment, anything they do, including anything illegal, carries the company's name. Therefore, the employer can be traced and held liable. Management in many firms fear that racist, sexually explicit, or other potentially offensive material accessed or traded by their employees could result in adverse publicity and even lawsuits for the firm. Even if the company is found not to be liable, responding to lawsuits could run up huge legal bills. Symantec's 2011 Social Media Protection Flash Poll found that the average litigation cost for companies with social media incidents ran over $650,000.

Companies also fear leakage of confidential information and trade secrets through e-mail or social networks. Another survey conducted by the American Management Association and the ePolicy Institute found that 14 percent of the employees polled admitted they had sent confidential or potentially embarrassing company e-mails to outsiders.

U.S. companies have the legal right to monitor what employees are doing with company equipment during business hours. The question is whether electronic surveillance is an appropriate tool for maintaining an efficient and positive workplace. Some companies try to ban all personal activities on corporate networks—zero tolerance. Others block employee access to specific Web sites or social sites, closely monitor e-mail messages, or limit personal time on the Web.

For example, P&G blocks Netflix and has asked employees to limit their use of Pandora. It still allows some YouTube viewing, and is not blocking access to social networking sites because staff use them for digital marketing campaigns. Ajax Boiler in Santa Ana, California, uses software from SpectorSoft Corporation that records all the Web sites employees visit, time spent at each site, and all e-mails sent. Financial services and investment firm Wedbush Securities monitors the daily e-mails, instant messaging, and social networking activity of its 1,000-plus employees. The firm's e-mail monitoring software flags certain types of messages and keywords within messages for further investigation.

A number of firms have fired employees who have stepped out of bounds. A Proofpoint survey found that one in five large U.S. companies fired an employee for violating e-mail policies in the past year. Among managers who fired employees for Internet misuse, the majority did so because the employees' e-mail contained sensitive, confidential, or embarrassing information.

No solution is problem free, but many consultants believe companies should write corporate policies on employee e-mail, social media, and Web use. The policies should include explicit ground rules that state, by position or level, under what circumstances employees can use company facilities for e-mail, blogging, or Web surfing. The policies should also inform employees whether these activities are monitored and explain why.

IBM now has "social computing guidelines" that cover employee activity on sites such as Facebook and Twitter. The guidelines urge employees not to conceal their identities, to remember that they are personally responsible for what they publish, and to refrain from discussing controversial topics that are not related to their IBM role.

The rules should be tailored to specific business needs and organizational cultures. For example, investment firms will need to allow many of their employees access to other investment sites. A company dependent on widespread information sharing, innovation, and independence could very well find that monitoring creates more problems than it solves.

Sources: "Workplace Privacy and Employee Monitoring," Privacy Rights Clearinghouse, June 2013; Samuel Greengard, "How Smartphone Addiction Hurts Productivity," *CIO Insight*, March 11, 2013; Emily Glazer, "P&G Curbs Employees' Internet Use," *The Wall Street Journal*, April 4, 2012; David L. Barron, "Social Media: Frontier for Employee Disputes," *Baseline*, January 19, 2012; Jennifer Lawinski, "Social Media Costs Companies Bigtime," *Baseline*, August 29, 2011; Don Reisinger, "March Madness: The Great Productivity Killer," *CIO Insight*, March 18, 2011; Catey Hill, "Things Your Boss Won't Tell You," *Smart Money*, January 12, 2011.

CASE STUDY QUESTIONS

1. Should managers monitor employee e-mail and Internet usage? Why or why not?

2. Describe an effective e-mail and Web use policy for a company.

3. Should managers inform employees that their Web behavior is being monitored? Or should managers monitor secretly? Why or why not?

Internet. Voice calls can be made and received with a computer equipped with a microphone and speakers or with a VoIP-enabled telephone.

Cable firms such as Time Warner and Cablevision provide VoIP service bundled with their high-speed Internet and cable offerings. Skype offers free VoIP worldwide using a peer-to-peer network, and Google has its own free VoIP service.

Although there are up-front investments required for an IP phone system, VoIP can reduce communication and network management costs by 20 to 30 percent. For example, VoIP saves Virgin Entertainment Group $700,000 per year in long-distance bills. In addition to lowering long-distance costs and eliminating monthly fees for private lines, an IP network provides a single voice-data infrastructure for both telecommunications and computing services. Companies no longer have to maintain separate networks or provide support services and personnel for each different type of network.

Unified Communications

In the past, each of the firm's networks for wired and wireless data, voice communications, and videoconferencing operated independently of each other and had to be managed separately by the information systems department. Now, however, firms are able to merge disparate communications modes into a single universally accessible service using unified communications technology. **Unified communications** integrates disparate channels for voice communications, data communications, instant messaging, e-mail, and electronic conferencing into a single experience where users can seamlessly switch back and forth between different communication modes. Presence technology shows whether a person is available to receive a call. Companies will need to examine how work flows and business processes will be altered by this technology in order to gauge its value.

CenterPoint Properties, a major Chicago area industrial real estate company, used unified communications technology to create collaborative Web sites for each of its real estate deals. Each Web site provides a single point for accessing structured and unstructured

Figure 7.10
A Virtual Private
Network Using the
Internet
*This VPN is a private
network of computers
linked using a secure
"tunnel" connection over
the Internet. It protects
data transmitted over
the public Internet by
encoding the data and
"wrapping" them within
the Internet Protocol (IP).
By adding a wrapper
around a network
message to hide its
content, organizations
can create a private
connection that travels
through the public
Internet.*

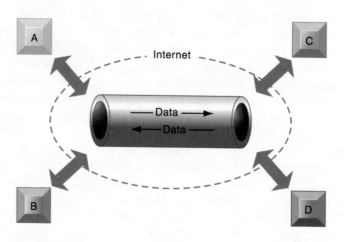

data. Integrated presence technology lets team members e-mail, instant message, call, or videoconference with one click.

Virtual Private Networks

What if you had a marketing group charged with developing new products and services for your firm with members spread across the United States? You would want them to be able to e-mail each other and communicate with the home office without any chance that outsiders could intercept the communications. In the past, one answer to this problem was to work with large private networking firms who offered secure, private, dedicated networks to customers. But this was an expensive solution. A much less-expensive solution is to create a virtual private network within the public Internet.

A **virtual private network (VPN)** is a secure, encrypted, private network that has been configured within a public network to take advantage of the economies of scale and management facilities of large networks, such as the Internet (see Figure 7.10). A VPN provides your firm with secure, encrypted communications at a much lower cost than the same capabilities offered by traditional non-Internet providers who use their private networks to secure communications. VPNs also provide a network infrastructure for combining voice and data networks.

Several competing protocols are used to protect data transmitted over the public Internet, including *Point-to-Point Tunneling Protocol (PPTP)*. In a process called tunneling, packets of data are encrypted and wrapped inside IP packets. By adding this wrapper around a network message to hide its content, business firms create a private connection that travels through the public Internet.

THE WEB

The Web is the most popular Internet service. It's a system with universally accepted standards for storing, retrieving, formatting, and displaying information using a client/server architecture. Web pages are formatted using hypertext with embedded links that connect documents to one another and that also link pages to other objects, such as sound, video, or animation files. When you click a graphic and a video clip plays, you have clicked a hyperlink. A typical **Web site** is a collection of Web pages linked to a home page.

Hypertext

Web pages are based on a standard Hypertext Markup Language (HTML), which formats documents and incorporates dynamic links to other documents and pictures stored in the same or remote computers (see Chapter 5). Web pages are accessible through the Internet because Web browser software operating your computer can request Web pages stored on an Internet host server using the **Hypertext Transfer Protocol (HTTP)**. HTTP is the communications standard used to transfer pages on the Web. For example, when you type a Web address in your browser, such as http://www.sec.gov, your browser sends an HTTP request to the sec.gov server requesting the home page of sec.gov.

HTTP is the first set of letters at the start of every Web address, followed by the domain name, which specifies the organization's server computer that is storing the document. Most companies have a domain name that is the same as or closely related to their official corporate name. The directory path and document name are two more pieces of information within the Web address that help the browser track down the requested page. Together, the address is called a **uniform resource locator (URL)**. When typed into a browser, a URL tells the browser software exactly where to look for the information. For example, in the URL *http://www.megacorp.com/content/features/082610.html*, *http* names the protocol used to display Web pages, *www.megacorp.com* is the domain name, *content/features* is the directory path that identifies where on the domain Web server the page is stored, and *082610.html* is the document name and the name of the format it is in (it is an HTML page).

Web Servers

A Web server is software for locating and managing stored Web pages. It locates the Web pages requested by a user on the computer where they are stored and delivers the Web pages to the user's computer. Server applications usually run on dedicated computers, although they can all reside on a single computer in small organizations.

The most common Web server in use today is Apache HTTP Server, which controls 65 percent of the market. Apache is an open source product that is free of charge and can be downloaded from the Web. Microsoft Internet Information Services (IIS) is the second most commonly used Web server, with 15 percent market share.

Searching for Information on the Web

No one knows for sure how many Web pages there really are. The surface Web is the part of the Web that search engines visit and about which information is recorded. For instance, Google visited an estimated 500 billion pages in 2013, and this reflects a large portion of the publicly accessible Web page population. But there is a "deep Web" that contains an estimated 1 trillion additional pages, many of them proprietary (such as the pages of the *Wall Street Journal Online*, which cannot be visited without a subscription or access code) or that are stored in protected corporate databases. Searching for information on Facebook is another matter. With an estimated one billion members, each with pages of text, photos, and media, the population of Web pages is larger than many estimates. But Facebook is a "closed" Web, and its pages are not searchable by Google or other search engines.

Search Engines Obviously, with so many Web pages, finding specific Web pages that can help you or your business, nearly instantly, is an important problem. The question is, how can you find the one or two pages you really want and need out of billions of indexed Web pages? **Search engines** attempt to solve the problem of finding useful information on the Web nearly instantly, and, arguably, they are the "killer app" of the Internet era. Today's search engines can sift through HTML files, files of Microsoft Office applications, PDF files, as well as audio, video, and image files. There are hundreds of different search engines in the world, but the vast majority of search results are supplied by Google, Yahoo!, and Microsoft's Bing. Bing has reached an all-time high of 17 billion monthly searches in 2013, while Google's share has shrunk slightly (see Figure 7.11).

Web search engines started out in the early 1990s as relatively simple software programs that roamed the nascent Web, visiting pages and gathering information about the content of each page. The first search engines were simple keyword indexes of all the pages they visited, leaving the user with lists of pages that may not have been truly relevant to their search.

In 1994, Stanford University computer science students David Filo and Jerry Yang created a hand-selected list of their favorite Web pages and called it "Yet Another Hierarchical Officious Oracle," or Yahoo. Yahoo was not initially a search engine but rather an edited

Figure 7.11
Top Web Search
Engines
*Google is the most
popular search engine,
handling 83 percent of
Web searches.*

*Sources: Based on data
from comScore Inc., July
2013.*

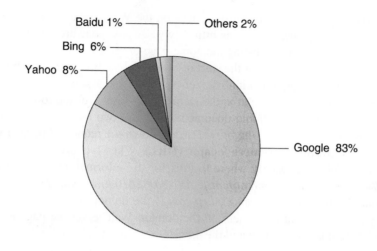

selection of Web sites organized by categories the editors found useful. Currently Yahoo relies on Microsoft's Bing for search results.

In 1998, Larry Page and Sergey Brin, two other Stanford computer science students, released their first version of Google. This search engine was different: Not only did it index each Web page's words but it also ranked search results based on the relevance of each page. Page patented the idea of a page ranking system (called PageRank System), which essentially measures the popularity of a Web page by calculating the number of sites that link to that page as well as the number of pages to which it links. The premise is that really popular Web pages are more "relevant" to users. Brin contributed a unique Web crawler program that indexed not only keywords on a page but also combinations of words (such as authors and the titles of their articles). These two ideas became the foundation for the Google search engine. Figure 7.12 illustrates how Google works.

Mobile Search With the growth of mobile smartphones and tablet computers, and with about 122 million Americans accessing the Internet via mobile devices, the nature of e-commerce and search is changing. Mobile search from smartphones and tablets made up about 26 percent of all searches in 2013, and according to Google will expand rapidly in the next few years. Both Google and Yahoo have developed new search interfaces to make searching and shopping from smartphones more convenient. Amazon, for instance, sold over $1 billion in goods in 2013 through mobile searches of its store (Search Agency, 2013)

Search Engine Marketing Search engines have become major advertising platforms and shopping tools by offering what is now called **search engine marketing**. Searching for information is one of the Web's most popular activities: 60% of American adult Internet users use a search engine at least once a day, generating about 17 billion queries a month. With this huge audience, search engines are the foundation for the most lucrative form of online marketing and advertising, search engine marketing. When users enter a search term at Google, Bing, Yahoo, or any of the other sites serviced by these search engines, they receive two types of listings: sponsored links, for which advertisers have paid to be listed (usually at the top of the search results page), and unsponsored "organic" search results. In addition, advertisers can purchase small text boxes on the side of search results pages. The paid, sponsored advertisements are the fastest growing form of Internet advertising and are powerful new marketing tools that precisely match consumer interests with advertising messages at the right moment. Search engine marketing monetizes the value of the search process. In 2012, search engine marketing generated $21 billion in revenue, over half of all online advertising ($41 billion). Google accounted for over 40% of all online advertising in 2013. About 97% of Google's revenue of $50 billion in 2012 came from online advertising, and 95% of the ad revenue came from search engine marketing (Google, 2012).

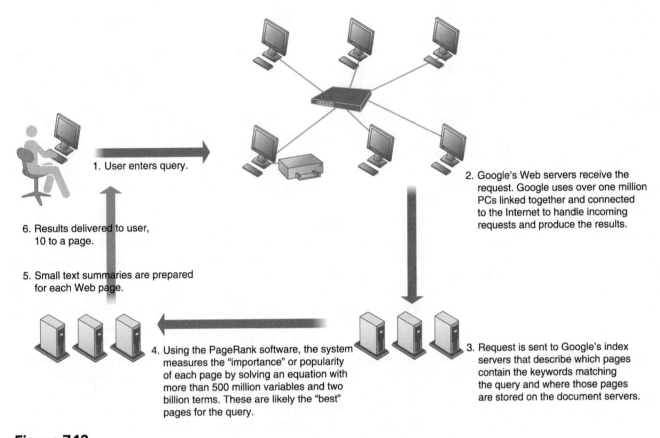

1. User enters query.

2. Google's Web servers receive the request. Google uses over one million PCs linked together and connected to the Internet to handle incoming requests and produce the results.

6. Results delivered to user, 10 to a page.

5. Small text summaries are prepared for each Web page.

4. Using the PageRank software, the system measures the "importance" or popularity of each page by solving an equation with more than 500 million variables and two billion terms. These are likely the "best" pages for the query.

3. Request is sent to Google's index servers that describe which pages contain the keywords matching the query and where those pages are stored on the document servers.

Figure 7.12
How Google Works
The Google search engine is continuously crawling the Web, indexing the content of each page, calculating its popularity, and storing the pages so that it can respond quickly to user requests to see a page. The entire process takes about one-half second.

Because search engine marketing is so effective (it has the highest click-through rate and the highest return on ad investment), companies seek to optimize their Web sites for search engine recognition. The better optimized the page is, the higher a ranking it will achieve in search engine result listings. **Search engine optimization (SEO)** is the process of improving the quality and volume of Web traffic to a Web site by employing a series of techniques that help a Web site achieve a higher ranking with the major search engines when certain keywords and phrases are put into the search field. One technique is to make sure that the keywords used in the Web site description match the keywords likely to be used as search terms by prospective customers. For example, your Web site is more likely to be among the first ranked by search engines if it uses the keyword "lighting" rather than "lamps" if most prospective customers are searching for "lighting." It is also advantageous to link your Web site to as many other Web sites as possible because search engines evaluate such links to determine the popularity of a Web page and how it is linked to other content on the Web. Search engines can be gamed by scammers who create thousands of phony Web site pages and link them altogether, or link them to a single retailer's site in an attempt to fool Google's search engine. Firms can also pay so-called "link farms" to link to their site. Google changed its search algorithm in 2012. Codenamed "Penguin," the new algorithm examines the quality of links more carefully with the intent of down ranking sites that have a suspicious pattern of sites linking to them. Penguin is updated annually and published.

In general, search engines have been very helpful to small businesses that cannot afford large marketing campaigns. Because shoppers are looking for a specific product or service when they use search engines, they are what marketers call "hot prospects"—people who are looking for information and often intending to buy. Moreover, search engines charge only for click-throughs to a site. Merchants do not have to pay for ads that don't work, only for ads that receive a click. Consumers benefit from search engine marketing because ads for merchants appear only when consumers are looking for a specific product. There are no pop-ups, Flash animations, videos, interstitials, e-mails, or other irrelevant communications to deal with. Thus, search engine marketing saves consumers cognitive energy and reduces search costs (including the cost of transportation needed to physically search for products). In a recent study, the global value of search to both merchants and consumers was estimated to be more than $800 billion, with about 65 percent of the benefit going to consumers in the form of lower search costs and lower prices (McKinsey, 2011). Google and Microsoft face challenges ahead as desktop PC search growth slows, and revenues decline because the price of search engine ads is declining slightly. The growth in mobile search does not make up for the loss of desktop search because mobile ads sell for generally half as much as desktop search ads.

Social Search One problem with Google and mechanical search engines is that they are so thorough: Enter a search for "ultra computers" and in .2 seconds you will receive over 300 million reponses! Search engines are not very discriminating. **Social search** is an effort to provide fewer, more relevant, and trustworthy search results based on a person's network of social contacts. In contrast to the top search engines that use a mathematical algorithm to find pages that satisfy your query, a social search Web site would review your friends' recommendations (and their friends'), their past Web visits, and their use of "Like" buttons.

In January 2013 Facebook launched Graph Search, a social network search engine that responds to user search queries with information from the user's social network of friends and connections. Graph Search relies upon the huge amount of data on Facebook that is, or can be, linked to individuals and organizations. You might use Graph Search to search for Boston restaurants that your friends like, alumni from the University of South Carolina who like Lady Gaga, or pictures of your friends before 2010. Google has developed Google +1 as a social layer on top of its existing search engine. Users can place a +1 next to the Web sites they found helpful, and their friends will be notified automatically. Subsequent searches by their friends would list the +1 sites recommended by friends higher up on the page. One problem with social search is that your close friends may not have intimate knowledge of topics you are exploring, or they may have tastes you don't appreciate. It's also possible your close friends don't have any knowledge about what you are searching for.

Semantic Search   Another way for search engines to become more discriminating and helpful is to make search engines that could understand what it is we are really looking for. Called "semantic search" the goal is to build a search engine that could really understand human language and behavior. For instance, in 2012 Google's search engine began delivering more than millions of links. It started to give users more facts and direct answers, and to provide more relevant links to sites based on the search engine's estimation of what the user intended, and even on the user's past search behavior. Google's search engine is trying to understand what people are most likely thinking about when they search for something. Google hopes to use its massive database of objects (people, places, things), and smart software to provide users better results than just millions of hits. For instance, do a search on "Lake Tahoe" and the search engine will return basic facts about Tahoe (altitude, average temperature, and local fish), a map, and hotel accommodations (Efrati, 2012).

Although search engines were originally designed to search text documents, the explosion of photos and videos on the Internet created a demand for searching and classifying these visual objects. Facial recognition software can create a digital version of a human face. In 2012 Facebook introduced its facial recognition software and combined it with tagging, to create a new feature called Tag Suggest. The software creates a digital facial print, similar to a finger print. Users can put their own tagged photo on their timeline, and their friend's timelines. Once a person's photo is tagged, Facebook can pick that person out of a group photo, and identify for others who is in the photo. You can also search for people on Facebook using their digital image to find and identify them.

Intelligent Agent Shopping Bots Chapter 11 describes the capabilities of software agents with built-in intelligence that can gather or filter information and perform other tasks to assist users. **Shopping bots** use intelligent agent software for searching the Internet for shopping information. Shopping bots such as MySimon or Google Product Search can help people interested in making a purchase filter and retrieve information about products of interest, evaluate competing products according to criteria the users have established, and negotiate with vendors for price and delivery terms. Many of these shopping agents search the Web for pricing and availability of products specified by the user and return a list of sites that sell the item along with pricing information and a purchase link.

Web 2.0

Today's Web sites don't just contain static content—they enable people to collaborate, share information, and create new services and content online. These second-generation interactive Internet-based services are referred to as **Web 2.0**. If you have shared photos over the Internet at Flickr or another photo site, pinned a photo on Pinterest, posted a video to YouTube, created a blog, or added an app to your Facebook page, you've used some of these Web 2.0 services.

Web 2.0 has four defining features: interactivity, real-time user control, social participation (sharing), and user-generated content. The technologies and services behind these features include cloud computing, software mashups and apps, blogs, RSS, wikis, and social networks.

Mashups, which we introduced in Chapter 5, are software services that enable users and system developers to mix and match content or software components to create something entirely new. For example, Yahoo's photo storage and sharing site Flickr combines photos with other information about the images provided by users and tools to make it usable within other programming environments. Web 2.0 tools and services have fueled the creation of social networks and other online communities where people can interact with one another in the manner of their choosing.

A **blog**, the popular term for a Weblog, is a personal Web site that typically contains a series of chronological entries (newest to oldest) by its author, and links to related Web pages. Blogging is a major activity for U.S. Internet users: 74 million read blogs, and 22 million write blogs or post to blogs. The blog may include a *blogroll* (a collection of links to other blogs) and *trackbacks* (a list of entries in other blogs that refer to a post on the first blog). Most blogs allow readers to post comments on the blog entries as well. The act of creating a blog is often referred to as "blogging." Blogs can be hosted by a third-party service such as Blogger. com, TypePad.com, and Xanga.com, and blogging features have been incorporated into social networks such as Facebook and collaboration platforms such as Lotus Notes. WordPress is a leading open source blogging tool and content management system. **Microblogging**, used in Twitter, is a type of blogging that features short posts of 140 characters or less.

Blog pages are usually variations on templates provided by the blogging service or software. Therefore, millions of people without HTML skills of any kind can post their own Web pages and share content with others. The totality of blog-related Web sites is often referred to as the **blogosphere**. Although blogs have become popular personal publishing tools, they also have business uses (see Chapters 2 and 10).

If you're an avid blog reader, you might use RSS to keep up with your favorite blogs without constantly checking them for updates. **RSS**, which stands for Really Simple Syndication or Rich Site Summary, pulls specified content from Web sites and feeds it automatically to users' computers. RSS reader software gathers material from the Web sites or blogs that you tell it to scan and brings new information from those sites to you. RSS readers are available through Web sites such as Google and Yahoo, and they have been incorporated into the major Web browsers and e-mail programs.

Blogs allow visitors to add comments to the original content, but they do not allow visitors to change the original posted material. **Wikis**, in contrast, are collaborative Web sites where visitors can add, delete, or modify content on the site, including the work of previous authors. Wiki comes from the Hawaiian word for "quick."

Wiki software typically provides a template that defines layout and elements common to all pages, displays user-editable software program code, and then renders the content into an HTML-based page for display in a Web browser. Some wiki software allows only basic text formatting, whereas other tools allow the use of tables, images, or even interactive elements, such as polls or games. Most wikis provide capabilities for monitoring the work of other users and correcting mistakes.

Because wikis make information sharing so easy, they have many business uses. The U.S. Department of Homeland Security's National Cyber Security Center (NCSC) deployed a wiki to facilitate collaboration among federal agencies on cybersecurity. NCSC and other agencies use the wiki for real-time information sharing on threats, attacks, and responses and as a repository for technical and standards information. Pixar Wiki is a collaborative community wiki for publicizing the work of Pixar Animation Studios. The wiki format allows anyone to create or edit an article about a Pixar film.

Social networking sites enable users to build communities of friends and professional colleagues. Members typically create a "profile," a Web page for posting photos, videos, MP3 files, and text, and then share these profiles with others on the service identified as their "friends" or contacts. Social networking sites are highly interactive, offer real-time user control, rely on user-generated content, and are broadly based on social participation and sharing of content and opinions. Leading social networking sites include Facebook, Twitter (with 1.1 billion and 200 million active users respectively in 2013), and LinkedIn (for professional contacts).

For many, social networking sites are the defining Web 2.0 application, and one that has radically changed how people spend their time online; how people communicate and with whom; how business people stay in touch with customers, suppliers, and employees; how providers of goods and services learn about their customers; and how advertisers reach potential customers. The large social networking sites are also morphing into application development platforms where members can create and sell software applications to other members of the community. Facebook alone has over 1 million developers who created over 550,000 applications for gaming, video sharing, and communicating with friends and family. We talk more about business applications of social networking in Chapters 2 and 10, and you can find social networking discussions in many other chapters of this book. You can also find a more detailed discussion of Web 2.0 in our Learning Tracks.

Web 3.0 and the Future Web

Every day, about 120 million Americans enter 600 million queries into search engines (about 17 billion per month). How many of these 600 million queries produce a meaningful result (a useful answer in the first three listings)? Arguably, fewer than half. Google, Yahoo, Microsoft, and Amazon are all trying to increase the odds of people finding meaningful answers to search engine queries. But with over 500 billion Web pages indexed, the means available for finding the information you really want are quite primitive, based on the words used on the pages, and the relative popularity of the page among people who use those same search terms. In other words, it's hit or miss.

To a large extent, the future of the Web involves developing techniques to make searching the 500 billion public Web pages more productive and meaningful for ordinary people. Web 1.0 solved the problem of obtaining access to information. Web 2.0 solved the problem of sharing that information with others and building new Web experiences. **Web 3.0** is the promise of a future Web where all this digital information, all these contacts, can be woven together into a single meaningful experience.

Sometimes this is referred to as the **Semantic Web**. "Semantic" refers to meaning. Most of the Web's content today is designed for humans to read and for computers to display, not for computer programs to analyze and manipulate. Semantic Search, described above, is a subset of a larger effort to make the Web more intelligent, more humanlike (W3C, 2012). Search engines can discover when a particular term or keyword appears in a Web document, but they do not really understand its meaning or how it relates to other information on the Web. You can check this out on Google by entering two searches.

First, enter "Paris Hilton". Next, enter "Hilton in Paris". Because Google does not understand ordinary English, it has no idea that you are interested in the Hilton Hotel in Paris in the second search. Because it cannot understand the meaning of pages it has indexed, Google's search engine returns the most popular pages for those queries where "Hilton" and "Paris" appear on the pages.

First described in a 2001 *Scientific American* article, the Semantic Web is a collaborative effort led by the World Wide Web Consortium to add a layer of meaning atop the existing Web to reduce the amount of human involvement in searching for and processing Web information (Berners-Lee et al., 2001). For instance, the New York Times launched a semantic application called Longitude which provides a graphical interface to access the Times content. For instance, you can ask for stories about Germany in the last 24 hours, or a city in the United States, to retrieve all recent stories in the Times (Donaldson, 2012).

Views on the future of the Web vary, but they generally focus on ways to make the Web more "intelligent," with machine-facilitated understanding of information promoting a more intuitive and effective user experience. For instance, let's say you want to set up a party with your tennis buddies at a local restaurant Friday night after work. One problem is that you are already scheduled to go to a movie with another friend. In a Semantic Web 3.0 environment, you would be able to coordinate this change in plans with the schedules of your tennis buddies and the schedule of your movie friend, and make a reservation at the restaurant all with a single set of commands issued as text or voice to your handheld smartphone. Right now, this capability is beyond our grasp.

Work proceeds slowly on making the Web a more intelligent experience, in large part because it is difficult to make machines, including software programs, that are truly intelligent like humans. But there are other views of the future Web. Some see a 3-D Web where you can walk through pages in a 3-D environment. Others point to the idea of a pervasive Web that controls everything from a city's traffic lights and water usage, to the lights in your living room, to your car's rear view mirror, not to mention managing your calendar and appointments. This is referred to as the "Internet of Things."

The Internet of Things includes the widespread use and distribution of sensors. Firms like IBM, HP, and Oracle are exploring how to build smart machines, factories, and cities through extensive use of remote sensors and fast cloud computing. We provide more detail on this topic in the following section.

The "App Internet" is another element in the future Web. The growth of apps within the mobile platform is astounding: Over 80% of mobile minutes in the United States are generated through apps, only 20% using browsers. Apps give users direct access to content and are much faster than loading a browser and searching for content.

The **visual Web** is another part of the future Web. The "visual Web" refers to Web sites like Pinterest where pictures replace text documents, where users search on pictures, and where pictures of products replace display ads for products. Pinterest is a social networking site that provides users (as well as brands) with an online board to which they can "pin" interesting pictures. Looking for a blue dress, or black dress shirt? Google will deliver thousands of links to sites that sell these items. Pinterest will deliver a much smaller collection of magazine quality photos linked subtly to vendor Web sites. Considered the fastest growing Web site in history, Pinterest has 25 million monthly users and was the 50th most popular Web destination in 2013. The Instagram app is another example of the visual Web. Instagram is a photo and video sharing site that allows users to take pictures, enhance them, and share them with friends on other social sites like Facebook, Twitter, Tumblr, and Google+. In 2013 Instagram had 130 million users.

Other complementary trends leading toward a future Web 3.0 include more widespread use of cloud computing and software as a service (SaaS) business models, ubiquitous connectivity among mobile platforms and Internet access devices, and the transformation of the Web from a network of separate siloed applications and content into a more seamless and interoperable whole. These more modest visions of the future Web 3.0 are more likely to be realized in the near term.

7.4 The Wireless Revolution

Welcome to the wireless revolution! Cell phones, smartphones, tablets, and wireless-enabled personal computers have morphed into portable media and computing platforms that let you perform many of the computing tasks you used to do at your desk, and a whole lot more. We introduced smartphones in our discussions of the mobile digital platform in Chapters 1 and 5. **Smartphones** such as the iPhone, Android phones, and BlackBerry combine the functionality of a cell phone with that of a mobile laptop computer with Wi-Fi capability. This makes it possible to combine music, video, Internet access, and telephone service in one device. A large part of the Internet is becoming a mobile, access-anywhere, broadband service for the delivery of video, music, and Web search.

CELLULAR SYSTEMS

In 2013, over 1.6 billion cell phones were sold worldwide. In the United States, there are 371 million cell phone subscriptions, and 140 million people have smartphones. About 143 million people access the Web using their phone (eMarketer, 2013). In a few years, smartphones will be the predominant source of searches, not the desktop PC. Digital cellular service uses several competing standards. In Europe and much of the rest of the world outside the United Sates, the standard is Global System for Mobile Communications (GSM). GSM's strength is its international roaming capability. There are GSM cell phone systems in the United States, including T-Mobile and AT&T.

A competing standard in the United States is Code Division Multiple Access (CDMA), which is the system used by Verizon and Sprint. CDMA was developed by the military during World War II. It transmits over several frequencies, occupies the entire spectrum, and randomly assigns users to a range of frequencies over time, making it more efficient than GSM.

Earlier generations of cellular systems were designed primarily for voice and limited data transmission in the form of short text messages. Today wireless carriers offer 3G and 4G networks. **3G networks**, with transmission speeds ranging from 144 Kbps for mobile users in, say, a car, to more than 2 Mbps for stationary users, offer fair transmission speeds for e-mail, browsing the Web, and online shopping, but are too slow for videos. **4G networks** have much higher speeds: 100 megabits/second download, and 50 megabits upload speed, with more than enough capacity for watching high definition video on your smartphone. Long Term Evolution (LTE) and mobile Worldwide Interoperability for Microwave Access (WiMax—see the following section) are the current 4G standards.

WIRELESS COMPUTER NETWORKS AND INTERNET ACCESS

An array of technologies provide high-speed wireless access to the Internet for PCs and mobile devices. These new high-speed services have extended Internet access to numerous locations that could not be covered by traditional wired Internet services, and have made ubiquitous computing, anywhere, anytime, a reality.

Bluetooth

Bluetooth is the popular name for the 802.15 wireless networking standard, which is useful for creating small **personal area networks (PANs)**. It links up to eight devices within a 10-meter area using low-power, radio-based communication and can transmit up to 722 Kbps in the 2.4-GHz band.

Wireless phones, pagers, computers, printers, and computing devices using Bluetooth communicate with each other and even operate each other without direct user intervention (see Figure 7.13). For example, a person could direct a notebook computer to send a document file wirelessly to a printer. Bluetooth connects wireless keyboards and mice to PCs or cell phones to earpieces without wires. Bluetooth has low power requirements, making it appropriate for battery-powered handheld computers or cell phones.

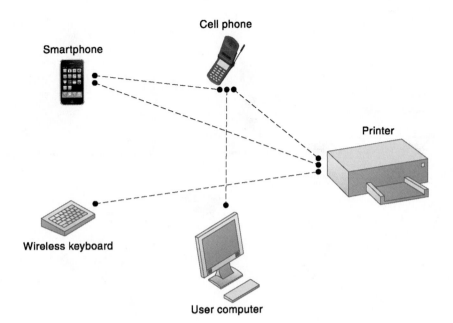

Smartphone

Cell phone

Printer

Wireless keyboard

User computer

Figure 7.13
A Bluetooth
Network (PAN)
*Bluetooth enables a
variety of devices,
including cell phones,
smartphones, wireless
keyboards and mice,
PCs, and printers, to
interact wirelessly with
each other within a small
30-foot (10-meter) area.
In addition to the links
shown, Bluetooth can be
used to network similar
devices to send data
from one PC to another,
for example.*

Although Bluetooth lends itself to personal networking, it has uses in large corporations. For example, FedEx drivers use Bluetooth to transmit the delivery data captured by their handheld PowerPad computers to cellular transmitters, which forward the data to corporate computers. Drivers no longer need to spend time docking their handheld units physically in the transmitters, and Bluetooth has saved FedEx $20 million per year.

Wi-Fi and Wireless Internet Access

The 802.11 set of standards for wireless LANs and wireless Internet access is also known as **Wi-Fi**. The first of these standards to be widely adopted was 802.11b, which can transmit up to 11 Mbps in the unlicensed 2.4-GHz band and has an effective distance of 30 to 50 meters. The 802.11g standard can transmit up to 54 Mbps in the 2.4-GHz range. 802.11n is capable of transmitting over 100 Mbps. Today's PCs and netbooks have built-in support for Wi-Fi, as do the iPhone, iPad, and other smartphones.

In most Wi-Fi communication, wireless devices communicate with a wired LAN using access points. An access point is a box consisting of a radio receiver/transmitter and antennas that links to a wired network, router, or hub. Mobile access points such as Verizon's Mobile Hotspots use the existing cellular network to create Wi-Fi connections.

Figure 7.14 illustrates an 802.11 wireless LAN that connects a small number of mobile devices to a larger wired LAN and to the Internet. Most wireless devices are client machines. The servers that the mobile client stations need to use are on the wired LAN. The access point controls the wireless stations and acts as a bridge between the main wired LAN and the wireless LAN. (A bridge connects two LANs based on different technologies.) The access point also controls the wireless stations.

The most popular use for Wi-Fi today is for high-speed wireless Internet service. In this instance, the access point plugs into an Internet connection, which could come from a cable service or DSL telephone service. Computers within range of the access point use it to link wirelessly to the Internet.

Hotspots typically consist of one or more access points providing wireless Internet access in a public place. Some hotspots are free or do not require any additional software to use; others may require activation and the establishment of a user account by providing a credit card number over the Web.

Businesses of all sizes are using Wi-Fi networks to provide low-cost wireless LANs and Internet access. Wi-Fi hotspots can be found in hotels, airport lounges, libraries, cafes, and

Figure 7.14
An 802.11 Wireless LAN
Mobile laptop computers equipped with network interface cards link to the wired LAN by communicating with the access point. The access point uses radio waves to transmit network signals from the wired network to the client adapters, which convert them into data that the mobile device can understand. The client adapter then transmits the data from the mobile device back to the access point, which forwards the data to the wired network.

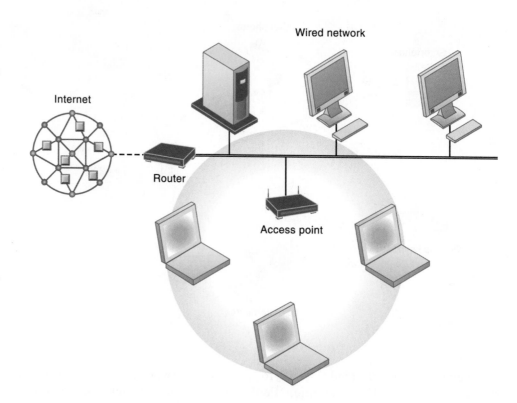

college campuses to provide mobile access to the Internet. Dartmouth College is one of many campuses where students now use Wi-Fi for research, course work, and entertainment.

Wi-Fi technology poses several challenges, however. One is Wi-Fi's security features, which make these wireless networks vulnerable to intruders. We provide more detail about Wi-Fi security issues in Chapter 8.

Another drawback of Wi-Fi networks is susceptibility to interference from nearby systems operating in the same spectrum, such as wireless phones, microwave ovens, or other wireless LANs. However, wireless networks based on the 802.11n standard are able to solve this problem by using multiple wireless antennas in tandem to transmit and receive data and technology called *MIMO* (multiple input multiple output) to coordinate multiple simultaneous radio signals.

WiMax

A surprisingly large number of areas in the United States and throughout the world do not have access to Wi-Fi or fixed broadband connectivity. The range of Wi-Fi systems is no more than 300 feet from the base station, making it difficult for rural groups that don't have cable or DSL service to find wireless access to the Internet.

The IEEE developed a new family of standards known as WiMax to deal with these problems. **WiMax**, which stands for Worldwide Interoperability for Microwave Access, is the popular term for IEEE Standard 802.16. It has a wireless access range of up to 31 miles and transmission speed of up to 75 Mbps.

WiMax antennas are powerful enough to beam high-speed Internet connections to rooftop antennas of homes and businesses that are miles away. Cellular handsets and laptops with WiMax capabilities are appearing in the marketplace. Mobile WiMax is one of the 4G network technologies we discussed earlier in this chapter.

RFID AND WIRELESS SENSOR NETWORKS

Mobile technologies are creating new efficiencies and ways of working throughout the enterprise. In addition to the wireless systems we have just described, radio frequency identification systems and wireless sensor networks are having a major impact.

Radio Frequency Identification (RFID)

Radio frequency identification (RFID) systems provide a powerful technology for tracking the movement of goods throughout the supply chain. RFID systems use tiny tags with embedded microchips containing data about an item and its location to transmit radio signals over a short distance to RFID readers. The RFID readers then pass the data over a network to a computer for processing. Unlike bar codes, RFID tags do not need line-of-sight contact to be read.

The RFID tag is electronically programmed with information that can uniquely identify an item plus other information about the item, such as its location, where and when it was made, or its status during production. Embedded in the tag is a microchip for storing the data. The rest of the tag is an antenna that transmits data to the reader.

The reader unit consists of an antenna and radio transmitter with a decoding capability attached to a stationary or handheld device. The reader emits radio waves in ranges anywhere from 1 inch to 100 feet, depending on its power output, the radio frequency employed, and surrounding environmental conditions. When a RFID tag comes within the range of the reader, the tag is activated and starts sending data. The reader captures these data, decodes them, and sends them back over a wired or wireless network to a host computer for further processing (see Figure 7.15). Both RFID tags and antennas come in a variety of shapes and sizes.

In inventory control and supply chain management, RFID systems capture and manage more detailed information about items in warehouses or in production than bar coding systems. If a large number of items are shipped together, RFID systems track each pallet, lot, or even unit item in the shipment. This technology may help companies such as Walmart improve receiving and storage operations by improving their ability to "see" exactly what stock is stored in warehouses or on retail store shelves. Continental Tires, described in the chapter-opening case, used RFID technology to precisely track the location of tire components as they moved through the production process.

Walmart has installed RFID readers at store receiving docks to record the arrival of pallets and cases of goods shipped with RFID tags. The RFID reader reads the tags a second time just as the cases are brought onto the sales floor from backroom storage areas. Software combines sales data from Walmart's point-of-sale systems and the RFID data regarding the number of cases brought out to the sales floor. The program determines

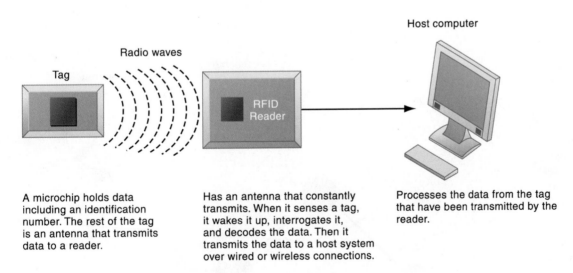

A microchip holds data including an identification number. The rest of the tag is an antenna that transmits data to a reader.

Has an antenna that constantly transmits. When it senses a tag, it wakes it up, interrogates it, and decodes the data. Then it transmits the data to a host system over wired or wireless connections.

Processes the data from the tag that have been transmitted by the reader.

Figure 7.15
How RFID Works
RFID uses low-powered radio transmitters to read data stored in a tag at distances ranging from 1 inch to 100 feet. The reader captures the data from the tag and sends them over a network to a host computer for processing.

which items will soon be depleted and automatically generates a list of items to pick in the warehouse to replenish store shelves before they run out. This information helps Walmart reduce out-of-stock items, increase sales, and further shrink its costs.

The cost of RFID tags used to be too high for widespread use, but now it starts at around 7 cents per tag in the United States. As the price decreases, RFID is starting to become cost-effective for many applications.

In addition to installing RFID readers and tagging systems, companies may need to upgrade their hardware and software to process the massive amounts of data produced by RFID systems—transactions that could add up to tens or hundreds of terabytes.

Software is used to filter, aggregate, and prevent RFID data from overloading business networks and system applications. Applications often need to be redesigned to accept large volumes of frequently generated RFID data and to share those data with other applications. Major enterprise software vendors, including SAP and Oracle PeopleSoft, now offer RFID-ready versions of their supply chain management applications.

Wireless Sensor Networks

If your company wanted state-of-the art technology to monitor building security or detect hazardous substances in the air, it might deploy a wireless sensor network. **Wireless sensor networks (WSNs)** are networks of interconnected wireless devices that are embedded into the physical environment to provide measurements of many points over large spaces. These devices have built-in processing, storage, and radio frequency sensors and antennas. They are linked into an interconnected network that routes the data they capture to a computer for analysis.

These networks range from hundreds to thousands of nodes. Because wireless sensor devices are placed in the field for years at a time without any maintenance or human intervention, they must have very low power requirements and batteries capable of lasting for years.

Figure 7.16 illustrates one type of wireless sensor network, with data from individual nodes flowing across the network to a server with greater processing power. The server acts as a gateway to a network based on Internet technology.

Wireless sensor networks are valuable in areas such as monitoring environmental changes, monitoring traffic or military activity, protecting property, efficiently operating and managing machinery and vehicles, establishing security perimeters, monitoring supply chain management, or detecting chemical, biological, or radiological material.

Figure 7.16
A Wireless Sensor Network
The small circles represent lower-level nodes and the larger circles represent high-end nodes. Lower-level nodes forward data to each other or to higher-level nodes, which transmit data more rapidly and speed up network performance.

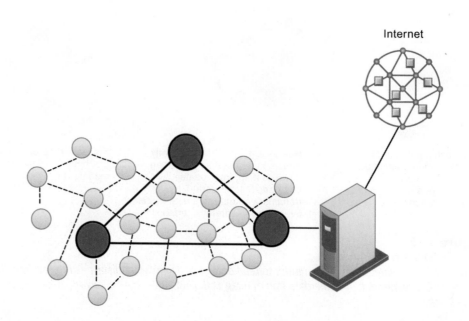

RFID systems and wireless sensor networks are major sources of "Big Data" that organizations are starting to analyze to improve their operations and decision making. Output from these systems is fueling what is called the Industrial Internet, also known as the **Internet of Things**, in which machines such as jet engines, power plant turbines, or agricultural sensors constantly gather data and send the data over the Internet for analysis. The data might signal the need to take action, such as replacing a part that's close to wearing out, restocking a product on a store shelf, starting the watering system for a soybean field, or slowing down a turbine. Over time, more and more everyday physical objects will be connected to the Internet and will be able to identify themselves to other devices, creating networks that can sense and respond as data changes. Another example is the "smart city," described in the Chapter 11 Interactive Session on Organizations. You'll see more examples of the Internet of Things in Chapter 11.

Review Summary

1 **What are the principal components of telecommunications networks and key networking technologies?** A simple network consists of two or more connected computers. Basic network components include computers, network interfaces, a connection medium, network operating system software, and either a hub or a switch. The networking infrastructure for a large company includes the traditional telephone system, mobile cellular communication, wireless local area networks, videoconferencing systems, a corporate Web site, intranets, extranets, and an array of local and wide area networks, including the Internet.

Contemporary networks have been shaped by the rise of client/server computing, the use of packet switching, and the adoption of Transmission Control Protocol/Internet Protocol (TCP/IP) as a universal communications standard for linking disparate networks and computers, including the Internet. Protocols provide a common set of rules that enable communication among diverse components in a telecommunications network.

2 **What are the different types of networks?** The principal physical transmission media are twisted copper telephone wire, coaxial copper cable, fiber-optic cable, and wireless transmission.

Local area networks (LANs) connect PCs and other digital devices together within a 500-meter radius and are used today for many corporate computing tasks. Wide area networks (WANs) span broad geographical distances, ranging from several miles to continents, and are often private networks that are independently managed. Metropolitan area networks (MANs) span a single urban area.

Digital subscriber line (DSL) technologies, cable Internet connections, and T1 lines are often used for high-capacity Internet connections.

3 **How do the Internet and Internet technology work, and how do they support communication and e-business?** The Internet is a worldwide network of networks that uses the client/server model of computing and the TCP/IP network reference model. Every computer on the Internet is assigned a unique numeric IP address. The Domain Name System (DNS) converts IP addresses to more user-friendly domain names. Worldwide Internet policies are established by organizations and government bodies, such as the Internet Architecture Board (IAB) and the World Wide Web Consortium (W3C).

Major Internet services include e-mail, newsgroups, chatting, instant messaging, Telnet, FTP, and the Web. Web pages are based on Hypertext Markup Language (HTML) and can display text, graphics, video, and audio. Web site directories, search engines, and RSS technology help users locate the information they need on the Web. RSS, blogs, social networking, and wikis are features of Web 2.0.

Firms are also starting to realize economies by using VoIP technology for voice transmission and by using virtual private networks (VPNs) as low-cost alternatives to private WANs.

4 **What are the principal technologies and standards for wireless networking, communication, and Internet access?** Cellular networks are evolving toward high-speed, high-bandwidth, digital packet-switched transmission. Broadband 3G networks are capable of transmitting data at speeds ranging from 144 Kbps to more than 2 Mbps. 4G networks capable of transmission speeds of 100 Mbps are starting to be rolled out.

Major cellular standards include Code Division Multiple Access (CDMA), which is used primarily in the United States, and Global System for Mobile Communications (GSM), which is the standard in Europe and much of the rest of the world.

Standards for wireless computer networks include Bluetooth (802.15) for small personal area networks (PANs), Wi-Fi (802.11) for local area networks (LANs), and WiMax (802.16) for metropolitan area networks (MANs).

5 **Why are radio frequency identification (RFID) and wireless sensor networks valuable for business?** Radio frequency identification (RFID) systems provide a powerful technology for tracking the movement of goods by using tiny tags with embedded data about an item and its location. RFID readers read the radio signals transmitted by these tags and pass the data over a network to a computer for processing. Wireless sensor networks (WSNs) are networks of interconnected wireless sensing and transmitting devices that are embedded into the physical environment to provide measurements of many points over large spaces.

Key Terms

3G Networks, 268
4G networks, 268
Bandwidth, 250
Blog, 265
Blogosphere, 265
Bluetooth, 268
Broadband, 244
Cable Internet connections, 251
Chat, 256
Digital subscriber line (DSL), 251
Domain name, 252
Domain Name System (DNS), 252
E-mail, 256
File Transfer Protocol (FTP), 256
Hertz, 250
Hotspots, 269
Hubs, 245
Hypertext Transfer Protocol (HTTP), 260
Instant messaging, 256
Internet of Things, 273

Internet Protocol (IP) address, 251
Internet service provider (ISP), 250
Internet2, 255
IPv6, 255
Local area network (LAN), 249
Metropolitan area network (MAN), 250
Microblogging, 265
Modem, 248
Network operating system (NOS), 245
Packet switching, 246
Peer-to-peer, 250
Personal area networks (PANs), 268
Protocol, 247
Radio frequency identification (RFID), 271
Router, 245
RSS, 265
Search engines, 261

Search engine marketing, 262
Search engine optimization (SEO), 263
Semantic Web, 266
Shopping bots, 265
Smartphones, 268
Social networking, 266
Social search, 264
Software-defined networking (SDN), 245
Switch, 245
T1 lines, 251
Telnet, 256
Transmission Control Protocol/Internet Protocol (TCP/IP), 247
Unified communications, 259
Uniform resource locator (URL), 261
Virtual private network (VPN), 260
Visual Web, 267
Voice over IP (VoIP), 257
Web 2.0, 265

Review Questions

7-1 What are the principal components of telecommunications networks and key networking technologies?
- Describe the features of a simple network and the network infrastructure for a large company.
- Describe one of the major problems facing corporations today with respect to telecommunications.
- Name and describe the principal technologies and trends that have shaped contemporary telecommunications systems.
- List and describe the four layers of the Department of Defense's reference model for TCP/IP.

7-2 What are the different types of networks?
- Distinguish between a LAN, MAN, and WAN.
- List and describe the different types of physical transmission media.

7-3 How do the Internet and Internet technology work, and how do they support communication and e-business?
- Define the Internet, describe how it works, and explain how it provides business value.
- Explain how the Domain Name System (DNS) and IP addressing system work.
- List and describe the principal Internet services.
- Define unified communications and explain how it provides value to businesses.
- List and describe alternative ways of locating information on the Web.
- Compare Web 2.0 and Web 3.0.

7-4 What are the principal technologies and standards for wireless networking, communications, and Internet access?
- Define Bluetooth, Wi-Fi, WiMax, and 3G and 4G networks.
- Describe the capabilities of each and for which types of applications each is best suited.

7-5 Why are RFID and wireless sensor networks (WSNs) valuable for business?
- Define RFID, explain how it works, and describe how it provides value to businesses.
- Define WSNs, explain how they work, and describe the kinds of applications that use them.

Discussion Questions

7-6 It has been said that within the next few years, smartphones will become the single most important digital device we own. Discuss the implications of this statement.

7-7 Does anyone own the Internet? Discuss how the Internet is currently governed and consider whether countries should be able to impose its own rules on the Internet within their own borders.

7-8 Compare Wi-Fi and high-speed cellular systems for accessing the Internet. What are the advantages and disadvantages of each?

Hands-On MIS Projects

The projects in this section give you hands-on experience evaluating and selecting communications technology, using spreadsheet software to improve selection of telecommunications services, and using Web search engines for business research.

MANAGEMENT DECISION PROBLEMS

7-9   Your company supplies ceramic floor tiles to Leroy Merlin, Bricorama, and other home improvement stores in France. You have been asked to start using radio frequency identification tags on each case of tiles you ship to help your customers improve the management of your products and those of other suppliers in their warehouses. Use the Web to identify the cost of hardware, software, and networking components for an RFID system for your company. What factors should be considered? What are the key decisions that have to be made in determining whether your firm should adopt this technology?

7-10 BD sells medical devices and instrument systems to hospitals, health clinics, medical offices, and laboratories in over 50 countries. The company employs over 30,000 people around the world, including account managers, customer service and support representatives, and warehouse staff. Management is considering adopting a system for unified communications. What factors should be considered? What are the key decisions that have to be made in determining whether to adopt this technology? Use the Web, if necessary, to find out more about unified communications and its costs.

IMPROVING DECISION MAKING: USING SPREADSHEET SOFTWARE TO EVALUATE WIRELESS SERVICES

Software skills: Spreadsheet formulas, formatting
Business skills: Analyzing telecommunications services and costs

7-11 In this project, you'll use the Web to research alternative wireless services and use spreadsheet software to calculate wireless service costs for a sales force.

You would like to equip your sales force of 35, based in Dublin, Ireland, with mobile phones that have capabilities for voice transmission, text messaging, and taking and sending photos. Use the Web to select a wireless service provider that provides international service as well as good service in your home area. Examine the features of the mobile handsets offered by each of these vendors. Assume that each of the 35 salespeople will need to spend three hours per weekday between 8 a.m. and 6 p.m. on mobile voice communication, send 30 text messages per weekday, and send five photos per week. Use your spreadsheet software to determine the wireless service and handset that will offer the best pricing per user over a two-year period. For the purposes of this exercise, you do not need to consider corporate discounts..

ACHIEVING OPERATIONAL EXCELLENCE: USING WEB SEARCH ENGINES FOR BUSINESS RESEARCH

Software skills: Web search tools
Business skills: Researching new technologies

7-12 This project will help develop your Internet skills in using Web search engines for business research.

Use Google and Bing to obtain information about the Internet of Things. If you wish, try some other search engines as well. Compare the volume and quality of information you find with each search tool. Which tool is the easiest to use? Which produced the best results for your research? Why?

Collaboration and Teamwork Project

7-13 In MyMISLab™, you will find a Collaboration and Teamwork Project dealing with the concepts in this chapter. You will be able to use Google Drive, Google Docs, Google Sites, Google+, or other open source collaboration tools to complete the assignment.

BUSINESS PROBLEM-SOLVING CASE

Google, Apple, and Facebook Struggle for Your Internet Experience

Three Internet titans—Google, Apple, and Facebook—are in an epic struggle to dominate your Internet experience, and caught in the crossfire are search, music, video, and other media, along with the devices you use for all of these things, cloud computing, and a host of other issues that are likely central to your life. The prize is a projected $400 billion retail e-commerce marketplace where the major access device will be a smartphone or tablet computer.

Mobile devices with advanced functionality and ubiquitous Internet access are rapidly overtaking traditional desktop machines as the most popular form of computing. Today, 63 percent of Internet access in the United States takes place using mobile devices. These smartphones and tablets take advantage of a growing cloud of computing capacity available to anyone with a smartphone and Internet connectivity. It's no surprise, then, that today's tech titans are so aggressively battling for control of this brave new mobile world.

Apple, which started as a personal computer company, quickly expanded into software and consumer electronics. Since upending the music industry with its MP3 player, the iPod, and the iTunes digital music service over a decade ago, Apple took mobile computing by storm with the iPhone, iPod Touch, and iPad, and it would like to be the computing platform of choice for the Internet. Apple is the leader in mobile software applications, thanks to the popularity of the App Store, with over 800,000 apps for mobile and tablet devices. Applications greatly enrich the experience of using a mobile device, and whoever creates the most appealing set of devices and applications will derive a significant competitive advantage over rival companies. Right now, that company is Apple.

Google, begun by Stanford computer science graduate students Larry Page and Sergey Brin as campus search engine BackRub in 1996, quickly attracted attention for its unrivaled ability to return relevant search results. It continues to be the world's leading search engine. Advertising dollars follow page views, and Google's search dominance quickly led to advertising ascendency. Between AdWords, its keyword-based search advertising product, AdSense, the most popular online advertising network, and DoubleClick, an intermediary between online publishers and ad networks that buys, sells, and conducts performance reporting on display advertising space, Goggle has controlled online advertising.

In 2005 Google had purchased the Android open source mobile operating system and founded the Open Handset Alliance in order to compete in mobile computing. Google provides Android at no cost to smartphone manufacturers, and many different manufacturers have adopted Android as a standard. In contrast, Apple only allows its own devices to use its proprietary operating system, and the hundreds of thousands of apps it sells can only run on Apple products. Since the first Android phone hit the market in October 2008, free, publicly available source code and permissive licensing have propelled Android to the top place in mobile operating systems. In 2013 Android was deployed on nearly 52% of handsets in the United States and over 68% worldwide. Android has also become the dominant operating system on tablets worldwide.

Aggressively following the eyeballs, Google purchased Motorola Mobility Holdings for $12.5 billion in August 2011. This move provided Google with 17,000 patents with another 7,000 in the pipeline to help defend Android from the smartphone patent wars.

In June 2012 Google released its Nexus 7 tablet. The sleek 7-inch tablet received rave reviews and grabbed market share from the iPad and Amazon's Kindle Fire. Google worked with Motorola to develop a smartphone, which focused on improving everyday usability features such as shatter and water resistance and battery life rather than packing the phone with increased specs and mounds of preloaded apps. Not interested in creating an oversized screen "phablet," the companies concentrated instead on optimizing the Android experience.

Command of the smartphone operating system market provides built-in channels for serving ads to mobile devices, for example, on Google-owned YouTube and the Google Maps app. Google had successfully tailored its search results to respond to mobile searchers' needs and accommodate smartphone functionality. But profit margins in the mobile device market are slim, and a $271 million first quarter 2013 operating loss in the Motorola division was not encouraging.

Google has to safeguard its advertising dominance. The cost-per-click paid for mobile ads consistently trails desktop ads, pushing the average down despite an increase in the number of paid clicks. Google instituted a design change to merge PC ads and mobile ads and present a cleaner mobile search page. Users were increasingly consenting to click mobile ads and shop from their smartphones and tablets. Both changes began to strengthen overall ad prices.

Furthermore, with its advertising networks still contributing 95% of its revenues, Google had to make sure that Facebook did not eclipse it as an advertising vehicle. It launched Google+ (Google Plus) in mid-2011, its fourth foray into social networking. With nearly 500 million registered users at the end of 2012, Google+ had passed Twitter and boasted half as many users as Facebook. Rather than a single Web site, Google hopes to meld the social experience across all of its sites.

With Google challenging it on every front, Apple recorded its first profit decline in a decade in the second quarter of its fiscal year 2013. Although Apple has a number of advantages in the battle for mobile supremacy, it may have to produce yet another market disrupting product in order to return to sales growth. Apple has on its side a loyal user base that has steadily grown and is very likely to buy future product and offerings. Declining profits are due to slowing iPhone sales while the share of sales from less profitable products such as the iPad mini is on the rise. Moreover, in order to compete with lower priced Android phones, particularly globally in huge markets such as India and China, Apple might need to develop a low-cost iPhone model.

Apple has a legacy of innovation on its side. In 2011, it unveiled the potentially market disrupting Siri (Speech Interpretation and Recognition Interface), a combination search/navigation tool and personal assistant. Siri uses Yelp for local business searches, tapping into its user recommendations and ratings. For factual and mathematical questions, it enlists Wolfram Alpha. Only referring to Google when stumped, it promises personalized recommendations that improve as it gains user familiarity—all from a verbal command. Customer response has been mixed. Google countered by quickly releasing its own AI tool, Google Now.

Facebook, founded by Mark Zuckerberg and a several Harvard friends in 2004, provided a way for local students to meet and share information online. Today it's the world's largest social networking service, with over a billion monthly active users. People use Facebook to stay connected with their friends and family and to express what matters most to them. Facebook Platform enables developers to build applications and Web sites that integrate with Facebook to reach its global network of users and to build personalized and social products.

Facebook always needed to find a way to convert its popularity and trove of user data into advertising dollars and it realized that these dollars would increasingly come from mobile devices. By the third quarter of 2012, Facebook's key mobile ad product, Sponsored Stories, had tripled its revenue. By the first quarter of 2013, nearly one out of every three dollars of Facebook revenue came from advertising on smartphones and tablets.

In March 2013 Facebook overhauled its home page to increase the size of both photos and links and allow users to create topical streams. Job Number 1 was to de-clutter smartphone screens. Marketers love larger pictures, both for their prominence and their greater persuasive impact. Job Number 2 was to give advertisers more opportunities, and more interest information, with which to target market. A "personalized newspaper" with, for example, an op-ed feed featuring followed commentary pages, a sports section tailored to preferred events and teams, and a hometown news feed, will swell Facebook's database with useful tidbits. Whether users oblige remains to be seen; a popular app, Flipboard, already serves users interested in creating topical and publication-based streams.

Next, Facebook introduced a mobile application suite to replace the typical smartphone home screen. Facebook Home is an interface running on top of the Android operating system that essentially turns an Android mobile device into a Facebook phone. Home replaces the smartphone's typical cover screen with Facebook content, such as photos, messages, and status updates. Home still provides access to apps on the phone, but the experience is centered around Facebook.

About the same time, Facebook also launched a new search tool to challenge Google dominance of search. Graph Search mines Facebook's vast repository of user data and delivers results based on social signals, such as Facebook "likes," and friend recommendations. It's a more "social" way of searching than Google. If the desire for friend-based recommendations outweighs users' reluctance to divulge more personal information, Graph Search will be a major revenue driver.

While users may be enticed to check-in, and then assign stars or review local restaurants and styling salons, they are unlikely to reveal sensitive data such as their doctors' identities or where their children go to school, let alone be subjected to the embarrassment of a public breakup. Moreover, entering "liked" movies, books, and music, etc., takes time. Will users disclose sufficient data for searches to accurately list and rank results? With time and responsiveness to user practices, Facebook may uncover niche areas at which it excels. Even if it cannot directly rival Google, it should be able to chip away at its dominance at the margins.

Facebook claims that using Graph Search to target market is forbidden, but no policy for supervision and sanctions has been revealed. Facebook is already under Federal Trade Commission (FTC) scrutiny, with independent privacy audits mandated for the next twenty years. Trust is the linchpin upon which Facebook's strategy depends. Eroding user trust means less data to generate relevant search results and less impetus to use Facebook Connect to connect to third-party sites and services. Facebook must tread carefully. But if Facebook can succeed in making itself synonymous with mobile access, the company could very well compete for global advertising dominance, with much of the world's population just coming on line—on inexpensive Android smartphones.

Sources: Eric Zeman, "Android Tablets Edge Out IPad: IDC," *Information Week*, May 2, 2013; Evelyn M. Rusli, "The Challenge of Facebook's Graph Search," *Wall Street Journal*, January 16, 2013 and "Facebook's Mobile Boom," *Wall Street Journal*, May 2, 2013; JoAnna Leach, "Facebook Home: Startups Show the Pros and Cons of 'Launchers'," *Wall Street Journal*, April 5, 2013; Matthew Lynley and Evelyn M. Rusli, "What Is Facebook 'Home'?", *Wall Street Journal*, April 4, 2013; Dan Graziano, "Motorola and Google Plan to Fight against the Rise of Phablets," BGR, April 16, 2013; Angela Moscaritolo, "Apple Leads U.S. Smartphone Market, But Android Is Top OS," PC Mag.com, April 4, 2013; Somini Sengupta, "Fortunes of Facebook May Hinge on Searches," *New York Times*, January 14, 2013; Somini Sengupta, "Facebook Shows Off New Home Page Design, Including Bigger Pictures," *New York Times*, March 7, 2013; Somini Sengupta, "Facebook Software Puts It Front and Center on Android Phones," *New York Times*, April 4, 2013; "Google internet ad revenue grows 23 per cent," Big News Network, April 19, 2013; Jeff Bercovici, "Wow, Facebook Is Already Making $3 Million A Day On Mobile Ads," *Forbes*, October 23, 2012; Amir Efrati and Spencer E. Ante, "Google's $12.5 Billion Gamble," *The Wall Street Journal*, August 16, 2011; John Letzing and Amir Efrati, "Google's New Role as Gadget Maker," *The Wall Street Journal*, June 28, 2012; Claire Cain Miller, "Google, a Giant in Mobile Search, Seeks New Ways to Make It Pay," *The New York Times*, April 24, 2011; and Evelyn M. Rusli, "Google's Big Bet on the Mobile Future," *The New York Times*, August 15, 2011.

Case Study Questions

7-14 Compare the business models and core competencies of Google, Apple, and Facebook.

7-15 Why is mobile computing so important to these three firms? Evaluate the mobile strategies of each firm.

7-16 What is the significance of search to the success or failure of mobile computing? How have Apple and Facebook attempted to compete with Google? Will their strategies succeed?

7-17 Which company and business model do you think is most likely to dominate the Internet and why?

7-18 What difference would it make to a business or to an individual consumer if Apple, Google, or Facebook dominated the Internet experience? Explain your answer.

Securing Information Systems

STUDENT LEARNING OBJECTIVES

After completing this chapter, you will be able to answer the following questions:

1. Why are information systems vulnerable to destruction, error, and abuse?

2. What is the business value of security and control?

3. What are the components of an organizational framework for security and control?

4. What are the most important tools and technologies for safeguarding information resources?

LEARNING TRACKS

1. The Booming Job Market in IT Security
2. The Sarbanes Oxley Act
3. Computer Forensics
4. General and Application Controls for Information Systems
5. Management Challenges of Security and Control
6. Software Vulnerability and Reliability

VIDEO CASES

Case 1: Stuxnet and Cyberwarfare

Case 2: Cyberespionage: The Chinese Threat

Case 3: IBM Zone Trusted Information Channel (ZTIC)

Instructional Video 1: Sony PlayStation Hacked; Data Stolen from 77 Million Users

Instructional Video 2: Zappos Working to Correct Online Security Breach

Instructional Video 3: Meet the Hackers: Anonymous Statement on Hacking SONY

CHAPTER OUTLINE

'MINIDUKE' EXPOSES EU CYBERSECURITY GAPS

When government computers in over 20 European countries, including Ukraine, Belgium, Portugal, Romania, the Czech Republic, and Ireland were infected with an unusual malware agent that combined malware writing techniques from the turn of the century with novel, new sandbox-evading techniques, security experts at Kaspersky Lab and CrySys Lab sounded the alarm. Dubbed MiniDuke, the social engineering exploit gained initial access by inducing targets to open infected PDF attachments that appeared legitimate and highly relevant to the recipient's work.

Sandboxing was developed as an alternative to traditional signature-based virus detection to find zero-day malware—unknown malware for which antivirus software signatures are not yet available. MiniDuke used a now patched Adobe Reader bug to avoid the sandbox, allowing it to install a dropper (small downloader) that provided the perpetrators with a customized backdoor unique to each system. Normal authentication procedures could then be bypassed and affected machines remotely accessed. What's more, the computer's unique fingerprint was then also used to encrypt communications back to the attackers. In hostile environments, MiniDuke goes dormant rather than proceeding to its next step—using Twitter to locate specific tweets from premade accounts created by its Command and Control (C2) operators. These tweets contain tags that

© Rafal Olechowski/Shutterstock

identify encrypted URLs for the C2s. The C2s in turn transmit encrypted files containing commands and infected GIF files to create a bigger backdoor on the system. In the absence of Twitter, MiniDuke can use Google Search to locate the C2s.

With geopolitical intelligence the goal, victims of the February 2013 attacks included a research institute, two think tanks, a prominent research foundation, and multiple government entities and institutions. But even though security researchers identified one command server in Panama and another in Turkey, the perpetrators, and the precise information they were seeking, remained unknown.

As 2013 continued, attacks on European government agencies became a recurring theme. In July, Trend Micro discovered that members of the diplomatic community in 16 European and several Asian countries had been targeted with malware-laden e-mail attachments suspected to have originated from China's defense ministry. Like MiniDuke, the malware exploited a vulnerability in widely-used business software (Microsoft Office 2003-2010), installed a dropper, and created a backdoor. It then collected e-mail user names and passwords from Outlook and Internet Explorer along with Web site login credentials and transmitted the data to two now defunct URLs in Hong Kong.

With the sophistication, efficacy, frequency, and geopolitical consequences of cyberattacks on the rise, ENISA, the European Union Agency for Network and Information Security, established in 2005, urged implementation of a common cybersecurity strategy. However, the fledgling European Cybercrime Centre (EC3) created in January 2013 was not even able to stipulate a clear definition for cyber security, let alone induce members to craft and implement coordinated policies. In July, its cybersecurity strategy presentation to the European Parliament merely defined the role of governments in combatting cybercrime, bolstering national defense, and effecting international cooperation along with setting general guidelines for fundamental rights, responsibilities, and access.

The 28 members are simply not willing to cede any part of their national security policy to the EU, and the EC3 did not challenge this entrenched outlook. Lack of a centralized and cohesive approach to cybersecurity makes for disjointed and disparate policies and procedures and unequal levels of protection. While members whose economies depend on Information and communications technology (ICT) stayed abreast of cybersecurity threats and defenses, others have not yet implemented the most basic protections. As MiniDuke demonstrated, having 28 different approaches to cybersecurity leaves all members vulnerable to national security breaches.

Sources: "Kaspersky Lab Identifies 'MiniDuke', a New Malicious Program Designed for Spying on Multiple Government Entities and Institutions Across the World," Kaspersky.com, February 27, 2013; "Hackers Attack European Governments Using 'MiniDuke' Malware," by Josh Halliday, theguardian.com, February 27, 2013; "MiniDuke Espionage Malware Uses Twitter to Infect PCs," by Mathew J. Schwartz, informationweek.com, February 28, 2013; "Malware Campaign Strikes Asian, European governments," by Jeremy Kirk, computerworld.com, July 16, 2013; "Microsoft DNS Servers Go Down for Some, Windows, Hotmail Sites Affected," by Bogdan Popa, softpedia.com, November 22nd, 2013; "Anonymous Claims Responsibility for Microsoft Website Crashes," by Anthony M Freed, tripwire.com, November 27, 2013; "Anonymous DDoS attack snowballs, affects several Microsoft services," by Adam Greenberg, scmagazine.com, November 27, 2013; "Hackers Hit European Bitcoin Payment Processor BIPS For $1 Million," by Anthony M Freed, tripwire.com, November 26, 2013;"Europe's Fragmented Approach towards Cyber Security," by Karine e Silva, policyreview.info, October 10, 2013; "EU Cyber Security Agency Issues Cloud Deployment Guide," by Medha Basu, futuregov.asia, November 25, 2013;

The problems created by malware such as MiniDuke and DDoS attacks illustrate why the EU and businesses operating there need to pay special attention to information system security. The fragmented approach to cybersecurity in the EU does not allocate responsibility among the stakeholders, and with no cohesive strategy, members are not encouraged to work together. Neither governments nor businesses are adequately protected.

In November 2013, ENISA, recognizing the switch to cloud computing, urged adoption of a unified strategy for public sector cloud security. Standard procedures for security certification of both services and providers, a shared framework for service-level agreements (SLAs), and a

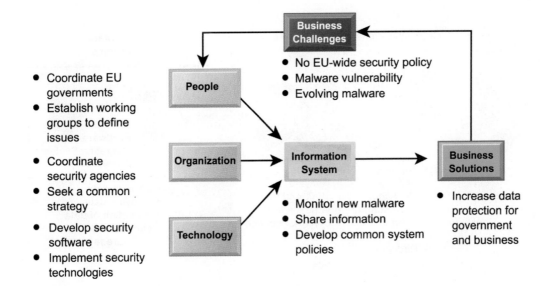

common certification and accreditation process were recommended as well as cloud deployment security measures to protect the integrity of the cloud supply chain.

The chapter-opening diagram calls attention to important points raised by this case and this chapter. While Web servers can never be completely secure from hackers who can steal sensitive public and private sector data, the EU must clearly do more to protect its member nations and the businesses that serve its citizens. While establishment of the EC3 was a start, member nations must be convinced to participate in a consistent, common cybersecurity strategy. This strategy must include the expert knowledge collected by private sector security companies such as Kaspersky Lab McAfee, CrySys Lab, Trend Micro and others as well as input from large business entities which are at the greatest risk due to the greater sensitivity and value of their stored data.

8.1 System Vulnerability and Abuse

Can you imagine what would happen if you tried to link to the Internet without a firewall or antivirus software? Your computer would be disabled in a few seconds, and it might take you many days to recover. If you used the computer to run your business, you might not be able to sell to your customers or place orders with your suppliers while it was down. And you might find that your computer system had been penetrated by outsiders, who perhaps stole or destroyed valuable data, including confidential payment data from your customers. If too much data were destroyed or divulged, your business might never be able to operate!

In short, if you operate a business today, you need to make security and control a top priority. **Security** refers to the policies, procedures, and technical measures used to prevent unauthorized access, alteration, theft, or physical damage to information systems. **Controls** are methods, policies, and organizational procedures that ensure the safety of the organization's assets, the accuracy and reliability of its records, and operational adherence to management standards.

WHY SYSTEMS ARE VULNERABLE

When large amounts of data are stored in electronic form, they are vulnerable to many more kinds of threats than when they existed in manual form. Through communications networks, information systems in different locations are interconnected. The potential for unauthorized access, abuse, or fraud is not limited to a single location but can occur at any access point in the network. Figure 8.1 illustrates the most common threats against contemporary information systems. They can stem from technical, organizational, and

Figure 8.1
Contemporary
Security Challenges
and Vulnerabilities
*The architecture of a
Web-based application
typically includes a Web
client, a server, and
corporate information
systems linked to
databases. Each of these
components presents
security challenges and
vulnerabilities. Floods,
fires, power failures, and
other electrical problems
can cause disruptions at
any point in the network.*

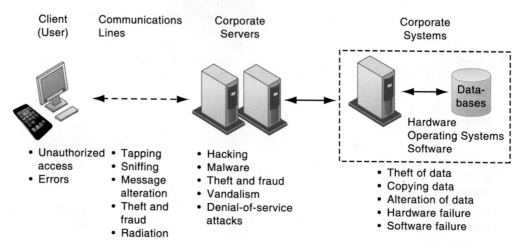

environmental factors compounded by poor management decisions. In the multi-tier client/ server computing environment illustrated here, vulnerabilities exist at each layer and in the communications between the layers. Users at the client layer can cause harm by introducing errors or by accessing systems without authorization. It is possible to access data flowing over networks, steal valuable data during transmission, or alter messages without authorization. Radiation may disrupt a network at various points as well. Intruders can launch denial-of-service attacks or malicious software to disrupt the operation of Web sites. Those capable of penetrating corporate systems can steal, destroy, or alter corporate data stored in databases or files.

Systems malfunction if computer hardware breaks down, is not configured properly, or is damaged by improper use or criminal acts. Errors in programming, improper installation, or unauthorized changes cause computer software to fail. Power failures, floods, fires, or other natural disasters can also disrupt computer systems.

Domestic or offshore partnering with another company adds to system vulnerability if valuable information resides on networks and computers outside the organization's control. Without strong safeguards, valuable data could be lost, destroyed, or could fall into the wrong hands, revealing important trade secrets or information that violates personal privacy.

The popularity of handheld mobile devices for business computing adds to these woes. Portability makes cell phones, smartphones, and tablet computers easy to lose or steal. Smartphones share the same security weaknesses as other Internet devices, and are vulnerable to malicious software and penetration from outsiders. Smartphones used by corporate employees often contain sensitive data such as sales figures, customer names, phone numbers, and e-mail addresses. Intruders may be able to access internal corporate systems through these devices.

Internet Vulnerabilities

Large public networks, such as the Internet, are more vulnerable than internal networks because they are virtually open to anyone. The Internet is so huge that when abuses do occur, they can have an enormously widespread impact. When the Internet becomes part of the corporate network, the organization's information systems are even more vulnerable to actions from outsiders.

Telephone service based on Internet technology (see Chapter 7) is more vulnerable than the switched voice network if it does not run over a secure private network. Most Voice over IP (VoIP) traffic over the public Internet is not encrypted, so anyone with a network can listen in on conversations. Hackers can intercept conversations or shut down voice service by flooding servers supporting VoIP with bogus traffic.

Vulnerability has also increased from widespread use of e-mail, instant messaging (IM), and peer-to-peer file-sharing programs. E-mail may contain attachments that serve as springboards for malicious software or unauthorized access to internal corporate systems. Employees may use e-mail messages to transmit valuable trade secrets, financial data, or confidential customer information to unauthorized recipients. Popular IM applications for consumers do not use a secure layer for text messages, so they can be intercepted and read by outsiders during transmission over the public Internet. Instant messaging activity over the Internet can in some cases be used as a back door to an otherwise secure network. Sharing files over peer-to-peer (P2P) networks, such as those for illegal music sharing, may also transmit malicious software or expose information on either individual or corporate computers to outsiders.

Wireless Security Challenges

Is it safe to log onto a wireless network at an airport, library, or other public location? It depends on how vigilant you are. Even the wireless network in your home is vulnerable because radio frequency bands are easy to scan. Both Bluetooth and Wi-Fi networks are susceptible to hacking by eavesdroppers. Local area networks (LANs) using the 802.11 standard can be easily penetrated by outsiders armed with laptops, wireless cards, external antennae, and hacking software. Hackers use these tools to detect unprotected networks, monitor network traffic, and, in some cases, gain access to the Internet or to corporate networks.

Wi-Fi transmission technology was designed to make it easy for stations to find and hear one another. The *service set identifiers (SSIDs)* that identify the access points in a Wi-Fi network are broadcast multiple times and can be picked up fairly easily by intruders' sniffer programs (see Figure 8.2). Wireless networks in many locations do not have basic protections against **war driving**, in which eavesdroppers drive by buildings or park outside and try to intercept wireless network traffic.

An intruder that has associated with an access point by using the correct SSID is capable of accessing other resources on the network. For example, the intruder could use the Windows operating system to determine which other users are connected to the network, access their computer hard drives, and open or copy their files.

Intruders also use the information they have gleaned to set up rogue access points on a different radio channel in physical locations close to users to force a user's radio network interface controller (NIC) to associate with the rogue access point. Once this association occurs, hackers using the rogue access point can capture the names and passwords of unsuspecting users.

MALICIOUS SOFTWARE: VIRUSES, WORMS, TROJAN HORSES, AND SPYWARE

Malicious software programs are referred to as **malware** and include a variety of threats, such as computer viruses, worms, and Trojan horses. A **computer virus** is a rogue software program that attaches itself to other software programs or data files in order to be executed, usually without user knowledge or permission. Most computer viruses deliver a "payload." The payload may be relatively benign, such as instructions to display a message or image, or it may be highly destructive—destroying programs or data, clogging computer memory, reformatting a computer's hard drive, or causing programs to run improperly. Viruses typically spread from computer to computer when humans take an action, such as sending an e-mail attachment or copying an infected file.

Most recent attacks have come from **worms**, which are independent computer programs that copy themselves from one computer to other computers over a network. Unlike viruses, worms can operate on their own without attaching to other computer program files and rely less on human behavior in order to spread from computer to computer. This explains why computer worms spread much more rapidly than computer viruses. Worms

Figure 8.2
Wi-Fi Security
Challenges
*Many Wi-Fi networks can
be penetrated easily by
intruders using sniffer
programs to obtain an
address to access the
resources of a network
without authorization.*

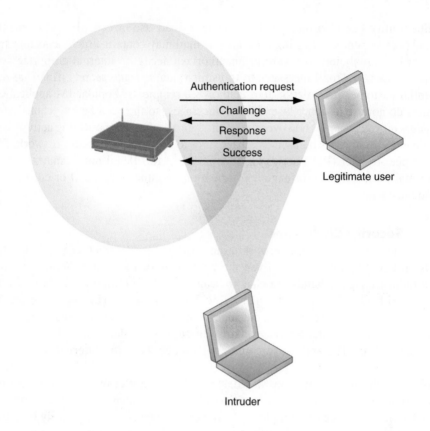

destroy data and programs as well as disrupt or even halt the operation of computer networks.

Worms and viruses are often spread over the Internet from files of downloaded software, from files attached to e-mail transmissions, or from compromised e-mail messages, online ads, or instant messaging. Viruses have also invaded computerized information systems from "infected" disks or infected machines. Especially prevalent today are **drive-by downloads**, consisting of malware that comes with a downloaded file that a user intentionally or unintentionally requests.

Hackers can do to a smartphone just about anything they can do to any Internet device: request malicious files without user intervention, delete files, transmit files, install programs running in the background to monitor user actions, and potentially convert the smartphone into a robot in a botnet to send e-mail and text messages to anyone. With smartphones starting to outsell PCs, and smartphones increasingly used as payment devices, they are becoming a major avenue for malware.

Malware targeting mobile devices is not yet as extensive as that targeting larger computers, but nonetheless is spreading rapidly using apps, e-mail, text messages, Bluetooth, and file downloads from the Web via Wi-Fi or cellular networks. In January 2013, the security firm McAfee found 36,699 different kinds of mobile malware, with 95 percent having first appeared during the previous twelve months (McAfee, 2013). Mobile device viruses pose serious threats to enterprise computing because so many wireless devices are now linked to corporate information systems.

Blogs, wikis, and social networking sites such as Facebook, Twitter, and LinkedIn have emerged as new conduits for malware or spyware. These applications allow users to post software code as part of the permissible content, and such code can be launched automatically as soon as a Web page is viewed. In the spring of 2013, a variant of TorRAT, a piece of malware often used by cybercriminals to steal users' online banking credentials, was used on Twitter to launch unauthorized spam campaigns targeting Dutch users (Kumar, 2013).

Panda Security reported it had detected over six and a half million new malware samples created in the first three months of 2013. Although many of those were probably slight variations of each other, the number of infections is still extremely high (Breedon, 2013). According to Internet security firm Symantec, 31 percent of malware today is being targeted at small businesses, because it is more difficult for such companies to protect themselves against so many different types of attacks (Symantec, 2013). Table 8.1 describes the characteristics of some of the most harmful worms and viruses that have appeared to date.

Over 80 percent of the infections Panda found were Trojan Horses. A **Trojan horse** is a software program that appears to be benign but then does something other than expected. The Trojan horse is not itself a virus because it does not replicate, but it is often a way for viruses or other malicious code to be introduced into a computer system. The term *Trojan horse* is based on the huge wooden horse used by the Greeks to trick the Trojans into opening the gates to their fortified city during the Trojan War. Once inside the city walls, Greek soldiers hidden in the horse revealed themselves and captured the city.

TABLE 8.1

Examples of Malicious Code

Name	Type	Description
Conficker (aka Downadup, Downup)	Worm	First detected in November 2008 and still prevalent. Uses flaws in Windows software to take over machines and link them into a virtual computer that can be commanded remotely. Had more than 5 million computers worldwide under its control. Difficult to eradicate.
Storm	Worm/ Trojan horse	First identified in January 2007. Spreads via e-mail spam with a fake attachment. Infected up to 10 million computers, causing them to join its zombie network of computers engaged in criminal activity.
Sasser.ftp	Worm	First appeared in May 2004. Spread over the Internet by attacking random IP addresses. Causes computers to continually crash and reboot, and infected computers to search for more victims. Affected millions of computers worldwide, disrupting British Airways flight check-ins, operations of British coast guard stations, Hong Kong hospitals, Taiwan post office branches, and Australia's Westpac Bank. Sasser and its variants caused an estimated $14.8 billion to $18.6 billion in damages worldwide.
MyDoom.A	Worm	First appeared on January 26, 2004. Spreads as an e-mail attachment. Sends e-mail to addresses harvested from infected machines, forging the sender's address. At its peak, this worm lowered global Internet performance by 10 percent and Web page loading times by as much as 50 percent. Was programmed to stop spreading after February 12, 2004.
Sobig.F	Worm	First detected on August 19, 2003. Spreads via e-mail attachments and sends massive amounts of mail with forged sender information. Deactivated itself on September 10, 2003, after infecting more than 1 million PCs and doing $5 to $10 billion in damage.
ILOVEYOU	Virus	First detected on May 3, 2000. Script virus written in Visual Basic script and transmitted as an attachment to e-mail with the subject line ILOVEYOU. Overwrites music, image, and other files with a copy of itself and did an estimated $10 billion to $15 billion in damage.
Melissa	Macro virus/ worm	First appeared in March 1999. Word macro script mailing infected Word file to first 50 entries in user's Microsoft Outlook address book. Infected 15 to 29 percent of all business PCs, causing $300 million to $600 million in damage.

An example of a modern-day Trojan horse is Odad.a, which disguises itself as a legitimate app in "alternative" app stores and fishy Web sites. Odad.a can download and install additional malware, infect nearby devices via Wi-Fi or Bluetooth and receive further instructions from the attacker. This Trojan can also send SMS text messages to premium phone numbers, thus generating revenue for attackers or their business associates. The Trojan exploits an Android operating system flaw to conceal itself so it can't be easily detected and removed.

SQL injection attacks have become a major malware threat. SQL injection attacks take advantage of vulnerabilities in poorly coded Web application software to introduce malicious program code into a company's systems and networks. These vulnerabilities occur when a Web application fails to properly validate or filter data entered by a user on a Web page, which might occur when ordering something online. An attacker uses this input validation error to send a rogue SQL query to the underlying database to access the database, plant malicious code, or access other systems on the network. Large Web applications have hundreds of places for inputting user data, each of which creates an opportunity for an SQL injection attack.

A large number of Web-facing applications are believed to have SQL injection vulnerabilities, and tools are available for hackers to check Web applications for these vulnerabilities. Such tools are able to locate a data entry field on a Web page form, enter data into it, and check the response to see if it shows vulnerability to a SQL injection.

Some types of spyware also act as malicious software. These small programs install themselves surreptitiously on computers to monitor user Web surfing activity and serve up advertising. Thousands of forms of spyware have been documented.

Many users find such **spyware** annoying, and some critics worry about its infringement on computer users' privacy. Some forms of spyware are especially nefarious. **Keyloggers** record every keystroke made on a computer to steal serial numbers for software, to launch Internet attacks, to gain access to e-mail accounts, to obtain passwords to protected computer systems, or to pick up personal information such as credit card numbers. For example, the Zeus Trojan stole financial and personal data from online banking and social networking sites by surreptitiously tracking users' keystrokes as they entered data into their computers. Other spyware programs reset Web browser home pages, redirect search requests, or slow performance by taking up too much memory.

HACKERS AND COMPUTER CRIME

A **hacker** is an individual who intends to gain unauthorized access to a computer system. Within the hacking community, the term *cracker* is typically used to denote a hacker with criminal intent, although in the public press, the terms hacker and cracker are used interchangeably. Hackers and crackers gain unauthorized access by finding weaknesses in the security protections employed by Web sites and computer systems, often taking advantage of various features of the Internet that make it an open system and easy to use.

Hacker activities have broadened beyond mere system intrusion to include theft of goods and information, as well as system damage and **cybervandalism**, the intentional disruption, defacement, or even destruction of a Web site or corporate information system. For example, a group of pro-Syrian regime hackers called the Syrian Electronic Army hacked the Associated Press Twitter feed on April 23, 2013, publishing a fake message which read, "Breaking: Two Explosions in the White House and Barack Obama is injured" (Smith-Spark and Van Heerden, 2013).

Spoofing and Sniffing

Hackers attempting to hide their true identities often spoof, or misrepresent, themselves by using fake e-mail addresses or masquerading as someone else. **Spoofing** may also involve redirecting a Web link to an address different from the intended one, with the site masquerading as the intended destination. For example, if hackers redirect customers to a fake Web site that looks almost exactly like the true site, they can then collect and process orders, effectively stealing business as well as sensitive customer information from the true site. We will provide more detail on other forms of spoofing in our discussion of computer crime.

A **sniffer** is a type of eavesdropping program that monitors information traveling over a network. When used legitimately, sniffers help identify potential network trouble spots or criminal activity on networks, but when used for criminal purposes, they can be damaging and very difficult to detect. Sniffers enable hackers to steal proprietary information from anywhere on a network, including e-mail messages, company files, and confidential reports.

Denial-of-Service Attacks

In a **denial-of-service (DoS) attack**, hackers flood a network server or Web server with many thousands of false communications or requests for services to crash the network. The network receives so many queries that it cannot keep up with them and is thus unavailable to service legitimate requests. A **distributed denial-of-service (DDoS)** attack uses numerous computers to inundate and overwhelm the network from numerous launch points.

For example, an anonymous group unhappy with Spamhaus, a volunteer organization that distributes a blacklist of spammers to e-mail providers, launched a massive retaliatory DDoS attack in March 2013. The attack harnessed a powerful botnet — a network of thousands of infected computers being controlled remotely—to try to overwhelm Spamhaus's Web site and later the Internet servers used by CloudFlare, a Silicon Valley company that Spamhaus hired to deflect its onslaught. The botnet fooled Internet servers into responding to requests for information sent simultaneously by a large group of computers. The Internet servers that answer the requests are tricked into sending blocks of data to the victims, in this case Spamhaus and CloudFlare. This was the largest DDoS attack ever mounted to date, causing hundreds of millions of people to experience delays and error messages across the Web (Markoff and Perlroth, 2013).

Although DoS attacks do not destroy information or access restricted areas of a company's information systems, they often cause a Web site to shut down, making it impossible for legitimate users to access the site. For busy e-commerce sites, these attacks are costly; while the site is shut down, customers cannot make purchases. Especially vulnerable are small and midsize businesses whose networks tend to be less protected than those of large corporations.

Perpetrators of DDoS attacks often use thousands of "zombie" PCs infected with malicious software without their owners' knowledge and organized into a **botnet**. Hackers create these botnets by infecting other people's computers with bot malware that opens a back door through which an attacker can give instructions. The infected computer then becomes a slave, or zombie, serving a master computer belonging to someone else. Once hackers infect enough computers, they can use the amassed resources of the botnet to launch DDoS attacks, phishing campaigns, or unsolicited "spam" e-mail.

Ninety percent of the world's spam and 80 percent of the world's malware are delivered via botnets. For example, the Grum botnet, once the world's third-largest botnet, was reportedly responsible for 18% of worldwide spam traffic (amounting to 18 billion spam messages per day) when it was shut down on July 19, 2012. At one point Grum had infected and controlled 560,000–840,000 computers.

Computer Crime

Most hacker activities are criminal offenses, and the vulnerabilities of systems we have just described make them targets for other types of **computer crime** as well. Computer crime is defined by the U.S. Department of Justice as "any violations of criminal law that involve a knowledge of computer technology for their perpetration, investigation, or prosecution." Table 8.2 provides examples of the computer as both a target and an instrument of crime. The Interactive Session on Organizations describes one of the largest computer crime cases reported to date.

No one knows the magnitude of the computer crime problem—how many systems are invaded, how many people engage in the practice, or the total economic damage. According to the Ponemon Institute's 2012 Annual Cost of Cyber Crime Study sponsored by HP Enterprise

INTERACTIVE SESSION: ORGANIZATIONS   The 21st Century Bank Heist

Six-shooters and masked gunmen, trench coats and machine guns, safe cracking, and sacks overflowing with mounds of cash: these images of 19th and 20th century bank robbers have been largely exiled to the realm of cinema. Twenty-first century technology has ushered in a new set of tools: laptops, bank databases, access codes, magnetic stripes, and ATM machines. One of the top ten bank heists of all time occurred in December 2012 and February 2013, when a worldwide network of cyber criminals appropriated a total of $45 million from two digital hacking operations.

Step one was to gain access to account information. In December, a company in India was targeted, and in February, a U.S. based firm. Both process transactions from Visa and MasterCard prepaid debit cards. Neither was named. Payment processors are known to employ less stringent network security than financial institutions. The hackers sought out prepaid debit cards issued by two Middle Eastern banks whose databases afforded another point of lax security: Rakbank (National Bank of Ras Al-Khaimah) in the United Arab Emirates and the Bank of Muscat in Oman.

In a new twist, rather than accumulating numerous account numbers, the hackers eliminated the withdrawal caps on just a handful of cards. There were two benefits to this strategy. First, just a few infiltrated cards could yield immense plunder. Information from just five Rakbank-issued cards generated the initial $5 million, with just twelve Bank of Muscat cards garnering the lion's share in the second strike. Second, no individual or business bank accounts were depleted. Instead, funds were extracted from pooled reserve accounts from which prepaid debit card transactions are immediately deducted with the individual subaccounts (the value associated with a card), reduced concurrently. Both tactics were designed to delay detection.

Next, the hackers created new PIN (personal identification) numbers for the cards. Then, using commercially-available card encoders attached via USB ports to laptops and PCs, a network of underlings simply used the built-in software to enter the account data, clicked Write or Encode, and swiped any plastic card with a magnetic stripe they could get their hands on, including old expired credit cards and hotel key cards. With counterfeit cards in hand, cashing crews in more than two dozen countries including Japan, Russia, Romania, Egypt, Colombia, Great Britain, Sri Lanka, Canada, and the United States began collecting the loot from ATM machines. The $45 million haul was accomplished through 36,000 bank transactions over ten hours time.

Each of the cells then took their cut and either flat out shipped the balance to the cybercrime mob leaders or sent them their share in the form of luxury goods. In May 2013, seven members of the New York cell were arrested; the eighth, and purported ringleader, had been found murdered in the Dominican Republic the month before. The global mob leaders were as yet uncaught and investigators justifiably tight-lipped about their whereabouts. A backpack increasingly teeming with cash, as seen in a progression of surveillance photos, helped to bring down the New York gang. Cell phone photos recording their jubilant cash-stoked spree bolstered the case against them.

Magnetic stripes are an over four decade old technology that much of the developed world has abandoned. They are so vulnerable to counterfeit replication and theft via handheld card skimmers that the credit card industry has had to adopt numerous corrective practices. For example, typical use patterns are collected so that purchases that do not fit the mold are either flagged for review or rejected. Nonetheless, according to the Aite Group research and advisory firm, $8.6 billion in payment card fraud occurs every year in the United States. Moreover, the Nilson Report found that with just 23 percent of total global card purchases, the United States registered 47 percent of the payment card fraud.

Other major regions of the world have been using EMV (Europay, MasterCard, and Visa) technology for nearly 20 years. EMV, first developed in 1994, is a global standard for IC (integrated circuit) cards and their attendant POS (point-of-sale) terminals and ATMs. Often referred to as the chip and PIN system, these smartcards store account information in an embedded chip, and, unlike magstripe cards, the data are encrypted with a strong cipher algorithm. Cryptography is used to authenticate the card, card issuer, and data stored on the card. For added security, the user must enter a PIN to verify that that person is the cardholder. As countries implemented EMV, their payment card fraud rates plummeted.

However, U.S. banks and merchants balked at the expense involved in switching payment processing systems. And it is not a trifling matter. Over 600 million credit cards and 520 million debit cards must be exchanged. Over 15 million POS card readers must be replaced. Over 350,000 ATM machines nationwide must all either be retrofitted or replaced. Every store, restaurant, hair salon, gas station, doctor's office, kiosk, and vending machine will be affected, as will the payment processing infrastructure at acquiring banks, where merchant accounts receive the deposits from credit card sales. Payment processors, which supply the software and tech systems to interface with the card associations (Visa, MasterCard, etc,) and process card transactions, will also be affected.

Meanwhile, in the name of global interoperability, the rest of the world had to continue issuing EMV cards with a magnetic stripe and retain magstripe infrastructure. But the U.S. switchover may finally be coming, just as many nations are setting deadlines for stopping production or acceptance of magstripe cards. April 1, 2013 was the deadline imposed by Visa and MasterCard for acquiring banks and payment processors to be EMV chip-compliant. Beginning in October 2015, and continuing through the end of 2017, on-EMV compliant card issuers, merchants, fuel dispensers, and ATMs will be subject to a liability transfer. If a merchant is not EMV-capable by the specified date, it will assume liability for fraudulent and disputed transactions. Compelling merchants to accept the risk for non-EMV cards was used successfully to incentivize European businesses to update their POS equipment in the past decade.

Stops and starts are expected. Merchant resistance has yet to be fully overcome. Still, within four to five years, the hacker-friendly magnetic stripe should finally meet its justly-deserved end. Just not in time to thwart the great $45 million cash machine heist of 2013, whose bloated sacks of cash are never expected to be recovered.

Sources: Colleen Long and Martha Mendoza, "Bloodless bank heist impressed cybercrime experts," *Associated Press*, May 10, 2013; Colleen Long, "Feds in NYC: Hackers stole $45M in ATM card breach," *Associated Press*, May 10, 2013; Marc Santora, "In Hours, Thieves Took $45 Million in A.T.M. Scheme, *New York Times*, May 9, 2013; Peter Svensson, Martha Mendoza, and Ezequiel Abiú López, "Global network of hackers steals $45M from ATMs," *Associated Press*, May 10, 2013; "EMV Chip Technology, Secure Electronic Payments," *Forbes*, March, 7, 2013; "EMV in the USA: After 8 Years of Foot-Dragging and Delays, What's the Real Timeline for Adoption Look Like?" *PRNewswire-iReach*, February 21, 2013.

CASE STUDY QUESTIONS

1. Describe the security vulnerabilities exploited by the hackers.

2. What people, organizational, and technology factors contributed to these problems?

3. What solutions are available for this problem? How difficult are they to implement? Why?

Computers as Targets of Crime

Breaching the confidentiality of protected computerized data

Accessing a computer system without authority

Knowingly accessing a protected computer to commit fraud

Intentionally accessing a protected computer and causing damage, negligently or deliberately

Knowingly transmitting a program, program code, or command that intentionally causes damage to a protected computer

Threatening to cause damage to a protected computer

Computers as Instruments of Crime

Theft of trade secrets

Unauthorized copying of software or copyrighted intellectual property, such as articles, books, music, and video

Schemes to defraud

Using e-mail for threats or harassment

Intentionally attempting to intercept electronic communication

Illegally accessing stored electronic communications, including e-mail and voice mail

Transmitting or possessing child pornography using a computer

TABLE 8.2

Examples of Computer Crime

Security, the median annualized cost of cybercrime for the organizations in the study was $8.9 million per year (Ponemon Institute, 2012). Many companies are reluctant to report computer crimes because the crimes may involve employees, or the company fears that publicizing its vulnerability will hurt its reputation. The most economically damaging kinds of computer crime are denial of service attacks, activities of malicious insiders, and Web-based attacks.

Identity Theft

With the growth of the Internet and electronic commerce, identity theft has become especially troubling. **Identity theft** is a crime in which an imposter obtains key pieces of personal information, such as social security identification numbers, driver's license numbers, or credit card numbers, to impersonate someone else. The information may be used to obtain credit, merchandise, or services in the name of the victim or to provide the thief with false credentials.

Identity theft has flourished on the Internet, with credit card files a major target of Web site hackers. According to the Identity Fraud Report by Javelin Strategy & Research, identity fraud affected 5.26 percent of U.S. adults. The total dolllar losses from identity theft increased to $21 billion, compared to $18 billion the previous year (Javelin, 2013). Moreover, e-commerce sites are wonderful sources of customer personal information—name, address, and phone number. Armed with this information, criminals are able to assume new identities and establish new credit for their own purposes.

One increasingly popular tactic is a form of spoofing called **phishing**. Phishing involves setting up fake Web sites or sending e-mail messages that look like those of legitimate businesses to ask users for confidential personal data. The e-mail message instructs recipients to update or confirm records by providing social security numbers, bank and credit card information, and other confidential data either by responding to the e-mail message, by entering the information at a bogus Web site, or by calling a telephone number. EBay, PayPal, Amazon.com, Walmart, and a variety of banks are among the top spoofed companies. In a more targeted form of phishing called *spear phishing,* messages appear to come from a trusted source, such as an individual within the recipient's own company or a friend.

Phishing techniques called evil twins and pharming are harder to detect. **Evil twins** are wireless networks that pretend to offer trustworthy Wi-Fi connections to the Internet, such as those in airport lounges, hotels, or coffee shops. The bogus network looks identical to a legitimate public network. Fraudsters try to capture passwords or credit card numbers of unwitting users who log on to the network.

Pharming redirects users to a bogus Web page, even when the individual types the correct Web page address into his or her browser. This is possible if pharming perpetrators gain access to the Internet address information stored by Internet service providers to speed up Web browsing and the ISP companies have flawed software on their servers that allows the fraudsters to hack in and change those addresses.

According to the Ponemon Institute's 2013 U.S. Cost of a Data Breach Study, data breach incidents cost U.S. companies $188 per compromised customer record in 2012. The average total organizational cost per incident in 2012 was $5.4 million (Ponemon, 2013). Moreover, brand damage can be significant, albeit hard to quantify. Table 8.3 describes other major data breaches.

The U.S. Congress addressed the threat of computer crime in 1986 with the Computer Fraud and Abuse Act, which makes it illegal to access a computer system without authorization. Most states have similar laws, and nations in Europe have comparable legislation. Congress passed the National Information Infrastructure Protection Act in 1996 to make malware distribution and hacker attacks to disable Web sites federal crimes.

U.S. legislation, such as the Wiretap Act, Wire Fraud Act, Economic Espionage Act, Electronic Communications Privacy Act, E-Mail Threats and Harassment Act, and Child Pornography Act, covers computer crimes involving intercepting electronic communication, using electronic communication to defraud, stealing trade secrets, illegally accessing stored electronic communications, using e-mail for threats or harassment, and transmitting

TABLE 8.3

Major Data Breaches

Data breach	Description
U.S. Veterans Affairs Department	In 2006, the names, birth dates, and social security numbers of 17.5 million military veterans and personnel were stolen from a laptop that a Department of Veterans Affairs employee had taken home. The VA spent at least $25 million to run call centers, send out mailings, and pay for a year of a credit-monitoring service for victims.
Heartland Payment Systems	In 2008, criminals led by Miami hacker Albert Gonzales installed spying software on the computer network of Heartland Payment Systems, a payment processor based in Princeton, NJ, and stole the numbers of as many as 100 million credit and debit cards. Gonzales was sentenced in 2010 to 20 years in federal prison, and Heartland paid about $140 million in fines and settlements.
TJX	A 2007 data breach at TJX, the retailer that owns national chains including TJ Maxx and Marshalls, cost at least $250 million. Cyber criminals took more than 45 million credit and debit card numbers, some of which were used later to buy millions of dollars in electronics from Walmart and elsewhere. Albert Gonzales, who played a major role in the Heartland hack, was linked to this cyberattack as well.
Epsilon	In March 2011, hackers stole millions of names and e-mail addresses from the Epsilon e-mail marketing firm, which handles e-mail lists for major retailers and banks like Best Buy, JPMorgan, TiVo, and Walgreens. Costs could range from $100 million to $4 billion, depending on what happens to the stolen data, with most of the costs from losing customers due to a damaged reputation.
Sony	In April 2011, hackers obtained personal information, including credit, debit, and bank account numbers, from over 100 million PlayStation Network users and Sony Online Entertainment users. The breach could cost Sony and credit card issuers up to a total of $2 billion.

or possessing child pornography. A proposed federal Data Security and Breach Notification Act would mandate organizations that possess personal information to put in place "reasonable" security procedures to keep the data secure and to notify anyone affected by a data breach, but it has not been enacted.

Click Fraud

When you click on an ad displayed by a search engine, the advertiser typically pays a fee for each click, which is supposed to direct potential buyers to its products. **Click fraud** occurs when an individual or computer program fraudulently clicks on an online ad without any intention of learning more about the advertiser or making a purchase. Click fraud has become a serious problem at Google and other Web sites that feature pay-per-click online advertising.

Some companies hire third parties (typically from low-wage countries) to fraudulently click on a competitor's ads to weaken them by driving up their marketing costs. Click fraud can also be perpetrated with software programs doing the clicking, and botnets are often used for this purpose. Search engines such as Google attempt to monitor click fraud but have been reluctant to publicize their efforts to deal with the problem.

Global Threats: Cyberterrorism and Cyberwarfare

The cyber criminal activities we have described—launching malware, denial-of-service attacks, and phishing probes—are borderless. China, South Korea, India, Japan, and

Hong Kong are believed to be responsible for 24 percent of malware attacks, while Russia, Romania, Poland, Ukraine, Kazakhstan, and Latvia account for 22 percent (Donohue, 2013). The global nature of the Internet makes it possible for cybercriminals to operate—and to do harm—anywhere in the world.

Internet vulnerabilities have also turned individuals and even entire nation states into easy targets for politically-motivated hacking to conduct sabotage and espionage. **Cyberwarfare** is a state-sponsored activity designed to cripple and defeat another state or nation by penetrating its computers or networks for the purposes of causing damage and disruption.

In general, cyberwarfare attacks have become much more widespread, sophisticated, and potentially devastating. There are 250,000 probes trying to find their way into the U.S. Department of Defense networks every hour, and cyberattacks on U.S. federal agencies have increased 150 percent since 2008. Over the years, hackers have stolen plans for missile tracking systems, satellite navigation devices, surveillance drones, and leading-edge jet fighters.

Cyberwarfare poses a serious threat to the infrastructure of modern societies, since their major financial, health, government, and industrial institutions rely on the Internet for daily operations. Cyberwarfare also involves defending against these types of attacks. The chapter-ending case discusses this topic in greater detail.

INTERNAL THREATS: EMPLOYEES

We tend to think the security threats to a business originate outside the organization. In fact, company insiders pose serious security problems. Employees have access to privileged information, and in the presence of sloppy internal security procedures, they are often able to roam throughout an organization's systems without leaving a trace.

Studies have found that user lack of knowledge is the single greatest cause of network security breaches. Many employees forget their passwords to access computer systems or allow co-workers to use them, which compromises the system. Malicious intruders seeking system access sometimes trick employees into revealing their passwords by pretending to be legitimate members of the company in need of information. This practice is called **social engineering**.

Both end users and information systems specialists are also a major source of errors introduced into information systems. End users introduce errors by entering faulty data or by not following the proper instructions for processing data and using computer equipment. Information systems specialists may create software errors as they design and develop new software or maintain existing programs.

SOFTWARE VULNERABILITY

Software errors pose a constant threat to information systems, causing untold losses in productivity, and sometimes endangering people who use or depend on systems. Growing complexity and size of software programs, coupled with demands for timely delivery to markets, have contributed to an increase in software flaws or vulnerabilities. On April 16, 2013, American Airlines had to cancel or delay 1,950 flights due to a faulty software patch from a vendor or internal software changes that were not properly tested. A systemwide network outage downed the airline's primary systems that manage airline operations, as well as backup systems that kick in when the primary systems fail (Boulton, 2013).

A major problem with software is the presence of hidden **bugs** or program code defects. Studies have shown that it is virtually impossible to eliminate all bugs from large programs. The main source of bugs is the complexity of decision-making code. A relatively small program of several hundred lines will contain tens of decisions leading to hundreds or even thousands of different paths. Important programs within most corporations are usually much larger, containing tens of thousands or even millions of lines of code, each with many times the choices and paths of the smaller programs.

Zero defects cannot be achieved in larger programs. Complete testing simply is not possible. Fully testing programs that contain thousands of choices and millions of paths would require thousands of years. Even with rigorous testing, you would not know for sure that a piece of software was dependable until the product proved itself after much operational use.

Flaws in commercial software not only impede performance but also create security vulnerabilities that open networks to intruders. Each year security firms identify thousands of software vulnerabilities in Internet and PC software.

To correct software flaws once they are identified, the software vendor creates small pieces of software called **patches** to repair the flaws without disturbing the proper operation of the software. An example is Microsoft's Windows 7 Service Pack 1, which features security, performance, and stability updates for Windows 7. It is up to users of the software to track these vulnerabilities, test, and apply all patches. This process is called *patch management.*

Because a company's IT infrastructure is typically laden with multiple business applications, operating system installations, and other system services, maintaining patches on all devices and services used by a company is often time-consuming and costly. Malware is being created so rapidly that companies have very little time to respond between the time a vulnerability and a patch are announced and the time malicious software appears to exploit the vulnerability.

8.2 Business Value of Security and Control

Many firms are reluctant to spend heavily on security because it is not directly related to sales revenue. However, protecting information systems is so critical to the operation of the business that it deserves a second look.

Companies have very valuable information assets to protect. Systems often house confidential information about individuals' taxes, financial assets, medical records, and job performance reviews. They also can contain information on corporate operations, including trade secrets, new product development plans, and marketing strategies. Government systems may store information on weapons systems, intelligence operations, and military targets. These information assets have tremendous value, and the repercussions can be devastating if they are lost, destroyed, or placed in the wrong hands. Systems that are unable to function because of security breaches, disasters, or malfunctioning technology can permanently impact a company's financial health. Some experts believe that 40 percent of all businesses will not recover from application or data losses that are not repaired within three days (Focus Research, 2010).

Inadequate security and control may result in serious legal liability. Businesses must protect not only their own information assets but also those of customers, employees, and business partners. Failure to do so may open the firm to costly litigation for data exposure or theft. An organization can be held liable for needless risk and harm created if the organization fails to take appropriate protective action to prevent loss of confidential information, data corruption, or breach of privacy. For example, BJ's Wholesale Club was sued by the U.S. Federal Trade Commission for allowing hackers to access its systems and steal credit and debit card data for fraudulent purchases. Banks that issued the cards with the stolen data sought $13 million from BJ's to compensate them for reimbursing card holders for the fraudulent purchases. A sound security and control framework that protects business information assets can thus produce a high return on investment. Strong security and control also increase employee productivity and lower operational costs.

LEGAL AND REGULATORY REQUIREMENTS FOR ELECTRONIC RECORDS MANAGEMENT

Recent U.S. government regulations are forcing companies to take security and control more seriously by mandating the protection of data from abuse, exposure, and unauthorized access. Firms face new legal obligations for the retention and storage of electronic records as well as for privacy protection.

If you work in the health care industry, your firm will need to comply with the Health Insurance Portability and Accountability Act (HIPAA) of 1996. **HIPAA** outlines medical security and privacy rules and procedures for simplifying the administration of health care billing and automating the transfer of health care data between health care providers, payers, and plans. It requires members of the health care industry to retain patient information for six years and ensure the confidentiality of those records. It specifies privacy, security, and electronic transaction standards for health care providers handling patient information, providing penalties for breaches of medical privacy, disclosure of patient records by e-mail, or unauthorized network access.

If you work in a firm providing financial services, your firm will need to comply with the Financial Services Modernization Act of 1999, better known as the **Gramm-Leach-Bliley Act** after its congressional sponsors. This act requires financial institutions to ensure the security and confidentiality of customer data. Data must be stored on a secure medium, and special security measures must be enforced to protect such data on storage media and during transmittal.

If you work in a publicly traded company, your company will need to comply with the Public Company Accounting Reform and Investor Protection Act of 2002, better known as the **Sarbanes-Oxley Act** after its sponsors Senator Paul Sarbanes of Maryland and Representative Michael Oxley of Ohio. This Act was designed to protect investors after the financial scandals at Enron, WorldCom, and other public companies. It imposes responsibility on companies and their management to safeguard the accuracy and integrity of financial information that is used internally and released externally. One of the Learning Tracks for this chapter discusses Sarbanes-Oxley in detail.

Sarbanes-Oxley is fundamentally about ensuring that internal controls are in place to govern the creation and documentation of information in financial statements. Because information systems are used to generate, store, and transport such data, the legislation requires firms to consider information systems security and other controls required to ensure the integrity, confidentiality, and accuracy of their data. Each system application that deals with critical financial reporting data requires controls to make sure the data are accurate. Controls to secure the corporate network, prevent unauthorized access to systems and data, and ensure data integrity and availability in the event of disaster or other disruption of service are essential as well.

ELECTRONIC EVIDENCE AND COMPUTER FORENSICS

Security, control, and electronic records management have become essential for responding to legal actions. Much of the evidence today for stock fraud, embezzlement, theft of company trade secrets, computer crime, and many civil cases is in digital form. In addition to information from printed or typewritten pages, legal cases today increasingly rely on evidence represented as digital data stored on portable storage devices, CDs, and computer hard disk drives, as well as in e-mail, instant messages, and e-commerce transactions over the Internet. E-mail is currently the most common type of electronic evidence.

In a legal action, a firm is obligated to respond to a discovery request for access to information that may be used as evidence, and the company is required by law to produce those data. The cost of responding to a discovery request can be enormous if the company has trouble assembling the required data or the data have been corrupted or destroyed. Courts now impose severe financial and even criminal penalties for improper destruction of electronic documents.

An effective electronic document retention policy ensures that electronic documents, e-mail, and other records are well organized, accessible, and neither retained too long nor discarded too soon. It also reflects an awareness of how to preserve potential evidence for computer forensics. **Computer forensics** is the scientific collection, examination, authentication, preservation, and analysis of data held on or retrieved from computer storage media in such a way that the information can be used as evidence in a court of law. It deals with the following problems:

- Recovering data from computers while preserving evidential integrity
- Securely storing and handling recovered electronic data
- Finding significant information in a large volume of electronic data
- Presenting the information to a court of law

Electronic evidence may reside on computer storage media in the form of computer files and as *ambient data*, which are not visible to the average user. An example might be a file that has been deleted on a PC hard drive. Data that a computer user may have deleted on computer storage media can be recovered through various techniques. Computer forensics experts try to recover such hidden data for presentation as evidence.

An awareness of computer forensics should be incorporated into a firm's contingency planning process. The CIO, security specialists, information systems staff, and corporate legal counsel should all work together to have a plan in place that can be executed if a legal need arises. You can find out more about computer forensics in the Learning Tracks for this chapter.

8.3 Establishing a Framework for Security and Control

Even with the best security tools, your information systems won't be reliable and secure unless you know how and where to deploy them. You'll need to know where your company is at risk and what controls you must have in place to protect your information systems. You'll also need to develop a security policy and plans for keeping your business running if your information systems aren't operational.

INFORMATION SYSTEMS CONTROLS

Information systems controls are both manual and automated and consist of general and application controls. **General controls** govern the design, security, and use of computer programs and the security of data files in general throughout the organization's information technology infrastructure. On the whole, general controls apply to all computerized applications and consist of a combination of hardware, software, and manual procedures that create an overall control environment.

General controls include software controls, physical hardware controls, computer operations controls, data security controls, controls over implementation of system processes, and administrative controls. Table 8.4 describes the functions of each of these controls.

Application controls are specific controls unique to each computerized application, such as payroll or order processing. They include both automated and manual procedures that ensure that only authorized data are completely and accurately processed by that application. Application controls can be classified as (1) input controls, (2) processing controls, and (3) output controls.

Input controls check data for accuracy and completeness when they enter the system. There are specific input controls for input authorization, data conversion, data editing, and error handling. *Processing controls* establish that data are complete and accurate during updating. *Output controls* ensure that the results of computer processing are accurate, complete, and properly distributed. You can find more detail about application and general controls in our Learning Tracks.

RISK ASSESSMENT

Before your company commits resources to security and information systems controls, it must know which assets require protection and the extent to which these assets are vulnerable. A risk assessment helps answer these questions and determine the most cost-effective set of controls for protecting assets.

A **risk assessment** determines the level of risk to the firm if a specific activity or process is not properly controlled. Not all risks can be anticipated and measured, but most

TABLE 8.4

General Controls

Type of General Control	Description
Software controls	Monitor the use of system software and prevent unauthorized access of software programs, system software, and computer programs.
Hardware controls	Ensure that computer hardware is physically secure, and check for equipment malfunction. Organizations that are critically dependent on their computers also must make provisions for backup or continued operation to maintain constant service.
Computer operations controls	Oversee the work of the computer department to ensure that programmed procedures are consistently and correctly applied to the storage and processing of data. They include controls over the setup of computer processing jobs and backup and recovery procedures for processing that ends abnormally.
Data security controls	Ensure that valuable business data files on either disk or tape are not subject to unauthorized access, change, or destruction while they are in use or in storage.
Implementation controls	Audit the systems development process at various points to ensure that the process is properly controlled and managed.
Administrative controls	Formalize standards, rules, procedures, and control disciplines to ensure that the organization's general and application controls are properly executed and enforced.

businesses will be able to acquire some understanding of the risks they face. Business managers working with information systems specialists should try to determine the value of information assets, points of vulnerability, the likely frequency of a problem, and the potential for damage. For example, if an event is likely to occur no more than once a year, with a maximum of a $1,000 loss to the organization, it is not wise to spend $20,000 on the design and maintenance of a control to protect against that event. However, if that same event could occur at least once a day, with a potential loss of more than $300,000 a year, $100,000 spent on a control might be entirely appropriate.

Table 8.5 illustrates sample results of a risk assessment for an online order processing system that processes 30,000 orders per day. The likelihood of each exposure occurring over a one-year period is expressed as a percentage. The next column shows the highest and lowest possible loss that could be expected each time the exposure occurred and an average loss calculated by adding the highest and lowest figures together and dividing by two. The

TABLE 8.5

Online Order Processing Risk Assessment

Exposure	Probability of Occurrence (%)	Loss Range/ Average ($)	Expected Annual Loss ($)
Power failure	30%	$5,000–$200,000 ($102,500)	$30,750
Embezzlement	5%	$1,000–$50,000 ($25,500)	$1,275
User error	98%	$200–$40,000 ($20,100)	$19,698

expected annual loss for each exposure can be determined by multiplying the average loss by its probability of occurrence.

This risk assessment shows that the probability of a power failure occurring in a one-year period is 30 percent. Loss of order transactions while power is down could range from $5,000 to $200,000 (averaging $102,500) for each occurrence, depending on how long processing is halted. The probability of embezzlement occurring over a yearly period is about 5 percent, with potential losses ranging from $1,000 to $50,000 (and averaging $25,500) for each occurrence. User errors have a 98 percent chance of occurring over a yearly period, with losses ranging from $200 to $40,000 (and averaging $20,100) for each occurrence.

Once the risks have been assessed, system builders will concentrate on the control points with the greatest vulnerability and potential for loss. In this case, controls should focus on ways to minimize the risk of power failures and user errors because anticipated annual losses are highest for these areas.

SECURITY POLICY

Once you've identified the main risks to your systems, your company will need to develop a security policy for protecting the company's assets. A **security policy** consists of statements ranking information risks, identifying acceptable security goals, and identifying the mechanisms for achieving these goals. What are the firm's most important information assets? Who generates and controls this information in the firm? What existing security policies are in place to protect the information? What level of risk is management willing to accept for each of these assets? Is it willing, for instance, to lose customer credit data once every 10 years? Or will it build a security system for credit card data that can withstand the once-in-a-hundred-year disaster? Management must estimate how much it will cost to achieve this level of acceptable risk.

The security policy drives other policies determining acceptable use of the firm's information resources and which members of the company have access to its information assets. An **acceptable use policy (AUP)** defines acceptable uses of the firm's information resources and computing equipment, including desktop and laptop computers, wireless devices, telephones, and the Internet. The policy should clarify company policy regarding privacy, user responsibility, and personal use of company equipment and networks. A good AUP defines unacceptable and acceptable actions for every user and specifies consequences for noncompliance. For example, security policy at Unilever, the giant multinational consumer goods company, requires every employee to use a company-specified device and employ a password or other method of identification when logging onto the corporate network.

Security policy also includes provisions for identity management. **Identity management** consists of business processes and software tools for identifying the valid users of a system and controlling their access to system resources. It includes policies for identifying and authorizing different categories of system users, specifying what systems or portions of systems each user is allowed to access, and the processes and technologies for authenticating users and protecting their identities.

Figure 8.3 is one example of how an identity management system might capture the access rules for different levels of users in the human resources function. It specifies what portions of a human resource database each user is permitted to access, based on the information required to perform that person's job. The database contains sensitive personal information such as employees' salaries, benefits, and medical histories.

The access rules illustrated here are for two sets of users. One set of users consists of all employees who perform clerical functions, such as inputting employee data into the system. All individuals with this type of profile can update the system but can neither read nor update sensitive fields, such as salary, medical history, or earnings data. Another profile applies to a divisional manager, who cannot update the system but who can read all employee data fields for his or her division, including medical history and salary. We provide more detail on the technologies for user authentication later on in this chapter.

Figure 8.3
Access rules for a
Personnel System
*These two examples
represent two security
profiles or data security
patterns that might be
found in a personnel
system. Depending on
the security profile, a
user would have certain
restrictions on access
to various systems,
locations, or data in an
organization.*

SECURITY PROFILE 1	
User: Personnel Dept. Clerk	
Location: Division 1	
Employee Identification Codes with This Profile:	00753, 27834, 37665, 44116
Data Field Restrictions	Type of Access
All employee data for Division 1 only	Read and Update
• Medical history data	None
• Salary	None
• Pensionable earnings	None

SECURITY PROFILE 2	
User: Divisional Personnel Manager	
Location: Division 1	
Employee Identification Codes with This Profile: 27321	
Data Field Restrictions	Type of Access
All employee data for Division 1 only	Read Only

DISASTER RECOVERY PLANNING AND BUSINESS CONTINUITY PLANNING

If you run a business, you need to plan for events, such as power outages, floods, earthquakes, or terrorist attacks that will prevent your information systems and your business from operating. **Disaster recovery planning** devises plans for the restoration of computing and communications services after they have been disrupted. Disaster recovery plans focus primarily on the technical issues involved in keeping systems up and running, such as which files to back up and the maintenance of backup computer systems or disaster recovery services.

For example, MasterCard maintains a duplicate computer center in Kansas City, Missouri, to serve as an emergency backup to its primary computer center in St. Louis. Rather than build their own backup facilities, many firms contract with disaster recovery firms, such as Comdisco Disaster Recovery Services in Rosemont, Illinois, and SunGard Availability Services, headquartered in Wayne, Pennsylvania. These disaster recovery firms provide hot sites housing spare computers at locations around the country where subscribing firms can run their critical applications in an emergency. For example, Champion Technologies, which supplies chemicals used in oil and gas operations, is able to switch its enterprise systems from Houston to a SunGard hot site in Scottsdale, Arizona, in two hours.

Business continuity planning focuses on how the company can restore business operations after a disaster strikes. The business continuity plan identifies critical business processes and determines action plans for handling mission-critical functions if systems go down. For example, Deutsche Bank, which provides investment banking and asset management services in 74 different countries, has a well-developed business continuity plan that it continually updates and refines. It maintains full-time teams in Singapore, Hong Kong, Japan, India, and Australia to coordinate plans addressing loss of facilities, personnel, or critical systems so that the company can continue to operate when a catastrophic event occurs. Deutsche Bank's plan distinguishes between processes critical for business survival and those critical to crisis support and is coordinated with the company's disaster recovery planning for its computer centers.

Business managers and information technology specialists need to work together on both types of plans to determine which systems and business processes are most critical to the company. They must conduct a business impact analysis to identify the firm's most critical systems and the impact a systems outage would have on the business. Management must determine the maximum amount of time the business can survive with its systems down and which parts of the business must be restored first.

THE ROLE OF AUDITING

How does management know that information systems security and controls are effective? To answer this question, organizations must conduct comprehensive and systematic audits. An **information systems audit** examines the firm's overall security environment as well as controls governing individual information systems. The auditor should trace the flow of sample transactions through the system and perform tests, using, if appropriate, automated audit software. The information systems audit may also examine data quality.

Security audits review technologies, procedures, documentation, training, and personnel. A thorough audit will even simulate an attack or disaster to test the response of the technology, information systems staff, and business employees.

The audit lists and ranks all control weaknesses and estimates the probability of their occurrence. It then assesses the financial and organizational impact of each threat. Figure 8.4 is a sample auditor's listing of control weaknesses for a loan system. It includes a section for notifying management of such weaknesses and for management's response. Management is expected to devise a plan for countering significant weaknesses in controls.

8.4 Technologies and Tools for Protecting Information Resources

Businesses have an array of technologies for protecting their information resources. They include tools for managing user identities, preventing unauthorized access to systems and data, ensuring system availability, and ensuring software quality.

Function: Loans Location: Peoria, IL	Prepared by: J. Ericson Date: June 16, 2014		Received by: T. Benson Review date: June 28, 2014	
Nature of Weakness and Impact	Chance for Error/Abuse		Notification to Management	
	Yes/No	Justification	Report date	Management response
User accounts with missing passwords	Yes	Leaves system open to unauthorized outsiders or attackers	5/10/14	Eliminate accounts without passwords
Network configured to allow some sharing of system files	Yes	Exposes critical system files to hostile parties connected to the network	5/10/14	Ensure only required directories are shared and that they are protected with strong passwords
Software patches can update production programs without final approval from Standards and Controls group	No	All production programs require management approval; Standards and Controls group assigns such cases to a temporary production status		

Figure 8.4
Sample Auditor's List of Control Weaknesses
This chart is a sample page from a list of control weaknesses that an auditor might find in a loan system in a local commercial bank. This form helps auditors record and evaluate control weaknesses and shows the results of discussing those weaknesses with management, as well as any corrective actions taken by management.

IDENTITY MANAGEMENT AND AUTHENTICATION

Midsize and large companies have complex IT infrastructures and many different systems, each with its own set of users. Identity management software automates the process of keeping track of all these users and their system privileges, assigning each user a unique digital identity for accessing each system. It also includes tools for authenticating users, protecting user identities, and controlling access to system resources.

To gain access to a system, a user must be authorized and authenticated. **Authentication** refers to the ability to know that a person is who he or she claims to be. Authentication is often established by using **passwords** known only to authorized users. An end user uses a password to log on to a computer system and may also use passwords for accessing specific systems and files. However, users often forget passwords, share them, or choose poor passwords that are easy to guess, which compromises security. Password systems that are too rigorous hinder employee productivity. When employees must change complex passwords frequently, they often take shortcuts, such as choosing passwords that are easy to guess or keeping their passwords at their workstations in plain view. Passwords can also be "sniffed" if transmitted over a network or stolen through social engineering.

New authentication technologies, such as tokens, smart cards, and biometric authentication, overcome some of these problems. A **token** is a physical device, similar to an identification card, that is designed to prove the identity of a single user. Tokens are small gadgets that typically fit on key rings and display passcodes that change frequently. A **smart card** is a device about the size of a credit card that contains a chip formatted with access permission and other data. (Smart cards are also used in electronic payment systems.) A reader device interprets the data on the smart card and allows or denies access.

Biometric authentication uses systems that read and interpret individual human traits, such as fingerprints, irises, and voices, in order to grant or deny access. Biometric authentication is based on the measurement of a physical or behavioral trait that makes each individual unique. It compares a person's unique characteristics, such as the fingerprints, face, or retinal image, against a stored profile of these characteristics to determine

This PC has a biometric fingerprint reader for fast yet secure access to files and networks. New models of PCs are starting to use biometric identification to authenticate users.

whether there are any differences between these characteristics and the stored profile. If the two profiles match, access is granted. Fingerprint and facial recognition technologies are just beginning to be used for security applications, with many PC laptops equipped with fingerprint identification devices and several models with built-in webcams and face recognition software.

FIREWALLS, INTRUSION DETECTION SYSTEMS, AND ANTIVIRUS SOFTWARE

Without protection against malware and intruders, connecting to the Internet would be very dangerous. Firewalls, intrusion detection systems, and antivirus software have become essential business tools.

Firewalls

Firewalls prevent unauthorized users from accessing private networks. A firewall is a combination of hardware and software that controls the flow of incoming and outgoing network traffic. It is generally placed between the organization's private internal networks and distrusted external networks, such as the Internet, although firewalls can also be used to protect one part of a company's network from the rest of the network (see Figure 8.5).

The firewall acts like a gatekeeper who examines each user's credentials before access is granted to a network. The firewall identifies names, IP addresses, applications, and other characteristics of incoming traffic. It checks this information against the access rules that have been programmed into the system by the network administrator. The firewall prevents unauthorized communication into and out of the network.

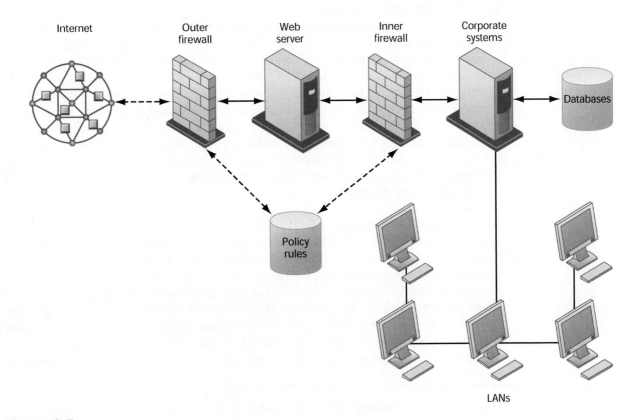

Figure 8.5

A Corporate Firewall

The firewall is placed between the firm's private network and the public Internet or another distrusted network to protect against unauthorized traffic.

In large organizations, the firewall often resides on a specially designated computer separate from the rest of the network, so no incoming request directly accesses private network resources. There are a number of firewall screening technologies, including static packet filtering, stateful inspection, Network Address Translation, and application proxy filtering. They are frequently used in combination to provide firewall protection.

Packet filtering examines selected fields in the headers of data packets flowing back and forth between the trusted network and the Internet, examining individual packets in isolation. This filtering technology can miss many types of attacks. *Stateful inspection* provides additional security by determining whether packets are part of an ongoing dialogue between a sender and a receiver. It sets up state tables to track information over multiple packets. Packets are accepted or rejected based on whether they are part of an approved conversation or whether they are attempting to establish a legitimate connection.

Network Address Translation (NAT) can provide another layer of protection when static packet filtering and stateful inspection are employed. NAT conceals the IP addresses of the organization's internal host computer(s) to prevent sniffer programs outside the firewall from ascertaining them and using that information to penetrate internal systems.

Application proxy filtering examines the application content of packets. A proxy server stops data packets originating outside the organization, inspects them, and passes a proxy to the other side of the firewall. If a user outside the company wants to communicate with a user inside the organization, the outside user first "talks" to the proxy application and the proxy application communicates with the firm's internal computer. Likewise, a computer user inside the organization goes through the proxy to talk with computers on the outside.

To create a good firewall, an administrator must maintain detailed internal rules identifying the people, applications, or addresses that are allowed or rejected. Firewalls can deter, but not completely prevent, network penetration by outsiders and should be viewed as one element in an overall security plan.

Intrusion Detection Systems

In addition to firewalls, commercial security vendors now provide intrusion detection tools and services to protect against suspicious network traffic and attempts to access files and databases. **Intrusion detection systems** feature full-time monitoring tools placed at the most vulnerable points or "hot spots" of corporate networks to detect and deter intruders continually. The system generates an alarm if it finds a suspicious or anomalous event. Scanning software looks for patterns indicative of known methods of computer attacks, such as bad passwords, checks to see if important files have been removed or modified, and sends warnings of vandalism or system administration errors. Monitoring software examines events as they are happening to discover security attacks in progress. The intrusion detection tool can also be customized to shut down a particularly sensitive part of a network if it receives unauthorized traffic.

Antivirus and Antispyware Software

Defensive technology plans for both individuals and businesses must include anti-malware protection for every computer. **Antivirus software** prevents, detects, and removes malware, including computer viruses, computer worms, Trojan horses, spyware, and adware. However, most antivirus software is effective only against malware already known when the software was written. To remain effective, the antivirus software must be continually updated, and even then it is not always effective. According to a report by Solutionary Security Engineering Research Team (SERT), 54 percent of malware evades anti-virus detection. Organizations need to use additional malware detection tools for better protection (Solutionary, 2013).

Unified Threat Management Systems

To help businesses reduce costs and improve manageability, security vendors have combined into a single appliance various security tools, including firewalls, virtual private networks, intrusion detection systems, and Web content filtering and antispam software. These comprehensive security management products are called **unified threat management (UTM)** systems. Although initially aimed at small and medium-sized businesses, UTM products are available for all sizes of networks. Leading UTM vendors include Blue Coat, Fortinent, and Check Point, and networking vendors such as Cisco Systems and Juniper Networks provide some UTM capabilities in their products.

SECURING WIRELESS NETWORKS

The initial security standard developed for Wi-Fi, called Wired Equivalent Privacy (WEP), is not very effective because its encryption keys are relatively easy to crack. WEP provides some margin of security, however, if users remember to enable it. Corporations can further improve Wi-Fi security by using it in conjunction with virtual private network (VPN) technology when accessing internal corporate data.

In June 2004, the Wi-Fi Alliance industry trade group finalized the 802.11i specification (also referred to as Wi-Fi Protected Access 2 or WPA2) that replaces WEP with stronger security standards. Instead of the static encryption keys used in WEP, the new standard uses much longer keys that continually change, making them harder to crack. It also employs an encrypted authentication system with a central authentication server to ensure that only authorized users access the network.

ENCRYPTION AND PUBLIC KEY INFRASTRUCTURE

Many businesses use encryption to protect digital information that they store, physically transfer, or send over the Internet. **Encryption** is the process of transforming plain text or data into cipher text that cannot be read by anyone other than the sender and the intended receiver. Data are encrypted by using a secret numerical code, called an encryption key, that transforms plain data into cipher text. The message must be decrypted by the receiver.

Two methods for encrypting network traffic on the Web are SSL and S-HTTP. **Secure Sockets Layer (SSL)** and its successor Transport Layer Security (TLS) enable client and server computers to manage encryption and decryption activities as they communicate with each other during a secure Web session. **Secure Hypertext Transfer Protocol (S-HTTP)** is another protocol used for encrypting data flowing over the Internet, but it is limited to individual messages, whereas SSL and TLS are designed to establish a secure connection between two computers.

The capability to generate secure sessions is built into Internet client browser software and servers. The client and the server negotiate what key and what level of security to use. Once a secure session is established between the client and the server, all messages in that session are encrypted.

There are two alternative methods of encryption: symmetric key encryption and public key encryption. In symmetric key encryption, the sender and receiver establish a secure Internet session by creating a single encryption key and sending it to the receiver so both the sender and receiver share the same key. The strength of the encryption key is measured by its bit length. Today, a typical key will be 128 bits long (a string of 128 binary digits).

The problem with all symmetric encryption schemes is that the key itself must be shared somehow among the senders and receivers, which exposes the key to outsiders who might just be able to intercept and decrypt the key. A more secure form of encryption called **public key encryption** uses two keys: one shared (or public) and one totally private as shown in Figure 8.6. The keys are mathematically related so that data encrypted with one key can be decrypted using only the other key. To send and receive messages, communicators first create separate pairs of private and public keys. The public key is kept in a directory and the private key must be kept secret. The sender encrypts a message with the recipient's public key. On receiving the message, the recipient uses his or her private key to decrypt it.

Digital certificates are data files used to establish the identity of users and electronic assets for protection of online transactions (see Figure 8.7). A digital certificate system uses a trusted third party, known as a certificate authority (CA, or certification authority), to

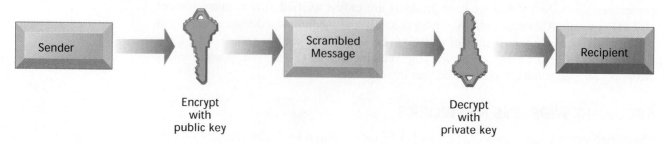

Figure 8.6
Public Key Encryption
A public key encryption system can be viewed as a series of public and private keys that lock data when they are transmitted and unlock the data when they are received. The sender locates the recipient's public key in a directory and uses it to encrypt a message. The message is sent in encrypted form over the Internet or a private network. When the encrypted message arrives, the recipient uses his or her private key to decrypt the data and read the message.

validate a user's identity. There are many CAs in the United States and around the world, including Symantec, GoDaddy, and Comodo.

The CA verifies a digital certificate user's identity offline. This information is put into a CA server, which generates an encrypted digital certificate containing owner identification information and a copy of the owner's public key. The certificate authenticates that the public key belongs to the designated owner. The CA makes its own public key available either in print or perhaps on the Internet. The recipient of an encrypted message uses the CA's public key to decode the digital certificate attached to the message, verifies it was issued by the CA, and then obtains the sender's public key and identification information contained in the certificate. Using this information, the recipient can send an encrypted reply. The digital certificate system would enable, for example, a credit card user and a merchant to validate that their digital certificates were issued by an authorized and trusted third party before they exchange data. **Public key infrastructure (PKI)**, the use of public key cryptography working with a CA, is now widely used in e-commerce.

Figure 8.7
Digital Certificates
Digital certificates help establish the identity of people or electronic assets. They protect online transactions by providing secure, encrypted, online communication.

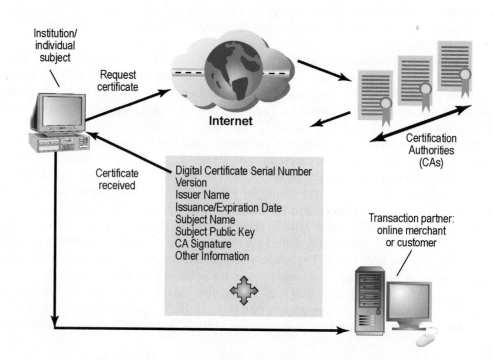

ENSURING SYSTEM AVAILABILITY

As companies increasingly rely on digital networks for revenue and operations, they need to take additional steps to ensure that their systems and applications are always available. Firms such as those in the airline and financial services industries with critical applications requiring online transaction processing have traditionally used fault-tolerant computer systems for many years to ensure 100 percent availability. In **online transaction processing**, transactions entered online are immediately processed by the computer. Multitudinous changes to databases, reporting, and requests for information occur each instant.

Fault-tolerant computer systems contain redundant hardware, software, and power supply components that create an environment that provides continuous, uninterrupted service. Fault-tolerant computers use special software routines or self-checking logic built into their circuitry to detect hardware failures and automatically switch to a backup device. Parts from these computers can be removed and repaired without disruption to the computer or downtime. **Downtime** refers to periods of time in which a system is not operational.

Researchers are exploring ways to make computing systems recover even more rapidly when mishaps occur, an approach called **recovery-oriented computing**. This work includes designing systems that recover quickly, and implementing capabilities and tools to help operators pinpoint the sources of faults in multi-component systems and easily correct their mistakes.

Controlling Network Traffic: Deep Packet Inspection

Have you ever tried to use your campus network and found it was very slow? It may be because your fellow students are using the network to download music or watch YouTube. Bandwith-consuming applications such as file-sharing programs, Internet phone service, and online video are able to clog and slow down corporate networks, degrading performance. For example, Ball State University in Muncie, Indiana, found its network had slowed because a small minority of students were using P2P file-sharing programs to download movies and music.

A technology called **deep packet inspection (DPI)** helps solve this problem. DPI examines data files and sorts out low-priority online material while assigning higher priority to business-critical files. Based on the priorities established by a network's operators, it decides whether a specific data packet can continue to its destination or should be blocked or delayed while more important traffic proceeds. Using a DPI system from Allot Communications, Ball State was able to cap the amount of file-sharing traffic and assign it a much lower priority. Ball State's preferred network traffic speeded up.

Security Outsourcing

Many companies, especially small businesses, lack the resources or expertise to provide a secure high-availability computing environment on their own. They can outsource many security functions to **managed security service providers (MSSPs)** that monitor network activity and perform vulnerability testing and intrusion detection. SecureWorks, BT Managed Security Solutions Group, and Symantec are leading providers of MSSP services.

SECURITY ISSUES FOR CLOUD COMPUTING AND THE MOBILE DIGITAL PLATFORM

Although cloud computing and the emerging mobile digital platform have the potential to deliver powerful benefits, they pose new challenges to system security and reliability. We now describe some of these challenges and how they should be addressed.

Security in the Cloud

When processing takes place in the cloud, accountability and responsibility for protection of sensitive data still reside with the company owning that data. Understanding how the cloud computing provider organizes its services and manages the data is critical.

Cloud computing is highly distributed. Cloud applications reside in large remote data centers and server farms that supply business services and data management for multiple corporate clients. To save money and keep costs low, cloud computing providers often distribute work to data centers around the globe where work can be accomplished most efficiently. When you use the cloud, you may not know precisely where your data are being hosted.

The dispersed nature of cloud computing makes it difficult to track unauthorized activity. Virtually all cloud providers use encryption, such as Secure Sockets Layer, to secure the data they handle while the data are being transmitted. But if the data are stored on devices that also store other companies' data, it's important to ensure these stored data are encrypted as well.

Companies expect their systems to be running 24/7, but cloud providers haven't always been able to provide this level of service. On several occasions over the past few years, the cloud services of Amazon.com and Salesforce.com experienced outages that disrupted business operations for millions of users (see the Chapter 5 ending case study).

Cloud users need to confirm that regardless of where their data are stored, they are protected at a level that meets their corporate requirements. They should stipulate that the cloud provider store and process data in specific jurisdictions according to the privacy rules of those jurisdictions. Cloud clients should find how the cloud provider segregates their corporate data from those of other companies and ask for proof that encryption mechanisms are sound. It's also important to know how the cloud provider will respond if a disaster strikes, whether the provider will be able to completely restore your data, and how long this should take. Cloud users should also ask whether cloud providers will submit to external audits and security certifications. These kinds of controls can be written into the service level agreement (SLA) before signing with a cloud provider.

Securing Mobile Platforms

If mobile devices are performing many of the functions of computers, they need to be secured like desktops and laptops against malware, theft, accidental loss, unauthorized access, and hacking attempts.

Mobile devices accessing corporate systems and data require special protection. Companies should make sure that their corporate security policy includes mobile devices, with additional details on how mobile devices should be supported, protected, and used. They will need mobile device management tools to authorize all devices in use; to maintain accurate inventory records on all mobile devices, users, and applications; to control updates to applications; and to lock down or erase lost or stolen devices so they can't be compromised. Data loss prevention technology can identify where critical data are saved, who is accessing the data, how data are leaving the company, and where the data are going. Firms should develop guidelines stipulating approved mobile platforms and software applications as well as the required software and procedures for remote access of corporate systems. The organization's mobile security policy should forbid employees from using unsecure, consumer-based applications for transferring and storing corporate documents and files, or sending such documents and files to oneself via e-mail without encryption.

Companies should encrypt communication whenever possible. All mobile device users should be required to use the password feature found in every smartphone. Mobile security products are available from Kaspersky, Symantec, Trend Micro, and McAfee.

Some companies insist that employees use only company-issued smartphones. BlackBerry devices are considered the most secure because they run within their own secure system. But, increasingly, companies are allowing employees to use their own devices, including iPhones, iPads, and Android phones, for work, to make employees more available and productive (see the Chapter 5 discussion of BYOD). Protective software products, such as the tools from Good Technology, are now available for segregating corporate data housed within personally owned mobile devices from the device's personal content.

INTERACTIVE SESSION: TECHNOLOGY   MWEB Business: Hacked

MWEB, launched in 1997, became South Africa's leading ISP in 1998. It has established itself as a company that provides a cutting-edge network and service infrastructure and outstanding customer service. Currently, MWEB's customer base of 320,000 includes home users; small, medium, and large business customers; and corporate clients. MWEB won the ISP of the Year award at the MyBroadband Conference in Johannesburg in 2010. The award was based on the performance of its various broadband services as well as on customer satisfaction.

Its business division, MWEB Business, was founded in January 1998. MWEB Business prides itself as being a business partner that is perfectly positioned to leverage the power of Web-based technologies in all areas of an organization. MWEB Business helps companies:

- Manage business data in ways that add real value and insight to their operations
- Integrate existing systems with the Internet so as to close the gap between technology, strategy, and the organization's bottom line
- Develop, manage, and maintain solutions that include all aspects of Internet connectivity, Web site development and hosting, broadband and wireless applications, e-commerce, and consultancy services
- Manage internal information among employees, as well as among business partners and suppliers

MWEB has moved forward in publicizing its plans for the South African Internet market. According to MWEB CEO Rudi Jansen, the company needs to improve the quality of their network, which is not only an MWEB problem, but also a Telkom network problem. Despite having a less-than-ideal network infrastructure, MWEB uses AVG Internet Security to offer its customers the best possible security while online. AVG Internet Security offers MWEB customers the following features:

- Identity protection for safe banking and shopping
- LinkScanner for safe surfing and searching
- WebShield for safe social networking, chatting, and downloading
- Antiphishing and antispam for a safe uncluttered inbox

- High-speed antivirus/antispyware software with automatic updates
- An enhanced firewall

In addition, MWEB automatically protects customers against junk email and viruses that are sent via email. Its virus filter ensures that only virus-free email is delivered to clients' inboxes by automatically cleaning e-mails from recognized malware sources.

Despite the multitude of security services offered by MWEB, a number of MWEB Business subscribers' account details were compromised when their logon and password details were published on the Internet by hackers. Initial reports indicated that as many as 2,390 users of MWEB's business digital subscriber lines were affected. The company disclosed the security breach on October 25, 2010. It appears that hackers gained access to the Internet Solutions' self-service management system that MWEB Business uses to provide and manage business accounts that have not yet been migrated to the MWEB network.

MWEB responded quickly to the hacking incident. According to Jansen, about 1,000 clients on the Internet Solutions network needed to be migrated from the old server which was attacked by hackers. Although the network was quickly secured, most customers had recently been moved to MWEB's IPC network. MWEB would also be contacting these customers to reset their passwords, as an added security measure. Jansen was quick to note that no personal information was lost and that none of MWEB's clients suffered any losses as their usernames and passwords had been recreated and changed. He further added that MWEB successfully repels 5,000 attacks a day.

Andre Joubert, general manager of MWEB Business, emphasized that only ADSL authentication usernames and passwords had been compromised. The integrity of the personal or private data related to the accounts remained intact, as did the access credentials for each customer's bundled onsite router. Joubert did acknowledge the seriousness of the hack, apologizing for any inconvenience the breach may have caused to MWEB's customers. As soon as the breach was identified, MWEB took immediate action to evaluate the extent of the breach and to limit any damage. In MWEB's defense, Jansen said that MWEB constantly advises its customers to be vigilant regarding their online data and security. In addition, MWEB was working closely with Internet Solutions to investigate the nature and source of the breach to ensure it doesn't happen again.

Sources: "2010 MyBroadband Awards: The Winners and Losers," MyBroadband, October 19, 2010; "About MWEB," MWEB (www.mweb.co.za/productspricing/MWEBBusiness/AboutMWEBB usiness.aspx, accessed November 17, 2010); "Hackers Target MWEB," NewsTime, October 25, 2010; "MWEB Business Tackles 'ADSL Hacking' Incident," MyBroadband, October 25, 2010; "MWEB Business Takes Action in 'Hacking' Incident," Moneyweb, October 25, 2010; "MWeb hacked, users' details exposed," TechCentral, October 26, 2010.

Case contributed by Upasana Singh, University of KwaZulu-Natal

CASE STUDY QUESTIONS

1. What technology issues led to the security breach at MWEB?

2. What is the possible business impact of this security breach for both MWEB and its customers?

3. If you were an MWEB customer, would you consider MWEB's response to the security breach to be acceptable? Why or why not?

4. What should MWEB do in the future to avoid similar incidents?

ENSURING SOFTWARE QUALITY

In addition to implementing effective security and controls, organizations can improve system quality and reliability by employing software metrics and rigorous software testing. Software metrics are objective assessments of the system in the form of quantified measurements. Ongoing use of metrics allows the information systems department and end users to jointly measure the performance of the system and identify problems as they occur. Examples of software metrics include the number of transactions that can be processed in a specified unit of time, online response time, the number of payroll checks printed per hour, and the number of known bugs per hundred lines of program code. For metrics to be successful, they must be carefully designed, formal, objective, and used consistently.

Early, regular, and thorough testing will contribute significantly to system quality. Many view testing as a way to prove the correctness of work they have done. In fact, we know that all sizable software is riddled with errors, and we must test to uncover these errors.

Good testing begins before a software program is even written by using a *walkthrough*— a review of a specification or design document by a small group of people carefully selected based on the skills needed for the particular objectives being tested. Once developers start writing software programs, coding walkthroughs can also be used to review program code. However, code must be tested by computer runs. When errors are discovered, the source is found and eliminated through a process called *debugging*. You can find out more about the various stages of testing required to put an information system into operation in Chapter 12. Our Learning Tracks also contain descriptions of methodologies for developing software programs that also contribute to software quality.

Review Summary

1 **Why are information systems vulnerable to destruction, error, and abuse?** Digital data are vulnerable to destruction, misuse, error, fraud, and hardware or software failures. The Internet is designed to be an open system and makes internal corporate systems more vulnerable to actions from outsiders. Hackers can unleash denial-of-service (DoS)

attacks or penetrate corporate networks, causing serious system disruptions. Wi-Fi networks can easily be penetrated by intruders using sniffer programs to obtain an address to access the resources of the network. Computer viruses and worms can disable systems and Web sites. The dispersed nature of cloud computing makes it difficult to track unauthorized activity or to apply controls from afar. Software presents problems because software bugs may be impossible to eliminate and because software vulnerabilities can be exploited by hackers and malicious software. End users often introduce errors.

2 **What is the business value of security and control?** Lack of sound security and control can cause firms relying on computer systems for their core business functions to lose sales and productivity. Information assets, such as confidential employee records, trade secrets, or business plans, lose much of their value if they are revealed to outsiders or if they expose the firm to legal liability. New laws, such as HIPAA, the Sarbanes-Oxley Act, and the Gramm-Leach-Bliley Act, require companies to practice stringent electronic records management and adhere to strict standards for security, privacy, and control. Legal actions requiring electronic evidence and computer forensics also require firms to pay more attention to security and electronic records management.

3 **What are the components of an organizational framework for security and control?** Firms need to establish a good set of both general and application controls for their information systems. A risk assessment evaluates information assets, identifies control points and control weaknesses, and determines the most cost-effective set of controls. Firms must also develop a coherent corporate security policy and plans for continuing business operations in the event of disaster or disruption. The security policy includes policies for acceptable use and identity management. Comprehensive and systematic information systems auditing helps organizations determine the effectiveness of security and controls for their information systems.

4 **What are the most important tools and technologies for safeguarding information resources?** Firewalls prevent unauthorized users from accessing a private network when it is linked to the Internet. Intrusion detection systems monitor private networks from suspicious network traffic and attempts to access corporate systems. Passwords, tokens, smart cards, and biometric authentication are used to authenticate system users. Antivirus software checks computer systems for infections by viruses and worms and often eliminates the malicious software, while antispyware software combats intrusive and harmful spyware programs. Encryption, the coding and scrambling of messages, is a widely used technology for securing electronic transmissions over unprotected networks. Digital certificates combined with public key encryption provide further protection of electronic transactions by authenticating a user's identity. Companies can use fault-tolerant computer systems or create high-availability computing environments to make sure that their information systems are always available. Use of software metrics and rigorous software testing help improve software quality and reliability.

Key Terms

Acceptable use policy (AUP), 299
Antivirus software, 304
Application controls, 297
Authentication, 302
Biometric authentication, 302
Botnet, 289
Bugs, 294
Business continuity planning, 300

Click fraud, 293
Computer crime, 289
Computer forensics, 296
Computer virus, 285
Controls, 283
Cybervandalism, 288
Cyberwarfare, 294
Deep packet inspection (DPI), 307

Denial-of-service (DoS) attack, 289
Digital certificates, 305
Disaster recovery planning, 300
Distributed denial-of-service (DDoS) attack, 289
Downtime, 307
Drive-by download, 286
Encryption, 305

Review Questions

8-1 Why are information systems vulnerable to destruction, error, and abuse?
- List and describe the most common threats against contemporary information systems.
- Define malware and distinguish among a virus, a worm, and a Trojan horse.
- Explain the challenges presented in securing wireless networks.
- Define computer crime. Provide two examples of crime in which computers are targets and two examples in which computers are used as instruments of crime.
- Define identity theft and phishing and explain why identity theft is such a big problem today.
- Define denial of service (DoS) attack, explain how it differs from a distributed denial of service (DDoS) attack, and discuss how DoS and DDoS attacks are related to the use of botnets.
- Explain how software defects affect system reliability and security.

8-2 What is the business value of security and control?
- Explain how security and control provide value for businesses.
- Define computer forensics and explain what it is used for.

8-3 What are the components of an organizational framework for security and control?
- Define general controls and describe each type of general control.
- Define application controls and describe each type of application control.
- Describe the function of risk assessment and explain how it is conducted for information systems.
- Define and describe the following: security policy, acceptable use policy, and identity management.
- Explain how information systems auditing promotes security and control.

8-4 What are the most important tools and technologies for safeguarding information resources?
- Name and describe three authentication methods.
- Describe the roles of firewalls, intrusion detection systems, and antivirus software in promoting security.
- Explain how encryption protects information.
- Describe the role of encryption and digital certificates in a public key infrastructure.
- Distinguish between disaster recovery planning and business continuity planning.
- Identify and describe the security problems posed by cloud computing.
- Explain the actions companies should take to secure mobile platforms

Discussion Questions

8-5 Security isn't simply a technology issue, it's a business issue. Discuss.

8-6 Who poses the biggest security threat – insiders or outsiders?

8-7 Suppose your business had an e-commerce Web site where it sold goods and accepted credit card pay-ments. Discuss the major security threats to this Web site and their potential impact. What can be done to minimize these threats?

Hands-On MIS Projects

The projects in this section give you hands-on experience analyzing security vulnerabilities, using spreadsheet software for risk analysis, and using Web tools to research security outsourcing services.

MANAGEMENT DECISION PROBLEMS

8-8 Gifty is an online e-tailer for handmade gifts. Customers can purchase either via its Web site or via a mobile app. Prepare a security analysis for this Internet-based business. What kinds of threats should it anticipate? What would be their impact on the business? What steps can it take to prevent damage to its Web sites and continuing operations?

8-9 A survey of your firm's IT infastructure has identified a number of security vulnerabilities. Review the data on these vulnerabilities, which can be found in a table in MyMISLab™. Use the table to answer the following questions:

- Calculate the total number of vulnerabilities for each platform. What is the potential impact of the security problems for each computing platform on the organization?
- If you only have one information systems specialist in charge of security, which platforms should you address first in trying to eliminate these vulnerabilities? Second? Third? Last? Why?
- Identify the types of control problems illustrated by these vulnerabilities and explain the measures that should be taken to solve them.
- What does your firm risk by ignoring the security vulnerabilities identified?

IMPROVING DECISION MAKING: USING SPREADSHEET SOFTWARE TO PERFORM A SECURITY RISK ASSESSMENT

Software skills: Spreadsheet formulas and charts
Business skills: Risk assessment

8-10 This project uses spreadsheet software to calculate anticipated annual losses from various security threats identified for a small company.

Mercer Paints is a paint manufacturing company located in Alabama that uses a network to link its business operations. A security risk assessment requested by manage-ment identified a number of potential exposures. These exposures, their associated prob-abilities, and average losses are summarized in a table, which can be found in MyMISLab. Use the table to answer the following questions:

- In addition to the potential exposures listed, identify at least three other potential threats to Mercer Paints, assign probabilities, and estimate a loss range.

- Use spreadsheet software and the risk assessment data to calculate the expected annual loss for each exposure.
- Present your findings in the form of a chart. Which control points have the greatest vulnerability? What recommendations would you make to Mercer Paints? Prepare a written report that summarizes your findings and recommendations.

IMPROVING DECISION MAKING: EVALUATING SECURITY OUTSOURCING SERVICES

Software skills: Web browser and presentation software
Business skills: Evaluating business outsourcing services

8-11 This project will help develop your Internet skills in using the Web to research and evaluate security outsourcing services.

You have been asked to help your company's management decide whether to outsource security or keep the security function within the firm. Search the Web to find information to help you decide whether to outsource security and to locate security outsourcing services.

- Present a brief summary of the arguments for and against outsourcing computer security for your company.

- Select two firms that offer computer security outsourcing services, and compare them and their services.

- Prepare an electronic presentation for management summarizing your findings. Your presentation should make the case on whether or not your company should outsource computer security. If you believe your company should outsource, the presentation should identify which security outsourcing service you selected and justify your decision.

Collaboration and Teamwork Project

8-12 In MyMISLab you will find a Collaboration and Teamwork Project dealing with the concepts in this chapter. You will be able to use GoogleDrive, Google Docs, Google Sites, Google+, or other open source collaboration tools to complete the assignment.

BUSINESS PROBLEM-SOLVING CASE

The Looming Threat of Cyberwarfare

"Now our enemies are also seeking the ability to sabotage our power grid, our financial institutions, and our air traffic control systems. We cannot look back years from now and wonder why we did nothing in the face of real threats to our security and our economy."

With these words in his 2013 State of the Union address, Barack Obama officially became the first US cyberwarfare president. Obama was about to sign the Improving Critical Infrastructure Cybersecurity executive order, which allows companies associated with the supervision of electrical grids, dams, and financial institutions to voluntarily join a program to receive classified and other cyber security threat information previously available only to government contractors. The main drawback is that only legislation can enforce minimum security requirements for private sector companies, which operate most U.S. critical infrastructure. Unfortunately, Congress in 2012 had failed to pass two cyber security bills that were much stronger, bowing to pressures from businesses worried about stepped-up security costs and concerns raised by privacy advocates.

Cyberwarfare is more complex than conventional warfare. Although many potential targets are military, a country's power grids, financial systems, and communications networks can also be crippled. Non-state actors such as terrorists or criminal groups can mount attacks, and it is often difficult to tell who is responsible. Nations must constantly be on the alert for new malware and other technologies that could be used against them, and some of these technologies developed by skilled hacker groups are openly for sale to interested governments.

The scale and speed of cyber attacks has escalated in the United States and other parts of the world. From September 2012 through March 2013, at least twelve U.S. financial institutions—Bank of America, Citigroup, Wells Fargo, U.S. Bancorp, PNC, Capital One, Fifth Third Bank, BB&T, HSBC, J.P. Morgan Chase, and American Express—were targeted in attacks that slowed their servers to a crawl and then shut them down. The severity of the attacks dwarfed previous distributed denial of service (DDoS) attacks. The data centers of these organizations had been infected with a long-available malware agent named Itsoknoproblembro, which creates botnets of slave servers, dubbed bRobots because they are so difficult to trace back to a command and control (C& C) server. The bRobots inundated the bank Web sites with encrypted data. A flood of encryption requests immensely intensifies attack effectiveness, enabling the attackers to take down a site with fewer requests.

The goal of the attacks was to inflict an unprecedented level of strain on as many financial institutions as possible. No account information was stolen and no financial gain sought, leading experts to think it was a state-sponsored attack. The hacker group Izzad-Din al-Qassam Cyber Fighters claimed responsibility, stating that it was retaliating for an anti-Islam video. U.S government officials believe the perpetrator is actually Iran, retaliating for economic sanctions imposed to halt its nuclear program and for what it believes were U.S. cyber attacks.

In August 2012, the Shamoon virus infected 30,000 machines at Saudi Arabian oil company, Aramco. It destroyed workstations by overwriting the master boot record (MBR), which stores key information about a hard disk drive to help a computer system start up. Shamoon also deleted data on servers, and overwrote certain files with an image of a burning American flag. U.S. officials attributed the attack to Iran.

Less than two weeks later, Qatari natural gas company, Rasgas, was forced to shut down its Web site and e-mail systems in an attack initially also attributed to Shamoon. An investigative team concluded it was likely a copycat attack trying to look like the same perpetrator. U.S. government officials blamed Iranian hackers. Israeli officials attributed both attacks to Iran's Cyber Corps, formed after Stuxnet.

Believed to have been developed by a secret joint United States-Israel operation, the Stuxnet worm was discovered in June 2010. It was designed to disable the software that controls Seimen centrifuges to enrich uranium, and it reportedly delayed Iran's ability to make nuclear arms by as much as five years. Iran has also been the target of other malware. The Duqu worm, discovered in September 2011, steals digital certificates used for authentication to help future viruses appear as secure software. In April 2012, other espionage malware closely related to Stuxnet and Duqu called Flame was discovered when hard drives at the Iranian Oil Ministry and National Iranian Oil Company were wiped clean. Four months later, investigators found that the data deletion agent they had been looking for when they discovered Flame was a separate malware agent they named Wiper. Investigators believe that Wiper's first objective is to eradicate the malware created by this group.

Cyber offensives come with a considerable downside. Previously released malware is recoverable and can be adapted and reused by both nation-state foes and unaffiliated cyber criminals. Stuxnet code has been adapted for use in financial cybercrime. Another drawback is uncontrollability. About 60 percent of known Stuxnet infections were in Iran, but 18 percent were in Indonesia, 8 percent in India, and the remaining 15 percent scattered around the world. In November 2012, Chevron admitted that its network had been infected with Stuxnet shortly after it spread beyond Iran.

To U.S. officials, the financial sector, Saudi Aramco, and Rasgas attacks signaled a shift in Iranian policy from cyber defense to cyber offense. After investing approximately $1 billion in its Cyber Corps in 2012 (still just a third of United States expenditures), Iran may have arrived as a first-tier cyber power.

China has been a first-tier cyber power for years. U.S. targets of suspected Chinese cyber attacks include federal departments (Homeland Security, State, Energy, Commerce); senior officials (Hillary Clinton, Adm. Mike Mullen); nuclear-weapons labs (Los Alamos, Oak Ridge); defense contractors (Northrup Grumman, Lockheed Martin); news organizations (the Wall Street Journal, the New York Times, Bloomberg), technology firms (Google, Adobe, Yahoo), multinationals (Coca-Cola, Dow Chemical), and just about every other node of American commerce, infrastructure or authority. Hackers have obtained sensitive information such as negotiation strategies of major corporations; designs of more than two dozen major U.S. weapons systems, including the advanced Patriot missile system, the Navy's Aegis ballistic missile defense systems, the F/A-18 fighter jet, the V-22 Osprey, the Black Hawk helicopter and the F-35 Joint Strike Fighter; and the workings of America's power grid, possibly laying groundwork for acts of sabotage. Cyberattacks from China and other nations have persisted because the U.S. has difficulty defending its information systems, cyberspace is not yet subject to international norms, and years of intrusions have provoked little American response.

Investigators believe that in September 2012, one of the elite hacking groups from China's People's Liberation Army (P.L.A.) attacked Telvent, a company that monitors utility companies, water treatment plants, and over half the oil and gas pipelines in North America. Six months later, Telvent and government investigators still didn't know if the motive was espionage or sabotage. U.S. intelligence experts believe that China's U.S. investments, particularly new, substantial investments in oil and gas, deter China from infrastructure attacks. China's economy could not escape the negative consequences from a significant shutdown of U.S. transportation systems or financial markets. Iran, with no U.S.

investments, is a much greater threat. Moreover, diplomatic channels are open with China.

Less than a week after Obama's State of the Union address, security firm Mandiant released details on a group it dubbed "APT1." Mandiant traced APT1 to a building in Shanghai that documents from China Telecom indicate was built at the same time as the General Staff Department's 3rd Department, 2nd Bureau—the military hacking unit, P.L.A. Unit 61398. Outfitted with a high-tech fiber optic infrastructure, this 12-story white office tower was said to be the origin of a six year offensive that infiltrated 141 companies across 20 industries.

The Obama administration's mounting concern with the economic and national security risks posed by cyber-intrusions has repeatedly been expressed to top Chinese officials. In May 2013, the Pentagon's annual report to Congress for the first time directly accused the Chinese government and P.L.A. of attacking U.S. government and defense contractor networks. Direct confrontation had been skirted because the United States wants China's help in dealing with the nuclear and military threat from North Korea and with sanctions against Iran. Obama again raised the issue during his informal summit with Chinese premier Xi Jinping in June 2013.

Two months earlier, however, North Korea, another budding cyberwarfare adversary, was accused of launching its most damaging attack to date. Despite obstacles limiting its ability to develop expertise, including sanctions, which restrict its access to technology, and a limited talent pool due to meager Internet penetration and restrictive access policies, North Korea is believed to have perpetrated attacks on both South Korean and American commercial, educational, governmental, and military institutions. In March 2013, 32,000 computers at three major South Korean banks and the two largest television broadcasters were affected. Internet banking sites were temporarily blocked, computer screens went blank, ATM machines failed, and commerce was disrupted.

The attackers used the Chinese-written Gondad exploit kit to infect PCs with a Trojan that provides an entryway for an attacker to take control of the machine, creating a bot or zombie computer. Once the digital backdoor is created, the controller can deposit a malware payload, in this case, a wiper agent named Dark Seoul. Like Shamoon, Dark Seoul overwrites the master boot record (MBR). There is no conclusive evidence implicating North Korea, but tensions had been escalating between the two countries. The Kim Jong-un administration had expressed fury in the days leading up to the attack over ongoing, routine joint Korea/United States military training exercises, exacerbated by South Korea's participation in U.S.-spearheaded United Nations sanctions against North Korea for its nuclear test the month before. Seoul contends that Pyongyang has committed six previous cyber attacks since 2009. Security experts at South Korea's newly formed cyber security command center believe it has been assembling and training a cyberwarrior team of thousands, and the United States agrees. For North Korea, the threat of cyber retaliation is negligible. Internet access is only now extending beyond a privileged few, businesses are just beginning to adopt online banking, and worthwhile targets are virtually nonexistent.

The Obama administration has begun helping Asian and Middle Eastern allies build up their computer network defenses against Iran and North Korea, including supplying advanced hardware and software and training programs. Future joint war games would include simulated cyber attacks. But deterring cyber attacks is a far more complex problem than conventional warfare, and US officials concede that this effort is an experiment.

While increased diplomatic pressure and the intertwined nature of the worlds' two largest economies may yield a practicable agreement between China and the United States, how to deal with the so-called "irrational actors," Iran and North Korea, is thornier. Since China is North Korea's biggest trading partner and most important ally, hammering out an agreement with China may be the first step towards managing North Korea. While Iran is diplomatically isolated, China depends on it to meet its energy needs. China walks a tightrope between exploiting the sanctioned Iranian economy and following the U.N. sanctions for which it voted. It just may be that the road to agreements with both Pyongyang and Tehran runs through Beijing. Meanwhile, the military command responsible for most U.S. cyber war efforts, U.S. Cyber Command (CYBERCOM), is slated for a 500 percent manpower increase between 2014 and 2016.

Sources: Julian E. Barnes, Siobhan Gorman, and Jeremy Page, "U.S., China Ties Tested in Cyberspace," *Wall Street Journal*, February 19, 2013; David Feith, "Why China Is Reading Your Email," *Wall Street Journal*, March 19, 2013; Thom Shanker and David E. Sanger, " U.S. Helps Allies Trying to Battle Iranian Hackers," *New York Times*, June 8, 2013; Mark Clayton , "New clue in South Korea cyberattack reveals link to Chinese criminals," *Christian Science Monitor*, March 21, 2013; Siobhan Gorman and Siobhan Hughes, "U.S. Steps Up Alarm Over Cyberattacks," Wall Street Journal, March 12, 2013; Siobhan Gorman and Julian E. Barnes, "Iran Blamed for Cyberattacks: U.S. Officials Say Iranian Hackers Behind Electronic Assaults on U.S. Banks, Foreign Energy Firms, *Wall Street Journal*, October 12, 2012;Choe Sang-Hun, "Computer Networks in South Korea Are Paralyzed in Cyberattacks," *New York Times*, March 20, 2013; Rachael King, "Stuxnet Infected Chevron's IT Network," *Wall Street Journal*, November 8, 2012; Mark Landler and David E. Sanger, "U.S. Demands China Block Cyberattacks and Agree to Rules," *New York Times*, March 11, 2013; Youkyung Lee, "Experts: NKorea training teams of 'cyber warriors," Associated Press, March 24, 2013;Nicole Perlroth, David E. Sanger and Michael S. Schmidt, "As Hacking Against U.S. Rises, Experts Try to Pin Down Motive," *New York Times*, March 3, 2013; Nicole Perlroth and Quentin Hardy, "Bank Hacking Was the Work of Iranians, Officials Say," *New York Times*, January 8, 2013; Nicole Perlroth and David E. Sanger, "Cyberattacks Seem Meant to Destroy, Not Just Disrupt," *New York Times*, March 28, 2013; David E. Sanger, David Barboza and Nicole Perlroth, "Chinese Army Unit Is Seen as Tied to Hacking Against U.S.," *New York Times*, February 18, 2013; David E. Sanger, "U.S. Blames China's Military Directly for Cyberattacks," *New York Times*, May 6, 2013; David E. Sanger and Nicole Perlroth, "Cyberattacks Against U.S. Corporations Are on the Rise," *New York Times*, May 12, 2013; Michael S. Schmidt and Nicole Perlroth, "Obama Order Gives Firms Cyberthreat Information," *New York Times*, February 12, 2013.

Case Study Questions

8-13 Is cyberwarfare a serious problem? Why or why not?

8-14 Assess the people, organization, and technology factors responsible for this problem.

8-15 What solutions are available for this problem? Do you think they will be effective? Why or why not?

Key System Applications for the Digital Age

PART III

Part III examines the core information system applications businesses are using today to improve operational excellence and decision making. These applications include enterprise systems; systems for supply chain management, customer relationship management, and knowledge management; e-commerce applications; and business intelligence systems to enhance decision making. This part answers questions such as these: How can enterprise applications improve business performance? How do firms use e-commerce to extend the reach of their businesses? How can systems improve decision making and help companies make better use of their knowledge assets?

Achieving Operational Excellence and Customer Intimacy: Enterprise Applications

CHAPTER 9

STUDENT LEARNING OBJECTIVES

After completing this chapter, you will be able to answer the following questions:

1. How do enterprise systems help businesses achieve operational excellence?

2. How do supply chain management systems coordinate planning, production, and logistics with suppliers?

3. How do customer relationship management systems help firms achieve customer intimacy?

4. What are the challenges posed by enterprise applications?

5. How are enterprise applications taking advantage of new technologies?

LEARNING TRACKS

1. SAP Business Process Map
2. Business Processes in Supply Chain Management and Supply Chain Metrics
3. Best-Practice Business Processes in CRM Software

VIDEO CASES

Case 1: Workday: Enterprise Cloud Software-as-a-Service (SaaS)

Case 2: Evolution Homecare Manages Patients with Microsoft Dynamics CRM

Instructional Video 1: GSMS Protects Products and Patients By Serializing Every Bottle of Drugs

CHAPTER OUTLINE

STATOIL FUEL AND RETAIL COMPETES USING ENTERPRISE SYSTEMS

When Alimentation Couche-Tard purchased Statoil Fuel and Retail (SFR) in April 2012, it was the Canadian convenience store giant's most ambitious acquisition to date (€2.058 billion). SFR, a division of Statoil, the Norwegian State Oil Company, had been spun off from its parent in October 2010. The purchase added 2,300 retail fuel stations—most full-service with a convenience store—to its over 6,200 stores throughout North America and expanded Couche-Tard's reach to eight European countries—Norway, Sweden, Denmark, Poland, Estonia, Latvia, Lithuania, and Russia.

SFR operates in both the B2C (sales to consumers) and B2B (sales to other businesses) sectors. 70% percent of its business derives from fuel products including gasoline blends, diesel fuels, biofuels, and LPG (liquefied petroleum gas). The full-service retail stations offer product lines that differ according to operator and location factors. Some prefer a product mix that concentrates on auto supplies and services while others focus on food-related products, beverages, and even fast-food. SFR's 12 terminals, 38 depots, and 400 road tankers provide bulk sales to commercial customers, including bus and car rental companies, road construction crews, and independent resellers. In

© markhall70/Fotolia

addition, SFR sells stationary energy, marine fuel, more than 750 lubricants, various chemicals, and it delivers aviation fuel to 85 airports in ten countries.

Couche-Tard welcomed both the opportunities and the challenges of its acquisition. While its increased size and global presence could be leveraged to exact cost savings from suppliers, retail fuel stations always operate on slim margins, necessitating continual cost savings efforts. Immediate synergies between Couche-Tard and SFR could not completely cover the remaining expenses from SFR's split from Statoil, rebranding efforts, and the replacement of an antiquated IT infrastructure and Enterprise Resource Planning (ERP) system. The old system used different processes in each country and market, resulting in over 5,000 custom software objects for the IT department to manage and massive operational inefficiencies.

SFR needed to maximize supply chain efficiency for its three closely related value chains—the fuel value chain, the grocery value chain, and the lubricants value chain. All corporate functions that provided shared services to the value chains had to be standardized and workplace activities coordinated for its 18,500 employees. Finally, SFR managers wanted an advanced pricing method for fuel sales to maximize profits in its core low-margin business.

Oracle's JD Edwards EnterpriseOne enterprise resource planning system was chosen as the basic platform, and a Web services interface developed within the ERP system to convert all data into a single format. Replacing numerous separate legacy systems with a single ERP force managers to develop common data definitions. This common source of master data now drives all transactions throughout the supply chains, as well as financial and other reports generated by the Oracle Business Intelligence Suite. Stock availability and average sales at each service station feed a real-time planning program that projects expected demand and feeds the data to a third-party distribution planning system. Onboard computers convey product types and quantities to tanker drivers at terminals and delivery locations. Fuel restocking, delivery, and confirmation occur automatically. Supplies are quickly transferred from depots or between stations to meet fluctuating demand. With the value chains optimized, inventory holding costs are minimized.

To coordinate workplace activities, Oracle Fusion Middleware integrates data management and communication across social, mobile, and cloud technologies and among multiple systems and regions. Called the "Connect Project," the software coordinates dozens of interfaces throughout the supply chain, implements a consistent fuel pricing structure, and manages multiple complicated excise taxes and regulations. The project was implemented in Sweden in June and in Denmark and Norway in October 2013. Scandinavia accounts for over 80% of SFR's revenue. Rollout is expected to be complete in 2014.

A series of Web portals created with Oracle WebCenter Portal provide access to all internal sales, distribution, and planning systems. Fuel stations all use a common interface to connect to the point-of-sale system, and a new e-commerce portal simplifies ordering from the depots and is expected to significantly strengthen e-commerce revenue. A proprietary demand-based pricing algorithm updates fuel prices several times daily based on nearby competitors in each micro-market. For managers and marketing personnel, this means most and least profitable stations and markets are identified and incentive and discounting initiatives can be accurately targeted.

Sources: "Our Operations," statoilfuelretail.com, Accessed January 15, 2014; "Statoil Fuel & Retail," statoil.com, Accessed January 15, 2014; "History," statoilfuelretail.com, Accessed January 15, 2014; "From well to wheel," Accessed January 15, 2014; "The Fuel and Retail Market," statoil.com, Accessed January 15, 2014; "Our Company," couche-tard.com, Accessed January 15, 2014; "2013 Annual Report," couche-tard.com, Accessed January 15, 2014; "Statoil Fuel & Retail Automates Planning and Distribution Operations in Eight Countries," by David Baum, oracle.com, November 2013

Statoil's efforts to standardize and integrate corporate functions into the supply chain, and coordinate workplace activity, illustrate the impact of ERP systems on supply chain management (SCM). SFR did not have a single source of business data nor uniform methods for

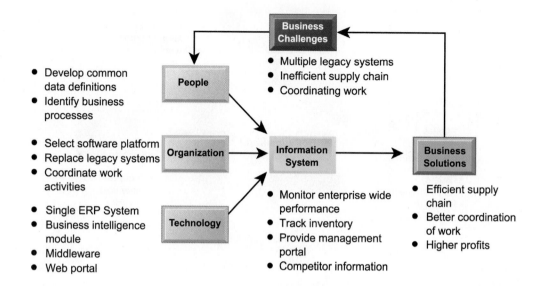

handling many critical SCM functions. Inventory holding costs were unnecessarily high, the IT department was strained, and lack of coordination was negatively impacting workplace productivity.

The chapter-opening diagram calls attention to important points raised by this case and this chapter. All transactions throughout SFR's supply chains are now in a common and consistent format that feeds directly into SFR's reporting software. The integrated ERP environment enables real-time planning based on stock availability and average sales at each service station, and a real-time fuel value chain can now accommodate variable demand from both consumer and business customers.

Benchmarks against which to assess future results by country, terminal, or market are being developed using the advanced pricing method developed by the Connect team. On the B2B side, managers will be able to quickly assess the effects of pricing structures and even sales reps will be able to evaluate the effects of purchasing terms.

Here are some questions to think about: How did SFR's lack of standardized processes affect its business operations? How were SFR's employees and supply chain management affected by the adoption of standardized interfaces? Why did SFR retain its legacy systems instead of replacing them entirely?

9.1 Enterprise Systems

Around the globe, companies are increasingly becoming more connected, both internally and with other companies. If you run a business, you'll want to be able to react instantaneously when a customer places a large order or when a shipment from a supplier is delayed. You may also want to know the impact of these events on every part of the business and how the business is performing at any point in time, especially if you're running a large company. Enterprise systems provide the integration to make this possible. Let's look at how they work and what they can do for the firm.

WHAT ARE ENTERPRISE SYSTEMS?

Imagine that you had to run a business based on information from tens or even hundreds of different databases and systems, none of which could speak to one another? Imagine your company had 10 different major product lines, each produced in separate factories, and each with separate and incompatible sets of systems controlling production, warehousing, and distribution.

Figure 9.1
How Enterprise
Systems Work
*Enterprise systems
feature a set of inte-
grated software modules
and a central database
that enables data to
be shared by many
different business
processes and functional
areas throughout the
enterprise.*

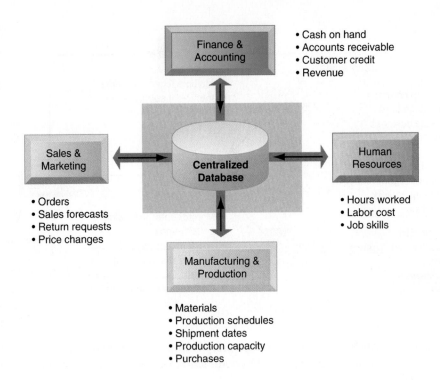

At the very least, your decision making would often be based on manual hard-copy reports, often out of date, and it would be difficult to really understand what is happening in the business as a whole. Sales personnel might not be able to tell at the time they place an order whether the ordered items are in inventory, and manufacturing could not easily use sales data to plan for new production. You now have a good idea of why firms need a special enterprise system to integrate information.

Chapter 2 introduced enterprise systems, also known as enterprise resource planning (ERP) systems, which are based on a suite of integrated software modules and a common central database. The database collects data from many different divisions and departments in a firm, and from a large number of key business processes in manufacturing and production, finance and accounting, sales and marketing, and human resources, making the data available for applications that support nearly all of an organization's internal business activities. When new information is entered by one process, the information is made immediately available to other business processes (see Figure 9.1).

If a sales representative places an order for tire rims, for example, the system verifies the customer's credit limit, schedules the shipment, identifies the best shipping route, and reserves the necessary items from inventory. If inventory stock is insufficient to fill the order, the system schedules the manufacture of more rims, ordering the needed materials and components from suppliers. Sales and production forecasts are immediately updated. General ledger and corporate cash levels are automatically updated with the revenue and cost information from the order. Users could tap into the system and find out where that particular order was at any minute. Management could obtain information at any point in time about how the business was operating. The system could also generate enterprise-wide data for management analyses of product cost and profitability.

ENTERPRISE SOFTWARE

Enterprise software is built around thousands of predefined business processes that reflect best practices. Table 9.1 describes some of the major business processes supported by enterprise software.

TABLE 9.1

Business Processes Supported by Enterprise Systems

Financial and accounting processes, including general ledger, accounts payable, accounts receivable, fixed assets, cash management and forecasting, product-cost accounting, cost-center accounting, asset accounting, tax accounting, credit management, and financial reporting

Human resources processes, including personnel administration, time accounting, payroll, personnel planning and development, benefits accounting, applicant tracking, time management, compensation, workforce planning, performance management, and travel expense reporting

Manufacturing and production processes, including procurement, inventory management, purchasing, shipping, production planning, production scheduling, material requirements planning, quality control, distribution, transportation execution, and plant and equipment maintenance

Sales and marketing processes, including order processing, quotations, contracts, product configuration, pricing, billing, credit checking, incentive and commission management, and sales planning

Companies implementing this software would have to first select the functions of the system they wished to use and then map their business processes to the predefined business processes in the software. (One of our Learning Tracks shows how SAP enterprise software handles the procurement process for a new piece of equipment.) A firm would use configuration tables provided by the software manufacturer to tailor a particular aspect of the system to the way it does business. For example, the firm could use these tables to select whether it wants to track revenue by product line, geographical unit, or distribution channel.

If the enterprise software does not support the way the organization does business, companies can rewrite some of the software to support the way their business processes work. However, enterprise software is unusually complex, and extensive customization may degrade system performance, compromising the information and process integration that are the main benefits of the system. If companies want to reap the maximum benefits from enterprise software, they must change the way they work to conform to the business processes defined by the software.

To implement a new enterprise system, Tasty Baking Company identified its existing business processes and then translated them into the business processes built into the SAP ERP software it had selected. To ensure it obtained the maximum benefits from the enterprise software, Tasty Baking Company deliberately planned for customizing less than 5 percent of the system and made very few changes to the SAP software itself. It used as many tools and features that were already built into the SAP software as it could. SAP has more than 3,000 configuration tables for its enterprise software.

Leading enterprise software vendors include SAP, Oracle, IBM, Infor Global Solutions, and Microsoft. There are versions of enterprise software packages designed for small and medium-sized businesses and on-demand versions, including software services running in the cloud (see Section 9.4).

BUSINESS VALUE OF ENTERPRISE SYSTEMS

Enterprise systems provide value both by increasing operational efficiency and by providing firmwide information to help managers make better decisions. Large companies with many operating units in different locations have used enterprise systems to enforce standard practices and data so that everyone does business the same way worldwide.

Coca-Cola, for instance, implemented a SAP enterprise system to standardize and coordinate important business processes in 200 countries. Lack of standard, company-wide business processes prevented the company from leveraging its worldwide buying power to obtain lower prices for raw materials and from reacting rapidly to market changes.

Enterprise systems help firms respond rapidly to customer requests for information or products. Because the system integrates order, manufacturing, and delivery data, manufacturing is better informed about producing only what customers have ordered, procuring exactly the right amount of components or raw materials to fill actual orders, staging production, and minimizing the time that components or finished products are in inventory.

Alcoa, the world's leading producer of aluminum and aluminum products with operations spanning 31 countries and over 200 locations, had initially been organized around lines of business, each of which had its own set of information systems. Many of these systems were redundant and inefficient. Alcoa's costs for executing requisition-to-pay and financial processes were much higher and its cycle times were longer than those of other companies in its industry. (Cycle time refers to the total elapsed time from the beginning to the end of a process.) The company could not operate as a single worldwide entity.

After implementing enterprise software from Oracle, Alcoa eliminated many redundant processes and systems. The enterprise system helped Alcoa reduce requisition-to-pay cycle time by verifying receipt of goods and automatically generating receipts for payment. Alcoa's accounts payable transaction processing dropped 89 percent. Alcoa was able to centralize financial and procurement activities, which helped the company reduce nearly 20 percent of its worldwide costs.

Enterprise systems provide much valuable information for improving management decision making. Corporate headquarters has access to up-to-the-minute data on sales, inventory, and production, and uses this information to create more accurate sales and production forecasts. Enterprise software includes analytical tools for using data captured by the system to evaluate overall organizational performance. Enterprise system data have common standardized definitions and formats that are accepted by the entire organization. Performance figures mean the same thing across the company. Enterprise systems allow senior management to easily find out at any moment how a particular organizational unit is performing, determine which products are most or least profitable, and calculate costs for the company as a whole.

For example, Alcoa's enterprise system includes functionality for global human resources management that shows correlations between investment in employee training and quality, measures the company-wide costs of delivering services to employees, and measures the effectiveness of employee recruitment, compensation, and training.

9.2 Supply Chain Management Systems

If you manage a small firm that makes a few products or sells a few services, chances are you will have a small number of suppliers. You could coordinate your supplier orders and deliveries using a telephone and fax machine. But if you manage a firm that produces more complex products and services, then you will have hundreds of suppliers, and each of your suppliers will have its own set of suppliers. Suddenly, you are in a situation where you will need to coordinate the activities of hundreds or even thousands of other firms in order to produce your products and services. Supply chain management (SCM) systems, which we introduced in Chapter 2, are an answer to the problems of supply chain complexity and scale.

THE SUPPLY CHAIN

A firm's **supply chain** is a network of organizations and business processes for procuring raw materials, transforming these materials into intermediate and finished products, and distributing the finished products to customers. It links suppliers, manufacturing plants, distribution centers, retail outlets, and customers to supply goods and services from source through consumption. Materials, information, and payments flow through the supply chain in both directions.

Goods start out as raw materials and, as they move through the supply chain, are transformed into intermediate products (also referred to as components or parts), and finally, into finished products. The finished products are shipped to distribution centers and from there to retailers and customers. Returned items flow in the reverse direction from the buyer back to the seller.

Let's look at the supply chain for Nike sneakers as an example. Nike designs, markets, and sells sneakers, socks, athletic clothing, and accessories throughout the world. Its primary suppliers are contract manufacturers with factories in China, Thailand, Indonesia, Brazil, and other countries. These companies fashion Nike's finished products.

Nike's contract suppliers do not manufacture sneakers from scratch. They obtain components for the sneakers—the laces, eyelets, uppers, and soles—from other suppliers and then assemble them into finished sneakers. These suppliers in turn have their own suppliers. For example, the suppliers of soles have suppliers for synthetic rubber, suppliers for chemicals used to melt the rubber for molding, and suppliers for the molds into which to pour the rubber. Suppliers of laces have suppliers for their thread, for dyes, and for the plastic lace tips.

Figure 9.2 provides a simplified illustration of Nike's supply chain for sneakers; it shows the flow of information and materials among suppliers, Nike, Nike's distributors, retailers, and customers. Nike's contract manufacturers are its primary suppliers. The suppliers of soles, eyelets, uppers, and laces are the secondary (Tier 2) suppliers. Suppliers to these suppliers are the tertiary (Tier 3) suppliers.

The *upstream* portion of the supply chain includes the company's suppliers, the suppliers' suppliers, and the processes for managing relationships with them. The *downstream* portion consists of the organizations and processes for distributing and delivering products to

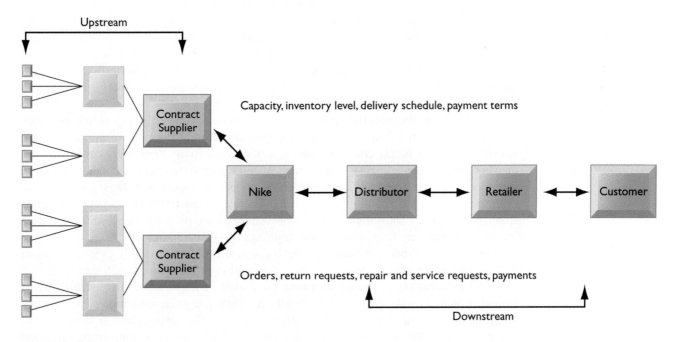

Figure 9.2
Nike's Supply Chain
This figure illustrates the major entities in Nike's supply chain and the flow of information upstream and downstream to coordinate the activities involved in buying, making, and moving a product. Shown here is a simplified supply chain, with the upstream portion focusing only on the suppliers for sneakers and sneaker soles.

the final customers. Companies doing manufacturing, such as Nike's contract suppliers of sneakers, also manage their own *internal supply chain* processes for transforming materials, components, and services furnished by their suppliers into finished products or intermediate products (components or parts) for their customers and for managing materials and inventory.

The supply chain illustrated in Figure 9.2 has been simplified. It only shows two contract manufacturers for sneakers and only the upstream supply chain for sneaker soles. Nike has hundreds of contract manufacturers turning out finished sneakers, socks, and athletic clothing, each with its own set of suppliers. The upstream portion of Nike's supply chain would actually comprise thousands of entities. Nike also has numerous distributors and many thousands of retail stores where its shoes are sold, so the downstream portion of its supply chain is also large and complex.

INFORMATION SYSTEMS AND SUPPLY CHAIN MANAGEMENT

Inefficiencies in the supply chain, such as parts shortages, underutilized plant capacity, excessive finished goods inventory, or high transportation costs, are caused by inaccurate or untimely information. For example, manufacturers may keep too many parts in inventory because they do not know exactly when they will receive their next shipments from their suppliers. Suppliers may order too few raw materials because they do not have precise information on demand. These supply chain inefficiencies waste as much as 25 percent of a company's operating costs.

If a manufacturer had perfect information about exactly how many units of product customers wanted, when they wanted them, and when they could be produced, it would be possible to implement a highly efficient **just-in-time strategy**. Components would arrive exactly at the moment they were needed and finished goods would be shipped as they left the assembly line.

In a supply chain, however, uncertainties arise because many events cannot be foreseen—uncertain product demand, late shipments from suppliers, defective parts or raw materials, or production process breakdowns. To satisfy customers, manufacturers often deal with such uncertainties and unforeseen events by keeping more material or products in inventory than what they think they may actually need. The *safety stock* acts as a buffer for the lack of flexibility in the supply chain. Although excess inventory is expensive, low fill rates are also costly because business may be lost from canceled orders.

One recurring problem in supply chain management is the **bullwhip effect**, in which information about the demand for a product gets distorted as it passes from one entity to the next across the supply chain. A slight rise in demand for an item might cause different members in the supply chain—distributors, manufacturers, suppliers, secondary suppliers (suppliers' suppliers), and tertiary suppliers (suppliers' suppliers' suppliers)—to stockpile inventory so each has enough "just in case." These changes ripple throughout the supply chain, magnifying what started out as a small change from planned orders, creating excess inventory, production, warehousing, and shipping costs (see Figure 9.3).

For example, Procter & Gamble (P&G) found it had excessively high inventories of its Pampers disposable diapers at various points along its supply chain because of such distorted information. Although customer purchases in stores were fairly stable, orders from distributors would spike when P&G offered aggressive price promotions. Pampers and Pampers' components accumulated in warehouses along the supply chain to meet demand that did not actually exist. To eliminate this problem, P&G revised its marketing, sales, and supply chain processes and used more accurate demand forecasting.

The bullwhip effect is tamed by reducing uncertainties about demand and supply when all members of the supply chain have accurate and up-to-date information. If all supply chain members share dynamic information about inventory levels, schedules, forecasts, and shipments, they have more precise knowledge about how to adjust their sourcing, manufacturing, and distribution plans. Supply chain management systems provide the kind of information that helps members of the supply chain make better purchasing and scheduling decisions.

SUPPLY CHAIN MANAGEMENT SOFTWARE

Supply chain software is classified as either software to help businesses plan their supply chains (supply chain planning) or software to help them execute the supply chain steps (supply chain execution). **Supply chain planning systems** enable the firm to model its existing supply chain, generate demand forecasts for products, and develop optimal sourcing and manufacturing plans. Such systems help companies make better decisions such as determining how much of a specific product to manufacture in a given time period; establishing inventory levels for raw materials, intermediate products, and finished goods; determining where to store finished goods; and identifying the transportation mode to use for product delivery.

For example, if a large customer places a larger order than usual or changes that order on short notice, it can have a widespread impact throughout the supply chain. Additional raw materials or a different mix of raw materials may need to be ordered from suppliers. Manufacturing may have to change job scheduling. A transportation carrier may have to reschedule deliveries. Supply chain planning software makes the necessary adjustments to production and distribution plans. Information about changes is shared among the relevant supply chain members so that their work can be coordinated. One of the most important—and complex—supply chain planning functions is **demand planning**, which determines

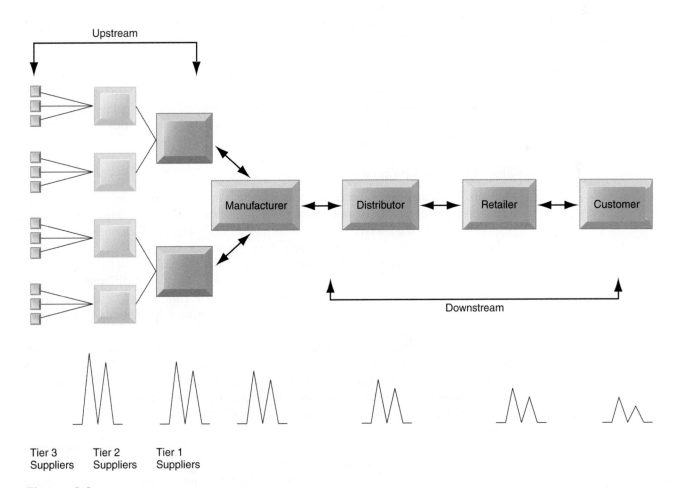

Figure 9.3
The Bullwhip Effect
Inaccurate information can cause minor fluctuations in demand for a product to be amplified as one moves further back in the supply chain. Minor fluctuations in retail sales for a product can create excess inventory for distributors, manufacturers, and suppliers.

how much product a business needs to make to satisfy all of its customers' demands (see the Interactive Session on Technology), JDA Software, SAP, and Oracle all offer supply chain management solutions.

Supply chain execution systems manage the flow of products through distribution centers and warehouses to ensure that products are delivered to the right locations in the most efficient manner. They track the physical status of goods, the management of materials, warehouse and transportation operations, and financial information involving all parties. The Oracle Transportation Management system used by Land O'Lakes (see the Interactive Session on Technology) is an example, as is the Warehouse Management System (WMS) used by Haworth Incorporated. Haworth is a world-leading manufacturer and designer of office furniture, with distribution centers in four different states. The WMS tracks and controls the flow of finished goods from Haworth's distribution centers to its customers. Acting on shipping plans for customer orders, the WMS directs the movement of goods based on immediate conditions for space, equipment, inventory, and personnel.

GLOBAL SUPPLY CHAINS AND THE INTERNET

Before the Internet, supply chain coordination was hampered by the difficulties of making information flow smoothly among disparate internal supply chain systems for purchasing, materials management, manufacturing, and distribution. It was also difficult to share information with external supply chain partners because the systems of suppliers, distributors, or logistics providers were based on incompatible technology platforms and standards. Enterprise and supply chain management systems enhanced with Internet technology supply some of this integration.

A manager uses a Web interface to tap into suppliers' systems to determine whether inventory and production capabilities match demand for the firm's products. Business partners use Web-based supply chain management tools to collaborate online on forecasts. Sales representatives access suppliers' production schedules and logistics information to monitor customers' order status.

Global Supply Chain Issues

More and more companies are entering international markets, outsourcing manufacturing operations, and obtaining supplies from other countries as well as selling abroad. Their supply chains extend across multiple countries and regions. There are additional complexities and challenges to managing a global supply chain.

Global supply chains typically span greater geographic distances and time differences than domestic supply chains and have participants from a number of different countries. Performance standards may vary from region to region or from nation to nation. Supply chain management may need to reflect foreign government regulations and cultural differences.

The Internet helps companies manage many aspects of their global supply chains, including sourcing, transportation, communications, and international finance. Today's apparel industry, for example, relies heavily on outsourcing to contract manufacturers in China and other low-wage countries. Apparel companies are starting to use the Web to manage their global supply chain and production issues. (Review the discussion of Li & Fung in Chapter 3.)

In addition to contract manufacturing, globalization has encouraged outsourcing warehouse management, transportation management, and related operations to third-party logistics providers, such as UPS Supply Chain Solutions and Schneider Logistics Services. These logistics services offer Web-based software to give their customers a better view of their global supply chains. Customers are able to check a secure Web site to monitor inventory and shipments, helping them run their global supply chains more efficiently.

INTERACTIVE SESSION: TECHNOLOGY — Land O'Lakes Butter Becomes Fresher with Demand Planning

Originally founded in 1921 by representatives from 320 individual creameries as the Minnesota Cooperative Creameries Association, Land O'Lakes has grown to one of the largest producers of butter and cheese in the United States. The company handles 12 billion pounds of milk annually and generates revenues of over $14 billion. The company also owns several other brands, such as Purina, a major producer of animal feed, which it acquired in 2001. Land O'Lakes also runs Winfield Solutions, which sells farm seeding and crop protection products.

All businesses dealing in consumer goods must deal with issues of supply chain efficiency and inventory management. For Land O'Lakes, the importance of those issues is heightened because its products are perishable and sales volume and product mix change greatly from season to season. In the winter, for example, Americans use more butter for baked goods, and demand spikes as high as 65 percent. The company must be prepared to adjust production and inventory accordingly.

Because of these fluctuations in demand and short product shelf life, Land O'Lakes needs to take special care to plan its inventory so that it can handle customers' needs in every season without incurring unnecessary costs. To that end, in 2010, Land O'Lakes implemented Oracle's Demantra Demand Management software to more effectively plan production on a weekly, monthly, and seasonal basis. Land O'Lakes hoped to reduce the amount of inventory it had on hand, simplify its supply chain, and predict demand before it develops. By improving its production planning, the company stood to reduce costs across the board.

The Land O'Lakes supply chain is complex, and involves several different entities. For example, when a stick of butter is made at a Land O'Lakes production plant in California or Pennsylvania, the company ships it to one of its distribution centers, and then on to the distribution centers of its customers, such as Shoprite Supermarkets or A&P. From there, the stick of butter travels to retail supermarket and grocery store locations, restaurants, and food service companies, but it's important that it travel as quickly as possible through Land O'Lakes's part of the supply chain so that it is still fresh when it arrives at its final destination. Supply chain efficiency is of the utmost importance.

Inventory management is similarly important. Land O'Lakes must keep a sufficient amount of store-ready product on hand, but any excess inventory that can't be sold before products start to spoil must be discarded, damaging the company's bottom line.

Additionally, the more inventory a company keeps on hand, the more that company must pay to maintain the inventory. Land O'Lakes sought to create a system where it would be able to predict shifts in demand and keep just enough inventory on hand to satisfy demand, but not so much that it was discarding a significant portion of its goods.

Land O'Lakes wanted to achieve this goal by implementing a demand-sensing solution to help predict and adjust to shifts in demand. The company had already installed Oracle's JD Edwards EnterpriseOne ERP system, so it relied on Demantra to extend the functionality of the ERP solution to improve demand sensing. Demantra's focus is exactly what Land O'Lakes had desired—getting the best possible value from a lean inventory. First, the system analyzes the optimal way to manage raw materials. It helps company managers determine how much milk is turned into butter, how much is turned into cheese, and what types of cheese to make.

Demantra extracts data on shipment history, open customer orders, and key master data on customers and products from the EnterpriseOne system to create models for future demand. Using these data with sophisticated statistical modeling and algorithms that calculate consumption, order lead time, and consumption allocation, Land O'Lakes is able to create accurate forecasts, especially for the next four weeks. Land O'Lakes uses EnterpriseOne to plan production of all of its goods to maintain a "just enough" inventory and keep costs as low as possible while ensuring that the right products are available for the right customer at the right time.

Demantra generates long-term, medium-term, and short-term reports that aid in the planning process. Long-term reports that forecast demand 18 to 24 months in the future help managers plan which type of product to make and ensure milk sheds will provide enough to satisfy demand at that time. Medium-term reports forecast demand 2 to 6 weeks out. Short-term reports are used to determine which customers need shipments immediately. Supply chain managers rely on Demantra for a combination of these reports to determine which Land O'Lakes facilities should be assigned to produce and distribute products. Reducing the distance between the factory and the customer lowers costs for fuel, transportation and overall production.

Demantra has helped Land O'Lakes cut their total inventory of finished product on hand by four full days, resulting in millions of dollars in savings. Adhering so closely to the "just enough" principle leaves Land

O'Lakes more vulnerable to sudden spikes in demand, but over the long run it saves the company much more. In the consumer packaged goods industry, the accuracy rate of demand forecasting is approximately 50 percent—thanks to Demantra, Land O'Lakes improved from 40 percent accuracy to 70 percent accuracy.

Land O'Lakes also relies on Oracle Transportation Management to plan its transportation, execution, freight payment, and business process automation. When Land O'Lakes trucks are loaded and ready to go, they have to get to the right destination as quickly and efficiently as possible. Shipments going bad because of inefficient routes or other unforeseen issues also hurt the company's bottom line. Oracle Transportation Management integrates with the EnterpriseOne system

and Demantra. Using information about which distribution centers need more goods and which need to unload goods, the system automatically plans the best routes for shipment trucks when they leave Land O'Lakes plants. Using this system, Land O'Lakes can pack its trucks with more goods, improving their average truck weight by 4 percent to 40,000 pounds. This saves the company money on transportation costs, and for a nation-wide business like Land O'Lakes, the total amount saved is significant. Land O'Lakes can rechannel these savings to expand into international markets.

Sources: Land O'Lakes, "Land O'Lakes Reports 2012 Results," February 26, 2013; Monica Mehta, "Milking Demand," *Profit Magazine*, February 2012; Monica Mehta, "Oracle Transportation Management," *Profit Magazine*, February 2012; www.landolakes.com, "About Us," accessed March 10, 2013.

CASE STUDY QUESTIONS

1. Why are inventory management and demand planning so important for Land O'Lakes? What is the business impact of not being able to manage inventory or predict demand for this company?

2. What people, organization, and technology issues had to be considered when selecting Oracle's Demantra as a solution for Land O'Lakes?

3. How did implementing Demantra change management decision making and the way that Land O'Lakes ran its business?

4. Describe two decisions that were improved by implementing Demantra.

Demand-Driven Supply Chains: From Push to Pull Manufacturing and Efficient Customer Response

In addition to reducing costs, supply chain management systems facilitate efficient customer response, enabling the workings of the business to be driven more by customer demand. (We introduced efficient customer response systems in Chapter 3.)

Earlier supply chain management systems were driven by a push-based model (also known as build-to-stock). In a **push-based model**, production master schedules are based on forecasts or best guesses of demand for products, and products are "pushed" to customers. With new flows of information made possible by Web-based tools, supply chain management more easily follows a pull-based model. In a **pull-based model**, also known as a demand-driven or build-to-order model, actual customer orders or purchases trigger events in the supply chain. Transactions to produce and deliver only what customers have ordered move up the supply chain from retailers to distributors to manufacturers and eventually to suppliers. Only products to fulfill these orders move back down the supply chain to the retailer. Manufacturers use only actual order demand information to drive their production schedules and the procurement of components or raw materials, as illustrated in Figure 9.4. Walmart's continuous replenishment system described in Chapter 3 is an example of the pull-based model.

The Internet and Internet technology make it possible to move from sequential supply chains, where information and materials flow sequentially from company to company, to concurrent supply chains, where information flows in many directions simultaneously among members of a supply chain network. Complex supply networks

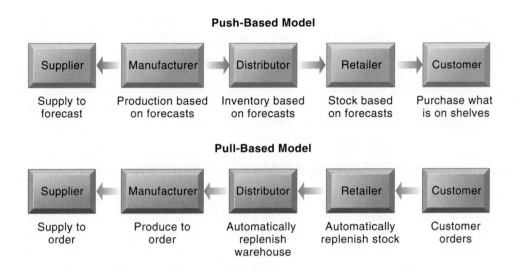

Figure 9.4
Push- Versus Pull-Based Supply Chain Models
The difference between push- and pull-based models is summarized by the slogan "Make what we sell, not sell what we make."

of manufacturers, logistics suppliers, outsourced manufacturers, retailers, and distributors are able to adjust immediately to changes in schedules or orders. Ultimately, the Internet could create a "digital logistics nervous system" throughout the supply chain (see Figure 9.5).

BUSINESS VALUE OF SUPPLY CHAIN MANAGEMENT SYSTEMS

You have just seen how supply chain management systems enable firms to streamline both their internal and external supply chain processes and provide management with more accurate information about what to produce, store, and move. By implementing a networked and integrated supply chain management system, companies match supply to demand, reduce inventory levels, improve delivery service, speed product time to market, and use assets more effectively.

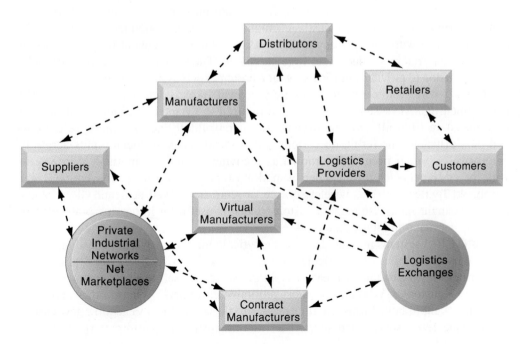

Figure 9.5
The emerging Internet-driven supply chain
The emerging Internet-driven supply chain operates like a digital logistics nervous system. It provides multidirectional communication among firms, networks of firms, and e-marketplaces so that entire networks of supply chain partners can immediately adjust inventories, orders, and capacities.

Total supply chain costs represent the majority of operating expenses for many businesses and in some industries approach 75 percent of the total operating budget. Reducing supply chain costs has a major impact on firm profitability.

In addition to reducing costs, supply chain management systems help increase sales. If a product is not available when a customer wants it, customers often try to purchase it from someone else. More precise control of the supply chain enhances the firm's ability to have the right product available for customer purchases at the right time.

9.3 Customer Relationship Management Systems

You've probably heard phrases such as "the customer is always right" or "the customer comes first." Today these words ring truer than ever. Because competitive advantage based on an innovative new product or service is often very short lived, companies are realizing that their most enduring competitive strength may be their relationships with their customers. Some say that the basis of competition has switched from who sells the most products and services to who "owns" the customer, and that customer relationships represent a firm's most valuable asset.

WHAT IS CUSTOMER RELATIONSHIP MANAGEMENT?

What kinds of information would you need to build and nurture strong, long-lasting relationships with customers? You'd want to know exactly who your customers are, how to contact them, whether they are costly to service and sell to, what kinds of products and services they are interested in, and how much money they spend on your company. If you could, you'd want to make sure you knew each of your customers well, as if you were running a small-town store. And you'd want to make your good customers feel special.

In a small business operating in a neighborhood, it is possible for business owners and managers to really know their customers on a personal, face-to-face basis. But in a large business operating on a metropolitan, regional, national, or even global basis, it is impossible to "know your customer" in this intimate way. In these kinds of businesses there are too many customers and too many different ways that customers interact with the firm (over the Web, the phone, e-mail, blogs, and in person). It becomes especially difficult to integrate information from all theses sources and to deal with the large numbers of customers.

A large business's processes for sales, service, and marketing tend to be highly compartmentalized, and these departments do not share much essential customer information. Some information on a specific customer might be stored and organized in terms of that person's account with the company. Other pieces of information about the same customer might be organized by products that were purchased. There is no way to consolidate all of this information to provide a unified view of a customer across the company.

This is where customer relationship management systems help. Customer relationship management (CRM) systems, which we introduced in Chapter 2, capture and integrate customer data from all over the organization, consolidate the data, analyze the data, and then distribute the results to various systems and customer touch points across the enterprise. A **touch point** (also known as a contact point) is a method of interaction with the customer, such as telephone, e-mail, customer service desk, conventional mail, Facebook, Twitter, Web site, wireless device, or retail store. Well-designed CRM systems provide a single enterprise view of customers that is useful for improving both sales and customer service (see Figure 9.6.)

Good CRM systems provide data and analytical tools for answering questions such as these: What is the value of a particular customer to the firm over his or her lifetime? Who are our most loyal customers? It can cost six times more to sell to a new customer than to an existing customer. Who are our most profitable customers? What do these profitable customers want to buy? Firms use the answers to these questions to acquire new customers, provide better service and support to existing customers, customize their offerings

Figure 9.6
Customer
Relationship
Management (CRM)
*CRM systems examine
customers from a
multifaceted perspec-
tive. These systems
use a set of integrated
applications to address
all aspects of the
customer relationship,
including customer
service, sales, and
marketing.*

more precisely to customer preferences, and provide ongoing value to retain profitable customers.

CUSTOMER RELATIONSHIP MANAGEMENT SOFTWARE

Commercial CRM software packages range from niche tools that perform limited functions, such as personalizing Web sites for specific customers, to large-scale enterprise applications that capture myriad interactions with customers, analyze them with sophisticated reporting tools, and link to other major enterprise applications, such as supply chain management and enterprise systems. The more comprehensive CRM packages contain modules for **partner relationship management (PRM)** and **employee relationship management (ERM)**.

PRM uses many of the same data, tools, and systems as customer relationship management to enhance collaboration between a company and its selling partners. If a company does not sell directly to customers but rather works through distributors or retailers, PRM helps these channels sell to customers directly. It provides a company and its selling partners with the ability to trade information and distribute leads and data about customers, integrating lead generation, pricing, promotions, order configurations, and availability. It also provides a firm with tools to assess its partners' performances so it can make sure its best partners receive the support they need to close more business.

ERM software deals with employee issues that are closely related to CRM, such as setting objectives, employee performance management, performance-based compensation, and employee training. Major CRM application software vendors include Oracle, SAP, Salesforce. com, and Microsoft Dynamics CRM.

Customer relationship management systems typically provide software and online tools for sales, customer service, and marketing. We briefly describe some of these capabilities.

Sales Force Automation (SFA)

Sales force automation modules in CRM systems help sales staff increase their productivity by focusing sales efforts on the most profitable customers, those who are good candidates for sales and services. CRM systems provide sales prospect and contact information, product information, product configuration capabilities, and sales quote generation capabilities. Such software can assemble information about a particular customer's past purchases to help the salesperson make personalized recommendations. CRM software enables sales, marketing, and delivery departments to easily share customer and prospect information. It increases each salesperson's efficiency by reducing the cost per sale as well as the cost of acquiring new customers and retaining old ones. CRM software also has capabilities for sales forecasting, territory management, and team selling.

Customer Service

Customer service modules in CRM systems provide information and tools to increase the efficiency of call centers, help desks, and customer support staff. They have capabilities for assigning and managing customer service requests.

One such capability is an appointment or advice telephone line: When a customer calls a standard phone number, the system routes the call to the correct service person, who inputs information about that customer into the system only once. Once the customer's data are in the system, any service representative can handle the customer relationship. Improved access to consistent and accurate customer information helps call centers handle more calls per day and decrease the duration of each call. Thus, call centers and customer service groups achieve greater productivity, reduced transaction time, and higher quality of service at lower cost. The customer is happier because he or she spends less time on the phone restating his or her problem to customer service representatives.

CRM systems may also include Web-based self-service capabilities: The company Web site can be set up to provide inquiring customers personalized support information as well as the option to contact customer service staff by phone for additional assistance.

Marketing

CRM systems support direct-marketing campaigns by providing capabilities for capturing prospect and customer data, for providing product and service information, for qualifying leads for targeted marketing, and for scheduling and tracking direct-marketing mailings or e-mail (see Figure 9.7). Marketing modules also include tools for analyzing marketing and customer data, identifying profitable and unprofitable customers, designing products and services to satisfy specific customer needs and interests, and identifying opportunities for cross-selling.

Cross-selling is the marketing of complementary products to customers. (For example, in financial services, a customer with a checking account might be sold a money market account or a home improvement loan.) CRM tools also help firms manage and execute marketing campaigns at all stages, from planning to determining the rate of success for each campaign.

Figure 9.8 illustrates the most important capabilities for sales, service, and marketing processes that would be found in major CRM software products. Like enterprise software, this software is business-process driven, incorporating hundreds of business processes

Figure 9.7
How CRM Systems
Support Marketing
Customer relationship management software provides a single point for users to manage and evaluate marketing campaigns across multiple channels, including e-mail, direct mail, telephone, the Web, and wireless messages.

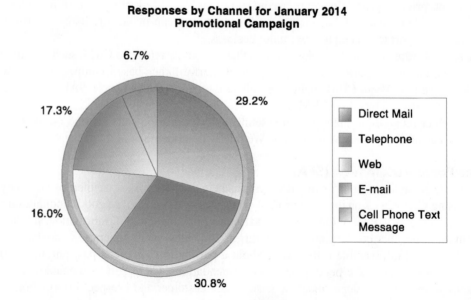

**Responses by Channel for January 2014
Promotional Campaign**

- Direct Mail
- Telephone
- Web
- E-mail
- Cell Phone Text Message

6.7%
29.2%
17.3%
16.0%
30.8%

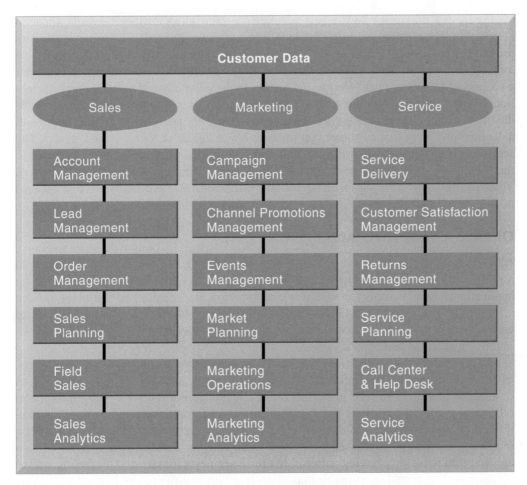

Figure 9.8
CRM Software Capabilities
The major CRM software products support business processes in sales, service, and marketing, integrating customer information from many different sources. Included is support for both the operational and analytical aspects of CRM.

thought to represent best practices in each of these areas. To achieve maximum benefit, companies need to revise and model their business processes to conform to the best-practice business processes in the CRM software.

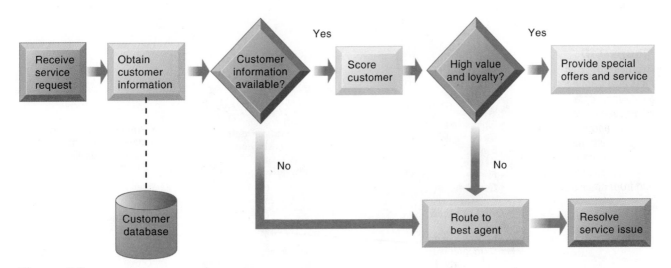

Figure 9.9
Customer Loyalty Management Process Map
This process map shows how a best practice for promoting customer loyalty through customer service would be modeled by customer relationship management software. The CRM software helps firms identify high-value customers for preferential treatment.

Figure 9.9 illustrates how a best practice for increasing customer loyalty through customer service might be modeled by CRM software. Directly servicing customers provides firms with opportunities to increase customer retention by singling out profitable long-term customers for preferential treatment. CRM software can assign each customer a score based on that person's value and loyalty to the company and provide that information to help call centers route each customer's service request to agents who can best handle that customer's needs. The system would automatically provide the service agent with a detailed profile of that customer that includes his or her score for value and loyalty. The service agent would use this information to present special offers or additional service to the customer to encourage the customer to keep transacting business with the company. You will find more information on other best-practice business processes in CRM systems in our Learning Tracks.

OPERATIONAL AND ANALYTICAL CRM

All of the applications we have just described support either the operational or analytical aspects of customer relationship management. **Operational CRM** includes customer-facing applications, such as tools for sales force automation, call center and customer service support, and marketing automation. **Analytical CRM** includes applications that analyze customer data generated by operational CRM applications to provide information for improving business performance.

Analytical CRM applications are based on data from operational CRM systems, customer touch points, and other sources that have been organized in data warehouses or analytic platforms for use in online analytical processing (OLAP), data mining, and other data analysis techniques (see Chapter 6). Customer data collected by the organization might be combined with data from other sources, such as customer lists for direct-marketing campaigns purchased from other companies or demographic data. Such data are analyzed to identify buying patterns, to create segments for targeted marketing, and to pinpoint profitable and unprofitable customers (see Figure 9.10 and the Interactive Session on Organizations).

Another important output of analytical CRM is the customer's lifetime value to the firm. **Customer lifetime value (CLTV)** is based on the relationship between the revenue produced by a specific customer, the expenses incurred in acquiring and servicing that customer, and the expected life of the relationship between the customer and the company.

Figure 9.10
Analytical CRM
Analytical CRM uses a customer data warehouse or analytic platform and tools to analyze customer data collected from the firm's customer touch points and from other sources.

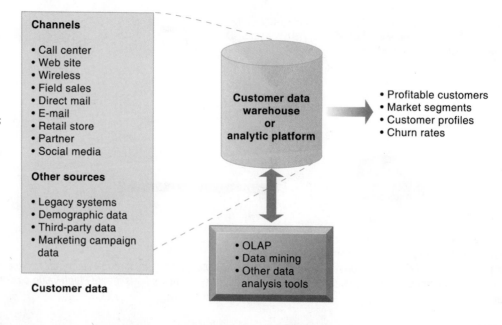

Channels

- Call center
- Web site
- Wireless
- Field sales
- Direct mail
- E-mail
- Retail store
- Partner
- Social media

Other sources

- Legacy systems
- Demographic data
- Third-party data
- Marketing campaign data

Customer data

Customer data warehouse or analytic platform

- Profitable customers
- Market segments
- Customer profiles
- Churn rates

- OLAP
- Data mining
- Other data analysis tools

INTERACTIVE SESSION: MANAGEMENT DP World Takes Port Management to the Next Level with RFID

DP (Dubai Ports) World has reason to be proud of its accomplishment of becoming one of the leading terminal operators in the world. Today, DP World has 60 terminals across 6 continents, and 11 new terminals are under development. The firm employs an international professional team of more than 30,000 people to serve customers in some of the most dynamic economies in the world.

DP World has adopted a customer-centric approach to enhancing its customers' supply chains by providing quality, innovative services to effectively manage container, bulk, and other terminal cargo. The firm invests heavily in terminal infrastructures, technologies, and people to best serve its customers.

Like other global port and terminal operators, DP World helps shippers around the world address the often complex and costly challenges of managing the supply chain. One of the typical problems encountered in container terminal operations is traffic congestion at port entry points. This congestion is often due to delays introduced by lengthy procedures and paper-based logistics. In response, DP World has introduced many IT-based solutions to enhance terminal capacity utilization. These solutions include the electronic custom release of cargo, Electronic Data Interchange (EDI) reporting, two-way digital radio communications, and the "e-token" advanced booking system.

DP World management wanted to take things a step further and decided to make the loading and unloading of containers operate on "just in time" principles to improve container turnaround. It found that Radio Frequency Identification (RFID) technology was an effective way of increasing the efficiency of truck movements through port access gates. Today, DP World uses RFID-enabled automatic gate systems at the port terminals it operates in Dubai and Australia. According to Mohammed Al Muallem, managing director of DP World UAE, the introduction of an automated gate system would not only eliminate traffic congestion but would also help to eliminate a number of lengthy procedures, increasing productivity at the ports, and improving customer satisfaction. This will in turn, increase the turn-around of shipping goods.

Prior to the RFID deployment, DP World spent several months performing proof-of-concept trials involving several competing RFID suppliers. Because of the rugged environmental conditions at the ports, DP World required that 99.5 percent of all tags be read successfully, which was a key challenge for many vendors. After extensive testing and evaluation, DP World selected Identec Solutions, a global leader in active wireless tracking solutions, as its RFID supplier.

How does the RFID tracking system work? Trucks that visit a port terminal are equipped with active RFID tags supplied by Identec Solutions that are fixed on the rear chassis. As a truck moves towards the gate, its unique tag ID number is read by an RFID reader, which is integrated with an automated gate system. At the gate, an optical character recognition (OCR) system determines if the truck is loaded with a container, identifies the ID number of the truck's container, and reads the truck license plate number as a backup identification. The system uses the supplied information to automatically issue a ticket to the driver that specifies the lane the truck should proceed to in order to load or unload the container. The system can also automatically determine if the truck is on time, which is essential information for the efficient pickup and drop off of containers. As the truck leaves the gate, the RFID tag is read once again, and the driver receives a receipt for the completed transaction.

RFID has enabled DP World to increase the productivity of container handoffs, speed the entry and exit of trucks through terminal gates, and increase fuel efficiency. Victoria Rose, regional office project coordinator at DP World Sydney maintained that RFID would improve gate efficiency through improved truck management, reducing queues and congestion around gates, and removing the number of trucks from public roads by streamlining procedures.

Identec's RFID-based solution has also enabled DP World to improve customer satisfaction by enhancing the efficiency of customers' supply chains through smoother, faster, and more effective delivery of their containers at terminal gates. The elimination of lengthy paper transactions and manual inspections at gates and the reduction in manual data input errors demonstrate DP World's customer-centric approach to delivering a superior level of service. The technology also allows transport companies to save time, increase revenues, and reduce costs.

DP World's use of RFID has also helped it to tighten security by providing better accuracy on inbound and outbound truck movements through the terminals. For instance, the system can automatically check whether a truck has a booking and whether it is authorized to enter the port.

As a next step, DP World will consider expanding its use of RFID-enabled scanning and tracking technology to further optimize supply chain flow. In the future, Rose hopes DP World will focus on investigating its use within the yard, and how data captured can be used.

Sources: Dave Friedlos, "RFID Boosts DP World's Productivity in Australia," RFID Journal, July 27, 2009 (www.rfidjournal.com/article/view/5086, accessed October 20, 2010); Rhea Wessel, "DP World Ramps Up Its Dubai Deployment," RFID Journal, August 13, 2009 (www.rfidjournal.com/article/view/5130, accessed October 20, 2010); "DP World UAE Implements Automated Gate System at Jebel Ali Port," The Zone, May-June 2008 (www.jafza.ae/mediafiles/ 2008/10/23/20081023_Issue-11.pdf, accessed October 20, 2010), p. 11; DP World (www.dpworld.com, accessed October 20, 2010); Identec Solutions (www.identecsolutions.com, accessed October 20, 2010).

Case contributed by Faouzi Kamoun, The University of Dubai

CASE STUDY QUESTIONS

1. How did Identec Solutions' RFID-based technology help DP World increase the efficiency and effectiveness of its customers' supply chains?

2. Describe two improvements that resulted from implementing the Identec RFID-based solution.

3. How does the concept of supply chain execution relate to this interactive session?

4. What managerial, organizational, and technological challenges might DP World have faced in the early stages of the RFID project's deployment?

BUSINESS VALUE OF CUSTOMER RELATIONSHIP MANAGEMENT SYSTEMS

Companies with effective customer relationship management systems realize many benefits, including increased customer satisfaction, reduced direct-marketing costs, more effective marketing, and lower costs for customer acquisition and retention. Information from CRM systems increases sales revenue by identifying the most profitable customers and segments for focused marketing and cross-selling.

Customer churn is reduced as sales, service, and marketing better respond to customer needs. The **churn rate** measures the number of customers who stop using or purchasing products or services from a company. It is an important indicator of the growth or decline of a firm's customer base.

9.4 Enterprise Applications: New Opportunities and Challenges

Many firms have implemented enterprise systems and systems for supply chain and customer relationship management because they are such powerful instruments for achieving operational excellence and enhancing decision making. But precisely because they are so powerful in changing the way the organization works, they are challenging to implement.

Let's briefly examine some of these challenges, as well as new ways of obtaining value from these systems.

ENTERPRISE APPLICATION CHALLENGES

Promises of dramatic reductions in inventory costs, order-to-delivery time, as well as more efficient customer response and higher product and customer profitability make enterprise systems and systems for supply chain management and customer relationship management very alluring. But to obtain this value, you must clearly understand how your business has to change to use these systems effectively.

Enterprise applications involve complex pieces of software that are very expensive to purchase and implement. It might take a large Fortune 500 company several years to complete a large-scale implementation of an enterprise system or a system for SCM or CRM. According to a 2013 survey of 172 companies conducted by Panorama Consulting, the average cost of an ERP project was US $7.1 million and completion would take 17.8 months, with 61 percent of respondents reporting the implementation would take longer than planned. Sixty percent of respondents said they had received 50 percent or less of the expected benefits of their project. Changes in project scope and additional customization work add to implementation delays and costs (Kanaracus, 2013 and 2012).

Enterprise applications require not only deep-seated technological changes but also fundamental changes in the way the business operates. Companies must make sweeping changes to their business processes to work with the software. Employees must accept new job functions and responsibilities. They must learn how to perform a new set of work activities and understand how the information they enter into the system can affect other parts of the company. This requires new organizational learning.

Supply chain management systems require multiple organizations to share information and business processes. Each participant in the system may have to change some of its processes and the way it uses information to create a system that best serves the supply chain as a whole.

Some firms experienced enormous operating problems and losses when they first implemented enterprise applications because they didn't understand how much organizational change was required. For example, Kmart had trouble getting products to store shelves when it first implemented i2 Technologies supply chain management software. The i2 software did not work well with Kmart's promotion-driven business model, which created sharp downward spikes in demand for products. Overstock.com's order tracking system went down for a full week when the company replaced a homegrown system with an Oracle enterprise system. The company rushed to implement the software, and did not properly synchronize the Oracle software's process for recording customer refunds with its accounts receivable system. These problems contributed to a third-quarter loss of $14.5 million that year.

Enterprise applications also introduce "switching costs." Once you adopt an enterprise application from a single vendor, such as SAP, Oracle, or others, it is very costly to switch vendors, and your firm becomes dependent on the vendor to upgrade its product and maintain your installation.

Enterprise applications are based on organization-wide definitions of data. You'll need to understand exactly how your business uses its data and how the data would be organized in a customer relationship management, supply chain management, or enterprise system. CRM systems typically require some data cleansing work.

Enterprise software vendors are addressing these problems by offering pared-down versions of their software and "fast-start" programs for small and medium-sized businesses and best-practice guidelines for larger companies.

Companies adopting enterprise applications can also save time and money by keeping customizations to a minimum. For example, Kennametal, a $2 billion metal-cutting tools company in Pennsylvania, had spent $10 million over 13 years maintaining an ERP system with over 6,400 customizations. The company has now replaced it with a "plain vanilla," noncustomized version of SAP enterprise software and changing its business processes to conform to the software.

NEXT-GENERATION ENTERPRISE APPLICATIONS

Today, enterprise application vendors are delivering more value by becoming more flexible, Web-enabled, and capable of integration with other systems. Stand-alone enterprise systems, customer relationship management systems, and supply chain management systems are becoming a thing of the past. The major enterprise software vendors have created what they call *enterprise solutions*, *enterprise suites*, or e-business suites to make their customer relationship management, supply chain management, and enterprise systems work closely with each other, and link to systems of customers and suppliers. SAP Business Suite, Oracle e-Business Suite, and Microsoft Dynamics suite (aimed at mid-sized companies) are examples, and they now utilize Web services and service-oriented architecture (SOA) (see Chapter 5).

SAP's next-generation enterprise applications incorporate SOA standards and are able to link SAP's own applications and Web services developed by independent software vendors. Oracle also has included SOA and business process management capabilities in its Fusion middleware products. Businesses can use these tools to create platforms for new or improved business processes that integrate information from multiple applications.

Next-generation enterprise applications also include open source and cloud solutions, as well as more functionality available on mobile platforms. Open source products such as Compiere, Apache Open for Business (OFBiz), and Openbravo do not offer as many capabilities as large commercial enterprise software, but are attractive to companies such as small manufacturers because of their low cost.

For small and medium-sized businesses in selected countries, SAP offers cloud-based versions of its Business One Cloud and Business ByDesign enterprise software solutions. Cloud-based enterprise systems are also offered by smaller vendors such as NetSuite and Plex Online, but they are not as popular as cloud-based CRM products, which account for 40% of CRM systems sold (Columbus, 2013). The undisputed global market leader in cloud-based CRM systems is Salesforce.com, with over 100,000 customers. Salesforce.com delivers its service through Internet-connected computers or mobile devices and it is widely used by small, medium, and large enterprises. As cloud-based products mature, more companies will be choosing to run all or part of their enterprise applications in the cloud on an as-needed basis.

Social CRM and Business Intelligence

CRM software vendors are enhancing their products to take advantage of social networking technologies. These social enhancements help firms identify new ideas more rapidly, improve team productivity, and deepen interactions with customers.

Employees who interact with customers via social networking sites such as Facebook and Twitter are often able to provide customer service functions much faster and at lower cost than by using telephone conversations or e-mail. Customers who are active social media users increasingly want—and expect—businesses to respond to their questions and complaints through this channel.

Social CRM tools enable a business to connect customer conversations and relationships from social networking sites to CRM processes. The leading CRM vendors now offer such tools to link data from social networks into their CRM software. Salesforce.com and Oracle CRM products are incorporating technology to monitor, track, and analyze social media activity in Facebook, LinkedIn, Twitter, YouTube, and other sites.

For example, Salesforce.com connected its system for tracking leads in the sales process with social-listening and social-media marketing tools, enabling users to tailor their social-marketing dollars to core customers and observe the resulting comments. If an ad agency wants to run a targeted Facebook or Twitter ad, these capabilities make it possible to aim the ad specifically at people in the client's lead pipeline, who are already being tracked in the CRM system. Users will be able to view tweets as they take place in real time and perhaps uncover new leads. They can also manage multiple campaigns and compare them all to figure out which ones generate the highest click-through rates and cost per click.

Business Intelligence in Enterprise Applications Enterprise application vendors have added business intelligence features to help managers obtain more meaningful information from the massive amounts of data generated by these systems. Included are tools for flexible reporting, ad hoc analysis, interactive dashboards, what-if scenario analysis, and data visualization. Rather than requiring users to leave an application and launch separate reporting and analytics tools, the vendors are starting to embed analytics within the context of the application itself. They are also offering complementary stand-alone analytics products, such as SAP Business Objects and Oracle Business Intelligence Enterprise Edition.

The major enterprise application vendors also offer portions of their products that work on mobile handhelds. You can find out more about this topic in our Chapter 7 Learning Track on Wireless Applications for Customer Relationship Management, Supply Chain Management, and Healthcare.

Review Summary

1 How do enterprise systems help businesses achieve operational excellence?
Enterprise software is based on a suite of integrated software modules and a common central database. The database collects data from and feeds the data into numerous applications that can support nearly all of an organization's internal business activities. When new information is entered by one process, the information is made available immediately to other business processes.

Enterprise systems support organizational centralization by enforcing uniform data standards and business processes throughout the company and a single unified technology platform. The firmwide data generated by enterprise systems helps managers evaluate organizational performance.

2 How do supply chain management systems coordinate planning, production, and logistics with suppliers? Supply chain management (SCM) systems automate the flow of information among members of the supply chain so they can use it to make better decisions about when and how much to purchase, produce, or ship. More accurate information from supply chain management systems reduces uncertainty and the impact of the bullwhip effect.

Supply chain management software includes software for supply chain planning and for supply chain execution. Internet technology facilitates the management of global supply chains by providing the connectivity for organizations in different countries to share supply chain information. Improved communication among supply chain members also facilitates efficient customer response and movement toward a demand-driven model.

3 How do customer relationship management systems help firms achieve customer intimacy? Customer relationship management (CRM) systems integrate and automate customer-facing processes in sales, marketing, and customer service, providing an enterprise-wide view of customers. Companies can use this customer knowledge when they interact with customers to provide them with better service or to sell new products and services. These systems also identify profitable or nonprofitable customers or opportunities to reduce the churn rate.

The major customer relationship management software packages provide capabilities for both operational CRM and analytical CRM. They often include modules for managing relationships with selling partners (partner relationship management) and for employee relationship management.

4   **What are the challenges posed by enterprise applications?** Enterprise applications are difficult to implement. They require extensive organizational change, large new software investments, and careful assessment of how these systems will enhance organizational performance. Enterprise applications cannot provide value if they are implemented atop flawed processes or if firms do not know how to use these systems to measure performance improvements. Employees require training to prepare for new procedures and roles. Attention to data management is essential.

5   **How are enterprise applications taking advantage of new technologies?** Enterprise applications are now more flexible, Web-enabled, and capable of integration with other systems, using Web services and service-oriented architecture (SOA). They also have open source and on-demand versions and are able to run in cloud infrastructures or on mobile platforms. CRM software has added social networking capabilities to enhance internal collaboration, deepen interactions with customers, and utilize data from social networking sites. Open source, mobile, and cloud versions of some of these products are becoming available.

Key Terms

Analytical CRM, 338
Bullwhip effect, 328
Churn rate, 340
Cross-selling, 336
Customer lifetime value (CLTV), 338
Demand planning, 329

Employee relationship management (ERM), 335
Enterprise software, 324
Just-in-time strategy, 328
Operational CRM, 338
Partner relationship management (PRM), 335
Pull-based model, 332

Push-based model, 332
Social CRM, 342
Supply chain, 326
Supply chain execution systems, 330
Supply chain planning systems, 329
Touch point, 334

Review Questions

9-1   How do enterprise systems help businesses achieve operational excellence?
- Define an enterprise system and explain how enterprise software works.
- List the business processes supported by enterprise systems.

9-2   How do supply chain management systems coordinate planning, production, and logistics with suppliers?
- Define a supply chain and identify each of its components.
- Describe some of the issues that arise with supply chains and explain what causes them.
- Define and compare supply chain planning systems and supply chain execution systems.
- Describe the challenges of global supply chains and how Internet technology can help companies manage them better.
- Distinguish between a push-based and a pull-based model of supply chain management and explain how contemporary supply chain management systems facilitate a pull-based model.

9-3   How do customer relationship management systems help firms achieve customer intimacy?
- Define customer relationship management and explain why customer relationships are so important today.
- Describe how partner relationship management (PRM) and employee relationship management (ERM) are related to customer relationship management (CRM).

- Describe the tools and capabilities of customer relationship management software for sales, marketing, and customer service.
- Explain the business value of customer relationship management systems.

9-4 What are the challenges posed by enterprise applications?
- List and describe the challenges posed by enterprise applications.
- Explain how these challenges can be addressed.

9-5 How are enterprise applications taking advantage of new technologies?
- How are enterprise applications taking advantage of SOA, Web services, open source software, and wireless technology?
- Describe how business intelligence features are being used in enterprise applications.

Discussion Questions

9-6 Supply chain management is less about managing the physical movement of goods and more about managing information. Discuss the implications of this statement.

9-7 If a company wants to implement an enterprise application, it had better do its homework. Discuss the implications of this statement.

9-8 What advantages does a firm gain by implementing a social CRM application?

Hands-On MIS Projects

The projects in this section give you hands-on experience analyzing business process integration, suggesting supply chain management and customer relationship management applications, using database software to manage customer service requests, and evaluating supply chain management business services.

MANAGEMENT DECISION PROBLEMS

9-9 Mercedes-Benz Retail Group UK Ltd, with a network of 18 retail sites, nine used car sites, and seven smart centers across London, Birmingham, and Manchester, wanted to learn more about its customers. How could CRM and PRM systems help solve this problem?

9-10 Office Depot is a global supplier of office supply products and services in 59 countries. The company tries to offer a wider range of office supplies at lower cost than other retailers by using just-in-time replenishment and tight inventory control systems. It uses information from a demand forecasting system and point-of-sale data to replenish its inventory in its 2,200 retail stores around the world. Explain how these systems help Office Depot minimize costs and any other benefits they provide. Identify and describe other supply chain management applications that would be especially helpful to Office Depot.

IMPROVING DECISION MAKING: USING DATABASE SOFTWARE TO MANAGE CUSTOMER SERVICE REQUESTS

Software skills: Database design; querying and reporting
Business skills: Customer service analysis

9-11 In this exercise, you'll use database software to develop an application that tracks customer service requests and analyzes customer data to identify customers meriting priority treatment.

Prime Service is a large service company that provides maintenance and repair services for close to 1,200 commercial businesses in New York, New Jersey, and Connecticut. Its customers include businesses of all sizes. Customers with service needs call into its customer service department with requests for repairing heating ducts, broken windows, leaky roofs, broken water pipes, and other problems. The company assigns each request a number and writes down the service request number, the identification number of the customer account, the date of the request, the type of equipment requiring repair, and a brief description of the problem. The service requests are handled on a first-come-first-served basis. After the service work has been completed, Prime calculates the cost of the work, enters the price on the service request form, and bills the client. This arrangement treats the most important and profitable clients—those with accounts of more than $70,000—no differently from its clients with small accounts. Managment would like to find a way to provide its best customers with better service. Management would also like to know which types of service problems occur most frequently so that it can make sure it has adequate resources to address them.

Prime Service has a small database with client account information, which can be found in MyMISLab™. Use database software to design a solution that would enable Prime's customer service representatives to identify the most important customers so that they could receive priority service. Your solution will require more than one table. Populate your database with at least 10 service requests. Create several reports that would be of interest to management, such as a list of the highest—and lowest—priority accounts and a report showing the most frequently occurring service problems. Create a report listing service calls that customer service representatives should respond to first on a specific date.

ACHIEVING OPERATIONAL EXCELLENCE: EVALUATING SUPPLY CHAIN MANAGEMENT SERVICES

Software skills: Web browser and presentation software
Business skills: Evaluating supply chain management services

9-12 Third party logistics providers provide transportation, consolidation, forwarding and customs brokerage, warehousing, fulfillment, distribution and virtually any logistics and trade-related services that their international customers need. In this project, you'll use the Web to research and evaluate two of these business services. Investigate the Web sites of two companies, U.K.-based Exel and Swiss-based Kuehne & Nagel, to see how these companies' services can be used for supply chain management. Then respond to the following questions:

- What supply chain processes can each of these companies support for their clients?
- How can customers use the Web sites of each company to help them with supply chain management?
- Compare the supply chain management services provided by these companies. Which company would you select to help your firm manage its supply chain? Why?

Collaboration and Teamwork Project

9-13 In MyMISLab, you will find a Collaboration and Teamwork Project dealing with the concepts in this chapter. You will be able to use Google Drive, Google Docs, Google Sites, Google+, or other open-source tools to complete the assignment.

BUSINESS PROBLEM-SOLVING CASE

Vodafone: A Giant Global ERP Implementation

Vodafone Group Plc is the largest mobile service provider by revenue in the world, with 400 million customers across Europe, the Middle East, Africa, Asia Pacific, and the United States. In 2012, it had revenues of $71.8 billion and over 86,000 employees working in over 40 countries. Since its founding 28 years ago, the business has experienced phenomenal growth, largely by establishing local operating companies that provided products and services to service their local markets.

As a result, the company was very decentralized, lacking common practices, centralized operations, and data sharing among its various operating companies. Most of Vodafone's mobile subsidiaries operated as independent companies with their own business processes. Vodafone was a network of individual businesses, but it wanted to function more like a single global firm to deal better with competitive pressures. Management called for a major business transformation to make this happen.

In 2006 Vodafone's board of directors approved the "Evolution Vodafone" Business Transformation Program" (EVO) designed to refashion Vodafone into a truly global company, with a centralized shared services organization and common worldwide business processes in finances, human resources, and supply chain management for all of the operating companies. (Shared services refers to the consolidation of business operations that are used by multiple parts of the same organization in order to reduce costs and redundancy.) A common SAP ERP (enterprise resource planning) system would provide the technology platform for these changes by supporting information-sharing and common business processes that would simplify and speed up work throughout the company. Additional software tools from Informatica, Opentext, Readsoft, Sabrix, Redwood, HP, and Remedy that could integrate with SAP were added to the mix.

Vodafone's system turned out to be one of the biggest SAP ERP implementations in the world. How did Vodafone pull it off? First of all, Vodafone's management realized the company lacked the expertise and resources to manage such a complex project entirely on its own. It enlisted the consulting firms Accenture and IBM to provide skills and services that this ambitious project required and which were not available inside the company.

The company spent a year identifying and designing its new business processes and establishing the scope of this project. The management team wanted to limit risks to non-customer-facing processes that were nevertheless important sources of value for the firm. Customer-facing front-end processes were excluded from the first phase of the rollout to keep the transformation more manageable.

Procurement was targeted as the first set of processes to be transformed using the new ERP system. Vodafone had been allowing each of its local companies to manage its own procurement, which prevented it from leveraging the massive purchasing power the company could obtain by managing relationships with material and service suppliers from a single entity. By generating savings from centralized procurement, the transformation project would be able to quickly show a return on investment and win further support. Vodafone did not establish a centralized procurement department but instead created a centralized procurement company based in Luxembourg that uses the SAP ERP platform. Most of the company's spending goes through this central organization. Suppliers benefit because the system helps them plan their sales to Vodafone and they only need to work with a single purchaser instead of many. This new way of doing business included a new purchase-to-pay process in which invoices are approved automatically for payment by matching them with purchase orders and receipts.

Once the new procurement process and organization were running, Vodafone started creating a centralized shared services organization based on the SAP ERP system. It selected Budapest, Hungary as the pilot location for this new arrangement. Vodafone Hungary is a mid-sized company with 2,000 employees with a small IT platform based on Oracle software. This made Vodafone Hungary more receptive to changing its information system and business processes than Vodafone organizations in larger countries, and Hungary had been using Oracle systems. There Vodafone built an entire shared services organization from scratch while simultaneously implementing the SAP ERP system. Vodafone then set up two more shared services organizations in India running on SAP.

After Hungary, Vodafone implemented the new procurement process and SAP software for its German operating company. Germany is Vodafone's largest market, and is responsible for more than 20 percent of Vodafone's total revenue. Vodafone Germany is a much larger organization than Vodafone Hungary, with 13,000 employees, over 130 local legacy systems, and many customized business processes to replace. Work habits were more deeply entrenched, and Vodafone encountered some employee resistance as it tried to implement the new systems and processes. To minimize risk, Vodafone used a phased, incremental implementation, did a tremendous amount of testing, and made all the necessary system modifications before the system went live.

Special support teams were dispatched to work with all the employees affected by the transition. These efforts helped address problems and employee resistance before they got out of hand. Once the German implementation was deemed successful, Vodafone rolled out the new system at many more operating companies, prioritizing the implementations based on each operating company's size, complexity, and willingness to change.

No two rollouts proceeded the same way because each operating company had unique challenges and demands. Many of these companies had grown rapidly, and had numerous legacy systems based on local requirements. There were large numbers of users, interfaces, and legal requirements to deal with. Vodafone's project team had to balance the need to proceed rapidly with the need to ensure that the system was implemented carefully.

Vodafone's implementation plan called for a core project team to visit each individual operating company and implement the new processes locally, assisted by a systems integrator and local resources. Local teams and senior management met with the global teams, IT consultants, and local IT vendors in a friendly environment to encourage knowledge-sharing and openness to change. The success of each rollout was based on multiple factors, including the number and complexity of each unit's legacy systems, the skills of each local project team, and the willingness of each local organization to embrace change. Vodafone enlisted the services of the global consulting firm Accenture to provide skills where needed and assist with change management in the local companies. Over time, the Vodafone project team and the Accenture consultants learned how to tailor their activities to the needs of each operating company. For example, if no representatives from an operating company showed up for the project launch meeting or they attended but showed little interest, the project team knew that company might be less cooperative. In such cases, the project would require more resources and attention.

The project team also had to be sensitive to local trends as system rollouts took place. For instance, if an operating company was located in a country experiencing economic downturn, its employees might be more resistant to the rollout. Some might see a major business and technology change as an improvement in their situation, while others might see it as another thing to cope with during a very stressful time.

As it finished rolling out the system to its remaining operating companies, the Vodafone project team used what it had learned to make improvements to its earlier ERP implementations. For example, testing and employee feedback revealed that more attention should be paid to usability. So the project team enhanced the system's interfaces to make them more user-friendly.

Given the nature of the business, Vodafone's management wants about 80% of the company's internal transactions to take place on a mobile device. According to Niall O'Sullivan, Vodafone's Global Finance Transformation Director, management believes mobile apps will be a major advantage in driving compliance, increasing ease of use, and reducing resistance to the actual processes themselves. The goal is to have the vast majority of user interactions with the system take place on a mobile phone. According to O'Sullivan, mobility provides easy access for employees who don't typically engage with the SAP system, so more employees are using the system. The more people use the system, the greater the return on investment. Over 60,000 employees around the world now use the new system, with 80,000 expected by the end of 2012.

Vodafone is now rolling out some of its enterprise applications for mobile devices, and so far, four have been selected. The first to go mobile was a travel and expense reporting application. Employees are able to take a photo of their receipts and get reimbursed without using any paper, and they can issue or approve requests for leave on their mobile phones all at one time.

Vodafone's business process transformation and ERP system have increased business efficiency and produced annual cost savings of $719 million. The total cost of ownership (TCO) of information technology has been lowered. Throughout the world, Vodafone has a consistent way of working and a more unified organizational structure. Getting the various operating companies to think and act more uniformly and to adopt a shared service model has produced benefits that are not immediately quantifiable, but should lead to further profitability in the long run.

Sources: Derek DuPreez, "Vodafone HANA Project Moves Beyond Trial Despite Skills Challenge," *TechWorld*, March 11, 2013; www.vodafone.com, accessed March 15, 2013; "Using SAP MaxAttention to Safeguard the Global Rollout of SAP ERP," www.mysap.com, accessed April 8, 2013; David Hannon, "Vodafone Walks the Talk," *SAP InsiderPROFILES*, October–December 2012; and Michaela Kresak, Lilian Corvington, Frits Wiegel, Guido Wokurka, Stephanie Teufel, and Peter Williamson, "Vodafone Answers Call to Transformation," 360-bt.com, Issue 2 (October 2011).

Case Study Questions

9-14 Identify and describe the problem discussed in this case. What people, organization, and technology factors contributed to the problem?

9-15 Why did Vodafone have to spend so much time dealing with change during its business transformation?

9-16 Why was an ERP system required for Vodafone's global business transformation?

9-17 What people, organization, and technology issues had to be addressed by the Vodafone project team to ensure the transformation would be successful?

9-18 What were the business benefits of Vodafone's global business transformation? How did it change decision making and the way the company operated?

E-commerce: Digital Markets, Digital Goods

CHAPTER 10

STUDENT LEARNING OBJECTIVES

After completing this chapter, you will be able to answer the following questions:

1. What are the unique features of e-commerce, digital markets, and digital goods?

2. What are the principal e-commerce business and revenue models?

3. How has e-commerce transformed marketing?

4. How has e-commerce affected business-to-business transactions?

5. What is the role of m-commerce in business and what are the most important m-commerce applications?

6. What issues must be addressed when building an e-commerce presence?

OTTO GROUP: PROFITS FROM PREDICTION

The Otto Group is the world's largest mail order company, the second largest online retailer in Europe behind Amazon, and the third largest online retailer in the world. In 2012 Otto Group generated €11.8 billion in total global revenue, and €5.7 billion in online global sales, nearly all of which is generated in Europe. By comparison, in 2012 Amazon had online sales in Europe of €15 billion, and total global sales of €45 billion. For perspective, China's online retail giant, Alibaba, generated €116 billion. Founded in 1949 in Hamburg by Werner Otto as a catalog merchant selling 28 styles of shoes, in 2013 Otto Group is composed of 123 companies operating in more than twenty countries, employing over 53,000 people. Otto carries more than 1.8 million items and 3600 brands on its sites every day.

Though Otto Group originated in Germany, in the 1990s, the company began an aggressive acquisition program throughout Europe, North America, and China. You may not recognize the Otto Group corporate name, but you will recognize some of its better known brands, including Crate and Barrel (U.S. furnishing), Bombay Co. (U.S.

z_amir/Fotolia.

furniture), s.Oliver (German fashion), Eddie Bauer (U.S. fashion), Tom Tailor (Europe fashion), and 3 Suisses (French mail order fashion).

Otto Group's aggressive acquisition growth strategy has created its own set of challenges. Purchasing over 100 companies in the past few decades, it has inherited a bewildering array of products, accounting systems, multiple sales channels, and market dynamics. Geography added additional complexity for managers trying to deliver products to consumers in a timely manner. Predicting demand became a major issue. The traditional retail marketing system was sometimes in error: shelves throughout the Otto Group could be filled with goods that did not sell, creating large losses. Other shelves could be empty because the traditional system could not respond to hot trends in a timely manner. In the traditional retail system, dynamic pricing (lowering prices to clear overstock items, or raising prices on really hot fashions) was impossible. In the past, Otto had used various off line regression analysis programs to predict demand, but they were often too late and slow to respond to real-time market changes.

The Otto Group turned to Big Data and predictive analytics to help it achieve real- time market decision making. It worked with Teradata Inc. (San Diego) to create a data warehouse containing literally terabytes of customer data from its online and catalog operations in twenty countries. The Teradata Portfolio for Hadoop software provides flexible Big Data storage for firms using SQL and non-SQL databases. It allows firms to analyze social media, documents, text, images, and other non-structured data. For instance, when yellow blouses are mentioned on thousands of Twitter posts followed by Otto's customers in France, based on prior knowledge of the relationship between Twitter posts and its own sales to followers, it may want to expand its inventory of yellow blouses in France.

To analyze and understand its huge collection of customer data, Otto Group purchased a software company now named Blue Yonder software, a leading provider of forecasting and data pattern recognition, or what is called "predictive analytics." Using an artificial intelligence program to recognize patterns in very large data sets, Blue Yonder's NeuroBayes software is used by firms to discover patterns in data by analyzing up to petabytes of information per second.

Using predictive analytics and Big Data repositories, Otto Group has been able to increase its ability to forecast demand by 40%, and it claims to have reaped tens of millions of euros in savings. Otto calculates annually over one billion individual consumer predictions which it aggregates to predict demand for its 40,000 online and catalog products. Leftover merchandise has been reduced by 20 percent. Predicting how many items will be returned has become more precise and has helped the company understand why items are returned. The firm can use the same systems to engage in dynamic pricing, changing prices in accordance with aggregate demand, as well as individual propensities to spend.

Implementing a data driven approach to marketing has also introduced cultural and organizational challenges. Otto's experienced merchandisers and buyers have a long history of making correct decisions when it comes to selecting products to sell, and the price points that motivate consumers. To ensure predictive analytics and data-driven decision making is used throughout the firm whenever possible, Otto Group created a central business intelligence team. This was a major cultural shift within the firm. Time will tell if the central business intelligence team can out perform Otto's human professionals, or if they will learn and work together to produce better results

Sources: Blue Yonder GmbH & Co., "Otto Improves its Prediction Quality by Up to 50% With Blue Yonder," blueyonder.com/solutions, December 11, 2013; Lindsay Clarke, "German Retailer Otto Invests in Neural Software to Net future Sales," Computer Weekly, November 9, 2012;Dan Conway, "Terradata Delivers Industry's First Flexible, Comprehensive Hadoop Portfolio," Terradata.com/News-Releases, June 26, 2013; and Lindsay Clarke, "Analysis" How Tesco and Otto Are Using Data to Forecast Demand," Retail Week, October 10, 2013.

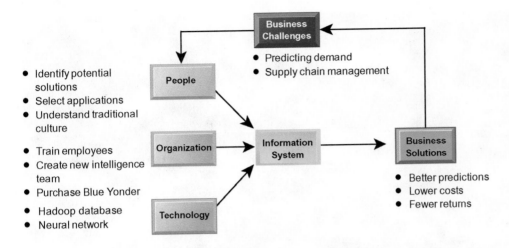

- Identify potential solutions
- Select applications
- Understand traditional culture

- Train employees
- Create new intelligence team
- Purchase Blue Yonder

- Hadoop database
- Neural network

People

Organization

Technology

Business Challenges
- Predicting demand
- Supply chain management

Information System

Business Solutions
- Better predictions
- Lower costs
- Fewer returns

The chapter-opening diagram calls attention to important points raised by this case and this chapter. Otto's primary challenge is understanding and predicting the demand for thousands of products it sells online and through catalogs in twenty countries. If it could solve this challenge it could make its supply chain more effective and responsive, reduce returns, lower overall costs, and increase its profit margins. To solve this challenge Otto turned to new database technology and new analytic software for analyzing non-structured customer data. To implement its new approach to demand prediction and buying, it created a new organizational unit and retrained employees in how to take advantage of the new technologies. These results allow the firm to make its supply chain more responsive and efficient.

Here are some questions to think about: How did the global nature of Otto's business present problems for the company? How did analyzing big data change the way the company ran its business?

10.1 E-commerce and the Internet

Bought an iTunes track lately, streamed a Netflix movie to your home TV, purchased a book at Amazon, or a diamond at Blue Nile? If so, you've engaged in e-commerce. In 2013, an estimated 189 million Americans went shopping online, and 155 million purchased something online as did millions of others worldwide. And although most purchases still take place through traditional channels, e-commerce continues to grow rapidly and to transform the way many companies do business. In 2013, e-commerce consumer sales of goods, services, and content will reach 419 billion, about 9 percent of all retail sales, and they are growing at 12 percent annually (compared to 3.5 percent for traditional retailers) (eMarketer, 2013a). In just the past two years, e-commerce has expanded from the desktop and home computer to mobile devices, from an isolated activity to a new social commerce, and from a Fortune 1000 commerce with a national audience to local merchants and consumers whose location is known to mobile devices. The key words for understanding this new e-commerce in 2013 are "social, mobile, local."

E-COMMERCE TODAY

E-commerce refers to the use of the Internet and the Web to transact business. More formally, e-commerce is about digitally enabled commercial transactions between and among organizations and individuals. For the most part, this means transactions that occur over the Internet and the Web. Commercial transactions involve the exchange of value (e.g., money) across organizational or individual boundaries in return for products and services.

E-commerce began in 1995 when one of the first Internet portals, Netscape.com, accepted the first ads from major corporations and popularized the idea that the Web

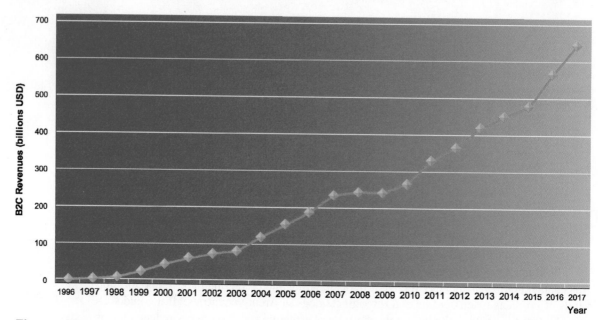

Figure 10.1

The Growth of E-Commerce

Retail e-commerce revenues grew 15–25 percent per year until the recession of 2008–2009, when they slowed measurably. In 2013, e-commerce revenues are growing again at an estimated 12 percent annually.

could be used as a new medium for advertising and sales. No one envisioned at the time what would turn out to be an exponential growth curve for e-commerce retail sales, which doubled and tripled in the early years. E-commerce grew at double-digit rates until the recession of 2008–2009 when growth slowed to a crawl. In 2009, e-commerce revenues were flat (Figure 10.1), not bad considering that traditional retail sales were shrinking by 5 percent annually. In fact, e-commerce during the recession was the only stable segment in retail. Some online retailers forged ahead at a record pace: Amazon's 2009 revenues were up 25 percent over 2008 sales. Despite the continuing slow growth in 2013, the number of online buyers increased by 5 percent to 155 million, and the number of online retail transactions was up 8 percent. Amazon's sales grew to $61 billion in 2012, up an incredible 50 percent from 2011!

Mirroring the history of many technological innovations, such as the telephone, radio, and television, the very rapid growth in e-commerce in the early years created a market bubble in e-commerce stocks. Like all bubbles, the "dot-com" bubble burst (in March 2001). A large number of e-commerce companies failed during this process. Yet for many others, such as Amazon, eBay, Expedia, and Google, the results have been more positive: soaring revenues, fine-tuned business models that produce profits, and rising stock prices. By 2006, e-commerce revenues returned to solid growth, and have continued to be the fastest growing form of retail trade in the United States, Europe, and Asia.

- Online consumer sales grew to an estimated $419 billion in 2013, an increase of more than 12 percent over 2012 (including travel services and digital downloads), with 155 million people purchasing online and an additional 39 million shopping and gathering information but not purchasing (eMarketer, 2013a).

- The number of individuals of all ages online in the United States expanded to 259 million in 2013, up from 147 million in 2004. In the world, over 2.6 billion people are now connected to the Internet. Growth in the overall Internet population has spurred growth in e-commerce (Internet World Stats, 2013).

- Approximately 85 million households have broadband access to the Internet in 2013, representing about 70 percent of all households.

- About 143 million Americans now access the Internet using a smartphone such as an iPhone, Droid, or BlackBerry. Mobile e-commerce has begun a rapid growth based on apps, ring tones, downloaded entertainment, and location-based services. Mobile commerce will add up to about $38.8 billion in 2013 (roughly double 2010's revenue). Amazon sold an estimated $4 billion in retail goods to mobile users in 2012. In a few years, mobile phones will be the most common Internet access device. Currently half of all mobile phone users access the Internet using their phones.

- On an average day, an estimated 212 million adult U.S. Internet users go online. About 152 million send e-mail, 152 million use a search engine, and 117 million get news. Around 124 million use a social network, 62 million do online banking, 73 million watch an online video, and 44 million look for information on Wikipedia (Pew Internet & American Life Project, 2013).

- B2B e-commerce use of the Internet for business-to-business commerce and collaboration among business partners expanded to more than $4.7 trillion. Table 10.1 highlights these new e-commerce developments.

THE NEW E-COMMERCE: SOCIAL, MOBILE, LOCAL

One of the biggest changes is the extent to which e-commerce has become more social, mobile, and local. Online marketing consisted largely of creating a corporate Web site, buying display ads on Yahoo, purchasing ad words on Google, and sending e-mails. The workhorse of online marketing was the display ad. It still is. Display ads from the very beginning of the Internet were based on television ads where brand messages were flashed before millions of users who were not expected to respond immediately, ask questions, or make observations. If the ads did not work, the solution was often to repeat the ad. The primary measure of success was how many "eyeballs" (unique visitors) a Web site produced, and how many "impressions" a marketing campaign generated. (An impression was one ad shown to one person.) Both of these measures were carry overs from the world of television, which measures marketing in terms of audience size and ad views.

From Eyeballs to Conversations

After 2007, all this changed with the rapid growth of Facebook and other social sites, the explosive growth of smartphones beginning with Apple iPhone, and the growing interest in local marketing. What's different about the new world of social-mobile-local e-commerce are the dual and related concepts of "conversations" and "engagement." Marketing in this new period is based on firms engaging in multiple online conversations with their customers, potential customers, and even critics. Your brand is being talked about on the Web and social media (that's the conversation part), and marketing your firm, building and restoring your brands, requires you to locate, identify, and participate in these conversations. Social marketing means all things social like listening, discussing, interacting, empathizing, and engaging. The emphasis in online marketing has shifted from a focus on eyeballs to a focus on participating in customer-oriented conversations. In this sense, social marketing is not simply a "new ad channel," but a collection of technology-based tools for communicating with shoppers.

In the past, firms could tightly control their brand messaging, and lead consumers down a funnel of cues that ended in a purchase. That is not true of social marketing. Consumer purchase decisions are increasingly driven by the conversations, choices, tastes, and opinions of their social network. Social marketing is all about firms participating in and shaping this social process.

From the Desktop to the Smartphone

By 2012, mobile marketing and advertising had already overtaken social marketing using traditional Web browsers on the Web, and by 2013, mobile was almost twice as large. By 2015, mobile marketing is estimated to be around $16 billion annually, while social marketing is just over $6 billion. While social marketing is growing at around 30 percent a year, mobile is growing at around 50 percent a year. Local marketing, estimated to be about $2.2 billion in 2013, has been growing by nearly 100 percent a year.

TABLE 10.1

The Growth of E-Commerce

Business Transformation

- E-commerce remains the fastest growing form of commerce when compared to physical retail stores, services, and entertainment.

- Social, mobile, and local commerce have become the fastest growing forms of e-commerce.

- The first wave of e-commerce transformed the business world of books, music, and air travel. In the second wave, nine new industries are facing a similar transformation scenario: marketing and advertising, telecommunications, movies, television, jewelry and luxury goods, real estate, online travel, bill payments, and software.

- The breadth of e-commerce offerings grows, especially in the services economy of social networking, travel, entertainment, retail apparel, jewelry, appliances, and home furnishings.

- The online demographics of shoppers broaden to match that of ordinary shoppers.

- Pure e-commerce business models are refined further to achieve higher levels of profitability, whereas traditional retail brands, such as Sears, JCPenney, L.L.Bean, and Walmart, use e-commerce to retain their dominant retail positions.

- Small businesses and entrepreneurs continue to flood the e-commerce marketplace, often riding on the infrastructures created by industry giants, such as Amazon, Apple, and Google, and increasingly taking advantage of cloud-based computing resources.

- Mobile e-commerce begins to take off in the United States with location-based services and entertainment downloads including e-books, movies, and television shows.

Technology Foundations

- Wireless Internet connections (Wi-Fi, WiMax, and 3G/4G smartphones) grow rapidly.

- Powerful smartphones, tablet computers, and mobile devices support music, Web surfing, and entertainment as well as voice communication. Podcasting and streaming take off as mediums for distribution of video, radio, and user-generated content.

- The Internet broadband foundation becomes stronger in households and businesses as transmission prices fall. More than 82 million households had broadband cable or DSL access to the Internet in 2012, about 69 percent of all households in the United States (eMarketer, 2013a).

- Social networking software and sites such as Facebook, MySpace, Twitter, LinkedIn, and thousands of others become a major new platform for e-commerce, marketing, and advertising. Facebook hits 1 billion users worldwide, and 142 million in the United States (comScore, 2013).

- New Internet-based models of computing, such as smartphone apps, cloud computing, software as a service (SaaS), and Web 2.0 software greatly reduce the cost of e-commerce Web sites.

New Business Models Emerge

- More than half the Internet user population have joined an online social network, contribute to social bookmarking sites, create blogs, and share photos. Together these sites create a massive online audience as large as television that is attractive to marketers. In 2013, social networking accounts for an estimated 25 percent of online time.

- The traditional advertising industry is disrupted as online advertising grows twice as fast as TV and print advertising; Google, Yahoo, and Facebook display nearly 1 trillion ads a year.

- Newspapers and other traditional media adopt online, interactive models but are losing advertising revenues to the online players despite gaining online readers. The New York Times adopts a paywall for its online edition and succeeds in capturing 850,000 subscribers.

- Online entertainment business models offering television, movies, music, sports, and e-books surge, with cooperation among the major copyright owners in Hollywood and New York and with Internet distributors like Apple, Amazon, Google, YouTube, and Facebook.

Traditional online marketing (browser based, search and display ads, e-mail, and games) still constitutes the majority (68 percent) of all online marketing ($41 billion), but it's growing much more slowly than social-mobile-local marketing. The marketing dollars are following customers and shoppers from the PC to mobile devices.

Social, mobile, and local e-commerce are connected. As mobile devices become more powerful, they are more useful for accessing Facebook and other social sites. As mobile devices become more widely adopted, they can be used by customers to find local merchants, and by merchants to alert customers in their neighborhood of special offers.

WHY E-COMMERCE IS DIFFERENT

Why has e-commerce grown so rapidly? The answer lies in the unique nature of the Internet and the Web. Simply put, the Internet and e-commerce technologies are much richer and more powerful than previous technology revolutions like radio, television, and the telephone. Table 10.2 describes the unique features of the Internet and Web as a commercial medium. Let's explore each of these unique features in more detail.

E-commerce Technology Dimension	Business Significance
Ubiquity. Internet/Web technology is available everywhere: at work, at home, and elsewhere via desktop and mobile devices. Mobile devices extend service to local areas and merchants.	The marketplace is extended beyond traditional boundaries and is removed from a temporal and geographic location. "Marketspace" anytime, is created; shopping can take place anywhere. Customer convenience is enhanced, and shopping costs are reduced.
Global reach. The technology reaches across national boundaries, around the earth.	Commerce is enabled across cultural and national boundaries seamlessly and without modification. The marketspace includes, potentially, billions of consumers and millions of businesses worldwide.
Universal Standards. There is one set of technology standards, namely Internet standards.	With one set of technical standards across the globe, disparate computer systems can easily communicate with each other.
Richness. Video, audio, and text messages are possible.	Video, audio, and text marketing messages are integrated into a single marketing message and consumer experience.
Interactivity. The technology works through interaction with the user.	Consumers are engaged in a dialog that dynamically adjusts the experience to the individual, and makes the consumer a co-participant in the process of delivering goods to the market.
Information Density. The technology reduces information costs and raises quality.	Information processing, storage, and communication costs drop dramatically, whereas currency, accuracy, and timeliness improve greatly. Information becomes plentiful, cheap, and more accurate.
Personalization/Customization. The technology allows personalized messages to be delivered to individuals as well as groups.	Personalization of marketing messages and customization of products and services are based on individual characteristics.
Social Technology. The technology supports content generation and social networking.	New Internet social and business models enable user content creation and distribution, and support social networks.

TABLE 10.2

Eight Unique Features of E-Commerce Technology

Ubiquity

In traditional commerce, a marketplace is a physical place, such as a retail store, that you visit to transact business. E-commerce is ubiquitous, meaning that is it available just about everywhere, at all times. It makes it possible to shop from your desktop, at home, at work, or even from your car, using smartphones. The result is called a **marketspace**—a marketplace extended beyond traditional boundaries and removed from a temporal and geographic location.

From a consumer point of view, ubiquity reduces **transaction costs**—the costs of participating in a market. To transact business, it is no longer necessary that you spend time or money traveling to a market, and much less mental effort is required to make a purchase.

Global Reach

E-commerce technology permits commercial transactions to cross cultural and national boundaries far more conveniently and cost effectively than is true in traditional commerce. As a result, the potential market size for e-commerce merchants is roughly equal to the size of the world's online population (estimated to be more than 2 billion).

In contrast, most traditional commerce is local or regional—it involves local merchants or national merchants with local outlets. Television, radio stations and newspapers, for instance, are primarily local and regional institutions with limited, but powerful, national networks that can attract a national audience but not easily cross national boundaries to a global audience.

Universal Standards

One strikingly unusual feature of e-commerce technologies is that the technical standards of the Internet and, therefore, the technical standards for conducting e-commerce are universal standards. They are shared by all nations around the world and enable any computer to link with any other computer regardless of the technology platform each is using. In contrast, most traditional commerce technologies differ from one nation to the next. For instance, television and radio standards differ around the world, as does cell telephone technology.

The universal technical standards of the Internet and e-commerce greatly lower **market entry costs**—the cost merchants must pay simply to bring their goods to market. At the same time, for consumers, universal standards reduce **search costs**—the effort required to find suitable products.

Richness

Information **richness** refers to the complexity and content of a message. Traditional markets, national sales forces, and small retail stores have great richness: They are able to provide personal, face-to-face service using aural and visual cues when making a sale. The richness of traditional markets makes them powerful selling or commercial environments. Prior to the development of the Web, there was a trade-off between richness and reach: The larger the audience reached, the less rich the message. The Web makes it possible to deliver rich messages with text, audio, and video simultaneously to large numbers of people.

Interactivity

Unlike any of the commercial technologies of the twentieth century, with the possible exception of the telephone, e-commerce technologies are interactive, meaning they allow for two-way communication between merchant and consumer. Television, for instance, cannot ask viewers any questions or enter into conversations with them, and it cannot request that customer information be entered into a form. In contrast, all of these activities are possible on an e-commerce Web site. Interactivity allows an online merchant to engage a consumer in ways similar to a face-to-face experience but on a massive, global scale.

Information Density

The Internet and the Web vastly increase **information density**—the total amount and quality of information available to all market participants, consumers, and merchants alike. E-commerce technologies reduce information collection, storage, processing, and communication costs while greatly increasing the currency, accuracy, and timeliness of information.

Information density in e-commerce markets make prices and costs more transparent. **Price transparency** refers to the ease with which consumers can find out the variety of prices in a market; **cost transparency** refers to the ability of consumers to discover the actual costs merchants pay for products.

There are advantages for merchants as well. Online merchants can discover much more about consumers than in the past. This allows merchants to segment the market into groups that are willing to pay different prices and permits the merchants to engage in **price discrimination**—selling the same goods, or nearly the same goods, to different targeted groups at different prices. For instance, an online merchant can discover a consumer's avid interest in expensive, exotic vacations and then pitch high-end vacation plans to that consumer at a premium price, knowing this person is willing to pay extra for such a vacation. At the same time, the online merchant can pitch the same vacation plan at a lower price to a more price-sensitive consumer. Information density also helps merchants differentiate their products in terms of cost, brand, and quality.

Personalization/Customization

E-commerce technologies permit **personalization**: Merchants can target their marketing messages to specific individuals by adjusting the message to a person's clickstream behavior, name, interests, and past purchases. The technology also permits **customization**—changing the delivered product or service based on a user's preferences or prior behavior. Given the interactive nature of e-commerce technology, much information about the consumer can be gathered in the marketplace at the moment of purchase. With the increase in information density, a great deal of information about the consumer's past purchases and behavior can be stored and used by online merchants.

The result is a level of personalization and customization unthinkable with traditional commerce technologies. For instance, you may be able to shape what you see on television by selecting a channel, but you cannot change the content of the channel you have chosen. In contrast, the *Wall Street Journal* Online allows you to select the type of news stories you want to see first and gives you the opportunity to be alerted when certain events happen.

Social Technology: User Content Generation and Social Networking

In contrast to previous technologies, the Internet and e-commerce technologies have evolved to be much more social by allowing users to create and share with their personal friends (and a larger worldwide community) content in the form of text, videos, music, or photos. Using these forms of communication, users are able to create new social networks and strengthen existing ones.

All previous mass media in modern history, including the printing press, use a broadcast model (one-to-many) where content is created in a central location by experts (professional writers, editors, directors, and producers) and audiences are concentrated in huge numbers to consume a standardized product. The new Internet and e-commerce empower users to create and distribute content on a large scale, and permit users to program their own content consumption. The Internet provides a unique many-to-many model of mass communications.

KEY CONCEPTS IN E-COMMERCE: DIGITAL MARKETS AND DIGITAL GOODS IN A GLOBAL MARKETPLACE

The location, timing, and revenue models of business are based in some part on the cost and distribution of information. The Internet has created a digital marketplace where millions of people all over the world are able to exchange massive amounts of information directly, instantly, and for free. As a result, the Internet has changed the way companies conduct business and increased their global reach.

The Internet reduces information asymmetry. An **information asymmetry** exists when one party in a transaction has more information that is important for the transaction than the other party. That information helps determine their relative bargaining power. In digital markets, consumers and suppliers can "see" the prices being charged for goods, and in that sense digital markets are said to be more "transparent" than traditional markets.

For example, before auto retailing sites appeared on the Web, there was a significant information asymmetry between auto dealers and customers. Only the auto dealers knew the manufacturers' prices, and it was difficult for consumers to shop around for the best price. Auto dealers' profit margins depended on this asymmetry of information. Today's consumers have access to a legion of Web sites providing competitive pricing information, and three-fourths of U.S. auto buyers use the Internet to shop around for the best deal. Thus, the Web has reduced the information asymmetry surrounding an auto purchase. The Internet has also helped businesses seeking to purchase from other businesses reduce information asymmetries and locate better prices and terms.

Digital markets are very flexible and efficient because they operate with reduced search and transaction costs, lower **menu costs** (merchants' costs of changing prices), greater price discrimination, and the ability to change prices dynamically based on market conditions. In **dynamic pricing**, the price of a product varies depending on the demand characteristics of the customer or the supply situation of the seller. For instance, online retailers from Amazon to Walmart change prices on many products based on time of day, demand for the product, and users' prior visits to their sites. Using Big Data analytics, some online firms can adjust prices at the individual level based on behavioral targeting parameters, such as whether the consumer is a price haggler (who will receive a lower price offer) versus a person who accepts offered prices and does not search for lower prices. Prices can also vary by zip code, with higher prices set for poor sections of a community.

These new digital markets may either reduce or increase switching costs, depending on the nature of the product or service being sold, and they may cause some extra delay in gratification. Unlike a physical market, you can't immediately consume a product such as clothing purchased over the Web (although immediate consumption is possible with digital music downloads and other digital products.)

Digital markets provide many opportunities to sell directly to the consumer, bypassing intermediaries, such as distributors or retail outlets. Eliminating intermediaries in the distribution channel can significantly lower purchase transaction costs. To pay for all the steps in a traditional distribution channel, a product may have to be priced as high as 135 percent of its original cost to manufacture.

Figure 10.2 illustrates how much savings result from eliminating each of these layers in the distribution process. By selling directly to consumers or reducing the number of intermediaries, companies are able to raise profits while charging lower prices. The removal of organizations or business process layers responsible for intermediary steps in a value chain is called **disintermediation**.

Disintermediation is affecting the market for services. Airlines and hotels operating their own reservation sites online earn more per ticket because they have eliminated travel agents as intermediaries. Table 10.3 summarizes the differences between digital markets and traditional markets.

Digital Goods

The Internet digital marketplace has greatly expanded sales of digital goods. **Digital goods** are goods that can be delivered over a digital network. Music tracks, video, Hollywood movies, software, newspapers, magazines, and books can all be expressed, stored, delivered, and sold as purely digital products. For the most part, digital goods are "intellectual property" which is defined as "works of the mind." Intellectual property is protected from misappropriation by copyright, patent, and trade secret laws (see Chapter 4). Today, all these products are delivered as digital streams or downloads, while their physical counterparts decline in sales.

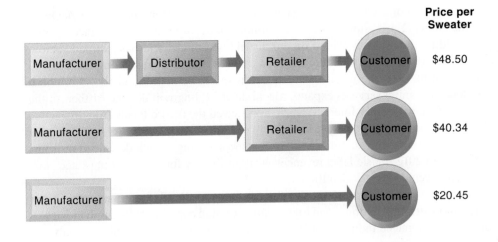

Figure 10.2
The Benefits of Disintermediation to the Consumer
The typical distribution channel has several intermediary layers, each of which adds to the final cost of a product, such as a sweater. Removing layers lowers the final cost to the customer.

In general, for digital goods, the marginal cost of producing another unit is about zero (it costs nothing to make a copy of a music file). However, the cost of producing the original first unit is relatively high—in fact, it is nearly the total cost of the product because there are few other costs of inventory and distribution. Costs of delivery over the Internet are very low, marketing costs often remain the same, and pricing can be highly variable. (On the Internet, the merchant can change prices as often as desired because of low menu costs.)

The impact of the Internet on the market for these kinds of digital goods is nothing short of revolutionary, and we see the results around us every day. Businesses dependent on physical products for sales—such as bookstores, music stores, book publishers, music labels, and film studios—face the possibility of declining sales and even destruction of their businesses. Newspapers and magazines subscriptions to hard copies are declining, while online readership and subscriptions are expanding.

Total record label industry revenues have fallen from $14 billion in 1999, to $7.1 billion estimated in 2012, a drop of 50 percent, due almost entirely to the decline in CD album

TABLE 10.3

Digital Markets Compared to Traditional Markets

	Digital Markets	**Traditional Markets**
Information asymmetry	Asymmetry reduced	Asymmetry high
Search costs	Low	High
Transaction costs	Low (sometimes virtually nothing)	High (time, travel)
Delayed gratification	High (or lower in the case of a digital good)	Lower: purchase now
Menu costs	Low	High
Dynamic pricing	Low cost, instant	High cost, delayed
Price discrimination	Low cost, instant	High cost, delayed
Market segmentation	Low cost, moderate precision	High cost, less precision
Switching costs	Higher/lower (depending on product characteristics)	High
Network effects	Strong	Weaker
Disintermediation	More possible/likely	Less possible/unlikely

sales, and the growth of digital music services (both legal and illegal music piracy). On the plus side, the Apple iTunes Store has sold 25 billion songs for 99 cents each since opening in 2003, providing the industry with a digital distribution model that has restored some of the revenues lost to digital music channels. Since iTunes, illegal downloading has been cut in half, and legitimate online music sales are estimated to be approximately $4 billion in 2013. As cloud streaming services expand, illegal downloading will decline further. In that sense, Apple, along with other Internet distributors, saved the record labels from extinction. In 2012, digital music sales accounted for over 50 percent of all music revenues for the first time. Yet the music labels make only about 32 cents from a single track download or from a streamed track. In 2012, music label revenues went up slightly for the first time since 2003, and worldwide revenues were $27 billion.

Hollywood has not been similarly disrupted by digital distribution platforms, in part because it is more difficult to download high-quality, pirated copies of full-length movies. To avoid the fate of the music industry, Hollywood has struck lucrative distribution deals with Netflix, Google, Amazon, and Apple, making it convenient to download and pay for high quality movies. Nevertheless, these arrangements are not enough to compensate entirely for the loss in DVD sales, which fell 50 percent from 2006 to 2012, although this is changing rapidly as the online distributors like Netflix are forced to pay billions for high-quality Hollywood content. In 2013, for the first time, consumers will view more and pay more for Web-based movie downloads, rentals, and streams than for DVDs or related physical products. As with television, the demand for feature-length Hollywood movies appears to be expanding in part because of the growth of smartphones and tablets making it easier to watch movies in more locations. In addition, the surprising resurgence of music videos, led by the Web site VEVO, is attracting millions of younger viewers on smartphones and tablets. Online movies began a growth spurt in 2010 as broadband services spread throughout the country. In 2011, movie viewing doubled in a single year. In 2013, about 73 million Internet users are expected to view movies, about one-third of the adult Internet audience. Online movie viewing is growing faster than all other video viewing (which includes TV shows). While this rapid growth will not continue forever, there is little doubt that the Internet is becoming a movie distribution channel that rivals cable television, and someday may replace cable television entirely. Table 10.4 describes digital goods and how they differ from traditional physical goods.

10.2 E-commerce: Business and Technology

E-commerce has grown from a few advertisements on early Web portals in 1995 to over 9 percent of all retail sales in 2013 (an estimated $419 billion), surpassing the mail order catalog

TABLE 10.4

How the Internet
Changes the Markets
for Digital Goods

	Digital Goods	Traditional Goods
Marginal cost/unit	Zero	Greater than zero , high
Cost of production	High (most of the cost)	Variable
Copying cost	Approximately zero	Greater than zero, high
Distributed delivery cost	Low	High
Inventory cost	Low	High
Marketing cost	Variable	Variable
Pricing	More variable (bundling, random pricing games)	Fixed, based on unit costs

business. E-commerce is a fascinating combination of business models and new information technologies. Let's start with a basic understanding of the types of e-commerce, and then describe e-commerce business and revenue models. We'll also cover new technologies that help companies reach over 189 million online shoppers in the United States, and an estimated 2.6 billion more worldwide.

TYPES OF E-COMMERCE

There are many ways to classify electronic commerce transactions—one is by looking at the nature of the participants. The three major electronic commerce categories are business-to-consumer (B2C) e-commerce, business-to-business (B2B) e-commerce, and consumer-to-consumer (C2C) e-commerce.

- **Business-to-consumer (B2C)** electronic commerce involves retailing products and services to individual shoppers. BarnesandNoble.com, which sells books, software, and music to individual consumers, is an example of B2C e-commerce.
- **Business-to-business (B2B)** electronic commerce involves sales of goods and services among businesses. ChemConnect's Web site for buying and selling chemicals and plastics is an example of B2B e-commerce.
- **Consumer-to-consumer (C2C)** electronic commerce involves consumers selling directly to consumers. For example, eBay, the giant Web auction site, enables people to sell their goods to other consumers by auctioning their merchandise off to the highest bidder, or for a fixed price. Craigslist is the most widely used platform used by consumers to buy from and sell directly to others.

Another way of classifying electronic commerce transactions is in terms of the platforms used by participants in a transaction. Until recently, most e-commerce transactions took place using a personal computer connected to the Internet over wired networks. Several wireless mobile alternatives have emerged: smartphones, tablet computers like iPads, dedicated e-readers like the Kindle, and smartphones and small tablet computers using Wi-Fi wireless networks. The use of handheld wireless devices for purchasing goods and services from any location is termed **mobile commerce** or **m-commerce**. Both business-to-business and business-to-consumer e-commerce transactions can take place using m-commerce technology, which we discuss in detail in Section 10.3.

E-COMMERCE BUSINESS MODELS

Changes in the economics of information described earlier have created the conditions for entirely new business models to appear, while destroying older business models. Table 10.5 describes some of the most important Internet business models that have emerged. All, in one way or another, use the Internet to add extra value to existing products and services or to provide the foundation for new products and services.

Portal

Portals are gateways to the Web, and are often defined as those sites which users set as their home page. Some definitions of a portal include search engines like Google and Bing even if few make these sites their home page. Portals such as Yahoo, Facebook, MSN, and AOL offer powerful Web search tools as well as an integrated package of content and services, such as news, e-mail, instant messaging, maps, calendars, shopping, music downloads, video streaming, and more, all in one place. Initially, portals were primarily "gateways" to the Internet. Today, however, the portal business model provides a destination site where users start their Web searching and linger to read news, find entertainment, meet other people, and, of course, be exposed to advertising which provides the revenues to support the portal. Portals generate revenue primarily by attracting very large audiences, charging advertisers for ad placement, collecting referral fees for steering customers to other sites, and charging for premium services. In 2013, portals (not including Google or Bing) generated an estimated $17.5 billion in display ad revenues. Although there are hundreds of portal/search engine sites, the top four portals

TABLE 10.5

Internet Business Models

Category	Description	Examples
E-tailer	Sells physical products directly to consumers or to individual businesses.	Amazon RedEnvelope.com
Transaction broker	Saves users money and time by processing online sales transactions and generating a fee each time a transaction occurs.	ETrade.com Expedia
Market creator	Provides a digital environment where buyers and sellers can meet, search for products, display products, and establish prices for those products. Can serve consumers or B2B e-commerce, generating revenue from transaction fees.	eBay Priceline.com Exostar Elemica
Content provider	Creates revenue by providing digital content, such as news, music, photos, or video, over the Web. The customer may pay to access the content, or revenue may be generated by selling advertising space.	WSJ.com GettyImages.com iTunes.com Games.com
Community provider	Provides an online meeting place where people with similar interests can communicate and find useful information.	Facebook Google+ iVillage, Twitter
Portal	Provides initial point of entry to the Web along with specialized content and other services.	Yahoo Bing Google
Service provider	Provides Web 2.0 applications such as photo sharing, video sharing, and user-generated content as services. Provides other services such as online data storage and backup.	Google Apps Photobucket.com Dropbox

(Yahoo, Facebook, MSN, and AOL) gather more than 95 percent of the Internet portal traffic because of their superior brand recognition (eMarketer, 2013e).

E-tailer

Online retail stores, often called **e-tailers**, come in all sizes, from giant Amazon with 2011 revenues of more than $60 billion, to tiny local stores that have Web sites. An e-tailer is similar to the typical bricks-and-mortar storefront, except that customers only need to connect to the Internet to check their inventory and place an order. Altogether, online retail will generate about $258 billion in revenues for 2013. The value proposition of e-tailers is to provide convenient, low-cost shopping 24/7, offering large selections and consumer choice. Some e-tailers, such as Walmart.com or Staples.com, referred to as "bricks-and-clicks," are subsidiaries or divisions of existing physical stores and carry the same products. Others, however, operate only in the virtual world, without any ties to physical locations. Amazon, BlueNile.com, and Drugstore.com are examples of this type of e-tailer. Several other variations of e-tailers—such as online versions of direct mail catalogs, online malls, and manufacturer-direct online sales—also exist.

Content Provider

While e-commerce began as a retail product channel, it has increasingly turned into a global content channel. "Content" is defined broadly to include all forms of intellectual property. **Intellectual property** refers to all forms of human expression that can be put into a tangible medium such as text, CDs, or DVDs, or stored on any digital (or other) media, including the Web. Content providers distribute information content, such as digital video, music, photos, text, and artwork, over the Web. The value proposition of online content providers is that consumers can find a wide range of content online, conveniently, and purchase this content inexpensively, to be played, or viewed, on multiple computer devices or smartphones.

Providers do not have to be the creators of the content (although sometimes they are, like Disney.com), and are more likely to be Internet-based distributors of content produced and created by others. For example, Apple sells music tracks at its iTunes Store, but it does not create or commission new music.

The phenomenal popularity of the iTunes Store, and Apple's Internet-connected devices like the iPhone, iPod, and iPad, have enabled new forms of digital content delivery from podcasting to mobile streaming. **Podcasting** is a method of publishing audio or video broadcasts via the Internet, allowing subscribing users to download audio or video files onto their personal computers or portable music players. **Streaming** is a publishing method for music and video files that flows a continuous stream of content to a user's device without being stored locally on the device.

Estimates vary, but total download, streaming, and subscription media revenues for 2012 are estimated at $19 billion annually. They are the fastest growing segment within e-commerce, growing at an estimated 20 percent annual rate.

Transaction Broker

Sites that process transactions for consumers normally handled in person, by phone, or by mail are transaction brokers. The largest industries using this model are financial services and travel services. The online transaction broker's primary value propositions are savings of money and time, as well as providing an extraordinary inventory of financial products and travel packages, in a single location. Online stock brokers and travel booking services charge fees that are considerably less than traditional versions of these services. Fidelity Financial Services, and Expedia, are the largest online financial and travel service firms based on a transaction broker model.

Market Creator

Market creators build a digital environment in which buyers and sellers can meet, display products, search for products, and establish prices. The value proposition of online market creators is that they provide a platform where sellers can easily display their wares and where purchasers can buy directly from sellers. Online auction markets like eBay and Priceline are good examples of the market creator business model. Another example is Amazon's Merchants platform (and similar programs at eBay) where merchants are allowed to set up stores on Amazon's Web site and sell goods at fixed prices to consumers. This is reminiscent of open air markets where the market creator operates a facility (a town square) where merchants and consumers meet. Crowdsource funding markets like Kickstarter. com and Mosaic Inc. bring together private equity investors and entrepreneurs in a funding marketplace (Cardwell, 2013). Both are examples of B2B financial market places.

Service Provider

While e-tailers sell products online, service providers offer services online. There's been an explosion in online services. Web 2.0 applications, photo sharing, and online sites for data backup and storage all use a service provider business model. Software is no longer a physical product with a CD in a box, but increasingly software as a service (SaaS) that you subscribe to online rather than purchase from a retailer, or an app that you download. Google has led the way in developing online software service applications such as Google Apps, Google Sites, Gmail, and online data storage services. Salesforce.com is a major provider of cloud-based software for customer management.

Community Provider (Social Networks)

Community providers are sites that create a digital online environment where people with similar interests can transact (buy and sell goods); share interests, photos, videos;

communicate with like-minded people; receive interest-related information; and even play out fantasies by adopting online personalities called avatars. The social networking sites Facebook, Google+, Tumblr, LinkedIn, and Twitter; online communities such as iVillage; and hundreds of other smaller, niche sites such as Doostang and Sportsvite all offer users community-building tools and services. Social networking sites have been the fastest growing Web sites in recent years, often doubling their audience size in a year. However, they are struggling to achieve profitability.

E-COMMERCE REVENUE MODELS

A firm's **revenue model** describes how the firm will earn revenue, generate profits, and produce a superior return on investment. Although there are many different e-commerce revenue models that have been developed, most companies rely on one, or some combination, of the following six revenue models: advertising, sales, subscription, free/freemium, transaction fee, and affiliate.

Advertising Revenue Model

In the **advertising revenue model**, a Web site generates revenue by attracting a large audience of visitors who can then be exposed to advertisements. The advertising model is the most widely used revenue model in e-commerce, and arguably, without advertising revenues, the Web would be a vastly different experience from what it is now. Content on the Web—everything from news to videos and opinions—is "free" to visitors because advertisers pay the production and distribution costs in return for the right to expose visitors to ads. Companies will spend an estimated $42 billion on online advertising in 2013, (in the form of a paid message on a Web site, paid search listing, video, app, game, or other online medium, such as instant messaging). About $8 billion of this will involve spending for mobile ads, the fastest growing ad platform. In the last five years, advertisers have increased online spending and cut outlays on traditional channels such as radio and newspapers. In 2013, online advertising will grow at 14 percent and constitute about 25 percent of all advertising in the United States. Television advertising has also expanded along with online advertising revenues and remains the largest advertising platform with about $66 billion in ad revenues in 2013 (eMarketer, 2013e).

Web sites with the largest viewership or that attract a highly specialized, differentiated viewership and are able to retain user attention ("stickiness") are able to charge higher advertising rates. Yahoo, for instance, derives nearly all its revenue from display ads (banner ads) and to a lesser extent search engine text ads. Ninety-five percent of Google's revenue derives from advertising, including selling keywords (AdWord), selling ad spaces (AdSense), and selling display ad spaces to advertisers (DoubleClick). Facebook will display one-third of the trillion display ads shown on all sites in 2013. Facebook's users spend an average of over 6 hours a week on the site, far longer than any of the other portal sites.

Sales Revenue Model

In the **sales revenue model**, companies derive revenue by selling goods, information, or services to customers. Companies such as Amazon (which sells books, music, and other products), LLBean.com, and Gap.com, all have sales revenue models. Content providers make money by charging for downloads of entire files such as music tracks (iTunes Store) or books or for downloading music and/or video streams (Hulu.com TV shows). Apple has pioneered and strengthened the acceptance of micropayments. **Micropayment systems** provide content providers with a cost-effective method for processing high volumes of very small monetary transactions (anywhere from 25 cents to $5.00 per transaction). The largest micropayment system on the Web is Apple's iTunes Store, which has more than 400 million credit customers who frequently purchase individual music tracks for 99 cents. MyMISLab™ has a Learning Track with more detail on micropayment and other e-commerce payment systems.

Subscription Revenue Model

In the **subscription revenue model**, a Web site offering content or services charges a subscription fee for access to some or all of its offerings on an ongoing basis. Content providers often use this revenue model. For instance, the online version of *Consumer Reports* provides access to premium content, such as detailed ratings, reviews, and recommendations, only to subscribers, who have a choice of paying a $6.95 monthly subscription fee or a $30.00 annual fee. Netflix is one of the most successful subscriber sites with more that 30 million subscribers in September 2013. The Wall Street Journal has the largest online subscription newspaper with more than 1.2 million online subscribers, followed by the New York Times with 800,000 paid digital only subscriptions. To be successful, the subscription model requires that the content be perceived as having high added value, differentiated, and not readily available elsewhere nor easily replicated. Companies successfully offering content or services online on a subscription basis include Match.com and eHarmony (dating services), Ancestry.com and Genealogy.com (genealogy research), Microsoft's Xbox Live, and Pandora.com (music).

Free/Freemium Revenue Model

In the **free/freemium revenue model**, firms offer basic services or content for free, while charging a premium for advanced or special features. For example, Google offers free applications but charges for premium services. Pandora, the subscription radio service, offers a free service with limited play time and advertising, and a premium service with unlimited play (see the Interactive Session on Organizations). The Flickr photo-sharing service offers free basic services for sharing photos with friends and family, and also sells a $24.95 "premium" package that provides users unlimited storage, high-definition video storage and playback, and freedom from display advertising. Spotify music service also uses a fremium business model. The idea is to attract very large audiences with free services, and then to convert some of this audience to pay a subscription for premium services. One problem with this model is converting people from being "free loaders" into paying customers. "Free" can be a powerful model for losing money. None of the fremium music streaming sites have earned a profit to date.

Transaction Fee Revenue Model

In the **transaction fee revenue model**, a company receives a fee for enabling or executing a transaction. For example, eBay provides an online auction marketplace and receives a small transaction fee from a seller if the seller is successful in selling an item. E*Trade, an online stockbroker, receives transaction fees each time it executes a stock transaction on behalf of a customer. The transaction revenue model enjoys wide acceptance in part because the true cost of using the platform is not immediately apparent to the user.

Affiliate Revenue Model

In the **affiliate revenue model**, Web sites (called "affiliate Web sites") send visitors to other Web sites in return for a referral fee or percentage of the revenue from any resulting sales. Referral fees are also referred to as "lead generation fees." For example, MyPoints makes money by connecting companies to potential customers by offering special deals to its members. When members take advantage of an offer and make a purchase, they earn "points" they can redeem for free products and services, and MyPoints receives a referral fee. Community feedback sites such as Epinions and Yelp receive much of their revenue from steering potential customers to Web sites where they make a purchase. Amazon uses affiliates who steer business to the Amazon Web site by placing the Amazon logo on their blogs. Personal blogs often contain display ads as a part of affiliate programs. Some bloggers are paid directly by manufacturers, or receive free products, for speaking highly of products and providing links to sales channels.

INTERACTIVE SESSION: ORGANIZATIONS   Can Pandora Succeed with Freemium?

Pandora is the Internet's most successful subscription radio service. In 2013, Pandora had 71 million users. It has been adding more than 1 million new subscribers a week—that's one new subscriber every second. Pandora accounts for more than 70 percent of all Internet radio listening hours. The music is delivered to users from a cloud server, and is not stored on user devices.

It's easy to see why Pandora is so popular. Users are able to hear only the music they like. Each user selects a genre of music based on a favorite musician or vocalist, and a computer algorithm puts together a "personal radio station" that plays the music of the selected artist plus closely-related music by different artists. Users do not control what they hear, and cannot repeat a selection. The algorithm uses more than 400 factors to help classify songs. Like Taylor Swift? You can create a radio station on Pandora with Taylor Swift as the artist and you can listen all day to some Taylor Swift tracks as well as to musically-related artists such as Carrie Underwood, Rascal Flatts, and Anna Nalick.

People love Pandora, but the question is whether this popularity can be translated into profits. How can Pandora compete with other online music subscription services and online stations that have been making music available for free, sometimes without advertising? "Free" illegally-downloaded music has also been a significant factor, as was iTunes, charging 99 cents per song with no ad support. At the time of Pandora's founding (2005), iTunes was already a roaring success.

Pandora's first business model was to give away 10 hours of free music and then ask subscribers to pay $36 per month for a year once they used up their 10 free hours. Result: 100,000 people listened to their 10 hours for free and then refused to pay for the annual service.

Facing financial collapse, in November 2005, Pandora introduced an ad-supported option. Subscribers could listen to a maximum of 40 hours of music in a calendar month for free. After the 40 hours were used up, subscribers had three choices: (a) pay 99 cents for the rest of the month; (b) sign up for a premium service offering unlimited usage; or (c) do nothing. If they chose (c), the music would stop, but users could sign up again the next month. The ad-supported business model was a risky move because Pandora had no ad server or accounting system, but it attracted so many users that Pandora was able to line up enough advertisers (including Apple) to pay for their infrastructure.

In 2006, Pandora added a "Buy" button to each song being played and struck deals with Amazon, iTunes, and other online retail sites. Pandora now gets an affiliate fee for directing listeners to Amazon where users can buy the music. In 2008, Pandora added an iPhone app to allow users to sign up from their smartphones and listen all day if they wanted. This added 35,000 new users a day. By 2009, this "free" ad-supported model had attracted 20 million users. After struggling for years showing nothing but losses, Pandora finally gained some breathing room.

In late 2009, the company launched Pandora One, a premium service that offered no advertising, higher quality streaming music, a desktop app, and fewer usage limits. The service cost $36 per year. By July 2010, this premium service had 600,000 subscribers, about 1 percent of Pandora's 60 million users. At the end of 2009, Pandora reported $55 million in annual revenue mostly from ads, with the remainder coming from subscriptions and payments when people bought music from iTunes and Amazon. In 2010, revenue more than doubled to $137 million, with about $120 million coming from advertising, and $18 million from subscriptions. For 2012, revenue again doubled to $274 million, with about 87 ($239 million) percent coming from advertising and the rest from subscriptions and other sources.

As impressive as these numbers are, Pandora (along with the other streaming subscription services) has yet to show a profit. It is unclear if streaming music is a viable business model for the recorded music industry. There are infrastructure costs and royalties to pay for content from the music labels. Pandora's royalty rates are less flexible than those of its competitor Spotify, which signed individual song royalty agreements with each record label, and Pandora could be paying even higher rates when its current royalty contracts expire in 2015. About 61 percent of Pandora's revenue is currently allocated to paying royalties, a rate comparable to music download stores and other subscription services. However, under Pandora's royalty arrangements, the more music Pandora customers listen to, the more the company must pay out in royalties—royalty costs are not fixed.

Pandora's user base is huge, representing 7 percent of the total radio listening audience, but only a small percentage (about 2 percent) choose to pay for subscriptions. The vast majority continue to opt for the free service with ads. Nearly 90 percent of Pandora's total revenue comes from advertising. Advertising can only be leveraged so far, because users who opt for free ad-supported services generally do not tolerate heavy ad loads. Investors have nevertheless poured money into

Pandora and Spotify hoping that their large audiences can be monetized. And Apple has announced its new iTunes radio service for the Fall of 2013 that will compete directly with Pandora. ITunes radio has both free ad-supported options, and a subscription service for $25 per year, undercutting Pandora's annual fee of $36.

Pandora is a leading example of the "freemium" revenue business model, in which a business gives away some services for free and relies on a small percentage of customers to pay for premium versions of the same service. If a market is very large, getting just 1 percent of that market to pay could be very lucrative—under certain circumstances. Although freemium is an efficient way of amassing a large group of potential customers, companies, including Pandora, have found that it's a challenge to convert people enjoying the free service into customers willing to pay. A freemium model works best when a business incurs very low marginal cost, approaching zero, for each free user of its services, when a business can be supported by the percentage of customers willing to pay, and when there are other revenues like advertising fees that can make up for shortfalls in subscriber revenues. Is this enough for Pandora's business model to succeed?

Sources: Glenn Peoples, "Pandora's Business Model: Is It Sustainable?" Billboard.com, August 7, 2013; Kylie Bylin, "Can Pandora Find A Business Model That Works?"Hypebot.com, accessed August 25, 2013; Paul Verna, "Internet Radio: Marketers Move In," *eMarketer*, February 2013;Jim Edwards, "This Crucial Detail In Spotify's Business Model Could Kill Pandora," Business Insider, July 11, 2012; Sarah E. Needleman and Angus Loten, "When Freemium Fails," *Wall Street Journal*, August 22, 2012; and Kenneth C. Laudon and Carol Guercio Traver, *E-Commerce 2013* (2013).

CASE STUDY QUESTIONS

1. Analyze Pandora using the value chain and competitive forces models. What competitive forces does the company have to deal with? What is its customer value proposition?

2. Explain how Pandora's "freemium" business model works. How does the company generate revenue?

3. Can Pandora succeed with its "freemium" model? Why or why not? What people, organization, and technology factors affect its success with this business model?

SOCIAL NETWORKING AND THE WISDOM OF CROWDS

One of the fastest growing areas of e-commerce revenues are social networking services, where people can meet their friends and their friends' friends. Every day over 124 million Internet users in the United States visit a social networking site like Facebook, Google+, Tumblr, MySpace, LinkedIn, and hundreds of others.

Social networking sites link people through their mutual business or personal connections, enabling them to mine their friends (and their friends' friends) for sales leads, job-hunting tips, or new friends. Google+, MySpace, Facebook, and Friendster appeal to people who are primarily interested in extending their friendships, while LinkedIn focuses on job networking for professionals.

At **social shopping** sites like Pinterest, Kaboodle, ThisNext, and Stylehive, you can swap shopping ideas with friends. Facebook offers the Like button and Google the +1 button to let your friends know you admire something, and in some cases, purchased something online. Online communities are also ideal venues to employ viral marketing techniques. Online viral marketing is like traditional word-of-mouth marketing except that the word can spread across an online community at the speed of light, and go much further geographically than a small network of friends.

The Wisdom of Crowds

Creating sites where thousands, even millions, of people can interact offers business firms new ways to market and advertise, and to discover who likes (or hates) their products. In a phenomenon called "the **wisdom of crowds**," some argue that large numbers of people can make better decisions about a wide range of topics or products than a single person or even a small committee of experts (Surowiecki, 2004).

Obviously this is not always the case, but it can happen in interesting ways. In marketing, the wisdom of crowds concept suggests that firms should consult with thousands of their customers first as a way of establishing a relationship with them, and second, to better understand how their products and services are used and appreciated (or rejected). Actively soliciting the comments of your customers builds trust and sends the message to your customers that you care what they are thinking, and that you need their advice.

Beyond merely soliciting advice, firms can be actively helped in solving some business problems using what is called **crowdsourcing**. For instance, in 2006, Netflix announced a contest in which it offered to pay $1 million to the person or team who comes up with a method for improving by 10 percent Netflix's prediction of what movies customers would like as measured against their actual choices. By 2009, Netflix received 44,014 entries from 5,169 teams in 186 countries. The winning team improved a key part of Netflix's business: a recommender system that recommends to its customers what new movies to order based on their personal past movie choices and the choices of millions of other customers who are like them (Howe, 2008; Resnick and Varian, 1997). By 2013, Netflix had attracted 30 million subscribers to its streaming service. In 2012, BMW launched a crowdsourcing project to enlist the aid of customers in designing an urban vehicle for 2025. Kickstarter.com is arguably one of the most famous e-commerce crowd funding sites where visitors invest in start-up companies. Other examples include Caterpillar working with customers to design better machinery, and Pepsico using Super Bowl 2013 viewers to build an online video (Boulton, 2013).

Firms can also use the wisdom of crowds in the form of prediction markets. **Prediction markets** are established as peer-to-peer betting markets where participants make bets on specific outcomes of, say, quarterly sales of a new product, designs for new products, or political elections. The world's largest commercial prediction market is Betfair, where you bet for or against specific outcomes on football games, horse races, and whether or not the Dow Jones will go up or down in a single day. Iowa Electronic Markets (IEM) is an academic market focused on elections. You can place bets on the outcome of local and national elections. In the United States, the largest prediction market is Intrade.com, where users can buy or sell shares in predictions.

E-COMMERCE MARKETING: SOCIAL, MOBILE, LOCAL

While e-commerce and the Internet have changed entire industries and enabled new business models, no industry has been more affected than marketing and marketing communications.

The Internet provides marketers with new ways of identifying and communicating with millions of potential customers at costs far lower than traditional media, including search engine marketing, data mining, recommender systems, and targeted e-mail. The Internet enables **long tail marketing**. Before the Internet, reaching a large audience was very expensive, and marketers had to focus on attracting the largest number of consumers with popular hit products, whether music, Hollywood movies, books, or cars. In contrast, the Internet allows marketers to inexpensively find potential customers for products where demand is very low. For instance, the Internet makes it possible to sell independent music profitably to very small audiences. There's always some demand for almost any product. Put a string of such long tail sales together and you have a profitable business.

The Internet also provides new ways—often instantaneous and spontaneous—to gather information from customers, adjust product offerings, and increase customer value. Table 10.6 describes the leading marketing and advertising formats used in e-commerce.

Many e-commerce marketing firms use behavioral targeting techniques to increase the effectiveness of banners, rich media, and video ads. **Behavioral targeting** refers to tracking the clickstreams (history of clicking behavior) of individuals on thousands of Web

Marketing Format	2013 Revenue	Description
Search engine	$19.5	Text ads targeted at precisely what the customer is looking for at the moment of shopping and purchasing. Sales oriented.
Display ads	$8.7	Banner ads (pop-ups and leave-behinds) with interactive features; increasingly behaviorally targeted to individual Web activity. Brand development and sales. Includes blog display ads.
Video	$4.1	Fastest growing format, engaging and entertaining; behaviorally targeted, interactive. Branding and sales.
Classified	$2.7	Job, real estate, and services ads; interactive, rich media, and personalized to user searches. Sales and branding.
Rich media	$2	Animations, games, and puzzles. Interactive, targeted, and entertaining. Branding orientation.
Lead generation	$1.9	Marketing firms that gather sales and marketing leads online, and then sell them to online marketers for a variety of campaign types. Sales or branding orientation.
Sponsorships	$1.9	Online games, puzzles, contests, and coupon sites sponsored by firms to promote products. Sales orientation.
E-mail	$.22	Effective, targeted marketing tool with interactive and rich media potential. Sales oriented.

TABLE 10.6

Online marketing and advertising formats (billions)

sites for the purpose of understanding their interests and intentions, and exposing them to advertisements that are uniquely suited to their behavior. Proponents believe this more precise understanding of the customer leads to more efficient marketing (the firm pays for ads only to those shoppers who are most interested in their products) and larger sales and revenues. Unfortunately, behavioral targeting of millions of Web users also leads to the invasion of personal privacy without user consent. When consumers lose trust in their Web experience, they tend not to purchase anything.

Behavioral targeting takes place at two levels: at individual Web sites and on various advertising networks that track users across thousands of Web sites. All Web sites collect data on visitor browser activity and store it in a database. They have tools to record the site that users visited prior to coming to the Web site, where these users go when they leave that site, the type of operating system they use, browser information, and even some location data. They also record the specific pages visited on the particular site, the time spent on each page of the site, the types of pages visited, and what the visitors purchased (see Figure 10.3). Firms analyze this information about customer interests and behavior to develop precise profiles of existing and potential customers. In addition, most major Web sites have hundreds of tracking programs on their home pages, which track your clickstream behavior across the Web by following you from site to site and re-target ads to you by showing you the same ads on different sites. The leading online advertising networks are Google's DoubleClick, Yahoo's RightMedia, and AOL's Ad Network. Ad networks represent publishers who have space to sell, and advertisers who want to market online. The lubricant of this trade is information on millions of Web shoppers, which helps advertisers target their ads to precisely the groups and individuals they desire.

Figure 10.3
Web Site Visitor
Tracking
*E-commerce Web
sites and advertising
platforms like Google's
DoubleClick have tools
to track a shopper's
every step through an
online store and then
across the Web as shop-
pers move from site to
site. Close examination
of customer behavior
at a Web site selling
women's clothing shows
what the store might
learn at each step and
what actions it could
take to increase sales.*

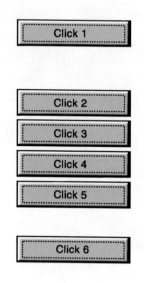

The shopper clicks on the home page. The store can tell that the shopper arrived from the Yahoo! portal at 2:30 PM (which might help determine staffing for customer service centers) and how long she lingered on the home page (which might indicate trouble navigating the site). Tracking beacons load cookies on the shopper's browser to follow her across the Web.

The shopper clicks on blouses, clicks to select a woman's white blouse, then clicks to view the same item in pink. The shopper clicks to select this item in a size 10 in pink and clicks to place it in her shopping cart. This information can help the store determine which sizes and colors are most popular. If the visitor moves to a different site, ads for pink blouses will appear from the same or different vendor.

From the shopping cart page, the shopper clicks to close the browser to leave the Web site without purchasing the blouse. This action could indicate the shopper changed her mind or that she had a problem with the Web site's checkout and payment process. Such behavior might signal that the Web site was not well designed.

This information enables firms to understand how well their Web site is working, create unique personalized Web pages that display content or ads for products or services of special interest to each user, improve the customer's experience, and create additional value through a better understanding of the shopper (see Figure 10.4). By using personalization technology to modify the Web pages presented to each customer, marketers achieve some of the benefits of using individual salespeople at dramatically lower costs. For instance, General Motors will show a Chevrolet banner ad to women emphasizing safety and utility, while men will receive different ads emphasizing power and ruggedness.

Figure 10.4
Web Site
Personalization
*Firms can create unique
personalized Web pages
that display content
or ads for products
or services of special
interest to individual
users, improving the
customer experience
and creating additional
value.*

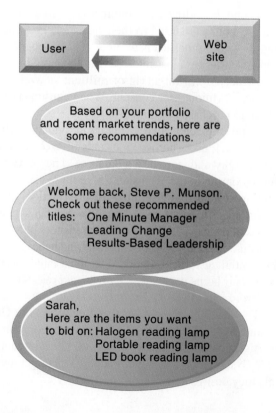

What if you are a large national advertising company with many different clients trying to reach millions of consumers? What if you were a large global manufacturer trying to reach potential consumers for your products? With millions of Web sites, working with each one would be impractical. Advertising networks solve this problem by creating a network of several thousand of the most popular Web sites visited by millions of people, tracking the behavior of these users across the entire network, building profiles of each user, and then selling these profiles to advertisers. Popular Web sites download dozens of Web tracking cookies, bugs, and beacons, which report user online behavior to remote servers without the users' knowledge. Looking for young, single consumers, with college degrees, living in the Northeast, in the 18–34 age range who are interested purchasing a European car? Not a problem. Advertising networks can identify and deliver hundreds of thousands of people who fit this profile and expose them to ads for European cars as they move from one Web site to another. Estimates vary, but behaviorally targeted ads are generally 10 times more likely to produce a consumer response than a randomly chosen banner or video ad (see Figure 10.5). So-called advertising exchanges use this same technology to auction access to people with very specific profiles to advertisers in a few milliseconds. In 2013, about 25 percent of online display ads are targeted, and the rest depend on the context of the pages shoppers visit, the estimated demographics of visitors, or so-called "blast and scatter" advertising, which is placed randomly on any available page with minimal targeting, such as time of day or season. Several surveys have reported that over 75 percent of American consumers do not approve of behaviorally targeted ads.

Two-thirds (68 percent) of Internet users disapprove of search engines and Web sites tracking their online behavior in order to aim targeted ads at them. Twenty-eight percent of those surveyed approve of behavioral targeting because they believe it produces more relevant ads and information (Pew Internet, 2012).

Social E-commerce and Social Network Marketing

Social e-commerce is commerce based on the idea of the digital **social graph**. The digital social graph is a mapping of all significant online social relationships. The social graph is synonymous with the idea of a "social network" used to describe offline relationships. You can map your own social graph (network) by drawing lines from yourself to the 10 closest people you know. If they know one another, draw lines between these people. If you are ambitious, ask these 10 friends to list and draw in the names of the 10 people closest to them. What emerges from this exercise is a preliminary map of your social network. Now imagine

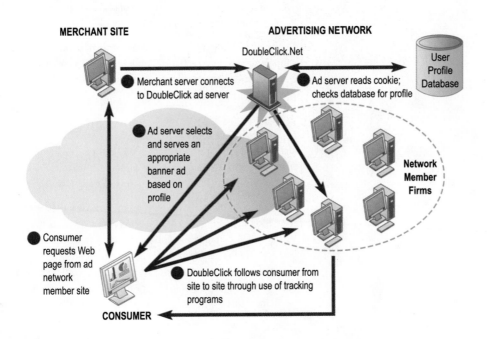

Figure 10.5
How an Advertising Network such as DoubleClick Works
Advertising networks and their use of tracking programs have become controversial among privacy advocates because of their ability to track individual consumers across the Internet.

if everyone on the Internet did the same, and posted the results to a very large database with a Web site. Ultimately, you would end up with Facebook or a site like it. The collection of all these personal social networks is called "the social graph."

According to small world theory, you are only six links away from any other person on earth. If you entered your personal address book, which has, say, 100 names in it, on to a list and sent it to your friends, and they in turn entered 50 new names of their friends, and so on, five times, the social network created would encompass 31 billion people! The social graph is therefore a collection of millions of personal social graphs (and all the people in them). So, it's a small world indeed, and we are all more closely linked than we ever thought.

Ultimately, you will find that you are directly connected to many friends and relatives, and indirectly connected to an even larger universe of indirect friends and relatives (your distant second and third cousins, and their friends). Theoretically, it takes six links for any one person to find another person anywhere on earth.

If you understand the inter-connectedness of people, you will see just how important this concept is to e-commerce: The products and services you buy will influence the decisions of your friends, and their decisions will in turn influence you. If you are a marketer trying to build and strengthen a brand, the implication is clear: Take advantage of the fact that people are enmeshed in social networks, share interests and values, and communicate and influence one another. As a marketer, your target audience is not a million isolated people watching a TV show, but the social network of people who watch the show, and the viewers' personal networks. Table 10.7 describes four features of social commerce that are driving its growth.

In 2013, one of the fastest growing media for branding and marketing is social media. In 2013, companies will spend $44 billion using social networks like Facebook to reach millions of consumers who spend hours a day on the Facebook site. Facebook accounts for 90 percent of all social marketing in the Untied States. Expenditures for social media marketing are much smaller than television, magazines, and even newspapers, but this will change in the future. Social networks in the offline world are collections of people who voluntarily

TABLE 10.7

Features of Social Commerce

Social Commerce Feature	Description
Social sign-on	Web sites allow users to sign into their sites through their social network pages on Facebook or another social site. This allows Web sites to receive valuable social profile information from Facebook and use it in their own marketing efforts.
Collaborative shopping	Creating an environment where consumers can share their shopping experiences with one another by viewing products, chatting, or texting. Friends can chat online about brands, products, and services.
Network notification	Creating an environment where consumers can share their approval (or disapproval) of products, services, or content, or share their geo-location, perhaps a restaurant or club, with friends. Facebook's ubiquitous Like button is an example. Twitter tweets and followers are another example.
Social search (recommendations)	Enabling an environment where consumers can ask their friends for advice on purchases of products, services, and content. While Google can help you find things, social search can help you evaluate the quality of things by listening to the evaluations of your friends, or their friends. For instance, Amazon's social recommender system can use your Facebook social profile to recommend products.

communicate with one another over an extended period of time. Online social networks, such as Facebook, MySpace, LinkedIn, Twitter, Tumblr, and Google+, along with other sites with social components, are Web sites that enable users to communicate with one another, form group and individual relationships, and share interests, values, and ideas. Individuals establish online profiles with text and photos, creating an online profile of how they want others to see them, and then invite their friends to link to their profile. The network grows by word of mouth and through e-mail links. One of the most ubiquitous graphical elements on Web sites is Facebook's Like button, which allows users to tell their friends they like a product, service, or content. Facebook processes around 50 million Likes a day, or 1.5 billion a year.

While Facebook, with 144 million U.S. monthly visitors, receives most of the public attention given to social networking, the other top four social sites are growing very rapidly with the exception of MySpace. LinkedIn has grown 58 percent in 2013 to reach 40 million monthly visitors; Twitter grew 13 percent in 2013 to reach 53 million; the social blogging site Tumblr reached 38 million people a month; and Pinterest hit the top 50 Web sites with 25 million. MySpace, in contrast, has been shrinking but nevertheless attracted 27 million visitors a month in 2013. According to ComScore, about 30 percent of the total time spent online in the United States was spent on social network sites, up from around 8 percent in 2007 (ComScore, 2013). The fastest growing smartphone applications are social network apps: about 30 percent of smartphone users use their phones to visit social sites. More than half of all visits to Facebook in 2013 come from smartphones.

Marketers cannot ignore these huge audiences which rival television and radio in size. In 2013, 77 percent of the U.S. Fortune 500 companies had a Twitter account, 70 percent had a Facebook account, 69 percent had a YouTube account, and 28 percent had a corporate blog. Marketers will spend over $4 billion on social network marketing in 2013 (twice the level of 2012), about 10 percent of all online marketing (eMarketer Inc., 2013e).

Marketing via social media is still in its early stages, and companies are experimenting in hopes of finding a winning formula. Social interactions and customer sentiment are not always easy to manage, presenting new challenges for companies eager to protect their brands. The chapter-ending case study provides specific examples of companies' social marketing efforts using Facebook and Twitter.

B2B E-COMMERCE: NEW EFFICIENCIES AND RELATIONSHIPS

The trade between business firms (business-to-business commerce or B2B) represents a huge marketplace. The total amount of B2B trade in the United States in 2013 is estimated to be about $10.8 trillion, with B2B e-commerce (online B2B) contributing about $4.4 trillion of that amount (U.S. Census Bureau, 2013; authors' estimates). By 2017, B2B e-commerce should grow to about $6.6 trillion in the United States. The process of conducting trade among business firms is complex and requires significant human intervention, and therefore, it consumes significant resources. Some firms estimate that each corporate purchase order for support products costs them, on average, at least $100 in administrative overhead. Administrative overhead includes processing paper, approving purchase decisions, spending time using the telephone and fax machines to search for products and arrange for purchases, arranging for shipping, and receiving the goods. Across the economy, this adds up to trillions of dollars annually being spent for procurement processes that could potentially be automated. If even just a portion of inter-firm trade were automated, and parts of the entire procurement process assisted by the Internet, literally trillions of dollars might be released for more productive uses, consumer prices potentially would fall, productivity would increase, and the economic wealth of the nation would expand. This is the promise of B2B e-commerce. The challenge of B2B e-commerce is changing existing patterns and systems of procurement, and designing and implementing new Internet-based B2B solutions.

Business-to-business e-commerce refers to the commercial transactions that occur among business firms. Increasingly, these transactions are flowing through a variety of different Internet-enabled mechanisms. About 80 percent of online B2B e-commerce is still based on proprietary systems for **electronic data interchange (EDI)**. Electronic data interchange enables the computer-to-computer exchange between two organizations of standard transactions such as invoices, bills of lading, shipment schedules, or purchase orders. Transactions are automatically transmitted from one information system to another through a network, eliminating the printing and handling of paper at one end and the inputting of data at the other. Each major industry in the United States and much of the rest of the world has EDI standards that define the structure and information fields of electronic documents for that industry.

EDI originally automated the exchange of documents such as purchase orders, invoices, and shipping notices. Although many companies still use EDI for document automation, firms engaged in just-in-time inventory replenishment and continuous production use EDI as a system for continuous replenishment. Suppliers have online access to selected parts of the purchasing firm's production and delivery schedules and automatically ship materials and goods to meet prespecified targets without intervention by firm purchasing agents (see Figure 10.6).

Although many organizations still use private networks for EDI, they are increasingly Web-enabled because Internet technology provides a much more flexible and low-cost platform for linking to other firms. Businesses are able to extend digital technology to a wider range of activities and broaden their circle of trading partners.

Take procurement, for example. Procurement involves not only purchasing goods and materials but also sourcing, negotiating with suppliers, paying for goods, and making delivery arrangements. Businesses can now use the Internet to locate the lowest-cost supplier, search online catalogs of supplier products, negotiate with suppliers, place orders, make payments, and arrange transportation. They are not limited to partners linked by traditional EDI networks.

The Internet and Web technology enable businesses to create new electronic storefronts for selling to other businesses with multimedia graphic displays and interactive features similar to those for B2C commerce. Alternatively, businesses can use Internet technology to create extranets or electronic marketplaces for linking to other businesses for purchase and sale transactions.

Private industrial networks typically consist of a large firm using a secure Web site to link to its suppliers and other key business partners (see Figure 10.7). The network is owned by the buyer, and it permits the firm and designated suppliers, distributors, and other business partners to share product design and development, marketing, production scheduling, inventory management, and unstructured communication, including graphics and e-mail. Another term for a private industrial network is a **private exchange**.

An example is VW Group Supply, which links the Volkswagen Group and its suppliers. VW Group Supply handles 90 percent of all global purchasing for Volkswagen, including all automotive and parts components.

Net marketplaces, which are sometimes called e-hubs, provide a single, digital marketplace based on Internet technology for many different buyers and sellers (see Figure 10.8). They are industry owned or operate as independent intermediaries between buyers and sellers. Net marketplaces generate revenue from purchase and sale transactions and other services provided to clients. Participants in Net marketplaces can establish prices through online negotiations, auctions, or requests for quotations, or they can use fixed prices.

Figure 10.6
Electronic Data Interchange (EDI)
Companies use EDI to automate transactions for B2B e-commerce and continuous inventory replenishment. Suppliers can automatically send data about shipments to purchasing firms. The purchasing firms can use EDI to provide production and inventory requirements and payment data to suppliers.

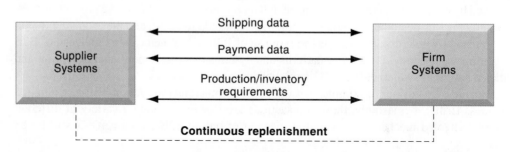

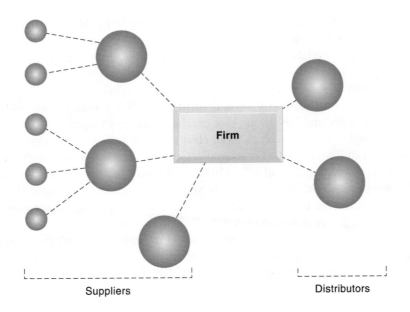

Figure 10.7
A Private Industrial Network
A private industrial network, also known as a private exchange, links a firm to its suppliers, distributors, and other key business partners for efficient supply chain management and other collaborative commerce activities.

Suppliers   Distributors

There are many different types of Net marketplaces and ways of classifying them. Some Net marketplaces sell direct goods and some sell indirect goods. **Direct goods** are goods used in a production process, such as sheet steel for auto body production. **Indirect goods** are all other goods not directly involved in the production process, such as office supplies or products for maintenance and repair. Some Net marketplaces support contractual purchasing based on long-term relationships with designated suppliers, and others support short-term spot purchasing, where goods are purchased based on immediate needs, often from many different suppliers.

Some Net marketplaces serve vertical markets for specific industries, such as automobiles, telecommunications, or machine tools, whereas others serve horizontal markets for goods and services that can be found in many different industries, such as office equipment or transportation.

Exostar is an example of an industry-owned Net marketplace, focusing on long-term contract purchasing relationships and on providing common networks and computing platforms for reducing supply chain inefficiencies. This aerospace and defense

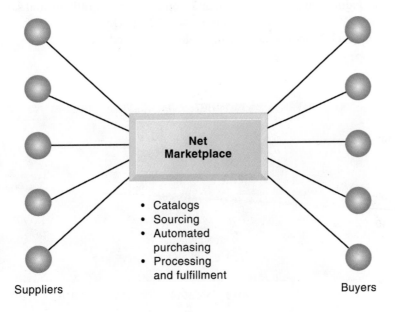

Figure 10.8
A Net Marketplace
Net marketplaces are online marketplaces where multiple buyers can purchase from multiple sellers.

- Catalogs
- Sourcing
- Automated purchasing
- Processing and fulfillment

Suppliers   Buyers

industry-sponsored Net marketplace was founded jointly by BAE Systems, Boeing, Lockheed Martin, Raytheon, and Rolls-Royce plc to connect these companies to their suppliers and facilitate collaboration. More than 70,000 trading partners in the commercial, military, and government sectors use Exostar's sourcing, e-procurement, and collaboration tools for both direct and indirect goods.

Exchanges are independently owned third-party Net marketplaces that connect thousands of suppliers and buyers for spot purchasing. Many exchanges provide vertical markets for a single industry, such as food, electronics, or industrial equipment, and they primarily deal with direct inputs. For example, Go2Paper enables a spot market for paper, board, and craft among buyers and sellers in the paper industries from over 75 countries.

Exchanges proliferated during the early years of e-commerce but many have failed. Suppliers were reluctant to participate because the exchanges encouraged competitive bidding that drove prices down and did not offer any long-term relationships with buyers or services to make lowering prices worthwhile. Many essential direct purchases are not conducted on a spot basis because they require contracts and consideration of issues such as delivery timing, customization, and quality of products.

10.3 Mobile E-commerce and Local E-commerce

Walk down the street in any major metropolitan area and count how many people are pecking away at their iPhones, Samsungs or BlackBerrys. Ride the trains, fly the planes, and you'll see your fellow travelers reading an online newspaper, watching a video on their phone, or reading a novel on their Kindle. In five years, the majority of Internet users in the United States will rely on mobile devices as their primary device for accessing the Internet. As the mobile audience expands in leaps and bounds, mobile advertising and M-commerce have taken off.

In 2013, m-commerce represented about 10 percent of all e-commerce, with about $38 billion in annual revenues generated by retail goods and services, apps, advertising, music, videos, ring tones, applications, movies, television, and location-based services like local restaurant locators and traffic updates. However, m-commerce is the fastest growing form of e-commerce, with some areas expanding at a rate of 50 percent or more per year, and is estimated to grow to $108 billion in 2017 (see Figure 10.9). It is becoming especially popular in the online travel industry, as discussed in the Interactive Session on Technology. In 2013, there were an estimated 4 billion cell phone users worldwide, with over 1 billion in China and 246 million in the United States (eMarketer, 2013g (M-commerce sales); eMarketer, 2013h (mobile phone users)).

The main areas of growth in mobile e-commerce are retail sales at the top Mobile 400 companies, including Amazon ($4 billion) and Apple (about $1.1 billion); and sales of digital content music, TV shows and movies (about $4 billion) (Internet Retailer, 2013). These estimates do not include mobile advertising or location-based services.

Figure 10.9
Consolidated Mobile Commerce Revenues

Mobile e-commerce is the fastest growing type of B2C e-commerce although it represents only a small part of all e-commerce in 2013.

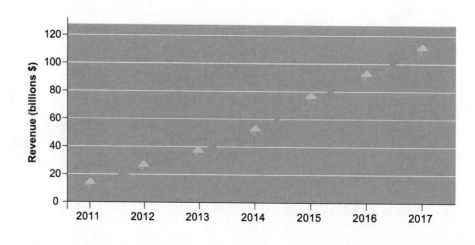

M-commerce applications have taken off for services that are time-critical, that appeal to people on the move, or that accomplish a task more efficiently than other methods. The Interactive Session on Technology describes how m-commerce is benefiting the online travel industry and the following sections provide other examples.

LOCATION-BASED SERVICES AND APPLICATIONS

Location-based services include geosocial services, geoadvertising, and geoinformation services. Seventy-four percent of smartphone owners use location-based services. What ties these activities together and is the foundation for mobile commerce is the global positioning system (GPS) enabled map services available on smartphones. A **geosocial service** can tell you where your friends are meeting. **Geoadvertising services** can tell you where to find the nearest Italian restaurant, and **geoinformation services** can tell you the price of a house you are looking at, or about special exhibits at a museum you are passing.

Wikitude.me is an example of a geoinformation service. Wikitude.me provides a special kind of browser for smartphones equipped with a built-in GPS and compass that can identify your precise location and where the phone is pointed. Using information from over 800,000 points of interest available on Wikipedia, plus thousands of other local sites, the browser overlays information about points of interest you are viewing, and displays that information on your smartphone screen, superimposed on a map or photograph that you just snapped. For example, users can point their smartphone cameras towards mountains from a tour bus and see the names and heights of the mountains displayed on the screen. Wikitude.me also allows users to geo-tag the world around them, and then submit the tags to Wikitude in order to share content with other users.

Foursquare, Loopt, and new offerings by Facebook and Google are examples of geosocial services. Geosocial services help you find friends, or be found by your friends, by "checking in" to the service, announcing your presence in a restaurant or other place. Your friends are instantly notified. About 20 percent of smartphone owners use geosocial services. The popularity of specialized sites like Foursquare has waned as Facebook and Google+ have moved into geosocial services and turned them into extensions of their larger social networks.

Loopt had 5 million users in 2013. The service doesn't sell information to advertisers, but does post ads based on user location. Loopt's target is to deal with advertisers at the walking level (within 200 to 250 meters). Foursquare provides a similar location-based social networking service to 22 million registered users, who may connect with friends and update their location. Points are awarded for checking in at designated venues. Users choose to have their check-ins posted on their accounts on Twitter, Facebook, or both. Users also earn badges by checking in at locations with certain tags, for check-in frequency, or for the time of check-in. More than 500,000 local merchants worldwide use the merchant platform for marketing.

Connecting people to local merchants in the form of geoadvertising is the economic foundation for mobile commerce. Mobile advertising reached $7.4 billion in 2013. Geoadvertising sends ads to users based on their GPS locations. Smartphones report their locations back to Google and Apple. Merchants buy access to these consumers when they come within range of a merchant. For instance, Kiehl Stores, a cosmetics retailer, sent special offers and announcements to customers who came within 100 yards of their store.

OTHER MOBILE COMMERCE SERVICES

Banks and credit card companies are rolling out services that let customers manage their accounts from their mobile devices. JPMorgan Chase and Bank of America customers can use their cell phones to check account balances, transfer funds, and pay bills.

Although the mobile advertising market is currently small, it is rapidly growing (up 75 percent from last year and expected to grow to over $22 billion by 2017), as more and more companies seek ways to exploit new databases of location-specific information. The largest providers of mobile display advertising are Apple's iAd platform and Google's AdMob

INTERACTIVE SESSION: TECHNOLOGY   Will Mobile Technology Put Orbitz in the Lead?

When it comes to mobile apps and gauging their impact on consumers and business, the online travel industry and its airline and hotel reservation systems are probably the best place to look. And there's no better company in this industry in developing mobile apps than Orbitz Worldwide Inc. Orbitz connects consumers to plane tickets from 400 airlines, hotel rooms from 80,000 hotels worldwide, as well as rental cars, cruises, and vacation packages.

Orbitz was launched in 2001 by five major airlines—Delta, United, Continental, Northwest, and American, to compete with Internet travel companies such as Priceline, Travelocity, and Expedia, which were upending the travel industry. These companies have remained formidable competitors.

From its very beginning, Orbitz distinguished itself as a leader in mobile technology. In 2006, it became the first Internet travel company to offer a mobile Web site where users could check flight status for 27 airlines, search for hotels in the US and Cancun, Mexico, and access a personal page with itineraries for Orbitz-booked trips.

During the years that followed, Orbiz made many enhancements to its mobile services. It enabled mobile users to view average wait times for airport security lines, locate available Wi-Fi services at airports, compute check-in delays and taxi line wait times, and view weather and traffic conditions. In 2010, Orbitz redesigned its mobile Web site so that users of any Web-enabled device could access capabilities similar to any full-screen e-commerce site, including the ability to purchase flight tickets, book car rentals, and obtain hotel reservations. Like the standard Orbitz Web site, the redesigned mobile site offers a Price Assurance service, which guarantees customers an automatic refund if another Orbitz customer books the same service for less. Orbitz also developed apps that ran on iPhones, iPads and later Android devices that could perform the same functions.

Orbitz went first-to-market with an m-commerce site designed specifically for business users. The opportunity was huge, since most business travelers carry smartphones or tablets. Corporate travelers typically must adhere to company rules specifying preferred vendors, cost limits, mandatory services, and expense documentation. Since each company has its own business "rules" for travel, the Orbitz m-commerce platform needed to be customized for each firm. Orbitz constructed a mobile Web site that could be accessed from any Web-enabled device. The Orbitz for Business mobile Web site delivers the same set of tools enjoyed by the consumer market while incorpo-

rating features that enable business travelers to adhere to company guidelines—the ability to enter and modify the purpose of the trip, search results that give precedence to preferred vendors, and access to company-specific reference data.

In 2011, the m-commerce site was again upgraded to respond to swiping gestures, expedite touch screen transactions, and accommodate the small screen size of any Web-enabled mobile device. Orbitz's new proprietary global online travel agency platform creates mobile HTML5 Web pages on the fly from standard e-commerce Web pages. Mobile users can book vacation packages, view the savings from simultaneously booking a flight and hotel room, and create an online profile linked to their credit card to expedite the checkout process. GPS and improved search capabilities enable consumers to locate nearby hotels and conduct price, distance, and rating comparisons; to compare flights and car rentals based on various criteria, including traveler type; and to access customer reviews. Orbitz also instituted mobile exclusive same-day deals, called Mobile Steals, available both on the m-commerce site and through the Hotels by Orbitz app available for iPhone and Android devices. Proprietors are able to fill rooms that might otherwise remain vacant, and consumers save up to 50 percent of the standard rate. While only 12 to 14 percent of traditional e-commerce Web site shoppers want to reserve a room for the day on which they are searching, smartphone and other mobile users book for the same night between 50 to 60 percent of the time because they are more likely to be traveling and need a room at the last minute.

Orbitz touts the ability to book a hotel room in just three taps. The new mobile Web site has produced a 110 percent increase in visits, a 145 percent increase in the conversion rate, and four times the number of transactions compared to the original Orbitz m-commerce site. Orbitz has been focusing on lodging because hotel bookings are more profitable than airline reservations. Priceline.com, the largest and most profitable online travel agency, generates approximately 90 percent of its sales from hotels. Orbitz only had 27 percent of revenue from hotels in 2011.

Orbitz further enhanced its iOS and Android apps to cut down the number of steps required to search for and make reservations so that the entire process can take place on the mobile device without redirecting the user to hotel, airline, or car rental Web sites to complete the transaction. Orbitz now has apps for the iPhone, IPad, iPod Touch, Kindle Fire, and Android devices.

Does all this investment in mobile technology make a difference? Chris Brown, Orbitz vice president in charge of product strategy, believes that although mobile transactions in 2012 accounted for less than 10 percent of total Orbitz bookings, the ability to be a major player in the rapidly escalating m-commerce market will pay off. Increased transaction speed provided by Orbitz mobile apps will attract new customers, especially those trying to book same-day reservations, which account for about 50 percent of Orbitz's mobile car rental purchases.

But the other online travel players also believe consumers will increasingly move to mobile to make their travel plans, and they also have been making large investments in mobile Web sites, search tools, and apps. Priceline and TripAdvisor have rated highest in providing an engaging, enjoyable experience on their sites, and both continue to enjoy much stronger growth in unique visitors and visits than Expedia and Orbitz. Travelers are increasingly planning trips on sites such as TripAdvisor, which aggregate offerings from a number of different online sources in one place. (TripAdvisor offers more than 100 million traveler reviews and obtains most of its revenue from ads and referrals to other travel sites.) TripAdvisor recently redesigned its Web site to show customers all the rates offered by online agents like Expedia, Priceline, and Travelocity in a single list on its site. By using this "metasearch" capability, customers are able to find the lowest prices on a single screen without having to click on several links.

Sources: Karen Jacobs, "Orbitz Profit Tops Forecasts, Hotel Booking Revenues Up," Reuters, August 8, 2013; Drew Fitzgerald, "Out of Nest, TripAdvisor Soars Past Expedia," *Wall Street Journal*, August 8, 2013; Karl Baker, "Orbitz Falls as CIO Exit Rekindles Hotel Growth Concerns," *Bloomberg Businessweek*, January 10, 2013; Ryan Peckyno, "How Mobile Will Impact Online Travel Companies, Motley Fool, July 29, 2013; Bill Siwicki, "Orbitz Spreads Its 'Mobile Magic' Throughout a Resdesigned M-commerce Site," Internet Retailer, October 10, 2012; Kenneth C. Laudon and Carol GuercioTraver, *E-Commerce 2013*, Pearson Education (2013).

CASE STUDY QUESTIONS

1. How important is mobile technology in Orbitz's business strategy? Why?

2. What people, organization, and technology issues did Orbitz need to address in its mobile strategy?

3. Why are mobile phone users much more likely to book same-day hotel room or airline reservations?

4. What role does Orbitz for Business play in the company's business strategy?

5. How successful is Orbitz's mobile strategy? Explain your answer.

---

platform (both with a 21 percent market share) followed by Millenial Media. Facebook is a distant fourth but moving rapidly to catch up. Alcatel-Lucent offers a new service to be managed by Placecast that will identify cell phone users within a specified distance of an advertiser's nearest outlet and notify them about the outlet's address and phone number, perhaps including a link to a coupon or other promotion. Placecast's clients include Hyatt, FedEx, and Avis Rent A Car.

Yahoo displays ads on its mobile home page for companies such as Pepsi, Procter & Gamble, Hilton, Nissan, and Intel. Google is displaying ads linked to cell phone searches by users of the mobile version of its search engine, while Microsoft offers banner and text advertising on its MSN Mobile portal in the United States. Ads are embedded in games, videos, and other mobile applications.

Shopkick is a mobile application that enables retailers such as Best Buy, Sports Authority, and Macy's to offer coupons to people when they walk into their stores. The Shopkick app automatically recognizes when the user has entered a partner retail store and offers a new virtual currency called "kickbucks," which can be redeemed for Facebook credits, iTunes Gift Cards, travel vouchers, DVDs, or immediate cash-back rewards at any of the partner stores.

Fifty-five percent of online retailers now have m-commerce Web sites—simplified versions of their Web sites that make it possible for shoppers to use cell phones to place orders. Clothing retailers Lilly Pulitzer and Armani Exchange, Home Depot, Amazon, Walmart, and 1–800 Flowers are among those companies with apps for m-commerce sales.

10.4 Building an E-commerce Presence

Building a successful e-commerce presence requires a keen understanding of business, technology, and social issues, as well as a systematic approach. Today, an e-commerce presence is not just a corporate Web site, but may also include a social network site on Facebook, a Twitter company feed, and smartphone apps where customers can access your services. Developing and coordinating all these different customer venues can be difficult. A complete treatment of the topic is beyond the scope of this text, and students should consult books devoted to just this topic (Laudon and Traver, 2013). The two most important management challenges in building a successful e-commerce presence are (1) developing a clear understanding of your business objectives and (2) knowing how to choose the right technology to achieve those objectives.

DEVELOP AN E-COMMERCE PRESENCE MAP

E-commerce has moved from being a PC-centric activity on the Web to a mobile and tablet-based activity. While 80 percent or more of e-commerce today is conducted using PCs, increasingly smartphones and tablets will be used for purchasing. Currently, smartphones and tablets are used by a majority of Internet users in the United States to shop for goods and services, look up prices, enjoy entertainment, and access social sites, less so to make purchases. Your potential customers use these various devices at different times during the day, and involve themselves in different conversations depending what they are doing—touching base with friends, tweeting, or reading a blog. Each of these are "touch points" where you can meet the customer, and you have to think about how you develop a presence in these different virtual places. Figure 10.10 provides a roadmap to the platforms and related activities you will need to think about when developing your e-commerce presence.

Figure 10.10 illustrates four different kinds of an e-commerce presence: Web sites, e-mail, social media, and offline media. For each of these types there are different platforms that you will need to address. For instance, in the case of Web site presence, there are three different platforms: traditional desktop, tablets, and smartphones, each with different

Figure 10.10
E-commerce
Presence Map
*An e-commerce pres-
ence requires firms
to consider the four
different types of pres-
ence, with specific
platforms and activities
associated with each.*

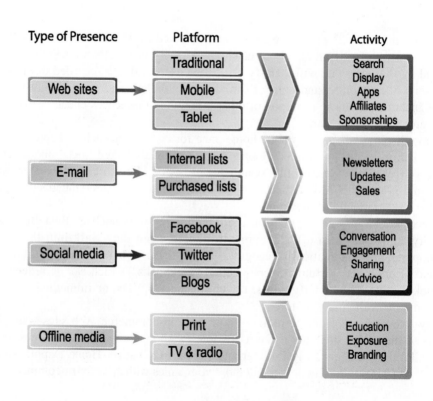

PHASE	ACTIVITY	MILESTONE
Phase 1: Planning	Envision Web presence; determine personnel	Web mission statement
Phase 2: Web site development	Acquire content; develop a site design; arrange for hosting the site	Web site plan
Phase 3: Web Implementation	Develop keywords and metatags; focus on search engine optimization; identify potential sponsors	A functional Web site
Phase 4: Social media plan	Identify appropriate social platforms and content for your products and services	A social media plan
Phase 5: Social media implementation	Develop Facebook, Twitter, and Pinterest presence	Functioning social media presence
Phase 6: Mobile plan	Develop a mobile plan; consider options for porting your Web site to smartphones	A mobile media plan

TABLE 10.8

E-Commerce Presence Timeline

capabilities. And for each type of e-commerce presence there are related activities you will need to consider. For instance, in the case of Web sites, you will want to engage in search engine marketing, display ads, affiliate programs, and sponsorships. Offline media, the fourth type of e-commerce presence, is included here because many firms use multiplatform or integrated marketing where print ads refer customers to Web sites.

DEVELOP A TIMELINE: MILESTONES

Where would you like to be a year from now? It's a good idea for you to have a rough idea of the time frame for developing your e-commerce presence when you begin. You should break your project down into a small number of phases that could be completed within a specified time. Table 10.8 illustrates a one-year timeline for the development of an e-commerce presence for a start-up company devoted to teenage fashions. You can also find more detail about developing an e-commerce Web site in the Learning Tracks for this chapter.

Review Summary

1. **What are the unique features of e-commerce, digital markets, and digital goods?** E-commerce involves digitally enabled commercial transactions between and among organizations and individuals. Unique features of e-commerce technology include ubiquity, global reach, universal technology standards, richness, interactivity, information density, capabilities for personalization and customization, and social technology. E-commerce is becoming increasingly social, mobile, and local.

Digital markets are said to be more "transparent" than traditional markets, with reduced information asymmetry, search costs, transaction costs, and menu costs, along with the ability to change prices dynamically based on market conditions. Digital goods, such as music, video, software, and books, can be delivered over a digital network. Once a digital product has been produced, the cost of delivering that product digitally is extremely low.

2. **What are the principal e-commerce business and revenue models?** E-commerce business models are e-tailers, transaction brokers, market creators, content providers, community providers, service providers, and portals. The principal e-commerce revenue models are advertising, sales, subscription, free/freemium, transaction fee, and affiliate.

3. **How has e-commerce transformed marketing?** The Internet provides marketers with new ways of identifying and communicating with millions of potential customers at costs far lower than traditional media. Crowdsourcing utilizing the "wisdom of crowds" helps companies learn from customers in order to improve product offerings and increase customer value. Behavioral targeting techniques increase the effectiveness of banner, rich media, and video ads. Social commerce uses social networks and social network sites to improve targeting of products and services.

4. **How has e-commerce affected business-to-business transactions?** B2B e-commerce generates efficiencies by enabling companies to locate suppliers, solicit bids, place orders, and track shipments in transit electronically. Net marketplaces provide a single, digital marketplace for many buyers and sellers. Private industrial networks link a firm with its suppliers and other strategic business partners to develop highly efficient and responsive supply chains.

5. **What is the role of m-commerce in business, and what are the most important m-commerce applications?** M-commerce is especially well-suited for location-based applications, such as finding local hotels and restaurants, monitoring local traffic and weather, and providing personalized location-based marketing. Mobile phones and handhelds are being used for mobile bill payment, banking, securities trading, transportation schedule updates, and downloads of digital content, such as music, games, and video clips. M-commerce requires wireless portals and special digital payment systems that can handle micropayments. The GPS capabilities of smartphones make possible geoadvertising, geosocial, and geoinformation services.

6. **What issues must be addressed when building an e-commerce presence?** Building a successful e-commerce presence requires a clear understanding of the business objectives to be achieved and selection of the right platforms, activities, and timeline to achieve those objectives. An e-commerce presence includes not only a corporate Web site but also a presence on Facebook, Twitter, and other social networking sites and smartphone apps.

Key Terms

Advertising revenue model, 366
Affiliate revenue model, 367
Behavioral targeting, 370
Business-to-business (B2B), 363
Business-to-consumer (B2C), 363
Community providers, 365
Consumer-to-consumer (C2C), 363
Cost transparency, 359
Crowdsourcing, 370
Customization, 359
Digital goods, 360
Direct goods, 377
Disintermediation, 360
Dynamic pricing, 360
Electronic data interchange (EDI), 376
E-tailer, 364

Exchanges, 378
Free/freemium revenue model, 367
Geoadvertising services, 379
Geoinformation services, 379
Geosocial services, 379
Indirect goods, 377
Information asymmetry, 360
Information density, 359
Intellectual property, 364
Location-based services, 379
Long tail marketing, 370
Market creator, 365
Market entry costs, 358
Marketspace, 358
Menu costs, 360
Micropayment systems, 366
Mobile commerce (m-commerce), 363
Net marketplaces, 376
Personalization, 359

Podcasting, 365
Prediction market, 370
Price discrimination, 359
Price transparency, 359
Private exchange, 376
Private industrial networks, 376
Revenue model, 366
Richness, 358
Sales revenue model, 366
Search costs, 358
Social graph, 373
Social shopping, 369
Streaming, 365
Subscription revenue model, 367
Transaction costs, 358
Transaction fee revenue model, 367
Wisdom of crowds, 369

Review Questions

10-1 What are the unique features of e-commerce, digital markets, and digital goods?
- Name and describe four business trends and three technology trends shaping e-commerce today.
- List and describe the eight unique features of e-commerce.
- Explain how e-commerce has become more social, mobile, and local.

10-2 What are the principal e-commerce business and revenue models?
- Summarize the three main types of e-commerce.
- Name and describe the principal e-commerce business models.
- Name and describe the e-commerce revenue models.

10-3 How has e-commerce transformed marketing?
- Explain how social networking and the "wisdom of crowds" help companies improve their marketing.
- Define behavioral targeting and explain how it works at individual Web sites and on advertising networks.
- Define the social graph and explain how it is used in e-commerce marketing.

10-4 How has e-commerce affected business-to-business transactions?
- Explain how Internet technology supports business-to-business electronic commerce.
- Define exchanges and explain how they differ from Net marketplaces.

10-5 What is the role of m-commerce in business, and what are the most important m-commerce applications?
- List and describe important types of m-commerce services and applications.
- Describe common location-based services and applications.

10-6 What issues must be addressed when building an e-commerce presence?
- List and describe the 4 types of e-commerce presence.

Discussion Questions

10-7 How does the Internet change consumer and supplier relationships?

10-8 The mobile platform may not make
desktop PCs obsolete, but corporations will have to change their business models to adjust to this shift.
Do you agree? Why or why not?

10-9 How have social technologies
changed e-commerce?

Hands-On MIS Projects

The projects in this section give you hands-on experience developing e-commerce strategies
for businesses, using spreadsheet software to research the profitability of an e-commerce
company, and using Web tools to research and evaluate e-commerce hosting services.

MANAGEMENT DECISION PROBLEMS

10-10 Columbiana is a small, independent island in the Caribbean that has many historical buildings, forts, and other sites, along with rain forests and striking mountains.
A few first-class hotels and several dozen less-expensive accommodations can be
found along its beautiful white sand beaches. The major airlines have regular flights
to Columbiana, as do several small airlines. Columbiana's government wants to
increase tourism and develop new markets for the country's tropical agricultural
products. How can a Web presence help? What Internet business model would be
appropriate? What functions should the Web site perform?

10-11 Explore the Web sites of the following companies: Eurosparkle, Promod, Kingfisher
plc, and ebookers.com. Determine which of these Web sites would benefit most from
adding a company-sponsored blog to the Web site. List the business benefits of the
blog. Specify the intended audience for the blog. Decide who in the company should
author the blog, and select some topics for the blog.

IMPROVING DECISION MAKING: USING SPREADSHEET
SOFTWARE TO ANALYZE A DOT-COM BUSINESS

Software skills: Spreadsheet downloading, formatting, and formulas
Business skills: Financial statement analysis

10-12 Pick one e-commerce company on the Internet—for example, Ashford, Buy.com,
Yahoo, or Priceline. Study the Web pages that describe the company and explain its
purpose and structure. Use the Web to find articles that comment on the company.
Then visit the Securities and Exchange Commission's Web site at www.sec.gov to
access the company's 10-K (annual report) form showing income statements and
balance sheets. Select only the sections of the 10-K form containing the desired
portions of financial statements that you need to examine, and download them
into your spreadsheet. (MyMISLab provides more detailed instructions on how to
download this 10-K data into a spreadsheet.) Create simplified spreadsheets of the
company's balance sheets and income statements for the past three years.
- Is the company a dot-com success, borderline business, or failure? What
information provides the basis of your decision? Why? When answering these
questions, pay special attention to the company's three-year trends in revenues,
costs of sales, gross margins, operating expenses, and net margins.

- Prepare an overhead presentation (with a minimum of five slides), including appropriate spreadsheets or charts, and present your work to your professor and classmates.

ACHIEVING OPERATIONAL EXCELLENCE: EVALUATING E-COMMERCE HOSTING SERVICES

Software skills: Web browser software
Business skills: Evaluating e-commerce hosting services

10-13 This project will help develop your Internet skills in commercial services for hosting an e-commerce site for a small start-up company.

You would like to set up a Web site to sell towels, linens, pottery, and tableware from Portugal and are examining services for hosting small business Internet storefronts. Your Web site should be able to take secure credit card payments and to calculate shipping costs and taxes. Initially, you would like to display photos and descriptions of 40 different products. Visit Verio Europe, Host Europe, and iPage and compare the range of e-commerce hosting services they offer to small businesses, their capabilities, and costs. Also examine the tools they provide for creating an e-commerce site. Compare these services and decide which you would use if you were actually establishing a Web store. Write a brief report indicating your choice and explaining the strengths and weaknesses of each.

Collaboration and Teamwork Project

10-14 In MyMISLab, you will find a Collaboration and Teamwork Project dealing with the concepts in this chapter. You will be able to use Google Drive, Google Docs, Google Sites, Google+, or other open-source tools to complete the assignment.

BUSINESS PROBLEM-SOLVING CASE

Cultivating Customers the Social Way

To most people, Facebook and Twitter are ways to keep in touch with friends and to let them know what you are doing. For companies of all shapes and sizes, however, Facebook, Twitter, and other social media have become powerful tools for engaging customers, amplifying product messages, discovering trends and influencers, building brand awareness, and taking action on customer requests and recommendations. Half of all Twitter users recommend products in their tweets. It has been said that social media are the world's largest focus group, with consumers telling you what they want every single day.

Nearly all Fortune 1000 companies and hundreds of thousands of smaller firms have Facebook Brand pages to develop "fans" of the brand by providing users opportunities to interact with the brand through blogs, comment pages, contests, and offerings on the brand page. The Like button gives users a chance to share with their social network their feelings about content and other objects they are viewing and Web sites they are visiting. With Like buttons on millions of Web sites, Facebook can track user behavior on other sites and then sell this information to marketers. Facebook also sells display ads to firms that show up in the right column of users' Homepages, and most other pages in the Facebook interface such as Photos and Apps.

Twitter has developed many new offerings to interested advertisers, like 'Promoted Tweets' and 'Promoted Trends'. These features give advertisers the ability to have their tweets displayed more prominently when Twitter users search for certain keywords.

Wrigleyville Sports—a small business with three retail stores and e-commerce sites selling sports-related clothing and novelties like a panini maker that puts the Chicago Cubs logo on your sandwich—has been building a Facebook following for over three years. Facebook page posts use much of the same content as its e-mail campaigns, but its Twitter campaigns have to be condensed to 140 characters. Some Wrigleyville promotions use all of these channels while others are more social-specific. For example, in 2011, the company ran a Mother's Day contest on its Facebook page exhorting visitors to post a picture of Mom demonstrating why she's the biggest Chicago Cubs fan. Wrigleyville tracks purchases related to its promotions with its NetSuite customer relationship management system and is able to tell which promotions yield the most profitable new customers. Wrigleyville knows which customers responded, how much they spent, and what they purchased, so it can measure conversion rates, the value of keyword buys, and the ultimate return on campaigns.

Even if the Facebook or Twitter postings show brands apologizing about missteps or customer complaints, companies may still benefit. Today, the more honest and human companies appear, the more likely consumers are to like them and stick with them. For example, JCD Repair, a six-year-old iPhone, iPad and Android repair business based in Chicago, found that encouraging customers to post reviews of its service on Facebook, Yelp, and Google Plus Local helped generate more business. Although the vast majority of the reviews are overwhelmingly positive, Matt McCormick, JCD's owner, believes that even the bad reviews can be useful. A bad review here and there not only helps you look more credible, it can also give you very valuable feedback on what you're doing wrong, McCormick believes. It also gives you a chance to set the situation right with the customer. If you deal with problems swiftly and set things right, people are impressed.

Companies have also gained from posting good comments about their competitors. General Mills has 30.1 percent share of the cold cereal market and maintains a strong social presence on Facebook, Twitter, Instagram, and Tumblr. Its Facebook group Hello, Cereal Lovers, has more than 366,000 followers. Although General Mill sprimarily uses these channels to discuss its own brands like Cheerios and Lucky Charms, it occasionally highlights rival cereals. For example, Hello, Cereal Lovers featured a recipe suggested by a user made with Post Honey Bunches of Oats, while on Twitter General Mills reposted a recipe made with Post Fruity Pebbles and Kelloggs Rice Krispies. Carla Vernón, marketing director for General Mills cereal, believes this "brand agnostic" approach makes the company appear more authentic and inspires better conversations with the people who buy and enjoy its products.

With cold cereal consumed by 92 percent of American households, the market for cold cereal is saturated. A common growth strategy for General Mills and other cereal companies is to increase what marketers call "usage occasions" by promoting how the cereals can be used in recipes, craft projects, or weight-loss programs. General Mills has been using its Web site and social network presence to encourage cereal consumption on these multiple fronts.

Still, the results of a social presence can be unpredictable, and not always beneficial, as a number of companies have learned. Businesses do not have much control in the placement of their Facebook ads, which are largely based on computer algorithms. In late May of 2013, after failing to get Facebook to remove pages glorifying violence against women, feminist activists waged a digital media campaign highlighting companies whose ads appeared alongside the offensive pages. Nissan and a number of small companies temporarily removed their ads from the site and Facebook removed the pages in question.

When Burger King's Twitter account was hacked in early 2013, its logo was replaced by a McDonald's logo and rogue announcements appeared, including one that Burger King had been sold to a competitor. Other posts were unprintable. Jeep was hacked a day later. Hackers replaced the company's thumbnail image with a one for Cadillac. (Cadillac is a division of General Motors, while Jeep is a division of Chrysler.) Nonsensical posts began to flow into the Jeep news feed.

Companies everywhere have rushed to create Facebook pages and Twitter accounts, but many still don't understand how to make effective use of these social media tools. Traditional marketing is all about creating and delivering a message using communication that is primarily one-way. Social media marketing is all about two-way communication and interaction. It enables businesses to receive an immediate response to a message—and to react and change the message, if necessary. Many companies still don't understand that difference. They flood social media sites with sales and marketing pitches touting themselves and don't engage in conversations with customers where they could collect customer feedback and input. According to Vala Afshar, Chief Customer Officer at Enterasys Networks, most companies are missing the mark with social media because they're too impatient. They want to bombard potential customers with "me, me, me" marketing and sales pitches instead of using social media slowly over time to have conversations and build relationships.

Vistaprint, a Netherlands-based online graphic design and printing firm with U.S. headquarters in Lexington,

Massachusetts, joined Twitter in 2008, but initially did not get the hang of how to use social media to reach customers. When Vistaprint's first tweets went out, the company learned that its message and tone were wrong. Vistaprint had thought social media were supposed to be used for public relations. The company gradually learned how to use social media to communicate with customers by creating conversations. Now Vistaprint poses marketing advice for small businesses. It does not expect that the people reading the posts will buy one of its products, such as business cards, right away, only that they will remember Vistaprint when they are ready to buy. Vistaprint is able to demonstrate that using Twitter and Facebook has directly increased profits because it keeps track of sales that come through links from social media sites.

Some companies have not been taking advantage of social media capabilities for capturing customer data for analysis. Even when they have the software tools for social media analytics, they might not know how to ask the right questions. According to Jill Dyche of Baseline Consulting, the problem with social media is when you get it to work, what do you do with it? A social community is buzzing about your flagship product? Great! But now what?

Companies may need to experiment. Pradeep Kumar, vice president and customer intelligence director at advertising firm DraftFCB, believes his social media analytics program will pay off eventually, though he's unsure of how or when. Kumar believes analyzing social media data requires multiple tools and the flexibility to experiment with those tools to see what works and what doesn't. Kumar and others warn that that existing tools for sentiment analysis aren't always accurate, often failing to pick up on sarcastic or colloquial language.

Best Western International, the world's largest hotel chain, has both a mobile and desktop Web site with social tools. Both sites pull in ratings from TripAdvisor to let users see what others are saying about a hotel. TripAdvisor, with 200 million monthly visitors worldwide, provides a place for people to share their experiences about hotels, flights, restaurants and rentals. It is a leading example of social feedback driving customer buying decisions. Additionally, visitors to the Best Western sites can "Like" specific hotel pages on the site.

Best Western worked with Medallia, Inc., a Palo Alto, California-based provider of customer experience management software, to create a tool that allows hotels to manage and respond to social feedback and to perform sentiment analysis (see Chapter 6). For example, a hotel's Internet speed might elicit the most comments, but the software can show that this has a limited impact on guest likelihood to recommend that hotel compared to the cleanliness of guest rooms. These findings help Best Western focus its resources on areas that have the greatest impact on recommendations.

Sources: Andrew Adam Newman, "Online, a Cereal Maker Takes an Inclusive Approach," *New York Times*, July 23, 2013; Aaron Lester, "Seeking Treasure from Social Media Tracking? Follow the Customer," Searchbusinessanalytics.techtarget.com, accessed May 17, 2013; Connor Marsden, "The Role of Social CRM: Changing Dynamics and a Bright Outlook," Destinationcrm.com, August 23, 2013; Tanzina Vega and Leslie Kaufman, "The Distasteful Side of Social Media Puts Advertisers on Their Guard," *New York Times*, June 3, 2013; Tanzina Vega and Nicole Perlroth, "Twitter Hackings Put Focus on Security for Brands," *New York Times*, February 24, 2013; Ashley Smith, "Social Media for Businesses Begs for More Listening and Less Marketing,"SearchCRM.com, January 22, 2013; Melinda F. Emerson, "Even Bad Reviews on the Web Can Help Your Business," *New York Times*, July 17, 2012; and Betsy Sigman, "Social Media Helps Build Strong Brands," *Baseline*, March 9, 2012.

Case Study Questions

10-15 Assess the people, organization, and technology issues for using social media to engage with customers.

10-16 What are the advantages and disadvantages of using social media for advertising, brand building, market research, and customer service?

10-17 Give some examples of management decisions that were facilitated by using social media to interact with customers.

10-18 Should all companies use Facebook and Twitter for customer service and marketing? Why or why not? What kinds of companies are best suited to use these platforms?

Improving Decision Making and Managing Knowledge

CHAPTER 11

STUDENT LEARNING OBJECTIVES

After completing this chapter, you will be able to answer the following questions:

1. What are the different types of decisions, and how does the decision-making process work?

2. How do business intelligence and business analytics support decision making?

3. How do information systems help people working in a group make decisions more efficiently?

4. What are the business benefits of using intelligent techniques in decision making and knowledge management?

5. What types of systems are used for enterprise-wide knowledge management and knowledge work, and how do they provide value for businesses?

CHAPTER OUTLINE

FIAT: REAL TIME MANAGEMENT WITH BUSINESS INTELLIGENCE

Few industries have experienced as much disruption due to the financial meltdown of 2007-2009 as the auto industry. Global production peaked in 2007 when 53 million cars were produced. Global production fell to 47 million two years later at the height of the global financial recession. Two large American firms, General Motors and Chrysler, required a financial bail out of €5.6 billion from the United States government. After filing for bankruptcy in 2009, Chrysler found a buyer in Fiat Automobiles S.p.A. who eventually purchased majority control by 2011, and has since attempted to purchase all the shares from the Canadian government, and employee unions in 2013.

Fiat was one of the global automotive companies to weather the financial storm of 2008- 2011 without significant government intervention. The 114 year old automaker is based in Turin, Italy, and is Italy's largest auto manufacturer, with 9% of the European market. It's second largest market is Brazil, where it has been the market leader for a decade. The combined Chrysler Fiat company has nearly 215,000 employees, 158 plants, and 77 R&D centers. Fiat's 2012 revenue approached €84 billion.

Vladimir Kramin/Fotolia.

Fiat faced several information system challenges resulting from its global expansion, and in particular its purchase of Chrysler. In the past, Fiat global production centers adopted their own database systems to manage their business, and these legacy systems evolved independently over many years. Even enterprise systems from a single vendor differed by country and market, making compatibility and reporting a challenge for executives. This meant that executives in Turin could not receive timely and complete information on the firm's key business processes and financial performance. A good deal of management decision making relied on manual spreadsheets using data from different systems, and this led to errors in the data. With Chrysler, Fiat inherited another set of enterprise systems. All business functions were impacted, from supply management and production to marketing, and finance. Financial managers required a detailed planning capability. Selling Fiat 500s in the United States and Jeeps throughout Europe made it very difficult to identify the potential cost savings of sharing parts and products across these brands.

Fiat decided it needed a new system that could provide near real-time information on its operations across the globe to integrate control and reporting, data definitions, pricing, and marketing campaigns for new vehicles. Working with Oracle's Hyperion database and reporting software, and the consulting firm TechEdge SpA, Fiat set out to build an enterprise performance management system with significant business intelligence capabilities based on current data from the divisions.

The new system allows Fiat managers to analyze automobile production across divisions, including the motors used, and vehicle options. In turn this enables executives to define the costs and budgets of production worldwide. Manual work with spreadsheets has been greatly reduced. Using Oracle's Hyperion Planning system, Fiat manages are able to develop a detailed understanding of local market conditions, and initiate marketing campaigns and incentive programs to ensure excess inventories of completed cars do not pile up.

Oracle's Hyperion Financial Management provided an integrated platform for managing government reporting requirements, and the ability to trace and audit assembly and sales by providing a detailed view of dealer sales to final customers. For marketing, the new system enabled Fiat managers to simulate sales volumes and costs, and compared marketing expenditures in each market to sales results. In contrast to previous legacy systems, the enterprise performance system is Web-enabled, and reduces reliance on individual PCs. An important element of the new system is making data and information more understandable by creating performance dashboards for managers which reflect their needs as decision makers. These new user interfaces are essential elements for using the data effectively in a competitive environment.

Sources: Worldometer, "Cars Produced in the World," December 15, 2013; Technology Reply, " Competitive Analysis: Second Generation Business Intelligence for Competitive Advantage." October 2013; Oracle Magazine, "Fiat Group Automobiles Aligns Operational Decisions with Strategy by Using End-to-End Enterprise Performance Management System," September 2013; David Baum, "Dashboard View: As Fiat Maneuvers Beyond Italy, New Analytics Help Steer Managers in the Right Direction, Oracle Magazine, May 2013;

The experiences of Fiat provide an excellent of example of the challenges which businesses face when increasing their scope of operations and move towards a truly global business. The existing legacy systems at Fiat made it very difficult to coordinate supply chain, production, financial, and marketing decisions on a global basis. Existing systems could not provide real-time data to central management in Turin, and did not have the analytical power to analyze the data from these legacy systems. In this traditional climate, management had a difficult time responding to changes in local conditions, and discovering potential synergies among their divisions.

The chapter-opening diagram calls attention to important points raised by this case and this chapter. To operate efficiently on a global scale, firms need more timely, and accurate data to make intelligent decisions. They also need sophisticated analytic packages that can make sense out of the data, provide capsule summaries to management, and provide interfaces that managers can easily use. With these systems, managers are able to see where

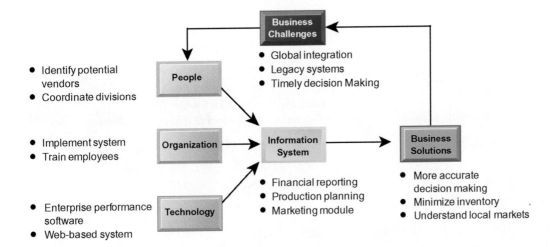

- Identify potential vendors
- Coordinate divisions

People

Business Challenges
- Global integration
- Legacy systems
- Timely decision Making

- Implement system
- Train employees

Organization → **Information System**

Business Solutions

- Enterprise performance software
- Web-based system

Technology

- Financial reporting
- Production planning
- Marketing module

- More accurate decision making
- Minimize inventory
- Understand local markets

production bottlenecks occur, understand how their various divisions can cooperate by sharing parts and designs, and respond to changes in demand and avoid excess inventories. Better decision making using business intelligence makes companies like Fiat more profitable.

Here are some questions to think about: Why is it important that global performance management be delivered using Web-based technologies rather than traditional software running on corporate servers and PCs? What people and organizational difficulties do you think firms will face when implementing these global systems? Do firms become too dependent on database firms like Oracle?

11.1 Decision Making and Information Systems

One of the main contributions of information systems has been to improve decision making, both for individuals and groups. Decision making in businesses used to be limited to management. Today, lower-level employees are responsible for some of these decisions, as information systems make information available to lower levels of the business. But what do we mean by better decision making? How does decision making take place in businesses and other organizations? Let's take a closer look.

BUSINESS VALUE OF IMPROVED DECISION MAKING

What does it mean to the business to be able to make a better decision? What is the monetary value to the business of better, improved decision making? Table 11.1 attempts to measure the monetary value of improved decision making for a small U.S. manufacturing firm with $280 million in annual revenue and 140 employees. The firm has identified a number of key decisions where new system investments might improve the quality of decision making. The table provides selected estimates of annual value (in the form of cost savings or increased revenue) from improved decision making in selected areas of the business.

We can see from Table 11.1 that decisions are made at all levels of the firm, and that some of these decisions are common, routine, and numerous. Although the value of improving any single decision may be small, improving hundreds of thousands of "small" decisions adds up to a large annual value for the business.

TYPES OF DECISIONS

Chapter 2 showed that there are different levels in an organization. Each of these levels has different information requirements for decision support and responsibility for different types of decisions (see Figure 11.1). Decisions are classified as structured, semistructured, and unstructured.

TABLE 11.1

Business Value of Enhanced Decision Making

Example Decision Value	Decision Maker	Number of Annual Decisions	Estimated Value to Firm of a Single Improved Decision	Annual
Allocate support to most-valuable customers	Accounts manager	12	$100,000	$1,200,000
Predict call center daily demand	Call Center management	4	150,000	600,000
Decide parts inventory levels daily	Inventory manager	365	5,000	1,825,000
Identify competitive bids from major suppliers	Senior management	1	2,000,000	2,000,000
Schedule production to fill orders	Manufacturing manager	150	10,000	1,500,000
Allocate labor to complete a job	Production floor manager	100	4,000	400,000

Unstructured decisions are those in which the decision maker must provide judgment, evaluation, and insight to solve the problem. Each of these decisions is novel, important, and nonroutine, and there is no well-understood or agreed-on procedure for making them.

Structured decisions, by contrast, are repetitive and routine, and they involve a definite procedure for handling them so that they do not have to be treated each time as if they were new. Many decisions have elements of both types and are **semistructured decisions**, where only part of the problem has a clear-cut answer provided by an accepted procedure. In general, structured decisions are more prevalent at lower organizational levels, whereas unstructured problems are more common at higher levels of the firm.

Figure 11.1
Information Requirements of Key Decision-Making Groups in a Firm
Senior managers, middle managers, operational managers, and employees have different types of decisions and information requirements.

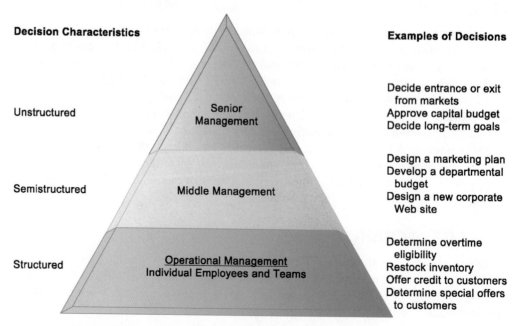

Decision Characteristics

Examples of Decisions

Unstructured — Senior Management
- Decide entrance or exit from markets
- Approve capital budget
- Decide long-term goals

Semistructured — Middle Management
- Design a marketing plan
- Develop a departmental budget
- Design a new corporate Web site

Structured — Operational Management / Individual Employees and Teams
- Determine overtime eligibility
- Restock inventory
- Offer credit to customers
- Determine special offers to customers

Senior executives face many unstructured decision situations, such as establishing the firm's 5- or 10-year goals or deciding new markets to enter. Answering the question "Should we enter a new market?" would require access to news, government reports, and industry views, as well as high-level summaries of firm performance. However, the answer would also require senior managers to use their own best judgment and poll other managers for their opinions.

Middle management faces more structured decision scenarios, but their decisions may include unstructured components. A typical middle-level management decision might be "Why is the reported order fulfillment showing a decline over the past six months at a distribution center in Minneapolis?" This middle manager could obtain a report from the firm's enterprise system or distribution management system on order activity and operational efficiency at the Minneapolis distribution center. This is the structured part of the decision. But before arriving at an answer, this middle manager will have to interview employees and gather more unstructured information from external sources about local economic conditions or sales trends.

Operational management and rank-and-file employees tend to make more structured decisions. For example, a supervisor on an assembly line has to decide whether an hourly paid worker is entitled to overtime pay. If the employee worked more than eight hours on a particular day, the supervisor would routinely grant overtime pay for any time beyond eight hours that was clocked on that day.

A sales account representative often has to make decisions about extending credit to customers by consulting the firm's customer database that contains credit information. If the customer met the firm's prespecified criteria for granting credit, the account representative would grant that customer credit to make a purchase. In both instances, the decisions are highly structured and are routinely made thousands of times each day in most large firms. The answer has been preprogrammed into the firm's payroll and accounts receivable systems.

THE DECISION-MAKING PROCESS

Making a decision is a multistep process. Simon (1960) described four different stages in decision making: intelligence, design, choice, and implementation (see Figure 11.2). These stages correspond to the four steps in problem-solving used throughout this book.

Intelligence consists of discovering, identifying, and understanding the problems occurring in the organization—why the problem exists, where, and what effects it is having on the firm. **Design** involves identifying and exploring various solutions to the problem. **Choice** consists of choosing among solution alternatives. **Implementation** involves making the chosen alternative work and continuing to monitor how well the solution is working.

What happens if the solution you have chosen does not work? Figure 11.2 shows that you can return to an earlier stage in the decision-making process and repeat it, if necessary. For instance, in the face of declining sales, a sales management team may decide to pay the sales force a higher commission for making more sales to spur on the sales effort. If this does not increase sales, managers would need to investigate whether the problem stems from poor product design, inadequate customer support, or a host of other causes that call for a different solution.

High Velocity Automated Decision Making

Today, many decisions made by organizations are not made by managers or any humans. For instance, when you enter a query into Google's search engine, Google's computer system has to decide which URLs to display in about half a second on average (500 milliseconds). High-frequency trading programs at electronic stock exchanges in the United States execute their trades in under 30 milliseconds. Humans are eliminated from the decision chain because they are too slow.

In these high-speed automated decisions, the intelligence, design, choice, and implementation parts of the decision-making process are captured by computer algorithms that precisely define the steps to be followed to produce a decision. The people who wrote the

Figure 11.2
Stages in Decision
Making
*The decision-making
process can be broken
down into four stages.*

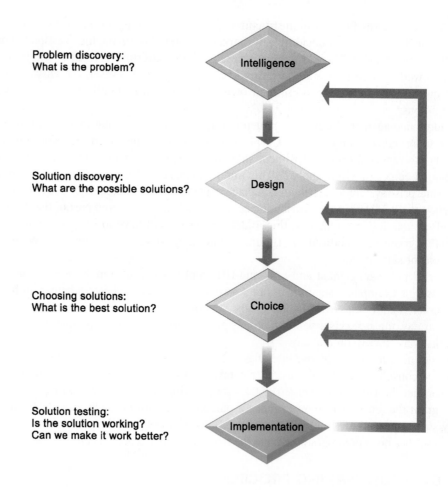

Problem discovery:
What is the problem?

Intelligence

Solution discovery:
What are the possible solutions?

Design

Choosing solutions:
What is the best solution?

Choice

Solution testing:
Is the solution working?
Can we make it work better?

Implementation

software identified the problem, designed a method for finding a solution, defined a range of acceptable solutions, and implemented the solution. In these situations, organizations are making decisions faster than what managers can monitor or control, and great care needs to be taken to ensure the proper operation of these systems to prevent significant harm.

QUALITY OF DECISIONS AND DECISION MAKING

How can you tell if a decision has become "better" or the decision-making process "improved"? Accuracy is one important dimension of quality: In general, we think decisions are "better" if they accurately reflect the real-world data. Speed is another dimension: We tend to think that the decision-making process should be efficient, even speedy. For instance, when you apply for car insurance, you want the insurance firm to make a fast and accurate decision. But there are many other dimensions of quality in decisions and the decision-making process to consider. Which is important for you will depend on the business firm where you work, the various parties involved in the decision, and your own personal values. Table 11.2 describes some quality dimensions for decision making. When we describe how systems "improve decisions and the decision-making process" in this chapter, we are referencing the dimensions in this table.

11.2 Business Intelligence in the Enterprise

Chapter 2 introduced you to different kinds of systems for supporting the levels and types of decisions we have just described. The foundation for all of these systems is a business

TABLE 11.2

Qualities of Decisions
and the Decision-
Making Process

Quality Dimension	Description
Accuracy	Decision reflects reality
Comprehensiveness	Decision reflects a full consideration of the facts and circumstances
Fairness	Decision faithfully reflects the concerns and interests of affected parties
Speed (efficiency)	Decision making is efficient with respect to time and other resources, including the time and resources of affected parties, such as customers
Coherence	Decision reflects a rational process that can be explained to others and made understandable
Due process	Decision is the result of a known process and can be appealed to a higher authority

intelligence and business analytics infrastructure that supplies data and the analytic tools for supporting decision making.

WHAT IS BUSINESS INTELLIGENCE?

"Business intelligence" (BI) is a term used by hardware and software vendors and information technology consultants to describe the infrastructure for warehousing, integrating, reporting and analyzing data that come from the business environment. The foundation infrastructure collects, stores, cleans, and makes available relevant data to managers. Think databases, data warehouses, and data marts described in Chapter 6. "Business analytics" (BA) is also a vendor-defined term that focuses more on tools and techniques for analyzing and understanding data. Think OLAP, statistics, models, and data mining, which we also introduced in Chapter 6.

Business intelligence and analytics are essentially about integrating all the information streams produced by a firm into a single, coherent enterprise wide set of data, and then using modeling, statistical analysis and data mining tools to make sense out of all these data so managers can make better decisions and better plans. The Oakland Athletics described in the chapter-opening case are using business intelligence applications to make some very fine-grained decisions about which players to recruit and how to build a winning baseball team.

It is important to remember that business intelligence and analytics are products defined by technology vendors and consulting firms. They consist of hardware and software suites sold primarily by large system vendors to very large Fortune 500 firms. The largest five providers of these products are SAP, Oracle, IBM, SAS Institute, and Microsoft. The size of worldwide business intelligence software sales reached $13.8 billion in 2013 (Gartner 2013). A number of BI and BA products now have cloud and mobile versions.

THE BUSINESS INTELLIGENCE ENVIRONMENT

Figure 11.3 gives an overview of a business intelligence environment, highlighting the kinds of hardware, software, and management capabilities that the major vendors offer and that firms develop over time. There are six elements in this business intelligence environment:

Data from the business environment: Businesses must deal with both structured and unstructured data from many different sources, including big data. The data need to be integrated and organized so that they can be analyzed and used by human decision makers.

Figure 11.3
Business Intelligence
and Analytics for
Decision Support
*Business intelligence
and analytics require a
strong database founda-
tion, a set of analytic
tools, and an involved
management team that
can ask intelligent ques-
tions and analyze data.*

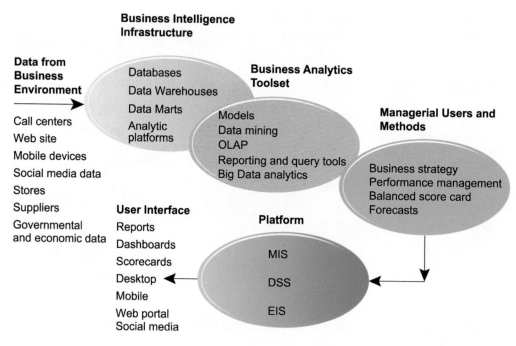

Business intelligence infrastructure: The underlying foundation of business intelligence is a powerful database system that captures all the relevant data to operate the business. The data may be stored in transactional databases or combined and integrated into an enterprise-data warehouse, series of interrelated data marts, or analytic platforms.

Business analytics toolset: A set of software tools are used to analyze data and produce reports, respond to questions posed by managers, and track the progress of the business using key indicators of performance.

Managerial users and methods: Business intelligence hardware and software are only as intelligent as the human beings who use them. Managers impose order on the analysis of data using a variety of managerial methods that define strategic business goals and specify how progress will be measured. These include business performance management and balanced scorecard approaches that focus on key performance indicators, with special attention to competitors.

Delivery platform—MIS, DSS, ESS: The results from business intelligence and analytics are delivered to managers and employees in a variety of ways, depending on what they need to know to perform their job. MIS, DSS, and ESS, which we introduced in Chapter 2, deliver information and knowledge to different people and levels in the firm—operational employees, middle managers, and senior executives. In the past, all these systems could not share data and operated as independent systems. Today, one suite of hardware and software tools in the form of a business intelligence and analytics package is able to integrate all this information and bring it to managers' desktop or mobile platforms.

User Interface: Business people are no longer tied to their desks and desktops. They often learn quicker from a visual representation of data than from a dry report with columns and rows of information. Today's business analytics software suites feature **data visualization** tools, such as rich graphs, charts, dashboards, and maps. They also are able to deliver reports on BlackBerrys, iPhones, and other mobile handhelds as well as on the firm's Web portal. BA software is adding capabilities to post information on Twitter, Facebook, or internal social media to support decision making in an online, group setting rather than in a face-to-face meeting.

BUSINESS INTELLIGENCE AND ANALYTICS CAPABILITIES

Business intelligence and analytics promise to deliver correct, nearly real-time information to decision makers, and the analytic tools help them quickly understand the information and take action. There are five analytic functionalities that BI systems deliver to achieve these ends:

Production reports: These are pre-defined reports based on industry-specific requirements (see Table 11.3).

Parameterized reports: Users enter several parameters as in a pivot table to filter data and isolate impacts of parameters. For instance, you might want to enter region and time of day to understand how sales of a product vary by region and time. If you were Starbucks, you might find that customers in the eastern United States buy most of their coffee in the morning, whereas in the northwest customers buy coffee throughout the day. This finding might lead to different marketing and ad campaigns in each region. (See the discussion of pivot tables later in this section.)

Dashboards/Scorecards: These are visual tools for presenting performance data defined by users.

Ad hoc query/search/ report creation: These allow users to create their own reports based on queries and searches.

Drill down: This is the ability to move from a high level summary to a more detailed view.

Forecasts, scenarios, models: These include capabilities for linear forecasting, "what if" scenario analysis, and analyzing data using standard statistical tools.

Predictive Analytics

An important capability of business intelligence analytics is the ability to model future events and behaviors, such as the probability that a customer will respond to an offer to purchase a product. **Predictive analytics** use statistical analysis, data mining techniques, historical data, and assumptions about future conditions to predict future trends and behavior patterns. Variables that can be measured to predict future behavior are identified. For example, an insurance company might use variables such as age, gender, and driving record as predictors of driving safety when issuing auto insurance policies. A collection of such predictors is combined into a predictive model for forecasting future probabilities with an acceptable level of reliability.

Business Functional Area	Production Reports
Sales	Sales forecasts, sales team performance, cross selling, sales cycle times
Service/Call Center	Customer satisfaction, service cost, resolution rates, churn rates
Marketing	Campaign effectiveness, loyalty and attrition, market basket analysis
Procurement and Support	Direct and indirect spending, off-contract purchases, supplier performance
Supply Chain	Backlog, fulfillment status, order cycle time, bill of materials analysis
Financials	General ledger, accounts receivable and payable, cash flow, profitability
Human Resources	Employee productivity, compensation, workforce demographics, retention

TABLE 11.3

Examples of Business Intelligence Pre-Defined Production Reports

FedEx has been using predictive analytics to develop models that predict how customers will respond to price changes and new services, which customers are most at risk of switching to competitors, and how much revenue will be generated by new storefront or drop-box locations. The accuracy rate of FedEx's predictive analytics system ranges from 65% to 90%.

Predictive analytics are being incorporated into numerous business intelligence applications for sales, marketing, finance, fraud detection, and health care. One of the most well-known applications is credit scoring, which is used throughout the financial services industry. When you apply for a new credit card, scoring models process your credit history, loan application, and purchase data to determine your likelihood of making future credit payments on time. Telecommunications companies use predictive analytics to identify which customers are most profitable, which are most likely to leave, and which new services and plans will be most likely to retain customers. Health care insurers have been analyzing data for years to identify which patients are most likely to generate high costs.

Many companies employ predictive analytics to predict response to direct marketing campaigns. By identifying customers less likely to respond, companies are able to lower their marketing and sales costs by bypassing this group and focusing their resources on customers who have been identified as more promising. For instance, the U.S. division of The Body Shop plc used predictive analytics and its database of catalog, Web, and retail store customers to identify customers who were more likely to make catalog purchases. That information helped the company build more precise and targeted mailing lists for its catalogs, improving the response rate for catalog mailings and catalog revenues.

Big Data Analytics

Predictive analytics are now taking advantage of big data accumulated in both private and public sectors, including data from social media, customer transactions, and ouput from sensors and machines. In e-commerce, many online retailers have capabilities for making personalized online product recommendations to their Web site visitors to help stimulate purchases and guide their decisions about what merchandise to stock. However, most of these product recommendations are based on the behaviors of similar groups of customers, such as those with incomes under $50,000 or whose ages are between 18–25. Now some are starting to analyze the tremendous quantities of online and in-store customer data they collect along with social media data to make these recommendations more individualized.

Major online companies such as Walmart, Netflix, and eBay are analyzing big data from their customer transactions and social media streams to create real-time personalized shopping experiences. These efforts are translating into higher customer spending and customer retention rates.

EBay uses Hunch.com, which it acquired in 2001, to deliver customized recommendations to individual users based on their specific set of tastes. Hunch has built a massive database that includes data from customer purchases, social networks, and signals from around the Web. Hunch is able to analyze the data to create a "taste graph" that maps users with their predicted affinity for products, services, Web sites, and other people, and use this information to create customized recommendations.

The Hunch "taste graph" includes predictions on about 500 million people, 200 million objects (such as videos, gadgets, or books), and 30 billion connections between people and objects. To generate accurate predictions in near real-time, Hunch transformed each person's tastes into a more manageable "taste fingerprint" extracted from the larger taste graph.

Hunch.com's prediction technology is helping eBay develop recommendations of items that might not be immediately obvious for users to purchase from its online marketplace. For example, for a coin collector purchasing on eBay, Hunch might recommend microscopes that are especially useful for coin analysis. Hunch could also become an important tool for eBay sellers if its customer profiles help them make better decisions about which items to offer, the content they use to describe their inventory, and perhaps even the advertising they use to promote their eBay listings (Grau, 2012).

In the public sector, big-data analytics are driving the movement toward "smart cities," which make intensive use of digital technology and data stores to make better decisions about running cities and serving their residents. Over two hundred years of public record-keeping has produced warehouses full of property transfers, tax records, corporate filings, environmental compliance audits, restaurant inspections, building maintenance reports, mass transit appraisals, crime data, health department stats, public education records, utility reviews, and more. The Big Data movement is not only harnessing the underutilized data, but adding to them through the use of sensors, location data from mobile phones, and targeted smartphone apps. Predictive modeling programs can now inform public policy decisions on utility management, transportation operation, healthcare delivery, and public safety. What's more, the ability to evaluate how changes in one service impact the operation and delivery of other services enables holistic problem solving that could only be dreamed of a generation ago. The Interactive Session on Organizations describes how big-data analytics are helping New York City become "smarter."

Location Analytics and Geographic Information Systems

Some of the applications described in the Interactive Session on Organizations deal with data and decisions based on location data. Big data analytics include **location analytics**, the ability to gain business insight from the location (geographic) component of data, including location data from mobile phones, output from sensors or scanning devices, and data from maps. For example, location analytics might help a marketer determine which people to target with mobile ads about nearby restaurants and stores, or quantify the impact of mobile ads on in-store visits. Location analytics would help a utility company view and measure outages and their associated costs as related to customer location to help prioritize marketing, system upgrades and customer service efforts. UPS's package tracking and delivery routing systems described in Chapter 1 uses location analytics, as does the application used by Starbucks to determine where to open new stores. (The system identifies geographic locations that will produce a high sales-to-investment ratio and per-store sales volume.)

The Starbucks application and some of the New York City systems described earlier are examples of **geographic information systems (GIS)**. GIS provide tools to help decision makers visualize problems that benefit from mapping. GIS software ties location data about the distribution of people or other resources to points, lines, and areas on a map. Some GIS have modeling capabilities for changing the data and automatically revising business scenarios.

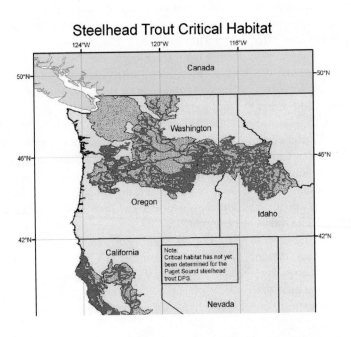

Steelhead Trout Critical Habitat

The U.S. National Marine Fisheries Service (NMFS) created a GIS for identifying critical habitat for steelhead trout on the U.S. west coast. Red areas show critical habitat. Pink-shaded areas indicate places where the steelhead trout are endangered, and dotted-yellow areas indicate places where the species is threatened.

INTERACTIVE SESSION: ORGANIZATIONS   Big Data Make Cities Smarter

New York City wants very much to be a "smart city." In the fall of 2013, New York University, with support from city government, opened the Center for Urban Science and Progress under the direction of Steven E. Koonin, a former Obama administration undersecretary for science in the Department of Energy. Koonin foresees work on a broad range of quality of life and urban efficiency projects ranging from traffic management to reducing water and electricity consumption by 30 to 50 percent in ten years' time.

The first target for a ten-member team of graduate students, music professors, and computer scientists is noise pollution. Starting with data from 311 (the non-emergency line for citizen complaints on a range of issues including noise disturbances), the researchers will gather additional data from wireless sensors on windows and buildings and noise meters on traffic lights and street corners. A smartphone app may also be employed in a crowd-sourcing effort to encourage citizen participation and gather even more comprehensive statistics. One possible outcome foreseen by Koonin is a noise limit ordinance for vehicles. Using a combination of incentives and violation fees, citizens will be persuaded to replace or repair malfunctioning mufflers. Computer simulations will inform decision-makers about the optimum combination of enforcement mechanisms and sequence of steps to maximize compliance.

Zoning, building classification, and traffic flow data, along with Department of Sanitation routes and pickup times will be used to optimize garbage collection. The goal will be to service as many commercial districts as possible in the middle of the night when traffic is lightest and the fewest residents will be disturbed. Next up is a plan to assemble thermal images of buildings across the city that will serve as the basis for energy use studies.

A terabyte of information (equivalent to 143 million printed pages) flows daily to New York's Office of Policy and Strategic Initiatives from every corner of the city, from death certificates to minutiae such as the type of boilers and sprinklers installed in the city's 900,000 buildings. The Office was tasked with reducing the number of illegal conversions—the creation of additional dwelling units in buildings that lack legally required infrastructure such as adequate means of egress and electrical wiring. The team combined data from 19 agencies and created a model to optimize building inspections. Building age, repair permits, foreclosure notices, late tax payments, and other similar data fed a program that fueled an increase from 13 percent to 70 percent of building inspections

identifying a hazardous dwelling. Previously, the city's 200 building inspectors had futilely attempted to respond to the more than 20,000 annual complaints based solely on sketchy grievance descriptions.

Michael Flowers is the Analytics Director for the Office. When the Department of Environmental Protection wanted to improve its efficiency in locating restaurants that illegally dump cooking oil into sewers—the primary cause of clogged city pipes—it turned to Flowers's team. Using restaurant location, geospatial sewer location, and certificates on file with the Business Integrity Commission, a data sifting program easily pinpointed restaurants that had not contracted with a grease-hauling service and their nearest storm drain. Health department inspectors sent to these locations registered a stunning 95% success rate in catching culprits.

Participants in a Big Apps competition, begun in 2009, use the more than 1,000 data sets now publicly available on the NYC Open Data Portal as their primary resource. In the 2013 Best Jobs and Economic Mobility category, the ChildCareDesk app garnered first place. Maps, Yelp reviews, and detailed reports from various city accreditation agencies assist parental decision-making, and an alert system notifies them when a vacancy has arisen. Other winning apps in previous years provide the locations of public restrooms and the safest routes for bicyclists.

Flowers sees even more data that can be mined— the hundreds of thousands of daily posts to Twitter, Facebook and other social media sites. Complaints that do not make it to city agencies concerning unhygienic restaurants, uncollected garbage, and unsafe streets can be gleaned from these sources to further the cause of enhancing a New Yorker's quality of life.

This may be a bridge too far for privacy advocates who have been watching the Big Data/Smart City movement with a wary eye. While recognizing the Smart Cities potential for improving services and helping citizens, groups such as the New York Civil Liberties Union worry about possible abuses. Safeguards, including removing names and tax identification numbers and installing employee keystroke logs, have proven vulnerable to reverse identification and tampering. Undoubtedly, the release of public data, even absent any surveillance intent, must include safeguards.

Ford is working on safety systems that will inform drivers of both internal (V2I: vehicle-to-infrastructure) and external (V2V: vehicle-to-vehicle) threats. The V2V system warns you if a car is speeding up to run a red light, for example. Ford has also developed an upgrade for stoplights to create "smart intersections" that monitor digital maps, GPS data, and traffic signal status and transmit that data to onboard computers. Drivers are then both visually and aurally alerted to potential hazards.

Intel research scientists foresee smart cities with drivers who not only know the velocity of the car in front of them, but can simultaneously see three cars to the right, left, and behind. What's more, cameras can detect if surrounding drivers are looking up, down, or forward, and if one of them is balancing a cup along with the steering wheel. These "driver states" will feed predictive modeling programs to calculate the odds of an accident occurring and which vehicles are best-positioned to avert calamity. Decreased collision rates and their attendant injuries and fatalities are no doubt a societal good, but many questions arise with this level of data-sharing. Will law enforcement have access to velocity information that could result in automatic speeding tickets? If you turn around to give a pacifier to the baby in the car seat, will the increase in accident probability garner you an automatic moving violation? While we might all want the information about the careless drivers around us, are we willing to share our own driving foibles?

Sources: Jeff Bertolucci, "Big Data: When Cars Can Talk," *Information Week*, June 11, 2013; Alan Feuer, "The Mayor's Geek Squad" *New York Times*, March 23, 2013; John Foley, "New York City Builds On Its Technology Base," *Information Week*, April 23, 2013; Steve Lohr, "SimCity, for Real: Measuring an Untidy Metropolis," *New York Times*, February 23, 2013; "Smarter, More Competitive Cities: Forward-thinking cities are investing in insight today," IBM, January 2012;

CASE STUDY QUESTIONS

1. What technologies is New York employing to improve the quality of life of its citizens?

2. What are the people, organization, and technology issues that should be addressed by "smart city" initiatives?

3. What problems are solved by "smart cities?" What are the drawbacks?

4. Give examples of 4 decisions that would be improved in a "smart city."

5. Would you be concerned if social media data were used to supplement public data to help improve the delivery of municipal services? Why or why not?

BUSINESS INTELLIGENCE USERS

Figure 11.4 shows that over 80 percent of the audience for BI consists of casual users. Senior executives tend use BI to monitor firm activities using visual interfaces like dashboards and scorecards. Middle managers and analysts are much more likely to be immersed in the data and software, entering queries and slicing and dicing the data along different dimensions. Operational employees will, along with customers and suppliers, be looking mostly at pre-packaged reports.

Support for Semistructured Decisions

Many BI pre-packaged production reports are MIS reports supporting structured decision making for operational and middle managers. We described operational and middle management, and the systems they use, in Chapter 2. However, some managers are "super users" and keen business analysts who want to create their own reports, and use more sophisticated analytics and models to find patterns in data, to model alternative business scenarios, or to test specific hypotheses. Decision-support systems (DSS) are the BI delivery platform for this category of users, with the ability to support semistructured decision making.

DSS rely more heavily on modeling than MIS, using mathematical or analytical models to perform what-if or other kinds of analysis. What-if analysis, working forward from known or assumed conditions, allows the user to vary certain values to test results to predict outcomes if changes occur in those values. What happens if we raise product prices by 5 percent or increase the advertising budget by $1 million? **Sensitivity analysis** models ask

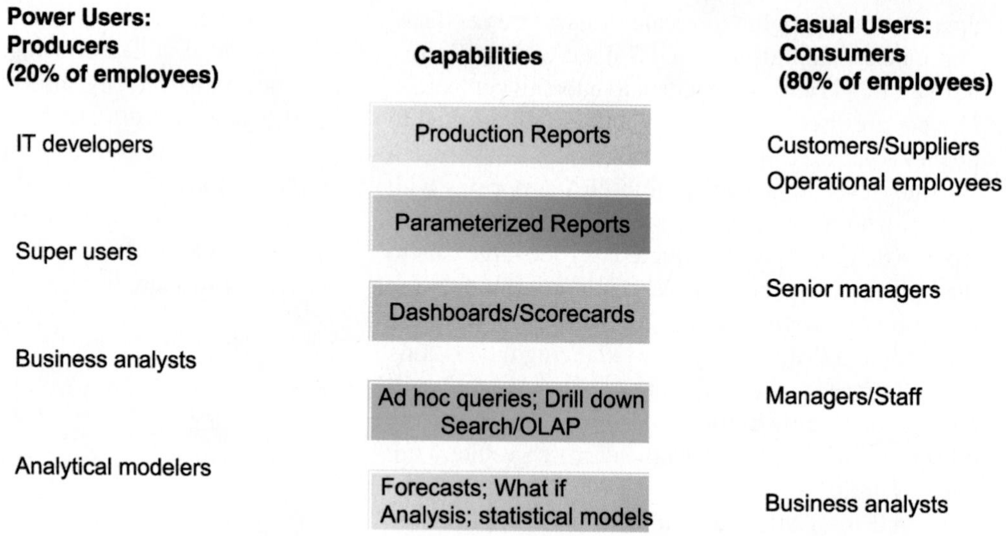

Figure 11.4
Business Intelligence
Users
*Casual users are
consumers of BI output,
while intense power
users are the producers
of reports, new analyses,
models, and forecasts.*

Power Users: Producers (20% of employees)	Capabilities	Casual Users: Consumers (80% of employees)
IT developers	Production Reports	Customers/Suppliers Operational employees
Super users	Parameterized Reports	
	Dashboards/Scorecards	Senior managers
Business analysts	Ad hoc queries; Drill down Search/OLAP	Managers/Staff
Analytical modelers	Forecasts; What if Analysis; statistical models	Business analysts

what-if questions repeatedly to predict a range of outcomes when one or more variables are changed multiple times (see Figure 11.5). Backward sensitivity analysis helps decision makers with goal seeking: If I want to sell 1 million product units next year, how much must I reduce the price of the product?

Chapter 6 described multidimensional data analysis and OLAP as one of the key business intelligence technologies. Spreadsheets have a similar feature for multidimensional analysis called a **pivot table**, which "super user" managers and analysts employ to identify and understand patterns in business information that may be useful for semistructured decision making.

Figure 11.6 illustrates a Microsoft Excel pivot table that examines a large list of order transactions for a company selling online management training videos and books. It shows the relationship between two dimensions: the sales region and the source of contact (Web banner ad or e-mail) for each customer order. It answers the question: does the source of the customer make a difference in addition to region? The pivot table in this figure shows that most customers come from the West and that banner advertising produces most of the customers in all the regions.

One of the Hands-on MIS projects for this chapter asks you to use a pivot table to find answers to a number of other questions using the same list of transactions for the online training company as we used in this discussion. The complete Excel file for these transactions is available in MyMISLab™. We have a Learning Track on creating pivot tables using Excel.

Figure 11.5
Sensitivity Analysis
*This table displays the
results of a sensitivity
analysis of the effect
of changing the sales
price of a necktie and
the cost per unit on the
product's break-even
point. It answers the
question, "What happens
to the break-even point
if the sales price and the
cost to make each unit
increase or decrease?"*

		Variable Cost per Unit				
Total fixed costs	19000					
Variable cost per unit	3					
Average sales price	17					
Contribution margin	14					
Break-even point	1357					
Sales	1357	2	3	4	5	6
Price	14	1583	1727	1900	2111	2375
	15	1462	1583	1727	1900	2111
	16	1357	1462	1583	1727	1900
	17	1267	1357	1462	1583	1727
	18	1188	1267	1357	1462	1583

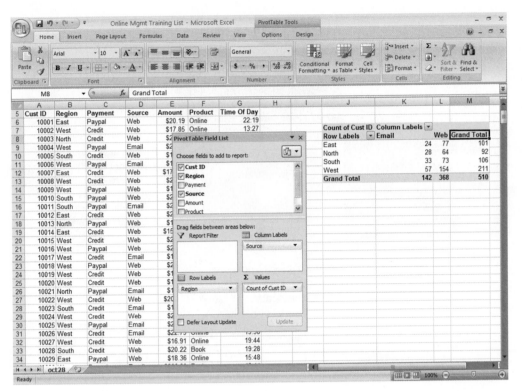

Figure 11.6
A Pivot Table that Examines Customer Regional Distribution and Advertising Source
In this pivot table, we are able to examine where an online training company's customers come from in terms of region and advertising source.

In the past, much of this modeling was done with spreadsheets and small stand-alone databases. Today these capabilities are incorporated into large enterprise BI systems, and they are able to analyze data from large corporate databases. BI analytics include tools for intensive modeling, some of which we described earlier. Such capabilities help Progressive Insurance identify the best customers for its products. Using widely available insurance industry data, Progressive defines small groups of customers, or "cells," such as motorcycle riders aged 30 or above with college educations, credit scores over a certain level, and no accidents. For each "cell," Progressive performs a regression analysis to identify factors most closely correlated with the insurance losses that are typical for this group. It then sets prices for each cell, and uses simulation software to test whether this pricing arrangement will enable the company to make a profit. These analytic techniques make it possible for Progressive to profitably insure customers in traditionally high-risk categories that other insurers would have rejected.

Decision Support for Senior Management: The Balanced Scorecard and Enterprise Performance Management

Business intelligence delivered in the form of executive support systems (ESS) helps senior executives focus on the really important performance information that affects the overall profitability and success of the firm. Currently, the leading methodology for understanding the most important information needed by a firm's executives is called the **balanced scorecard method** (Kaplan and Norton, 2004; Kaplan and Norton, 1992). The balanced score card is a framework for operationalizing a firm's strategic plan by focusing on measurable outcomes on four dimensions of firm performance: financial, business process, customer, and learning and growth (see Figure 11.7).

Performance on each dimension is measured using **key performance indicators (KPIs)**, which are the measures proposed by senior management for understanding how well the firm is performing along any given dimension. For instance, one key indicator of how well an online retail firm is meeting its customer performance objectives is the average length of time required to deliver a package to a consumer. If your firm is a bank, one KPI of business

Figure 11.7
The Balanced Scorecard Framework
In the balanced scorecard framework, the firm's strategic objectives are operationalized along four dimensions: financial, business process, customer, and learning and growth. Each dimension is measured using several KPIs.

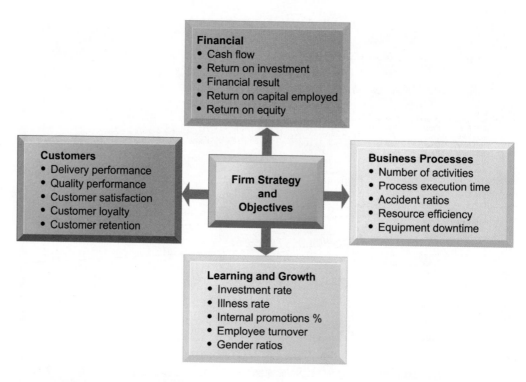

process performance is the length of time required to perform a basic function like creating a new customer account.

The balanced scorecard framework is thought to be "balanced" because it causes managers to focus on more than just financial performance. In this view, financial performance is past history—the result of past actions—and managers should focus on the things they are able to influence today, such as business process efficiency, customer satisfaction, and employee training. Once a scorecard is developed by consultants and senior executives, the next step is automating a flow of information to executives and other managers for each of the key performance indicators.

Another closely related management methodology is **business performance management (BPM).** Originally defined by an industry group in 2004 (led by the same companies that sell enterprise and database systems like Oracle, SAP, and IBM), BPM attempts to systematically translate a firm's strategies (e.g., differentiation, low-cost producer, market share growth, and scope of operation) into operational targets. Once the strategies and targets are identified, a set of key performance indicators are developed to measure progress toward the targets. The firm's performance is then measured with information drawn from the firm's enterprise database systems. (BPM Working Group, 2004).

Corporate data for contemporary ESS are supplied by the firm's existing enterprise applications (enterprise resource planning, supply chain management, and customer relationship management). ESS also provide access to news services, financial market databases, economic information, and whatever other external data senior executives require. ESS have significant **drill-down** capabilities if managers need more detailed views of data.

Well-designed ESS help senior executives monitor organizational performance, track activities of competitors, recognize changing market conditions, and identify problems and opportunities. Employees lower down in the corporate hierarchy also use these systems to monitor and measure business performance in their areas of responsibility. For these and other business intelligence systems to be truly useful, the information must be "actionable"—it must be readily available and also easy to use when making decisions. If users have difficulty identifying critical metrics within the reports they receive, employee productivity and business performance will suffer.

GROUP DECISION-SUPPORT SYSTEMS

The systems we have just described focus primarily on helping you make a decision acting alone. But what if you are part of a team and need to make a decision as a group? You would use a special category of systems called group decision-support systems (GDSS) for this purpose.

A **group decision-support system (GDSS)** is an interactive computer-based system for facilitating the solution of unstructured problems by a set of decision makers working together as a group in the same location or in different locations. Groupware and Web-based tools for videoconferencing and electronic meetings described earlier in this text support some group decision processes, but their focus is primarily on communication. GDSS, however, provide tools and technologies geared explicitly toward group decision making.

GDSS-guided meetings take place in conference rooms with special hardware and software tools to facilitate group decision making. The hardware includes computer and networking equipment, overhead projectors, and display screens. Special electronic meeting software collects, documents, ranks, edits, and stores the ideas offered in a decision-making meeting. The more elaborate GDSS use a professional facilitator and support staff. The facilitator selects the software tools and helps organize and run the meeting.

A sophisticated GDSS provides each attendee with a dedicated desktop computer under that person's individual control. No one will be able to see what individuals do on their computers until those participants are ready to share information. Their input is transmitted over a network to a central server that stores information generated by the meeting and makes it available to all on the meeting network. Data can also be projected on a large screen in the meeting room.

GDSS make it possible to increase meeting size while at the same time increasing productivity because individuals contribute simultaneously rather than one at a time. A GDSS promotes a collaborative atmosphere by guaranteeing contributors' anonymity so that attendees can focus on evaluating the ideas themselves without fear of personally being criticized or of having their ideas rejected based on the contributor. GDSS software tools follow structured methods for organizing and evaluating ideas and for preserving the results of meetings, enabling nonattendees to locate needed information after the meeting. The effectiveness of GDSS depends on the nature of the problem and the group and on how well a meeting is planned and conducted.

11.3 Intelligent Systems for Decision Support

Decision making is also enhanced by intelligent techniques and knowledge management systems. **Intelligent techniques** consist of expert systems, case-based reasoning, genetic algorithms, neural networks, fuzzy logic, and intelligent agents. These techniques are based on **artificial intelligence (AI)** technology, which consists of computer-based systems (both hardware and software) that attempt to emulate human behavior and thought patterns. Intelligent techniques aid decision makers by capturing individual and collective knowledge, discovering patterns and behaviors in very large quantities of data, and generating solutions to problems that are too large and complex for human beings to solve on their own.

Knowledge management systems, which we introduced in Chapter 2, and knowledge work systems provide tools for knowledge discovery, communication, and collaboration that make knowledge more easily available to decision makers and integrate it into the business processes of the firm.

EXPERT SYSTEMS

What if employees in your firm had to make decisions that required some special knowledge, such as how to formulate a fast-drying sealing compound or how to diagnose and repair a malfunctioning diesel engine, but all the people with that expertise had left the firm? Expert systems are one type of decision-making aid that could help you out. An **expert system** captures human expertise in a limited domain of knowledge as a set of rules in a software system that can be used by others in the organization. These systems typically perform a limited number of tasks that can be performed by professionals in a few minutes or hours, such as diagnosing a malfunctioning machine or determining whether to grant credit for a loan. They are useful in decision-making situations where expertise is expensive or in short supply.

How Expert Systems Work

Human knowledge must be modeled or represented in a form that a computer can process. Expert systems model human knowledge as a set of rules that collectively are called the **knowledge base**. Expert systems can have from 200 to as many as 10,000 of these rules, depending on the complexity of the decision-making problem. These rules are much more interconnected and nested than in a traditional software program (see Figure 11.8).

The strategy used to search through the collection of rules and formulate conclusions is called the **inference engine**. The inference engine works by searching through the rules and "firing" those rules that are triggered by facts gathered and entered by the user.

Expert systems provide businesses with an array of benefits, including improved decisions, reduced errors, reduced costs, reduced training time, and improved quality and

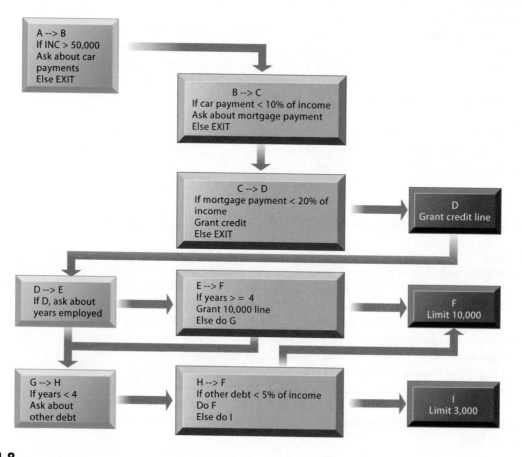

Figure 11.8
Rules in an Expert System

An expert system contains a set of rules to be followed when used. The rules are interconnected, the number of outcomes is known in advance and is limited, there are multiple paths to the same outcome, and the system can consider multiple rules at a single time. The rules illustrated are for a simple credit-granting expert system.

service. For example, Con-Way Transportation built an expert system called Line-haul to automate and optimize planning of overnight shipment routes for its nationwide freight-trucking business. The expert system captures the business rules that dispatchers follow when assigning drivers, trucks, and trailers to transport 50,000 shipments of heavy freight each night across 25 U.S. states and Canada and when plotting their routes. Line-haul runs on a Sun platform and uses data on daily customer shipment requests, available drivers, trucks, trailer space, and weight stored in an Oracle database. The expert system uses thousands of rules and 100,000 lines of program code written in C++ to crunch the numbers and create optimum routing plans for 95 percent of daily freight shipments. Con-Way dispatchers tweak the routing plan provided by the expert system and relay final routing specifications to field personnel responsible for packing the trailers for their nighttime runs. Con-Way recouped its $3 million investment in the system within two years by reducing the number of drivers, packing more freight per trailer, and reducing damage from rehandling. The system also reduces dispatchers' arduous nightly tasks.

Although expert systems lack the robust and general intelligence of human beings, they can provide benefits to organizations if their limitations are well understood. Only certain classes of problems can be solved using expert systems. Virtually all successful expert systems deal with problems of classification in which there are relatively few alternative outcomes and in which these possible outcomes are all known in advance. Expert systems are much less useful for dealing with unstructured problems typically encountered by managers.

CASE-BASED REASONING

Expert systems primarily capture the knowledge of individual experts, but organizations also have collective knowledge and expertise that they have built up over the years. This organizational knowledge can be captured and stored using case-based reasoning. In **case-based reasoning (CBR)**, knowledge and past experiences of human specialists are represented as cases and stored in a database for later retrieval when the user encounters a new case with similar parameters. The system searches for stored cases with problem characteristics similar to the new one, finds the closest fit, and applies the solutions of the old case to the new case. Successful solutions are tagged to the new case and both are stored together with the other cases in the knowledge base. Unsuccessful solutions also are appended to the case database along with explanations as to why the solutions did not work (see Figure 11.9).

You'll find case-based reasoning in diagnostic systems in medicine or customer support where users can retrieve past cases whose characteristics are similar to the new case. The system suggests a solution or diagnosis based on the best-matching retrieved case.

FUZZY LOGIC SYSTEMS

Most people do not think in terms of traditional IF-THEN rules or precise numbers. Humans tend to categorize things imprecisely, using rules for making decisions that may have many shades of meaning. For example, a man or a woman may be *strong* or *intelligent*. A company may be *large, medium,* or *small* in size. Temperature may be *hot, cold, cool,* or *warm.* These categories represent a range of values.

Fuzzy logic is a rule-based technology that represents such imprecision by creating rules that use approximate or subjective values. It describes a particular phenomenon or process linguistically and then represents that description in a small number of flexible rules.

Let's look at the way fuzzy logic would represent various temperatures in a computer application to control room temperature automatically. The terms (known as *membership functions*) are imprecisely defined so that, for example, in Figure 11.10, cool is between 45 degrees and 70 degrees, although the temperature is most clearly cool between about 60 degrees and 67 degrees. Note that *cool* is overlapped by *cold* or *norm*. To control the room environment using this logic, the programmer would develop similarly imprecise definitions for humidity and other factors, such as outdoor wind and temperature. The rules might include one that says, "If the temperature is *cool* or *cold* and the humidity is low while the

Figure 11.9
How Case-Based
Reasoning Works
*Case-based reasoning
represents knowledge as
a database of past cases
and their solutions. The
system uses a six-step
process to generate
solutions to new
problems encountered
by the user.*

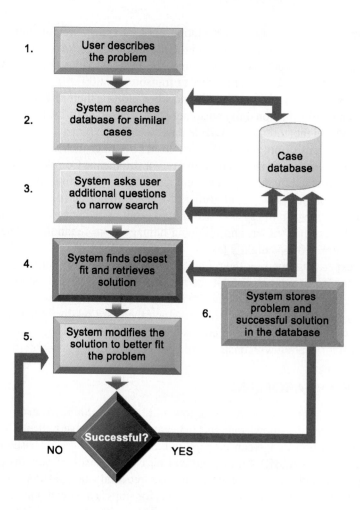

outdoor wind is high and the outdoor temperature is low, raise the heat and humidity in the room." The computer would combine the membership function readings in a weighted manner and, using all the rules, raise and lower the temperature and humidity.

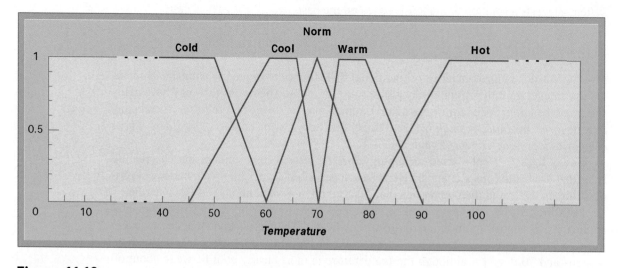

Figure 11.10
Fuzzy Logic for Temperature Control
The membership functions for the input called "temperature" are in the logic of the thermostat to control the room temperature. Membership functions help translate linguistic expressions, such as warm, into numbers that the computer can manipulate.

Fuzzy logic provides solutions to problems requiring expertise that is difficult to represent in the form of crisp IF-THEN rules. In Japan, Sendai's subway system uses fuzzy logic controls to accelerate so smoothly that standing passengers need not hold on. Fuzzy logic allows incremental changes in inputs to produce smooth changes in outputs instead of discontinuous ones, making it useful for consumer electronics and engineering applications.

NEURAL NETWORKS

Neural networks are used for solving complex, poorly understood problems for which large amounts of data have been collected. They find patterns and relationships in massive amounts of data that would be too complicated and difficult for a human being to analyze. Neural networks discover this knowledge by using hardware and software that parallel the processing patterns of the biological or human brain. Neural networks "learn" patterns from large quantities of data by sifting through data, searching for relationships, building models, and correcting over and over again the model's own mistakes.

A neural network has a large number of sensing and processing nodes that continuously interact with each other. Figure 11.11 represents one type of neural network comprising an input layer, a hidden processing layer, and an output layer. Humans "train" the network by feeding it a set of training data for which the inputs produce a known set of outputs or conclusions. This helps the computer learn the correct solution by example. As the computer is fed more data, each case is compared with the known outcome. If it differs, a correction is calculated and applied to the nodes in the hidden processing layer. These steps are repeated until a condition, such as corrections being less than a certain amount, is reached. The neural network in Figure 11.11 has learned how to identify a fraudulent credit card purchase. Also, self-organizing neural networks can be trained by exposing them to large amounts of data and allowing them to discover the patterns and relationships in the data.

Whereas expert systems seek to emulate or model a human expert's way of solving problems, neural network builders claim that they do not program solutions and do not aim to solve specific problems. Instead, neural network designers seek to put intelligence into the hardware in the form of a generalized capability to learn. In contrast, the expert system is highly specific to a given problem and cannot be retrained easily.

Neural network applications in medicine, science, and business address problems in pattern classification, prediction, financial analysis, and control and optimization. In medicine, neural network applications are used for screening patients for coronary artery disease, for diagnosing patients with epilepsy and Alzheimer's disease, and for performing pattern recognition of pathology images. The financial industry uses neural networks to discern patterns in vast pools of data that might help investment firms predict the performance of equities, corporate bond ratings, or corporate bankruptcies. Visa International uses

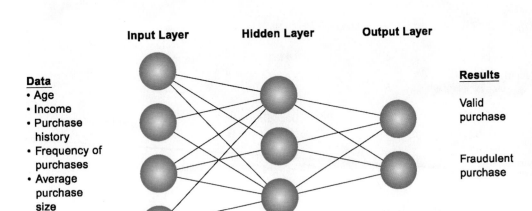

Input Layer **Hidden Layer** **Output Layer**

Data
- Age
- Income
- Purchase history
- Frequency of purchases
- Average purchase size

Results

Valid purchase

Fraudulent purchase

Figure 11.11
How a Neural Network Works
A neural network uses rules it "learns" from patterns in data to construct a hidden layer of logic. The hidden layer then processes inputs, classifying them based on the experience of the model. In this example, the neural network has been trained to distinguish between valid and fraudulent credit card purchases.

a neural network to help detect credit card fraud by monitoring all Visa transactions for sudden changes in the buying patterns of cardholders.

There are many puzzling aspects of neural networks. Unlike expert systems, which typically provide explanations for their solutions, neural networks cannot always explain why they arrived at a particular solution. They may not perform well if their training covers too little or too much data. In most current applications, neural networks are best used as aids to human decision makers instead of substitutes for them.

GENETIC ALGORITHMS

Genetic algorithms are useful for finding the optimal solution for a specific problem by examining a very large number of alternative solutions for that problem. They are based on techniques inspired by evolutionary biology, such as inheritance, mutation, selection, and crossover (recombination).

A genetic algorithm works by representing a solution as a string of 0s and 1s. The genetic algorithm searches a population of randomly generated strings of binary digits to identify the right string representing the best possible solution for the problem. As solutions alter and combine, the worst ones are discarded and the better ones survive to go on to produce even better solutions.

In Figure 11.12, each string corresponds to one of the variables in the problem. One applies a test for fitness, ranking the strings in the population according to their level of desirability as possible solutions. After the initial population is evaluated for fitness, the algorithm then produces the next generation of strings, consisting of strings that survived the fitness test plus offspring strings produced from mating pairs of strings, and tests their fitness. The process continues until a solution is reached.

Genetic algorithms are used to solve problems that are very dynamic and complex, involving hundreds or thousands of variables or formulas. The problem must be one where the range of possible solutions can be represented genetically and criteria can be established for evaluating fitness. Genetic algorithms expedite the solution because they can evaluate many solution alternatives quickly to find the best one. For example, General Electric engineers used genetic algorithms to help optimize the design for jet turbine aircraft engines, where each design

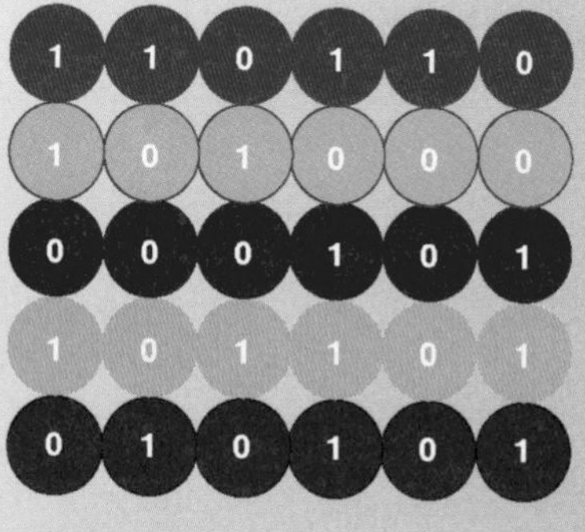

		Length	Width	Weight	Fitness
	1	Long	Wide	Light	55
	2	Short	Narrow	Heavy	49
	3	Long	Narrow	Heavy	36
	4	Short	Medium	Light	61
	5	Long	Medium	Very light	74
A population of chromosomes			Decoding of chromosomes		Evaluation of chromosomes

Figure 11.12
The Components of a Genetic Algorithm
This example illustrates an initial population of "chromosomes," each representing a different solution. The genetic algorithm uses an iterative process to refine the initial solutions so that the better ones, those with the higher fitness, are more likely to emerge as the best solution.

change required changes in up to 100 variables. The supply chain management software from i2 Technologies uses genetic algorithms to optimize production-scheduling models, incorporating hundreds of thousands of details about customer orders, material and resource availability, manufacturing and distribution capability, and delivery dates.

INTELLIGENT AGENTS

Intelligent agent technology helps businesses and decision makers navigate through large amounts of data to locate and act on information that is considered important. **Intelligent agents** are software programs that work in the background without direct human intervention to carry out specific, repetitive, and predictable tasks for an individual user, business process, or software application. The agent uses a limited built-in or learned knowledge base to accomplish tasks or make decisions on the user's behalf, such as deleting junk e-mail, scheduling appointments, or finding the cheapest airfare to California.

There are many intelligent agent applications today in operating systems, application software, e-mail systems, mobile computing software, and network tools. Of special interest to business are intelligent agents that search for information on the Internet. Chapter 7 describes how shopping bots help consumers find products they want and assist them in comparing prices and other features.

Procter & Gamble (P&G) used intelligent agent technology to make its supply chain more efficient (see Figure 11.13). It modeled a complex supply chain as a group of semiautonomous "agents" representing individual supply chain components, such as trucks, production facilities, distributors, and retail stores. The behavior of each agent is programmed to follow rules that mimic actual behavior, such as "order an item when it is out of stock." Simulations using the agents enable the company to perform what-if analyses on inventory levels, in-store stockouts, and transportation costs.

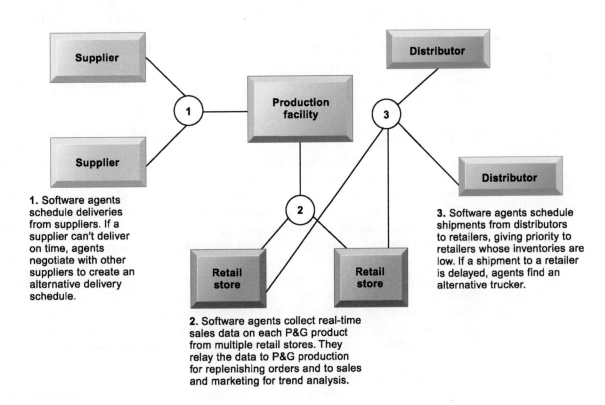

1. Software agents schedule deliveries from suppliers. If a supplier can't deliver on time, agents negotiate with other suppliers to create an alternative delivery schedule.

2. Software agents collect real-time sales data on each P&G product from multiple retail stores. They relay the data to P&G production for replenishing orders and to sales and marketing for trend analysis.

3. Software agents schedule shipments from distributors to retailers, giving priority to retailers whose inventories are low. If a shipment to a retailer is delayed, agents find an alternative trucker.

Figure 11.13
Intelligent Agents in P&G's Supply Chain Network
Intelligent agents are helping Procter & Gamble shorten the replenishment cycles for products, such as a box of Tide.

Using intelligent agent models, P&G discovered that trucks should often be dispatched before being fully loaded. Although transportation costs would be higher using partially loaded trucks, the simulation showed that retail store stockouts would occur less often, thus reducing the amount of lost sales, which would more than make up for the higher distribution costs. Agent-based modeling has saved P&G $300 million annually on an investment of less than 1 percent of that amount.

Although artificial intelligence technology plays an important role in contemporary knowledge management, it still does not exhibit the breadth, complexity, and originality of human intelligence. Computer scientists and neurologists alike have come to realize how sophisticated our brains actually are, and how complicated certain tasks like recognizing language, identifying objects, and making informed decisions can be for computers.

Solving what's known as the "Paris Hilton problem"—determining whether the phrase "Paris Hilton" refers to the celebrity socialite or a hotel in Paris—has been one of the toughest problems for developers of AI systems. Human beings solve ambiguities like this using context, but computers don't have that option.

11.4 Systems for Managing Knowledge

Systems for knowledge management improve the quality and utilization of knowledge used in the decision-making process. **Knowledge management** refers to the set of business processes developed in an organization to create, store, transfer, and apply knowledge. Knowledge management increases the ability of the organization to learn from its environment and to incorporate knowledge into its business processes and decision making.

Knowledge that is not shared and applied to the problems facing firms and managers does not add any value to the business. Knowing how to do things effectively and efficiently in ways that other organizations cannot duplicate is a major source of profit and competitive advantage. Why? Because the knowledge you generate about your own production processes, and about your customers, usually stays within your firm and cannot be sold or purchased on the open market. In this sense, self-generated business knowledge is a strategic resource and can provide strategic advantage. Businesses will operate less effectively and efficiently if this unique knowledge is not available for decision making and ongoing operations. There are two major types of knowledge management systems: enterprise-wide knowledge management systems and knowledge work systems.

ENTERPRISE-WIDE KNOWLEDGE MANAGEMENT SYSTEMS

Firms must deal with at least three kinds of knowledge. Some knowledge exists within the firm in the form of structured text documents (reports and presentations). Decision makers also need knowledge that is semistructured, such as e-mail, voice mail, chat room exchanges, videos, digital pictures, brochures, or bulletin board postings. In still other cases, there is no formal or digital information of any kind, and the knowledge resides in the heads of employees. Much of this knowledge is **tacit knowledge** and is rarely written down.

Enterprise-wide knowledge management systems deal with all three types of knowledge. Enterprise-wide knowledge management systems are general-purpose, firmwide systems that collect, store, distribute, and apply digital content and knowledge. These systems include capabilities for searching for information, storing both structured and unstructured data, and locating employee expertise within the firm. They also include supporting technologies such as portals, search engines, collaboration tools, and learning management systems.

Enterprise Content Management Systems

Businesses today need to organize and manage both structured and semistructured knowledge assets. **Structured knowledge** is explicit knowledge that exists in formal documents, as well as in formal rules that organizations derive by observing experts and their decision-making behaviors. But, according to experts, at least 80 percent of an organization's business content is semistructured or unstructured—information in folders, messages, memos, proposals, e-mails, graphics, electronic slide presentations, and even videos created in different formats and stored in many locations.

Enterprise content management (ECM) systems help organizations manage both types of information. They have capabilities for knowledge capture, storage, retrieval, distribution, and preservation to help firms improve their business processes and decisions. Such systems include corporate repositories of documents, reports, presentations, and best practices, as well as capabilities for collecting and organizing semistructured knowledge such as e-mail (see Figure 11.14). Major enterprise content management systems also enable users to access external sources of information, such as news feeds and research, and to communicate via e-mail, chat/instant messaging, discussion groups, and videoconferencing.

A key problem in managing knowledge is the creation of an appropriate classification scheme to organize information into meaningful categories. Once the categories for classifying knowledge have been created, each knowledge object needs to be "tagged," or classified, so that it can be easily retrieved. Enterprise content management systems have capabilities for tagging, interfacing with corporate databases where the documents are stored, and creating an enterprise portal environment for employees to use when searching for corporate knowledge. Open Text, EMC Documentum, IBM, and Oracle are leading vendors of enterprise content management software.

The City of Denver implemented Alfresco, a Web-based open-source enterprise content management system to replace 14 different document management systems used by more than 70 agencies of the consolidated city-county government, none of which could communicate or interact with each other. The Alfresco ECM system features document, record, and image management; document versioning; multi-language support; support for multiple client operating systems; Web content management; and integration with MySQL, which Denver used for its relational database management system. Implementation of a single ECM system has increased security, document sharing, and the ability to audit scanned contracts and financial records. Employee productivity has risen, and management believes the Alfresco system is saving Denver $1.5 million over five years.

Firms in publishing, advertising, broadcasting, and entertainment have special needs for storing and managing unstructured digital data such as photographs, graphic images, video, and audio content. **Digital asset management systems** help them classify, store, and distribute these digital objects.

Knowledge Network Systems

Knowledge network systems, address the problem that arises when the appropriate knowledge is not in the form of a digital document but instead resides in the memory of expert individuals in the firm. Knowledge network systems provide an online directory of corporate

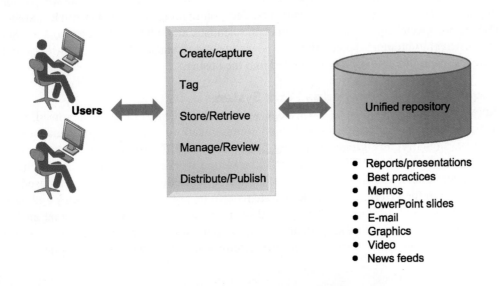

Figure 11.14
An Enterprise Content Management System
An enterprise content management system has capabilities for classifying, organizing, and managing structured and semistructured knowledge and making it available throughout the enterprise.

experts and their profiles, with details about their job experience, projects, publications, and educational degrees. Search tools make it easy for employees to find the appropriate expert in a company. Knowledge network systems such as Hivemine's AskMe include repositories of expert-generated content. Some knowledge networking capabilities are included in the leading enterprise content management, social networking, and collaboration software products.

Collaboration Tools and Learning Management Systems

We have already discussed the role of collaboration tools in information sharing and teamwork in Chapters 2 and 7. Social bookmarking and learning management systems feature additional capabilities for sharing and managing knowledge.

Social bookmarking makes it easier to search for and share information by allowing users to save their bookmarks to Web pages on a public Web site and tag these bookmarks with keywords. These tags can be used to organize and search for the documents. Lists of tags can be shared with other people to help them find information of interest. The user-created taxonomies created for shared bookmarks and social tagging are called **folksonomies**. Delicious and Digg are two popular social bookmarking sites.

Suppose, for example, that you are on a corporate team researching wind power. If you did a Web search and found relevant Web pages on wind power, you would click on a bookmarking button on a social bookmarking site and create a tag identifying each Web document you found to link it to wind power. By clicking on the "tags" button at the social networking site, you would be able to see a list of all the tags you created and select the documents you need.

Companies need ways to keep track of and manage employee learning and to integrate it more fully into their knowledge management and other corporate systems. A **learning management system (LMS)** provides tools for the management, delivery, tracking, and assessment of various types of employee learning and training.

Businesses run their own learning management systems, but they are also turning to publicly-available **massive open online courses (MOOCs)** to educate their employees. A MOOC is an online course made available via the Web to a very large numbers of participants. For example, in March, 2013, employees from General Electric, Johnson & Johnson, Samsung, and Walmart were among over 90,000 learners from 143 countries enrolled in Foundations of Business Strategy, a MOOC offered through the Coursera online learning platform by the University of Virginia's Darden School of Business. The course explored the frameworks and theories underlying successful business strategies (Nurmohamed, Gillani, and Lenox, 2013).

KNOWLEDGE WORK SYSTEMS

The enterprise-wide knowledge systems we have just described provide a wide range of capabilities used by many, if not all, the workers and groups in an organization. Firms also have specialized systems for knowledge workers to help them create new knowledge for improving the firm's business processes and decision making. **Knowledge work systems (KWS)** are specialized systems for engineers, scientists, and other knowledge workers that are designed to promote the creation of knowledge and to ensure that new knowledge and technical expertise are properly integrated into the business.

Requirements of Knowledge Work Systems

Knowledge work systems give knowledge workers the specialized tools they need, such as powerful graphics, analytical tools, and communications and document management. These systems require great computing power to handle the sophisticated graphics or complex calculations necessary for such knowledge workers as scientific researchers, product designers, and financial analysts. Because knowledge workers are so focused on knowledge in the external world, these systems also must give the worker quick and easy access to external databases. They typically feature user-friendly interfaces that enable users to perform needed tasks without having to spend a lot of time learning how to use the computer. Figure 11.15 summarizes the requirements of knowledge work systems.

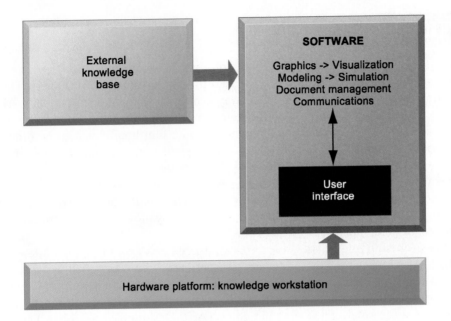

Figure 11.15
Requirements of Knowledge Work Systems
Knowledge work systems require strong links to external knowledge bases in addition to specialized hardware and software.

Knowledge workstations often are designed and optimized for the specific tasks to be performed. Design engineers need graphics with enough power to handle three-dimensional CAD systems. However, financial analysts are more interested in access to a myriad of external databases and technology for efficiently storing and accessing massive amounts of financial data.

Examples of Knowledge Work Systems

Major knowledge work applications include CAD systems (which we introduced in Chapter 3), virtual reality systems for simulation and modeling, and financial workstations.

Contemporary CAD systems are capable of generating realistic-looking three-dimensional graphic designs that can be rotated and viewed from all sides. The CAD software produces design specifications for manufacturing, reducing both errors and production time. The Interactive Session on Technology illustrates some of these benefits and shows how they can be sources of competitive advantage.

Virtual reality systems use interactive graphics software to create computer-generated simulations that are so close to reality that users almost believe they are participating in a real-world situation. In many virtual reality systems, the user dons special clothing, headgear, and equipment, depending on the application. The clothing contains sensors that record the user's movements and immediately transmit that information back to the computer. For instance, to walk through a virtual reality simulation of a house, you would need garb that monitors the movement of your feet, hands, and head. You also would need goggles containing video screens and sometimes audio attachments and feeling gloves so that you are immersed in the computer feedback.

Ford Motor Company has been using virtual reality to help design its vehicles. In one example of Ford's Immersive Virtual Environment, a designer was presented with a car seat, steering wheel, and blank dashboard. Wearing virtual reality glasses and gloves with sensors, the designer was able to "sit" in the seat surrounded by the vehicle's 3-D design to experience how a proposed interior would look and feel. The designer would be able to identify blind spots or see if knobs were in an awkward place. Ford's designers could also use this technology to see the impact of a design on manufacturing. For example, is a bolt that assembly line workers need to tighten too hard to reach (Murphy, 2012)?

Augmented reality (AR) is a related technology for enhancing visualization. AR provides a live direct or indirect view of a physical real-world environment whose

INTERACTIVE SESSION: TECHNOLOGY   Firewire Surfboards Lights Up with CAD

Nev Hyman had been building surfboards in Australia for 35 years. In 2005, he teamed up with Mark Price and a group of longtime surfing friends in Carlsbad, CA, to form Firewire Surfboards. This company thrives on innovation and was responsible for the first major change in surfboard composition and assembly methods in 40 years. Rather than polyurethane resin and polyurethane foam, Firewire's boards were composed of expanded polystyrene (EPS) foam and epoxy resins. Hyman and Price believed that this composition for the surfboard core, along with aerospace composites for the deck skin and balsa wood rails (the outside edge), created a more flexible and maneuverable product that would attract top surfers and set Firewire apart from its competitors.

FireWire is competing in a crowded field that includes Isle Surfboards, Surftech, Aviso Surf, Boardworks Surf, Channel Island, and Lost Enterprises. FireWire is alone in the reintroduction of balsa wood to the board rails for added flex response time and the ability to maintain speed during precarious maneuvers. Firewire believes it can compete successfully because its surf boards are far lighter, stronger, and more flexible than those of competitors. An additional selling point is the reduced environmental impact: Firewire's materials emit only 2 percent of the harmful compounds of traditional boards and recycling excess expanded polystyrene (EPS) foam has earned Firewire international awards and acclaim.

But that isn't enough. To make sure it stays ahead of the competition, Firewire decided to start making custom surfboards instead of just the usual off-the-rack sizes. For the everyday surfer, the durability and flexibility of Firewire's materials was a key selling point. However, custom boards made to surfer specifications are critical in the elite surfboard market, and the ability to claim top-level competitive surfers as customers drives the broader surfboard market as well.

Traditionally, skilled craftsman, called shapers, designed and built surfboards by hand, but Firewire started doing some of this work using computer-aided designs (CAD) sent to cutting facilities. The company's computer-aided manufacturing process returned to the shaper a board that was 85–90 percent complete, leaving the artisan to complete the customization and the lamination process.

According to Price, who became Firewire's CEO, there are 29 time-consuming and labor intensive steps in the surfboard manufacturing process. Initially, the multifaceted manufacturing process made it impossible to offer personalized CAD to the average consumer. Customized boards could only be produced for elite competitive customers. There was no way to offer customization to a wider market without overburdening Firewire's CAD system. Moreover, most custom boards had to be ordered by filling out a piece of paper with various dimensions for the requested changes. There was no way to see a visual representation of these adjustments or assess their impact on the board's volume, which directly affects buoyancy, paddling ability, and performance.

Firewire needed a system that would allow customers to experiment with established designs, feed the CAD process, and integrate it with its computer numerical control (CNC) manufacturing process. Enter ShapeLogic Design-to-Order Live! For NX, which provides an online customization system with a Web-based user interface and advanced 3D CAD tools.

Firewire started working with the ShapeLogicNX software in 2009 to develop its own Firewire Surfboards' Custom Board Design (CBD) system, which allows users to easily manipulate board dimensions of established models within design parameters. Any registered customer can choose a standard Firewire model and use drag-and-drop tools to adjust the board's length, midpoint width, nose width, tail width, and thickness, as long as these changes don't degrade the board's design integrity. CBD generates a precise three-dimensional model of the stock model used as the base design along with a 3D portable document format (PDF) file of the customized board. The PDF file documents the board's dimensions and volume. A customer can manipulate the model from all angles and compare the customized board to the standard board to fully understand the design before placing an order. When the customer uses the system to order a custom board, CBD generates a precise solid CAD model of the board that is transmitted directly to the Firewire factory for driving the CNC machines that manufacture the board.

This combination of technologies results in a board that is 97 percent complete, minimizing the manufacturing time, finishing process, and thus, costs to the consumer. In contrast to the earlier CAD assisted, 10–15 percent hand-finished boards, once a surfer has designed the board of his or her dreams, it can be remade to those exact specifications time and again. Neither the ideal handmade board nor a shaper-finished board can be replicated with this degree of precision.

An additional benefit of Firewire's online design system is the social networking engendered by the sharing of customers' unique design files. Before placing an order, customers can show their modifications to fellow surfers and ask for opinions and advice. After placing an order and using the product, they can report their experiences and (hopefully) tout their design or suggest improvements to other customers. Interactive communication such as this drives customers to the Firewire site, creating a marketing buzz that boosts sales.

Sources: "Case Study: NX CAD Technology Drives Custom Surfboard Design," http://www.plm.automation.siemens.com/en_us, accessed August 9, 2013; www.firewiresurfboards.com, accessed August 9, 2013; "Firewire Partners with NanoTune 'Board Tuning Technology,'" www.surfnewsdaily.com, February 22, 2012; "Firewire Surfboards Custom Board Design Blends Replicability of Machine Made Boards With Uniqueness of Custom Boards," http://surfingnewsdaily.com, October 12, 2011; and William Atkinson, "How Firewire Surfboards Refined Its 3D Order Customization," www.cioinsight.com, November 21, 2011.

CASE STUDY QUESTIONS

1. Analyze Firewire using the value chain and competitive forces models.

2. What strategies is Firewire using to differentiate its product, reach its customers, and persuade them to buy its products?

3. What is the role of CAD in Firewire's business model?

4. How did the integration of online custom board design software (CBD), CAD, and computer numerical control (CNC) improve Firewire's operations?

elements are augmented by virtual computer-generated imagery. The user is grounded in the real physical world, and the virtual images are merged with the real view to create the augmented display. The digital technology provides additional information to enhance the perception of reality, making the surrounding real world of the user more interactive and meaningful. The yellow first-down markers shown on televised football games are examples of augmented reality as are medical procedures like image-guided surgery, where data acquired from computerized tomography (CT) and magnetic resonance imaging (MRI) scans or from ultrasound imaging are superimposed on the patient in the operating room. Google Glass, a hands-free, head-mounted wearable computer that can be worn as eyewear, includes augmented reality applications such as specifying the height of a building the user is viewing at the moment and translating a sign into another language.

Virtual reality applications developed for the Web use a standard called **Virtual Reality Modeling Language (VRML)**. VRML is a set of specifications for interactive, three-dimensional modeling on the World Wide Web that organizes multiple media types, including animation, images, and audio, to put users in a simulated real-world environment. VRML is platform independent, operates over a desktop computer, and requires little bandwidth.

DuPont, the Wilmington, Delaware, chemical company, created a VRML application called HyperPlant, which enables users to access three-dimensional data over the Internet using Web browser software. Engineers can go through three-dimensional models as if they were physically walking through a plant, viewing objects at eye level. This level of detail reduces the number of mistakes they make during construction of oil rigs, oil plants, and other structures.

The financial industry is using specialized **investment workstations** to leverage the knowledge and time of its brokers, traders, and portfolio managers. Firms such as Merrill Lynch and UBS Financial Services have installed investment workstations that integrate a wide range of data from both internal and external sources, including contact management data, real-time and historical market data, and research reports. Previously, financial professionals had to spend considerable time accessing data from separate systems and piecing together the information they needed. By providing one-stop information faster and with fewer errors, the workstations streamline the entire investment process from stock selection to updating client records.

Review Summary

1 **What are the different types of decisions, and how does the decision-making process work?** Decisions may be structured, semistructured, or unstructured, with structured decisions clustering at the operational level of the organization and unstructured decisions at the strategic level. Decision making can be performed by individuals or groups and includes employees as well as operational, middle, and senior managers. There are four stages in decision making: intelligence, design, choice, and implementation.

2 **How do business intelligence and business analytics support decision making?** Business intelligence and analytics promise to deliver correct, nearly real-time information to decision makers, and the analytic tools help them quickly understand the information and take action. A business intelligence environment consists of data from the business environment, the BI infrastructure, a BA toolset, managerial users and methods, a BI delivery platform (MIS, DSS, or ESS), and the user interface. There are six analytic functionalities that BI systems deliver to achieve these ends: pre-defined production reports, parameterized reports, dashboards and scorecards, ad hoc queries and searches, the ability to drill down to detailed views of data, and the ability to model scenarios and create forecasts. BI analytics are starting to handle big data. Predictive analytics and location analytics are important analytic capabilities.

Management information systems (MIS) producing prepackaged production reports are typically used to support operational and middle management, whose decision making is fairly structured. For making unstructured decisions, analysts and "super users" employ decision-support systems (DSS) with powerful analytics and modeling tools, including spreadsheets and pivot tables. Senior executives making unstructured decisions use dashboards and visual interfaces displaying key performance information affecting the overall profitability, success, and strategy of the firm. The balanced scorecard and business performance management are two methodologies used in designing executive support systems (ESS).

3 **How do information systems help people working in a group make decisions more efficiently?** Group decision-support systems (GDSS) help people meeting together in a group arrive at decisions more efficiently. GDSS feature special conference room facilities where participants contribute their ideas using networked computers and software tools for organizing ideas, gathering information, ranking and setting priorities, and documenting meeting sessions.

4 **What are the business benefits of using intelligent techniques in decision making and knowledge management?** Expert systems capture tacit knowledge from a limited domain of human expertise and express that knowledge in the form of rules. The strategy to search through the knowledge base is called the inference engine. Case-based reasoning represents organizational knowledge as a database of cases that can be continually expanded and refined.

Fuzzy logic is a software technology for expressing knowledge in the form of rules that use approximate or subjective values. Neural networks consist of hardware and software that attempt to mimic the thought processes of the human brain. Neural networks are notable for their ability to learn without programming and to recognize patterns in massive amounts of data.

Genetic algorithms develop solutions to particular problems using genetically-based processes, such as fitness, crossover, and mutation. Intelligent agents are software programs with built-in or learned knowledge bases that carry out specific, repetitive, and predictable tasks for an individual user, business process, or software application.

5 **What types of systems are used for enterprise-wide knowledge management and knowledge work, and how do they provide value for businesses?** Enterprise content management systems feature databases and tools for organizing and storing structured documents and semistructured knowledge, such as e-mail or rich media. Knowledge network systems provide directories and tools for locating firm employees with special expertise who are important sources of tacit knowledge. Often these systems include group collaboration tools, portals to simplify information access, search tools, and tools for classifying information based on a taxonomy that is appropriate for the organization. Learning management systems provide tools for the management, delivery, tracking, and assessment of various types of employee learning and training.

Knowledge work systems (KWS) support the creation of new knowledge and its integration into the organization. KWS require easy access to an external knowledge base; powerful computer hardware that can support software with intensive graphics, analysis, document management, and communications capabilities; and a user-friendly interface.

Key Terms

Artificial intelligence (AI), 407
Augmented reality, 417
Balanced scorecard method, 405
Business performance management (BPM), 406
Case-based reasoning (CBR), 409
Choice, 395
Data visualization, 398
Design, 395
Digital asset management systems, 415
Drill down, 406
Enterprise content management systems, 415
Enterprise-wide knowledge management systems, 414
Expert system, 408

Folksonomies, 416
Fuzzy logic, 409
Genetic algorithms, 412
Geographic information systems (GIS), 401
Group decision-support systems (GDSS), 407
Implementation, 395
Intelligence, 395
Inference engine, 408
Intelligent agents, 413
Intelligent techniques, 407
Investment workstations, 419
Key performance indicators (KPIs), 405
Knowledge base, 408
Knowledge management, 414
Knowledge network systems, 415

Knowledge work systems (KWS), 416
Learning management system (LMS), 416
Location analytics, 401
Massive open online course (MOOC), 416
Neural networks, 411
Pivot table, 404
Predictive analytics, 399
Semistructured decisions, 394
Sensitivity analysis, 403
Social bookmarking, 416
Structured decisions, 394
Structured knowledge, 414
Tacit knowledge, 414
Unstructured decisions, 394
Virtual reality systems, 417
Virtual Reality Modeling Language (VRML), 419

Review Questions

11-1 What are the different types of decisions and how does the decision-making process work?
- List and describe the different decision-making levels and decision-making groups in organizations, and their decision-making requirements.
- Distinguish between an unstructured, semistructured, and structured decision.
- List and describe the stages in decision making.
- Explain how you can determine the quality of decisions and decision making.
- Describe some of the issues involved with high velocity automated decision making.

11-2 How do business intelligence and business analytics support decision making?
- Define and describe business intelligence and business analytics.
- List and describe the elements of a business intelligence environment.
- List and describe the analytic functionalities provided by BI systems.
- Define predictive analytics and location analytics and give 2 examples of each.
- Describe Big Data analytics and provide 2 examples.
- List each of the types of business intelligence users and describe the kinds of systems that provide decision support for each type of user.

11-3 How do information systems help people working in a group make decisions more efficiently?

- Define a group decision support system (GDSS), and explain how it works and how it supports organizational decision making.

11-4 What are the business benefits of using intelligent techniques in decision making and knowledge management?

- Define an expert system, describe how it works, and explain its value to business.
- Define case-based reasoning and explains how it differs from an expert system.
- Define a neural network, and describe how it works and how it benefits businesses.
- Define and describe fuzzy logic, genetic algorithms, and intelligent agents. Explain how each works and the kinds of problems for which each is suited.

11-5 What types of systems are used for enterprise-wide knowledge management and knowledge work, and how do they provide value for businesses?

- Define knowledge management and explain its value to businesses.
- Define and describe the various types of enterprise-wide knowledge systems and explain how they provide value for businesses.
- Define knowledge work systems and describe the generic requirements of these systems.
- Describe how the following systems support knowledge work: computer-aided design (CAD), virtual reality, and investment workstations.
- Provide examples of collaboration tools and learning management systems.

Discussion Questions

11-6 Why is the balanced scorecard method a leading methodology for understanding the most important information needed a firm's executives? How is related to business performance management?

11-7 Describe various ways that knowledge management systems could help firms with sales and marketing or with manufacturing and production.

11-8 How much can business intelligence and business analytics help companies refine their business strategy? Explain your answer.

Hands-On MIS Projects

The projects in this section give you hands-on experience designing a knowledge portal, identifying opportunities for business intelligence, using a spreadsheet pivot table to analyze sales data, and using intelligent agents to research products for sale on the Web.

MANAGEMENT DECISION PROBLEMS

11-9 British Pharma Corporation Corporation is headquartered in London but has research sites in Germany, France, Switzerland, and Australia. Research and development of new pharmaceuticals is key to ongoing profits, and British Pharma researches and tests thousands of possible drugs. The company's researchers need to share information with others within and outside the company, including the the World Health Organization, and the International Federation of Pharmaceutical Manufacturers & Associations. Also critical is access to health information sites, such as the and to industry conferences and professional journals. Design a knowledge portal for British Pharma's researchers. Include in your design specifications relevant internal systems and databases, external sources of information, and internal and external communication and collaboration tools. Design a home page for your portal.

11-10 Applebee's is the largest casual dining chain in the world, with over 1,800 locations in 21 countries throughout the world. The menu features beef, chicken, and pork items, as well as burgers, pasta, and seafood. Applebee's CEO wants to make the restaurant more profitable by developing menus that are tastier and contain more items that customers want and are willing to pay for despite rising costs for gasoline and agricultural products. How might business intelligence help management implement this strategy? What pieces of data would Applebee's need to collect? What kinds of reports would be useful to help management make decisions on how to improve menus and profitability?

IMPROVING DECISION MAKING: USING PIVOT TABLES TO ANALYZE SALES DATA

Software skills: Pivot tables
Business skills: Analyzing sales data

11-11 This project gives you an opportunity to learn how to use Excel's PivotTable functionality to analyze a database or data list. Use the data file for Online Management Training Inc. described earlier in the chapter. This is a list of the sales transactions at OMT for one day. You can find this spreadsheet file at MyMISLab. Use Excel's PivotTable to help you answer the following questions:

- Where are the average purchases higher? The answer might tell managers where to focus marketing and sales resources, or pitch different messages to different regions.
- What form of payment is the most common? The answer could be used to emphasize in advertising the most preferred means of payment.
- Are there any times of day when purchases are most common? Do people buy products while at work (likely during the day) or at home (likely in the evening)?
- What's the relationship between region, type of product purchased, and average sales price?

We provide instructions on how to use Excel PivotTables in our Learning Tracks.

IMPROVING DECISION MAKING: USING INTELLIGENT AGENTS FOR COMPARISON SHOPPING

Software skills: Web browser and shopping bot software
Business skills: Product evaluation and selection

11-12 This project will give you experience using shopping bots to search online for products, find product information, and find the best prices and vendors. Select a LCD flat screen television you might want to purchase, such as a 46-inch LG or a similar Samsung model. Visit Kelkoo (kelkoo.co.uk), Shopzilla, and Google Shopping to do price comparisons for you. Evaluate these shopping sites in terms of their ease of use, number of offerings, speed in obtaining information, thoroughness of information offered about the product and seller, and price selection. Which site or sites would you use and why? Which camera would you select and why? How helpful were these sites for making your decision?

Collaboration and Teamwork Project

11-13 In MyMISLab, you will find a Collaboration and Teamwork Project dealing with the concepts in this chapter. You will be able to use Google Drive, Google Docs, Google Sites, Google+, or other open-source tools to complete the assignment.

BUSINESS PROBLEM-SOLVING CASE

Should a Computer Grade Your Essays?

Would you like your college essays graded by a computer? Well, you just might find that happening in your next course. In April 2013, EdX, a Harvard/MIT joint venture to develop massively open online courses (MOOCs), launched an essay scoring program. Using artificial intelligence technology, essays and short answers are immediately scored and feedback tendered, allowing students to revise, resubmit, and improve their grade as many times as necessary. The non-profit organization is offering the software free to any institution that wants to use it. From a pedagogical standpoint—if the guidance is sound—immediate feedback and the ability to directly act on it is an optimal learning environment. But while proponents trumpet automated essay grading's superiority to students waiting days or weeks for returned papers—which they may or may not have the opportunity to revise—as well as the time-saving benefit for instructors, critics doubt that humans can be replaced.

In 2012, Les Perelman, the former director of writing at MIT, countered a paper touting the proficiency of automated essay scoring (AES) software. University of Akron College of Education dean, Mark Shermis, and co-author, data scientist Ben Hamner used AES programs from nine companies, including Pearson and McGraw-Hill, to rescore over 16,000 middle and high school essays from six different state standardized tests. Their Hewlett Foundation sponsored study found that machine scoring closely tracked human grading, and in some cases, produced a more accurate grade. Perelman, however, found that no direct statistical comparison between the human graders and the programs was performed. While Shermis concedes that appropriate statistical analysis was not performed—because the software companies imposed this condition in order to allow him and Hamner to test their products—he unsurprisingly accuses Perelman of evaluating their work without performing research of his own.

Perelman has in fact conducted studies on the Electronic Essay Rater (e-Rater) developed by the Educational Testing Service (ETS)—the only organization that would allow him access. The e-rater uses syntactic variety, discourse structure and content analysis and is based on natural language processing technology. It applies statistical analysis to linguistic features like argument formation and syntactic variety to determine scores, but also gives weight to vocabulary and topical content. In the month granted him, Perelman analyzed the algorithms and toyed with the e-Rater, confirming his prior critiques. The major problem with AES programs (so far) is that they cannot distinguish fact from fiction. For example, in response to an essay prompt about the causes for the steep rise in the cost of higher education, Perelman wrote that the main driver was greedy teaching assistants whose salaries were six times that of college presidents with exorbitant benefits packages including South Seas vacations, private jets, and movie contracts. He supplemented the argument with a line from Allen Ginsberg's "Howl," and received the top score of 6. The metrics that merited this score included overall length, paragraph length, number of words per sentence, word length, and the use of conjunctive adverbs such as "however" and "moreover." Since computer programs cannot divine meaning, essay length is a proxy for writing fluency, conjunctive adverb use for complex thinking, and big words for vocabulary aptitude.

Program vendors such as Pearson and Vantage Learning defend these parameters, asserting that they are highly correlated. Good writers have acquired skills that enable them to write more under time constraints; they use more complex vocabulary, and they understand how to introduce, interrupt, connect, and conclude complex ideas—the jobs of conjunctive adverbs. AES programs also recognize sentence fragments and dock students for sentences that begin with "and" or "or." However, professional writers know how to employ both to great effect. And Perelman and a newly formed group of educators, Professionals Against Machine Scoring of Student Essays in High-Stakes Assessment, warn that writing instruction will be dumbed down to meet the limited and rigid metrics machines are capable of measuring.

The productivity gains from using automated essay-grading software will undoubtedly take away some of the jobs of the graders hired by the standardized test companies. Pearson, for example, ostensibly pays its graders between $40 and $60 per hour. In that hour, a grader is expected to score between 20 and 30 essays—that's two to three minutes (and dollars) per essay. Clearly graders must use some type of shorthand metrics in order to score this quickly. But at least they can recognize as false the statement that on July 4, 2013, the United States observed its 2,013th birthday, even if it is contained in a well-constructed sentence. While the e-Rater can score 16,000 essays in 20 seconds, it cannot. And presumably, a 716 word essay containing multiple nonsense sentences will not receive a 6 from a human grader while a 150 word shorter, factual, well-reasoned essay scores a 5, as Perelman was able to demonstrate.

ETS, developer of the SAT, GRE, Praxis, and K-12 standardized tests for multiple states, counters that the e-Rater is not replacing human graders in high-stakes tests; it is supplementing them. Essays are scored by both human and machine and when the scores do not match, a second human breaks the impasse. Furthermore, they posit that the test prep course Perelman developed to teach students how to beat AES software requires higher-order thinking skills—precisely those the tests seek to measure. Thus, if students can master Perelman's techniques, they have likely earned their 6. Pearson adds that its Intelligent Essay Assessor is primarily a classroom tool, allowing students to revise their essays multiple times before turning them in to a teacher to be graded. But for many states looking to introduce writing sections to their battery of K-12 standardized tests, and for those that abandoned the effort due to the cost, eliminating graders altogether will make them affordable. And the stakes are not insubstantial for failure to achieve passing grades on state standardized tests, ranging from retesting, to remedial programs, to summer school, to non-promotion.

The free EdX tool appears to be more sophisticated than some vendor offerings in that it is "trainable" with at least some ability to develop grading standards and to adapt to grading preferences. First, instructors grade 100 essays or essay questions, and these are input to the program. Using these guidelines, the tool develops customized grading metrics and follows the scoring method preferred by the instructor, either a numerical system or letter grade. As noted by Shermis, in many lesser-ranked colleges than those of the critics, classes are now so large as to render comprehensive writing feedback infeasible. Moreover, at top universities, the instructional level is higher with fewer students in need of remediation. Down in the educational trenches, a tool that can adequately simulate human scoring, with no greater variation than that seen from instructor to instructor, and that provides immediate guidance, is a welcome addition to the instructional toolbox. But as demands on instructor's time decrease, will university administrators push staff cutbacks to meet budgetary constraints? Will fewer and fewer instructors be teaching more and more students?

As MOOC and AES proliferate, the answer is: most likely. Ed X is quickly becoming controversial in academic circles. Presently, its course offerings are free and students earn a certificate of completion, but not course credit. To become self-sustaining, however, the non-profit plans to offer its MOOC platform as a "self-service" system, which faculty members can use to develop courses specifically branded for their universities. EdX will then receive the first $50,000 in revenue

generated from the course or $10,000 for a recurring course. Thereafter, revenue will be split 50-50 between the university and EdX. A second revenue-generating model offers universities "production help" with course development, charging them $250,000 for a new course and $50,000 each term the course is offered again. If a course is successful, the university receives 70 percent of the revenue, as long as EdX has been fully compensated for any self-service courses. However, in order to generate enough revenue to share with its 12 university partners, which now include University of California, Berkeley, Wellesley, Georgetown, and the University of Texas, a licensing model is likely. Tested at no charge at San Jose State University in 2012, an EdX MOOC served as the basis for a blended online engineering course. The enriched curriculum resulted in an increased passing rate from 60 percent to 91 percent. If course licensing becomes the key revenue stream, Anant Agarwal, the electrical engineer president of EdX, foresees this happening in closed classrooms with limited enrollment.

But some members of the San Jose State faculty are nonetheless alarmed. When a second EdX MOOC, JusticeX, was considered, the Philosophy department sent a sharply worded letter addressed to Harvard course developer, Michael Sandel, but actually leveled at university administrators. Asserting that the department did not have an academic problem in need of remediation and was not lacking faculty to teach its equivalent course, it did not shy from attacking the economic motives behind public universities' embrace of MOOCs. The authors further asserted that MOOCs represented a decline in educational quality and noted the irony involved when a social justice course was the vehicle for perpetrating a social injustice—a long-term effort to "dismantle departments and replace professors." Sandel's conciliatory response expressed his desire to share free educational resources, his aversion to undercutting colleagues, and a call for a serious debate at both EdX and in the higher education community.

Other universities are similarly pushing back, against both EdX and other new MOOC ventures such as Coursera and Udacity, founded by Stanford faculty members. MOOCs and AES are inextricably linked. Massive online courses require automated assessment systems. And both Coursera and Udacity have expressed their commitment to using them due to the value of immediate feedback. Amherst College faculty voted against joining the EdX consortium. Duke University faculty members thwarted administration attempts to join nine other universities and educational technology company 2U in a venture to develop a collection of for-credit undergraduate courses.

But EdX was founded by two of the most prominent universities in the United States, has gathered prestigious partners, and is already shaping educational standards.

Stanford, for one, has decided to get on board; it adopted the OpenEdX open-source platform and began offering a summer reading program for freshman and two public courses in the summer of 2013. Stanford will collaborate with EdX on the future development of OpenEdX and will offer both public and university classes on it.

So while Professor Perelman jokes that his former computer science major students could develop an Android app capable of spitting out formulaic essays that would get a 6 from e-Rater, cutting humans completely out of the equation, he knows that serious issues are in play. What educational outcomes will result from diminishing human interaction and input? Will AI develop to the point that truth, accuracy, effective organization, persuasiveness, argumentation and supporting evidence can be evaluated? And how many more jobs in education will disappear as a result?

Sources: Michael Gonchar, "How Would You Feel About a Computer Grading Your Essays?" New York Times, April 5, 2013; Steve Kolowich, "How EdX Plans to Earn, and Share, Revenue From Its Free Online Courses," The Chronicle of Higher Education, February 21, 2013; John Markoff, "Essay-Grading Software Offers Professors a Break," *New York Times*, April 4, 2013; Ry Rivard, "Humans Fight Over Robo-Readers," Inside Higher Ed, March 15, 2013; David Rotman, "How Technology Is Destroying Jobs, MIT Technology Review, June 12, 2013; Randall Stross, "The Algorithm Didn't Like My Essay, *New York Times*, June 9, 2012; Michael Winerip, "Facing a Robo-Grader? Just Keep Obfuscating Mellifluously," *New York Times*, April 22, 2012; Paul Wiseman, Bernard Condon, and Jonathan Fahey, "Can smart machines take your job? Middle class jobs increasingly being replaced by technology," *The Associated Press*, January 24, 2013; "San Jose State University Faculty Pushes Back Against EdX," Inside Higher Ed, May 3, 2013.

Case Study Questions

11-14 How "intelligent" is automated essay grading? Explain your answer.

11-15 How effective is automated essay grading?

11-16 What are the benefits of automated essay grading? What are the drawbacks?

11-17 What people, organization, and technology factors should be considered when deciding whether to use AES?

11-18 Would you be suspicious of a low grade you received on a paper graded by AES software? Why or why not? Would you request a review by a human grader?

Building and Managing Systems

PART IV

Part IV shows how to use the knowledge acquired in earlier
chapters to analyze and design information system solutions to
business problems. This part answers questions such as these:
How can I develop a solution to an information system problem
that provides genuine business benefits? How can the firm adjust
to the changes introduced by the new system solution? What
alternative approaches are available for building system solutions?

Building Information Systems and Managing Projects

CHAPTER 12

STUDENT LEARNING OBJECTIVES

After completing this chapter, you will be able to answer the following questions:

1. What are the core problem-solving steps for developing new information systems?

2. What are the alternative methods for building information systems?

3. What are the principal methodologies for modeling and designing systems?

4. How should information systems projects be selected and evaluated?

5. How should information systems projects be managed?

CHAPTER OUTLINE

A NEW ORDERING SYSTEM FOR GIRL SCOUT COOKIES

Thin Mints, Samoas, and Trefoils may be fun to eat, but selling Girl Scout cookies is a serious business. During the 2012 sales season, the Girl Scouts sold about 215 million boxes of cookies, bringing in $785 million in revenue. Cookie sales are a major source of funding for the Girl Scouts, and an opportunity for the 1.5 million girls who do the selling to develop valuable sales and money management skills. However, collecting, counting, and organizing the annual avalanche of cookie orders has become a tremendous challenge.

The Girl Scouts' traditional cookie-ordering process depends on mountains of paperwork. During the peak sales period in January, each Girl Scout marked her sales on an individual order card and turned the card in to the troop leader when she was finished. The troop leader would transfer the information onto a five-part form and give this form to a community volunteer who tabulated the orders. From there, the orders data passed to a regional council headquarters, where they would be batched into final orders for the manufacturer, ABC Cookies. In addition to ordering, Girl Scout

© LES BREAULT/Alamy.

volunteers and troop members had to coordinate cookie deliveries, from the manufacturer to regional warehouses, to local drop-off sites, to each scout, and to the customers themselves.

The paperwork was overwhelming. Order transactions changed hands too many times, creating many opportunities for error. All the added columns, multiple prices per box, and calculations had to be made by different people, all on a deadline.

The Patriots' Trail Girl Scout Council, representing 65 communities and 18,000 Girl Scouts in the greater Boston area, was one of the first councils to tackle this problem. The council sells over 1.5 million boxes of cookies each year. The council initially investigated building a computerized system using Microsoft Access database management and application development tools. But this alternative would have cost $25,000 to develop and would have taken at least three to four months to get the system up and running. It was too time-consuming, complex, and expensive for the Girl Scouts. In addition to Microsoft Access software, the Girl Scouts would have to purchase a server to run the system plus pay for networking and Web site maintenance services so the system could be made available on the Web.

After consulting with management consultants Dovetail Associates, the council selected Intuit's QuickBase for Corporate Workgroups. QuickBase is a hosted Web-based software service for small businesses and corporate workgroups. It is especially well suited for building simple database applications very quickly and does not require a great deal of training to use. QuickBase is customizable and designed to collect, organize, and share data among teams in many different locations.

A Dovetail consultant created a working QuickBase prototype with some basic functions for the Girl Scouts within a few hours. It only took two months to build, test, and implement the entire system using this software. The cost for developing the entire system was a fraction of the Microsoft Access solution. The Girl Scouts do not have to pay for any hardware, software, or networking services because QuickBase runs everything for them on its servers. QuickBase costs about $500 per month for organizations with 100 users and $1,500 per month for organizations with up to 500 users. It is very easy to use.

The QuickBase solution eliminates paperwork and calculation errors by providing a clear central source of data for the entire council and easy online entry of cookie orders over the Web. Troop leaders collect the Girl Scouts' order cards and enter them directly into the QuickBase system using their home computers linked to the Web. With a few mouse clicks, the council office consolidates the unit totals and transmits the orders electronically to ABC Cookies. As local orders come in, local section leaders can track the data in real time.

The Patriots' Trail Girl Scouts also uses the QuickBase system to manage the Cookie Cupboard warehouse, where volunteers pick up their cookie orders. Volunteers use the system to make reservations so that the warehouse can prepare the orders in advance, saving time and inventory management costs. The trucking companies that deliver cookie shipments now receive their instructions electronically through QuickBase so that they can create efficient delivery schedules.

Since its implementation, the Patriots' Trail QuickBase system has cut paperwork by more than 90 percent, reduced errors to 1 percent, and reduced the time spent by volunteers by 50 percent. The old system used to take two months to tally the orders and determine which Scouts should be rewarded for selling the most cookies. Now that time has been cut to 48 hours.

Other Girl Scout councils have implemented similar QuickBase systems to track sales and achieved similar benefits. The Girl Scouts of Greater Los Angeles, serving Los Angeles County and parts of Kern and San Bernardino counties, has reduced the paperwork associated with the sales for 3.5 million boxes of cookies annually by 95 percent.

Sources: Ron Lieber, "More Than Pushing Cookies," New York Times, February 8, 2013; www.girlscouts.org, accessed August 19, 2013; Liz McCann, "Texting + QuickBase Make Selling Girl Scout Cookies Easier in LA, "March 8, 2010, www.quickbase.intuit.com, www.girlscoutseasternmass.org/cookies, accessed July 15, 2011; and "Girl Scouts Unite Behind Order Tracking," Customer Relationship Management, May 2005.

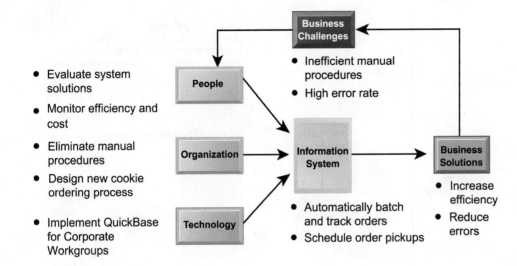

- Evaluate system solutions
- Monitor efficiency and cost
- Eliminate manual procedures
- Design new cookie ordering process
- Implement QuickBase for Corporate Workgroups

Business Challenges
- Inefficient manual procedures
- High error rate

People

Organization

Technology

Information System
- Automatically batch and track orders
- Schedule order pickups

Business Solutions
- Increase efficiency
- Reduce errors

The experience of the Patriots' Trail Girl Scout Council illustrates some of the steps required to design and build new information systems. It also illustrates some of the benefits of a new system solution. The Girl Scouts had an outdated manual paper-based system for processing cookie orders that was excessively time-consuming and error ridden. The Girl Scouts tried several alternative solutions before opting for a new ordering system based on the QuickBase software service. In this chapter, we will examine the Girl Scouts' search for a system solution as we describe each step of building a new information system using the problem-solving process.

12.1 Problem Solving and Systems Development

We have already described the problem-solving process and how it helps us analyze and understand the role of information systems in business. This problem-solving process is especially valuable when we need to build new systems. A new information system is built as a solution to a problem or set of problems the organization perceives it is facing. The problem may be one in which managers and employees believe that the business is not performing as well as expected, or it may come from the realization that the organization should take advantage of new opportunities to perform more effectively.

Let's apply this problem-solving process to system building. Figure 12.1 illustrates the four steps we would need to take: (1) define and understand the problem, (2) develop alternative solutions, (3) choose the best solution, and (4) implement the solution.

Before a problem can be solved, it first must be properly defined. Members of the organization must agree that a problem actually exists and that it is serious. The problem must be investigated so that it can be better understood. Next comes a period of devising alternative solutions, then one of evaluating each alternative and selecting the best solution. The final stage is one of implementing the solution, in which a detailed design for the solution is specified, translated into a physical system, tested, introduced to the organization, and further refined as it is used over time.

In the information systems world, we have a special name for these activities. Figure 12.1 shows that the first three problem-solving steps, where we identify the problem, gather information, devise alternative solutions, and make a decision about the best solution, are called **systems analysis**.

Figure 12.1
Developing an
Information System
Solution
*Developing an informa-
tion system solution is
based on the problem-
solving process.*

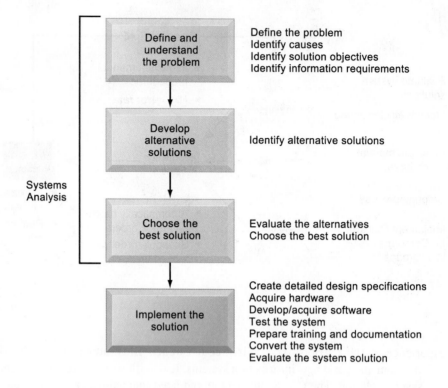

```
Systems
Analysis
```

Define and
understand
the problem
— Define the problem
Identify causes
Identify solution objectives
Identify information requirements

Develop
alternative
solutions
— Identify alternative solutions

Choose the
best solution
— Evaluate the alternatives
Choose the best solution

Implement the
solution
— Create detailed design specifications
Acquire hardware
Develop/acquire software
Test the system
Prepare training and documentation
Convert the system
Evaluate the system solution

DEFINING AND UNDERSTANDING THE PROBLEM

Defining the problem may take some work because various members of the company may have different ideas about the nature of the problem and its severity. What caused the problem? Why is it still around? Why wasn't it solved long ago? Systems analysts typically gather facts about existing systems and problems by examining documents, work papers, procedures, and system operations, and by interviewing key users of the system.

Information systems problems in the business world typically result from a combination of people, organization, and technology factors. When identifying a key issue or problem, ask what kind of problem it is: Is it a people problem, an organizational problem, a technology problem, or a combination of these? What people, organizational, and technological factors contributed to the problem?

Once the problem has been defined and analyzed, it is possible to make some decisions about what should and can be done. What are the objectives of a solution to the problem? Is the firm's objective to reduce costs, increase sales, or improve relationships with customers, suppliers, or employees? Do managers have sufficient information for decision making? What information is required to achieve these objectives?

At the most basic level, the **information requirements** of a new system identify who needs what information, where, when, and how. Requirements analysis carefully defines the objectives of the new or modified system and develops a detailed description of the functions that the new system must perform. A system designed around the wrong set of requirements will either have to be discarded because of poor performance or will need to undergo major modifications. Section 12.2 describes alternative approaches to eliciting requirements that help minimize this problem.

Let's return to our opening case about the Girl Scouts. The problem here is that the Girl Scout ordering process is heavily manual and cannot support the large number of volunteers and cookie orders that must be coordinated. As a result, cookie ordering is extremely inefficient with high error rates and volunteers spending excessive time organizing orders and deliveries.

Organizationally, the Girl Scouts is a volunteer organization distributed across a large area, with cookie sales as the primary source of revenue. The Scouts rely on volunteers with little or no business or computer experience for sales and management of orders and deliveries. They have almost no financial resources and volunteers are strapped for time. The Girl Scout cookie-ordering process requires many steps and coordination of multiple groups and organizations—individual Girl Scouts, volunteers, the council office, the cookie manufacturing factory, trucking companies, and the Cookie Cupboard warehouse.

The objectives of a solution for the Girl Scouts would be to reduce the amount of time, effort, and errors in the cookie-ordering process. Information requirements for the solution include the ability to rapidly total and organize order transactions for transmittal to ABC Cookies; the ability to track orders by type of cookie, troop, and individual Girl Scout; the ability to schedule deliveries to the Cookie Cupboard; and the ability to schedule order pickups from the Cookie Cupboard.

DEVELOPING ALTERNATIVE SOLUTIONS

What alternative solutions are possible for achieving these objectives and meeting these information requirements? The systems analysis lays out the most likely paths to follow given the nature of the problem. Some possible solutions do not require an information system solution but instead call for an adjustment in management, additional training, or refinement of existing organizational procedures. Some, however, do require modifications to the firm's existing information systems or an entirely new information system.

EVALUATING AND CHOOSING SOLUTIONS

The systems analysis includes a **feasibility study** to determine whether each proposed solution is feasible, or achievable, from a financial, technical, and organizational standpoint. The feasibility study establishes whether each alternative solution is a good investment, whether the technology needed for the system is available and can be handled by the firm's information systems staff, and whether the organization is capable of accommodating the changes introduced by the system.

A written systems proposal report describes the costs and benefits, and advantages and disadvantages of each alternative solution. Which solution is best in a financial sense? Which works best for the organization? The systems analysis will detail the costs and benefits of each alternative and the changes that the organization will have to make to use the solution effectively. We provide a detailed discussion of how to determine the business value of systems and manage change in the following section. On the basis of this report, management will select what it believes is the best solution for the company.

The Patriots' Trail Girl Scouts had three alternative solutions. One was to streamline existing processes, continuing to rely on manual procedures. However, given the large number of Girl Scouts and cookie orders, as well as relationships with manufacturers and shippers, redesigning and streamlining a manual ordering and delivery process would not have provided many benefits. The Girl Scouts needed an automated solution that accurately tracked thousands of order and delivery transactions, reduced paperwork, and created a central real-time source of sales data that could be accessed by council headquarters and individual volunteers.

A second alternative was to custom-build a cookie-ordering system using Microsoft Access. This alternative was considered too time-consuming, expensive, and technically challenging for the Girl Scouts. It required $25,000 in initial programming costs, plus the purchase of hardware and networking equipment to run the system and link it to the Internet, as well as trained staff to run and maintain the system.

The third alternative was to rapidly create a system using a software service provider. QuickBase provides templates and tools for creating simple database systems in very short periods, provides the hardware for running the application and Web site, and can be accessed by many different users over the Web. This solution did not require the Girl Scouts to purchase any hardware, software, or networking technology or to maintain any information system staff to support the system. This last alternative was the most feasible for the Girl Scouts.

IMPLEMENTING THE SOLUTION

The first step in implementing a system solution is to create detailed design specifications. **Systems design** shows how the chosen solution should be realized. The system design is the model or blueprint for an information system solution and consists of all the specifications that will deliver the functions identified during systems analysis. These specifications should address all of the technical, organization, and people components of the system solution. Table 12.1 shows some of the design specifications for the Girl Scouts' new system, which were based on information requirements for the solution that was selected.

TABLE 12.1

Design Specifications for the Girl Scout Cookie System

Output	Online reports
	Hard-copy reports
	Online queries
	Order transactions for ABC Cookies
	Delivery tickets for the trucking firm
Input	Order data entry form
	Troop data entry form
	Girl Scout data entry form
	Shipping/delivery data entry form
User interface	Graphical Web interface
Database	Database with cookie order file, delivery file, troop contact file
Processing	Calculate order totals by type of cookie and number of boxes
	Track orders by troop and individual Girl Scout
	Schedule pickups at the Cookie Cupboard
	Update Girl Scout and troop data for address and member changes
Manual procedures	Girl Scouts take orders with paper forms
	Troop leaders collect order cards from Scouts and enter the order data online
Security and controls	Online passwords
	Control totals
Conversion	Input Girl Scout and troop data
	Transfer factory and delivery data
	Test system
Training and documentation	System guide for users
	Online practice demonstration
	Online training sessions
	Training for ABC Cookies and trucking companies to accept data and instructions automatically from the Girl Scout system
Organizational changes	Job design: Volunteers no longer have to tabulate orders
	Process design: Take orders on manual cards but enter them online into the system
	Schedule order pickups from the Cookie Cupboard online

Completing Implementation

In the final steps of implementing a system solution, the following activities would be performed:

- *Hardware selection and acquisition.* System builders select appropriate hardware for the application. They would either purchase the necessary computers and networking hardware or lease them from a technology provider.
- *Software development and programming.* Software is custom programmed in-house or purchased from an external source, such as an outsourcing vendor, an application software package vendor, or a software service provider.

The Girl Scouts did not have to purchase additional hardware or software. QuickBase offers templates for generating simple database applications. Dovetail consultants used the QuickBase tools to rapidly create the software for the system. The system runs on QuickBase servers.

- *Testing.* The system is thoroughly tested to ensure it produces the right results. The **testing process** requires detailed testing of individual computer programs, called **unit testing**, as well as **system testing**, which tests the performance of the information system as a whole. **Acceptance testing** provides the final certification that the system is ready to be used in a production setting. Information systems tests are evaluated by users and reviewed by management. When all parties are satisfied that the new system meets their standards, the system is formally accepted for installation.

The systems development team works with users to devise a systematic test plan. The **test plan** includes all of the preparations for the series of tests we have just described. Figure 12.2 shows a sample from a test plan that might have been used for the Girl Scout cookie system. The condition being tested is online access of an existing record for a specific Girl Scout troop.

- *Training and documentation.* End users and information system specialists require training so that they will be able to use the new system. Detailed **documentation** showing how the system works from both a technical and end-user standpoint must be prepared.

The Girl Scout cookie system provides an online practice area for users to practice entering data into the system by following step-by-step instructions. Also available on the Web is a step-by-step instruction guide for the system that can be downloaded and printed as a hard-copy manual.

Figure 12.2
A Sample Test Plan for the Girl Scout Cookie System
When developing a test plan, it is imperative to include the various conditions to be tested, the requirements for each condition tested, and the expected results. Test plans require input from both end users and information systems specialists.

Test Case Number: GS02-010

Prepared by: A. Nelson | Date: February 15, 2014

Objective: This subtest checks for accessing an existing troop record

Specific Environment: QuickBase for WorkGroups

Procedure Description:
Click on My Troop Summary link.
Enter Troop Number

Expected Result:
When user clicks on My Troop Summary, the Troop Summary screen appears.
When user enters the correct Troop Number, the Troop record appears.
When user enters the wrong Troop Number, the error message "Wrong Troop Number" appears.

Test Results:
All OK.

- *Conversion* is the process of changing from the old to the new system. There are three main conversion strategies: the parallel strategy, the direct cutover strategy, and the phased approach strategy.

  In a **parallel strategy**, both the old system and its potential replacement are run together for a time until everyone is assured that the new one functions correctly. The old system remains available as a backup in case of problems. The **direct cutover strategy** replaces the old system entirely with the new system on an appointed day, carrying the risk that there is no system to fall back on if problems arise. A **phased approach** introduces the system in stages (such as first introducing the modules for ordering Girl Scout cookies and then introducing the modules for transmitting orders and instructions to the cookie factory and shipper).

- *Production and maintenance.* After the new system is installed and conversion is complete, the system is said to be in **production**. During this stage, users and technical specialists review the solution to determine how well it has met its original objectives and to decide whether any revisions or modifications are in order. Changes in hardware, software, documentation, or procedures to a production system to correct errors, meet new requirements, or improve processing efficiency are termed **maintenance.**

The Girl Scouts continued to improve and refine their QuickBase cookie system. The system was made more efficient for users with slow Internet connections. Other recent enhancements include capabilities for paying for orders more rapidly, entering troop information and initial orders without waiting for a specified starting date, and receiving online confirmation for reservations to pick up orders from the Cookie Cupboard.

Managing the Change

Developing a new information systems solution is not merely a matter of installing hardware and software. The business must also deal with the organizational changes that the new solution will bring about—new information, new business processes, and perhaps new reporting relationships and decision-making power. A very well-designed solution may not work unless it is introduced to the organization very carefully. The process of planning change in an organization so that it is implemented in an orderly and effective manner is so critical to the success or failure of information system solutions that we devote Section 12.4 to a detailed discussion of this topic.

To manage the transition from the old manual cookie-ordering processes to the new system, the Girl Scouts would have to inform troop leaders and volunteers about changes in cookie-ordering procedures, provide training, and provide resources for answering any questions that arose as parents and volunteers started using the system. They would need to work with ABC Cookies and their shippers on new procedures for transmitting and delivering orders.

12.2 Alternative Systems-Building Approaches

There are alternative methods for building systems using the basic problem-solving model we have just described. These alternative methods include the traditional systems lifecycle, prototyping, end-user development, application software packages, and outsourcing.

TRADITIONAL SYSTEMS DEVELOPMENT LIFECYCLE

The **systems development lifecycle (SDLC)** is the oldest method for building information systems. The lifecycle methodology is a phased approach to building a system, dividing systems development into a series of formal stages, as illustrated in Figure 12.3. Although systems builders can go back and forth among stages in the lifecycle, the systems lifecycle is predominantly a "waterfall" approach in which tasks in one stage are completed before work for the next stage begins.

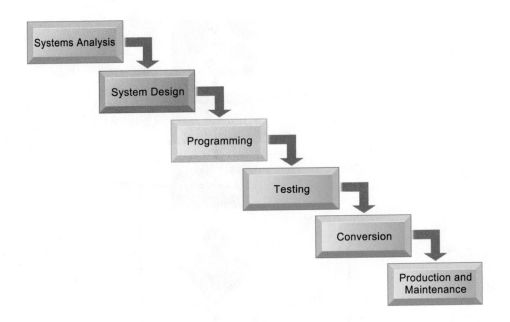

Figure 12.3
The Traditional
Systems
Development
Lifecycle
*The systems develop-
ment lifecycle partitions
systems development
into formal stages, with
each stage requiring
completion before the
next stage can begin.*

This approach maintains a very formal division of labor between end users and information systems specialists. Technical specialists, such as system analysts and programmers, are responsible for much of the systems analysis, design, and implementation work; end users are limited to providing information requirements and reviewing the technical staff's work. The lifecycle also emphasizes formal specifications and paperwork, so many documents are generated during the course of a systems project.

The systems lifecycle is still used for building large complex systems that require rigorous and formal requirements analysis, predefined specifications, and tight controls over the systems-building process. However, this approach is also time-consuming and expensive to use. Tasks in one stage are supposed to be completed before work for the next stage begins. Activities can be repeated, but volumes of new documents must be generated and steps retraced if requirements and specifications need to be revised. This encourages freezing of specifications relatively early in the development process. The lifecycle approach is also not suitable for many small desktop systems, which tend to be less structured and more individualized.

PROTOTYPING

Prototyping consists of building an experimental system rapidly and inexpensively for end users to evaluate. The prototype is a working version of an information system or part of the system, but it is intended as only a preliminary model. Users interact with the prototype to get a better idea of their information requirements, refining the prototype multiple times. (The chapter-opening case describes how Dovetail Associates used QuickBase to create a prototype that helped the Patriots' Trail Girl Scout Council refine the specifications for their cookie-ordering system.) When the design is finalized, the prototype will be converted to a polished production system. Figure 12.4 shows a four-step model of the prototyping process.

Step 1: *Identify the user's basic requirements.* The system designer (usually an information systems specialist) works with the user only long enough to capture the user's basic information needs.

Step 2: *Develop an initial prototype.* The system designer creates a working prototype quickly, using tools for rapidly generating software.

Step 3: *Use the prototype.* The user is encouraged to work with the system to determine if the prototype meets his or her needs and to suggest improvements for the prototype.

Figure 12.4
The Prototyping
Process
The process of developing a prototype consists of four steps. Because a prototype can be developed quickly and inexpensively, systems builders can go through several iterations, repeating steps 3 and 4, to refine and enhance the prototype before arriving at the final operational one.

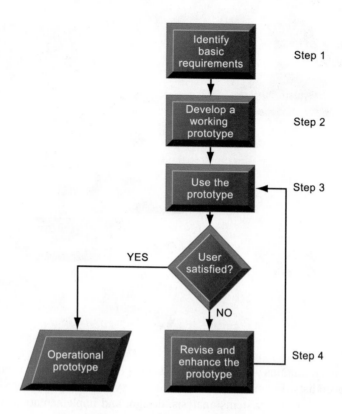

Step 1

Step 2

Step 3

Step 4

Step 4: *Revise and enhance the prototype.* The system builder notes all changes the user requests and refines the prototype accordingly. After the prototype has been revised, the cycle returns to Step 3. Steps 3 and 4 are repeated until the user is satisfied.

Prototyping is especially useful in designing an information system's user interface. Because prototyping encourages intense end-user involvement throughout the systems development process, it is more likely to produce systems that fulfill user requirements.

However, rapid prototyping may gloss over essential steps in systems development, such as thorough testing and documentation. If the completed prototype works reasonably well, management may not see the need to build a polished production system. Some hastily constructed systems do not easily accommodate large quantities of data or a large number of users in a production environment.

END-USER DEVELOPMENT

End-user development allows end users, with little or no formal assistance from technical specialists, to create simple information systems, reducing the time and steps required to produce a finished application. Using user-friendly query, reporting, Web site development, graphics, and PC software tools, end users can access data, create reports, and develop simple applications on their own, with little or no help from professional systems analysts or programmers.

For example, Neways Enterprise, a multinational firm which designs, manufactures, and sells personal care, household and nutritional products that are free of harmful ingredients, used Information Builders WEBFOCUS to create an online self-service reporting system for its thousands of independent distributors and its business analysts. The business analysts use the self-service reports to monitor finances, anticipate trends, and predict results based on current insights. Neways' globally dispersed independent distributors use the system to access real-time production data to support sales efforts and track qualification for monthly bonuses. The system's reporting tools let them decide how deeply they want to drill into the data (Information Builders, 2013).

On the whole, end-user-developed systems are completed more rapidly than those developed with conventional programming tools. Allowing users to specify their own business needs improves requirements gathering and often leads to a higher level of user involvement and satisfaction with the system. However, end-user development tools still cannot replace conventional tools for some business applications because they cannot easily handle the processing of large numbers of transactions or applications with extensive procedural logic and updating requirements.

End-user development also poses organizational risks because systems are created rapidly, without a formal development methodology, testing, and documentation. To help organizations maximize the benefits of end-user applications development, management should require cost justification of end-user information system projects and establish hardware, software, and quality standards for user-developed applications.

PURCHASING SOLUTIONS: APPLICATION SOFTWARE PACKAGES AND OUTSOURCING

Chapter 5 points out that the software for most systems today is not developed in-house but is purchased from external sources. Firms may choose to purchase a software package from a commercial vendor, rent the software from a service provider, or outsource the development work to another firm. Selection of the software or software service is often based on a **Request for Proposal (RFP)**, which is a detailed list of questions submitted to external vendors to see how well they meet the requirements for the proposed system.

Application Software Packages

Most new information systems today are built using an application software package or preprogrammed software components. Many applications are common to all business organizations—for example, payroll, accounts receivable, general ledger, or inventory control. For such universal functions with standard processes that do not change a great deal over time, a generalized system will fulfill the requirements of many organizations.

If a software package can fulfill most of an organization's requirements, the company does not have to write its own software. The company saves time and money by using the prewritten, predesigned, pretested software programs from the package.

Many packages include capabilities for customization to meet unique requirements not addressed by the package software. **Customization** features allow a software package to be modified to meet an organization's unique requirements without destroying the integrity of the packaged software. However, if extensive customization is required, additional programming and customization work may become so expensive and time-consuming that it negates many of the advantages of software packages. If the package cannot be customized, the organization will have to adapt to the package and change its procedures.

Outsourcing

If a firm does not want to use its internal resources to build or operate information systems, it can outsource the work to an external organization that specializes in providing these services. Software service providers, which we describe in Chapter 5, are one form of outsourcing. An example is the Girl Scouts leasing the software and hardware from QuickBase to run their cookie-ordering system. Subscribing companies use the software and computer hardware of the service provider as the technical platform for their systems. In another form of outsourcing, a company hires an external vendor to design and create the software for its system, but that company operates the system on its own computers.

The outsourcing vendor might be domestic or in another country. Domestic outsourcing is driven primarily by the fact that outsourcing firms possess skills, resources, and assets that their clients do not have. Installing a new supply chain management system in a very large company might require hiring an additional 30 to 50 people with specific expertise in supply chain management software. Rather than hire permanent new employees, and then release them after the new system is built, it makes more sense, and is often less expensive, to outsource this work for a 12-month period.

In the case of offshore outsourcing, the decision tends to be driven by cost. A skilled programmer in India or Russia earns about U.S. $10,000 per year, compared to $73,000 per year for a comparable programmer in the United States. The Internet and low-cost communications technology have drastically reduced the expense and difficulty of coordinating the work of global teams in faraway locations. In addition to cost savings, many offshore outsourcing firms offer world-class technology assets and skills. Wage inflation outside the United States has eroded some of these advantages, and some jobs have moved back to the United States.

For example, leading companies such as Hilton, NBC, Fox News, and Yahoo have outsourced Web site design and development work to India-based Profit By Outsourcing. Profit By Outsourcing provides expertise in areas such as Ajax programming, custom programmed content management and e-commerce solutions, mobile application development, and application development using Adobe Flash, Adobe Flex, and Microsoft Silverlight, that is not available internally in most companies.

There is a very strong chance that at some point in your career, you'll be working with offshore outsourcers or global teams. Your firm is most likely to benefit from outsourcing if it takes the time to evaluate all the risks and to make sure outsourcing is appropriate for its particular needs. Any company that outsources its applications must thoroughly understand the project, including its requirements, method of implementation, source of expected benefits, cost components, and metrics for measuring performance.

Many firms underestimate costs for identifying and evaluating vendors of information technology services, for transitioning to a new vendor, for improving internal software development methods to match those of outsourcing vendors, and for monitoring vendors to make sure they are fulfilling their contractual obligations. Outsourcing offshore incurs additional costs for coping with cultural differences that drain productivity and dealing with human resources issues, such as terminating or relocating domestic employees. These hidden costs undercut some of the anticipated benefits from outsourcing. Firms should be especially cautious when using an outsourcer to develop or to operate applications that give some type of competitive advantage.

Figure 12.5 shows best- and worst-case scenarios for the total cost of an offshore outsourcing project. It shows how much hidden costs affect the total project cost. The best case reflects the lowest estimates for additional costs, and the worst case reflects the highest estimates for these costs. As you can see, hidden costs increase the total cost of an offshore

Figure 12.5
Total Cost of Offshore Outsourcing
If a firm spends $10 million on offshore outsourcing contracts, that company will actually spend 15.2 percent in extra costs even under the best-case scenario. In the worst-case scenario, where there is a dramatic drop in productivity along with exceptionally high transition and layoff costs, a firm can expect to pay up to 57 percent in extra costs on top of the $10 million outlay for an offshore contract.

TOTAL COST OF OFFSHORE OUTSOURCING				
Cost of outsourcing contract			**$10,000,000**	
Hidden Costs	Best Case	Additional Cost ($)	Worst Case	Additional Cost ($)
1. Vendor selection	0.2%	20,000	2%	200,000
2. Transition costs	2%	200,000	3%	300,000
3. Layoffs & retention	3%	300,000	3%	300,000
4. Lost productivity/cultural issues	3%	300,000	5%	500,000
5. Improving development processes	1%	100,000	27%	2,700,000
6. Managing the contract	6%	600,000	10%	1,000,000
Total additional costs		1,520,000		5,700,000
	Outstanding Contract ($)	Additional Cost ($)	Total Cost ($)	Additional Cost
Total cost of outsourcing (TCO) best case	10,000,000	1,520,000	11,520,000	15.2%
Total cost of outsourcing (TCO) worst case	10,000,000	5,700,000	15,700,000	57.0%

outsourcing project by an extra 15 to 57 percent. Even with these extra costs, many firms will benefit from offshore outsourcing if they manage the work well.

MOBILE APPLICATION DEVELOPMENT: DESIGNING FOR A MULTI-SCREEN WORLD

Today, employees and customers expect, and even demand, to be able to use a mobile device of their choice to obtain information or perform a transaction anywhere and at any time. To meet these needs, companies will need to develop mobile Web sites, mobile apps, and native apps as well as traditional information systems. According to digital advertising agency Vertic, mobile app development projects will outnumber native PC projects by a 4-to-1 ratio by 2015 (Greengard, 2013)

A **mobile Web site** is a version of a regular Web site that is scaled down in content and navigation for easy access and search on a small mobile screen. (Access Amazon's Web site from your computer and then from your smartphone to see the difference from a regular Web site.) Most large firms today have mobile Web sites.

A **mobile Web app** is an application which resides on a server and is accessed via the the mobile Web browser built into a smartphone or tablet computer. For instance, Apple smartphones and tablets use the Safari browser, and these devices would be able to run mobile apps built for Safari. Mobile apps can support complex interactions used in games and rich media, perform real-time on-the-fly calculations, and show location-sensitivity using the smartphone's built-in global positioning system.

A **native app** is a standalone application designed to run on a specific mobile platform and it must be installed directly onto the device. These standalone programs can connect to the Internet to download and upload data, and they can also operate on these data even when not connected to the Internet. For example, an e-book reading app such as Kindle software can download a book from the Internet, disconnect from the Internet, and present the book for reading. Different native apps need to be developed for different mobile operating systems and hardware.

Developing applications for mobile platforms is quite different from development for PCs and their much larger screens. The reduced size of mobile devices makes using fingers and multi-touch gestures much easier than typing and using keyboards. Mobile apps need to be optimized for the specific tasks they are to perform; they should not try to carry out too many tasks; and they should be designed for usability. The user experience for mobile interaction is fundamentally different from using a desktop or laptop PC. Saving resources—bandwidth, screen space, memory, processing, data entry, and user gestures—is a top priority.

When a full Web site created for the desktop shrinks to the size of a smartphone screen, it is difficult for the user to navigate through the site. The user must continually zoom in and out and scroll to find relevant material. Therefore, companies need to design Web sites specifically for mobile interfaces and create multiple mobile sites to meet the needs of smartphones, tablets, and desktop browsers. This equates to at least three sites with separate content, maintenance, and costs. Currently, Web sites know what device you are using because your browser will send this information to the server when you logon. Based on this information, the server will deliver the appropriate screen.

One solution to the problem of having multiple Web sites is to use **responsive Web design**. Responsive Web design enables Web sites to automatically change layouts according to the visitor's screen resolution, whether on a desktop, laptop, tablet, or smartphone. Responsive design uses tools such as flexible grid-based layouts, flexible images, and media queries, to optimize the design for different viewing contexts. This eliminates the need for separate design and development work for each new device. HTML5, which we introduced in Chapter 5, is also used for mobile application development because it can support cross-platform mobile applications.

The Interactive Session on Technology describes how some companies have addressed the challenges of mobile development we have just identified.

INTERACTIVE SESSION: TECHNOLOGY   What Does It Take to Go Mobile?

How should we go mobile? What should we do? Where should we start? With smartphones and tablets going mainstream, almost every company today is asking these questions.

Developing mobile apps or a mobile Web site has some special challenges. The user experience on a mobile device is fundamentally different from that on a PC. There are special features on mobile devices such as location-based services that that give firms the potential to interact with customers in meaningful new ways. Firms need to be able to take advantage of those features while delivering an experience that is appropriate to a small screen. There are multiple mobile platforms to work with, including iOS, Android, and Windows 8, and a firm may need a different version of an application to run on each of these. You can't just port a Web site or desktop application to a smartphone or tablet. It's a different systems development process.

It's important to understand how, why, and where customers use mobile devices and how these mobile experiences change business interactions and behavior. For example, do customers who use an app handle a greater number of transactions on their own and use the phone less? Do they spend more or less time researching products and shopping from a mobile device?

Deckers Outdoor Corporation, the parent company of brands such as UGG Australia, Teva, and Simple Shoes, spent considerable time studying its customers' mobile behavior. It looked at how customers use their mobile devices while shopping and researching brands to find out how consumers would connect with its brand through the mobile channel. When people use mobile devices, how do they research the products? What information do they want about brand? Are they looking for information about product features, product reviews, or retail store locations?

Decker's customer analysis showed that when consumers use mobile devices inside a Deckers store, what is most important is a seamless interaction. The customer wants to be able to look at a product on his or her mobile device and see the same information on that device as that person would obtain in the store, plus some additional information, such as consumer reviews.

A mobile strategy involves much more than selecting mobile devices, operating systems, and applications. It also involves changes to business processes, changing the way people work and the way a firm interacts with its customers. Mobile technology can streamline processes, make them more portable, and enhance them with capabilities such as touch interfaces, location and mapping features, alerts, texting, cameras, and video functionality. The technology can also create less efficient processes or fail to deliver benefits if the mobile application is not properly designed.

USAA, the giant financial services company serving members of the U.S. military and their families, is acutely aware of the need to ensure that mobile technology is aligned with its customer-facing business processes and leads to genuine improvements. The company is using mobile technology to refine its business processes and provide simpler and more powerful ways for customers to interact with the company.

USAA launched its Web site in 2007, and went mobile ten years later, with about 90 percent of its interactions with customers taking place on these two self-service channels. In 2011, USAA handled 183 million customer contacts through the mobile channel alone, and expects the mobile channel will be its primary point of contact with customers in the next two years. USAA has 100 dedicated mobile developers writing apps for devices using the iPhone, iPad, and Android operating systems, along with apps for the BlackBerry and Windows Phone.

USAA developed a smartphone accident report and claims app that enables customers to snap a photo and submit a claim directly from the site of an accident. The app is also able to send geographic information system (GIS) data to a towing service and display nearby car rental locations. Another mobile app supports photo deposits: a customer can capture an image of a check with a smartphone and automatically submit it to the bank. The money is instantly deposited in the customer's account. This system eliminates the labor and expense of processing paper checks, and the time required to mail the check and wait three days for the deposit to clear. In 2011, USAA Federal Savings Bank processed $6.4 billion in deposits through this mobile app.

The mobile app also displays loan and credit card balances, shopping services, homeowners and auto insurance policy information, Home Circle and Auto Circle buying services, retirement products and information, ATM and taxi locators, and a communities feature that lets users see what others are posting about USAA on Twitter, Facebook, and YouTube.

Denver-based Markwest Energy Partners, a 1,000-person company that gathers, processes, and transports oil and gas products to refineries, had been shackled with cumbersome manual approval processes further complicated by traveling executives and field operations that weren't always in touch with the company headquarters.

Obtaining an authorization for expenditure (AFE) document had become a huge bottleneck that was affecting the company's efficiency and profits. In December 2011, Markwest deployed K2's BlackPearl, a visual design tool for building process-driven applications and began supporting iPads and iPhones in the field. The company worked with telecom providers to install cell towers near worksites that lacked cellular service. This solution enabled Markwest to automate workflows, standardize processes, and expedite signatures. Managers can now view pending AFEs within a task queue, and are able to review and electronically sign documents from a PC, laptop or a mobile device. Markwest's accounting team can view the status of everything from a central dashboard.

Markwest supports only iOS devices and has a BYOD policy in place. The company is now looking to push mobile business processes out to additional groups of employees.

Sources: Samuel Greengard, "Pervasive Mobility Creates New Business Challenges," *Baseline*, June 28, 2013 and "Mobility Transforms the Customer Relationship," *Baseline*, February 2012; "K2 Blackpearl," www.pinpoint. Microsoft.com, accessed August 18. 2013; William Atkinson, "How Deckers Used a Mobile Application to Build Customer Traffic," *CIO Insight*, November 9, 2011; and "Going Mobile: A Portable Approach to Process Improvement," *Business Agility Insights*, June 2012.

CASE STUDY QUESTIONS

1. What people, organization, and technology issues need to be addressed when building mobile applications?

2. How does user requirement definition for mobile applications differ from that in traditional systems analysis?

3. Describe the business processes changed by USAA's mobile applications before and after the applications were deployed.

RAPID APPLICATION DEVELOPMENT FOR E-BUSINESS

Technologies and business conditions are changing so rapidly that agility and scalability have become critical elements of system solutions. Companies are adopting shorter, more informal development processes for many of their e-commerce and e-business applications, processes that provide fast solutions that do not disrupt their core transaction processing systems and organizational databases. In addition to using software packages, application service providers, and other outsourcing services, they are relying more heavily on fast-cycle techniques, such as joint application design (JAD), prototypes, and reusable standardized software components that can be assembled into a complete set of services for e-commerce and e-business.

The term **rapid application development (RAD)** refers to the process of creating workable systems in a very short period of time. RAD includes the use of visual programming and other tools for building graphical user interfaces, iterative prototyping of key system elements, the automation of program code generation, and close teamwork among end users and information systems specialists. Simple systems often can be assembled from prebuilt components (see Section 12.3). The process does not have to be sequential, and key parts of development can occur simultaneously.

Sometimes a technique called **joint application design (JAD)** will be used to accelerate the generation of information requirements and to develop the initial systems design. JAD brings end users and information systems specialists together in an interactive session to discuss the system's design. Properly prepared and facilitated, JAD sessions can significantly speed up the design phase and involve users at an intense level.

12.3 Modeling and Designing Systems

We have just described alternative methods for building systems. There are also alternative methodologies for modeling and designing systems. The two most prominent are structured methodologies and object-oriented development.

STRUCTURED METHODOLOGIES

Structured methodologies have been used to document, analyze, and design information systems since the 1970s. **Structured** refers to the fact that the techniques are step by step, with each step building on the previous one. Structured methodologies are top-down, progressing from the highest, most abstract level to the lowest level of detail—from the general to the specific.

Structured development methods are process-oriented, focusing primarily on modeling the processes, or actions, that capture, store, manipulate, and distribute data as the data flow through a system. These methods separate data from processes. A separate programming procedure must be written every time someone wants to take an action on a particular piece of data. The procedures act on data that the program passes to them.

The primary tool for representing a system's component processes and the flow of data between them is the **data flow diagram (DFD)**. The data flow diagram offers a logical graphic model of information flow, partitioning a system into modules that show manageable levels of detail. It rigorously specifies the processes or transformations that occur within each module and the interfaces that exist between them.

Figure 12.6 shows a simple data flow diagram for a mail-in university course registration system. The rounded boxes represent processes, which portray the transformation of data. The square box represents an external entity, which is an originator or receiver of information located outside the boundaries of the system being modeled. The open rectangles represent data stores, which are either manual or automated inventories of data. The arrows represent data flows, which show the movement between processes, external entities, and data stores. They always contain packets of data with the name or content of each data flow listed beside the arrow.

This data flow diagram shows that students submit registration forms with their names, identification numbers, and the numbers of the courses they wish to take. In Process 1.0, the system verifies that each course selected is still open by referencing the university's

Figure 12.6
Data Flow Diagram for Mail-in University Registration System
The system has three processes: Verify availability (1.0), enroll student (2.0), and confirm registration (3.0). The name and content of each of the data flows appear adjacent to each arrow. There is one external entity in this system: the student. There are two data stores: the student master file and the course file.

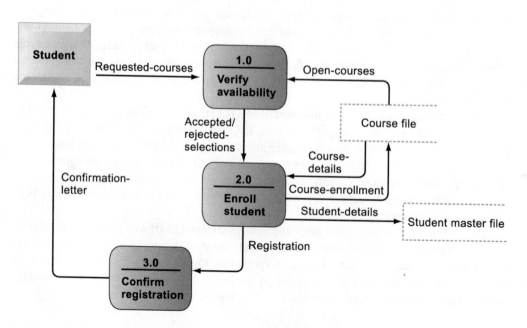

course file. The file distinguishes courses that are open from those that have been canceled or filled. Process 1.0 then determines which of the student's selections can be accepted or rejected. Process 2.0 enrolls the student in the courses for which he or she has been accepted. It updates the university's course file with the student's name and identification number and recalculates the class size. If maximum enrollment has been reached, the course number is flagged as closed. Process 2.0 also updates the university's student master file with information about new students or changes in address. Process 3.0 then sends each student applicant a confirmation-of-registration letter listing the courses for which he or she is registered and noting the course selections that could not be fulfilled.

Through leveled data flow diagrams, a complex process can be broken down into successive levels of detail. An entire system can be divided into subsystems with a high-level data flow diagram. Each subsystem, in turn, can be divided into additional subsystems with lower-level data flow diagrams, and the lower-level subsystems can be broken down again until the lowest level of detail has been reached. **Process specifications** describe the transformation occurring within the lowest level of the data flow diagrams, showing the logic for each process.

In structured methodology, software design is modeled using hierarchical structure charts. The **structure chart** is a top-down chart, showing each level of design, its relationship to other levels, and its place in the overall design structure. The design first considers the main function of a program or system, then breaks this function into subfunctions, and decomposes each subfunction until the lowest level of detail has been reached. Figure 12.7 shows a high-level structure chart for a payroll system. If a design has too many levels to fit onto one structure chart, it can be broken down further on more detailed structure charts. A structure chart may document one program, one system (a set of programs), or part of one program.

OBJECT-ORIENTED DEVELOPMENT

Structured methods treat data and processes as logically separate entities, whereas in the real world such separation seems unnatural. Different modeling conventions are used for analysis (the data flow diagram) and for design (the structure chart).

Object-oriented development addresses these issues. Object-oriented development uses the object, which we introduced in Chapter 5, as the basic unit of systems analysis and design. An object combines data and the specific processes that operate on those data. Data encapsulated in an object can be accessed and modified only by the operations, or methods, associated with that object. Instead of passing data to procedures, programs send a message for an object to perform an operation that is already embedded in it. The system is modeled

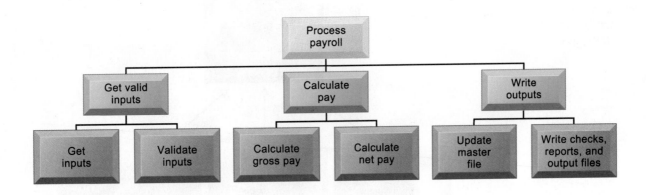

Figure 12.7
High-Level Structure Chart for a Payroll System
This structure chart shows the highest or most abstract level of design for a payroll system, providing an overview of the entire system.

as a collection of objects and the relationships among them. Because processing logic resides within objects rather than in separate software programs, objects must collaborate with each other to make the system work.

Object-oriented modeling is based on the concepts of *class* and *inheritance*. Objects belonging to a certain class, or general categories of similar objects, have the features of that class. Classes of objects in turn inherit all the structure and behaviors of a more general class and then add variables and behaviors unique to each object. New classes of objects are created by choosing an existing class and specifying how the new class differs from the existing class, instead of starting from scratch each time.

We can see how class and inheritance work in Figure 12.8, which illustrates the relationships among classes concerning employees and how they are paid. Employee is the common ancestor, or superclass, for the other three classes. Salaried, Hourly, and Temporary are subclasses of Employee. The class name is in the top compartment, the attributes for each class are in the middle portion of each box, and the list of operations is in the bottom portion of each box. The features that are shared by all employees (ID, name, address, date hired, position, and pay) are stored in the Employee superclass, whereas each subclass stores features that are specific to that particular type of employee. Specific to Hourly employees, for example, are their hourly rates and overtime rates. A solid line from the subclass to the superclass is a generalization path showing that the subclasses Salaried, Hourly, and Temporary have common features that can be generalized into the superclass Employee.

Object-oriented development is more iterative and incremental than traditional structured development. During systems analysis, systems builders document the functional requirements of the system, specifying its most important properties and what the proposed system must do. Interactions between the system and its users are analyzed to identify objects, which include both data and processes. The object-oriented design phase describes how the objects will behave and how they will interact with one another. Similar objects are grouped together to form a class, and classes are grouped into hierarchies in which a subclass inherits the attributes and methods from its superclass.

The information system is implemented by translating the design into program code, reusing classes that are already available in a library of reusable software objects and adding new ones created during the object-oriented design phase. Implementation may also involve the creation of an object-oriented database. The resulting system must be thoroughly tested and evaluated.

Figure 12.8
Class and
Inheritance
*This figure illustrates
how classes inherit the
common features of
their superclass.*

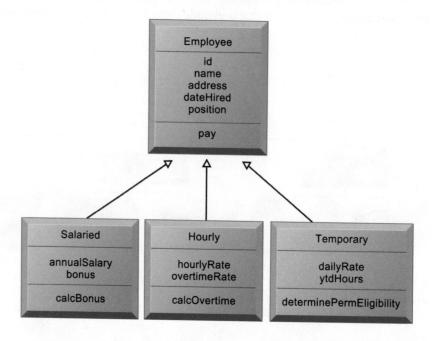

Because objects are reusable, object-oriented development could potentially reduce the time and cost of writing software if organizations reuse software objects that have already been created as building blocks for other applications. New systems can be created by using some existing objects, changing others, and adding a few new objects.

Component-Based Development, Web Services, and Cloud-Based Development

To further expedite software creation, groups of objects have been assembled into software components for common functions, such as a graphical user interface or online ordering capability, and these components can be combined to create large-scale business applications. This approach to software development is called **component-based development**. Businesses are using component-based development to create their e-commerce applications by combining commercially available components for shopping carts, user authentication, search engines, and catalogs with pieces of software for their own unique business requirements.

Chapter 5 introduced Web services as loosely coupled, reusable software components based on Extensible Markup Language (XML) and other open protocols and standards that enable one application to communicate with another with no custom programming required. In addition to supporting internal and external integration of systems, Web services provide nonproprietary tools for building new information system applications or enhancing existing systems.

Platform as a service (PaaS), introduced in the Chapter 5 discussion of cloud computing, also holds considerable potential for helping system developers quickly write and test customer- or employee-facing Web applications. These online development environments come from a range of vendors, including Oracle, IBM, Salesforce.com (Force.com), and Microsoft (Azure). These platforms automate tasks such as setting up a newly composed application as a Web service or linking to other applications and services. Some also offer a cloud infrastructure service, or links to cloud vendors such as Amazon, so that developers can launch what they build in a cloud infrastructure.

COMPUTER-AIDED SOFTWARE ENGINEERING (CASE)

Computer-aided software engineering (CASE)—sometimes called computer-aided systems engineering—provides software tools to automate the methodologies we have just described to reduce the amount of repetitive work in systems development. CASE tools provide automated graphics facilities for producing charts and diagrams, screen and report generators, data dictionaries, extensive reporting facilities, analysis and checking tools, code generators, and documentation generators. CASE tools also contain features for validating design diagrams and specifications.

CASE tools facilitate clear documentation and coordination of team development efforts. Team members can share their work by accessing each other's files to review or modify what has been done. Modest productivity benefits are achieved if the tools are used properly. Many CASE tools are PC based, with powerful graphical capabilities.

12.4 Project Management

Your company might have developed what appears to be an excellent system solution. Yet when the system is in use, it does not work properly or it doesn't deliver the benefits that were promised. If this occurs, your firm is not alone. There is a very high failure rate among information systems projects because they have not been properly managed. The Standish Group consultancy, which monitors IT project success rates, found that only 32 percent of all technology investments were completed on time, on budget, and with all features and functions originally specified (McCafferty, 2010). Firms may have incorrectly assessed the business value of the new system or were unable to manage the organizational change

Austin Energy's Billing System Can't Light Up

Austin Energy handles electrical, water, and waste disposal for the city of Austin, Texas and surrounding counties, serving more than 1 million residents. It is a publicly owned company and an arm of city government, and returns its profits to the community each year. The company has provided $1.5 billion in dividends back to Austin since 1976, which help fund city services such as fire, police, emergency medical services, parks, and libraries.

Austin Energy has one of the largest renewable energy programs in the country, but its legacy billing systems did not integrate with smart meters and other newer technologies. It also lacked newer customer assistance options, like the ability to choose the time of the month that a customer prefers to pay bills. To modernize the billing system and to bring its information systems up to date with newer energy conservation methods, Austin Energy contracted with IBM in 2009 to create a centralized billing system and to run the system for five years. Austin agreed to pay IBM $55 million, with $38 million allocated for building and installing the new billing system, and $17 million for operating the system for five years after its completion. The new billing system was slated to handle electricity, water, trash, and recycling. Austin was optimistic that a successful installation would eventually pay for itself in savings.

To date, the project has been a disappointment at best. The system was supposed to go live in early 2011, but is still not fully operational. Software bugs have led to errors in thousands of bills. Over 65,000 customers have not received bills entirely, and another 35,000 have received inaccurate bills. For example, one business that owed Austin Energy $3,000 was instead charged $300,000. Although Austin was able to identify affected accounts and work with customers individually to correct the problems, the company was ill-prepared to handle the outpouring of customer dissatisfaction with the new system, and their customer service department was in danger of being overrun.

According to Austin Energy manager Larry Weiss, "Instability issues …. continue to have serious and costly impacts on our business and our customers." Persistent system errors prevented the company from billing apartment residents for water, balancing its books, and filing audit reports. Without the ability to bill for utilities properly, the City of Austin was losing revenue.

Officials with Austin Energy put the blame for the project's woes squarely on IBM. Austin's CIO Alan Claypool stated in an interview that "we have yet to reach a stable system (and) we are extremely disap-

pointed and continue to have serious concerns about the quality of service we have received from IBM to date." He noted in a September 2011 message that IBM was repeating mistakes as it tried to implement the system. Two separate errors of IBM cost the project 37 hours of delay, and one of the errors was the same type of error made by the same team in December 2010. "We continue to be gravely disappointed in the delays and seemingly ad hoc methods toward managing this project," Claypool stated.

The company now plans to include provisions in future contracts with IBM that guard against similar mishaps, with a particular focus on system availability, and Austin is withholding $3.8 million in payments currently owed to IBM until the system meets baseline performance benchmarks.

Claypool and other Austin Energy executives have made numerous direct appeals to IBM officials, ranging from the managers of the billing system project all the way up to IBM CEO Sam Palmisano. Claypool first wrote directly to Marc Lautenbach, the head of IBM's Global Business Services unit in North America, which was responsible for the billing system project. He explained that thousands of customers required one-on-one assistance to access their accounts or correct billing errors. Lautenbach was then replaced as Global Business head by Frank Kern, who wrote back to Austin and described a five-step plan to fix the problems with the billing system.

Kern's plan was to improve communications on business impacts caused by known defects, to ensure that problems with the system are delegated to the correct people, to implement best practice processes to ensure repeatable success, to work more closely with third-party vendors like Oracle, and to identify gaps outside the project's scope and recommend solutions. Since that time, Kern has since retired, and Claypool wrote back to IBM yet again to report that no progress had been made since the five-step plan was first developed for Austin's billing system. Austin Energy officials also objected to IBM's suggestion to add more powerful servers to help fix the problem because that would force the utility to pay more than originally planned on the project.

Despite all of the blunders, Austin Energy continues to hold out hope for a successful and amicable solution to the problem. Austin has a relationship with IBM dating back several years, when the companies contracted together to develop an inventory management system for the city. Though that system also experienced problems, they pale in comparison to the billing system fiasco. Austin also claims that IBM's errors have cost the company $8 million since the project's outset, so switching vendors might simply make matters worse for Austin with so much invested in IBM's project development already. When asked for comment, IBM has only said that it is working with Austin Energy to resolve the billing system issues.

IBM has successfully managed other projects like this one in the past. The IBM billing system consists of Oracle databases running atop IBM's Websphere middleware and Tivoli management tools. The problems with the system have not stemmed from one root cause. The new billing system is complex, with 73 different interfaces, and getting them all to work seamlessly with one another has been an arduous process. Customers have been unable to access the system's online portal, and Austin Energy employees have described their experience with the system as if they are 'alpha testers', meaning they have encountered bugs and issues that should never have made it to a live version.

Roughly one in four Austin customers has had problems with IBM's system. Some customers had their accounts canceled and could only correct the errors after several different phone calls. The billing system woes have come at a bad time for Austin Energy, which was preparing to institute its first rate increase in 17 years. In the wake of the public relations disaster brought about by the botched billing system, the company has had to rethink those plans.

As of February 2012, most—but not all—of the billing system errors had been fixed. Claypool remained hopeful that Austin Energy would be able to maintain an amicable relationship with IBM and finish the work successfully. IBM has been responsive, Claypool noted, but Claypool felt its response was too "incremental...We would like to see a faster response." Claypool was not Austin Energy's CIO at the time the utility contracted with IBM. Going forward, Austin Energy's outsourcing contracts will include stronger penalties for vendor nonperformance, including the question of system availability.

Sources: www.austinenergy.com, accessed August 17, 2013; Paul McDougall, "Chronology of an Outsourcing Disaster," *Information Week*, February 23, 2012; "Austin Energy Fixes Billing System Bug," MyFoxAustin.com, February 22, 2012; and IBM, "Austin Energy," 2012.

CASE STUDY QUESTIONS

1. Is the Austin Energy project a failure? Explain your answer.

2. Describe the business impact of the faltering Austin Energy project.

3. How much was IBM responsible for the problems countered by the Austin Energy billing project? Austin Energy? Explain your answer.

4. What were the specific organizational or technical factors as well as people factors involved in this project failure?

5. Describe the steps Austin Energy and IBM should have taken to better manage this project.

required by the new technology. That's why it's essential to know how to manage information systems projects and the reasons why they succeed or fail.

The Interactive Session on Organizations provides an example of a problem-ridden information systems project. As you read this case, try to determine why this project was not successful and the role of project management in the outcome.

PROJECT MANAGEMENT OBJECTIVES

A **project** is a planned series of related activities for achieving a specific business objective. Information systems projects include the development of new information systems, enhancement of existing systems, or projects for replacement or upgrading of the firm's information technology (IT) infrastructure.

Project management refers to the application of knowledge, skills, tools, and techniques to achieve specific targets within specified budget and time constraints. Project management activities include planning the work, assessing risk, estimating resources required to accomplish the work, organizing the work, acquiring human and material resources, assigning tasks, directing activities, controlling project execution, reporting progress, and analyzing the results. As in other areas of business, project management for information systems must deal with five major variables: scope, time, cost, quality, and risk.

Scope defines what work is or is not included in a project. For example, the scope of a project for a new order processing system might include new modules for inputting orders and transmitting them to production and accounting but not any changes to related accounts receivable, manufacturing, distribution, or inventory control systems. Project management defines all the work required to complete a project successfully, and should ensure that the scope of a project does not expand beyond what was originally intended.

Time is the amount of time required to complete the project. Project management typically establishes the amount of time required to complete major components of a project. Each of these components is further broken down into activities and tasks. Project management tries to determine the time required to complete each task and establish a schedule for completing the work.

Cost is based on the time to complete a project multiplied by the daily cost of human resources required to complete the project. Information systems project costs also include the cost of hardware, software, and work space. Project management develops a budget for the project and monitors ongoing project expenses.

Quality is an indicator of how well the end result of a project satisfies the objectives specified by management. The quality of information systems projects usually boils down to improved organizational performance and decision making. Quality also considers the accuracy and timeliness of information produced by the new system and ease of use.

Risk refers to potential problems that would threaten the success of a project. These potential problems might prevent a project from achieving its objectives by increasing time and cost, lowering the quality of project outputs, or preventing the project from being completed altogether. We discuss the most important risk factors for information systems projects later in this section.

SELECTING PROJECTS: MAKING THE BUSINESS CASE FOR A NEW SYSTEM

Companies typically are presented with many different projects for solving problems and improving performance. There are far more ideas for systems projects than there are resources. You will need to select the projects that promise the greatest benefit to the business.

Determining Project Costs and Benefits

As we pointed out earlier, the systems analysis includes an assessment of the economic feasibility of each alternative solution—whether each solution represents a good investment for the company. In order to identify the information systems projects that will deliver the most business value, you'll need to identify their costs and benefits and how they relate to the firm's information systems plan.

Table 12.2 lists some of the more common costs and benefits of systems. **Tangible benefits** can be quantified and assigned a monetary value. **Intangible benefits**, such as more efficient customer service or enhanced decision making, cannot be immediately quantified. Yet systems that produce mainly intangible benefits may still be good investments if they produce quantifiable gains in the long run.

To determine the benefits of a particular solution, you'll need to calculate all of its costs and all of its benefits. Obviously, a solution where costs exceed benefits should be rejected. But even if the benefits outweigh the costs, some additional financial analysis is required to determine whether the investment represents a good return on the firm's invested capital. Capital budgeting methods, such as net present value, internal rate of return (IRR), or accounting rate of return on investment (ROI), would typically be employed to evaluate the proposed information system solution as an investment. You can find out more about how

TABLE 12.2

Costs and Benefits of
Information Systems

Implementation Costs
Hardware
Telecommunications
Software
Personnel costs

Operational Costs
Computer processing time
Maintenance
Operating staff
User time
Ongoing training costs
Facility costs

Tangible Benefits
Increased productivity
Lower operational costs
Reduced workforce
Lower computer expenses
Lower outside vendor costs
Lower clerical and professional costs
Reduced rate of growth in expenses
Reduced facility costs
Increased sales

Intangible Benefits
Improved asset utilization
Improved resource control
Improved organizational planning
Increased organizational flexibility
More timely information
More information
Increased organizational learning
Legal requirements attained
Enhanced employee goodwill
Increased job satisfaction
Improved decision making
Improved operations
Higher client satisfaction
Better corporate image

these capital budgeting methods are used to justify information system investments in our Learning Tracks.

Some of the tangible benefits obtained by the Girl Scouts were increased productivity and lower operational costs resulting from automating the ordering process and from reducing errors. Intangible benefits included enhanced volunteer job satisfaction and improved operations.

The Information Systems Plan

An **information systems plan** shows how specific information systems fit into a company's overall business plan and business strategy. Table 12.3 lists the major components of such a plan. The plan contains a statement of corporate goals and specifies how information technology will help the business attain these goals. The report shows how general goals will be achieved by specific systems projects. It identifies specific target dates and milestones that can be used later to evaluate the plan's progress in terms of how many objectives were actually attained in the time frame specified in the plan. The plan indicates the key management decisions concerning hardware acquisition; telecommunications; centralization/decentralization of authority, data, and hardware; and required organizational change.

The plan should describe organizational changes, including management and employee training requirements, changes in business processes, and changes in authority, structure, or management practice. When you are making the business case for a new information system project, you show how the proposed system fits into that plan.

Portfolio Analysis and Scoring Models

Once you have determined the overall direction of systems development, **portfolio analysis** will help you evaluate alternative system projects. Portfolio analysis inventories all of

TABLE 12.3

Information Systems
Plan

1. **Purpose of the Plan**
   Overview of plan contents
   Current business organization and future organization
   Key business processes
   Management strategy

2. **Strategic Business Plan Rationale**
   Current situation
   Current business organization
   Changing environments
   Major goals of the business plan
   Firm's strategic plan

3. **Current Systems**
   Major systems supporting business functions and processes
   Current infrastructure capabilities
     Hardware
     Software
     Database
     Telecommunications and the Internet
   Difficulties meeting business requirements
   Anticipated future demands

4. **New Developments**
   New system projects
     Project descriptions
     Business rationale
     Applications' role in strategy
   New infrastructure capabilities required
     Hardware
     Software
     Database
     Telecommunications and the Internet

5. **Management Strategy**
     Acquisition plans
     Milestones and timing
     Organizational realignment
     Internal reorganization
     Management controls
     Major training initiatives
     Personnel strategy

6. **Implementation of the Plan**
     Anticipated difficulties in implementation
     Progress reports

7. **Budget Requirements**
     Requirements
     Potential savings
     Financing
     Acquisition cycle

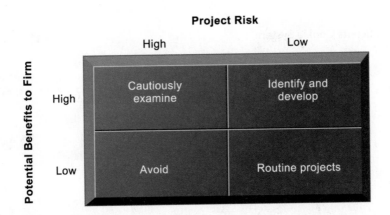

Project Risk

Figure 12.9
A System Portfolio
Companies should examine their portfolio of projects in terms of potential benefits and likely risks. Certain kinds of projects should be avoided altogether and others developed rapidly. There is no ideal mix. Companies in different industries have different information systems needs.

the firm's information systems projects and assets, including infrastructure, outsourcing contracts, and licenses. This portfolio of information systems investments can be described as having a certain profile of risk and benefit to the firm (see Figure 12.9), similar to a financial portfolio. Each information systems project carries its own set of risks and benefits. Firms try to improve the return on their information system portfolios by balancing the risk and return from their systems investments.

Obviously, you begin first by focusing on systems of high benefit and low risk. These promise early returns and low risks. Second, high-benefit, high-risk systems should be examined; low-benefit, high-risk systems should be totally avoided; and low-benefit, low-risk systems should be reexamined for the possibility of rebuilding and replacing them with more desirable systems having higher benefits. By using portfolio analysis, management can determine the optimal mix of investment risk and reward for their firms, balancing riskier, high-reward projects with safer, lower-reward ones.

Another method for evaluating alternative system solutions is a **scoring model**. Scoring models give alternative systems a single score based on the extent to which they meet selected objectives. Table 12.4 shows part of a simple scoring model that could have been used by the Girl Scouts in evaluating their alternative systems. The first column lists the criteria that decision makers use to evaluate the systems. Table 12.4 shows that the Girl Scouts attach the most importance to capabilities for sales order processing, ease of use, ability to support users in many different locations, and low cost. The second column in Table 12.4 lists the weights that decision makers attached to the decision criteria. Columns 3 and 5 show the percentage of requirements for each function that each alternative system meets. Each alternative's score is calculated by multiplying the percentage of requirements met for each function by the weight attached to that function. The QuickBase solution has the highest total score.

MANAGING PROJECT RISK AND SYSTEM-RELATED CHANGE

Some systems development projects are more likely to run into problems or to suffer delays because they carry a much higher level of risk than others. The level of project risk is influenced by project size, project structure, and the level of technical expertise of the information systems staff and project team. The larger the project—as indicated by the dollars spent, project team size, and how many parts of the organization will be affected by the new system—the greater the risk. Very large-scale systems projects have a failure rate that is 50 to 75 percent higher than that for other projects because such projects are complex and difficult to control. Risks are also higher for systems where information requirements are not clear and straightforward or the project team must master new technology.

TABLE 12.4

Example of a Scoring Model for the Girl Scouts Cookie System

Criteria	Weight	Microsoft Access System (%)	Microsoft Access System Score	QuickBase System (%)	QuickBase System Score
1.1 Order processing					
1.2 Online order entry	5	67	335	83	415
1.3 Order tracking by troop		81	405	87	435
1.4 Order tracking by individual Girl Scout	5	72	360	80	400
1.5 Reserving warehouse pickups	3	66	198	79	237
Total order processing			1,298		1,487
2.1 Ease of use					
2.2 Web access from multiple locations	5	55	275	92	460
2.3 Short training time	4	79	316	85	340
2.4 User-friendly screens and data entry forms	4	65	260	87	348
Total ease of use			851		1,148
3.1 Costs					
3.2 Software costs	3	51	153	65	195
3.3 Hardware (server) costs	4	57	228	90	360
3.4 Maintenance and support costs	4	42	168	89	356
Total costs			549		911
Grand Total			2,698		3,546

Implementation and Change Management

Dealing with these project risks requires an understanding of the implementation process and change management. A broader definition of **implementation** refers to all the organizational activities working toward the adoption and management of an innovation, such as a new information system. Successful implementation requires a high level of user involvement in a project and management support.

If users are heavily involved in the development of a system, they have more opportunities to mold the system according to their priorities and business requirements, and more opportunities to control the outcome. They also are more likely to react positively to the completed system because they have been active participants in the change process.

The relationship between end users and information systems specialists has traditionally been a problem area for information systems implementation efforts because of differing backgrounds, interests, and priorities. These differences create a **user-designer communications gap**. Information systems specialists often have a highly technical orientation to problem solving, focusing on technical solutions in which hardware and software efficiency is optimized at the expense of ease of use or organizational effectiveness. End users prefer systems that are oriented toward solving business problems or facilitating organizational tasks. Often the orientations of both groups are so at odds that they appear to speak in different tongues. These differences are illustrated in Table 12.5.

If an information systems project has the backing and commitment of management at various levels, it is more likely to receive higher priority from both users and the technical information systems staff. Management backing also ensures that a systems project receives sufficient funding and resources to be successful. Furthermore, to be enforced effectively, all the changes in work habits and procedures and any organizational realignments associated with a new system depend on management backing.

Controlling Risk Factors

There are strategies you can follow to deal with project risk and increase the chances of a successful system solution. If the new system involves challenging and complex technology, you can recruit project leaders with strong technical and administrative experience. Outsourcing or using external consultants are options if your firm does not have staff with the required technical skills or expertise.

Large projects benefit from appropriate use of **formal planning and tools** for documenting and monitoring project plans. The two most commonly used methods for documenting project plans are Gantt charts and PERT charts. A **Gantt chart** lists project activities and their corresponding start and completion dates. The Gantt chart visually represents the timing and duration of different tasks in a development project as well as their human resource requirements (see Figure 12.10). It shows each task as a horizontal bar whose length is proportional to the time required to complete it.

Although Gantt charts show when project activities begin and end, they don't depict task dependencies, how one task is affected if another is behind schedule, or how tasks should be ordered. That is where **PERT charts** are useful. PERT stands for Program Evaluation and Review Technique, a methodology developed by the U.S. Navy during the 1950s to manage the Polaris submarine missile program. A PERT chart graphically depicts project tasks and their interrelationships. The PERT chart lists the specific activities that make up a project and the activities that must be completed before a specific activity can start, as illustrated in Figure 12.11.

The PERT chart portrays a project as a network diagram consisting of numbered nodes (either circles or rectangles) representing project tasks. Each node is numbered and shows

User Concerns	Designer Concerns
Will the system deliver the information I need for my work?	What demands will this system put on our servers?
Can we access the data on our iPhones, Blackberrys, tablets, and PCs?	What kind of programming demands will this place on our group?
What new procedures do we need to enter data into the system?	Where will the data be stored? What's the most efficient way to store them?
How will the operation of the system change employees' daily routines?	What technologies should we use to secure the data?

TABLE 12.5

The User-Designer Communications Gap

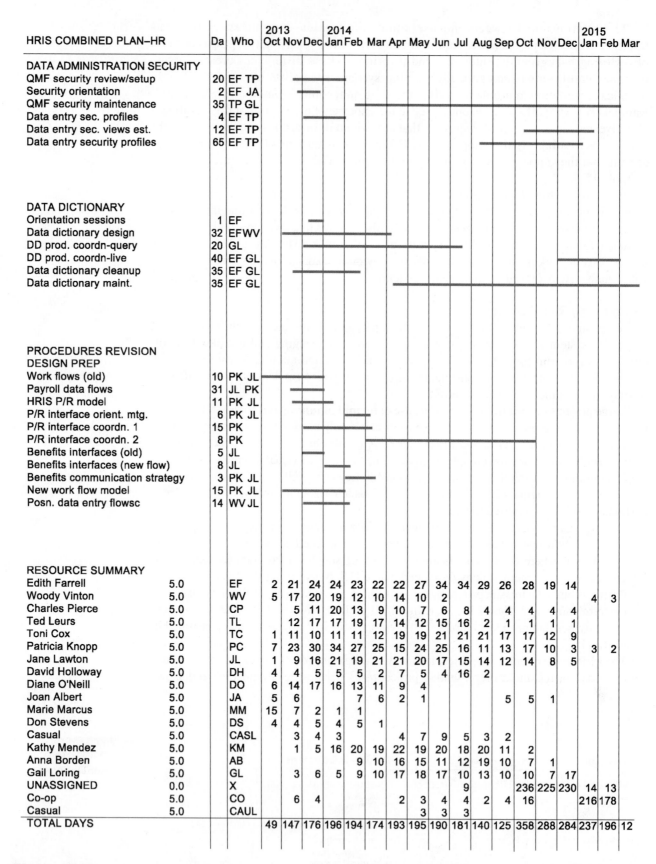

HRIS COMBINED PLAN–HR

Task	Da	Who
DATA ADMINISTRATION SECURITY		
QMF security review/setup	20	EF TP
Security orientation	2	EF JA
QMF security maintenance	35	TP GL
Data entry sec. profiles	4	EF TP
Data entry sec. views est.	12	EF TP
Data entry security profiles	65	EF TP
DATA DICTIONARY		
Orientation sessions	1	EF
Data dictionary design	32	EFWV
DD prod. coordn-query	20	GL
DD prod. coordn-live	40	EF GL
Data dictionary cleanup	35	EF GL
Data dictionary maint.	35	EF GL
PROCEDURES REVISION / **DESIGN PREP**		
Work flows (old)	10	PK JL
Payroll data flows	31	JL PK
HRIS P/R model	11	PK JL
P/R interface orient. mtg.	6	PK JL
P/R interface coordn. 1	15	PK
P/R interface coordn. 2	8	PK
Benefits interfaces (old)	5	JL
Benefits interfaces (new flow)	8	JL
Benefits communication strategy	3	PK JL
New work flow model	15	PK JL
Posn. data entry flowsc	14	WV JL

RESOURCE SUMMARY

Name		Who	2013 Oct	Nov	Dec	2014 Jan	Feb	Mar	Apr	May	Jun	Jul	Aug	Sep	Oct	Nov	Dec	2015 Jan	Feb	Mar
Edith Farrell	5.0	EF	2	21	24	24	23	22	22	27	34	34	29	26	28	19	14			
Woody Vinton	5.0	WV	5	17	20	19	12	10	14	10	2							4	3	
Charles Pierce	5.0	CP		5	11	20	13	9	10	7	6	8	4	4	4	4	4			
Ted Leurs	5.0	TL		12	17	17	19	17	14	12	15	16	2	1	1	1	1			
Toni Cox	5.0	TC	1	11	10	11	11	12	19	19	21	21	21	17	17	12	9			
Patricia Knopp	5.0	PC	7	23	30	34	27	25	15	24	25	16	11	13	17	10	3	3	2	
Jane Lawton	5.0	JL	1	9	16	21	19	21	21	20	17	15	14	12	14	8	5			
David Holloway	5.0	DH	4	4	5	5	5	2	7	5	4	16	2							
Diane O'Neill	5.0	DO	6	14	17	16	13	11	9	4										
Joan Albert	5.0	JA	5	6			7	6	2	1				5	5	1				
Marie Marcus	5.0	MM	15	7	2	1	1													
Don Stevens	5.0	DS	4	4	5	4	5	1												
Casual	5.0	CASL		3	4	3			4	7	9	5	3	2						
Kathy Mendez	5.0	KM		1	5	16	20	19	22	19	20	18	20	11	2					
Anna Borden	5.0	AB					9	10	16	15	11	12	19	10	7	1				
Gail Loring	5.0	GL		3	6	5	9	10	17	18	17	10	13	10	10	7	17			
UNASSIGNED	0.0	X												9		236	225	230	14	13
Co-op	5.0	CO		6	4				2	3	4	4	2	4	16			216	178	
Casual	5.0	CAUL									3	3	3							
TOTAL DAYS			49	147	176	196	194	174	193	195	190	181	140	125	358	288	284	237	196	12

Figure 12.10
A Gantt Chart
The Gantt chart in this figure shows the task, person-days, and initials of each responsible person, as well as the start and finish dates for each task. The resource summary provides a good manager with the total person-days for each month and for each person working on the project to manage the project successfully. The project described here is a data administration project.

the task, its duration, the starting date, and the completion date. The direction of the arrows on the lines indicates the sequence of tasks and shows which activities must be completed before the commencement of another activity. In Figure 12.11, the tasks in nodes 2, 3, and 4 are not dependent on each other and can be undertaken simultaneously, but each is dependent on completion of the first task.

Project Management Software Commercial software tools are available to automate the creation of Gantt and PERT charts and to facilitate the project management process. Project management software typically features capabilities for defining and ordering tasks, assigning resources to tasks, establishing starting and ending dates for tasks, tracking progress, and facilitating modifications to tasks and resources. The most widely used project management tool today is Microsoft Office Project. We should also point out that these traditional project management tools are being supplemented with some of the social business tools described in Chapter 2. For example, projects might use collaborative shared workspaces, where project tasks are updated in real time, or let activity streams inform team members of events taking place on a project as they occur.

Overcoming User Resistance

You can overcome user resistance by promoting user participation (to elicit commitment as well as to improve design), by making user education and training easily available, and by providing better incentives for users who cooperate. End users can become active members of the project team, take on leadership roles, and take charge of system installation and training.

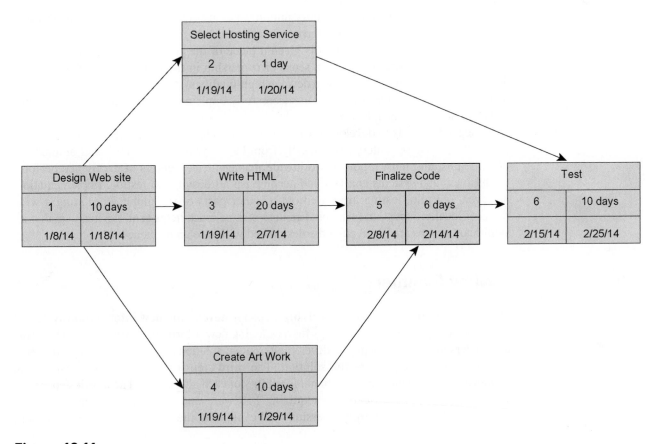

Figure 12.11
A PERT Chart
This is a simplified PERT chart for creating a small Web site. It shows the ordering of project tasks and the relationship of a task with preceding and succeeding tasks.

You should pay special attention to areas where users interface with the system, with sensitivity to ergonomics issues. **Ergonomics** refers to the interaction of people and machines in the work environment. It considers the design of jobs, health issues, and the end-user interface of information systems. For instance, if a system has a series of complicated online data entry screens that are extremely difficult or time-consuming to work with, users will reject the system if it increases their work load or level of job stress.

Users will be more cooperative if organizational problems are solved prior to introducing the new system. In addition to procedural changes, transformations in job functions, organizational structure, power relationships, and behavior should be identified during systems analysis using an **organizational impact analysis**.

MANAGING PROJECTS ON A GLOBAL SCALE

As globalization proceeds, companies will be building many more new systems that are global in scale, spanning many different units in many different countries. The project management challenges for global systems are similar to those for domestic systems, but they are complicated by the international environment. User information requirements, business processes, and work cultures differ from country to country. It is difficult to convince local managers anywhere in the world to change their business processes and ways of working to align with units in other countries, especially if this might interfere with their local performance.

Involving people in change, and assuring them that change is in the best interests of the company and their local units, is a key tactic for convincing users to adopt global systems and standards. Information systems projects should involve users in the design process without giving up control over the project to parochial interests.

One tactic is to permit each country unit in a global corporation to develop one transnational application first in its home territory, and then throughout the world. In this manner, each major country systems group is given a piece of the action in developing a transnational system, and local units feel a sense of ownership in the transnational effort. On the downside, this assumes the ability to develop high-quality systems is widely distributed, and that, a German team, for example, can successfully implement systems in France and Italy. This will not always be the case.

A second tactic is to develop new transnational centers of excellence, or a single center of excellence. These centers draw heavily from local national units, are based on multinational teams, and must report to worldwide management. Centers of excellence perform the business and systems analysis and accomplish all design and testing. Implementation, however, and pilot testing are rolled out to other parts of the globe. Recruiting a wide range of local groups to transnational centers of excellence helps send the message that all significant groups are involved in the design and will have an influence.

Review Summary

1 **What are the core problem-solving steps for developing new information systems?** The core problem-solving steps for developing new information systems are: (1) define and understand the problem, (2) develop alternative solutions, (3) evaluate and choose the solution, and (4) implement the solution. The third step includes an assessment of the technical, financial, and organizational feasibility of each alternative. The fourth step entails finalizing design specifications, acquiring hardware and software, testing, providing training and documentation, conversion, and evaluating the system solution once it is in production.

2 **What are the alternative methods for building information systems?** The systems lifecycle requires that information systems be developed in formal stages. The stages

must proceed sequentially and have defined outputs; each requires formal approval before the next stage can commence. The system lifecycle is rigid and costly but nevertheless useful for large projects.

Prototyping consists of building an experimental system rapidly and inexpensively for end users to interact with and evaluate. The prototype is refined and enhanced until users are satisfied that it includes all of their requirements and can be used as a template to create the final system. End-user-developed systems can be created rapidly and informally using fourth-generation software tools. End-user development can improve requirements determination and reduce application backlog.

Application software packages eliminate the need for writing software programs when developing an information system. Application software packages are helpful if a firm does not have the internal information systems staff or financial resources to custom-develop a system.

Outsourcing consists of using an external vendor to build (or operate) a firm's information systems. If it is properly managed, outsourcing can save application development costs or enable firms to develop applications without an internal information systems staff.

Rapid application design, joint application design (JAD), cloud-based platforms, and reusable software components (including Web services) can be used to speed up the systems development process. Mobile application development must address multiple platforms, small screen sizes, and the need to conserve resources.

3 **What are the principal methodologies for modeling and designing systems?** The two principal methodologies for modeling and designing information systems are structured methodologies and object-oriented development. Structured methodologies focus on modeling processes and data separately. The data flow diagram is the principal tool for structured analysis, and the structure chart is the principal tool for representing structured software design. Object-oriented development models a system as a collection of objects that combine processes and data.

4 **How should information systems projects be selected and evaluated?** To determine whether an information system project is a good investment, one must calculate its costs and benefits. Tangible benefits are quantifiable, and intangible benefits cannot be immediately quantified but may provide quantifiable benefits in the future. Benefits that exceed costs should then be analyzed using capital budgeting methods to make sure they represent a good return on the firm's invested capital.

Organizations should develop information systems plans that describe how information technology supports the company's overall business plan and strategy. Portfolio analysis and scoring models can be used to evaluate alternative information systems projects.

5 **How should information systems projects be managed?** Information systems projects and the entire implementation process should be managed as planned organizational change using an organizational impact analysis. Management support and control of the implementation process are essential, as are mechanisms for dealing with the level of risk in each new systems project. Project risks are influenced by project size, project structure, and the level of technical expertise of the information systems staff and project team. Formal planning and control tools (including Gantt and PERT charts) track the resource allocations and specific project activities. Users can be encouraged to take active roles in systems development and become involved in installation and training. Global information systems projects should involve local units in the creation of the design without giving up control of the project to parochial interests.

Key Terms

Acceptance testing, 435

Component-based
development, 447

Computer-aided software
engineering (CASE), 447

Conversion, 436

Customization, 439

Data flow diagram (DFD),
444

Direct cutover strategy, 436

Documentation, 435

End-user development, 450

Ergonomics, 458

Feasibility study, 433

Formal planning and tools,
455

Gantt chart, 455

Implementation, 454

Information requirements,
432

Information systems plan,
451

Intangible benefits, 450

Joint application design
(JAD), 443

Maintenance, 436

Mobile Web app, 441

Mobile Web site, 441

Native app, 441

Object-oriented development,
445

Organizational impact
analysis, 458

Parallel strategy, 436

PERT charts, 455

Phased approach, 436

Portfolio analysis, 451

Process specifications, 445

Production, 436

Project, 449

Project management, 449

Prototyping, 437

Rapid application
development (RAD), 443

Request for Proposal (RFP),
439

Responsive Web design, 441

Scope, 438

Scoring model, 453

Structure chart, 445

Structured, 444

System testing, 435

Systems analysis, 431

Systems design, 434

Systems development
lifecycle (SDLC), 436

Tangible benefits, 450

Test plan, 435

Testing, 435

Unit testing, 435

User-designer
communications gap, 455

Review Questions

12-1 What are the core problem-solving steps for developing new information systems?
- List and describe the problem-solving steps for building a new system.
- Define information requirements and explain why they are important for developing a system solution.
- List the various types of design specifications required for a new information system.
- Describe the roles of documentation, conversion, production, and maintenance in systems development.
- Explain why managing change is an important part of developing a new information system.

12-2 What are the alternative methods for building information systems?
- Define the traditional systems lifecycle and describe its advantages and disadvantages for systems building.
- Define information system prototyping and describe its benefits and limitations. List and describe the steps in the prototyping process.
- Define end-user development and explain its advantages and disadvantages.
- Describe the advantages and disadvantages of developing information systems based on application software packages.
- Define outsourcing. Describe the circumstances in which it should be used for building information systems. List and describe the hidden costs of offshore software outsourcing.
- Explain how businesses can rapidly develop e-business applications.
- Explain the differences between mobile Web sites, mobile Web apps, and native apps.

12-3 What are the principal methodologies for modeling and designing systems?
- Compare object-oriented and traditional structured approaches for modeling and designing systems.

12-4 How should information systems projects be selected and evaluated?
- Define a project and describe the five major variables of project management and their effects.
- Explain the difference between tangible and intangible benefits.
- List six tangible benefits and six intangible benefits.
- List and describe the major components of an information systems plan.

12-5 How should information systems projects be managed?
- Explain the importance of implementation for managing the organizational change surrounding a new information system.
- Define the user-designer communications gap and explain the kinds of implementation problems it creates.
- List and describe the factors that influence project risk and describe strategies for minimizing project risks.
- Describe ways that firms can overcome user resistance to new project implementations.
- Describe tactics for managing global projects.

Discussion Questions

12-6 Evaluating an information systems' worth can be a difficult task. What are some ways to do this?

12-7 What are some of the ways a firm overcome user resistance to new project implementations?

12-8 Why is building a system a form of organizational problem-solving?

Hands-On MIS Projects

The projects in this section give you hands-on experience evaluating information systems projects, designing a customer system for auto sales, and analyzing Web site information requirements.

MANAGEMENT DECISION PROBLEMS

12-9 The Warm and Toasty Heating Oil Company in Glasgow, Scotland, used to deliver heating oil by sending trucks that printed out a ticket with the number of gallons of oil delivered and that was placed on customers' doorsteps. Customers received their oil delivery bills in the mail two weeks later. The company recently revised its oil delivery and billing system so that oil truck drivers can calculate and print out a complete bill for each delivery and leave customers with the bill and a return envelope at the time the delivery takes place. Evaluate the business impact of the new system and the people and organizational changes required to implement the new technology.

12-10 Caterpillar is the world's leading maker of earth-moving machinery and supplier of agricultural equipment. The software for its Dealer Business System (DBS), which it licenses to its dealers to help them run their businesses, is becoming outdated. Senior management wants its dealers to use a hosted version of the software supported by Accenture Consultants so Caterpillar can concentrate on its core business. The system had become a de-facto standard for doing business with the company. The majority of the Caterpillar dealers in North America use some version of DBS, as do about half of the Caterpillar dealers in the rest of the world. Before Caterpillar turns the product over to Accenture, what factors and issues should it consider? What questions should it ask? What questions should its dealers ask?

IMPROVING DECISION MAKING: USING DATABASE SOFTWARE TO DESIGN A CUSTOMER SYSTEM FOR AUTO SALES

Software skills: Database design, querying, reporting, and forms
Business skills: Sales lead and customer analysis

12-11 This project requires you to perform a systems analysis and then design a system solution using database software.

Ace Auto Dealers specializes in selling new vehicles from Subaru in Portland, Oregon. The company advertises in local newspapers and is also listed as an authorized dealer on the Subaru Web site and other major Web sites for auto buyers. The company benefits from a good local word-of-mouth reputation and name recognition.

Ace does not believe it has enough information about its customers. It cannot easily determine which prospects have made auto purchases, nor can it identify which customer touch points have produced the greatest number of sales leads or actual sales so it can focus advertising and marketing more on the channels that generate the most revenue. Are purchasers discovering Ace from newspaper ads, from word of mouth, or from the Web?

Prepare a systems analysis report detailing Ace's problem and a system solution that can be implemented using PC database management software. Then use database software to develop a simple system solution. In MyMISLab™, you will find more information about Ace and its information requirements to help you develop the solution.

ACHIEVING OPERATIONAL EXCELLENCE: ANALYZING WEB SITE DESIGN AND INFORMATION REQUIREMENTS

Software skills: Web browser software
Business skills: Information requirements analysis, Web site design

12-12 Visit the Web site of your choice and explore it thoroughly. Prepare a report analyzing the various functions provided by that Web site and its information requirements. Your report should answer these questions: What functions does the Web site perform? What data does it use? What are its inputs, outputs, and processes? What are some of its other design specifications? Does the Web site link to any internal systems or systems of other organizations? What value does this Web site provide the firm?

Collaboration and Teamwork Project

12-13 In MyMISLab, you will find a Collaboration and Teamwork Project dealing with the concepts in this chapter. You will be able to use Google Drive, Google Docs, Google Sites, Google+, or other open-source tools to complete the assignment.

BUSINESS PROBLEM-SOLVING CASE

NYCAPS and CityTime: A Tale of Two New York City IS Projects

Soon after taking office, New York City Mayor Michael Bloomberg announced the development of the New York City Automated Personnel System, or NYCAPS with an initial budget of $66 million. The goal of the project was to create a modern automated system for managing and updating the personal information for New York City's work force, including employee benefit information. The city had been using eight individual citywide systems, 200 systems within individual agencies, and a maze of paperwork for handling employee benefits and job changes. Successful implementation of the NYCAPS project stood to save the city millions of dollars per year in labor and IT costs. To date, the implementation has been anything but timely, and the total expenditures of the project have grown to over $363 million, nearly six times the original budget.

Project monitors' reports described chronic misman-agement, cost overruns, and general waste, but the city continued ahead with the project without making any significant changes. These reports indicated that the primary reason for the project's ballooning costs and myriad delays was lack of strong leadership.

The NYCAPS project was controlled by government officials who did not have the authority or expertise to make important project decisions, and therefore missed many opportunities to lower development costs. Early on, in 2002, NYCAPS's lone functionality was as a Web site where people could apply to take civil service exams. But less than two weeks after the launch of the site, a user found that he could obtain other users' personal information by exploiting a security flaw, and the site was immediately shut down. Officials in charge of the project then vowed to fix the flaw and get the project right.

However, instead of taking charge of more facets of the project, the Bloomberg administration delegated more of the project to Accenture, a prominent consulting firm. The city tasked Accenture with both defining the specifications of the system as well as putting it together themselves. Companies and government agencies building a new system rarely do this, since splitting those roles keeps the costs from any one contractor from exploding unchecked.

Accenture consultants charged the city up to $400 an hour, and the company earned $8 million from the city in 2004, then $26 million in 2005, $29 million in 2006, and a whopping $53 million in 2007. Raj Agarwal, the city's appointed project manager, openly criticized Accenture's billing techniques, claiming that they were billing at rates that reflected many more consultants than were actually on the job, and that the company was using recent college graduates and interns to perform the work, while billing the city at much higher rates typi-cally used for experienced workers. Agarwal has long since quit his post, and the city has struggled to attract experienced and capable managers from the private sector. The city was eventually able to switch Accenture to fixed-price billing.

Accenture blamed the city for increasing the scope and functionality of the project beyond the original specifications. As time passed and the city grew desperate for a functioning version of the system, the city abandoned development on many of the capabili-ties that the system was intended to have. Nearly ten years after the project was launched, the city has a live version of NYCAPS, but thousands of retirees still cannot access the site, and thousands more current workers are not included in the system. Even worse, NYCAPS was built to run on the same old legacy systems that used the previous patchwork system, despite the fact that upgrading legacy technology was a major reason for the project's development in the first place.

An earlier, even more ambitious New York City project makes NYCAPS look tame. The CityTime payroll system project, first conceived in 1998, has seen its budget grow from approximately $65 million to well over $700 million as of 2012. CityTime was created to automate payroll timekeeping once dependent on pen and paper, and in the process to curb undeserved over-time payments to city workers and improve account-ability throughout the government. In an ironic twist, the project has instead been permeated with fraud at every level, and engineers from the main consulting organiza-tion, Science Applications International Corporation (SAIC) were charged with fraud.

A June 2011 press release from Manhattan US Attorney Preet Bharara stated that contractors and subcontractors systematically inflated costs, overbilled for consultants' time, and artificially extended the completion date. Again, the biggest reason for the proj-ect's unheard-of budget increases was lack of qualified oversight. The few government employees constantly monitoring the project turned a seemingly blind eye on the ballooning costs incurred by SAIC and the lack of progress in the project. Belief that the software devel-oped for the system could be sold to other governments was perhaps another reason why the city let costs run wild.

Bloomberg's budget director, Mark Page, was reportedly the strongest voice in favor of CityTime. He had hoped to stop the trend of police officers, firefighters, and other aging city workers receiving unnecessary overtime at the end of their careers, presumably to increase their pensions. Page also wanted to limit lawsuits against the city from workers claiming their pay was too low for the hours they had worked. But Page's background was in law, not information systems, making him a poor choice to oversee CityTime. Other government branches, like the city comptroller, left the project mostly to Page. William C. Thompson, the city comptroller from 2002 to 2009, never audited CityTime despite numerous warnings about the project from staffers. An aide for the mayor did suggest that the comptroller's office had raised concerns about the project to the mayor, but those concerns too were ignored or dismissed by Page.

In 2000, work on the project was transferred to SAIC from the first contractor, a subsidiary of MCI. Instead of the usual competitive bidding process for contracts, the city opted simply to pass it off to SAIC. Shortly after SAIC took control of the contract, work on CityTime was switched from fixed-price to hourly billing. This, in turn, inflated costs from $224 million in 2006 to a total of $628 million by 2009. Thanks to the hourly contracts, the city was on the hook for all of the waste incurred by SAIC. The terms of contracts were also constantly changing: another consulting company hired to provide quality assurance for CityTime had its contract amended 11 times, increasing its value to almost $50 million from its original $3.4 million figure.

SAIC delegated most of the work on CityTime to subcontractors, further complicating the chain of command involved in the project. The most prominent of these, Technodyne, received $450 million in funds from the city. Today, over 150,000 city workers use CityTime to keep track of attendance and leave of absence requests, but the cost per user for the project is estimated to be approximately $4,000. The industry standard for projects of this size is between $200 and $1,000. New York State has developed a system to perform similar tasks for only $217 million, which makes CityTime's $720 million price tag look even worse by comparison.

In March 2012, the city received some good news – SAIC agreed to repay $500 million in restitution and penalties back to the city to avoid federal prosecution for various instances of fraud involving the CityTime project. The city recovered most of that money and, according to Mayor Bloomberg, the SAIC repayment meant that taxpayers only had to pay $100 million for CityTime. The scandal nevertheless is a black mark for Bloomberg and his goals to modernize city information systems.

The New York City Council also called a hearing to respond to the budget-crippling cost overruns of both projects. The Bloomberg administration vowed once again to review the way it handles complex, multi-million dollar technology projects. Proposed changes included first looking for commercial software before developing customized software without a real need for it. The city also stated that it would bill contractors as functional benchmarks for projects are achieved instead of hourly, to avoid future partnerships like Accenture and SAIC, and would ensure that multi-million dollar technology projects are overseen by qualified experts, instead of government administrators from other areas with no project management experience.

Sources: Jennifer Fermino, "Bloomberg Says New York City 'Lucky' It Had $500 Million CityTime Fraud," New York Daily News, July 26, 2013; www.nyc.gov, accessed August 17, 2013; "CityTime," The New York Times, March 14, 2012; Michael M. Grynbaum, "Contractor Strikes $500 Million Deal in City Payroll Scandal," The New York Times, March 14, 2012; David M. Halbfinger, "For Mayor, Waste Mars Another Digital Project," The New York Times, September 23, 2011 and "City Hall Admits Mishandling Technology Projects," The New York Times, October 31, 2011; Josh Margolin, "277M Overrun a City 'Soar' Point," The New York Post, August 11, 2011, Robert Charette, "New York City's $720 Million CityTime Project a Vehicle for Unprecedented Fraud Says US Prosecutor," IEEE Spectrum, June 21, 2011, David W. Chen, Serge F. Kovaleski and John Eligon, Behind Troubled City Payroll Project, Lax Oversight and One Powerful Insider," The New York Times, March 27, 2011.

Case Study Questions

12-14 How important were the NYCAPS and CityTime projects for New York City? What were their objectives? What would have been their business benefits?

12-15 Evaluate the key risk factors in both projects.

12-16 Classify and describe the problems each project encountered as the NYCAPS and CityTime systems were being implemented. What people, organization, and technology factors were responsible for these problems?

12-17 What were the similarities and differences in the management of both projects?

12-18 What was the business impact of these botched implementations? Explain your answer.

12-19 Describe the steps that should have been taken to prevent negative outcomes in these projects.

Glossary

3-D printing: Uses machines to make solid objects, layer by layer, from specifications in a digital file. Also known as additive manufacturing.

3G networks: High-speed cellular networks based on packet-switched technology, enabling users to transmit video, graphics, and other rich media, in addition to voice.

4G networks: Ultra high-speed wireless networks that are entirely packet switched, with speeds between 1 Mbps and 1 Gbps.

acceptable use policy (AUP): Defines acceptable uses of the firm's information resources and computing equipment, including desktop and laptop computers, wireless devices, telephones, and the Internet, and specifies consequences for noncompliance.

acceptance testing: Provides the final certification that the system is ready to be used in a production setting.

accountability: The mechanisms for assessing responsibility for decisions made and actions taken.

accumulated balance digital payment systems: Systems enabling users to make micropayments and purchases on the Web, accumulating a debit balance on their credit card or telephone bills.

advertising revenue model: Web site generating revenue by attracting a large audience

affiliate revenue model: E-commerce revenue mode in which Web sites are paid as "affiliates" for sending their visitors to other sites in return for a referral fee.

agile development: Rapid delivery of working software by breaking a large project into a series of small sub-projects that are completed in short periods of time using iteration and continuous feedback.

analytic platform: Preconfigured hardware-software system that is specifically designed for high-speed analysis of large datasets.

analytical CRM: Customer relationship management applications dealing with the analysis of customer data to provide information for improving business performance.

Android: Open source operating system for mobile devices developed by Google and the Open Handset Alliance. Currently the most popular smartphone operating system worldwide.

antivirus software: Software designed to detect, and often eliminate, computer viruses from an information system.

application controls: Specific controls unique to each computerized application that ensure that only authorized data are completely and accurately processed by that application.

application proxy filtering: Firewall screening technology that uses a proxy server to inspect and transmit data packets flowing into and out of the organization so that all the organization's internal applications communicate with the outside using a proxy application.

application server: Software that handles all application operations between browser-based computers and a company's back-end business applications or databases.

application software: Programs written for a specific application to perform functions specified by end users.

apps: Small pieces of software that run on the Internet, on a computer, or on a mobile phone and are generally delivered over the Internet.

artificial intelligence (AI): The effort to develop computer-based systems that can behave like humans, with the ability to learn languages, accomplish physical tasks, use a perceptual apparatus, and emulate human expertise and decision making.

attributes: Pieces of information describing a particular entity.

augmented reality: Technology for enhancing visualization that provides a live view of a physical world environment whose elements are augmented by virtual computer-generated imagery.

authentication: The ability of each party in a transaction to ascertain the identity of the other party.

authorization management systems: Systems for allowing each user access only to those portions of a system or the Web that person is permitted to enter, based on information established by a set of access rules.

authorization policies: Determine differing levels of access to information assets for different levels of users in an organization.

autonomic computing: Effort to develop systems that can manage themselves without user intervention.

backbone: Part of a network handling the major traffic and providing the primary path for traffic flowing to or from other networks.

balanced scorecard method: Framework for operationalizing a firms strategic plan by focusing on measurable financial, business process, customer, and learning and growth outcomes of firm performance.

bandwidth: The capacity of a communications channel as measured by the difference between the highest and lowest frequencies that can be transmitted by that channel.

banner ad: A graphic display on a Web page used for advertising. The banner is linked to the advertiser's Web site so that a person clicking on it will be transported to the advertiser's Web site.

behavioral targeting: Tracking the click-streams (history of clicking behavior) of individuals across multiple Web sites for the purpose of understanding their interests and intentions, and exposing them to advertisements which are uniquely suited to their interests.

benchmarking: Setting strict standards for products, services, or activities and measuring organizational performance against those standards.

best practices: The most successful solutions or problem-solving methods that have been developed by a specific organization or industry.

big data: Datasets with volumes so huge that they are beyond the ability of typical relational DBMS to capture, store, and analyze. The data are often unstructured or semi-structured.

biometric authentication: Technology for authenticating system users that compares a person's unique characteristics such as fingerprints, face, or retinal image, against a stored set profile of these characteristics.

bit: A binary digit representing the smallest unit of data in a computer system. It can only have one of two states, representing 0 or 1.

blog: Popular term for Weblog, designating an informal yet structured Web site where individuals can publish stories, opinions, and links to other Web sites of interest.

blogosphere: The totality of blog-related Web sites.

Bluetooth: Standard for wireless personal area networks that can transmit up to 722 Kbps within a 10-meter area.

botnet: A group of computers that have been infected with bot malware without users' knowledge, enabling a hacker to use the amassed resources of the computers to launch distributed denial-of-service attacks, phishing campaigns or spam.

broadband: High-speed transmission technology. Also designates a single communications medium that can transmit multiple channels of data simultaneously.

bugs: Software program code defects.

bullwhip effect: Distortion of information about the demand for a product as it passes from one entity to the next across the supply chain.

bundling: Cross-selling in which a combination of products is sold as a bundle at a price lower than the total cost of the individual products.

business continuity planning: Planning that focuses on how the company can restore business operations after a disaster strikes.

business intelligence (BI): Applications and technologies to help users make better business decisions.

business model: An abstraction of what an enterprise is and how the enterprise delivers a product or service, showing how the enterprise creates wealth.

business performance management: Methodology for measuring firm performance using key performance indicators based on the firm's strategies.

business process management: Tools and methodologies for continuously improving and managing business processes.

business process reengineering (BPR): The radical redesign of business processes to maximize the benefits of information technology.

business processes: The unique ways in which organizations coordinate and organize work activities, information, and knowledge to produce a product or service.

business strategy: Set of activities and decisions that determine the products and services the firm produces, the industries in which the firm competes, firm competitors, suppliers, and customers, and the firm's long-term goals.

business: A formal organization whose aim is to produce products or provide services for a profit

business-to-business (B2B) electronic commerce: Electronic sales of goods and services among businesses.

business-to-consumer (B2C) electronic commerce: Electronic retailing of products and services directly to individual consumers.

BYOD: Allowing employees to use their personal mobile devices in the workplace.

C: A powerful programming language with tight control and efficiency of execution; is portable across different microprocessors and is used primarily with PCs.

cable Internet connections: Use digital cable coaxial lines to deliver high-speed Internet access to homes and businesses.

call center: An organizational department responsible for handling customer service issues by telephone and other channels.

campus area network (CAN): An interconnected set of local area networks in a limited geographical area such as a college or corporate campus.

capacity planning: The process of predicting when a computer hardware system becomes saturated to ensure that adequate computing resources are available for work of different priorities and that the firm has enough computing power for its current and future needs.

carpal tunnel syndrome (CTS): Type of RSI in which pressure on the median nerve through the wrist's bony carpal tunnel structure produces pain.

case-based reasoning (CBR): Artificial intelligence technology that represents knowledge as a database of cases and solutions.

cathode ray tube (CRT): Electronic gun that shoots a beam of electrons illuminating pixels on a display screen.

CD-ROM (compact disk read-only memory): Read-only optical disk storage used for imaging, reference, and database applications with massive amounts of unchanging data and for multimedia.

CD-RW (CD-ReWritable): Optical disk storage that can be rewritten many times by users.

cellular telephones (cell phones): A device that transmits voice or data, using radio waves to communicate with radio antennas placed within adjacent geographic areas called cells.

central processing unit (CPU): Area of the computer system that manipulates symbols, numbers, and letters, and controls the other parts of the computer system.

centralized processing: Processing that is accomplished by one large central computer.

change agent: In the context of implementation, the individual acting as the catalyst during the change process to ensure successful organizational adaptation to a new system or innovation.

change management: Giving proper consideration to the impact of organizational change associated with a new system or alteration of an existing system.

chat: Live, interactive conversations over a public network.

chief information officer (CIO): Senior manager in charge of the information systems function in the firm.

chief knowledge officer (CKO): Responsible for the firm's knowledge management program.

chief privacy officer (CPO): Responsible for ensuring the company complies with existing data privacy laws.

chief security officer (CSO): Heads a formal security function for the organization and is responsible for enforcing the firm's security policy.

choice: Simon's third stage of decision making, when the individual selects among the various solution alternatives.

Chrome OS: Google's lightweight operating system for cloud computing using a Web-connected computer or mobile device.

churn rate: Measurement of the number of customers who stop using or purchasing products or services from a company. Used as an indicator of the growth or decline of a firm's customer base.

click fraud: Fraudulently clicking on an online ad in pay per click advertising to generate an improper charge per click.

clickstream tracking: Tracking data about customer activities at Web sites and storing them in a log.

client/server computing: A model for computing that splits processing between clients and servers on a network, assigning functions to the machine most able to perform the function.

client: The user point-of-entry for the required function in client/server computing. Normally a desktop computer, workstation, or laptop computer.

cloud computing: Model of computing that provides acess to a shared pool of computing resources over a network, often the Internet.

coaxial cable: A transmission medium consisting of thickly insulated copper wire; can transmit large volumes of data quickly.

COBOL (Common Business Oriented Language): Major programming language for business applications because it can process large data files with alphanumeric characters.

collaboration: Working with others to achieve shared and explicit goals.

collaborative filtering: Tracking users' movements on a Web site, comparing the information gleaned about a user's behavior against data about other customers with similar interests to predict what the user would like to see next.

co-location: Web hosting approach in which the firm actually purchases and owns the server computer housing its Web site but locates the server in the physical facility of the hosting service.

community provider: Web site business model that creates a digital online environment where people with similar interests can transact; share interests, photos, and videos; and receive interest-related information.

competitive forces model: Model used to describe the interaction of external influences, specifically threats and opportunities, that affect an organization's strategy and ability to compete.

component-based development: Building large software systems by combining pre-existing software components.

computer abuse: The commission of acts involving a computer that may not be illegal but are considered unethical.

computer crime: The commission of illegal acts through the use of a computer or against a computer system.

computer forensics: The scientific collection, examination, authentication, preservation, and analysis of data held on or retrieved from computer storage media in such a way that the information can be used as evidence in a court of law.

computer hardware: Physical equipment used for input, processing, and output activities in an information system.

computer literacy: Knowledge about information technology, focusing on understanding of how computer-based technologies work.

computer software: Detailed, preprogrammed instructions that control and coordinate the work of computer hardware components in an information system.

computer virus: Rogue software program that attaches itself to other software programs or data files in order to be executed, often causing hardware and software malfunctions.

computer vision syndrome (CVS): Eyestrain condition related to computer display screen use; symptoms include headaches, blurred vision, and dry and irritated eyes.

computer: Physical device that takes data as an input, transforms the data by executing stored instructions, and outputs information to a number of devices.

computer-aided design (CAD) system: Information system that automates the creation and revision of designs using sophisticated graphics software.

computer-aided software engineering (CASE): Automation of step-by-step methodologies for software and systems development to reduce the amounts of repetitive work the developer needs to do.

consumerization of IT: New information technology originating in the consumer market that spreads to business organizations.

consumer-to-consumer (C2C) electronic commerce: Consumers selling goods and services electronically to other consumers.

controls: All of the methods, policies, and procedures that ensure protection of the organization's assets, accuracy and reliability of its records, and operational adherence to management standards.

conversion: The process of changing from the old system to the new system.

cookies: Tiny file deposited on a computer hard drive when an individual visits certain Web sites. Used to identify the visitor and track visits to the Web site.

copyright: A statutory grant that protects creators of intellectual property against copying by others for any purpose during the life of the author plus an additional 70 years after the author's death.

core competency: Activity at which a firm excels as a world-class leader.

cost transparency: The ability of consumers to discover the actual costs merchants pay for products.

cost-benefit ratio: A method for calculating the returns from a capital expenditure by dividing total benefits by total costs.

cracker: A hacker with criminal intent.

critical thinking: Sustained suspension of judgment with an awareness of multiple perspectives and alternatives.

cross-selling: Marketing complementary products to customers.

crowdsourcing: Using large Internet audiences for advice, market feedback, new ideas and solutions to business problems. Related to the 'wisdom of crowds' theory.

culture: Fundamental set of assumptions, values, and ways of doing things that has been accepted by most members of an organization.

customer lifetime value (CLTV): Difference between revenues produced by a specific customer and the expenses for acquiring and servicing that customer minus the cost of promotional marketing over the lifetime of the customer relationship, expressed in today's dollars.

customer relationship management (CRM) systems: Information systems that track all the ways in which a company interacts with its customers and analyze these interactions to optimize revenue, profitability, customer satisfaction, and customer retention.

customization: In e-commerce, changing a delivered product or service based on a user's preferences or prior behavior.

customization: The modification of a software package to meet an organization's unique requirements without destroying the package software's integrity.

cyberlocker: Online file-sharing service that allows users to upload files to a secure online storage site from which the files can be synchronized and shared with others.

cybervandalism: Intentional disruption, defacement, or even destruction of a Web site or corporate information system.

cyberwarfare State-sponsored activity designed to cripple and defeat another state or nation by damaging or disrupting its computers or networks.

cycle time: The total elapsed time from the beginning of a process to its end.

data administration: A special organizational function for managing the organization's data resources, concerned with information policy, data planning, maintenance of data dictionaries, and data quality standards.

data center: Facility housing computer systems and associated components, such as telecommunications, storage and security systems and backup power supplies.

data cleansing: Activities for detecting and correcting data in a database or file that are incorrect, incomplete, improperly formatted, or redundant. Also known as data scrubbing.

data definition: Specifies the structure of the content of a database.

data dictionary: An automated or manual tool for storing and organizing information about the data maintained in a database.

data flow diagram (DFD): Primary tool for structured analysis that graphically illustrates a system's component process and the flow of data between them.

data management software: Software used for creating and manipulating lists, creating files and databases to store data, and combining information for reports.

data management technology: Software governing the organization of data on physical storage media.

data manipulation language: A language associated with a database management system that end users and programmers use to manipulate data in the database.

data mart: A small data warehouse containing only a portion of the organization's data for a specified function or population of users.

data mining: Analysis of large pools of data to find patterns and rules that can be used to guide decision making and predict future behavior.

data quality audit: A survey and/or sample of files to determine accuracy and completeness of data in an information system.

data visualization: Technology for helping users see patterns and relationships in large amounts of data by presenting the data in graphical form.

data warehouse: A database, with reporting and query tools, that stores current and historical data extracted from various operational systems and consolidated for management reporting and analysis.

data workers: People such as secretaries or bookkeepers who process the organization's paperwork.

data: Streams of raw facts representing events occurring in organizations or the physical environment before they have been organized and arranged into a form that people can understand and use.

database administration: Refers to the more technical and operational aspects of managing data, including physical database design and maintenance.

database management system (DBMS): Special software to create and maintain a database and enable individual business applications to extract the data they need without having to create separate files or data definitions in their computer programs.

database server: A computer in a client/server environment that is responsible for running a DBMS to process SQL statements and perform database management tasks.

database: A group of related files.

decision-support systems (DSS): Information systems at the organization's management level that combine data and sophisticated analytical models or data analysis tools to support semistructured and unstructured decision making.

deep packet inspection (DPI): Technology for managing network traffic by examining data packets, sorting out low-priority data

from higher priority business-critical data, and sending packets in order of priority.

demand planning: Determining how much product a business needs to make to satisfy all its customers' demands.

denial of service (DoS) attack: Flooding a network server or Web server with false communications or requests for services in order to crash the network.

Descartes' rule of change: A principle that states that if an action cannot be taken repeatedly, then it is not right to be taken at any time.

design: Simon's second stage of decision making, when the individual conceives of possible alternative solutions to a problem.

digital asset management systems: Classify, store, and distribute digital objects such as photographs, graphic images, video, and audio content.

digital certificates: Attachments to an electronic message to verify the identity of the sender and to provide the receiver with the means to encode a reply.

digital checking: Systems that extend the functionality of existing checking accounts so they can be used for online shopping payments.

digital dashboard: Displays all of a firm's key performance indicators as graphs and charts on a single screen to provide one-page overview of all the critical measurements necessary to make key executive decisions

digital divide: Large disparities in access to computers and the Internet among different social groups and different locations.

digital goods: Goods that can be delivered over a digital network.

digital market: A marketplace that is created by computer and communication technologies that link many buyers and sellers.

Digital Millennium Copyright Act (DMCA): Adjusts copyright laws to the Internet Age by making it illegal to make, distribute, or use devices that circumvent technology-based protections of copy-righted materials.

digital signature: A digital code that can be attached to an electronically transmitted message to uniquely identify its contents and the sender.

digital subscriber line (DSL): A group of technologies providing high-capacity transmission over existing copper telephone lines.

digital video disk (DVD): High-capacity optical storage medium that can store full-length videos and large amounts of data.

digital wallet: Software that stores credit card, electronic cash, owner identification, and address information and provides this data automatically during electronic commerce purchase transactions.

direct cutover: A risky conversion approach where the new system completely replaces the old one on an appointed day.

disaster recovery planning: Planning for the restoration of computing and communications services after they have been disrupted.

disintermediation: The removal of organizations or business process layers responsible for certain intermediary steps in a value chain.

disruptive technologies: Technologies with disruptive impact on industries and businesses, rendering existing products, services and business models obsolete.

distributed denial-of-service (DDoS) attack: Uses numerous computers to inundate and overwhelm a network from numerous launch points.

distributed processing: The distribution of computer processing work among multiple computers linked by a communications network.

documentation: Descriptions of how an information system works from either a technical or end-user standpoint.

Domain Name System (DNS): A hierarchical system of servers maintaining a database enabling the conversion of domain names to their numeric IP addresses.

domain name: English-like name that corresponds to the unique 32-bit numeric Internet Protocol (IP) address for each computer connected to the Internet.

domestic exporter: Form of business organization characterized by heavy centralization of corporate activities in the home county of origin.

downtime: Period of time in which an information system is not operational.

drill down: The ability to move from summary data to lower and lower levels of detail.

drive-by download: Malware that comes with a downloaded file a user intentionally

due process: A process in which laws are well-known and understood and there is an ability to appeal to higher authorities to ensure that laws are applied correctly.

dynamic pricing: Pricing of items based on real-time interactions between buyers and sellers that determine what a item is worth at any particular moment.

efficient customer response system: System that directly links consumer behavior back to distribution, production, and supply chains.

e-government: Use of the Internet and related technologies to digitally enable government and public sector agencies' relationships with citizens, businesses, and other arms of government.

electronic billing presentment and payment systems: Systems used for paying routine monthly bills that allow users to view their bills electronically and pay them through electronic funds transfers from banks or credit card accounts.

electronic business (e-business): The use of the Internet and digital technology to execute all the business processes in the enterprise. Includes e-commerce as well as processes for the internal management of the firm and for coordination with suppliers and other business partners.

electronic commerce (e-commerce): The process of buying and selling goods and services electronically involving transactions using the Internet, networks, and other digital technologies.

electronic data interchange (EDI): The direct computer-to-computer exchange between two organizations of standard business transactions, such as orders, shipment instructions, or payments.

electronic mail (e-mail): The computer-to-computer exchange of messages.

electronic records management (ERM): Policies, procedures, and tools for managing the retention, destruction, and storage of electronic records.

employee relationship management (ERM): Software dealing with employee issues that are closely related to CRM, such as setting objectives, employee performance management, performance-based compensation, and employee training.

encryption: The coding and scrambling of messages to prevent their being read or accessed without authorization.

end users: Representatives of departments outside the information systems group for whom applications are developed.

end-user development: The development of information systems by end users with little or no formal assistance from technical specialists.

end-user interface: The part of an information system through which the end user interacts with the system, such as on-line screens and commands.

enterprise applications: Systems that can coordinate activities, decisions, and knowledge across many different functions, levels, and business units in a firm. Include enterprise systems, supply chain management systems, customer relationship management systems, and knowledge management systems.

enterprise content management systems: Help organizations manage structured and semistructured knowledge, providing corporate repositories of documents, reports, presentations, and best practices and capabilities for collecting and organizing e-mail and graphic objects.

enterprise systems: Integrated enterprise-wide information systems that coordinate key internal processes of the firm. Also known as enterprise resource planning (ERP).

enterprise-wide knowledge management systems: General-purpose, firmwide systems that collect, store, distribute, and apply digital content and knowledge.

entity: A person, place, thing, or event about which information must be kept.

entity-relationship diagram: A methodology for documenting databases illustrating the relationship between various entities in the database.

ergonomics: The interaction of people and machines in the work environment, including the design of jobs, health issues, and the end-user interface of information systems.

e-tailer: Online retail stores from the giant Amazon to tiny local stores that have Web sites where retail goods are sold.

Ethernet: The dominant LAN standard at the physical network level, specifying the physical medium to carry signals between computers; access control rules; and a standardized set of bits to carry data over the system.

ethical "no free lunch" rule: Assumption that all tangible and intangible objects are owned by someone else, unless there is a specific declaration otherwise, and that the creator wants compensation for this work.

ethics: Principles of right and wrong that can be used by individuals acting as free moral agents to make choices to guide their behavior.

evil twins: Wireless networks that pretend to be legitimate Wi-Fi networks to entice participants to log on and reveal passwords or credit card numbers.

exchanges: Third-party Net marketplaces that are primarily transaction oriented and that connects many buyers and suppliers for spot purchasing.

executive support systems (ESS): Information systems at the organization's strategic level designed to address unstructured decision making through advanced graphics and communications.

expert systems: Knowledge-intensive computer programs that capture the expertise of a human in limited domains of knowledge.

Extensible Markup Language (XML): A more powerful and flexible markup language than hypertext markup language (HTML) for Web pages, allowing data to be manipulated by the computer.

extranets: Private intranets that are accessible to authorized outsiders.

Fair Information Practices (FIP): A set of principles originally set forth in 1973 that governs the collection and use of information about individuals and forms the basis of most U.S. and European privacy laws.

fault-tolerant computer systems: Systems that contain extra hardware, software, and power supply components that can back a system up and keep it running to prevent system failure.

feasibility study: As part of the systems analysis process, the way to determine whether the solution is achievable, given the organization's resources and constraints.

feedback: Output that is returned to the appropriate members of the organization to help them evaluate or correct input.

fiber-optic cable: A fast, light, and durable transmission medium consisting of thin strands of clear glass fiber bound into cables. Data are transmitted as light pulses.

field: A grouping of characters into a word, a group of words, or a complete number, such as a person's name or age.

file transfer protocol (FTP): Tool for retrieving and transferring files from a remote computer.

finance and accounting information systems: Systems keep track of the firm's financial assets and fund flows.

firewalls: Hardware and software placed between an organization's internal network and an external network to prevent outsiders from invading private networks.

FLOPS: Stands for floating point operations per second and is a measure of computer processing speed.

folksonomies: User-created taxonomies for classifying and sharing information.

foreign key: Field in a database table that enables users to find related information in another database table.

formal planning and control tools: Improve project management by listing the specific activities that make up a project, their duration, and the sequence and timing of tasks.

fourth-generation languages: Programming languages that can be employed directly by end users or less-skilled programmers to develop computer applications more rapidly than conventional programming languages.

franchiser: Form of business organization in which a product is created, designed, financed, and initially produced in the home country, but for product-specific reasons relies heavily on foreign personnel for further production, marketing, and human resources.

free/freemium revenue model: E-commerce revenue mode in which a firm offers basic services or content for free, while charging a premium for advanced or high value features.

fuzzy logic: Rule-based AI that tolerates imprecision by using nonspecific terms called membership functions to solve problems.

Gantt chart: Visually represents the timing, duration, and human resource requirements of project tasks, with each task represented as a horizontal bar whose length is proportional to the time required to complete it.

general controls: Overall control environment governing the design, security, and use of computer programs and the security of data files in general throughout the organization's information technology infrastructure.

genetic algorithms: Problem-solving methods that promote the evolution of solutions to specified problems using the model of living organisms adapting to their environment.

geoadvertising: Delivering ads to users based on their GPS location.

geographic information systems (GIS): Systems with software that can analyze and display data using digitized maps to enhance planning and decision-making.

geoinformation services: Information on local places and things based on the GPS position of the user.

geosocial services: Social networking based on the GPS location of users.

gigabyte: Approximately one billion bytes.

Google Apps: Google's cloud-based productivity suite for businesses.

Golden Rule: Putting oneself in the place of others as the object of a decision.

Gramm-Leach-Bliley Act: Requires financial institutions to ensure the security and confidentiality of customer data.

graphical user interface (GUI): The part of an operating system users interact with that uses graphic icons and the computer mouse to issue commands and make selections.

green computing: Practices and technologies for producing, using, and disposing of computers and associated devices to minimize impact on the environment.

grid computing: Applying the resources of many computers in a network to a single problem.

group decision-support system (GDSS): An interactive computer-based system to facilitate the solution to unstructured problems by a set of decision makers working together as a group.

hacker: A person who gains unauthorized access to a computer network for profit, criminal mischief, or personal pleasure.

Hadoop: Open-source software framework that enables distributed parallel processing of huge amounts of data across many inexpensive computers.

hertz: Measure of frequency of electrical impulses per second, with 1 Hertz equivalent to 1 cycle per second.

high-availability computing: Tools and technologies ,including backup hardware resources, to enable a system to recover quickly from a crash.

HIPAA: Law outlining medical security and privacy rules and procedures for simplifying the administration of healthcare billing and automating the transfer of healthcare data between healthcare providers, payers, and plans.

home page: A World Wide Web text and graphical screen display that welcomes the user and explains the organization that has established the page.

hotspots: Specific geographic locations in which an access point provides public Wi-Fi network service.

HTML (Hypertext Markup Language): Page description language for creating Web pages.

HTML5: Next evolution of HTML, which will make it possible to embed images, video, and audio directly into a document without using add-on software.

hubs: Very simple devices that connect network components, sending a packet of data to all other connected devices.

hybrid cloud: Computing model where firms use both their own IT infrastructure and also public cloud computing services.

hypertext markup language (HTML): Page description language for creating Web pages and other hypermedia documents.

hypertext transport protocol (HTTP): The communications standard used to transfer pages on the Web. Defines how messages are formatted and transmitted.

identity management: Business Processes and software tools for identifying the valid users of a system and controlling their access to system resources.

identity theft: Theft of key pieces of personal information, such as credit card or Social Security numbers, in order to obtain merchandise and services in the name of the victim or to obtain false credentials.

Immanuel Kant's Categorical Imperative: A principle that states that if an action is not right for everyone to take it is not right for anyone.

implementation: All the organizational activities surrounding the adoption, management, and routinization of an innovation, such as a new information system.

implementation: Simon's final stage of decision-making, when the individual puts the decision into effect and reports on the progress of the solution.

inference engine: The strategy used to search through the rule base in an expert system; can be forward or backward chaining.

information appliance: Device that has been customized to perform a few specialized computing tasks well with minimal user effort.

information asymmetry: Situation where the relative bargaining power of two parties in a transaction is determined by one party in the transaction possessing more information essential to the transaction than the other party.

information density: The total amount and quality of information available to all market participants, consumers, and merchants

information policy: Formal rules governing the maintenance, distribution, and use of information in an organization.

information requirements: A detailed statement of the information needs that a new system must satisfy; identifies who needs what information, and when, where, and how the information is needed.

information rights: The rights that individuals and organizations have with respect to information that pertains to themselves.

information system: Interrelated components working together to collect, process, store, and disseminate information to support decision making, coordination, control, analysis, and visualization in an organization.

Information systems audit: Identifies all the controls that govern individual information systems and assesses their effectiveness.

information systems department: The formal organizational unit that is responsible for the information systems function in the organization.

information systems literacy: Broad-based understanding of information systems that includes behavioral knowledge about organizations and individuals using information systems as well as technical knowledge about computers.

information systems managers: Leaders of the various specialists in the information systems department.

information systems plan: A road map indicating the direction of systems development: the rationale, the current situation, the management strategy, the implementation plan, and the budget.

information technology (IT) infrastructure: Computer hardware, software, data, storage technology, and networks providing a portfolio of shared IT resources for the organization.

information technology (IT): All the hardware and software technologies that a firm needs to use in order to achieve its business objectives.

information: Data that have been shaped into a form that is meaningful and useful to human beings.

informed consent: Consent given with knowledge of all the facts needed to make a rational decision.

in-memory computing: Technology for very rapid analysis and processing of large quantities of data by storing the data in the computer's main memory rather than in secondary storage.

input devices: Device which gathers data and converts them into electronic form for use by the computer.

input: The capture or collection of raw data from within the organization or from its external environment for processing in an information system.

instant messaging: Chat service that allows participants to create their own private chat channels so that a person can be alerted whenever someone on his or her private list is on-line to initiate a chat session with that particular individual.

intangible benefits: Benefits that are not easily quantified; they include more efficient customer service or enhanced decision making.

intellectual property: Intangible property created by individuals or corporations that is subject to protections under trade secret, copyright, and patent law.

intelligence: The first of Simon's four stages of decision making, when the individual collects information to identify problems occurring in the organization.

intelligent agents: Software programs that use a built-in or learned knowledge base to carry out specific, repetitive, and predictable tasks for an individual user, business process, or software application.

intelligent techniques: Technologies that aid decision makers by capturing individual and collective knowledge, discovering patterns and behaviors in very large quantities of data, and generating solutions to problems that are too large and complex for human beings to solve on their own.

Internet Protocol (IP) address: Four-part numeric address indicating a unique computer location on the Internet.

Internet service provider (ISP): A commercial organization with a permanent connection to the Internet that sells temporary connections to subscribers.

Internet telephony: Technologies that use the Internet Protocol's packet-switched connections for voice service.

Internet: global network of networks using univeral standards to connect millions of different networks.

Internet2: Research network with new protocols and transmission speeds that provides an infrastructure for supporting high-bandwidth Internet applications.

Internet of Things: Pervasive Web in which each object or machine has a unique identity and is able to use the Internet to link with other machines or send data. Also known as the Industrial Internet

internetworking: The linking of separate networks, each of which retains its own identity, into an interconnected network.

interorganizational system: Information systems that automate the flow of information across organizational boundaries and link a company to its customers, distributors, or suppliers.

intranets: Internal networks based on Internet and World Wide Web technology and standards.

intrusion detection systems: Tools to monitor the most vulnerable points in a network to detect and deter unauthorized intruders.

investment workstations: Powerful desktop computers for financial specialists, which are optimized to access and manipulate massive amounts of financial data.

iOS: Operating system for the Apple iPad, iPhone, and iPod Touch

IPv6: New IP addressing system using 128-bit IP addresses. Stands for Internet Protocol version 6.

IT governance: Strategy and policies for using information technology within an organization, specifying the decision rights and accountabilities to ensure that information technology supports the organization's strategies and objectives.

Java: An operating system–independent, processor-independent, object-oriented programming language that has become a leading interactive programming environment for the Web.

Joint application design (JAD): Process to accelerate the generation of information requirements by having end users and information systems specialists work together in intensive interactive design sessions.

just-in-time: Scheduling system for minimizing inventory by having components arrive exactly at the moment they are needed and finished goods shipped as soon as they leave the assembly line.

key field: A field in a record that uniquely identifies instances of that record so that it can be retrieved, updated, or sorted.

key loggers: Spyware that records every keystroke made on a computer.

key performance indicators: Measures proposed by senior management for understanding how well the firm is performing along specified dimensions.

knowledge base: Model of human knowledge that is used by expert systems.

knowledge management systems (KMS): Systems that support the creation, capture, storage, and dissemination of firm expertise and knowledge.

knowledge management: The set of processes developed in an organization to create, gather, store, maintain, and disseminate the firm's knowledge.

knowledge network systems: Online directory for locating corporate experts in well-defined knowledge domains.

knowledge work systems: Information systems that aid knowledge workers in the creation and integration of new knowledge in the organization.

knowledge workers: People such as engineers or architects who design products or services and create knowledge for the organization.

learning management system (LMS): Tools for the management, delivery, tracking, and assessment of various types of employee learning.

legacy systems: System that have been in existence for a long time and that continue to be used to avoid the high cost of replacing or redesigning them.

liability: The existence of laws that permit individuals to recover the damages done to them by other actors, systems, or organizations.

Linux: Reliable and compactly designed operating system that is an open-source offshoot of UNIX and that can run on many different hardware platforms and is available free or at very low cost.

local area network (LAN): A telecommunications network that requires its own dedicated channels and that encompasses a limited distance, usually one building or several buildings in close proximity.

location analytics: Ability to gain insight from the location (geographic) component of data, including location data from mobile phones, output from sensors or scanning devices, and data from maps.

long tail marketing: Ability of firms to profitably market goods to very small online audiences, largely because of the lower costs of reaching very small market segments.

magnetic disk: A secondary storage medium in which data are stored by means of magnetized spots on a hard or floppy disk.

magnetic tape: Inexpensive, older secondary-storage medium in which large volumes of information are stored sequentially by means of magnetized and nonmagnetized spots on tape.

mainframe: Largest category of computer, used for major business processing.

maintenance: Changes in hardware, software, documentation, or procedures to a production system to correct errors, meet new requirements, or improve processing efficiency.

malware: Malicious software programs such as computer viruses, worms, and Trojan horses.

managed security service providers (MSSPs): Companies that provide security management services for subscribing clients.

management information systems (MIS): Specific category of information system providing reports on organizational performance to help middle management monitor and control the business.

management information systems (MIS): The study of information systems focusing on their use in business and management..

manufacturing and production information systems: Systems that deal with the planning, development, and production of products and services and with controlling the flow of production.

market creator: E-commerce business model in which firms provide a digital online environment where buyers and sellers can meet, search for products, and engage in transactions.

market entry costs: The cost merchants must pay simply to bring their goods to market.

marketspace: A marketplace extended beyond traditional boundaries and removed from a temporal and geographic location.

mashups: Composite software applications that depend on high-speed networks, universal communication standards, and open source code and are intended to be greater than the sum of their parts.

mass customization: The capacity to offer individually tailored products or services on a large scale.

menu prices: Merchants' costs of changing prices.

metropolitan area network (MAN): Network that spans a metropolitan area, usually a city and its major suburbs. Its geographic scope falls between a WAN and a LAN.

microblogging: Blogging featuring very short posts, such as those using Twitter.

microbrowser: Web browser software with a small file size that can work with low-memory constraints, tiny screens of handheld wireless devices, and low bandwidth of wireless networks.

micropayment: Payment for a very small sum of money, often less than $10.

microprocessor: Very large scale integrated circuit technology that integrates the computer's memory, logic, and control on a single chip.

microwave: A high-volume, long-distance, point-to-point transmission in which high-frequency radio signals are transmitted through the atmosphere from one terrestrial transmission station to another.

middle management: People in the middle of the organizational hierarchy who are responsible for carrying out the plans and goals of senior management.

middleware: Software that connects two disparate applications, allowing them to communicate with each other and to exchange data.

midrange computers: Middle-size computers that are capable of supporting the computing needs of smaller organizations or of managing networks of other computers.

minicomputers: Middle-range computers used in systems for universities, factories, or research laboratories.

mobile commerce (m-commerce): The use of wireless devices, such as cell phones or handheld digital information appliances, to conduct both business-to-consumer and business-to-business e-commerce transactions over the Internet.

mobile device management: Software that monitors, manages, and secures mobile devices being used by the organization.

mobile Web app: Application residing on a server and accessed through the mobile Web browser built into a smartphone or tablet computer.

mobile Web site: Version of a regular Web site that is scaled down in content and navigation for easy access and search on a small mobile screen.

model: An abstract representation that illustrates the components or relationships of a phenomenon.

modem: A device for translating a computer's digital signals into analog form or for translating analog signals back into digital form for reception by a computer.

mouse: Handheld input device with point-and-click capabilities that is usually connected to the computer by a cable.

MP3 (MPEG3): Standard for compressing audio files for transfer over the Internet.

multicore processor: Integrated circuit to which two or more processors have been attached for enhanced performance, reduced power consumption and more efficient simultaneous processing of multiple tasks.

multinational: Form of business organization that concentrates financial management and control out of a central home base while decentralizing production, sales, and marketing.

multitouch: Interface that features the use of one or more finger gestures to manipulate lists or objects on a screen without using a mouse or keyboard.

nanotechnology: Technology that builds structures and processes based on the manipulation of individual atoms and molecules.

native app: Standalone application specifically designed to run on a mobile platform

natural languages: Nonprocedural languages that enable users to communicate with the computer using conversational commands resembling human speech.

net marketplaces: Digital marketplaces based on Internet technology linking many buyers to many sellers.

netbook: Small low-cost lightweight subnotebooks optimized for wireless communication and Internet access,

network address translation (NAT): Conceals the IP addresses of the organization's internal host computer(s) to prevent sniffer programs outside the firewall from ascertaining them and using that information to penetrate internal systems.

network economics: Model of strategic systems at the industry level based on the concept of a network where adding another participant entails zero marginal costs but can create much larger marginal gains.

network interface card (NIC): Expansion card inserted into a computer to enable it to connect to a network.

network operating system (NOS): Special software that routes and manages communications on the network and coordinates network resources.

network: The linking of two or more computers to share data or resources, such as a printer.

networking and telecommunications technology: Physical devices and software that link various pieces of hardware and transfer data from one physical location to another.

neural networks: Hardware or software that attempts to emulate the processing patterns of the biological brain.

nonobvious relationship awareness (NORA): Technology that can find obscure hidden connections between people or other entities by analyzing information from many different sources to correlate relationships.

non-relational database management system: Database management system for working with large quantities of structured and unstructured data that would be difficult to analyze with a relational model.

normalization: The process of creating small stable data structures from complex groups of data when designing a relational database.

n-tier client/server architecture: Client/server arrangement which balances the work of the entire network over multiple levels of servers.

object: Software building block that combines data and the procedures acting on the data.

object-oriented development: Approach to systems development that uses the object as the basic unit of systems analysis and design. The system is modeled as a collection o objects and the relationship between them.

Office 2010: Microsoft desktop software suite with capabilities for supporting collaborative work on the Web or incorporating information from the Web into documents.

offshore outsourcing: Outsourcing systems development work or maintenance of existing systems to external vendors in another country.

offshore software outsourcing: Outsourcing systems development work or maintenance of existing systems to external vendors in another country.

on-demand computing: Firms off-loading peak demand for computing power to remote, large-scale data processing centers, investing just enough to handle average processing loads and paying for only as much additional computing power as they need. Also called utility computing.

online analytical processing (OLAP): Capability for manipulating and analyzing large volumes of data from multiple perspectives.

online processing: A method of collecting and processing data in which transactions are entered directly into the computer system and processed immediately.

online transaction processing: Transaction processing mode in which transactions entered on-line are immediately processed by the computer.

open source software: Software that provides free access to its program code, allowing users to modify the program code to make improvements or fix errors.

operating system: The system software that manages and controls the activities of the computer.

operational CRM: Customer-facing applications, such as sales force automation, call center and customer service support, and marketing automation.

operational management: People who monitor the day-to-day activities of the organization.

opt-in: Model of informed consent permitting prohibiting an organization from collecting any personal information unless the individual specifically takes action to approve information collection and use.

opt-out: Model of informed consent permitting the collection of personal information until the consumer specifically requests that the data not be collected.

organizational impact analysis: Study of the way a proposed system will affect organizational structure, attitudes, decision making, and operations.

output devices: Device that displays data after they have been processed.

output: The distribution of processed information to the people who will use it or to the activities for which it will be used.

outsourcing: The practice of contracting computer center operations, telecommunications networks, or applications development to external vendors.

P3P: Industry standard designed to give users more control over personal information gathered on Web sites they visit. Stands for Platform for Privacy Preferences Project.

packet filtering: Examines selected fields in the headers of data packets flowing back and forth between the trusted network and the Internet

packet switching: Technology that breaks messages into small, fixed bundles of data and routes them in the most economical way through any available communications channel.

parallel processing: Type of processing in which more than one instruction can be processed at a time by breaking down a problem into smaller parts and processing them simultaneously with multiple processors.

parallel strategy: A safe and conservative conversion approach where both the old system and its potential replacement are run together for a time until everyone is assured that the new one functions correctly.

partner relationship management (PRM): Automation of the firm's relationships with its selling partners using customer data and analytical tools to improve coordination and customer sales.

password: Secret word or string of characters for authenticating users so they can access a resource such as a computer system.

patches: Small pieces of software that repair flaws in programs without disturbing the proper operation of the software.

patent: A legal document that grants the owner an exclusive monopoly on the ideas behind an invention for 17 years; designed to ensure that inventors of new machines or methods are rewarded for their labor while making widespread use of their inventions.

peer-to-peer: Network architecture that gives equal power to all computers on the network; used primarily in small networks.

people perspective: Consideration of the firm's management, as well as employees as individuals and their interrelationships in workgroups.

personal computer (PC): Small desktop or portable computer.

Personal digital assistants (PDA): Small, pen-based, handheld computers with built-in wireless telecommunications capable of entirely digital communications transmission.

personal-area networks (PANs): Computer networks used for communication among digital devices (including telephones and PDAs) that are close to one person.

personalization: Ability of merchants to target their marketing messages to specific individuals by adjusting the message to a person's name, interests, and past purchases.

PERT chart: Graphically depicts project tasks and their interrelationships, showing the specific activities that must be completed before others can start.

pharming: Phishing technique that redirects users to a bogus Web page, even when the individual types the correct Web page address into his or her browser.

phased approach: Introduces the new system in stages either by functions or by organizational units.

phishing: A form of spoofing involving setting up fake Web sites or sending e-mail messages that look like those of legitimate businesses to ask users for confidential personal data.

pilot study: A strategy to introduce the new system to a limited area of the organization until it is proven to be fully functional; only then can the conversion to the new system across the entire organization take place.

pivot table: Spreadsheet tool for reorganizing and summarizing two or more dimensions of data in a tabular format.

podcasting: Method of publishing audio broadcasts via the Internet, allowing subscribing users to download audio files onto their personal computers or portable music players.

pop-up ads: Ads that open automatically and do not disappear until the user clicks on them.

portal: Web interface for presenting integrated personalized content from a variety of sources. Also refers to a Web site service that provides an initial point of entry to the Web.

portfolio analysis: An analysis of the portfolio of potential applications within a firm to determine the risks and benefits, and to select among alternatives for information systems.

prediction markets: Peer-to-peer betting markets where participants make bets on specific outcomes of events.

predictive analytics: Use of data mining techniques, historical data, and assumptions about future conditions to predict outcomes of events.

presentation graphics: Software to create professional-quality graphics presentations that can incorporate charts, sound, animation, photos, and video clips.

price discrimination: Selling the same goods, or nearly the same goods, to different targeted groups at different prices.

price transparency: the ease with which consumers can find out the variety of prices in a market.

primary activities: Activities most directly related to the production and distribution of a firm's products or services.

primary key: Unique identifier for all the information in any row of a database table.

privacy: The claim of individuals to be left alone, free from surveillance or interference from other individuals, organizations, or the state.

private cloud: Proprietary network or data center that ties together servers, storage, networks, data, and applications as a set of virtualized services that are shared by users inside a company.

private exchange: Another term for a private industrial network.

private industrial networks: Web-enabled networks linking systems of multiple firms in an industry for the coordination of trans-organizational business processes.

process specifications: Describe the logic of the processes occurring within the lowest levels of a data flow diagram.

processing: The conversion, manipulation, and analysis of raw input into a form that is more meaningful to humans.

procurement: Sourcing goods and materials, negotiating with suppliers, paying for goods, and making delivery arrangements.

product differentiation: Competitive strategy for creating brand loyalty by developing new and unique products and services that are not easily duplicated by competitors.

production or service workers: People who actually produce the products or services of the organization.

production: The stage after the new system is installed and the conversion is complete; during this time the system is reviewed by users and technical specialists to determine how well it has met its original goals.

profiling: The use of computers to combine data from multiple sources and create electronic dossiers of detailed information on individuals.

program: Series of instructions for the computer.

programmers: Highly trained technical specialists who write computer software instructions.

programming: The process of translating the system specifications prepared during the design stage into program code.

project management: Application of knowledge, skills, tools and techniques to achieve specific targets within specified budget and time constraints. **project portfolio management software:** Helps organizations evaluate and manage portfolios of projects and dependencies among them.

project: A planned series of related activities for achieving a specific business objective.

protocol: A set of rules and procedures that govern transmission between the components in a network.

prototyping: The process of building an experimental system quickly and inexpensively for demonstration and evaluation so that users can better determine information requirements.

Public cloud: Cloud maintained by an external service provider, accessed through the Internet, and available to the general public.

public key encryption: Uses two keys: one shared (or public) and one private.

public key infrastructure (PKI): System for creating public and private keys using a certificate authority (CA) and digital certificates for authentication.

pull-based model: Supply chain driven by actual customer orders or purchases so that members of the supply chain produce and deliver only what customers have ordered.

pure-play: Business models based purely on the Internet.

push-based model: Supply chain driven by production master schedules based on forecasts or best guesses of demand for products, and products are "pushed" to customers.

quality: Product or service's conformance to specifications and standards.

quantum computing: Use of principles of quantum physics to represent data and perform operations on the data, with the ability to be in many different states at once and to perform many different computations simultaneously.

query languages: Software tools that provide immediate online answers to requests for information that are not predefined.

radio frequency identification (RFID): Technology using tiny tags with embedded microchips containing data about an item and its location to transmit short-distance radio signals to special RFID readers that then pass the data on to a computer for processing.

Rapid application development (RAD): Process for developing systems in a very short time period by using prototyping, fourth-generation tools, and close teamwork among users and systems specialists.

rationalization of procedures: The streamlining of standard operating procedures, eliminating obvious bottlenecks, so that automation makes operating procedures more efficient.

reach: Measurement of how many people a business can connect with and how many products it can offer those people.

records: Groups of related fields.

recovery-oriented computing: Computer systems designed to recover rapidly when mishaps occur.

referential integrity: Rules to ensure that relationships between coupled database tables remain consistent.

relational database: A type of logical database model that treats data as if they were stored in two-dimensional tables. It can relate data stored in one table to data in another as long as the two tables share a common data element.

repetitive stress injury (RSI): Occupational disease that occurs when muscle groups are forced through repetitive actions with high-impact loads or thousands of repetitions with low-impact loads.

Request for Proposal (RFP): A detailed list of questions submitted to vendors of software or other services to determine how well the vendor's product can meet the organization's specific requirements.

responsibility: Accepting the potential costs, duties, and obligations for the decisions one makes.

responsive Web design: Ability of a Web site to automatically change screen resolution and image size as a user switches to devices of different sizes, such as a laptop, tablet computer, or smartphone. Eliminates the need for separate design and development work for each new device.

revenue model: Description of how a firm will earn revenue, generate profits, and produce a return on investment.

richness: Measurement of the depth and detail of information that a business can supply to the customer as well as information the business collects about the customer.

ringtones: Digitized snippets of music that play on mobile phones when a user receives or places a call.

risk assessment: Determining the potential frequency of the occurrence of a problem and the potential damage if the problem were to occur. Used to determine the cost/benefit of a control.

Risk Aversion Principle: Principle that one should take the action that produces the least harm or incurs the least cost.

router: Specialized communications processor that forwards packets of data from one network to another network.

RSS: Technology using aggregator software to pull content from Web sites and feed it automatically to subscribers' computers.

SaaS (Software as a Service): Services for delivering and providing access to software remotely as a Web-based service.

safe harbor: Private self-regulating policy and enforcement mechanism that meets the objectives of government regulations but does not involve government regulation or enforcement.

sales and marketing information systems: Systems that help the firm identify customers for the firm's products or services, develop products and services to meet their needs, promote these products and services, sell the products and services, and provide ongoing customer support.

sales revenue model: Selling goods, information, or services to customers as the main source of revenue for a company.

Sarbanes-Oxley Act: Law passed in 2002 that imposes responsibility on companies and their management to protect investors by safeguarding the accuracy and integrity of financial information that is used internally and released externally.

satellites: The transmission of data using orbiting satellites that serve as relay stations for transmitting microwave signals over very long distances.

scalability: The ability of a computer, product, or system to expand to serve a larger number of users without breaking down.

Scope: Defines what work is or is not included in a project.

scoring model: A quick method for deciding among alternative systems based on a system of ratings for selected objectives.

search costs: The time and money spent locating a suitable product and determining the best price for that product.

search engine marketing: Use of search engines to deliver sponsored links, for which advertisers have paid, in search engine results.

Search engine optimization (SEO): Process of changing a Web site's content, layout, and format in order to increase the site's ranking on popular search engines, and to generate more site visitors.

search engines: Tools for locating specific sites or information on the Internet.

secondary storage: Relatively long term, nonvolatile storage of data outside the CPU and primary storage.

Secure Hypertext Transfer Protocol (S-HTTP): Protocol used for encrypting data flowing over the Internet; limited to individual messages.

Secure Sockets Layer (SSL): Enables client and server computers to manage encryption and decryption activities as they communicate with each other during a secure Web session.

security policy: Statements ranking information risks, identifying acceptable security goals, and identifying the mechanisms for achieving these goals.

security: Policies, procedures, and technical measures used to prevent unauthorized access, alteration, theft, or physical damage to information systems.

Semantic Web: Ways of making the Web more "intelligent," with machine-facilitated understanding of information so that searches can be more intuitive, effective, and executed using intelligent software agents.

semistructured decisions: Decisions in which only part of the problem has a clear-cut answer provided by an accepted procedure.

semistructured knowledge: Information in the form of less structured objects, such as e-mail, chat room exchanges, videos, graphics, brochures, or bulletin boards.

senior management: People occupying the topmost hierarchy in an organization who are responsible for making long-range decisions.

sensitivity analysis: Models that ask "what-if" questions repeatedly to determine the impact of changes in one or more factors on the outcomes.

sensors: Devices that collect data directly from the environment for input into a computer system.

sentiment analysis: Mining text comments in an e-mail message, blog, social media

server: Computer specifically optimized to provide software and other resources to other computers over a network.

service level agreement (SLA): Formal contract between customers and their service providers that defines the specific responsibilities of the service provider and the level of service expected by the customer.

service level agreement (SLA): Formal contract between customers and their service providers that defines the specific responsibilities of the service provider and the level of service expected by the customer.

service-oriented architecture (SOA): Software architecture of a firm built on a collection of software programs that communicate with each other to perform assigned tasks to create a working software application.

shopping bots: Software with varying levels of built-in intelligence to help electronic commerce shoppers locate and evaluate products or service they might wish to purchase.

six sigma: A specific measure of quality, representing 3.4 defects per million opportunities; used to designate a set of methodologies and techniques for improving quality and reducing costs.

smart card: A credit-card-size plastic card that stores digital information and that can be used for electronic payments in place of cash.

smartphones: Wireless phones with voice, messaging, scheduling, e-mail, and Internet capabilities.

sniffer: A type of eavesdropping program that monitors information traveling over a network.

social bookmarking: Capability for users to save their bookmarks to Web pages on a public Web site and tag these bookmarks with keywords to organize documents and share information with others.

social business: Use of social networking platforms, including Facebook, Twitter, and internal corporate social tools, to engage employees, customers, and suppliers.

social CRM: Tools enabling a business to link customer conversations, data, and relationships from social networking sites to CRM processes.

social engineering: Tricking people into revealing their passwords by pretending to be legitimate users or members of a company in need of information.

social graph: Map of all significant online social relationships, comparable to a social network describing offline relationships.

social networking: Online community for expanding users' business or social contacts by making connections through their mutual business or personal connections.

social search: Effort to provide more relevant and trustworthy search results based on a person's network of social contacts.

social shopping: Use of Web sites featuring user-created Web pages to share knowledge about items of interest to other shoppers.

software localization: Process of converting software to operate in a second language.

software package: A prewritten, precoded, commercially available set of programs that eliminates the need to write software programs for certain functions.

software-defined networking (SDN): Using a central control program separate from network devices to manage the flow of data on a network.

solid state drive (SSD): Storage device that stores data on an array of semiconductor memory organized as a disk drive.

spam: Unsolicited commercial e-mail.

spamming: A form of abuse in which thousands and even hundreds of thousands of unsolicited e-mail and electronic messages are sent out, creating a nuisance for both businesses and individual users.

spoofing: Tricking or deceiving computer systems or other computer users by hiding one's identity or faking the identity of another user on the Internet.

spreadsheet: Software displaying data in a grid of columns and rows, with the capability of easily recalculating numerical data.

spyware: Technology that aids in gathering information about a person or organization without their knowledge.

SQL injection attack: Attack against a Web site that takes advantage of vulnerabilities in poorly coded SQL applications in order to introduce malicious program code into a company's systems and networks.

stateful inspection: Provides additional security by determining whether packets are part of an ongoing dialogue between a sender and a receiver.

Storage area networks (SAN): High-speed networks dedicated to storage that connects different kinds of storage devices, such as tape libraries and disk arrays so they can be shared by multiple servers.

strategic information system: Information system that changes the goals, operations, products, services, or environmental relationships of an organization to help gain a competitive advantage.

structure chart: System documentation showing each level of design, the relationship among the levels, and the overall place in the design structure; can document one program, one system, or part of one program.

structured decisions: Decisions that are repetitive, routine, and have a definite procedure for handling them.

structured knowledge systems: Systems for organizing structured knowledge in a repository where it can be accessed throughout the organization. Also known as content management systems.

structured knowledge: Knowledge in the form of structured documents and reports.

Structured Query Language (SQL): The standard data manipulation language for relational database management systems.

structured: Refers to the fact that techniques are carefully drawn up, step by step, with each step building on a previous one.

subscription revenue model: Web site charging a subscription fee for access to some or all of its content or services on an ongoing basis.

supercomputer: Highly sophisticated and powerful computer that can perform very complex computations extremely rapidly.

supply chain execution systems: Systems to manage the flow of products through distribution centers and warehouses to ensure that products are delivered to the right locations in the most efficient manner.

supply chain management (SCM) systems: Information systems that automate the flow of information between a firm and its suppliers in order to optimize the planning, sourcing, manufacturing, and delivery of products and services.

supply chain planning systems: Systems that enable a firm to generate demand forecasts for a product and to develop sourcing and manufacturing plans for that product.

supply chain: Network of organizations and business processes for procuring materials, transforming raw materials into intermediate and finished products, and distributing the finished products to customers.

support activities: Activities that make the delivery of a firm's primary activities possible. Consist of the organization's infrastructure, human resources, technology, and procurement.

switch: Device to connect network components that has more intelligence than a hub and can filter and forward data to a specified destination.

switching costs: The expense a customer or company incurs in lost time and expenditure of resources when changing from one supplier or system to a competing supplier or system.

syndicators: Business aggregating content or applications from multiple sources, packaging them for distribution, and reselling them to third-party Web sites.

system software: Generalized programs that manage the computer's resources, such as the central processor, communications links, and peripheral devices.

system testing: Tests the functioning of the information system as a whole in order to determine if discrete modules will function together as planned.

systems analysis: The analysis of a problem that the organization will try to solve with an information system.

systems analysts: Specialists who translate business problems and requirements into information requirements and systems, acting as liaison between the information systems department and the rest of the organization.

systems design: Details how a system will meet the information requirements as determined by the systems analysis.

systems development life cycle (SDLC): A traditional methodology for developing an information system that partitions the systems development process into formal stages that must be completed sequentially with a very formal division of labor between end users and information systems specialists.

systems development: The activities that go into producing an information systems solution to an organizational problem or opportunity.

systems integration: Ensuring that a new infrastructure works with a firm's older, so-called legacy systems and that the new elements of the infrastructure work with one another.

T lines: High-speed data lines leased from communications providers, such as T-1 lines (with a transmission capacity of 1.544 Mbps).

tablet computer: Mobile handheld computer that is larger than a mobile phone and operated primarily by touching a flat screen

tacit knowledge: Expertise and experience of organizational members that has not been formally documented.

tangible benefits: Benefits that can be quantified and assigned a monetary value; they include lower operational costs and increased cash flows.

taxonomy: Method of classifying things according to a predetermined system.

teams: Formal groups whose members collaborate to achieve specific goals.

technostress: Stress induced by computer use; symptoms include aggravation, hostility toward humans, impatience, and enervation.

telepresence: Technology that allows a person to give the appearance of being present at a location other than his or her true physical location.

terabyte: Approximately one trillion bytes.

test plan: Prepared by the development team in conjunction with the users; it includes all of the preparations for the series of tests to be performed on the system.

testing: The exhaustive and thorough process that determines whether the system produces the desired results under known conditions.

text mining: Discovery of patterns and relationships from large sets of unstructured data.

token: Physical device, similar to an identification card, that is designed to prove the identity of a single user.

Total cost of ownership (TCO): Designates the total cost of owning technology resources, including initial purchase costs, the cost of hardware and software upgrades, maintenance, technical support, and training.

Total quality management (TQM): A concept that makes quality control a responsibility to be shared by all people in an organization.

touch point: Method of firm interaction with a customer, such as telephone, e-mail, customer service desk, conventional mail, or point-of-purchase.

touch screen: Device that allows users to enter limited amounts of data by touching the surface of a sensitized video display monitor with a finger or a pointer.

trade secret: Any intellectual work or product used for a business purpose that can be classified as belonging to that business, provided it is not based on information in the public domain.

transaction fee revenue model: E-commerce revenue model where the firm receives a fee for enabling or executing transactions.

transaction processing systems (TPS): Computerized systems that perform and record the daily routine transactions necessary to conduct the business; they serve the organization's operational level.

Transmission Control Protocol/Internet Protocol (TCP/IP): Dominant model for achieving connectivity among different networks. Provides a universally agree-on method for breaking up digital messages into packets, routing them to the proper addresses, and then reassembling them into coherent messages.

transnational: Truly global form of business organization where value-added activities are managed from a global perspective without reference to national borders, optimizing sources of supply and demand and local competitive advantage.

Trojan horse: A software program that appears legitimate but contains a second hidden function that may cause damage.

tuples: Rows or records in a relational database.

twisted wire: A transmission medium consisting of pairs of twisted copper wires; used to transmit analog phone conversations but can be used for data transmission.

unified communications: Integrates disparate channels for voice communications, data communications, instant messaging, e-mail, and electronic conferencing into a single experience where users can seamlessly switch back and forth between different communication modes.

unified threat management (UTM): Comprehensive security management tool that combines multiple security tools, including firewalls, virtual private networks, intrusion detection systems, and Web content filtering and anti-spam software.

Uniform Resource Locator (URL): The address of a specific resource on the Internet.

unit testing: The process of testing each program separately in the system. Sometimes called program testing.

UNIX: Operating system for all types of computers, which is machine independent and supports multiuser processing, multitasking, and networking. Used in high-end workstations and servers.

unstructured decisions: Nonroutine decisions in which the decision maker must provide judgment, evaluation, and insights into the problem definition; there is no agreed-upon procedure for making such decisions.

up-selling: Marketing higher-value products or services to new or existing customers.

user interface: The part of the information system through which the end user interacts with the system; type of hardware and the series of on-screen commands and responses required for a user to work with the system.

user-designer communications gap: The difference in backgrounds, interests, and priorities that impede communication and problem solving among end users and information systems specialists.

Utilitarian Principle: Principle that assumes one can put values in rank order and understand the consequences of various courses of action.

utility computing: Model of computing in which companies pay only for the information technology resources they actually use during a specified time period. Also called on-demand computing or usage-based pricing.

value chain model: Model that highlights the primary or support activities that add a margin of value to a firm's products or services where information systems can best be applied to achieve a competitive advantage.

value web: Customer-driven network of independent firms who use information technology to coordinate their value chains to collectively produce a product or service for a market.

virtual company: Uses networks to link people, assets, and ideas, enabling it to ally with other companies to create and distribute products and services without being limited by traditional organizational boundaries or physical locations.

Virtual private network (VPN): A secure connection between two points across the Internet to transmit corporate data. Provides a low-cost alternative to a private network.

Virtual Reality Modeling Language (VRML): A set of specifications for interactive three-dimensional modeling on the World Wide Web.

virtual reality systems: Interactive graphics software and hardware that create computer-generated simulations that provide sensations that emulate real-world activities.

virtual world: Computer-based simulated environment intended for its users to inhabit and interact via graphical representations called avatars.

virtualization: Presenting a set of computing resources so that they can all be accessed in ways that are not restricted by physical configuration or geographic location.

visual programming language: Allows users to manipulate graphic or iconic elements to create programs.

Visual Web: Refers to Web linking visual sites such as Pinterest where pictures replace text documents and where users search on pictures and visual characteristics.

Voice over IP (VoIP): Facilities for managing the delivery of voice information using the Internet Protocol (IP).

voice portals: Capability for accepting voice commands for accessing Web content, e-mail, and other electronic applications from a cell phone or standard telephone and for translating responses to user requests for information back into speech for the customer.

war driving: An eavesdropping technique in which eavesdroppers drive by buildings or park outside and try to intercept wireless network traffic.

Web 2.0: Second-generation, interactive Internet-based services that enable people to collaborate, share information, and create new services online, including mashups, blogs, RSS, and wikis.

Web 3.0: Future vision of the Web where all digital information is woven together with intelligent search capabilities.

Web beacons: Tiny objects invisibly embedded in e-mail messages and Web pages that are designed to monitor the behavior of the user visiting a Web site or sending e-mail.

Web browsers: Easy-to-use software tool for accessing the World Wide Web and the Internet.

Web hosting service: Company with large Web server computers to maintain the Web sites of fee-paying subscribers.

Web mining: Discovery and analysis of useful patterns and information from the World Wide Web.

Web server: Software that manages requests for Web pages on the computer where they are stored and that delivers the page to the user's computer.

Web services: Set of universal standards using Internet technology for integrating different applications from different sources without time-consuming custom coding. Used for linking systems of different organizations or for linking disparate systems within the same organization.

Web site: All of the World Wide Web pages maintained by an organization or an individual.

Webmaster: The person in charge of an organization's Web site.

Wide area networks (WANs): Telecommunications networks that span a large geographical distance. May consist of a variety of cable, satellite, and microwave technologies.

Wi-Fi: Standards for Wireless Fidelity and refers to the 802.11 family of wireless networking standards.

wiki: Collaborative Web site where visitors can add, delete, or modify content on the site, including the work of previous authors.

WiMax: Popular term for IEEE Standard 802.16 for wireless networking over a range of up to 31 miles with a data transfer rate of up to 75 Mbps. Stands for Worldwide Interoperability for Microwave Access.

Windows 7: Recent Windows operating system for end users, with improved usability, taskbar, performance, and security, as well as support for multitouch interfaces.

Windows 8: Most recent Microsoft client operating system, which runs on tablets as well as PCs, and includes multitouch capabilities.

Windows Server 2012: Most recent Windows operating system for servers.

wireless portals: Portals with content and services optimized for mobile devices to steer users to the information they are most likely to need.

wireless sensor networks (WSNs): Networks of interconnected wireless devices with built-in processing, storage, and radio frequency sensors and antennas that are embedded into the physical environment to provide measurements of many points over large spaces.

wisdom of crowds: Belief that large numbers of people can make better decisions about a wide range of topics and products than a single person or even a small committee of experts.

Word processing software: Software for electronically creating, editing, formatting, and printing documents.

workflow management: The process of streamlining business procedures so that documents can be moved easily and efficiently from one location to another.

workstation: Desktop computer with powerful graphics and mathematical capabilities and the ability to perform several complicated tasks at once.

World Wide Web: A system with universally accepted standards for storing, retrieving, formatting, and displaying information in a networked environment.

worms: Independent software programs that propagate themselves to disrupt the operation of computer networks or destroy data and other programs.

References

CHAPTER 1

BEA. "Table 5.5.5. Private Fixed Investment in Equipment and Software by Type." Bureau of Economics Analysis (2013).

Brynjolfsson, Erik. "VII Pillars of IT Productivity." *Optimize* (May 2005).

Bureau Of Labor Statistics. *Occupational Outlook Handbook 2012-2013 Edition.* United States Department of Labor (2013).

Dean, David, Sebastian DiGrande, Dominic Field, and Paul Zwillenberg. "The Connected World." BCG (January 27, 2012).

FedEx Corporation. "SEC Form 10-K For the Fiscal Year Ended 2012."

Friedman, Thomas. *The World is Flat.* New York: Picador (2007).

Gartner Research. "Information Technology Expenditures World Wide." (July 12, 2012).

Greengard, Samuel. "Pervasive Mobility Creates New Business Challenges." Baseline (June 28, 2013).

_____. "Ten Tech Trends that Will Change IT in 2013." Baseline (December 2 2012).

Murphy, Chris. "Goodbye IT, Hello Digital Business." *Information Week* (March 18, 2013).

Pew Internet and American Life Project. "What Internet Users Do Online." (May 2013)

Ross, Jeanne W. And Peter Weill. "Four Questions Every CEO Should Ask About IT." *Wall Street Journal* (April 25, 2011).

Tuomi, Ilkka. "Data Is More Than Knowledge. *Journal of Management Information Systems* 16, no. 3 (Winter 1999–2000).

U.S. Census. "Statistical Abstract of the United States 2013." Department of Commerce (2013).

Weill, Peter and Jeanne Ross. *IT Savvy: What Top Executives Must Know to Go from Pain to Gain.* Boston: Harvard Business School Press (2009).

CHAPTER 2

Aral, Sinan; Erik Brynjolfsson; and Marshall Van Alstyne, "Productivity Effects of Information Diffusion in Networks," MIT Center for Digital Business (July 2007).

Banker, Rajiv D., Nan Hu, Paul A. Pavlou, and Jerry Luftman. "CIO Reporting Structure, Strategic Positioning, and Firm Performance ." *MIS Quarterly* 35. No. 2 (June 2011).

Bughin, Jacques, Angela Hung Byers, and Michael Chui. " How Social Technologies Are Extending the Organization." *McKinsey Quarterly* (November 2011).

Deiser, Roland and Sylvain Newton. "Six Social-Media Skills Every Leader Needs." *McKinsey Quarterly* (February 2013).

Forrester Consulting, "Total Economic Impact of IBM Social Collaboration Tools" (September 2010).

Forrester Research. "Social Business: Delivering Critical Business Value" (April 2012).

Frost & White. "Meetings Around the World II: Charting the Course of Advanced Collaboration." (October 14, 2009).

Guillemette, Manon G. and Guy Pare. "Toward a New Theory of the Contribution of the IT Function in Organizations." *MIS Quarterly* 36, No. 2 (June 2012).

Healey, Michael. "Why Enterprise Social Networking Falls Short." *Information Week* (March 4, 2013).

IBM Corporation. "Aarhus University Hospital Enhances Compliance." (August 2, 2012).

Kiron, David, Doug Palmer, Anh Nguyen Phillips and Robert Berkman. "The Executive's Role in Social Business."*MIT Sloan Management Review* 54, No. 4 (Summer 2013).

Kiron, David, Doug Palmer, Anh Nguyen Phillips and Nina Kruschwitz . "What Managers Really Think About Social Business." *MIT Sloan Management Review* 53, No. 4 (Summer 2012).

Kolfschoten, Gwendolyn L. , Niederman, Fred , Briggs, Robert O. and Vreede, Gert-Jan De. "Facilitation Roles and Responsibilities for Sustained Collaboration Support in Organizations." *Journal of Management Information Systems* 28, No. 4 (Spring 2012).

Li, Charlene. "Making the Business Case for Enterprise Social Networks." Altimeter Group (February 22, 2012).

Majchrzak, Ann, Christian Wagner, and Dave Yates. " The Impact of Shaping on Knowledge Reuse for Organizational Improvement with Wikis ." *MIS Quarterly* 37, No. 2 (June 2013).

Malone, Thomas M., Kevin Crowston, Jintae Lee, and Brian Pentland. "Tools for Inventing Organizations: Toward a Handbook of Organizational Processes." *Management Science* 45, no. 3 (March 1999).

McKinsey & Company. "Evolution of the Networked Enterprise. " (2013).

McKinsey Global Institute. "The Social Economy: Unlocking Value and Productivity Through Social Technologies." McKinsey & Company (July 2012).

Microsoft Corporation, "Bank Innovates Work Environment, Boosts Performance with Social Collaboration." (November 9, 2012).

Morgan, Jacob. "How to Market Collaboration to Employees." *Information Week* (March 21, 2013).

Poltrock, Steven and Mark Handel. "Models of Collaboration as the Foundation for Collaboration Technologies. *Journal of Management Information Systems* 27, No. 1 (Summer 2010).

Raice, Shayndi. "Social Networking Heads to the Office." *Wall Street Journal* (April 2, 2012).

Sarker, Saonee, Manju Ahuja , Suprateek Sarker and Sarah Kirkeby. "The Role of Communication and Trust in Global Virtual Teams: A Social Network Perspective." *Journal of Management Information Systems* 28, No. 1 (Summer 2011).

Saunders, Carol, A. F. Rutkowski, Michiel van Genuchten, Doug Vogel, and Julio Molina Orrego. "Virtual Space and Place: Theory and Test." *MIS Quarterly* 35, No. 4 (December 2011).

Weill, Peter and Jeanne W. Ross. *IT Governance.* Boston: Harvard Business School Press (2004).

CHAPTER 3

Boulton, Clint. "Printing Out Barbies and Ford Cylinders." *Wall Street Journal* (June 5, 2013).

Bunkley, Nick. "Piecing Together a Supply Chain." *New York Times* (May 12, 2011).

Chen, Daniel Q., Martin Mocker, David S. Preston, and Alexander Teubner. "Information Systems Strategy: Reconceptualization, Measurement, and Implications." *MIS Quarterly 34, no. 2* (June 2010).

Christensen, Clayton. "The Past and Future of Competitive Advantage." *Sloan Management Review* 42, no. 2 (Winter 2001).

Davenport, Thomas H. and Jeanne G. Harris. *Competing on Analytics: The New Science of Winning.* Boston: Harvard Business School Press (2007).

De Jong, Jeroen P.J. and Erik de Bruijn "Innovation Lessons from 3-D Printing." *MIT Sloan Management Review* 54, No. 2 (Winter 2013).

Dedrick , Jason, Kenneth L. Kraemer and Eric Shih. "Information Technology and Productivity in Developed and Developing Countries." *Journal of Management Information Systems* 30, No. 1 (Summer 2013).

Downes, Larry and Paul F.Nunes."Big-Bang Disruption."*Harvard Business Review* (March 2013).

Drnevich, Paul L.and David C. Croson . "Information Technology and Business-Level Strategy: Toward an Integrated Theoretical Perspective." *MIS Quarterly* 37, No. 2 (June 2013).

El Sawy, Omar A. *Redesigning Enterprise Processes for E-Business.* New York: McGraw-Hill (2001).

Engardio, Pete. " Mom-and-Pop Multinationals." Business Week (July 3, 2008).

Hammer, Michael, and James Champy. *Reengineering the Corporation.* New York: HarperCollins (1993).

Hammer, Michael. "Process Management and the Future of Six Sigma." *Sloan Management Review* 43, no.2 (Winter 2002).

Iansiti, Marco, and Roy Levien. "Strategy as Ecology." *Harvard Business Review* (March 2004).

Kauffman, Robert J., and Yu-Ming Wang. "The Network Externalities Hypothesis and Competitive Network Growth." *Journal of Organizational Computing and Electronic Commerce* 12, no. 1 (2002).

Luftman, Jerry. *Competing in the Information Age: Align in the Sand,*. Oxford University Press , USA; 2 edition (August 6, 2003).

Mattera, Savatore "Sam." "Google's Ecosystem Could be More Profitable Than Apple's." Motley Fool (May 18, 2013).

McAfee, Andrew and Erik Brynjolfsson. "Investing in the IT That Makes a Competitive Difference." *Harvard Business Review* (July/August 2008).

McLaren, Tim S., Milena M. Head, Yufei Yuan, and Yolande E. Chan. *"*A Multilevel Model for Measuring Fit Between a Firm's Competitive Strategies and Information Systems Capabilities." *MIS Quarterly* 35, No. 4 (December 2011).

Mithas, Sunil, Ali Tafti, and Will Mitchell. "How a Firm's Competitive Environment and Digital Strategic Posture Influence Digital Business Strategy ." *MIS Quarterly* 37, No. 2 (June 2013).

Osawa, Juro. "Next to Use 3-D Printing: Your Surgeon." *Wall Street Journal* (April 8, 2013).

Piccoli, Gabriele, and Blake Ives. "Review: IT-Dependent Strategic Initiatives and Sustained Competitive Advantage: A Review and Synthesis of the Literature." *MIS Quarterly* 29, no. 4 (December 2005).

Porter, Michael E., and Scott Stern. "Location Matters." *Sloan Management Review* 42, no. 4 (Summer 2001).

Porter, Michael. *Competitive Advantage.* New York: Free Press (1985).

_____. "Strategy and the Internet." *Harvard Business Review* (March 2001).

_____. "The Five Competitive Forces that Shape Strategy." *Harvard Business Review* (January 2008).

Shapiro, Carl, and Hal R. Varian. *Information Rules.* Boston: Harvard Business School Press (1999).

Von Hippel, Eric, Susumu Ogawa, and Jeroen P.J. DeJong. "The Age of the Customer-Innovator." *MIT Sloan Management Review* 53, No. 1 (Fall 2011).

CHAPTER 4

Angwin, Julia. "Online Tracking Ramps Up." *Wall Street Journal* (June 17, 2012).

Ante, Spencer E. "Online Ads Can Follow You Home." *Wall Street Journal* (April 29, 2013).

Austen, Ian. "With Apologies, Officials Say Blackberry Service is Restored." *New York Times* (October 13, 2011).

Belanger, France and Robert E. Crossler. "Privacy in the Digital Age: A Review of Information Privacy Research in Information Systems." *MIS Quarterly* 35, No. 4 (December 2011).

Bertolucci, Jeff. "Big Data Firm Chronicles Your Online, Offline Lives." *Information Week* (May 7, 2013).

Bilski v. Kappos, 561 US, (2010).

Brown Bag Software vs. Symantec Corp. 960 F2D 1465 (Ninth Circuit, 1992).

Brynjolfsson, Erik and Andrew McAfee. *Race Against the Machine.* Digital Frontier Press (2011).

Business Software Alliance, "Shadow Market: 2011 BSA Global Software Piracy Study," Ninth edition (May 2012).

Computer Security Institute. "CSI Computer Crime and Security Survey 2012." (2012).

Culnan, Mary J. and Cynthia Clark Williams. "How Ethics Can Enhance Organizational Privacy." *MIS Quarterly* 33, No. 4 (December 2009).

European Parliament. "Directive 2009/136/EC of the European Parliament and of the Council of November 25, 2009." European Parliament (2009).

Fowler, Geoffrey A. "Tech Giants Agree to Deal on Privacy Policies for Apps." *Wall Street Journal* (February 23, 2012).

Federal Trade Commission. "Protecting Consumer Privacy In an Era of Rapid Change." Washington D.C. (2012).

Frank, Adam. "Big Data and Its Big Problems." NPR (September 18, 2012).

Goldfarb, Avi, and Catherine Tucker. "Why Managing Consumer Privacy Can Be an Opportunity." *MIT Sloan Management Review* 54, No. 3 (Spring 2013).

Hsieh, J.J. Po-An, Arun Rai, and Mark Keil. "Understanding Digital Inequality: Comparing Continued Use Behavioral Models of the Socio-Economically Advantaged and Disadvantaged." *MIS Quarterly* 32, no. 1 (March 2008).

Laudon, Kenneth C. and Carol Guercio Traver. *E-Commerce: Business, Technology, Society* 9th Edition. Upper Saddle River, NJ: Prentice-Hall (2013).

Laudon, Kenneth C. *Dossier Society: Value Choices in the Design of National Information Systems.* New York: Columbia University Press (1986b).

Lee, Dong-Joo, Jae-Hyeon Ahn, and Youngsok Bang. "Managing Consumer Privacy Concerns in Personalization: A Strategic Analysis of Privacy Protection." *MIS Quarterly* 35, No. 2 (June 2011).

National White Collar Crime Center and the Federal Bureau of Investigation. "Internet Crime Complaint Center 2012 Internet Crime Report. (2013).

Rifkin, Jeremy. "Watch Out for Trickle-Down Technology." *New York Times* (March 16, 1993).

Robinson, Francis. "EU Unveils Web-Privacy Rules." *Wall Street Journal* (January 26, 2012).

Singer, Natasha. "When the Privacy Button Is Already Pressed." *New York Times* (September 15, 2012).

Smith, H. Jeff. "The Shareholders vs. Stakeholders Debate." *MIS Sloan Management Review* 44, no. 4 (Summer 2003).

Symantec. "Symantec Intelligence Report: August 2013 Report" (August 2013).

United States Department of Health, Education, and Welfare. *Records, Computers, and the Rights of Citizens.* Cambridge: MIT Press (1973).

U.S. Senate. "Do-Not-Track Online Act of 2011." Senate 913 (May 9, 2011).

U.S. Sentencing Commission. "Sentencing Commission Toughens Requirements for Corporate Compliance Programs. " (April 13, 2004).

CHAPTER 5

Andersson, Henrik, James Kaplan, and Brent Smolinski. "Capturing Value from IT Infrastructure Innovation." *McKinsey Quarterly* (October 2012).

Babcock, Charles. "Cloud's Thorniest Question: Does It Pay Off?" *Information Week* (June 4, 2012).

Benlian , Alexander, Marios Koufaris and Thomas Hess. "Service Quality in Software-as-a-Service: Developing the SaaS-Qual Measure and Examining Its Role in Usage Continuance." *Journal of Management Information Systems*, 28, No. 3 (Winter 2012).

Bensinger, Greg. "The Evolving Economics of the App." *Wall Street Journal* (March 3, 2013).

Bott, Ed. "Latest OS share data shows Windows still dominating in PCs." ZDNet (April 1, 2013).

Carr, Nicholas. *The Big Switch.* New York: Norton (2008).

Choi, Jae, Derek L. Nazareth, and Hemant K. Jain. "Implementing Service-Oriented Architecture in Organizations." *Journal of Management Information Systems* 26, No. 4 (Spring 2010).

David, Julie Smith, David Schuff, and Robert St. Louis. "Managing Your IT Total Cost of Ownership." *Communications of the ACM* 45, no. 1 (January 2002).

Davis, Michael A. "BYOD." *Information Week* (December 3, 2012).

Fitzgerald, Brian. "The Transformation of Open Source Software." *MIS Quarterly* 30, No. 3 (September 2006).

Ganek, A. G., and T. A. Corbi. "The Dawning of the Autonomic Computing Era." *IBM Systems Journal* 42, no 1, (2003).

Gartner Inc, "Worldwide IT Outsourcing Services Spending to Hit US \$251bn in 2012 ." siliconrepublic.com (August 8, 2012).

Gartner, Inc." Gartner Says Worldwide IT Spending On Pace to Surpass \$3.6 Trillion in 2012 ." (July 9, 2012).

Hamblen, Matt. "Consumerization Trends Driving IT Shops Crazy." CIO (May 2, 2012).

Hardy, Quentin. "A Strange Computer Promises Great Speed." *New York Times* (March 21, 2013).

Kern, Justin. "How to Determine Cloud TCO." Information Management (March 7, 2013).

Lohr, Steve. "I.B.M. Mainframe Evolves to Serve the Digital World. *New York Times* (August 28, 2012).

_____. "Sizing Up Big Data." *New York Times* (June 19, 2013).

Lyman, Peter and Hal R. Varian. "How Much Information 2003?" University of California at Berkeley School of Information Management and Systems (2003).

Mann, Andi, Kurt Milne and Jeanne Morain. "Calculting the Cost Advantages of a Private Cloud. " Cloud Computing Review 1, No. 1 (June 2011).

Markoff, John. "New Storage Device Is Very Small, at 12 Atoms." *New York Times* (January 12, 2012).

McAfee, Andrew. "What Every CEO Needs to Know about the Cloud." *Harvard Business Review* (November 2011).

Mell, Peter and Tim Grance. "The NIST Definition of Cloud Computing" Version 15. NIST (October 17, 2009).

Mueller, Benjamin, Goetz Viering, Christine Legner, and Gerold Riempp. "Understanding the Economic Potential of Service-Oriented Architecture." *Journal of Management Information Systems* 26, No. 4 (Spring 2010).

Murphy, Chris. "FedEx's Strategic Tech Shift." *Information Week* (May 20, 2013).

Schuff, David and Robert St. Louis. "Centralization vs. Decentralization of Application Software." *Communications of the ACM* 44, no. 6 (June 2001).

Strom, David. "Shopping Around for Cloud Computing Services." Cloud Computing Review 1, No. 1 (June 2011).

Taft, Darryl K. "Application Development: Java Death Debunked: 10 Reasons Why It's Still Hot." eWeek (February 22, 2012).

Tibken, Shara. "Here Come Tablets. Here Come Problems." *Wall Street Journal* (April 2, 2012).

_____ "Smartphones Challenge Chip Limits." *Wall Street Journal* (August 27, 2012).

Torode, Christine, Linda Tucci and Karen Goulart. "Managing the Next-Generation Data Center." Modern Infrastructure CIO Edition (January 2013).

Vance, Ashlee. "Behind the 'Internet of Things' Is Android—and It's Everywhere." Business Week (May 30, 2013).

"Wintel PCs Down to 50% Share of All Personal Computing," Electronista (January 16, 2012).

CHAPTER 6

Barth, Paul S. "Managing Big Data: What Every CIO Needs to Know." CIO Insight (January 12, 2012).

Barton, Dominic and David Court. "Making Advanced Analytics Work for You." *Harvard Business Review* (October 2012).

Baum, David. "Flying High with a Private Database Cloud." Oracle Magazine (November/December 2011).

Beath, Cynthia, , Irma Becerra-Fernandez, Jeanne Ross and James Short. "Finding Value in the Information Explosion." *MIT Sloan Management Review* 53, No. 4 (Summer 2012).

Bughin, Jacques, John Livingston, and Sam Marwaha."Seizing the Potential for Big Data." The *McKinsey Quarterly* (October 2011).

Clifford, James, Albert Croker, and Alex Tuzhilin. "On Data Representation and Use in a Temporal Relational DBMS." *Information Systems Research* 7, no. 3 (September 1996).

Davenport, Thomas H. and D.J. Patil. "Data Scientist: The Sexiest Job of the 21st Century." *Harvard Business Review* (October 2012).

Davenport, Thomas H., Paul Barth, and Randy Bean. "How Big Data Is Different." *MIT Sloan Management Review* 54, No 1(Fall 2012).

Dunn & Bradstreet. "The Big Payoff of Quality Data" (May 2012).

Eckerson, Wayne W. "Analytics in the Era of Big Data: Exploring a Vast New Ecosystem." TechTarget (2012).

_____. "Data Quality and the Bottom Line." The Data Warehousing Institute (2002).

Greengard, Samuel. "Big Data Unlocks Business Value." Baseline (January 2012).

Henschen, Doug. " MetLife Uses NoSQL for Customer Service Breakthrough." *Information Week* (May 13, 2013).

Hoffer, Jeffrey A., Ramesh Venkataraman, and Heikki Toppi. *Modern Database Management*, 11th ed. Upper Saddle River, NJ: Prentice-Hall (2013).

Jinesh Radadia. "Breaking the Bad Data Bottlenecks." *Information Management* (May/June 2010).

Kajepeeta, Sreedhar. "How Hadoop Tames Enterprises' Big Data." *Information Week* (February 2012).

Klau, Rick. "Data Quality and CRM." Line56. com, accessed March 4, 2003.

Kroenke, David M. and David Auer. *Database Processing* 12e. Upper Saddle River, NJ: Prentice-Hall (2012).

Lee, Yang W., and Diane M. Strong. "Knowing-Why about Data Processes and Data Quality." *Journal of Management Information Systems* 20, no. 3 (Winter 2004).

Lohr, Steve. "The Age of Big Data." *New York Times* (February 11, 2012).

Loveman, Gary. "Diamonds in the Datamine." *Harvard Business Review* (May 2003).

McAfee, Andrew and Erik Brynjolfsson. "Big Data: The Management Revolution." *Harvard Business Review* (October 2012).

McKinsey Global Institute. "Big Data: The Next Frontier for Innovation, Competition, and Productivity." McKinsey & Company (2011).

Morrison, Todd and Mark Fontecchio, "In-memory Technology Pushes Analytics Boundaries, Boosts BI Speeds," SearchBusinessAnalytics.techtarget.com, accessed May 17, 2013.

Morrow, Rich. "Apache Hadoop: The Swiss Army Knife of IT." Global Knowledge (2013).

Mulani, Narendra. "In-Memory Technology: Keeping Pace with Your Data." Information Management (February 27, 2013).

Pant, Prashant. "Data Mining and Predictive Analytics." Information Management (January 24, 2013).

Redman, Thomas. *Data Driven: Profiting from Your Most Important Business Asset.* Boston: Harvard Business Press (2008).

Rosenbush, Steven and Michael Totty. "How Big Data Is Transforming Business." *Wall Street Journal* (March 10, 2013).

Vizard, Michael. "McLaren Has a Need for Hana Speed." CIO Insight (May 28, 2013).

Wallace, David J. "How Caesar's Entertainment Sustains a Data-Driven Culture." DataInformed (December 14, 2012).

CHAPTER 7

Boutin, Paul. "Search Tool on Facebook Puts Network to Work." *New York Times* (March 20, 2013).

Cain Miller, Claire. "Seeking to Weed Out Drivel, Google Adjusts Search Engine." *New York Times* (February 25, 2011).

Donaldson, Sonya. "*New York Times* Launches Semantic Web Experiment." *New York Times* (September 3, 2012).

Efrati, Amir. "Google's Search Revamp: A Step Closer to AI." *Wall Street Journal* (March 14, 2012).

Flynn, Laurie J. "New System to Add Internet Addresses as Numbers Run Out." *New York Times* (February 14, 2011).

Google, Inc. "Form 10K for the Fiscal Year 2011." Securities and Exchange Commission, filed February 11, 2012.

Holmes, Sam and Jeffrey A. Trachtenberg. "Web Addresses Enter New Era." *Wall Street Journal* (June 21, 2011).

ICANN. "ICANN Policy Update." 10, No. 9 (September 2010).

Lahiri, Atanu, I. "The Disruptive Effect of Open Platforms on Markets for Wireless Services." *Journal of Management Information Systems* 27, No. 3 (Winter 2011).

Lohr, Steve. "Can Microsoft Make You Bing?" *New York Times* (July 30, 2011).

Lohr, Steve. "The Internet Gets Physical." *New York Times* (December 17, 2011).

Marin Software, Inc. "The State of Mobile Search Advertising in the US: How the Emergence of Smartphones and Tablets Changes Paid Search." Marin Software Inc. (2012).

McKinsey & Company. "The Impact of Internet Technologies: Search (July 2011).

Miller, Claire Cain. "Google, a Giant in Mobile Search, Seeks New Ways to Make It Pay," *New York Times* (April 24, 2011).

Miller, Miranda. "Mobile to Account for 25% of Paid Search Clicks on Google in 2012." Searchenginewatch.com (March 28, 2012).

Murphy, Chris. "The Internet of Things." *Information Week* (August 13, 2012).

Panko, Raymond R. and Julia Panko. *Business Data Networks and Telecommunications* 8e. Upper Saddle River, NJ: Prentice-Hall (2011).

Shaw, Tony. "Innovation Web 3.0." Baseline (March/April 2011).

Simonite, Tom. "Social Indexing." Technology Review (May/June 2011).

"The Internet of Things." *McKinsey Quarterly* (March 2010).

Troianovski, Anton. "Optical Delusion? Fiber Booms Again, Despite Bust," *Wall Street Journal*, (April 3, 2012).

Wittman, Art. "Here Comes the Internet of Things" *Information Week* (July 22, 2013).

Worldwide Web Consortium, " Semantic Web." w3.org/standards/semanticweb (October 18, 2012).

Worthen, Ben and Cari Tuna. "Web Running Out of Addresses." *Wall Street Journal* (Feb 1, 2011).

Xiao, Bo and Izak Benbasat. "E-Commerce Product Recommendation Agents: Use, Characteristics, and Impact." *MIS Quarterly* 31, No. 1 (March 2007).

CHAPTER 8

"Android Malware Spreading for First Time Via Hacked Sites." CIO Insight (May 4, 2012).

"Devastating Downtime: The Surprising Cost of Human Error and Unforeseen Events." Focus Research (October 2010).

Boulton, Clint. "American Airlines Outage Likely Caused by Software Quality Issues." *Wall Street Journal* (April 17, 2013).

Boyle, Randy J. and Raymond Panko. *Corporate Computer Security 3e.* Upper Saddle River, NJ: Prentice Hall (2013).

Bray, Chad. "Global Cyber Scheme Hits Bank Accounts." *Wall Street Journal* (October 1, 2010.)

Breedon, John II. "Trojans Horses Gain Inside Track as Top Form of Malware." GCN (May 6, 2013).

Cavusoglu, Huseyin, Birendra Mishra, and Srinivasan Raghunathan. "A Model for Evaluating IT Security Investments." *Communications of the ACM* 47, no. 7 (July 2004).

Donohue, Brian. "Malware C&C Servers Found in 184 Countries." ThreatPost.com (August 2, 2013).

Fowler, Geoffrey A. "What's a Company's Biggest Security Risk? YOU." *Wall Street Journal* (September 26, 2011).

Galbreth, Michael R. and Mikhael Shor. "The Impact of Malicious Agents on the Enterprise Software Industry." *MIS Quarterly 34, no. 3* (September 2010).

Graziano, Dan. "Study Says Malware Attacks Are on the Rise, Mobile Threats Becoming More Serious," BGR.com (September 4, 2012).

Hui , Kai Lung, Wendy Hui and Wei T. Yue. "Information Security Outsourcing with System Interdependency and Mandatory Security Requirement." *Journal of Management Information Systems* 29, No. 3 (Winter 2013).

IBM. "Secure By Design: Building Identity-Based Security into Today's Information Systems." (March 2010).

Javelin Strategy & Research. "2013 Identity Fraud Report." (2013).

Kaplan, James, Chris Rezek, and Kara Sprague. "Protecting Information in the Cloud." *McKinsey Quarterly* (January 2013).

King, Ivory. "The United States, a Top Source and Target of Malware." *L'Atelier* (August 13, 2012).

Kumar, Mohit. "Twitter Malware Spotted in the Wild Stealing Banking Credentials, The Hacker News (April 22, 2013).

Markoff, John and Nicole Perlroth. "Attacks Used the Internet Against Itself to Clog Traffic." *New York Times* (March 27, 2013).

McAfee."Mobile Malware Growth Continuing in 2013." (February 21, 2013).

Nachenberg, Carey. "A Window into Mobile Device Security." Symantec (2011).

Osterman Research. "The Risks of Social Media and What Can Be Done to Manage Them. Commvault (June 2011).

Panko, Raymond R. and Julia Panko. *Business Data Networks and Security 9e.* Upper Saddle River NJ: Prentice-Hall (2013).

Ponemon Institute. "2012 Cost of Cybercrime Study: United States (October 2012).

_____. "2013 Cost of Data Breach Study: United States." (May 2013).

_____. "Global Study on Mobility Risks." Websense Inc. (February 2012).

Rashid, Fahmida. Y. "Anonymous Avenges Megaupload Shutdown With Attacks on FBI, Hollywood Websites. eWeek (January 20, 2012).

Roche, Edward M., and George Van Nostrand. *Information Systems, Computer Crime and Criminal Justice.* New York: Barraclough Ltd. (2004).

Sadeh, Norman M. "Phish Isn't Spam." *Information Week* (June 25, 2012).

Schwartz, Matthew J. "Android Trojan Looks, Acts Like Windows Malware." *Information Week* (June 7, 2013).

Sengupta, Somini. "Machines that Know You without Using a Password." *New York Times* (September 10, 2013).

Smith-Spark, Laura and Dominique Van Heerden. "What Is the Syrian Electronic Army?" CNN.com (April 25, 2013).

Solutionary. "Solutionary Security Engineering Research Team Unveils Annual Global Threat Intelligence Report ." (March 12, 2013).

Spears. Janine L. and Henri Barki. "User Participation in Information Systems Security Risk Management." *MIS Quarterly* 34, No. 3 (September 2010).

Strom, David. "Cost of a Data Breach Declines For First Time, According to Ponemon," ReadWriteWeb/Enterprise (March 20, 2012).

Symantec. "More Than a Third of Global Cyber Attacks Aimed at Small Businesses, Research Shows. " SupplyChainBrain.com (July 17, 2012).

_____. "State of Mobility Global Results 2013." (2013).

_____. "Symantec Internet Security Threat Report." (2013).

Temizkan , Orcun, Ram L. Kumar , Sungjune Park and Chandrasekar Subramaniam. "Patch Release Behaviors of Software Vendors in Response to Vulnerabilities: An Empirical Analysis . " *Journal of Management Information Systems* 28, No. 4 (Spring 2012).

Vance , Anthony, Paul Benjamin Lowry and Dennis Eggett. "Using Accountability to Reduce Access Policy Violations in Information Systems ." *Journal of Management Information Systems* Volume 29 Number 4 Spring 2013.

Westerman, George. *IT Risk: Turning Business Threats into Competitive Advantage.* Harvard Business School Publishing (2007)

Yan Chen , K. Ram Ramamurthy and Kuang- Wei Wen. " Organizations' Information Security Policy Compliance: Stick or Carrot Approach?"*Journal of Management Information Systems* 29, No. 3 (Winter 2013).

Zhao, Xia, Ling Xue and Andrew B. Whinston ."Managing Interdependent Information Security Risks: Cyberinsurance, Managed Security Services, and Risk Pooling Arrangements ." *Journal of Management Information Systems* 30, No. 1 (Summer 2013).

CHAPTER 9

"Building the Supply Chain of the Future." SupplyChainBrain (March 29, 2012).

"Social and Mobile CRM Boost Productivity by 26.4 Percent." DestinationCRM (March 8, 2012).

"What is Social CRM?" CRM Magazine (April 2012).

Bozarth, Cecil and Robert B. Handfield. *Introduction to Operations and Supply Chain Management* 3e. Upper Saddle River, NJ: Prentice-Hall (2013).

Carew, Joanne. "Most Companies Failing at CRM." IT Web Business (February 14, 2013).

Chickowski, Ericka. "5 ERP Disasters Explained."www.Baselinemag.com, accessed October 8, 2009.

Columbus, Louis. "2013 CRM Market Share Update: 40% Of CRM Systems Sold Are SaaS-Based.".Forbes (April 26, 2013).

D'Avanzo, Robert, Hans von Lewinski, and Luk N. Van Wassenhove. "The Link between Supply Chain and Financial Performance." *Supply Chain Management Review* (November 1, 2003).

Davenport, Thomas H. *Mission Critical: Realizing the Promise of Enterprise Systems.* Boston: Harvard Business School Press (2000).

Davenport, Thomas H., Leandro Dalle Mule, and John Lucke. "Know What Your Customers Want Before They Do." *Harvard Business Review* (December 2011).

Hitt, Lorin, D. J. Wu, and Xiaoge Zhou. "Investment in Enterprise Resource Planning: Business Impact and Productivity Measures." *Journal of Management Information Systems* 19, no. 1 (Summer 2002).

IBM Institute for Business Value. "Customer Analytics Pay Off." IBM Corporation (2011).

Kalakota, Ravi, and Marcia Robinson. E-Business 2.0. Boston: Addison-Wesley (2001).

Kanaracus, Chris. "ERP Project Overruns 'Distressingly Common': Survey." IDG News Service (July 12, 2012).

_____. "ERP Software Project Woes Continue to Mount, Survey Says." IT World (February 20, 2013).

Klein, Richard and Arun Rai. "Interfirm Strategic Information Flows in Logistics Supply Chain Relationships. *MIS Quarterly* 33, No. 4 (December 2009).

Kopczak, Laura Rock, and M. Eric Johnson. "The Supply-Chain Management Effect." *MIT Sloan Management Review* 44, no. 3 (Spring 2003).

Laudon, Kenneth C. "The Promise and Potential of Enterprise Systems and Industrial Networks." Working paper, The Concours Group. Copyright Kenneth C. Laudon (1999).

Lee, Hau, L., V. Padmanabhan, and Seugin Whang. "The Bullwhip Effect in Supply Chains." *Sloan Management Review* (Spring 1997).

Lee, Hau. "The Triple-A Supply Chain." *Harvard Business Review* (October 2004).

Li, Xinxin and Lorin M. Hitt. "Price Effects in Online Product Reviews: An Analytical Model and Empirical Analysis." *MIS Quarterly* 34, No. 4 (December 2010).

Liang, Huigang, Nilesh Sharaf, Quing Hu, and Yajiong Xue. "Assimilation of Enterprise Systems: The Effect of Institutional Pressures and the Mediating Role of Top Management." *MIS Quarterly* 31, no. 1 (March 2007).

Maklan, Stan, Simon Knox, and Joe Peppard. "When CRM Fails." *MIT Sloan Management Review* 52, No. 4 (Summer 2011).

Malik, Yogesh, Alex Niemeyer, and Brian Ruwadi. "Building the Supply Chain of the Future." *McKinsey Quarterly* (January 2011).

Mehta, Krishna."Best Practices for Developing a Customer Lifetime Value Program." Information Management (July 28, 2011).

Novet, Jordan. "New Salesforce.com Features Meld Social Media, Marketing, and CRM."Gigaom (April 23, 2013).

Oracle Corporation. "Alcoa Implements Oracle Solution 20% below Projected Cost, Eliminates 43 Legacy Systems." www.oracle.com, accessed August 21, 2005.

Rai, Arun, Paul A. Pavlou, Ghiyoung Im, and Steve Du. "Interfirm IT Capability Profiles and Communications for Cocreating Relational Value: Evidence from the Logistics Industry." *MIS Quarterly* 36, No. 1 (March 2012).

Rai, Arun, Ravi Patnayakuni, and Nainika Seth. "Firm Performance Impacts of Digitally Enabled Supply Chain Integration Capabilities." *MIS Quarterly* 30 No. 2 (June 2006).

Ranganathan, C. and Carol V. Brown. "ERP Investments and the Market Value of Firms: Toward an Understanding of Influential ERP Project Variables." *Information Systems Research* 17, No. 2 (June 2006).

Sarker, Supreteek, Saonee Sarker, Arvin Sahaym, and Bjørn-Andersen. "Exploring Value Cocreation in Relationships Between an ERP Vendor and its Partners: A Revelatory Case Study." *MIS Quarterly* 36, No. 1 (March 2012).

Seldon, Peter B., Cheryl Calvert, and Song Yang. "A Multi-Project Model of Key Factors Affecting Organizational Benefits from Enterprise Systems." *MIS Quarterly 34, No. 2* (June 2010).

Strong, Diane M. and Olga Volkoff. "Understanding Organization-Enterprise System Fit: A Path to Theorizing the Information Technology Artifact." *MIS Quarterly* 34, No.4 (December 2010).

"Why Social CRM Is Important to Business. Ziff-Davis (2012).

Wong, Christina W.Y. , Lai, Kee-hung and Cheng, T.C.E.. "Value of Information Integration to Supply Chain Management: Roles of Internal and External Contingencies." *Journal of Management Information Systems* 28, No. 3 (Winter 2012).

Ziff Davis. "Top 5 Reasons ERP Implementations Fail and What You Can Do About It." (2013).

CHAPTER 10

Arazy, Ofer and Ian R. Gallatly. "Corporate Wikis: The Effects of Owners' Motivation and Behavior on Group Members' Engagement" *Journal of Management Information Systems* 29, No. 3 (Winter 2013).

Bakos, Yannis. "The Emerging Role of Electronic Marketplaces and the Internet." *Communications of the ACM* 41, no. 8 (August 1998).

Barnes, Brooks. "Disney, Struggling to Find Its Digital Footing, Overhauls Disney.com." *New York Times"* (October 21, 2012).

Bell, David R., Jeonghye Choi and Leonard Lodish."What Matters Most in Internet Retailing." *MIT Sloan Management Review* 54, No. 1 (Fall 2012).

Boulton, Clint. "Crowdsourcing Takes Center Stage in Businesses." *Wall Street Journal*, (February 1, 2013).

Brynjolfsson, Erik, Yu Jeffrey Hu, and Mohammad S. Rahman. "Competing in the Age of Multichannel Retailing." *MIT Sloan Management Review* (May 2013).

Brynjolfsson, Erik,Yu Hu, and Michael D. Smith. "Consumer Surplus in the Digital Economy: Estimating the Value of Increased Product Variety at Online Booksellers." *Management Science* 49, no. 11 (November 2003).

Cardwell, Diane. "A Bet on the Environment." *New York Times* (September 2, 2013).

Clemons, Eric K. "Business Models for Monetizing Internet Applications and Web Sites: Experience, Theory, and Predictions. "*Journal of Management Information Systems* 26, No. 2 (Fall 2009).

comScore Inc. "ComScore Media Metrix Ranks Top 50 U.S. Web Properties for July 2013." (August 14, 2013a).

comScore Inc. "ComScore 2013 US Digital Future in Focus." [Nick Mulligan]. (February 28, 2013b).

eMarketer . "US Ad Spending Mid 2013 Forecast." (July 2013e).

eMarketer chart, "US Mobile Phone Users and Penetration, 2012-2017 (millions and % of population)" (March 2013g).

eMarketer. "US Digital Content Users." (March 2013f).

eMarketer. "US Fixed Broadband Households, 2011-2017. (February 2013c).

eMarketer. "US Internet Users 2013." (February 2013b).

eMarketer. "US Retail E-commerce 2013 Forecast." (April 2013a).

eMarketer. "US Retail Mcommerce Sales, 2011-2017" (April 2013h).

eMarketer. "US Time Spent With Media." (August 2013d)

eMarketer. "Facebook Advertising: Why the Marketplace Ad Platform Deserves a Second Look." (June 2012).

eMarketer. "Mobile Phone Users Worldwide, by Region and Country, 2010-2016." (April 17, 2012).

Evans, Philip and Thomas S. Wurster. *Blown to Bits: How the New Economics of Information Transforms Strategy.* Boston, MA: Harvard Business School Press (2000).

Fuller, Johann, Hans Muhlbacher, Kurt Matzler, and Gregor Jawecki. "Customer Empowerment Through Internet-Based Co-Creation." *Journal of Management Information Systems* 26, No. 3 (Winter 2010).

Gast, Arne and Michele Zanini. "The Social Side of Strategy." *McKinsey Quarterly* (May 2012).

Giamanco, Barbara and Kent Gregoire. "Tweet Me, Friend Me, Make Me Buy." *Harvard Business Review* (July-August 2012).

Grau, Jeffery. "US Retail E-commerce Forecast: Entering the Age of Omnichannel Retailing." eMarketer. (March 1, 2012).

Gupta, Sunil. "For Mobile Devices, Think Apps, Not Ads." *Harvard Business Review* (March 2013).

Haughney,, Christine. "Under Pressure, Stewart Shifts Company's Focus." *New York Times* (June 16, 2013).

Hinz, Oliver , Jochen Eckert, and Bernd Skiera. "Drivers of the Long Tail Phenomenon: An Empirical Analysis." *Journal of Management Information Systems* 27, No. 4 (Spring 2011).

Hinz, Oliver, Il-Horn Hann, and Martin Spann. Price Discrimination in E-Commerce? An Examination of Dynamic Pricing in Name-Your-Own Price Markets." *MIS Quarterly* 35, No 1 (March 2011).

Howe, Heff. *Crowdsourcing: Why the Power of the Crowd Is Driving the Future of Business.* New York: Random House (2008).

Internet Retailer. "Mobile Commerce Top 400 2013." (2013).

Internet World Stats. "Internet Users in the World." (Internetworldstats.com, 2013).

Khan, Mickey. "*Wall Street Journal* Debuts Mobile Site With Intentional Design Approach." *Wall Street Journal* (February 15, 2013).

Koch, Hope and Ulrike Schultze. " Stuck in the Conflicted Middle: A Role-Theoretic Perspective on B2B E-Marketplaces." *MIS Quarterly* 35, No. 1 (March 2011).

Kumar, V. and Rohan Mirchandan "Increasing the ROI of Social Media Marketing." *MIT Sloan Management Review* 54, No. 1 (Fall 2012).

Laudon, Kenneth C. and Carol Guercio Traver. *E-Commerce: Business, Technology, Society*, 9th edition. Upper Saddle River, NJ: Prentice-Hall (2013).

Leimeister, Jan Marco, Michael Huber, Ulrich Bretschneider, and Helmut Krcmar." Leveraging Crowdsourcing: Activation-Supporting Components for IT-Based Ideas Competition." *Journal of Management Information Systems* 26, No. 1 (Summer 2009).

Li, Xinxin and Lorin M. Hitt. "Price Effects in Online Product Reviews: An Analytical Model and Empirical Analysis." *MIS Quarterly* 34, No. 4 (December 2010).

Limelight Networks. "Websites are Dead: Long Live Digital Presence." (October 2012).

Lin, Mei , Ke, Xuqing and Whinston, Andrew B. "Vertical Differentiation and a Comparison of Online Advertising Models . " *Journal of Management Information Systems* 29, No. 1 (Summer 2012).

Moe, Wendy W., David A. Schweidel, and Michael Trusov. '"What Influences Customers' Online Comments." *MIT Sloan Management Review* 53, No. 1 (Fall 2011).

Oestreicher-Singer, Gal and Arun Sundararajan. " Recommendation Networks and the Long Tail of Electronic Commerce." *MIS Quarterly* 36, No. 1 (March 2012).

Pew Internet and American Life Project. "Daily Internet Activities." (January 6, 2013.)

Pew Internet and American Life Project. " Internet Users Don't like Targeted Ads." (March 13, 2012).

Piskorski, Mikolaj Jan. "Social Strategies that Work." *Harvard Business Review* (November 2011).

Resnick, Paul and Hal Varian. "Recommender Systems." *Communications of the ACM* (March 2007).

Schoder, Detlef and Alex Talalavesky. "The Price Isn't Right." *MIT Sloan Management Review* (August 22, 2010).

Silverman, Rachel Emma. "Big Firms Try Crowdsourcing," *Wall Street Journal*, January 17, 2012.

Smith, Michael D. and Rahul Telang. "Competing with Free: The Impact of Movie Broadcasts on DVD Sales and Internet Piracy." *MIS Quarterly* 33, No. 2 (June 2009).

Smith, Michael D. and Rahul Telang. "Why Digital Media Require a Strategic Rethink." *Harvard Business Review* (October 2012).

Smith, Michael D., Joseph Bailey and Erik Brynjolfsson. "Understanding Digital Markets: Review and Assessment" in Erik Brynjolfsson and Brian Kahin, ed. *Understanding the Digital Economy.* Cambridge, MA: MIT Press (1999).

Surowiecki, James. The Wisdom of Crowds: *Why the Many Are Smarter Than the Few and How Collective Wisdom Shapes Business, Economies, Societies and Nations.* Boston: Little, Brown (2004).

US Bureau of the Census. "E-Stats." http://www.census.gov/econ/index.html (May 28, 2013).

"US M-Commerce Sales, 2010-2015" in "Mobile Commerce Forecast: Capitalizing on Consumers' Urgent Needs." eMarketer (January 2012).

Wilson, H. James, PJ. Guinan, Salvatore Parise, and Bruce D. Weinberg. "What's Your Social Media Strategy?" *Harvard Business Review* (July 2011).

Yang, James. "When Freemium Fails." *Wall Street Journal* (August 22, 2012).

Zhao, Xia and Ling Xue. "Competitive Target Advertising and Consumer Data Sharing." *Journal of Management Information Systems* 29, No. 3 (Winter 2013).

CHAPTER 11

Alavi, Maryam and Dorothy Leidner. "Knowledge Management and Knowledge Management Systems: Conceptual Foundations and Research Issues," *MIS Quarterly* 25, No. 1 (March 2001).

Animesh Animesh, Alain Pinsonneault, Sung-Byung Yang, and Wonseok Oh. " An Odyssey into Virtual Worlds: Exploring the Impacts of Technological and Spatial Environments." *MIS Quarterly* 35, No. 3 (September 2011).

Bertolucci, Jeff. "Did You Really Buy A Snowmobile? Big Data Knows." *Information Week* (May 13,2013).

Booth, Corey and Shashi Buluswar. "The Return of Artificial Intelligence," *The McKinsey Quarterly* No. 2 (2002).

Breuer, Peter, Jessica Moulton, and Robert Turtle. "Applying Advanced Analytics in Consumer Companies. McKinsey & Company (May 2013).

Burtka, Michael. "Genetic Algorithms." *The Stern Information Systems Review* 1, no. 1 (Spring 1993).

Clark, Thomas D., Jr., Mary C. Jones, and Curtis P. Armstrong. "The Dynamic Structure of Management Support Systems: Theory Development, Research Focus, and Direction." *MIS Quarterly* 31, no. 3 (September 2007).

Davenport, Thomas H. and Jim Hagemann Snabe. "How Fast and Flexible to You Want Your Information, Really?" *MIT Sloan Management Review* 52, No. 3 (Spring 2011).

Davenport, Thomas H., and Lawrence Prusak. *Working Knowledge: How Organizations Manage What They Know.* Boston, MA: Harvard Business School Press (1997).

Davenport, Thomas H., Jeanne Harris, and Robert Morison. Analytics at Work: Smarter Decisions, Better Results. Boston: Harvard Business Press (2010).

Davenport, Thomas H., Robert J. Thomas and Susan Cantrell. "The Mysterious Art and Science of Knowledge-Worker Performance." *MIT Sloan Management Review* 44, no. 1 (Fall 2002).

Davis, Gordon B. "Anytime/ Anyplace Computing and the Future of Knowledge Work." *Communications of the ACM* 42, no.12 (December 2002).

Dennis, Alan R., Randall K. Minas and Akshay P. Bhagwatwar. "Sparking Creativity: Improving Electronic Brainstorming with Individual Cognitive Priming." *Journal of Management Information Systems* 29, No. 4 (Spring 2013).

Dennis, Alan R., Jay E. Aronson, William G. Henriger, and Edward D. Walker III. "Structuring Time and Task in Electronic Brainstorming." *MIS Quarterly* 23, no. 1 (March 1999).

DeSanctis, Geraldine, and R. Brent Gallupe. "A Foundation for the Study of Group Decision Support Systems." *Management Science* 33, no. 5 (May 1987).

Dhar, Vasant, and Roger Stein. *Intelligent Decision Support Methods: The Science of Knowledge Work.* Upper Saddle River, NJ: Prentice Hall (1997).

Fisher, Lauren T. "Data Management Platforms: Using Big Data to Power Marketing Performance." eMarketer (May 2013).

Gartner Inc., " Gartner Says Worldwide Business Intelligence Software Revenue to Grow 7 Percent in 2013" (February 19, 2013)

Gast, Arne and Michele Banini. "The Social Side of Strategy." *McKinsey Quarterly* (May 2012).

Grau, Jeffrey. "How Retailers Are Leveraging 'Big Data' to Personalize Ecommerce." eMarketer (2012).

Holland, John H. "Genetic Algorithms." *Scientific American* (July 1992).

Housel Tom and Arthur A. Bell. *Measuring and Managing Knowledge.* New York: McGraw-Hill (2001).

IBM Corporation. "Extending Business Intelligence with Dashboards." (2010).

Hurst, Cameron with Michael S. Hopkins and Leslie Brokaw. "Matchmaking With Math: How Analytics Beats Intuition to Win Customers." *MIT Sloan Management Review* 52, No. 2 (Winter 2011).

Jarvenpaa, Sirkka L. and D. Sandy Staples. "Exploring Perceptions of Organizational Ownership of Information and Expertise." *Journal of Management*

Information Systems 18, no. 1 (Summer 2001).

Johns, Tammy and Lynda Gratton. "The Third Wave of Virtual Work." *Harvard Business Review* (January-February 2013).

King, William R., Peter V. Marks, Jr. and Scott McCoy. "The Most Important Issues in Knowledge Management." *Communications of the ACM* 45, no.9 (September 2002).

Kiron, David, Pamela Kirk, and Renee Boucher Ferguson. "Innovating with Analytics." *MIT Sloan Management Review* 54, No. 1 (Fall 2012).

Kiron, David And Rebecca Schockley. "Creating Business Value With Analytics." *MIT Sloan Management Review* 53, No 1 (Fall 2011).

Lanier, Jaron. "The First Church of Robotics." *New York Times* (August 9, 2010).

LaValle, Steve, Michael S Hopkins, Eric Lesser, Rebecca Shockley, and Nina Kruschwitz. "Analytics: The New Path to Value." *MIT Sloan Management Review* and IBM Institute for Business Value (Fall 2010).

LaValle, Steve, Eric Lesser, Rebecca Shockley, Michael S. Hopkins and Nina Kruschwitz. "Big Data, Analytics, and the Path from Insights to Value." *MIT Sloan Management Review* 52, No. 2 (Winter 2011).

Leonard-Barton, Dorothy and Walter Swap. "Deep Smarts.' *Harvard Business Review* (September 1, 2004).

Lev, Baruch. "Sharpening the Intangibles Edge." *Harvard Business Review* (June 1, 2004).

Lohr, Steve. "When There's No Such Thing as Too Much Information." *New York Times* (April 23, 2011).

Malone, Thomas. "Rethinking Knowledge Work: A Strategic Approach." *McKinsey Quarterly* (February 2011).

Marchand, Donald A. and Joe Peppard. "Why IT Fumbles Analytics." *Harvard Business Review* (January-February 2013).

Markoff, John. "A Fight to Win the Future: Computers vs. Humans." *New York Times* (February 14, 2011).

Markoff, John. "How Many Computers to Identify a Cat? 16,000." *New York Times* (June 26, 2012).

Markus, M. Lynne. "Toward a Theory of Knowledge Reuse: Types of Knowledge Reuse Situations and Factors in Reuse Success." *Journal of Management Information Systems* 18, no. 1 (Summer 2001).

McKnight, William. "Predictive Analytics: Beyond the Predictions." Information Management (July/August 2011).

Murphy, Chris "4 Ways Ford Is Exploring Next-Gen Car Tech." *Information Week* (July 27, 2012).

Nichols, Wes. "Advertising Analytics 2.0." *Harvard Business Review* (March 2013).

Nunamaker, Jay, Robert O. Briggs, Daniel D. Mittleman, Douglas R. Vogel, and Pierre A. Balthazard. "Lessons from a Dozen Years of Group Support Systems Research: A Discussion of Lab and Field Findings." *Journal of Management Information Systems* 13, no. 3 (Winter 1997).

Nurmohamed, Zafrin, Nabeel Gillani, and Michael Lenox "A New Use for MOOCs: Real-World Problem Solving." *Harvard Business Review* (July 14, 2013).

Pugh, Katrina and Lawrence Prusak. "Designing Effective Knowledge Networks." *MIT Sloan Management Review* (Fall 2013).

Robertson, Jordan. "IBM Pursues Chips that Behave Like Brains" Associated Press (August 18, 2011).

Samuelson, Douglas A. and Charles M. Macal. "Agent-Based Simulation." OR/MS Today (August 2006).

Sanders, Peter. "Boeing 787 Training Takes Virtual Path" *Wall Street Journal* (September 2, 2010).

Schultze, Ulrike and Dorothy Leidner."Studying Knowledge Management in Information Systems Research: Discourses and Theoretical Assumptions." *MIS Quarterly* 26, no. 3 (September 2002).

Simon, H. A. *The New Science of Management Decision.* New York: Harper & Row (1960).

Singer, Natasha. "The Virtual Anatomy, Ready for Dissection." *New York Times* (January 7, 2012).

Sommer, Dan and Bhavish Sood. "Market Share Analysis: Business Intelligence, Analytics and Performance Management, Worldwide, 2010." Gartner Inc. (April 18, 2011).

Ukelson, Jacob. "Trends in Knowledge Work." Information Management (May/June 2011).

Viaene, Stijn. and Annabel Van den Bunder "The Secrets to Managing Business Analytics Projects." Sloan Management Review 52, No. 1 (Fall 2011).

Wang, Yinglei, Darren B. Meister, and Peter H. Gray. "Social Influence and Knowledge Management Systems Use: Evidence from Panel Data." *MIS Quarterly* 37, No. 1 (March 2013).

Wayner, Peter. "Illustrating Your Life in Graphs and Charts.: *New York Times* (April 20, 2011).

Wheatley, Malcolm. "Data-Driven Location Choices Drive Latest Starbucks Surge." Data Informed (January 10, 2013).

Zadeh, Lotfi A. "The Calculus of Fuzzy If/Then Rules." *AI Expert* (March 1992).

CHAPTER 12

Appan, Radha and Glenn J. Browne. "The Impact of Analyst-Induced Misinformation on the Requirements Elicitation Process ." *MIS Quarterly* 36, No 1 (March 2012).

Armstrong, Deborah J. and Bill C. Hardgrove. "Understanding Mindshift Learning: The Transition to Object-Oriented Development." *MIS Quarterly 31,* no. 3 (September 2007).

Aron, Ravi, Eric K.Clemons, and Sashi Reddi. "Just Right Outsourcing: Understanding and Managing Risk." *Journal of Management Information Systems* 22, no. 1 (Summer 2005).

Ashrafi Noushin and Hessam Ashrafi. *Object-Oriented Systems Analysis and Design.* Upper Saddle River, NY: Prentice-Hall (2009).

Bloch, Michael, Sen Blumberg, and Jurgen Laartz. "Delivering Large-Scale IT Projects on Time, on Budget, and on Value." *McKinsey Quarterly* (October 2012).

Biehl, Markus. "Success Factors For Implementing Global Information Systems." *Communications of the ACM* 50, No. 1 (January 2007).

Chickowski, Ericka. "Projects Gone Wrong." *Baseline* (May 15, 2009).

Delone, William H., and Ephraim R. McLean. "The Delone and McLean Model of Information Systems Success: A Ten-Year Update. *Journal of Management nformation Systems* 19, no. 4 (Spring 2003).

Dibbern, Jess, Jessica Winkler, and Armin Heinzl. "Explaining Variations in Client Extra Costs between Software Projects Offshored to India." *MIS Quarterly* 32, no. 2 (June 2008).

Esposito, Dino. "A Whole New Ball Game: Aspects of Mobile Application Development." *Information Week* (March 12, 2011).

Feeny, David, Mary Lacity, and Leslie P. Willcocks. "Taking the Measure of Outsourcing Providers." *MIT Sloan Management Review* 46, no. 3 (Spring 2005).

Flyvbjerg, Bent and Alexander Budzier. "Why Your IT Project May Be Riskier Than You Think." *Harvard Business Review* (September 2011).

Vaidyanathan, Ganesh. *Project Management: Process, Technology and Practice.* Upper Saddle River, NJ: Prentice Hall (2013).

Gefen, David and Erarn Carmel. "Is the World Really Flat? A Look at Offshoring in an Online Programming Marketplace." *MIS Quarterly* 32, no. 2 (June 2008).

Goff, Stacy A. "The Future of IT Project Management Software." CIO (January 6, 2010).

Goo, Jahyun, Rajive Kishore, H. R. Rao, and Kichan Nam. The Role of Service Level Agreements in Relational Management of Information Technology Outsourcing: An Empirical Study." *MIS Quarterly* 33, No. 1 (March 2009).

Hahn, Eugene D., Jonathan P. Doh, and Kraiwinee Bunyaratavej. "The Evolution of Risk in Information Systems Offshoring: The Impact of Home Country Risk, Firm Learning, and Competitive Dynamics. *MIS Quarterly* 33, No. 3 (September 2009).

Han, Kunsoo and Sunil Mithas. "Information Technology Outsourcing and Non-IT Operating Costs: An Empirical Investigation." *MIS Quarterly* 37, No. 1 (March 2013).

Hickey, Ann M., and Alan M. Davis. "A Unified Model of Requirements Elicitation." *Journal of Management Information Systems* 20, no. 4 (Spring 2004).

Hoffer, Jeffrey, Joey George, and Joseph Valacich. *Modern Systems Analysis and Design*, 7th ed. Upper Saddle River, NJ: Prentice Hall (2013).

Information Builders. "WebFOCUS Turns Neways Into a Cleaner, Data-Driven Company." www.informationbuilders.com, accessed August 19, 2013.

Jeffrey, Mark, and Ingmar Leliveld. "Best Practices in IT Portfolio Management." *MIT Sloan Management Review* 45, no. 3 (Spring 2004).

Kendall, Kenneth E., and Julie E. Kendall. *Systems Analysis and Design,* 9th ed. Upper Saddle River, NJ: Prentice Hall (2013).

Kim, Hee Woo and Atreyi Kankanhalli. "Investigating User Resistance to Information Systems Implementation: A Status Quo Bias Perspective." *MIS Quarterly* 33, No. 3 (September 2009).

Kirsch, Laurie J. "Deploying Common Systems Globally: The Dynamic of Control." *Information Systems Research* 15, no. 4 (December 2004).

Koh, Christine, Song Ang, and Detmar W. Straub. "IT Outsourcing Success: A Psychological Contract Perspective." *Information Systems Research* 15 no. 4 (December 2004).

Lapointe, Liette, and Suzanne Rivard. "A Multilevel Model of Resistance to Information Technology Implementation." *MIS Quarterly* 29, no. 3 (September 2005).

Lee, Jong Seok , Keil, Mark and Kasi, Vijay . "The Effect of an Initial Budget and Schedule Goal on Software Project Escalation." *Journal of Management Information Systems* 29, No. 1 (Summer 2012).

Levina, Natalia, and Jeanne W. Ross. "From the Vendor's Perspective: Exploring the Value Proposition in Information Technology Outsourcing." *MIS Quarterly* 27, no. 3 (September 2003).

Majchrzak, Ann, Cynthia M. Beath, and Ricardo A. Lim. "Managing Client Dialogues during Information Systems Design to Facilitate Client Learning." *MIS Quarterly* 29, no. 4 (December 2005).

McCafferty, Dennis. "How Social IT Tools Killed 'Business as Usual." Baseline (August 19, 2013).

McCafferty, Dennis. "What Dooms IT Projects." Baseline (June 10, 2010).

McDougall, Paul. "Outsourcing's New Reality: Choice Beats Costs." *Information Week* (August 29, 2012).

McGrath, Rita. "Six Problems Facing Large Government IT Projects (and Their Solutions)." *Harvard Business Review* Online (October 10, 2008).

McMahan, Ty. "The Ins and Outs of Mobile Apps." *Wall Street Journal* (June 13, 2011).

Nelson, H. James, Deborah J. Armstrong, and Kay M. Nelson. Patterns of Transition: The Shift from Traditional to Object-Oriented Development." *Journal of Management Information Systems* 25, No. 4 (Spring 2009).

Overby, Stephanie. "The Hidden Costs of Offshore Outsourcing," *CIO Magazine* (September 1, 2003).

Polites, Greta L. and Elena Karahanna. "Shackled to the Status Quo: The Inhibiting Effects of Incumbent System Habit, Switching Costs, and Inertia on New System Acceptance." *MIS Quarterly* 36, No. 1 (March 2012).

Rai, Arun, Sandra S. Lang, and Robert B. Welker. "Assessing the Validity of IS Success Models: An Empirical Test and Theoretical Analysis." *Information Systems Research* 13, no. 1 (March 2002).

Reinecke, Katharina and Abraham Bernstein. "Knowing What a User Likes: A Design Science Approach to Interfaces that Automatically Adapt to Culture." *MIS Quarterly* 37, No. 2 (June 2013).

Ryan, Sherry D., David A. Harrison, and Lawrence L Schkade. "Information Technology Investment Decisions: When Do Cost and Benefits in the Social Subsystem Matter?" *Journal of*

Management Information Systems 19, no. 2 (Fall 2002).

Sharma, Rajeev and Philip Yetton. "The Contingent Effects of Training, Technical Complexity, and Task Interdependence on Successful Information Systems Implementation." *MIS Quarterly 31*, no. 2 (June 2007).

Silva, Leiser and Rudy Hirschheim. "Fighting Against Windmills: Strategic Information Systems and Organizational Deep Structures." *MIS Quarterly 31*, no. 2 (June 2007).

Sircar, Sumit, Sridhar P. Nerur, and Radhakanta Mahapatra. "Revolution or Evolution? A Comparison of Object-Oriented and Structured Systems Development Methods." *MIS Quarterly* 25, no. 4 (December 2001).

Smith, H. Jeff, Mark Keil, and Gordon Depledge. "Keeping Mum as the Project Goes Under." *Journal of Management Information Systems* 18, no. 2 (Fall 2001).

Vaidyanathan, Ganesh. *Project Management: Process, Technology and Practice.* Upper Saddle River, NJ: Prentice-Hall (2013).

Venkatesh, Viswanath, Michael G. Morris, Gordon B Davis, and Fred D. Davis. "User Acceptance of Information Technology: Toward a Unified View." *MIS Quarterly* 27, no. 3 (September 2003).

Whitaker , Jonathan, Sunil Mithas and M.S. Krishnan. "Organizational Learning and Capabilities for Onshore and Offshore Business Process Outsourcing." *Journal of Management Information Systems* 27, No. 3 (Winter 2011).

Wulf, Volker, and Matthias Jarke. "The Economics of End-User Development." *Communications of the ACM* 47, no. 9 (September 2004).

Zhu, Kevin, Kenneth L. Kraemer, Sean Xu, and Jason Dedrick. "Information Technology Payoff in E-Business Environments: An International Perspective on Value Creation of E-business in the Financial Services Industry." *Journal of Management Information Systems* 21, no. 1 (Summer 2004).

Index

Name Index

Afshar, Vala, 388

Bloomberg, Michael, 463
Brin, Sergey, 262, 277
Brown, Chris, 381
Brynjolfsson, Erik, 157
Buchanan, Brooke, 98

Claypool, Alan, 448

D'Ambrosio, Lou, 237
Dyche, Jill, 389

Filo, David, 261
Flowers, Michael, 402
Ford, Bill, Jr., 107
Ford, Henry, 79
Friedman, Thomas, 32

Gates, Bill, 79
Gonzalez, Albert, 293
Gupta, Rajat, 134

Heyman, Nev, 418
Horan, Jeanette, 196
Hunt, Neil, 204

Jackson, Eric, 30
Jobs, Steve, 79

Kant, Immanuel, 140
Kern, Frank, 448
Klipper, Michael, 128
Koonin, Steven E., 402
Kumar, Pradeep, 389

Lautenbach, Marc, 448

McAfee, Andrew P., 157
McCann, Chris, 116
McCann, Jim, 116
McCormick, Matt, 388
McDonald, Bob, 73
McIntosh, Madeline, 128

Obama, Barack, 315, 316, 317
Oberwager, Brad, 113, 114
Olson, Cliff, 203
Orwell, George, 154
O'Sullivan, Niall, 348
Oxley, Michael, 296

Page, Larry, 262, 277
Perelman, Les, 424, 425, 426
Pontefract, Dan, 60
Porter, Michael, 99, 100
Price Mark, 418
Ratliff, John, 30
Rockefeller, Jay D., 143, 144
Roman, Eugene, 197

Sandel, Michael, 425
Sarbanes, Paul, 296

Schlough, Bill, 26
Scott, Tsehai, 98
Shermis, Mark, 424
Simon, Herbert, 397
Snowden, Edward, 138
Soloway, Robert, 157
Sullivan, Jim, 238

Thomas, Wendell, 204
Thompson, Scott, 134

Wallace, Sanford, 157

Yach, David, 152
Yang, Jerry, 261

Zuckerberg, Mark, 164, 278

Organizations Index

A&P, 331
Aarhus University, 84
ABC Cookies, 429-431, 434, 436
Accenture, 55, 461, 463-464
Acorda, 182
Ad Council, 132
Adobe, 316
Advanced Micro Design (AMD), 32
Aetna, 56
Airborne Express, 41
AirWatch, 31
Aite Group, 290
Ajax Boiler, 258
AKM Semiconductor, 113
Alcatel-Lucent, 381
Alcoa, 326
Amazon.com, 33, 64, 99, 103, 104, 127, 128, 144, 145, 153, 154, 180, 187, 202-203, 204, 237, 266, 292, 308, 353, 354, 356, 360, 362, 364, 365, 366, 367, 368, 374, 378, 381, 441
America Online (AOL), 127, 363, 364
American Airlines, 380
American Bar Association (ABA), 141
American Express, 315
American Library Association, 254
American Management Association (AMA), 258
American Medical Association (AMA), 141
American Water, 231
Amherst College, 425
Ancestry.com, 367
Ann Taylor, 111
Apache Software Foundation, 221
Apple Inc., 33, 79, 103, 104, 113, 128, 144, 146-147, 150, 151, 154, 277-278, 356, 362, 365, 369, 379

Applebee's, 423
Aramco, 315, 316
Armani Exchange, 381
ASB Bank, 84
Association for Computing Machinery (ACM), 141
Association of Information Technology Professionals (AITP), 141
AT&T, 243, 251, 254, 268
Austin Energy, 448-449
AutoZone, 236
Avis Rent A Car, 381

B. Dalton, 128
BAE Systems, 207-209, 378
Bank of America, 110, 134, 315, 379
Bank of Muscat, 290
Barclays Bank, 134
Barnes & Noble (B&N), 127-128
Baseline Consulting, 389
Basex, 258
BB&T, 315
Bell Laboratories, 34, 185
Bertelsmann, 127
Best Buy, 293, 381
Best Western International, 389
Betfair, 370
BJ's Wholesale Club, 295
Blackburn Rovers, 158-159
Bloomberg, 316
Blue Nile, 353, 364
BMW, 107, 108
The Body Shop plc, 400
Boeing Corp., 237, 378
Books-A-Million, 127
Borders Group, 127, 128
BrightStar Partners, 226
British Airways, 287
Broadcom, 113
Burger King, 388
Business Software Alliance, 151

Cablevision, 244, 259
Cadillac, 388
Caesars Entertainment, 225
Canadian Tire, 196-197
Capital One, 315
Caterpillar Corp., 114, 370, 461
CenterPoint Properties, 259-260
Champion Technologies, 300
Charles Schwab, 225
Chevrolet, 372
Chevron, 316
ChoicePoint, 138
Christian Coalition, 254
Chrysler Corp., 388
Cincinnati Zoo, 225, 226-227
Cisco, 242
Cisco Systems, 220
CitiBank, 34, 112
Citigroup, 114, 315
City of Denver, 415

CloudFlare, 289
Coca-Cola, 316, 325-326
Coca-Cola Enterprises Inc. (CCE), 31
Colloquy, 237, 238
ComCast, 132, 147, 244, 254, 255
Comdisco Disaster Recovery Services, 300
Comodo, 306
Con-Way Transportation, 409
Continental AG, 241
Continental Airlines, 380
Continental Tires, 241-242, 243
Countrywide Financials, 110
Coursera, 425
Crown Books, 128
CYBERCOM, 317

Daimler, 107-108
Dartmouth College, 270
Deckers Outdoor Corp., 442
Defense Information Systems Agency (DISA), 170
Dell Inc., 186, 196
Delta Airlines, 117, 380
Deutsche Bank, 300-301
Dialog Semiconductor, 113
Dollar General Corp., 54
Dollar Rent-A-Car, 190
Dovetail Associates, 430, 437
Dow Chemical, 32, 316
DP World, 339-340
DraftFCB, 389
Dropbox, 177, 364
Drugstore.com, 364
Duke University, 425
DuPont, 419

E*Trade, 186, 367
EarthLink, 250-251
Eastman Kodak, 66
eBay, 104, 111, 292, 354, 364, 365, 367, 400
Educational Testing Service (ETS), 424, 425
EdX, 424-426
eHarmony, 367
800-Flowers, 116, 381
Electronic Privacy Information Center (EPIC), 165
Elemica, 364
EMC Documentum, 415
Enron, 296
Enterasys Networks, 388
EP International, Inc., 203
Epinions, 367
ePolicy Institute, 258
Epsilon, 293
ETrade.com, 364
Etsy, 203
Europay, 290
Exostar, 364, 377-378
Expedia, 354, 364, 365, 380, 381

487

Subject Index

BUSINESS CASES AND INTERACTIVE SESSIONS

Here are the cases and Interactive Sessions you'll find in the eleventh edition of Essentials of Management Information Systems. These cases and Interactive Sessions cover new developments in information systems and real-world company applications of systems.

Chapter 1: Business Information Systems in Your Career

Rugby Football Union Tries Big Data
Meet the New Mobile Workers
UPS Competes Globally with Information Technology
A New Look at Electronic Medical Records

Chapter 2: Global E-business and Collaboration

Social Networking Takes Off at Kluwer
Vail Ski Resorts Goes High-Tech for High Touch
Piloting Procter and Gamble from Decision Cockpits
Modernization of NTUC Income

Chapter 3: Achieving Competitive Advantage with Information Systems

Grupo Modelo: Competing on Processes
Auto Makers Become Software Companies
New Systems and Business Processes Put MoneyGram "On the Money"
Can This Bookstore Be Saved?

Chapter 4: IT Ethical and Social Issues in Information Systems

Content Pirates Sail the Web
Big Data Gets Personal: Behavioral Targeting
Monitoring in the Workplace
Facebook: It's About the Money

Chapter 5: IT Infrastructure: Hardware and Software

Portugal Telecom Offers IT Infrastructure For Sale
The Greening of the Data Center
The Pleasures and Pitfalls of BYOD
Is It Time for Cloud Computing?

Chapter 6: Foundation of Business Intelligence: Databases and Information Management

BAE Systems
Business Intelligence Helps the Cincinnati Zoo Know Its Customers
American Water Keeps Data Flowing
Does Big Data Bring Big Rewards?